CU01019188

PRECEDENT IN ENGLISH LAW
and other Essays

PRECEDENT
IN ENGLISH LAW
and other Essays

by

JAMES LOUIS MONTROSE

LL B (LOND) HON LL D (T C D)

Honorary Fellow of University College London;
Dean of the Faculty of Law and Professor of Law, Queen's University,
Belfast 1934-1963; Barstow Scholar 1924

edited by

HAROLD GREVILLE HANBURY

Q C D C L

Vinerian Professor Emeritus of English Law in the University of
Oxford; Honorary Fellow of Lincoln College, Oxford; Honorary
Master of the Bench, Inner Temple; Sometime Fellow of All Souls
College; Vinerian Scholar and Rhodes Travelling Fellow; Assistant
Reader in Equity to the Council of Legal Education

SHANNON · IRELAND

1968

SBN 7165 0503 7

Microfilm, microfiche and other forms of micro-publishing
© *Irish University Microforms Shannon Ireeand*

Irish University Press Shannon Ireland

DUBLIN CORK BELFAST LONDON NEW YORK

Captain T M MacGlinchey publisher
Robert Hogg printer

PRINTED IN THE REPUBLIC OF IRELAND
BY CAHILL AND COMPANY LIMITED DUBLIN

Contents

Chapter

INTRODUCTION 1

1 PRECEDENT IN ENGLISH LAW 9

2 ADDRESS QUEEN'S UNIVERSITY BELFAST TO MATRICULATION STUDENTS, 1955 20

3 EDMUND BURKE AND THE NATURAL LAW 23

4 RETURN TO AUSTIN'S COLLEGE 49

5 GENERAL PRINCIPLES OF LAW 65

6 THE USE OF LEGAL CATEGORIES IN PROBLEMS CONCERNING COMPILATION OF CUSTOMS AND CODIFICATION 74

7 LAW, SCIENCE AND THE HUMANITIES 89

8 THE SCOPE OF JURISPRUDENCE 103

9 THE TREATMENT OF STATUTES BY LORD DENNING .. 129

10 RATIO DECIDENDI AND THE HOUSE OF LORDS 151

11 SOME PROBLEMS ABOUT FUNDAMENTAL TERMS 158

12 THE CONTRACT OF SALE IN SELF-SERVICE STORES .. 189

13 THE BASIS OF THE POWER OF AN AGENT IN CASES OF ACTUAL AND APPARENT AUTHORITY 195

14 LIABILITY OF PRINCIPAL FOR ACTS EXCEEDING ACTUAL AND APPARENT AUTHORITY 224

15 THE APPARENT AUTHORITY OF AN AGENT OF A COMPANY 244

16 THE CHEQUES ACT, 1957 263

17 THE *Ostime* CASE 275

18 BASIC CONCEPTS OF THE LAW OF EVIDENCE 286

19 *Broom* v. *Morgan* AND THE NATURE OF JURISTIC DISCOURSE 312

APPENDIX: LIST OF OTHER WORKS BY THE AUTHOR .. 365

INTRODUCTION

James Louis Montrose was born in London on 6 May, 1904. He was educated first at the Central Foundation School, and afterwards at University College, London, of which he was destined to become a Fellow. His academic career was brilliant, and he was *facile princeps* in the First Class in the examination for LL.B. His performance in Bar Examinations was uniformly excellent, and in 1924 he won the greatest of all distinctions that the Council of Legal Education has to offer, the Barstow Scholarship. He was called to the Bar by Gray's Inn in 1926, and spent a brief period in the Chambers of Kenneth Carpmael, a master in the law and practice of Admiralty. But he reached an early decision to devote his life to teaching, and in 1927, at the age of 23, he was appointed Head of the Department of Law in the University College of Hull (now raised to University status). There he performed the first of his works of magic, in making " something out of nothing ". The present condition of flourishing prosperity which the Law Faculty, and indeed the whole University, of Hull now enjoys, is due in the largest measure to his untiring energy, and genius for organisation. In 1934 he took up his life-work, as Dean of the new Faculty of Law at Queen's University, Belfast. This post he filled for thirty years. At first he was alone, with everything to create. He acquired the services, as part-time assistant, of the present Lord Chief Justice of Northern Ireland, Lord Macdermott, and he was fortunate in the effective encouragement of Sir Frederick Ogilvie, the greatest of the Vice-Chancellors of Queen's, and one of the outstanding academic figures of all time. It must never be forgotten that in Northern Ireland the University looms larger than in almost any other part of the world, and the selection of those who are to direct its destinies is a matter of supreme importance. Jimmy trod the path of a pioneer in legal education, formerly trodden by Edward Jenks, and his contributions to it were as weighty as those of that great writer and teacher. " Precept upon precept, line upon line " he built up the edifice of the institution, and not many years had passed before he had erected a Faculty of Law second to none in Great Britain. The secret of the success of the Dean lay in the character of the man. To say that he took the greatest interest in his students is a ridiculous understatement; rather should it be said, that he identified himself with the aspirations of each and every one of them. He loved them all, and they repaid him with unfailing loyalty, pent up in a stream which burst its banks at the farewell dinner

1

given in his honour by the Students' Law Society on 11th June, 1964.

As a teacher he was most inspiring, as a scholar most profound. Not only did he devour every law book extant, but he accomplished considerable study of allied subjects, such as philosophy, logic and economics. Of him might justly be said, what has been sung by many Irish voices of the legendary Father O'Flynn:

> " Come, I venture to give ye my word,
> Never the likes of his logic was heard,
> Down from mythology into thayology,
> Troth! and conchology if he'd the call."

His mind was continually receptive of new ideas, and he had that priceless attribute of a great jurist, humility. Generous, almost to a fault, to colleagues inside and outside his own Faculty, he kept before him always the conviction that no man's knowledge can be complete, that a teacher never ceases to be a learner. Of the function of law in life he had the loftiest views; he regarded it, not as a narrow backwater, but as a bountiful spring of fresh water, irrigating the vast country of human relations.

I have compared him to Edward Jenks in his ability to create a flourishing garden out of virgin soil; he resembled him again in his services to the Society of Public Teachers of Law. Of this institution, now world-famed, Jenks was the founder; the title of the second founder must be conferred on Judge Raleigh Batt, its President throughout the Second World War. But the third founder was surely Jimmy Montrose. It is worth while, at this point, to insert an enumeration of his activities in this regard. He achieved, in 1965, the recognition of the Society by the first Commonwealth Conference Organisation. He submitted a paper, attended as the Society's representative, and in the course of discussion advanced proposals for the combined education of barristers and solicitors, and the provision of facilities for interchange between the two branches of the profession. This, though stopping short of fusion, must necessarily be controversial, and will doubtless so remain for many years to come; but Montrose never flinched from fearless advocacy of that which he believed to be right. On the vital subject of Law Libraries, he secured the adoption of his cherished plan for a questionnaire, the answers to which produced a " minimum library list ".

In 1956-57 he was the Society's President. In that capacity, he persuaded Lord Chancellor Kilmuir to appoint the Criminal Law Reform Committee, whose recommendations have been, and continue to be, far-reaching, and several are finding their way to the Statute Book. Thus he made his mark as a law reformer, as befitted an *alumnus* of the College whereof Jeremy Bentham is still the presiding genius. Other useful activities were the memoranda, and in some cases delegations, to the Robbins Committee on Higher Education, the National

Incomes Committee, and the Heyworth Committee on social study. He was the principal draftsman of the memorandum supporting the project of the survey of Legal Education in the United Kingdom. To his initiative and enterprise must be attributed the success of conferences of law teachers in the United States, Canada and Australia. In the history of legal education no name stands higher than his. Nor were his sympathies confined to his own subjects. He played a prominent part in the activities of the Association of University Teachers, to whose efforts teachers in all fields owe it that their salaries have kept pace with rises in the cost of living.

The width of his sympathies was shown on the large canvas of Ireland. He was not an Irishman, and neither a Catholic nor a Protestant, and perhaps for these very reasons he won the confidence, not only of persons of moderate opinions, but even of those whose views were extremist to the point of bigotry. I was privileged to act as External Examiner, at intervals, for a quarter of a century, and was, on each visit, increasingly impressed by the harmony pervading the entire student body. All seemed to feel that anything approaching rancour among them would be as abhorrent to their beloved Dean as would disloyalty to himself and his colleagues, and to their University. He was indeed the father of a happy family. Though the students were, for the most part, naturally drawn from the Six Counties, there was no lack of them from other parts of the world. He especially encouraged West Africans, and two who passed through his hands were elected to the Faculties of Nigerian Universities, Jerome Okolo at Enugu/Nsukka, and Arthur Okunniga at Ife. In two other ways he rendered magnificent service to Northern Ireland : (a) by playing a large part in the formation of the Poor Man's Lawyer's Scheme in 1937; he encouraged his students to enter fully into it, and himself gave unsparing assistance to it as consultant; (b) by his assistance in the establishment of the Marriage Guidance Council in 1947.

Thirty years, broken only by his distinguished war service in the R.A.F., is a long time to spend in one position; as Deirdre of the Sorrows put it, " there's no place to stay always ". But I am sure that there is not one of his students but would echo Albert Chevalier in the line " it don't seem a day too much ". His retirement in 1964 by no means meant his retirement from legal education. Almost immediately he went to lecture in the Free University of Berlin, proceeding thence, by way of a visiting professorship in the Hebrew University of Jerusalem, to the University of Singapore, where he became Dean of the Law Faculty. Here, for the first time, he found an institution ready-made, and for the first time, had a predecessor, and an able one, in Professor Groves, formerly Dean of Texas Southern University Law School. Though his stay there was short, he could not fail to leave his mark upon it, and he has shown, in some of his writings, the voracity of his appetite for learning in the manners and customs of the people, whether Chinese or Malay, among whom his lot had now been cast. From Singapore he passed, by way of Australia, to New Zealand, where he enjoyed what proved to be his last earthly assignment, as visiting professor in the University of Auckland, where all that was mortal of him now rests.

It is not surprising, in the case of a man of the calibre of Montrose, that his many friends should desire to preserve his memory in a fitting manner. A Committee was soon formed, with Judge James A. Brown, as chairman, James Elliott, an old pupil, as secretary, and Mr. T. Leslie Adamson, as treasurer. Two projects were mooted: (a) the foundation of a Montrose scholarship or prize; (b) the publication of a volume of his collected papers. From the start, project (b) found most favour, and I felt enormously honoured when invited to act as editor. Montrose was so preoccupied with the administration of his other multifarious activities, that he had never had time to write a *magnum opus*. This is to be regretted, as he was admirably equipped to write an epoch-making work, either on jurisprudence or on commercial law. But of essays, reviews and speeches there is no stint. The number of those that have been traced is 92, and the process of inclusion and exclusion has proved very difficult. Eventually I made a choice of 19, the rest being relegated to a list, inserted as an appendix to this volume. It is hoped that some of these may at some time be published in a second volume, but the resolution to omit some of them from the present volume, in obedience to the exigencies of space, has not been formed without much reluctance.

It is from the first essay that the title of the volume has been drawn. Though Montrose nowhere mentions Matthew Arnold, he must, in his reviews, have been animated by the philosophy of his essay on the function of criticism, in which, while conceding that the critical power is of lower rank than the creative, he yet insists that the one is the necessary complement of the other. Without the critical faculty, the creative artist will lack that sense of discrimination which is essential if he is to make a real contribution to contemporary thought. Arnold aptly laid down that " a false or malicious criticism had better never have been written ". But yet more deserving of censure is the critic who concentrates on *minutiae*, which are the proper subjects for a private letter to the author, and yet worse still is the critic who uses a review as a vehicle for the advertisement of his own brilliance, or the exercise of his own wit. These two faults are as alien to Montrose as to Holdsworth. He was lavish of praise where praise was due, sparing of polemics where he merely disagreed, gentle in condemnation where he detected error. Not that error can be detected in Professor Cross' great work on judicial precedent, that subject which is at once so elementary and so complex. Montrose estimates the book at its true worth, while pointing out, as a good reviewer, the points which he regards as open to question, and in which improvement might be effected.

The second is a gem, which it would be unthinkable to consign to oblivion. As an introduction to those standing on the threshold of a great profession, couched in beautiful language, with sincerity sparkling in every word, it is a model of what such an oration should be. No student who heard it could possibly forget it throughout his life.

The third place is taken by another review, concerning a figure who must inevitably have attracted Montrose as a magnet a steel rapier. He has been immortalised by many, the two encomiums which most readily spring to mind being those of Matthew Arnold, to whose felicity in phrasing I must again turn, and of Disraeli. The former wrote of him, that " he saturates politics with thought ". Disraeli relates that Rockingham, " a virtuous magnifico ", was " fortunate to enlist in his service the supreme genius of Edmund Burke ". The book was written by a professor, not of law but of literature, Peter J. Stanlis, of the University of Michigan. Montrose, while according full recognition to the value of the book, considered from its own angle, makes skilful use of it from another. He comments on the neglect of Burke by juristic writers, and demonstrates irrefutably that he was in truth a member of their supreme hierarchy. In this review Montrose reveals his belief in (a) the creative value of enlightened criticism—his thesis might stand as a convincing refutation of the cynical estimate *la critique est facile, l'art difficile*; (b) the high standards to which undergraduate reading should attain—based on his own standards, they might be regarded as almost impossibly high.

The fourth chapter is of especial interest in view of the place of its origin. I was myself most honoured in 1954-55 to be President of the Bentham Club at his own beloved University College, and I know that I took more trouble over the composition of my address than over anything that I have ever written. Doubly and trebly must this have been true of Montrose, an academic son of the great law reformer himself. He here brings into prominence two facets of Austin which often escape notice : (a) the part played by Mrs. Sarah Austin, as wife and widow, in preserving him from undeserved oblivion; (b) the influence exercised on him by Kant—this is by no means the only place in which Montrose expressed his own interest in the great author of the *Critique of Pure Reason,* and *Philosophy of Law.*

The fifth and sixth chapters were contributions by Montrose to the deliberations of the Sixth International Congress of Comparative Law, held in Hamburg in the summer of 1962. Chapter 7 is his Presidential address to the Society of Public Teachers of Law in 1956, and, as the title indicates, displays the immensity of Montrose's conception of the proper field of law. In the ensuing discussion, not here reproduced, the participants, while commending the splendour of their President's vision, yet tended to express scepticism of the practical possibility of basing upon it a students' curriculum. Chapter 8 reads almost as if written under a presentiment of approaching death. It is, in effect, a ramble in retrospect through the thoughts of a life, in every moment of which thought played so large a part. It stands out, even among Montrose's works, as a perfect example of his vast learning in many fields.

Characteristically, it pays generous tributes to that greatest of all law teachers, Roscoe Pound, and to Julius Stone, Montrose's lifelong friend.

In Chapter 9 we leave general jurisprudence for more specialised topics. Montrose always insisted on the vital importance of the Interpretation of Statutes, which he regarded as lying at the very roots of legal studies. Lord Denning, who has described himself as an iconoclast, naturally attracted Montrose, whose mind always reached out beyond the law as it is, towards the law as it ought to be. Chapter 10 is short, but raises a matter of the utmost importance, the status of decisions of the House of Lords, on appeals from the English Appeal Court, as authorities for the Courts of Northern Ireland. Chapter 11 consists of two articles in the *Cambridge Law Journal*, on the subject of Fundamental Terms, which is assuming an ever-increasing importance in the law of sale and hire-purchase. Montrose always emphasised the importance of linguistic analysis as the only road towards essential precision.

I included, as Chapter 12, an article prompted by a paper in a German legal journal, on a subject which has received too little attention from English writers. Montrose was a good German scholar, and it would be interesting to know whether he wrote the German version of his article, which was included among the papers handed over to me. The crucial question which it raises is, which of the parties is offeror, and which acceptor, in self-service stores?

The next three chapters are concerned with the law of agency, in which Montrose took a very great interest. The branch of mercantile law has the peculiar attraction, that it has been built up, for the most part, by judges, especially by Lord Ellenborough at the beginning of the nineteenth century, without much aid from the legislature except for the series of Factors Acts. The articles which form Chapters 13 and 14 were published in 1938 and 1939 respectively. At that time Bowstead's *Digest,* the article in Halsbury's *Laws of England,* and the almost forgotten works of Paley and Wilshere, were virtually the only text-book authorities. By 1965, when the article forming Chapter 15 appeared, there were three or four new books. It must never be forgotten that the duties of instructing students, and of presenting a panorama of the law, are incumbent on writers of text-books rather than on judges, whose primary function is to decide the case before them, and who may be excused, so long as they do justice in it, from a certain looseness of expression. Thus Montrose is at pains to disentangle, in judicial pronouncements, the phrases " apparent authority ", " ostensible authority ", and " agency by estoppel ", whose frontiers have tended to become undefined. In Chapter 15, Montrose boldly tackles a problem which need not have arisen but for the lack of precision among judges, who perhaps are not to be blamed overmuch for it. It is elementary equity, that the doctrine of constructive notice applies only to land, not to chattels, or commercial transactions. This was made clear in *Joseph* v. *Lyons* [1884], 15 Q.B.D. 280, which was used by Maitland as an illustration of its non-application to chattels, and which was reinforced by *County Laboratories* v. *Mindel* [1957] Ch. 295, an interpretation of section 25 of the Restrictive Trade Practices Act, 1956. But judges have been unable to escape the necessity, in some commercial cases, of building up a kindred doctrine, to which they, and especially in cases involving the apparent authority of the agent of a company, have unfortunately given the same name. Really, in speaking of " constructive notice " in this connotation, they have merely employed a loose method of indicating that a person is " put on inquiry "; this is implicit in the speech of Lord Herschell in *London Joint Stock Bank* v. *Simmons* [1892] A.C. 201, 221. Montrose's article is an admirable guide to clarity.

Chapters 16 and 17 were included in that both cheques and taxes are cardinal facts of life. Chapter 17, moreover, raises, without solving, the question whether Dicey's doctrine that Parliament cannot bind its successors can be reconciled with the application of the Interpretation Act. Chapter 18, as proclaimed by its title, probes thoroughly the basic concepts of the law of evidence, which it approaches from a similar standpoint to that of Gulson in his *Philosophy of Proof*. Montrose acts as umpire, on the vexed question, whether relevancy is a question of law or fact, between the theory of Thayer in favour of the former, and Wigmore in favour of the latter.

I had intended that the book should consist of these eighteen chapters and no more, but I was pressed by members of the Committee with the claims of the analysis of *Broom* v. *Morgan* [1953] 1 All E.R. 849. I had underestimated the generosity of the publishers as to space, and was very pleased to include it, the more so in that I agreed with the opinion of some of his old students, which may have been shared by the learned author himself, that it was the best thing he had ever written. The problem posed by the case was—can the master be liable for the servant's tort, for which the servant cannot be sued? Montrose used it as a lever, wherewith to prize open the chest of riddles, as to the basis of vicarious liability in tort. He did not break new ground, for it had previously been trodden by Dr. Baty in his brilliant, though sardonic monograph, and of course by Holdsworth, who treated the subject thoroughly, but in conjunction with tortious liability in general. Montrose treats it from every angle, and the article is one which it is difficult to lay down, when once embarked on its perusal.

Reviewers of this volume may well quarrel with my choice of essays, which I necessarily found invidious, when faced with an *embarras de richesse*. The essays were written, and lectures delivered, at intervals spread over a considerable period, but through them all the same steadfast purpose can be clearly traced. They are here presented almost exactly as they first appeared, footnotes having been added here and there, so as to avoid the presentation, as existing law, of that which is law no longer.

The editor's warmest thanks are due to several good friends. First they must be rendered to Lord Denning, Lord Chorley, Lord Justice Edmund Davies, and Dr. Kenneth Urwin, General Secretary of the Association of University Teachers, who have encouraged me by continual help and advice. Judge Brown was a tower of strength in launching the project; and an especial meed of praise is owed to Mr. Stewart O'Fee, who made an elaborate search among Montrose's papers, arranged them in order and transmitted them to me with much valuable information. Heartfelt thanks must also be paid to the numerous and generous subscribers to the Montrose Memorial Fund, which made the publication of the volume possible, and to those members of the Committee who corrected the proofs. Secondly, I must mention that I am no longer engaged in teaching, and cannot claim to have kept *au courant* with the development of the law, which appears, in every field, to advance by geometrical progression. Fortunately, I have been able to tap the limitless erudition of two Oxford friends and former colleagues, Dr. D. C. M. Yardley and Mr. G. Treitel; to both I am more than grateful. But the project could never have been launched, much less have seen the light, without the initiative and enterprise of my old friend and former pupil, Mr. J. H. S. Elliott, whose devotion to Montrose's memory, coupled with his own learning and technical skill, has impelled him to smooth out every obstacle in our path.

The task of editing has been indeed a labour of love; my wife and I counted as one of the happiest periods of each year, our visit to the fairyland of Crawfordsburn, where we enjoyed the privilege of the society of two of the finest people in this imperfect world, Jimmy and Mabel Montrose.

H. G. HANBURY

Marlborough House
Falmouth

I

Precedent in English Law*

Case law is often regarded as the most distinctive feature of the English legal system. Precedent is an attendant, though, in my view, logically independent doctrine. Consequently the absence of any major study of the character of case law and of the doctrine of precedent is surprising, even if one accepts the thesis, for which case law may be adduced as evidence, that the pragmatism of Englishmen makes them averse from consideration of fundamental principles in their various tasks of industry, commerce and government. Such studies as have been made are mainly to be found within books on " jurisprudence ". Thus monographs and articles on the subjects are generally classified under that heading. Moreover, in British universities, the subjects usually follow the books, and are included in courses on jurisprudence. True, they are subjects which are in great need of terminological clarification, conceptual analysis, and synthesis of principles, to name but tasks of analytical jurisprudence. But they are branches of English law, and other branches, which also need jurisprudential treatment, are expounded in separate treatises. It is true that case law and precedent are topics which pervade all other branches of law, and so have a degree of generality not possessed by subjects like contract, still less by such narrower topics as compulsory acquisition of land. Nevertheless, such pervasiveness has not inhibited the publication of works on statute law and its " interpretation ".

We now have an important book on precedent : its sole predecessor has been out of print for a century.[1] It is one of the Clarendon Law Series, and, though it will add to the high reputation of the Oxford law school, it is, accordingly, a general introduction to the subject, rather than a " text-book ". Its author presents it as " an essay in analytical jurisprudence ", though he does not rigidly confine himself to " analysis " : his description of judicial practice and his evaluation of legal rules are no insignificant part of the work. However, he does not

---

*A review of " Precedent in English Law ", by Professor Rupert Cross. It is reprinted from *Malaya Law Review*, 1965, by kind permission. [Professor Montrose's interest in this subject is shown by the fact that it dominates Chapters 10 and 17. Ed.]

[1] [It is thought that the author had in mind Wambaugh's "Study of Cases". Ed.]

attempt a comprehensive survey of judicial practices as does Karl
Llewellyn in his book on the work of the U.S. appellate courts : he is
mainly concerned with matters previously discussed in the jurisprudence books and articles.   But though the author calls the book a work
on " particular jurisprudence " dealing with " fundamental assumptions ", its appearance is a major event in the history of English law.
It brings together a number of basic problems which have hitherto
been separately considered, and in his lucid exposition the author presents
his own stimulating views.   His solutions of some problems are contributions both to jurisprudence and to general theory of English law.   For
example, he answers the riddle set by Glanville Williams, and echoed by
Lord Reid in *Scruttons* v. *Midland Silicones, Ltd.*[2] as to the possibility,
under the doctrine of precedent, of making binding changes in the
doctrine.   He lifts the doctrine, not however by its own bootstraps, on
to the level of constitutional law.   Nor does he deal merely with problems previously agitated.   Thus, he discusses the relationship of precedent to the definition of law, and he considers how far the limitations in
Young v. *Bristol Aeroplane Company*[3] are of general application, and
affect decisions of the House of Lords.   Above all, he has demonstrated
the existence of an independent subject of precedent.   It is to be hoped
that on this foundation the author in a larger work, or some other
scholar, may build that substantial structure which is called for by the
importance of the subject.

My admiration for what has been attempted and accomplished by
the author is, however, qualified by two sets of doubts.   Was it not
possible to provide a more adequate exposition of some of the topics
covered?   Was it not possible to have provided a more rigorous analysis
of the language and concepts involved?

Two examples of the attenuated character of the exposition are
to be found in the treatment on the one hand of comparative law and
on the other of the interpretation of statutes.   In the former the author
omits consideration of the Justinian text, *Non exemplis sed legibus
judicandum est,* and of its derivatives in modern legal systems.   In the
latter he regards what is, in effect, Willis's treatment, afforced by a
reference to the problem of vagueness, as a sufficient survey.   Of course,
this brief treatment can be explained on the ground that the book is
on precedent and not on statute law, and the section serves but as an
introduction to the interrelation of the doctrine of precedent with that
of the interpretation of statutes.   Nevertheless, the student needs surely
to be brought into touch with the modern attitude of the courts.   It is a
minor matter that Willis's terminology is not in accordance with judicial
practice.   The " golden rule " is not the rule that the grammatical
and ordinary sense of words may be modified so as to avoid an absurdity
or inconsistency, if, indeed, such a rule is recognised today.   The

---

[2] [1962] A.C. 446.
[3] [1944] K.B. 718.

" golden rule " is that words be given their ordinary and grammatical meaning. Are we, with some judges, to invoke the Rule in *Heydon's Case* only after consideration of the statutory words has disclosed an ambiguity, or may we, with other judges, first look at the social reasons for a statute, and then read the text in the light of that history?

The absence of uniformity of practice in connection with the interpretation of statutes, and the related variety of rules and doctrines, is paralleled in the field of precedent. Goodhart tells us that " there is no actual *uniform* operation of English courts concerning the operation of precedents " and Lord Reid finds " no invariable practice with regard to *rationes decidendi* ". But the impression I received from this book, which a more careful reading may correct, is of some " brooding omnipresence in the sky " of a coherent body of principles forming *the* doctrine of precedent, and needing but the illustration of a few cases. Certainly we are referred to but few cases. It may well be that the principles expounded are derived from a survey of many cases: the author from time to time speaks of the practice of the courts. Once again, the needs of an introduction for students may call for a telescope and not a microscope. Or is it that a " jurisprudential " approach blurs the distinction between an ideal of consistency and a reality which depicts our lady the common law warts and all? I see the cases as revealing various patterns of doctrine, some maintained by one group of judges, some by another; some belong to a past era, some to the present, and perhaps some to the future; some declining, some rising. Some doctrines exist concurrently, without conscious recognition of their diversity by counsel or judges: and it is not easy to predict which will be submitted or applied in a particular case, though it is plausible to suppose some relation between submission and application. Judges will sometimes speak in terms of the *ratio decidendi* of a precedent, sometimes in terms of distinguishing cases, sometimes in terms of an " explanation " of the precedent. Karl Llewellyn sees the conflict of doctrines as providing a rich choice of weapons in the armoury of justice, and discerns the existence of patterns of decision based on factors other than doctrines of precedent. I find the conflict disturbing, and am soothed by belief in the existence of dominating patterns of doctrines. But the discovery of such patterns requires a patient survey of the corpus of cases, not a recital of a selection of dicta.

Let me turn now to consideration of the book as a contribution to analytical jurisprudence. Despite the conventional name, the major tasks of this jurisprudence appear to be those of analysis of the language and concepts of legal discourse, and synthesis of the concepts and doctrines of legal systems. If the analysis discloses ambiguity of language or inadequacy of concepts, then the jurist may recommend a different terminology or a new conceptual framework. In the course

B

of attempted synthesis the jurist may discover inconsistencies of practices
and rules, but he cannot in this event make suggestions without
becoming a sociologist and stating trends towards the rise of one or
the decline of another doctrine, or becoming a politician and evaluating
the opposed doctrines.   My uneasiness is concerned more with the
preliminary examination of words and processes, rather than with
statements the author makes about trends and values.   May I become
less abstract by abstracting for consideration two pairs of related topics?
(1a) The analysis of the phrase " applying a decision ", and (1b) the
related problem of the distinction between the creative power of case
law and the restrictive effect of precedent. (2a) The analysis of the
phrase " *ratio decidendi* " and (2b) the related problem of the comparison in the examination of a precedent to see whether or not it
contains a *ratio decidendi* applicable to the instant case, with the process
of examining a precedent to see whether or no its facts are such that
it can be distinguished from the instant case.

Both pairs are of course interrelated.   Thus (1a) and (2b) are connected when the author links the phrase " applying a decision " with
the existence of " a reasonable distinction between [a previous decision]
and the instant case [which nevertheless] is not regarded as one which
should be acted on ".   He finds in Lord Halsbury's dictum in *Quinn
v. Leathem*[4] about the " logic " of precedent both a procedure for distinguishing cases on the ground of the " objective " materiality of their
facts and a procedure for deriving a *ratio decidendi* from all the material
facts before the court.

Both terms of the phrase " applying a decision " call for consideration.   It is well to remember, as our author tells us, that " the words
' decision ' and ' precedent ' are often used synonymously ", but we need
also to be reminded that the word " decision " may refer to a number of
distinct matters. (i) " Decision " is sometimes used as synonymous with
" precedent " or, indeed, " case " (precedent or subsequent): (ii)
" decision " is sometimes used as referring to the final order of the
court: e.g., that an appeal be dismissed.   It is to such an ultimate
decision that the verb refers in the phrase *ratio decidendi*.   In this sense
it may sometimes be synonymous with judgment, another ambiguous
word: (iii) " decision " is sometimes used as referring to the terms in
which an issue between the parties is resolved.   In this sense it is
synonymous with " holding ".   The ambiguity of " decision " obscures
the distinction, made by Viscount Dunedin in *The Mostyn,*[5] between
being bound by a precedent in the sense that one must apply to the
instant case the decision of an issue in the precedent case (the rule of
law adopted in the precedent), and being bound by a precedent in the
sense that one must not apply in the instant case a rule, which if

[4] [1901] A.C. 495.
[5] [1928] A.C. 57.

applied in the precedent, would have led to a different (final) decision in that precedent case. When we speak of a past decision applying to the instant case analysis will often disclose that we refer to the application of the decision in the precedent of an issue of law in the precedent case: i.e. to the application of a rule of law propounded in the precedent case.

If the facts in the instant case do not fall under the rule adopted in the precedent case, its " decision ", then we could well say the " decision " does not apply. But there is sanction in judicial usage, for saying that a decision " applies ", even though the rule propounded in it was stated in such a manner as to exclude the facts of the instant case. Cross refers the reader to the following *dictum* of Roxburgh J. in his brief discussion of the distinction between " applying " and " following " in *Re House Property and Investment Ltd.*[6] " It has often become material to consider whether a decision of the House of Lords should be applied in a case which can be distinguished but is analogous ". There is a need for further analysis. It is provided by considering some *dicta* of Devlin L.J. in *Berry* v. *British Transport Commission.*[7] There he examines various precedents from which he concludes that there is a rule that a party who had been awarded costs in civil cases can not allege that he has suffered damage by reason of the fact that the costs he recovered were less than he actually incurred. Devlin L.J. then speaks of seeing " whether [the rule] is equally applicable to criminal costs ". He also phrases that notion in the words " The question is whether [the rule] should be extended to costs in criminal cases ". Analysis discloses that in judicial language the word " apply " is ambiguous: sometimes it refers to the process of stating that particular facts are comprehended in the general words of a rule: sometimes it applies to the process of constructing a rule wider than the one given in the precedent case, so that the new rule may comprehend both the facts of the precedent case and the facts of the instant case.

Is it not desirable that there should be appropriate terminological distinctions to mark such very different concepts as that of law making —the extension of a rule, and law applying—the subsumption of facts under a rule? It seems to me plausible that if such a terminology existed we should see more clearly that Lord Halsbury's dictum in *Quinn* v. *Leathem*[4] is " really " a plea against extending rules merely by analogy. The ambiguity of " applies " may induce the error that the new law made by extension is identical with the old law. If we eliminate that error, may we not see more clearly that the declaratory theory of precedent reflects a practice of judges to make new law on the analogy of old law? This practice, however, may diminish as judges become more conscious of the dangers of arguing by analogy.

The distinction between case law in general and a doctrine of

---

[6] [1954] Ch. 576.
[7] [1962] 1 Q.B. 306.

precedent in particular is indeed made by the author. But, in my view, it could have been made more sharply. The discussion of law making is to be found in a chapter entitled " Precedent and Judicial Reasoning ". In the middle of a discussion about reasoning by analogy we find important additions to the earlier examination of the character of *ratio decidendi*. Of course, the sharpness of the conceptual distinction does not mean that in practice law making and law applying are not intertwined, that it may not be difficult to disentangle arguments for " following " precedents from argument in favour of principles and policies. Is not " following " an old rule in new circumstances the making of a new rule? Perhaps my general doubts derive from my particular doubt about the assertion made by the author in his introduction that " in a system based on case-law, judges in subsequent cases *must* have regard to . . . the rules laid down by judges in giving decisions ". A system of case-law appears to me to be a system of rules for which there is no legislative authority. I cannot see why such a system necessarily involves later judges in consideration of the rules propounded by earlier judges. And, even within a system incorporating a doctrine of precedent, the problem of deciding cases, in the absence of binding judicial authority, is different from that of determining whether a precedent is binding. But this is to take sides on the problem of the existence of " gaps in the law ", a problem doubtless wisely omitted from the book.

An analysis of the use of the words " *ratio decidendi* " is to me subordinate to an examination of the manner in which, in fact, judges treat precedent cases and of the evaluation of that judicial process. Nevertheless, its importance is considerable. Cross quotes statements of mine to the effect that the expression " *ratio decidendi* " is used in two senses. I have indicated a third sense other than the two cited, *viz.*, any reason, including a finding of fact, stated by the judge as being a ground of his final decision: and I can give instances of such usage. Cross however tells us that " by common consent the *ratio decidendi* is a proposition of law ". It is either " (i) The rule of law for which a case is of binding authority. (ii) The rule of law to be found in the actual opinion of the judge forming the basis of his decision." He appears to me, particularly in his " description " of the *ratio decidendi*, to use the phrase in the second sense. He says : " The *ratio decidendi* is any rule of law expressly or impliedly treated by the judge as a necessary step in reaching his conclusion, having regard to the line of reasoning adopted by him." If this sentence be considered in isolation, it may be regarded not as providing a nominal definition of " *ratio decidendi* ", but as asserting that the rule for which a case is of binding authority is any rule of law expressly or impliedly treated by a judge as a necessary step, and thus as providing an illustration of the use of *ratio decidendi* in the first sense. But later we are told : " The *ratio decidendi* of a case is generally the proposition of law for which that case may be cited as authority . . ." Here it would be self-contradictory to substitute for " *ratio decidendi* " the rule of law for which a case is of binding authority. Though the author refers to Llewellyn's statement in his *Bramble Bush* of two meanings of the phrase " *ratio decidendi* ", which, in substance, are my two senses, he does not, however, cite Goodhart's characterisation of my second sense as " a novel sense which I find it difficult to understand, singularly unhelpful and unnecessary ", or Goodhart's assertion that " other writers " never use the phrase in that sense. Nor does he quote Simpson's epithet " very eccentric ", and his assertion that the two cases are " not separable ". It does not appear that his use of the phrase " *ratio decidendi* " is always consistent. In his exegesis of Lord Halsbury's dictum in *Quinn* v. *Leathem*,[4] he surely uses the phrase in the sense of the rule of law for which a case is of binding authority. In his elaborate analysis of Goodhart's essay he nowhere suggests that Goodhart's use of the phrase " *ratio decidendi* " is in any way different from his own, though he does not accept Goodhart's method of determining the principle for which a case is " authoritative ". However, if his terminological analysis, as opposed to his substantial description, of *ratio decidendi* is correct, then there is no need to bother about two different senses. That analysis is found in his comment on my two senses: " If our description of the *ratio decidendi* is correct, there is no distinction between these two senses of the phrase until a decision has been interpreted in subsequent cases. Up to that moment the rule of law for which the decision is of binding authority is to be found in the actual opinion of the judge, forming the basis of his decision ". But this statement fails to distinguish adequately between the meanings of words and empirical description, between " what the description means " and " the thing which a description describes ", between " meaning " and " referring ". It happens to be empirically true that Sir Walter Scott was the author of " Waverley ", but it is not true that the meaning of " Sir Walter Scott " is the meaning of " the author of Waverley ". The meaning of " the evening star " is not identical with meaning of " the morning star ", though both phrases refer to the same planet. There is a distinction between the sense of " the victor of Austerlitz " and the sense of " the prisoner of St. Helena," though it was the victor of Austerlitz who became the prisoner of St. Helena. There is a distinction between the sense of " *ratio decidendi* " as a rule for which a decision is of binding authority and its sense as the rule found in the opinion of the judge, even though it be always true that the rule for which a decision is of binding authority is that found in the opinion. Moreover, if Simpson were correct, so that as a matter of empirical usage the element of binding authority always appears as part of the usage of the phrase " *ratio decidendi* ", then not only would it be odd, because self-contradictory, to say that a *ratio decidendi* is not binding, it would also be odd, because tautologous, to say that a *ratio decidendi* is binding.   However, such or similar, phrases are by no means uncommon.

It would be well, in view of the sterile character of merely terminological disputes, if one could turn to the examination of the substance of the doctrine of precedent unencumbered by the phrase " ratio decidendi ".   One can certainly ask how far it is true to say with Goodhart that the underlying principle which forms a precedent's authority is not found in the rule of law set forth in the opinion.   In my opinion, such a proposition can be supported by reference to cases in which the technique has been adopted of asking whether or not a precedent can be distinguished " on the facts ".   On the other hand, it is opposed to cases in which the technique has been adopted of asking whether the ratio decidendi of a precedent falls to be " applied " in the instant case.   There is no uniform and coherent doctrine at present of handling precedents, but, broadly speaking, two procedures involving opposed doctrine, though I perceive a trend in favour of seeking for the ratio decidendi.   (The technique of " explaining " cases, castigated by Hamson as " making nonsense of case law ", is perhaps best " explained " as a variant of distinguishing cases.)   Moreover, just as Lord Reid has said that " there is no invariable practice with regard to rationes decidendi ", so I find no invariable practice with regard to distinguishing cases on the facts.   Some of the practices can be reconciled with the technique of seeking for the binding principle in the rule of law set forth in the opinion: but some cannot.   The examination of the judicial procedures of distinguishing, however, leads us back to the language of ratio decidendi, for some of the judgments use both terms and sometimes both procedures.   Thus Lord Reid has said we may " limit " a " ratio decidendi " if " it is much wider than was necessary for the decision so that it becomes a question of how far it is proper to distinguish the earlier decision ".   We need to compare the technique of examining a precedent to see whether it contains a ratio decidendi that must be applied to the instant case with the technique of examining a precedent to see whether or not its facts are such that it can be distinguished from the instant case.

In the passage dealing with Lord Halsbury's dictum in Quinn v. Leathem,[4] Cross does indeed discuss the distinguishing of cases in relation to " ratio decidendi ".   He appears to regard the process of distinguishing, indicated by Lord Halsbury, as leading to the view " the ratio decidendi is derived from the material facts of the case ".   This is not Goodhart's doctrine, though in this sentence " ratio decidendi " is used as Goodhart uses it.   The " material facts " are not those " treated by the judge as material ".   " The basis of Lord Halsbury's pronouncement ", says the author, " seems to have been that every case has certain facts which every lawyer would regard to be material, quite apart from what the judge says about them.   In order to determine the ratio decidendi of a case it is, on the view under consideration, only necessary to eliminate objectively immaterial facts, *i.e.* those facts which all lawyers would agree could not reasonably be made a ground for distinguishing the case in subsequent litigation ". This legal mystique of the agreement of lawyers is surely the author's conception rather than Lord Halsbury's. It shouts for analysis. The author only spends a few more sentences, later in the book, on the process of distinguishing, indicated by Lord Halsbury, as leading to the view that the process is not reconcilable with that of considering the rule set forth in the precedent as binding.

On the other hand, Glanville Williams does reconcile the process of distinguishing with that of applying a judge's *ratio decidendi*. We should note first that he employs the terminology of " expressed *ratio decidendi* " as meaning " the rule that the judge who decided the case intended to lay down and apply to the facts ". Thus " expressed *ratio decidendi* " is synonymous with " *ratio decidendi* " in my second sense. I shall employ the phrase " *ratio decidendi* " henceforth in this second sense. Glanville Williams tells us that " Genuine . . . distinguishing occurs where a court accepts the expressed *ratio decidendi* of the earlier case . . . but finds that the case before it does not fall within the *ratio decidendi* because of some material differences of fact ". It is but a short step from this to saying that an instant case is distinguished from the precedent case if the *ratio decidendi* of the precedent case does not apply to the facts of the instant case. Such a proposition would eliminate all antithesis between the procedures of applying *rationes decidendi* and of distinguishing cases.

But what about the " authorities "? Lord Halsbury's dictum is a weak peg on which to hang a thesis of opposing " distinguishing " to " *ratio decidendi* ". Glanville Williams supplies none for his view. What is required is a comprehensive survey of cases. The impression I have is that neither Cross nor Glanville Williams has given an adequate account of the actual procedures used in distinguishing, and that some cases support one account and some the other. It is not possible here to justify that impression. It is, however, instructive both in relation to the comparison of the two procedures of " distinguishing " and " *ratio decidendi* ", and to their relation with the problem of analogical extension, to look at a case previously cited, which was referred to by Cross in his account of applying cases.

In *Re House Property and Investment, Ltd.*[6] the two techniques of distinguishing and determining the *ratio decidendi* are pursued by the same judge in one judgment. A landlord leased shops to L, who assigned the lease to H, who went into voluntary liquidation. In the course of the winding up H assigned the lease to B. An assignor remains liable in English law on the covenant to pay rent. The landlord claimed that the liquidator should set aside funds to meet H's liability as assignor (sufficient, indeed, to pay every instalment of rent as it fell due). The authority on which he relied was *Elphinstone* v. *Monkland Iron and Coal*

Co.[8] Roxburgh J. said: " If it decides the point before me—in other words if I cannot distinguish that case from the present case—I conceive myself to be bound by it ". In it a lessee, who had purported to assign, went into voluntary liquidation, and the landlord, in effect, succeeded in having a sum set aside to meet the rent. In Scots law an assignor ceases after assignment to be liable to pay rent. The difference in law was for Roxburgh J. "a fundamental difference ". The purported assignment was invalid, and, consequently, the assignor remained liable, but his liability, unlike the liability of the assignor in the *House Property* case,[6] was a sole liability : there could not in Scots law be liability of both assignor and assignee. Accordingly, Roxburgh J. said of the *Elphinstone* case :[8] " I regard the case as of no authority whatever on what the position would have been if the decision had been that the old company [the purported assignors] and the new company [the purported assignees] were both liable ". The case was distinguished from the instant case.

Roxburgh J. then proceeded to consider whether, even though the *Elphinstone* case could be distinguished, he should extend it on the ground that the instant case was analogous. But this question was soon transformed into asking " ought I to follow some of the things that were said in the course of the speeches? " : and this question became one of considering whether the *dicta* were *obiter*. If they were *obiter* Roxburgh J. "was not willing to adopt" them. Apparently, therefore, if they formed part of the *ratio* he thought himself bound. The question arose thus : there being no valid assignment the lessee was liable to pay rent, but that was only a future liability, since it was to pay the future instalments, and it was a contingent liability since it would cease on assignment. The Court of Session had said that the landlord's claim to have funds set aside could not be made as of right because there was no present liability. This view was rejected in the House of Lords. Lord Herschell said : " If any liability existed . . . he was entitled to have provision made for it by the liquidators," and Lord Watson made it clear that " any liability " included "future or contingent liabilities ". The contention was that these *dicta* involved the generalisation that any landlord is entitled to have funds set aside in a liquidation to meet any future or contingent liabilities. This would cover the position in England of an assignor of a lease, and it was maintained that Roxburgh J. should apply that principle. But he rejected the contention. In the first place he resolved, what our author calls the " psychological problem " of what the *dicta* meant, by saying that they were not intended to apply " without any regard to the circumstances ", to cover cases other than those of " sole liability ". And, secondly, if they said anything more then they were " *obiter* ". No *ratio decidendi* in *Elphinstone's* case applied to the instant case.

---

[8] 1886 11 App. Cas. 332.

The consideration given in the past few pages to the analysis of aspects of the doctrine of precedent is evidence of the stimulating power of the author, which extends over a far wider range of topics than those selected by me. Nor as I have already said are those topics confined to analytical jurisprudence. Even this " review " must have an end, and I would, in conclusion, support the proposal suggested by the author in his conclusions, that statutory power should be given to the House of Lords to overrule its past decisions.[9] The value of this book can indeed be assessed by the impressive manner in which the author marshals arguments and authorities in support of his proposal. His empirical realism is shown by his recognition of the fact that the adoption of the practice might not make much difference in practice, and his sense of values by his appreciation of the greater need for a partnership between courts and legislature with regard to statute law than for changes in the doctrine of precedent. Throughout, the book is informed by a spirit of reasoned discussion and broad perspectives. The future of our legal system will perhaps be most influenced by the education of lawyers and citizens. The author has made a notable contribution to law as a medium of liberal education, which is one of the aims of the Clarendon Law Series.

---

[9] [The power was assumed by the House in 1966; Practice Statement (H.L.) (Judicial Prceedent), [1966] 1 W.L.R. 1234. Ed.].

2

Address to Queen's University Belfast Matriculation Students, 1955*

This afternoon we observe the ceremony of incorporation of a new body of students into our fellowship of learning. This is what is meant by matriculation into a university. A university is a fellowship of those dedicated to searching for and guarding the knowledge that our ancestors have gained for us, to researching into that knowledge to free it from error and researching around the universe to extend the boundaries of knowledge, conscious of a duty to transmit our learning to posterity. Through the ceremony of matriculation we acquire that status of students in the university which is the first and permanent degree therein, making it possible for the university to be both a hierarchy and a fellowship of equals. Many of you will proceed to higher degrees which have a transitory nature. The status and the degree of bachelor is lost when he becomes a master; mastery ends when a doctorate is obtained. But we always remain students. You enter a republic as full and adult citizens. However you may differ in innate character or personal attainment, whether or no you are university scholars, whether or no you are champions in sport—and we are very proud that there are such among you—you are equals in this republic of learning. You are equal with your contemporary fellow-students of staff and class, of lecture room bench and lecture room rostrum, of women's hall, students' union, and academic " front ". You are, moreover, equal with those who have gone before, and not only of Queen's. You are of the company of the great minds of all the ages; and it is primarily with them, and only secondarily with us, that you should live what is essentially the life of a university, the reasoned discussion of man's perennial problems.

You may have already observed that in our entrance hall the window brings to the mind, that it may perdure in the memory, the lesson that Queen's men and Queen's women are sons and daughters of an *alma mater,* herself the servant of an ancient and everlasting republic. The light shines through and makes visible symbols of the

---

* Hitherto unpublished.

qualities which Plato in his *Republic* taught were the elements of the true society which makes real the true nature of man—qualities of courage, temperance, wisdom and justice. The republic of learning derives so much from Plato's *Republic* that a modern judge could describe a university as a continuing Socratic dialogue. It is well for us to remember that if wisdom is to be respected and justice to reign we must serve them with all our powers of courage and temperance.

We are the heirs of many ages. The torch lit in Greece by whose light men sought for the justice in laws served to kindle flames in which the Republic of France was born. From their light we see that fellowship and equality are joined with liberty. Academic freedom is a precious thing: it is the freedom to reach the highest by universal and unrestricted inquiry into the most profound. That freedom is yours. It is for the Arts student to inquire not only into man's history and destiny, his glory and his failure—it is for him to consider the character of the spiritual triumph of man in the realm of science. It is for the student of science not only to consider the nature of science, but also to seek understanding of the arduous enterprise of philosophical endeavour. Yet freedom without responsibility is freedom betrayed— it is the licence of beasts, not the liberty of man. Yours is the responsibility for the welfare of Queen's, for each university renews its life through its young men and women. Above all, yours is the responsibility for your education, for the sharpening of critical faculties, for the development of powers of judgment—the responsibility to array yourselves in the vestments of science and philosophy that you may live the life of reason, not alone in the pursuit of your particular discipline, but in all your doings for all time. Here in the company of fellow students, with the many facilities of libraries and laboratories, you will find aid and comfort in your effort—but strength of mind and purpose will be fully tested in that effort.

Freedom brings with it not only responsibility but, too often and too late, remorse for ill-used responsibility. Evil, and temptation to evil, are not banished by the invocation even of a vice-chancellor. You will find much that is wrong within the walls of a university. I believe, and I hope, that less moral sin exists here than outside—but you will need all your courage and restraint to resist what there is. I refer to one, perhaps mean, type of immorality, because it comes closer to intellectual sin, in which I can claim to be doubly expert. The stealing of library books is surely *trahison des clercs,* the betrayal of all for which a university stands—not only to be avoided by each of you, but which each of you should suppress in others. Intellectual sin too is mortal, both pride and sloth. Intellectual arrogance and snobbery are the easier to overcome—they are the mark of the half-educated—humility is the badge of the scholar. But intellectual sloth is insidious—the temptations are often subtle, the betraying shrewdness mocking the voice of reason with a cry of practicality. It can readily be seen that the exclusive use of cram books and lecture notes is like reading the classics out of picture comics, but from all quarters will come suggestions for the avoiding of hard reading and hard questioning. Our examination system with its apparent premium on learning by rote is perhaps the greatest seducer from mental vigour. There are, however, examiners who look for understanding not memory. To learn merely the ideas of others is to shirk the task of solving problems for oneself. To repeat the ideas of others without full understanding is like putting down, as your answers to sums, those culled from the back of the arithmetic book.

I trust that I have not overstressed the gloomy side of university life. May it be to you like the dark side of the moon—inferred but unseen. There is all the fun of the fair side of the world in a university. Somehow or other you must determine for yourselves how you will balance what, in our polysyllabic fashion, we call intra- and extra-curricular activity. This would be a poorer university if there were no games or student societies, and each student is poorer who does not play his part in them. In them you will not only find relaxation from, and refreshment for, more narrowly termed academic work—you will also find that cultural and intellectual development take place in such activities. But the fun is not only on playing field or in society debate: within the classroom and the laboratory there is both intellectual enjoyment and spiritual excitement, belonging to the adventure of ideas, which afford refreshment for the whole adventure of life.

I come to the conclusion of this part of the ceremony of matriculation: " *O ceremony, show me but thy worth* ". This ceremony is a formal and outward act of entry into a university. Perhaps little is gained through the formality of to-day beyond what was achieved by the more informal entry into your studies following interviews with deans and advisers of studies. It is certain that nothing can be gained by the outward show of this goodly company unless there is an inward act of dedication to the mission of universities made by each of you in the private retreat of conscience. In the faith that you are " highly resolved " to pursue our corporate purpose I add my sincere welcome of you to the Queen's University of Belfast. I trust that your days here will be days of gladness and fulfilment, and that in the wider world there will be for you many years of rich and rewarding achievement. Here, and in the community of which we are part, may you always be, as sons and daughters of this University, witnesses to the value of the life of the intellect. Along that way of life we all may walk with " *modest stillness and humility* ", but ever uprightly and with proper pride.

3

Edmund Burke and the Natural Law*

Most readers of this journal are presumably aware of two connected doctrines, one philosophical and one educational. The philosophical doctrine asserts that there is a unity, at least of method, between the natural sciences and the social sciences. The educational doctrine calls for greater movement across those artificial frontiers of the various disciplines which have resulted from pedagogical wars and peace treaties. The present work invokes both these doctrines. A professor of English has written a book of more than three hundred pages on a great literary figure,[1] with less than fifty words devoted to the style of writing.[2] His subject matter is Burke's political philosophy, which may be epitomised by saying that the principles of social control must not be divorced from the facts of social life. This did not make him an opponent of natural law; on the contrary, he was a supporter, the unity of the natural and the social sciences being part of the age-old tradition of natural law.

The author appears to have had two main purposes in view in writing this book. The major part of the book is devoted to a demonstration of where Burke stands in relation to the theory of natural law: this is the significance of the title. The thesis formulated in the nineteenth century proclaimed Burke as an opponent of natural law beliefs: this was based on his empirical approach to political and social affairs. The author controverts this thesis. He shows that Burke was a steadfast supporter of the " classical " natural law theory—a theory calling for an empirical approach to the solution of particular problems. Earlier commentators, says our author,

---

* A review of *Edmund Burke and the Natural Law*, by Professor Peter J. Stanlis. It is reprinted from the Natural Law *Forum*, vol. 6, 1961, by kind permission.

[1] Much of what Burke wrote is in his speeches. He is often described as an orator, and his orations had contemporary as well as later influence. But they emptied the House of Commons: they appeal to the eye and the mind more than to the ear and the heart. Lawyers are, of course, accustomed to spoken writing: in England the ritual of reading written judgments is still practised.

[2] STANLIS, *Edmund Burke and the Natural Law* 229. Where no other reference is given, a page reference is to the work being reviewed. References to quotations from Burke are given as they are presented by the author. He does not, however, provide a complete bibliography of Burke's own writings, with the result that one cannot be certain of the edition he uses for his quotations.

23

sensed the validity and profundity of his answers to man's eternal problems concerning the uses of power, the rule of law, and the moral and prudent means of achieving good order, civil liberty, and social justice, [but they] did not recognise the vital element of the Natural Law in Burke's political philosophy.[3]

The other purpose of the author, to the statement of which little space is given, but which is implicit throughout the book, has coordinate stature by reason of its importance. The author maintains the "vocation" of the present age for the theory of natural law. Even many supporters of its many doctrines may have thought that the greatest achievements have lain in the past, and that the theory no longer has any vital significance. Maine thought that natural law died in giving birth to international law. Our author himself says " with the triumph of the American and French revolutions the Natural Law at once achieved its greatest practical significance in modern affairs, and lost its hold upon the minds of men ".[4] But he has no doubt of the contemporary need for the theory or of its further victories: " If the commonwealth of Christian Europe is to survive and form the ethical norms of civilisation throughout the world, all men, but particularly Americans, will have to learn the great lessons of Burke's political philosophy." One of these lessons is that Burke teaches us the vital role played in human affairs by the classical natural law theory.

It is, of course, a commonplace that the term "natural law" covers many different doctrines. The difference between "classical" natural law and later versions has already been made by saying that Burke supported the "classical" doctrine. An analysis of what the differences are between the various theories is, of course, involved in the exposition of Burke's attitude. It is also involved in that revival of natural law theory which has been so marked a feature of juristic thought throughout this century. The revival began in Europe and spread to the United States.[5] Signs of more widespread acceptance of the theory in the United Kingdom exist, and it is noteworthy that in his address to the American Bar Association in 1957 the Lord Chancellor of Great Britain declared his adherence to the view that the common law demonstrated the validity of natural law beliefs.[6] The account which modern natural law lawyers give of the failure of the nineteenth century criticism is accepted by Professor Stanlis. The assault of the positivists was concentrated on the doctrines of natural law expounded in the seventeenth and eighteenth centuries by writers like Wolff and

---

[3] *Id.* at 247.

[4] *Id.* at 13.

[5] The titles of the following works are significant in this respect: Charmont, *La Renaissance du Droit Naturel* (1910); Haines, *Revival of Natural Law Concepts* (1930).

[6] Referring to the doctrine of the law of nature as "one of the noblest conceptions in the history of jurisprudence," the Lord Chancellor added: "Our two nations socially and legally are highly evolved, and the law of nature is so firmly embedded in our jurisprudence that it only occasionally shows above the surface." *The Times* (London), July 25, 1957.

Pufendorf and the proponents of natural rights. These doctrines, however, diverged in essential respects from older doctrines of natural law, and in particular from those of Aristotle and St. Thomas, which are regarded as forming the " classical " natural law. The positivist criticism, in so far as it had validity, was directed to the divergences of the later theories. Thus the classical natural law emerged unscathed from the fire of the nineteenth century. It is not so much that, in Gilson's phrase, natural law once again buried its undertakers,[7] but that the nineteenth century writers of the obituary notices mistook the identity of the corpse.[8] Later writers have sought to exclude the nineteenth century's victim from the family of natural law by calling it " ideal " law.[9] But in the nineteenth century " ideal law " was mistaken for natural law. Burke's criticism of the natural law doctrine of his age was concerned with its abstract and absolute character, i.e., its " ideal law " characteristics. Not only is this criticism logically consistent with support of classical natural law doctrine, but, as our author shows, express support for the classical doctrine is to be found widespread throughout Burke's writings. It was the positivism of his commentators which led to their regarding him an an opponent instead of a supporter of natural law.

As a background to his examination of Burke, Stanlis provides an introductory sketch of natural law theory. This account is derived from recent Catholic writers, and presents the " classical " natural law in a theological garb with dogmatic and rigid principles. The result is to obscure the basic distinction between " ideal law " and natural law, and to present a doctrine to which it is doubtful whether Burke would subscribe. Yet in his commentary on Burke's writings our author

---

[7] Lord Kilmuir in his address to the American Bar Association quoted Horace for this thesis: *Naturam furca, expellas tamen usque recurret.*

[8] Rommen points out that the victim of the nineteenth century had been the aggressor who disparaged the traditional doctrine. " From the time of Pufendorf fun began to be poked at the ' fancies of the Scholastics.' From here on, an anti-Aristotelian nominalism became, expressly or tacitly, the basis of philosophy . . . Indeed the same failure to understand tradition then led the nineteenth century to assume that, by refuting this natural law doctrine of the seventeenth and eighteenth centuries, it had overthrown the natural law with its philosophical tradition of over two thousand years." *The Natural Law* 82 (transl. Hanley, 1947).

[9] "Pour les philosophes du xviiie siecle le substantif ' droit ' avait la même signification dans les deux expressions ' droit positif ' et ' droit naturel,' savoir un système complet des normes destinées a regir les rapports sociaux . . . la notion d'un droit idéal est parfaitement plausible; seulement, ce n'est pas le droit naturel." RENARD, *Le Droit, L'Ordre et La Raison* 134 (1927). In this brilliant, but not widely known, work Renard ascribes the distinction between natural law and ideal law to Gèny. Even in the first edition (1899) of his *Mèthode d'Interprétation*, Gèny describes the error of the schools of the 17th and 18th centuries. " Portant de l'idée de la puissance absolue de la raison humaine, par découvrir, dans leurs principes comme dans leurs détails, les lois assignées a notre nature, l'École du Droit naturel pretendait constituer, par les seules forces de la pensée, un système complet de droit absolu, immuable, immediatement et universellement applicable, que le législateur n'eût qu' à mettre en formules" (p. 474). But he calls the writers " L'École du Droit naturel." He acknowledges for this account his indebtedness to Stammler. In the latter's *Rechtsphilosophie* (1921), this notion of a detailed blueprint of laws ready for enactment, elaborated by pure reason, is described as *Idealrecht* and condemned as fallacious. " Es ist wohl versuchtworden gegenuber dem geschichtslich gewordenen Recht . . . ein volkommenes Gesetzbuch mit Gültigkeit für alle Völker und Zeiten auszuführen. Das ist unmoglich." (Art. 4).

correctly states the basic distinction between the absoluteness of ideal laws and the flexibility of the natural law to which Burke subscribes. The classical natural law insists on full operation being given to human experience and refuses to attribute " divine " authority to the results of human reason. But before a fuller examination is given of natural law theory it is advisable to deal first with our author's full examination of Burke's contribution to legal philosophy.

It has to be borne in mind that Burke did not set out to expound a philosophy of law in abstract systematic fashion.[10] He did reflect deeply on the problems of government, but his views are expressed in relation to the political issues of his time. It is in the course of " propaganda " about the American and the French Revolutions, and about the conditions which led to the Irish Rebellion of 1798, that he expresses his opinions about natural law and natural rights. Nevertheless our author is able to demonstrate their coherence as deriving from a consistent philosophy. That Burke favoured the American and Irish " rebels ", but came to oppose those who seized political power in France, is to be explained not by the fact that Irish and Americans fought to throw off an " alien " yoke while the French Revolution had no such element, but by reference to the principles of government espoused by those who rebelled.[11] It is indeed this consideration of general principles in relation to specific practical affairs and his insistence that sound principles take account of changing circumstances which are Burke's distinction as a philosopher, and which have led many mistakenly to characterise him as an empiricist.[12] These doctrines are, however, not only consistent with natural law, but mark Burke as a supporter of that theory. Both Plato and Aristotle insist on the impossibility of dealing with political matters without taking all the circumstances into account.[13]

---

[10] His *Reflections on the French Revolution* is, of course, the nearest approach to a treatise on political theory.

[11] The unsuccessful rebellion of 1798 inspired another member of Trinity College, Dublin (Burke's college), James Kells Ingram, to write the poem, called by its first line, " Who fears to speak of ninety-eight?" Undergraduates of Trinity interrupted the recitation of the poem by interjecting at the end of that first line: " The author! " Burke sympathised with the opening stages of the French Revolution, but his change of attitude was in no way due to a timid lapse into conventionality.

[12] Thus HALÉVY, *The Growth of Philosophic Radicalism* 103 (Beacon ed.) : " To sum up, Burke's political philosophy is an empiricism." Halèvy makes Burke's conservatism logically dependent on his empiricism: " This essentially empirical and therefore conservative political philosophy" (p. 159). A " philosophy of experience " is made one which asserts: " the duration whether of an idea or an institution, its mere persistence through time, is a presumption in favour of that idea or institution."

[13] It is, of course, John Wild who has stressed so much Plato's attitude as that of the " practical philosopher." *Plato's Theory of Man* 11. He emphasises the " synthetic practical nature of Plato's approach " by elaborating Plato's distinction between what we now call " technology " and " technique." Philosophical understanding does not separate the theoretical from the practical. The handling of practical details in a blind and routine fashion is an " empiricism " to be avoided. On the other hand, " empeiria " is essential: " The way to guiding knowledge is through practice or direct experience with the matter itself." *Id.* at 52. Theory must be integrated with practice. The philosopher-king would not need laws, because these might limit him in his consideration of all the circumstances.

It is perhaps the absence of any work specifically entitled as one on
philosophy of law (or employing one of the many synonyms of that
phrase) which has led to the exclusion of Burke from the list of jurists
dealt with by expositors of legal philosophy.   Neither Berolzheimer in
The World's Legal Philosophies nor Stone in his encyclopaedic *Province
and Function of Law* deals with Burke.   He is ignored by Austin, and
in Maine's few references he is regarded as a rhetorician.   Allen in a
short statement presents the " orthodox " view of Burke as an empiricist
and traditionalist.   He is regarded as the leader of a revolt against
rationalism, one who " anticipates the historical school of the nineteenth
century ".[14]   Gurvitch likewise says in a description, which the present
work seeks to correct, " The reaction of the nineteenth century against
natural law formulae is traceable ultimately to Edmund Burke."[15]
Considering myself as a representative sample, I say that the ordinary
British lawyer would think of Burke, despite his political association
with Fox, as the philosopher of conservatism : not the new English
" conservatism " which has assumed the liberal doctrine of the limited
authority of the state, confining its powers to the maintenance of order
and the protection of property, but the older theory which accepted the
Aristotelian doctrine that the end of the state is the promotion of the
good life.   Indeed, Burke's own statement to this effect is one which
" everybody knows ":[16] " Society is not a partnership in things sub-
servient only to the gross animal existence of a temporary and perishable
nature.   It is a partnership in all science; a partnership in all arts; a
partnership in every virtue and in all perfection."[17]   The English
academic lawyer is also acquainted with Burke's panegyric about the
study of law, and I must confess to misquoting it in the form " Law
is . . . the first and noblest of human sciences: a science which does
more to quicken and invigorate the understanding than all other kinds
of learning put together."[18]

It is to the political scientists that one must turn for a discussion
of Burke's views and a recognition of his importance.   But political
science is today dominated by positivism,[19] and its writers have gener-

[14] *Law in the Making* 14 (1st ed., 1927).
[15] STANLIS 5. In the first article directly on natural law in the *Modern Law Reviews* there
is no reference to Burke. Chloros, *What is Natural Law*, 21, *Modern Law Review* 609 (1958).
[16] " Everyone knows " also Burke's repudiation of the view that a member of parliament
is but a delegate elected to express the views of his electors. (Expressed in his address to
his Bristol constituents.)
[17] The passage from which the above is an extract is set out at length at p. 72 and
at p. 207. On the latter occasion Stanlis says the passage has been much misunderstood,
since some commentators have regarded it as showing Burke's adherence to a " social
contract " doctrine. This, however, is not the only passage which may be cited as showing
Burke's support for some " social contract ". See HALÉVY, *op. cit. supra* note 12, at 158.
[18] The passage is quoted correctly at p. 35. I have suppressed (law is) " one of " (the
first) and the conclusion, " But it is not apt to open and liberate the mind exactly in the
same proportion."
[19] BERNARD CRICK seeks to demonstrate this for the United States in his *American
Science of Politics* (1959), but it is also true for the United Kingdom, though here " scientism "
may not be so widespread.

C

ally mistaken the significance of his views. A representative is Sabine, author of perhaps the most widely read undergraduate textbook on both sides of the Atlantic, viz., *A History of Political Theory*. He portrays Burke as a disciple of Hume, denying " that social institutions depend on reason and nature, and far more than Hume he reversed the scheme of values implied by the system of natural law ".[20] Our author traces this assessment of Burke back to his earliest expositors, Buckle and Morley, who saw him as an advocate of expediency and utility. As has already been stated, the aim of the present work is to re-assess Burke's views, and to present him as one who fully accepted " the sovereignty of natural law ".[21]

It is not possible for me to summarise adequately the elaborate arguments of Stanlis. He examines Burke's views from many aspects, and supports his contentions by a great many quotations. I shall not follow the plan of his treatment. Instead I posit three main theses as underlying Burke's adherence to a theory of natural law, and I shall endeavour to show his support of these propositions. I shall not, however, consider the many problems involved in an evaluation of the validity of the propositions. The theses are as follows:

(1) There are objective principles for the government of societies which ought to be observed by those who have political authority. A corollary to this is that the laws of a state are not justified solely by the authority of the lawmakers: it is the nature of human societies, not the will of the sovereign, which justifies the action of those possessed of power. There is an assumption, of course, that the concepts of " ought " and " justify " are meaningful.

(2) The principles of government are to be discussed by reason reflecting on experience of the nature of men in society. An alternative formulation is that the principles are not the product of quasi-mathematical intuition: such intuition creates but speculative hypotheses; and however much their authors claim that they are rational, they remain dogmatic abstractions There are, of course, problems about the nature of reason.

(3) The principles of government are not simple prescriptions which can be applied to the determination of human affairs *more geometrico;* in their application they call for that prudence which requires human judgment as to the effect of the multiplicity of circumstances on the operation of principles. This proposition involves perhaps more philosophic problems than the others, extending to the character of scientific laws and metaphysical doctrines, involving considerations like the distinction between " pragmatism " and utility.[22] It is hoped, however, that a discussion which does not consider all those problems will not be too obscure.

---

[20] GEORGE H. SABINE, *A History of Political Theory* 614 (New York, 1937). (STANLIS 34.)

[21] This phrase is the title of the last chapter.

[22] The theories of Körner (in *Conceptual Thinking*) about the nature of rules and metaphysical and scientific directives based on his doctrine of " interpretative levels " seem particularly relevant. The theories cannot, however, be simply stated: the book is a tightly knit argument involving many new original ideas. The chapters which deal with moral rules and metaphysical directives (ch. 29 and 30) cannot be detached from the rest of the book.

The third proposition merits the fuller consideration, quite apart from the philosophical involvement. It is the doctrine which perhaps most clearly serves as a criterion for distinguishing the classical natural law from the eighteenth century ideal law. It is the proposition which is most fully elaborated by Burke. It is his insistence on prudence which has probably led to the misstatement that his belief was in expediency and utility. But comment on the first two propositions is also called for.

The first proposition asserts the objectivity of principles. This is to be distinguished from the assertion of the universal acceptance of principles. But the assertion that there are principles universally applicable does imply belief in the objectivity of principles. Burke would not have accepted the relativism thus described by Robert Bridges:

> Ask what is reasonable! See how time and clime
> Conform mind more than body in their environment;
> What then and there was Reason, is here and now absurd;[23]

for Burke's own view was more objective:

> Against this geographical morality [by which the duties of men are not to be governed by their relations to one another but by climates] I do protest . . . the laws of morality are the same everywhere; and actions that are stamped with the character of peculation, extortion, oppression, and barbarity in England, are so in Asia, and the world over.[24]

He rejects the positivism to be found in some versions of the imperative theory of law.[25] This is what he says in condemnation of the misgovernment of Ireland:

> It would be hard to point to any error more truly subversive of all the order and beauty, of all the peace and happiness, of human society than the position that any body of men have a right to make what laws they please; or that laws can derive any authority from their institution merely and independent of the quality of the subject-matter.[26]

---

[23] *The Testament of Beauty*, lines 465-7. The conformity of varying detailed rules and particular institutions with common principles is explained by Burke's third proposition. The explanation goes back, of course, to Book V of the *Nichomachean Ethics*.

[24] *Speech Against Warren Hastings*, in 4 SPEECHES 34 (STANLIS 63).

[25] Insofar as Austin was merely setting out characteristics by which " rules " could be recognised as being " laws " (i.e., providing an ostensible definition in Bassin's use of that phrase, in DAVID HUME 133, Penguin ed.), he is not a positivist. Rommen explains thus: [According to moderate positivism] " law is not something pertaining to reason, but mere actual will in the psychological sense. It does not depend upon the essential being of things or upon the nature of the case, which L. von Baer, following here the Anglo-Saxon judicial tradition, designated as the basis of law." *The Natural Law* 129 (St. Louis, 1947). Stanlis shows that Burke was much influenced through his study of English law by the " Anglo-Saxon judicial tradition." Austin, of course, was a utilitarian influenced, however, by Hobbes's views that " authority " was justified as serving the ideal of peace and order, and laws as ensuring certainty.

[26] *Tract on Popery Laws* 21 (STANLIS 43).

Applied to the judicial process the doctrine of the first proposition produces this noteworthy statement of the declaratory theory:

> If the judgment makes the law, and not the law directs the judgment, it is impossible that there should be such a thing as an illegal judgment given . . . [this] is to corrupt judicature into legislature.[27]

The second of Burke's theses, viz., that principles are to be derived by reflection on experience, underlies much of his attack on the "natural rights" doctrine of his age. This he regarded as based on arbitrary fancy, not grounded on human nature. He was not an opponent of the "real rights" of man, but of what he called the "pretended rights".[28] These latter, he said, were created by abstract "human reasonings", not tested by the facts of "human nature", facts which were not, in his view, in accord with a Procrustean doctrine of equal rights. "Government was . . . not to furnish out a spectacle of uniformity, to gratify the schemes of visionary politicians."[29] "Abstract principles of natural right . . . annihilated . . . natural rights."[30] The real natural rights were derived from reason tested by experience.

> I do not vilify theory and speculation—no, because that would be to vilify reason itself . . . No, whenever I speak against theory, I mean always a weak, erroneous, . . . or imperfect theory; and one of the ways of discovering that it is a false theory is by comparing it with practice.[31]

But experience points to relations which have objective existence. Burke emphasised the existence of duties as well as rights, and the following passage deals with the reality of duties. The first proposition that principles of government have objective existence is linked with the second, which says that it is man's reason and not his fancy which discerns those principles. They may be hypotheses, but they are not, as some moderns would have it, mere "postulates".

> We have obligations to mankind at large, which . . . arise from the relation of man to man, and the relation of man to God, which relations are not matters of choice . . . The instincts which give rise to this mysterious process of nature are not of our making. But out of physical causes, unknown to us,

---

[27] 1 *Speeches* 78 (STANLIS 52). Burke was speaking in the debate on Wilkes's right to be admitted to the House of Commons on election despite the existence of a conviction. The House of Commons in such a situation was, in Burke's view, a judicial assembly. (It has no independent lawmaking powers, being but a branch of the legislature.) Stanlis, however, sees in Burke's speech an expression of the view that even when sitting as a legislative body Parliament ought to proceed in accordance with "principles of law," conceived as being "the ethical code of Natural Law."

[28] "Far am I from denying theory . . . or from withholding in practice . . . the *real* rights of men." "The pretended rights of man . . . cannot be the rights of the people." (STANLIS 130.)

[29] *Letter to the Sheriffs of Bristol* 29 (STANLIS 105). The theme was the abstraction of the "unity of empire" on which it was sought to found identical institutions for all parts of the empire.

[30] 3 *Speeches* 476 (STANLIS 131).

[31] 3 *Speeches* 48 (STANLIS 103).

perhaps unknowable, arise moral duties, which, as we are able perfectly to comprehend, we are bound indispensably to perform.[32]

Just as the first thesis is linked with the second, so is the second linked with the third. The principles of government have to be tested by experience, and they have no vitality in isolation from the problems of human life to which they have to be applied. If they are considered in isolation from social realities " their abstract perfection is their practical defect ".[33] Principles indeed exist, must be sought for, and held to: "without the light of sound well-understood principles, all reasoning in politics, as in everything else, would be a confused jumble of particular facts and details, without a means of drawing out any sort of theoretical or practical conclusion ". But inherent in sound principles is a flexibility to provide for their effective operation: the function of principles is to be applied to varying circumstances. Burke emphasises again and again the need to consider different circumstances: " the statesman has a number of circumstances to combine with those general ideas. . . . Circumstances are infinite, are infinitely combined; are variable and transient; he who does not take them into account is not erroneous but stark mad."[34] It is for this reason, as Aristotle pointed out long ago, that uniformity of principles is consistent with many different political institutions, the " diversity of forms " as Burke terms it. " These metaphysical rights entering into common life, like rays of light which pierce into a dense medium, are by the laws of nature refracted from their straight line."[35] And " social and civil freedom, like all other things in common life, are variously mixed and modified, enjoyed in very different degrees, and shaped into an infinite diversity of forms, according to the temper and circumstance of every community ".[36] Burke is aware of the two variables which are involved in the handling of practical affairs. On the one hand, there are the different environments of societies, such as their climates and natural resources, their created wealth and institutions; on the other hand, there are, in addition to the qualities common to all men, the varying characteristics of different men.[37]

> It is our duty . . . to conform our government to the character and circumstances of the several people who composed this mighty and strangely diversified mass. I never was wild enough to conceive that one method would serve

---

[32] *New to the Old Whigs* 79 (STANLIS 78).

[33] *Reflections on the French Revolution* 332 (STANLIS 107).

[34] 4 *Speeches* 55 (STANLIS 109). The immediately preceding quotation is from this same source and page.

[35] *Reflections on the French Revolution* 334 (STANLIS 76).

[36] *Letter to the Sheriffs of Bristol* 25 (STANLIS 106).

[37] Stanlis describes as the " touchstone " of all Burke's political theory the following test: " does it suit his nature in general? does it suit his nature as modified by his habits?" 3 SPEECHES 48 (STANLIS 103).

for the whole; that the natives of Hindostan and those of Virginia could be ordered in the same manner.[38]

The legislators . . . had to do with men, and they were obliged to study human nature. They had to do with citizens, and they were obliged to study the effects of those habits which are communicated by the circumstances of human life. . . . thence arose many diversities amongst men, according to their birth, their education, their professions, the period of their lives, their residence in towns or in the country, their several ways of acquiring and fixing property . . . all of which rendered them as it were so many different species of animals . . . [they] attended to the different kinds of citizens, and combined them into one commonwealth.[39]

It is not surprising that Burke presents no clear analysis of the manner in which principles are related to circumstances. He insists on a distinction between mathematical principles and political principles.

The lines of morality are not like ideal lines of mathematics. They are broad and deep as well as long. They admit of exceptions; they demand modifications. These exceptions and modifications are not made by the process of logic, but by the rules of prudence. Prudence is not only the first in rank of the virtues political and moral, but she is the director, the regulator, the standard of them all.[40]

Political principles are not applied by mere processes of deductive logic like those of mathematics. "In politics the most fallacious of all things was geometrical demonstration."[41] The thought behind this appears to be that political principles in their formulation appear as abstract propositions, which in their abstraction are capable of application to varieties of particulars. This is, of course, the character of mathematical propositions: Pythagoras demonstrated that the proposition about the square on the hypotenuse did not apply only to the well-known triangles with sides in the ratio of 3 : 4 : 5 used in practical buildings, but to right-angled triangles of all ratios. Euclid's theorems apply to figures of all sizes and shapes, without any modifications or exceptions. But when political principles come to be applied to actual affairs then Burke appears to say that account has to be taken of factors not contained in the principles: account has to be taken of prudence which operates *ab extra,* and which is superior to the principles, for it controls their application.

A fuller examination of Burke's writings shows, however, that he is not committed to such a view. Indeed he presents the contrary view of regarding true political principles as embodying in themselves a reference to varying circumstances. It is the false principles on which pretended natural rights are founded which are expressed in uncondi-

---

[38] *Letter to the Sheriffs of Bristol* 27 (STANLIS 105).

[39] *Reflections on the French Revolution* 454 (STANLIS 107, 108).

[40] *New to the Old Whigs* 16 (STANLIS 115).

[41] *Reflections on the French Revolution* 444 (STANLIS 76).

tional and indefeasible form:[42] they are described as "metaphysical abstractions" concerned with "metaphysical liberty and necessity". On the contrary, Burke affirms: "Nothing universal can be rationally affirmed on any moral or political subject. Pure metaphysical abstraction does not belong to these matters."[43] Thus, while Burke always supports freedom as a proper object of government, "The extreme of liberty (which is its real perfection) obtains nowhere, nor ought to obtain anywhere." If there were no restraints on liberty a common-sense view of human nature suggests that the exercise of freedom for social impulses would be imperilled by the licence afforded to anti-social impulses. Thus Burke avers: "Liberty . . . must be limited in order to be possessed,"[44] and again, "In a sense the restraints on men, as well as their liberties, are to be reckoned among their rights."[45] Any absolute right, whether of kings or subjects, may do social harm: real rights are not absolute.

> You can hardly state to me a case to which legislature is the most confessedly competent, in which, if the rules of benignity and prudence are not observed, the most mischievous and oppressive things may not be done. So that after all, it is a moral and virtuous discretion, and not any abstract theory of right, which keeps governments faithful to their ends.[46]

The point is that wise principles are so formulated that those who apply them have constantly in mind the policy to be served by them, which may be frustrated by mechanical application to varying circumstances. The formulation of a principle may for the sake of convenience or simplicity be in unconditional terms, but those who come to apply such a principle will seek for the implied conditions: this is no more than the Aristotelian doctrine restated by St. Paul when he said: "The

---

[42] Hart in his essay on *Ascription of Responsibility and Rights* has shown the importance of adequate consideration being given to the nature of what he calls "defeasible concepts." In law there are many situations in which certain factors give rise to particular legal relations *unless* other unspecified factors are present. For example, an exchange of promises gives rise to a contract *unless* there is fraud or illegality or some other circumstance recognised as entitling the court to refuse to enforce a promise. In Hart's apt language, the notion of a contract is a defeasible concept. As he points out, defeasible concepts exist outside the law. *Logic and Language* 147 *et seq.* (First Series, ed. Flew.)

[43] *New to the Old Whigs* 16 (STANLIS 115).

[44] *Letter to the Sheriffs of Bristol* 30 (STANLIS 106). The immediately preceding quotation is from the same source and page.

[45] *Reflections on the French Revolution* 333 (STANLIS 107).

[46] 4 *Speeches* 55 (STANLIS 115).
The nature and operation of rules which are not absolute in their application have recently been the subject of fuller study by logicians and philosophers. Ross discusses them under the terminology of "*prima facie* duties." THE RIGHT AND THE GOOD 19 *et seq.* Edel calls them "phase rules." *Ethical Judgment* 42 *et seq.* Toulmin deals with them in connection with the theories of probability, and his distinction between "analytical" and "substantial" arguments. *The Uses of Argument* 141 *et seq.* Toulmin's work is devoted to the theme that logicians have universally looked at all reasoning *more geometrico*, and that legal reasoning furnishes a more useful basis for the logical examination of the actual reasoning employed in human affairs.

letter killeth but the spirit giveth life." As our author points out,[47] Burke's thought is essentially similar to St. Thomas's doctrine of "determinatio". Indeed St. Thomas himself uses the notion of prudence, under the name of *sapientia*.

According to St. Thomas the utility of principles which are not of universal application lies in their application to "the majority of cases". But how is one to determine which is the ordinary and which the exceptional case? Must one go all the way with Holmes when he said : "General propositions do not decide concrete cases. The decision will depend on a judgment or intuition more subtle than any articulate major premise"?[48] His term "judgment" on which decision depends is equivalent to Burke's "prudence". Are both to be equated with "intuition", and opposed in consequence to "reason"? This certainly would contradict the first two theses which I have submitted Burke upheld. The solution I have suggested above in terms of policy directives needs much more refinement. Perhaps that analysis may come by considering not pure mathematics but physics; confusion between the two is common though it was stigmatised by St. Thomas as "a sin against the intellect". Nor, of course, should engineering be neglected, particularly when regard is had to the slogan of "social engineering". The physicist and the engineer may use mathematical models, but their principles do not neglect the varying conditions of the real world. The laws of motion in a frictionless model are not the principles of motion in the real world where friction exists. Motion on an inclined plane, to take a simple case, is based on "principles" of gravity and friction. The engineer may be able to compute the resultant of forces which he knows, but he must use "prudence" in dealing with situations where precise knowledge is wanting. The lawyer is required to use prudence because of the existence of competing principles[49] and because he must

---

[47] STANLIS 114. He draws attention to the distinction between speculative and practical reason drawn by Aristotle and adopted by St. Thomas, and says "in contingent matters and details there can be no general or necessary laws." The Thomistic language of "*determinatio*" is used in *Summa Theologica* (Prima Secundae Qu. 95. 2) in connection with the derivation of human law from natural law. But the same idea is used in Qu. 94. 4 in the application of natural law to particular cases. In considering the relation of principles of natural law to human behaviour it must, of course, be remembered that they are prescriptive not descriptive. The existence of uniform principles of natural law is not controverted by differences in human practices (i) because of the doctrine of *determinatio* quoted by Stanlis. "The determination of those things that are just must needs be different according to the differing states of mankind" ; (ii) because practices may be in breach of the principles of natural law. That people ought not to drink alcohol is not controverted by the fact that they do: indeed the "proof" of the normative proposition may be based on the observation of the empiric practice.

[48] *Lochner* v. *U.S.* 198 U.S. 45 at 76.

[49] In the light of the knowledge of competing principles we may obtain fuller understanding of Burke's statement: "But as the liberties and the restrictions vary with times and circumstances, and admit of infinite modifications, they cannot be settled upon any abstract rule." *Reflection on the French Revolutions* 333 (STANLIS 107).
    Liberties are not absolute, because the principles that give rise to them have so to be framed as not to contradict the principles which give rise to the restrictions; and *vice versa*. The principle of freedom of contract has to be stated so as to allow scope for the operation of the principle that laws bind without consent. The principle of freedom of action has

proceed qualitatively in the absence of the precise quantitative relations which are so often available to the physical technologist.[50]

The three theses which have been discussed are adequate to establish Burke's adherence to a belief in natural law. But they serve as an introduction also to many controversies which have been associated with that phrase. There are diverse theories which have been called by that name whose very existence has led to a denial of the central thesis of all " properly " called theories of natural law, viz., that there are objective principles of government. Instead of the various theories being regarded as different attempts to attain the objectivity of the principles, different approximations thereto, they have been considered as being essentially but historically conditioned ideologies.[51] The existence of a " classical " natural law theory associated with Aristotle

---

to be stated so as to allow scope for the operation of the principle that persons who suffer harm may receive compensation. Difficulties of formulating principles fully are paralleled by difficulties of decision in particular cases where principles appear to compete with each other for application. It may be possible to articulate the major premises, and yet still have to decide whether a premise of liberty or a premise of restriction applies. Folk wisdom provides us with many examples of principles couched in unconditional forms so that they appear to be in competition at least in borderline cases. " Look before you leap " is apparently contradicted by " He who hesitates is lost." But the real problem is to decide in a particular case how much looking amounts to hesitation. " Many hands make light work " is not contradicted by " Too many cooks spoil the broth." The question is obviously, What is " too many " ? But even were the adjective " too " omitted, there would always remain the general problems of whether the cost of additional labour (in all its aspects, not merely those of wages) is balanced by extra productivity, and at what stage additional labour lowers productivity.

[50] In many crafts problems of where to draw the line are solved by " prudence ". We may take the homely example of the cook who decides by " judgment or intuition " how much salt will enrich the flavour and not spoil it. But, of course, quantitative recipes are being replaced by scientific formulas: the modern housewife uses a specified weight, not a pinch of salt. In the chemical industry precise conditions are prescribed for many operations. But even in manufacturing processes there are many situations where there are so many variables and unknowns that precise calculation is impossible: the judgment of the skilled worker is still required as well as the computer of the scientist. In the social sciences we operate, perhaps of necessity, with situations where there is great complexity and little exact knowledge of modes of interaction. We are compelled to act with prudence. But this is not a duty imposed *ab extra* on the operation of principles. It is a necessity arising from limitations of human knowledge and the requirement of human decision which is written into a fully formulated principle.

[51] Pound has asserted that what " in practice . . . usually goes by the name of natural law, is an idealised version of the positive law of the time and place." This he would have us call " positive natural law." See *Natural Natural Law and Positive Natural Law*, 68 LAW QUARTERLY REVIEW 330 (1952). Such " positive natural law " is clearly but an ideology. Pound, however, both in this essay and more clearly in his *Introduction to the Philosophy of Law*, asserts that the juristic theories of " natural natural law " are but responses to the problems of the time and place when and where they are formulated. This doctrine is one aspect of a nineteenth-century reaction of " history " to " philosophy " which has been thus summarized by Croce:

> historical thought has played a nasty trick on this respectable transcendental philosophy . . . the trick of turning it into history by interpreting all its concepts, doctrines, disputes, and even its disconsolate sceptical renunciations, as historical facts and affirmations, which arise out of certain requirements, and were thus partly satisfied and partly unsatisfied. *History as the Story of Liberty* 35.

It may be noted that this relativism is not inconsistent with objectivity. The needs of time and place, the requirements of historical conditions, are not subjective fantasies of the theorist: they are the particular circumstances to which the classical natural law theory requires that full consideration should be given.

and St. Thomas[52] opposed to an ideal law theory of the seventeenth and eighteenth centuries has already been considered to some extent. Some further attention needs to be given to the differences between the classical and later theories; the account previously given has ignored other versions which our author in places tends to support. Again, in recent years, the doctrine has been asserted both by opponents and supporters of natural law, that acceptance of natural law involves belief in the permeation of the rules and processes of positive law by principles of natural law.[53] While it is not appropriate to enlarge upon this debate in this review, it is worth-while to consider Burke's position in relation to it. Finally, some attention must be given to what may be considered a central issue. The principles of government, says the second proposition suggested as underlying Burke's views, are obtained by " reason reflecting on experience ". What is the nature of this process? What are the conclusions which are reached by it? Have we any assurances

---

[52] Stanlis in one place (p. 7) tells us " the most profound and all-inclusive statements of the Natural Law are probably those of Cicero and St. Thomas Aquinas. Cicero supplied the touchstone for the classical conception of Natural Law: St. Thomas supplied it for the Scholastics." This appears to me to attach undue importance to Cicero. He is not generally regarded as a creative thinker, but as an expositor of Greek Stoic thought modified by Platonic influence. (Stoic thought, of course, itself followed after Plato.) The origins of natural law thinking surely lie in the early Greek philosophers. The basis is the Socratic doctrine that there can be objective knowledge of justice. This is developed by Plato, and, of course, by Aristotle, who is the supreme authority for St. Thomas. Aristotle himself purports largely to expound established theory. A major part of the task undertaken by St. Thomas is the systematisation of Aristotelian thought and its reconciliation with Christian doctrine.

It should also be noted that St. Thomas was not generally regarded as the dominant scholastic philosopher until the nineteenth century. The scholastic philosophers had important differences. Stanlis writes usually as if God's reason and God's will need not be distinguished; but while St. Thomas emphasised reason, Scotus emphasised will.

[53] It is now a commonplace of realistic description of legal systems to note how widespread is the operation of ethical ideas. Many of the rules themselves direct the employment of such ideas through the use of ethical terms: the Rules of the Supreme Court of England often require the judge to do what is " just," and, as Pollock has observed, the words " just " and " justice " have not lost their ethical connotation even in a technical context. Even where the rules are not phrased in ethical language the nature of application very often compels the judge to exercise a discretion, and here his ethical notions may determine his choice. Again, " gaps in the law " require the formulation of a new legal rule, and a legislative process necessarily provides scope for ethics. Where statutes are ambiguously drawn there is a conceded gap, for the judge may have to select an interpretation which conforms to his notion of justice. (The dominant practice in England, however, permits this to be done only after it is discovered that the ambiguity cannot be resolved by recourse to the intention of Parliament.) Moreover, there is general agreement that large sections of the rules of positive law are just, and in the language of Justinian " consist of precepts belonging to natural law". *Institutes* ii. 4.

But granted this, it does not follow that there is not a basic conceptual distinction between the *is* and the *ought*. Certainly " classical natural law " does not accord with Fuller's account of natural law as " the view which denies the possibility of a rigid separation of the *is* and the *ought*, and which tolerates a confusion of them in legal discussion". *Law in Quest of Itself* 5. One of the functions of classical natural law is to criticise the ideas of justice actually utilised in the administration of justice. There can be no marriage between the *is* and the *ought* unifying them. The language of a temporary divorce between the *is* and the *ought* used by Llewellyn and McDougal, may be misleading. 50 YALE LAW JOURNAL 535. On the other hand, I do not accept the exaggerated conclusions drawn from what appears to me a triviality, viz., Hume's doctrine that the conclusion of the traditional analytical syllogism cannot contain an *ought* if none was found in the premises. Nevertheless, the establishment of an ethical proposition may involve the demonstration of facts. See also *infra* notes 74 and 76.

that we have thereby attained " eternal, unchangeable and universal " principles?[54]

The doctrine supported by our author as to the difference between the classical natural law and " modern " thought is professedly derived from the works of Leo Strauss.[55] Hobbes's philosophy, we are told, is the great dividing line between medieval and modern secular thought: his revolutionary break with the past, his destruction of the primacy of " law " or " reason " in favour of " power " or " will ", is the fountain head of revolutionary social thought.[56] The result was to produce a natural law creating rights reflecting the wills of selfish men seeking as much arbitrary power as they could attain, derived from men's private reason divorced from any theistic support, and dependent only on mathematical logic. It may be doubted, however, whether the revolution is quite as widespread as is suggested: whether all the writers of the " ideal law " school accepted all these notions, and whether the classical writers present a complete antithesis to them.

A difference between " natural law " and " natural rights " may be no more than one of language and aspect. Whereas " laws " are concerned with abstract possibilities of application, " rights " are concerned with the application of legal propositions to specific individuals. A law which forbids any person to inflict harm on any other person gives John Doe a right not to be injured.[57] The Bill of Rights derives as much from classical natural law as from later writing. If there be a substantial difference it must be found in the nature of the contents of the laws and rights.[58] Here, too, the view sometimes put forward that natural law looked to the common good, as appears in the Thomistic definition,[59] while natural rights are concerned with the welfare of

---

[54] It is worth stressing that the problem here posed is whether there are immutable principles from which varying rules may be derived by a process of "determination". It was only the eighteenth-century rationalists who thought that detailed rules, valid for all time and places, could be deduced with certitude from basic principles. Chloros's opening sentence in his article, *What is Natural Law*, 21 *Modern Law Review* 609, may be misleading. He says: "The traditional view of natural law is that it is a body of immutable rules superior to positive law," but he does not make any distinction in the article between " principles " and " rules ". Thomistic natural law distinguishes between first principles and secondary derivations therefrom. Only the first principles are claimed to have universality.

[55] STANLIS 16.

[56] *Id.* at 17.

[57] This is surely the essence of the theory of " rights " expounded by Hart in his inaugural lecture. *Definition and Theory in Jurisprudence*, 70 *Law Quarterly Review* 37 (1954).

[58] Hobbes, however, says: " Right consisteth in liberty to do, or to forbear: whereas law determineth and bindeth to one of them: so that law and right differ as much as obligation and liberty." D'Entrèves *Natural Law* 59 arrives at the generalisation that the modern theory of natural law was not, properly speaking, a theory of law at all. It was a theory of rights. It is going far to suggest that lawyers before Hohfeld were unaware of the link between rights and duties, or lost sight of the way in which *jus* (droit subjectif) depended on *lex* (droit objectif).

[59] " *Rationis ordinatio ad bonum commune.*"

individuals, is an inadequate distinction. The classical writers were
well aware that the common good is the good of individuals, and the
modern writers are aware that the welfare of individuals depends on
limitation of individual claims in order to assure the good of all. The
difference is again largely one of aspects: both are found in classical
theory. There is, of course, a change of emphasis from the " rights of
governments " to the " rights of citizens ". But Jefferson, as well as
Hamilton, recognises both.

The view of natural law and natural right as merely the recognition of a balance which arises in a struggle for power between
government and citizens, and between man and man, as represented in
the approach of Machiavelli and Hobbes, is, of course, opposed to
classical theory, which adopts the Aristotelian view of man as both a
rational and a social animal. But Grotius founded his theory on a
social appetite, and the writings of Pufendorf and Wolff, of Locke and
Rousseau, are not easily reconciled with Hobbes's doctrine of a war of
all against all. The rejection of " natural law " by the nineteenth
century was not a rejection merely of Hobbes's theory of human nature.
Indeed the Hobbesian view of man's egoism, the nominalism with
which Stanlis connects it,[60] the empiricist philosophy of Locke which he
sees as fundamentally similar to that of Hobbes,[61] were all developed
in the century which produced the economics of *laissez faire,* Darwin's
Origin of Species, with its theory of a struggle for existence, and the new
science of sociology.

Nor is an antithesis between " reason " and " will " convincing—
unless " will " be regarded as the equivalent of " *arbitrium* ", of mere
power. Reason and will were in traditional psychology parts of the
" *psyche* ", and the good will was subject to reason: indeed " practical
reason " was the reason which controlled the will. Both " reason " and
" will " were known to classical natural law. Moreover, an opposition
between reason and will antedates the eighteenth century, and is to be
found among the scholastics. The social qualities of man, according to
Scotus, result from man's will having a *nisus affectionis.* Divine Law,
according to Scotus, is an emanation of Divine Will. Long before
Hobbes there was already the debate as to how far God's will was tied
to the nature of things. Mohammedan teaching produced the doctrine
that justice is what it is because God so willed it. Were He to will the
reverse, this would be just.

It needs, however, no recourse to Scotus or Calvin to show that
the classical natural law of reason was not a consequence of theistic

---

[60] " Historically, the foundations of Hobbes's individual ' natural rights ' are to be
found in nominalism." (STANLIS 17.)

[61] " The fundamental similarity between Locke and Hobbes is their common empirical
theory of knowledge and mechanistic conception of human nature." STANLIS 21. Stanlis
accepts Strauss's doctrine that " Locke deviated considerably from the traditional natural
law teaching and followed the lead given by Hobbes." *Id.* at 21.

doctrine. The views of our author on this subject[62] are surely a contradiction of the basic character of natural law, and fail to recognise the Thomistic distinction between divine law and natural law. The distinction of what is just by nature and just by convention was sufficient for Aristotle to show the existence of natural law " which bound all men " and of " various positive laws and customs " which are " the product of man's reason and will."[63] Yet our author appears to base the universality of natural law on the fact that " Natural Law comes from God ". A uniform reason in man, as was the teaching of Plato and Aristotle, or uniformity in nature, as was the teaching of the Stoics, can produce a natural law " independent of theological presuppositions ".[64] If man's reason, or a cosmic nature, be regarded as theistic conceptions, then the difference between humanism and pantheism (*Deus sive Natura*) on the one hand, and theism on the other, is gone. St. Thomas regarded reason as a gift of God, and for him the *lex aeterna* embraced all forms of law. But he drew a clear distinction between divine law, in which God has directly revealed his wishes for their conduct to men, and natural law, where man must elaborate the rules of conduct for himself. St. Thomas set himself the task of showing that the natural law of the pagans was consistent with divine law. A belief in natural law was not inconsistent with faith in Christian doctrines, and the divine law justified and supplied a basis for belief in natural law. The divine law also served as a means of verifying the fallible working of human reason.[65] Nevertheless, since divine law did not provide a complete code of conduct, much of social life fell to be regulated by principles of natural law.

What is, perhaps, common to Hobbes and Grotius and the members of the " ideal law " school is the belief in a " mathematical "

---

[62] " Natural law came from God and bound all men." STANLIS 7. " Until the time of Hobbes the tradition of Natural Law had been essentially theistic. The natural rights introduced by Hobbes and popularised by Locke exalted man's private reason and will above any eternal and unchangeable divine law." *Id.* at 23. " Every philosopher from Aristotle to Hooker had posited as the basis of his faith in Natural Law a belief in God's being and beneficence. Grotius was the first modern to say . . . that Natural Law would be valid even if God did not exist." *Id.* at 23.

[63] STANLIS 7.

[64] " Grotius . . . proved that it was possible to build up a theory of laws independent of theological presuppositions." D'ENTRÈVES, *Natural Law* 12. But he continues: " The natural law which they elaborated was entirely ' secular.' They sharply divided what the Schoolmen had taken great pains to reconcile." But reconciliation of different doctrines shows their consistency, not their identity.

[65] In his commentaries on Burke, Stanlis presents him as accepting my version of the Thomistic relationship between natural law and divine law. " Through ' right reason ' and free will, even without the special grace of divine revelation, every man was capable of obeying the imperative ethical norms of the Natural Law." STANLIS 17. " When the Natural Law was perceived only by individual reason, unaided by corporate religion, there was a danger that men would construct a false antithesis between reason and faith, between words and contemplation and man and God." *Id.* at 180. This presents Burke as not merely accepting the claim of the Church to interpret divine law so as to see whether it confirms a suggested principle of natural law, but supporting the claim of the Church to say what is truly natural law within the sphere of morals as opposed to faith.

natural law, " wherein the whole body of the law was deduced by inexorable logic from eternally true first principles derived from an analysis of human reason itself ".[66] It is this " deductive, arrogant, or naively romantic . . . doctrine of rationalism which attempted to set up detailed norms deduced from reason and valid for all men and all times ",[67] which is the characteristic differentiating the ideal law school from the earlier classical natural law. The derivation of rules from the classical natural law is by application to varying circumstances, and thus the classical theory is one of " nature with changing and progressive application ".[68] It is a prescription for rule-making, not a catalogue of rules.[69]

There is a division among the theories of natural law which is perhaps of even greater importance than that between the classical and the " ideal " versions of natural law. They are both alike in being " normative and deontological " in their character: in prescribing what ought to be the law and not describing what is the law. Indeed it was their critics who misrepresented them as historical and empirical theories about positive law. It was to the will of the legislator and to the conscience of the citizen, and not to the judge or administrator as mere executants of positive law, that the precepts of these systems of natural law were directed. Natural law and positive law, strictly speaking, never conflicted, though they might prescribe different courses of action which could loosely be described as conflict. The legislator could violate a precept of natural law by his enactment of positive law, and by ellipsis the rule of positive law may be said to violate natural law. Stanlis speaks in this sense when he says that one of the basic principles of natural law theory " until the time of Hobbes " was that " no positive law or social convention was morally valid if it violated the Natural Law ".[70] But it is its *moral* validity which is here categorised. The rule of positive law retains its empiric character, and its validity according to its own criteria of validity, notwithstanding the " conflict "

---

[66] This is the description given by Thomas A. Cowan to Wolff's *Jus Naturae* (*The American Jurisprudence Reader*, p. 211). He traces this " mathematical " outlook back to Descartes, and Spinoza's *Ethica More Geometrico*. Stanlis, following Strauss, favours Hobbes: " Hobbes rejected traditional law because it was not based upon infallible mathematics." (p. 25.) D'Entrèves traces it to Grotius: " Mathematics . . . provides the new methodological assumption which Grotius prides himself on having introduced into the study of law." *Natural Law* 53.

[67] ROMMEN, *The Natural Law* 228.

[68] This is preferred by Rommen (*Natural Law* 229, n. 25) to Stammler's " natural law with a changing content " and Renard's " natural law with a progressive content." But both Stammler and Renard agree with the character of the process of derivation.

[69] The nature of the prescription is discussed when the " principles " are further considered. Maritain reduces it to the first of St. Thomas's " first principles." " Natural Law is not a written law. Men know it with greater or less difficulty, and in different degrees, running the risk of error here as elsewhere . . . the only practical knowledge all men have naturally and infallibly in common is that we must do good and avoid evil" (quoted in ROMMEN, *The Natural Law* 227, n. 18).

[70] STANLIS 7.

with natural law.[71] Thus the affirmation of the doctrine that a rule of positive law was valid notwithstanding its " violation " of natural law did not constitute a rejection of natural law. Nor is the pursuit of the study of legal history or legal sociology necessarily inconsistent with acceptance of natural law. But the assertion that " values " are to be found only within historically given systems of positive law, and are to be obtained by mere " descriptive generalisation ",[72] without distinction between the " just " and the " unjust ", is, of course, a denial of natural law, and is the basis of much of the nineteenth-century reaction. The accounts of history which saw actual governments as being based on nothing but force and lawlessness and denied the reality of all else, are but extreme views of essentially the same doctrine.[73]

The twentieth century produced its own repudiation of natural law. The nineteenth-century form of positivism was empirical or historical: the later century asserted a " logical " positivism. Hume had emphasised the " logical " distinction between the categories of " ought " and " is ", and had stated the logical impossibility of establishing " ought " propositions from premises which consisted in " is " propositions. When to Hume's logic was added the doctrine that only statements capable of empirical verification were " meaningful ", a new basis for the repudiation of natural law was established. A number of replies to this attack are possible. Hume left open the problem of the valid establishment of " ought " propositions, and also the problem of the exact relation between " is " and " ought " propositions.[74] The verification theory calls for examination of its concept of " meaningful ". But one reply was to deny that there was a valid conceptual distinction

---

[71] An important Thomistic doctrine of the moral duty of a citizen to obey " unjust " rules of positive law is often overlooked. St. Thomas says that a rule of positive law is morally binding, notwithstanding conflict with natural law, if disobedience would jeopardise the system of positive law, producing public disorder and impeding obedience to just positive laws. On the other hand, a positive law which requires disobedience to divine law is never binding on the conscience.

[72] This is designedly a vague term used to avoid detailed consideration of the problem of distinguishing between, in Stammler's language, the " idea " and the " concept ", between Kant's transcendental presuppositions and secondary scientific generalisations. In one sense, everything exists in nature and is nature, cancer and the Bay of Naples, the unjust and the just.

[73] " Law . . . does not tell us what ought to be, but is merely an indication of how far the power, the material and psychological power, of the ruling class extends. The law indicates what the sociological situation is. This is the extreme form of materialist jurisprudence. In this view law is neither the reason nor the will: it is but the line of demarcation of the relations of social power. Therefore real force, whether physical or psychical, is of necessity the essential role of law. Law is merely what is actually enforced, not what is enforceable. Jurisprudence is an inept expression, handed down from a metaphysico-theological age, for the materialist sociology of purely experimental science that tells how the power pattern of the groups within a society stands at the moment in the struggle for the machinery of political control." ROMMEN, *The Natural Law* 127-8.

[74] Hume's teaching is that no number of descriptive propositions entails a value proposition. This is admittedly so at the level of the formal argument of the analytical syllogism. It is, however, a triviality to observe that *if* a value concept is " logically " of a different type from empirical concepts one cannot proceed from facts to values. But the analysis of the nature of a value concept may yield a connection with " facts." See also *supra* note 53.

between the " is " and the " ought ", and, indeed, to assert that such a denial was the essence of a belief in natural law.[75] What results is a theory of natural law which is a theory of history, a theory which instead of reducing philosophy to history with Croce, elevates history to philosophy with Hegel. It would appear, however, that the doctrine of Fuller[76] is limited to the character of legal institutions. It is within them that *what ought to be* is said to have actual existence. Society without law could be conceived; but in fact law exists, and in truth " law " involves what ought to be. The institutions of society, which are usually termed " legal ", cannot be accurately described in terms of mere force and power: the ordinary legal process—and, above all, the judicial process—is no mere mechanical application of authoritatively established precepts, but constantly requires reference to ideas of what ought to be law. The existence of bare power fiats is not, however, denied. Fuller is no Blackstonian optimist whom every prospect of the castle of law pleases, who equates all what is with what ought to be. The result appears to be that under the different terminology[77] of distinguishing " power " from " law ", we have the older concept of distinguishing what is from what ought to be.

For Burke the word " law " signified institutions that conformed to some moral requirements: and he used the word with that significa-tion in order to support his own theory of government. " Law and arbitrary power are at eternal hostility . . . He that would substitute will in the place of law is a public enemy to the world."[78] Moreover, he did not merely assert that " law " was to be found under the British

---

[75] Cf. the Thomistic doctrine that it is a sin against the intellect to confuse the mathe-matical, the physical and the metaphysical.

[76] In the well-known passage in *The Law in Quest of Itself*, Fuller says: " Natural law . . . is the view which denies the possibility of a rigid separation of the *is* and the *ought* and which tolerates a confusion of them in legal discussion." (p. 5) It is, of course, grammatically possible that the words "in legal discussion " do not qualify the clause pre-ceding the comma. But the other interpretation (which permits the possibility of a separa-tion in discussion of matters other than law, e.g., in the field of logic) is also possible. It is more consistent with Fuller's examination of American Legal Realism in Lecture II of his book. Indeed the employment of the language of *is* and *ought* surely presupposes the acceptance of a *conceptual* distinction between " is " and " ought ". " Is " and " ought " are conceptually outside the permitted degrees of matrimonial relations: the temporary divorce, suggested by Llewellyn and McDougal, is not possible. That which logic has put asunder no realist or naturalist can join together. See also *supra* note 53.

[77] I do not wish to minimise the importance of precise terminology. The discussions about natural law are often carried on with the use of words which are at any rate poten-tially ambiguous. The same word " law " is used not only for natural law and positive law, but also for the abstract concept unifying and characterising the rules and principles of positive law, and for the particular rules themselves. The same words are used to signify the different kinds of " existence " of natural law and positive law propositions and practices. The same word, "validity", is used for both conformity to natural law and conformity to positive law. Thus confusion does sometimes arise between a theory of justice and a theory of law, between the characteristics of ideals and the characteristics of empirical phenomena. But terminological devices do not solve all problems. What are the charac-teristics of particular governmental situations is not decided by terminology. No doubt with proper definitions the phrases " law " and " good law " may be used to refer to the same objects. For propaganda purposes there are advantages and disadvantages in either terminology.

[78] 4 *Speeches* 374 (STANLIS 63).

constitution, which he so often praised. On the contrary, " law " was a universal phenomenon. In his speech against Warren Hastings he denied that arbitrary power could be justified under some other " legal " system.

> Let him fly where he will—from law to law—law, thank God, meets him everywhere—arbitrary power cannot secure him against law; and I would as soon have him tried on the Koran, or any other eastern code of laws, as on the common law of this kingdom.[79]

But he is quite aware that actual rules and institutions may not conform to what he considers to be " truly " law. He does not consider that the principles of " law ", of " good rules ", are to be discovered by a mere examination of the historically given rules and institutions. The principles of good government are not for him sociological generalisations. When Warren Hastings sought to justify himself by saying he acted in accordance with the standards of other Indian rulers, Burke rebutted the defence by saying:

> Men . . . are to conform their practice to principles, and not to derive their principles from the wicked, corrupt, and abominable practices of any man whatever. Where is the man that ever before dared to mention the practice of all the villains, of all the notorious depredators, as his justification?[80]

Elsewhere he stated:

> My principles enable me to form my judgment upon men and actions in history, just as they do in common life, and are not formed out of events or characters, either present or past. History is a preceptor of prudence, not of principles. The principles of true politics are those of morality enlarged.[81]

We cannot expect from Burke any philosophical analysis showing how the principles of morality are derived. This, nevertheless, remains the major problem for our age and, doubtless, for succeeding ages. Before, however, we examine this for ourselves, some consideration may be given to the relation between " law " and " morals " suggested by the last quotation. The reference to " morality enlarged " has a Platonic echo; justice is identical with virtue in general, the justice of the state is but justice of the individual soul enlarged, and laws are the

---

[79] *Id.* at 366 (STANLIS 64). It will be noted that Burke uses " law " in two senses: in the first place, to refer to actual rules in force, irrespective of their moral quality; in the second place, to refer to rules which are derived from reason rather than will. Ordinary language, it would appear, uses the word " law " both in the sense recommended by Hart and in the sense recommended by Fuller, in that stimulating exchange between them in the *Harvard Law Review*, Vol. 71. In so far as " law " is used in the more morally neutral sense, men are not tempted to equate actual social institutions with good law. In so far as " law " is used in the more morally qualified sense, men may be more ready, through doubt as to the application of the word, to inquire whether particular institutions are morally justified. Would the uniform adoption of one usage rather than another have led more Germans to resist Hitler? (Incidentally, how many people refused to call Hitler's regime one of " law " ?)

[80] 4 *Speeches* 357 (STANLIS 62).

[81] 1 *Correspondence* 331. (STANLIS 176.) Stanlis uses this quotation in an argument which concludes with the statement that Burke believed " Ultimately, the acceptance of Natural Law and belief in man's capability to fulfil its ethical norms is an act of religious faith." (STANLIS 176.)

D

teachers of virtue. Bentham, too, equates principles of law with those of morality: he who could assert a distinction would suggest one arithmetic for large numbers and another for small numbers.[82] But Bentham's " felicific calculus " required the evil attendant upon every rule of law to be taken into account, so that every rule of morality is not paralleled by a legal rule. Traditional natural law recognised the distinction asserted by Aristotle between moral rules of conduct for the individual as such, and legal rules of conduct for the individual as a citizen. Natural law was but a branch of morality, consisting in those moral principles pertaining to social life and capable of practical implementation as governmental institutions, as means of social control. Burke certainly accepted this doctrine through his concept of prudence. His recognition of the limited scope of laws as contrasted with morals is shown in these words:

> Manners are of more importance than laws. Upon them, in a great measure, the laws depend. The law touches us but here and there, and now and then. Manners are what vex or soothe, corrupt or purify, exalt or debase, barbarise or refine us, by a constant, steady, uniform, insensible operation, like that of the air we breathe in.[83]

It is no doubt possible from an examination of Burke's writings to discover what are the various specific principles to which he subscribed as being those of morality enlarged and adapted to the processes of government. This is a task, however, which our author does not perform. His consideration of Burke's view of human nature is directed to its more general characteristics of being moral and rational, which the classical natural law assumed it to be, rather than egoistic and aggressive, as it is depicted in the accounts of Hobbes and his followers. He does not tell us how far Burke's view corresponded with St. Thomas's account of the more specific qualities of human nature on which he founded those precepts of natural law which gave effect to the logically prior principle that good was to be done and evil avoided. Nor does he examine the philosophical problems associated with Burke's

---

[82] Bentham, it is true, speaks not of " law " but of "politics", but he identifies politics with government and law. His own words are worth quoting in full:

> Those who, for the sake of accommodation, are willing to distinguish between politics and morals, to assign utility as the principle of one, and justice as the foundation of the other, announce nothing but confused ideas. The only difference between politics and morals is, that one directs the operation of governments, and the other the actions of individuals; but their object is common; it is happiness. That which is politically good cannot be morally bad, unless we suppose that the rules of arithmetic, true for large numbers, are false for small ones. *Theory of Legislation* 16. (transl. Hildreth.)

[83] *Letters on a Regicide Peace* 208 (STANLIS 223). The reference is to *mores*, actual practice, rather than to *mos*, ethical principle. The contrast is between custom and law rather than morals and law. But the limited scope of law is assumed as in the poet's couplet:

> Of all the ills that human heart endure
> How small the part that laws can cause or cure.

It is because most theories of natural law accept the doctrine that it is concerned not with morality in general but only that part capable of institutional implementation that I would not accept Goodhart's recommendation in his valuable Hamlyn lectures that the phrase " natural law " should be replaced by "moral law". *English Law and Moral Law* 30.

assumption of a distinction between " wicked, abominable and corrupt practices " and other presumably beneficial practices.

As I have indicated before, the method of arriving at principles of natural law and the criteria for their validity form the central issue of our debate about natural law today. There are not wanting jurists who term themselves opponents of natural law, and yet are ardent critics of aspects of existing law and advocates of its reform. They do not consider their views as being no more than subjective sentiments of personal approval or disapproval. But they are not prepared to accept propositions which have been advanced as principles of natural law as correct and unchangeable. There is, indeed, a vital problem whether belief in natural law involves acceptance of specific principles as incontrovertible dogma. A belief in the existence of objective, immutable principles of the just ordering of social relations, so far from entailing a belief that some specific set of propositions represents those principles, requires examination of those propositions. However much a particular author seeks to discover objective principles and endeavours to demonstrate that he has ascertained them, he may yet be subject to human error. How is error to be minimised ?

The answer of natural law theories has been the reliance on reason as opposed to emotion or will. The concept of reason, as well as the principles allegedly based on reason, must be subject to that " free and open scrutiny " which Kant said that reason required to be given to religion and law.[84] The merit of reason as opposed to emotion lies in its universal quality in contrast to the particularism of emotion. Reason judges one situation in relation to others, and its technique of an order of propositions serves the purpose of assuring that a comprehensive set of relations is considered. The schemes of both classical natural law and rationalist ideal law provide a *system* of principles for the evaluation of legal rules which obviate dependence on isolated and desultory invocations of sentiment. The coherence of principles and their derived propositions which evaluate particular rules, support the elimination of error from individual judgment, though they do not provide a guarantee of correspondence with some objective order. Consistency of conclusions with premises, and of premises with each other, may be demonstrated by logical reasoning, but this method is inappropriate for ultimate premises. But here, too, the superiority of " reason " may lie in its wider range. The reaction of an individual to particular circumstances unintegrated into the totality of his own personality and his reactions to other situations, and not related to the existence of other selves and their reactions, may be designated as a mere " emo-

---

[84] KANT, *Critique of Pure Reason*, Preface. The reference is to the well-known passage in the Preface to the First Edition where Kant said law would lose its claims to obedience if it were based solely on authority. The mainspring of Kant's production of his Critiques of reason is to subject reason itself to criticism. This is specifically stated in the Preface to the Second Edition of the *Critique of Pure Reason* : " Our opposition is to *dogmatism* . . . the dogmatical procedure of pure reason, *without a previous criticism of its own powers*."

tional " response, as opposed to the reaction of a human self in all its aspects with full consciousness of other selves. It may be that the test of a value judgment is derived from the latter kind of reaction. It would be dogmatism to assert that it is dogmatism to accept the conclusions of a judgment " purged of prejudice ". Certainly many have claimed that there are propositions which are self-evident to reason.

On the other hand, many assert that the principles which appear as self-evident statements of reason are but ideologies of a time and place. Pound has set forth as a major task of jurisprudence the elucidation of jural postulates which are but statements in ideal form of the generalisations derived from observation of the specific civilisations of the time and place. He has seen the various theories of natural law as themselves arising from the needs of time and place.[85] Others, though they consider the principles of natural law as not necessarily so tied to particular institutions, nevertheless consider them but as postulates having no authority or validity higher than that of subjective moral sentiment. The classical natural law, however, sought to derive its propositions from a total judgment which considered the entirety of experience. It was able to discern uniformities because it discovered that some modes of experience were closely related to life and happiness, to rich variety and harmony, while others were related to decay and misery, to monotony and discord. Its exponents felt impelled to distinguish these modes of experience as desirable and repelling, to be promoted and to be repressed. Thus they framed principles for doing good and avoiding evil. It may be that the judgment thus involved is that of " moral sentiment ". But it has close parallels with that attitude of the human spirit which has so far reached its highest attainment in the physical sciences, the " scientific " attitude of objective truth. It may be claimed for St. Thomas that he was not only the first Whig but the first social scientist.

The physical scientist assumes that there is an objective order sustaining the multiplicity of changing phenomena in which he participates through his bodily sensations, enlarged in their operation by his created instruments and techniques. By patient consideration of experience and experiment he accepts primary principles which through further experience and experiment yield general, but less comprehensive, uniformities. In all this he uses " reason " through imaginative formulation of possibilities, logical elaboration through mathematical manipulation of consequences of those possibilities, and examination of the conformity of his " laws " to the phenomena of his experience and experiment. The laws he thus discovers and creates are but hypotheses, which remain open to falsification by new evidence or further consideration of old evidence or argument. The " applied scientist ", seeking to control or exploit the natural resources of our physical environ-

---

[85] See *supra* note 51.

ment through human effort, converts the descriptive laws of the " pure scientist " into prescriptive statements. But his prescription must often take account not only of scientifically established laws but also of more empirically formed hypotheses dealing with features of the matter he handles which are still beyond the scope of the scientist. Both scientific and empiric hypotheses are complex in their nature, requiring judgment in relation to the particular situations dealt with by the applied scientist.

So, too, the natural law lawyer relies on principles of an objective order for humanity which require prudence in their conversion into more specific prescriptive laws for social control. If he be a theist, he assumes that this objective order exists because it is created by God, whose Nature or Will ordains and sustains a cosmos and not a chaos. If he be a pantheist, then this objective order, extending not only through humanity but beyond it to the universe in which it is maintained, is his god. If he be an atheist, it exists because it is a heuristic necessity required by the nature of man's mind or existing because it exists. The principles of this objective order are the uniformities of man's thinking and feeling and doing that he seeks to discern. And for this purpose he employs the same " reason " of imagination and logic and observation that forms the scientific attitude. The principles which he both propounds and applies are thus hypotheses or postulates in the sense that " laws " of the physical scientist are so: they do not seek to relate to a subjective framework or to particular states, but to an objective order, universal and eternal. They are, nevertheless, conditioned by the range of experience considered, by the fallibility of the reasoning employed. The " social scientist " of today may rightly modify the doctrines of Aristotle or St. Thomas; but this is so because he employs a wider range of experience, a deeper examination of the logic of the discussion, than was available to them. In view of the infancy of the social sciences we may well hesitate before rejecting old and substituting new hypotheses. On the other hand, we may, both in the spirit of social science and natural law, prefer the " principles " of Marx or Lenin, of Pareto or Toynbee, if they also be treated as hypotheses, to be confirmed or rejected by new thinking and further experience.

The range of experience to be considered in arriving at basic principles extended in classical natural law to all aspects of man's life, though, as has been seen, their content and operation took into account the limitations required for governmental implementation. Stammler advocates that the principles for the ordering of social life are to be derived from consideration of legal institutions.[86] They, of course, form

[86] " The judgment concerning the objective justice of a certain legal content must not be brought in from outside, but must be derived solely from the immanent unity of the law itself. Just law must, therefore, neither be constituted outside of the content of positive law, nor must another discipline be brought in as a criterion." *Theory of Justice* 38 (trans. Husik).

an important element of experience, particularly within the sphere of determination of the possibilities 'of implementation of social ideals by legal means. Doubtless Stammler's doctrine involves consideration of legal institutions within their social framework, for he held that law embraces all aspects of social life. Nevertheless, the formulation appears narrowing, and may appear to others as legal monopoly. But restrictive practice in dealing with experience does not contradict the assumption of an objective ordering of all experience: that order appears in all parts. It *may* be discerned within legal institutions as the character of gold may be ascertained from one specimen.[87] But restrictive practices do contradict the doctrine that postulated principles are hypotheses to be tested by every aspect of experience. Lawyers must cooperate with all other social scientists in the development of a natural law which bases itself on " social science ": the latter phrase is but a noun of collection for the various social sciences. Nor should we disregard the labours of those, who, though they may disdain or not aspire to the epithet of social scientist, yet examine and describe human nature, pursuing their inquiries and proclaiming their opinions under the banner of the humanities. Foolish, also, should we be to neglect the " insights " of a Shakespeare or a Goethe, a Dostoievsky or a Dickens. The literature of the world is a great storehouse of knowledge of human nature.[88] Too often, however, the adherents of other disciplines have thought that they may dispense with the cooperation of lawyers, and many neglect legal philosophy. The work under review, however, is an example of the different attitude which now appears to be developing. Every lawyer concerned with the relation between law and justice is greatly indebted to our author, who has conceived it to be part of his task as a professor of English to enable us to see more truly the character of the judgments, both profound and circumspect, expressed by a philosophic statesman about the aims and achievements of law. Were all students imbued with the spirit of the author and of his hero, law would indeed be the first and noblest of the human sciences, quickening and invigorating the understanding, liberating the mind from mechanical adherence to prejudice and convention, and opening it to the wider perspectives and the higher ideals of the human spirit.

[87] Cf. Holland's criticism of the term "particular jurisprudence". " It may mean: a science derived from an observation of the laws of one country only. If so, the particularity attached, not to the science itself, which is the same science whencesoever derived, but to the source whence the materials for it are gained. A science of law might undoubtedly be constructed from a knowledge of the law of England alone, as a science of geology might be, and in great part was, constructed from an observation of the strata in England only . . . Principles of Geology elaborated from the observation of England alone hold good all over the globe, in so far as the same substances and forces are everywhere present; and the principles of Jurisprudence, if arrived at entirely from English data, could be true if applied to the particular laws of any other community of human beings; assuming them to resemble in essentials the human beings who inhabit England." *Jurisprudence* 10 (13th ed.).

[88] Compare, however, Jerome Hall's pertinent comments to be found in his *Principles of Criminal Law* 564: "Literature, however suggestive, is not social science."

4

Return to Austin's College*

The journey on which I invite you to accompany me is to the dream college which John Austin described probably at the end of the first law lecture ever given in these buildings 130 years ago. He drew a picture of what he thought was involved in a " complete legal education " and proclaimed that London possessed peculiar advantages for the setting up of a Law Faculty, where such an education could be given. But in order to commence this journey with you, I have had physically to return to my own college where my ever incomplete legal education was begun, and our spiritual return to Austin's college should perhaps take us first through the fields of his jurisprudence. It is at the end of the two volumes of his *Lectures on Jurisprudence,* or *The Philosophy of Positive Law,* as she sub-titled them, that Sarah Austin placed his introductory lectures on the study of law.

My physical return is in itself a sentimental journey to the University of London of Austin's days. The College Christmas card reminded us that the twin lodges by Gower Street, which formed the only entrance for me as an undergraduate, were there in 1835. My path when a student to the law lecture rooms took me past the statue of John Stuart Mill, and at least once a term I made a pilgrimage to the Science Library where another of my heroes, Jeremy Bentham, then sat in his glass case. John Stuart Mill and Jeremy Bentham were the physical neighbours for a time of John Austin. Both were his spiritual teachers. Though John Stuart Mill sat at Austin's feet at his lectures and later supplied Sarah with the notes which enabled those lectures to be posthumously published, John Austin acknowledged his indebtedness to Mill's *Logic.*

The so-called Austinian theory of law was the dominant doctrine of my student days, and our jurisprudence course was exclusively analytical. It is true that the Quain Professor of Comparative Law of those days was rather an historical jurist, but his was but a part-time chair and he rarely came into contact with undergraduates. The law students of the University were formed into one intercollegiate society, for there were

---

* An address delivered to the Bentham Club, as its President. It is reprinted from *Current Legal Problems,* 1960, by kind permission.

hardly a hundred in all. But it was a great honour to be chairman of the society which, of course, met in this college, and to introduce as president of our first moot court Lord Atkin, a great friend of the University, who also had a vision of a great Institute of Legal Studies for London.

What great developments have occurred since my student days! There have, of course, been great strides forward in law teaching throughout the United Kingdom since those days just after the First World War. There were giants of earlier generations, Maine and Maitland; Austin whom we honour tonight, and Pollock, who, with his great correspondent Holmes, lived on to overawe my generation. I still remember that neither the monotone of his delivery nor the tiny size of the audience, in that English lecture theatre where Pollock majestically dramatised the evolution of Parliament, could dull the liberal spirit and scholarly genius of his lecture on the Judge as Man of Valour and Man of Caution. But despite those giants faculties of law have become substantial parts of universities only since my student days.

Nowhere else have the changes been so great as in this Faculty of Law of " Gower St. U.C.L." I should like to pay my respectful tribute to the great contribution made to legal education here, and through this college to the world, by the Head of our law school, George Keeton. I select two accomplishments for especial mention. The first is the production of *Current Legal Problems,* which, surely, ought in its title to bear a reference to this Faculty of Law. The name " Jeremiads " might, however, prove too elusive an illusion though not necessarily too false a description. Moreover, Jeremy Bentham is perhaps sufficiently commemorated in that other accomplishment, the Bentham Club. The academic lawyer does not seek the glittering prizes open to the professional lawyer : it was no such ambition that led John Austin to the Chair of Jurisprudence here. But he is greatly rewarded and encouraged, as John Austin was not, if his students appreciate the values he has endeavoured to maintain and advance by his teaching. The Bentham Club has many admirable qualities, but not least is its actuality and potentiality as a contribution to legal scholarship through its support of the Faculty. It is, indeed, a very great honour that has been conferred in electing me President.

AUSTIN'S JURISPRUDENCE

What of Austin's contribution to legal scholarship? It is still largely true, as I have said it was in my own student days, that he is regarded as the great expositor of the imperative theory of law. Indeed, because he is connected both with that theory and with analytical jurisprudence, a popular conception is that analytical jurisprudence is in some way tied to the imperative theory. Thus, Sir Hartley Shawcross[1] in his historic plea at the Nuremberg trials that international law was capable of juristic

---

[1] [Now Lord Shawcross. Ed.]

evolution through the elaboration of fundamental principles of justice, referred to the opposed theory that development could only take place by the enactment of a sovereign, as the doctrine of analytical jurisprudence. That it certainly is not : analytical jurisprudence is not tied to any theory of law, whether of legal institutions as a whole, or of the rule element in law which sometimes goes by the name of lawyer's law. Whether Austin was committed to the imperative theory of law is another question.

It is not easy to describe that theory. Is there any such theory in the abstract, or must one speak of Jones' or Smith's theory? It is, of course, amusing to satirise much jurisprudential discussion, as, indeed, other discussions also in the humanities, as hair-splitting debate about what Jones said about what Smith said about what Brown said, and so on, without ever seeking to criticise the basic theory by reference to some criterion other than some author's literary pronouncement. Buckland has told us how in his student days the study of jurisprudence was conceived largely as pin-pricking Austin. But the desire and ability to state accurately another person's views are precious virtues, not only in scholarship but in citizenship, and essential for toleration and true understanding on which internal and international peace ultimately depend.

One view of Austin's theory of law makes him not the logical analyst of positive law but a positivist philosopher of political government. The state is based on power politics and law is force. In every state there is a concentration of power : law is the instrument whereby this power is exercised; it is the apparatus of coercion for giving effect to the will of the sovereign. Such a doctrine is as old as Plato's Republic, where its exposition is put into the mouth of Thrasymachus, and as modern as the Marxist critique of capitalist society. In Marxist language, it is a " scientific " theory. More precisely, it is a sociological doctrine. This is not the occasion for a refutation of its accuracy : nor even for a full examination of whether it represents Austin's views. I do suggest, however, that the association of such a theory with Austin arose from the disassociation of his analysis of the word " law " from his examination of rules of law. We owe much to Sarah Austin's faith in the value of her husband's work. It is due to her that we have the posthumous publication of his *Lectures*. It may, however, be surmised that it was her influence which led to the publication of his construction of a definition of law under what I conceive to be the misleading title of *The Province of Jurisprudence Determined*. It was through this work alone that Austin's views were known to the world for many years. Doubtless a power doctrine of society can be read into some passages from this work. But if the *Province* is read in the context of the *Lectures* the argument, which can be supported from the *Province* itself, is strengthened, that what Austin was seeking to do was to isolate the concept of a legal rule which would serve for the purpose of the particular scope of the task of what he called " general jurisprudence ".

As I seek to show later, I do not think Austin fully realised the complexity of the many ideas associated with the word " law ", but he did realise how ambiguous and vague ordinary usage was, and he sought to eliminate some of the confusion. It is not surprising that he was not wholly successful : much confusion of the different basic notions of logic, fact and value is still found in the treatment of the subject. I think that when he spoke of " law properly so called ", he was merely seeking to emphasise the need for the construction of a concept which would adequately distinguish different things ordinarily denoted by the same word. He does, however, write at times, for example, as if the relation between a rule of law and a sanction were not the result of a stipulative definition, but of an inductive generalisation derived from examination of particular rules. However, Austin contributed a powerful impetus to the task of adequate discrimination of the complex aggregate of law, and his critics have often been no more clear sighted than he in distinguishing the logical differences between the various fields of legal scholarship.

The major task to which Austin sought to devote himself, as appears from his *Lectures,* was that of civilising English law. He saw it as an incoherent assembly of particular rules expressed in a language which, while technical, was largely imprecise, so that lawyers failed to state clearly and use systematically their basic concepts and principles. He contrasted this with the civil law. He expressed great admiration for the Roman jurists who seemed to him to possess a genius for logical manipulation of ideas. But it would appear that he looked at Roman law through the eyes of expositors of that system whom he had studied in Bonn during the years of preparation for his professorship. There, it is clear from his library, he came under the influence of Kantian epistemology.

He conceived the task of a philosophy of positive law to be the search for transcendental notions. These were not Platonic transcendent ideas of justice laid up in heaven though mixed with earthly experience in human laws, but the categories of concepts and principles which " logical " analysis may show are presupposed by the actual rules of a legal system or of a number of legal systems. Austin discerned the need for the comparative study of legal systems, but thought that its main value lay in facilitating the task of discovering general concepts and principles. It was this task of logical exploration of Roman law with which the glossators and commentators had been concerned since the birth of European universities with the institutions of legal studies at Bologna in the eleventh century. It had been carried to its culmination with the Pandectists of Germany, who were still dominant at Bonn when Austin was there. It had led to a systematic restatement of Roman law even by those who were opposed to the enactment of a systematic code of law which had been the culmination in France of civil law studies.

It was such a logical exploration and systematisation of English law that Austin conceived as his chief task at the outset of his academic career, and to this he gave the name of general jurisprudence. It was the view of Maitland that little came of it all in the end, and Dicey in 1880 wrote that " Jurisprudence is a word which stinks in the nostrils of the practising barrister." But Maitland's views can be controverted, and it must be remembered that Dicey's remark was basically a criticism of the education of the barrister. Much that was good, and much that I consider bad, did come from Austin's work. I would attribute to his influence the transformation of legal textbooks which Pollock with Oxford filialty ascribed to Maine. They ceased to be largely unorganised collections of abbreviated digests of authorities and became, much more, systematic expositions of principles with illustrations from cases.

I attribute also to Austin the divorce of law from justice, which was for a long time characteristic of English legal education: this was the unintended consequence of his construction of " general jurisprudence ". That it was unintended, I think, can be shown by another task of integration. I have hitherto stressed the need for bringing into relation with each other the content of the *Province* with its definition of law, and the content of the *Lectures* with their elaboration of general jurisprudence. It is also necessary for a balanced presentation of Austin's views to see the place that he ascribed to jurisprudence in the entire field of " a complete legal education ".

It is still requisite, however, to comment more particularly on one aspect of Austin's jurisprudence in order to bring out more clearly one interpretation of his definition of a law and one theory of his idea of a just legal order. A leading characteristic of Austin's treatment of jurisprudence is his separation of the categories of *what is* and *what ought to be* the law. For in order to carry out the task of ascertaining the highest generalisations of legal rules by the use of basic concepts, it did not appear necessary to examine the content of the legal rules and to evaluate them in terms of goodness. The task of evaluation was part of what Bentham had called critical jurisprudence, and what Austin called the science of legislation. The only criticism permitted in general jurisprudence was in terms of " logical " consistency.

The aspect of the entire complex of law to be studied was the rule element. Thus, all that was needed was the notion of a legal rule, and for this two defining characteristics were necessary—one of the genus rule and one of the differentia of " legal ". Legal rules belong to the class of prescriptive statements, said Austin: they were general commands. And they were legal rules as opposed to moral rules because they proceeded from some official source, though he was not content to stop at what Bryce called legal sovereignty, but ventured on empirical speculation to suggest a doctrine of political sovereignty. It was, moreover, necessary for Austin's purpose to state the characteristic of a legal rule in terms of a mode of creation rather than of its content or purpose. For a belief that law could be defined *a priori* by reference to such factors led to a doctrine of transcendent, non-empirical, rational law, which was contrary to Austin's theory of justice.

For Austin did have a theory of justice. True, anticipating the cheer word and sneer word language of modern semanticists, he said that the words " just " and " unjust " either meant conformity with or a departure from a set of laws, or had better be signified by a grunt or a groan than by such a mischievous and detestable abuse of language. But what he was criticising in that statement was the use of the words " justice " and " injustice " to express some vague yearning for an ideal, or some emotional disgust for a practice which, even when expressed in lyrical poem or incisive satire, needs to be supplemented by a rational evaluation of evidence.

Austin was a European radical who saw justice in terms of human happiness, to be achieved in a society where order was reconciled with freedom. This was to be attained by the age-old ideal of a government of laws. Laws ought to be made by a legislature accepted by the people on the basis of a science of legislation which established utility as the criterion of goodness of law, and thus directed the scientific use of experience. These enacted laws were to form an integrated system capable of application to the varying situations of life by some objective and deductive method. For Austin, as for Bryan King,[2] the ideal judicial function consisted in the logical application of previously clearly formulated rules; his spiritual descendants today are seeking to employ electronic computers in the discharge of that function.

But Austin, unlike Bentham, saw that the limitation of legislative foresight and linguistic symbolism in our world of kaleidoscopic change would always require judges to have some legislative power, and to employ discretion in judicial administration. However, for Austin, as opposed to Bryan King and to Kelsen, the tension between the ideal judicial function and the actual judicial process should be so little that it could be resolved by reference to analogy. Austin was quite aware of the defects of analogy, and he devoted some space to its analysis and to the problem of competing analogies. Yet he thought that the problems for courts were, to use Holmes' language, interstitial, so that the method of analogy, of " widening from precedent to precedent ", was adequate. Whether he would have adhered to such a view had his studies continued is doubtful.

Austin failed to establish permanently the terminology whereby " jurisprudence " was limited to the " logical " treatment of rules of positive law. At Oxford Maine was successful in extending its province beyond the analytical to the historical. But it was in this college mainly that " jurisprudence ", which Austin had conceived of as a philosophical enterprise, was extended to embrace a pursuit always associated

---

[2] [Fellow of Pembroke College, Cambridge. Ed.]

with philosophy, namely, an evaluation of the ends of law. First, before the First World War, Sir John Macdonnell, who was fully aware of the need for sociological inquiry into legal institutions for the purposes of determining whether they were phenomena of power, and of connecting law with society, nevertheless insisted that sociology of law is not enough: " any theory which does not account for the *ought* " is insufficient. Then Friedmann, after the Second World War, despite his belief in the relativity of ideal notions, brought policy considerations and theory of justice into the field of jurisprudence.

Nevertheless, Austin's terminological recommendation about the use of the word " jurisprudence " played its part, together with the strong professional influence, in largely confining the study of law in British universities to the rationalisation of the products of parliaments and courts. The attitude was one in which natural law expressed " but well meaning sloppiness of thought ",[3] and " policy " was a naughty, or still worse, an American word.

It is important, however, to consider whether Austin's own process of so-called logical systematisation of rules of positive law was as free from value judgments as he thought it to be. In my submission, Austinian analysis and synthesis concealed the employment of ideals of justice in the apparent exposition of what the law is. The actual pronouncements of parliaments and courts contain many inconsistencies. Certainly the influence of legal institutions has a strong tendency to produce uniformity, but there are also influences of a contrary character to be found not only in the nature of human personality, but within law itself. The task of systematisation of Austinian jurisprudence both simplifies and idealises. The complexities of actual statements are replaced by generalisations. These, at best, represent but dominant patterns discernible amid the varied pronouncements. More often they are but the writers' views as to what the law ought to be, expressed in language which speaks of principles of what the law is, because they are thought to be presupposed by the particular rules of law. This is indeed a time-honoured practice of juristic legislation, for which Asquith used the name " jurisprudence " and described as Rome's great contribution to the world. It is, indeed, not very different from the practice of much judicial legislation, and has much to commend it in the manner in which it hews close to facts. Nevertheless, it suffers from the defect which Holmes saw : to adapt his language, no generalisation is worth a straw which is not fully supported by the articulation of the premises on which it depends. Or perhaps the language of a recent writer may be adopted in saying that " the visible effect of [legal] education is to enable people to articulate more ingeniously their snap

---

[3] [This phrase was the description given by Scrutton L.J. to Lord Mansfield's theory that restitution is based, not on implied contract, but on unjustified enrichment: *Holt* v. *Markham* (1923) 1 K.B. 504, 513. Ed.]

judgments based on prejudice." The actual particulars of legal phenomena may, in accordance with logical doctrine, be classified under many different principles. A purely *a posteriori* process cannot yield a unique principle of systematisation: for that same *a priori* element is involved. The selection of the one principle propounded as the statement of what the law is must be based on some value judgment.

Hitherto, hurrying through the field of Austin's jurisprudence *en route* for his ideal law school, I have not attempted to relieve the dogmatism of my remarks by any illustration. Perhaps I may be permitted to pause for a moment to view recent controversy over the doctrine of precedent against this background of rationalisation and idealisation. I have carefully read the English cases of the last ten years in relation to this doctrine. It has been noteworthy that the phrase *ratio decidendi* occurs with very much greater frequency in that decade than ever before, and nearly always with the significance of referring to the actual reasoning of a judge. It is also noteworthy that judges have often expressed themselves as bound, authoritatively and not persuasively, by the actual reasoning of earlier judges. Many of the cases are concerned with the interpretation of a statute, and judges have dealt with the problem of resolution of ambiguities by seeing how earlier judges dealt with the words of the statute without regard to the facts of earlier cases. But judges have also spoken of being bound by the " decisions " of earlier cases, and, though sometimes it is clear that they are referring to the actual determination by a judge of a specific point of law, this is not always so, and the later judge engages in a task of logical construction and not of linguistic analysis, in stating what was decided in the earlier case. Moreover, judges still " distinguish " and " explain " earlier cases by reference to their facts, though I am not aware of any *dictum* by a judge in which he referred to what facts were considered material by an earlier court except for the purpose of specifying the true character of the reasoning *secundum subjectam materiam*. The dominant pattern of the past decade, nevertheless, has been that of accepting the actual judicial reasoning as of binding authority.

However, writing much earlier in what is the classical exposition of the problem of determining the *ratio decidendi* of a case, Professor Goodhart preferred as the recommended usage of the phrase *ratio decidendi* the concept of the rule for which a case is of binding authority, and warned against being misled by the term to associate it with " the reason which the judge gives for his decision ". Professor Goodhart also rejected the doctrine that what the judge said is of binding authority in so far as the statement is of a general rule of law. But what the judge says are the material facts of the case before him is binding on the later judge whose task it is to construct the *ratio decidendi* (in Goodhart's sense of the term) from the earlier judge's selection of the facts. Before I comment on these matters may I say that this account, while I believe it to be accurate, is only a summary intended but as mnemonic for an historic theory which I assume is already deservedly widely known. Goodhart is, of course, perfectly entitled to adopt a definition of the phrase *ratio decidendi* which does not accord with judicial usage. He stipulates precisely how he proposes to use the term, and his recommendation is in accord with the usage of most jurists. Nevertheless, I prefer judicial usage.

But is Goodhart entitled to say that the doctrine of precedent *is* based on the judge's selection of the material facts? I do not think so : but Goodhart is in no way departing from juristic practice in so doing. What he has done is to rationalise the various judicial pronouncements. He has indeed produced in excellent fashion, with great originality, a brilliant compromise, which some would term synthesis, between the dominant pattern of United States judicial practice which, as Edward Levi has shown, rejects completely the reasoning of the earlier court, and what I consider the dominant pattern of English judicial practice, which Goodhart, in my opinion, believes unduly fetters an English judge. His theory is really a recommendation of what judicial practice should be. I must add that it does not necessarily represent his view of what ideal judicial practice ought to be. In his later writings Goodhart has power-fully argued against the value of a doctrine which accepts the binding force of a single precedent.[4]

AUSTIN'S COLLEGE

It is my suggestion that a more accurate account of Austin's views, as expressed in the *Province* and the *Lectures,* may be achieved if those

---

[4] It is interesting to compare the manner in which Austin in his procedure of generalisation failed to adhere rigorously to the distinction between " is " and " ought " with the manner in which Hohfeld in his scheme of fundamental legal conceptions failed to adhere rigorously to the distinction between empirical fact and legal relation. Just as Austin rightly insisted on the distinction between " is " and " ought ", so Hohfeld rightly insisted on the distinction between " fact " and " law." Indeed, this distinction, in the character of presenting the formal character of a legal rule as a logical operation relating antecedent facts to legal consequences, is considered by many as Hohfeld's enduring contribution to legal scholarship. But Hohfeld, like Austin, has suffered from a fragmentary treatment of his writings. His essay on a " Vital School of Jurisprudence " has remained unread; his "anatomy of rights " has been regarded either as nothing more than a dictionary, or as an apparatus for solving legal problems. It was stated by its author to be a legal chemistry presenting the elements whose various combinations were to be found in all legal situations. His basic error was in failing to see, what Bentham had seen, that his " privilege: no-right " relation was derived not from the consideration of a legal relation, but from attention to the facts involved in a situation where law did not operate. A man's ability to walk on his own land is not a legal relation but a fact. It is possible to envisage a situation in which a man's actions are subject to no rule of law, where he may act without infringing another's rights or involving another's duties. To such an area of freedom from law the word " right " is often applied. But the legal aspects of such a situation are fully described by saying that there is an absence of rights and duties. To create a positive legal relation out of a negation is to indulge in unnecessary hypostatisation, which only attains plausibility through a confusion of fact and law. A more rigorous use of logic, which Hohfeld so rightly insisted was a prerequisite to the effective solution of legal problems, has exposed a flaw in his scheme of legal conceptions.

writings are read in the perspective of the curriculum which in the Essay on the Uses of Jurisprudence he sketched for an ideal law faculty. It is true that in the *Province* and the *Lectures* there are many passages which show that Austin was a disciple of Bentham: he accepted his theory of utility and he supported his plea for law reform. Like Bentham, he repudiated the doctrine of the Age of Enlightenment which sought to construct legal rules by a process of quasi-mathematical intuition. Logic was not enough even for the intellectual task of understanding law, still less for the pragmatic objective of reform of the law. Experience was a necessary guide. It was the basis of the theory of utility, and it was the foundation of the " political sciences ", as Austin termed them, to which Austin also adverted as when he discussed current work in psychology. Nor was history excluded. Austin was aware of Savigny's thesis: and he classified Bentham with Savigny as belonging to a single historical school. Nevertheless, the most explicit statement of the need to examine legal rules, not only in the light of logic but also in the light of the social sciences, is to be found in Austin's plans for legal education. I shall use modern names for the various disciplines. For example, Austin speaks of political sciences, of moral sciences and even of ethics, as he says in the largest sense. But John Stuart Mill has taught us to speak of the social sciences, and Comte of sociology. Again Austin refers to " philosophy of the human mind ", where today we usually refer to psychology.

This is not the only change I make. I believe that implicit in Austin's statement are three theses, and I make these explicit, conscious, however, that this attempt at rationalisation may not accurately represent Austin's educational theory.

In the first place, though he pays particular regard to the rule element, Austin sees this as but one aspect of the ultimate problem of the organisation of man in society. One branch of this organisation is the process of government by legal institutions, and rules of law are the specific characteristic of lawyer's law. But to understand fully even lawyer's law, one must also understand what Lord Kilmuir has happily called politician's law and administrator's law. The science of legislation was an integral part of the curriculum of Austin's college, side by side with jurisprudence and other subjects. Austin's command theory of law and his doctrine of absolute duties emphasise, indeed, public law rather than private law, which has hitherto been the main concern of lawyer's law.

In the second place, though Austin stresses the prescriptive quality of rules of law, he does regard them as instruments for human happiness. Consequently, law is seen by him as an applied science, a technology, for whose understanding and efficient development a knowledge is required of the pure sciences, the basic disciplines, on which law depends. He envisaged these disciplines as twofold: on the one side stood the empirical sciences of man and society, on the other stood logic.

Finally, since there existed a "science" of law, Austin considered that it was properly a university subject, and its study was to be distinguished from purely professional training. The latter should follow on the theoretical study at a university, and should consist in the acquisition of practical skills, and of knowledge of legal rules which were to be directly utilised in practice.

It is clear that Austin placed the highest value on the study of logic. It discharged one of the essential features of a university education in serving as a mental discipline. It was prerequisite to the study of law and ethics and of the social sciences, for without such knowledge the student could not fully realise the problems arising from the ambiguity of language and the character of abstract terms, nor properly appreciate the reasoning process involved. Austin kept himself abreast of developments in logic, and was aware of Mill's criticism of the syllogistic argument. He cannot be blamed for failing to anticipate the developments of this century. Yet it is necessary to mention two important tasks which modern logic specifies, which Austin omits in his utilisation of logic in law.

Austin does advert to "the elliptical form in which the reasoning is expressed" in the moral sciences: but he fails to make explicit the need for the expression of inarticulate premises in order that they together, with articulated premises, may be examined as to their logical type. Such an examination may reveal that they fall within the province of, say, economics or ethics so that they may be evaluated in the light of the theories of social science or justice.

Secondly, as has already been observed, while Austin recognises the need for the distinction between what is and what ought to be, he does not rigorously observe it. One of the great merits of linguistic analysis is the rigorous manner in which statements are examined in order to see to what realm of discourse they belong without being misled by grammatical appearances. Austin obviously had great talents for such analysis: for example, he shows that though we speak of rights over things, the logical force of the statement is that of rights against persons.

Nevertheless, without the specific guidance of modern logic, he does fail adequately to distinguish between logic, fact and value in his theory of law. He speaks at times of commands constituting law as if they were historic events. The distinction between token words and type words would have been sufficient to remind him that " rules " need not exist as physical events. He assumes that threats of evil control human actions without adequately considering the psychological and ethical questions involved. He does not fully stress how even the professional lawyer is concerned not only with rules of law but with problems of behaviour, both of officials and of citizens, and also with problems of justice, both of actual moral beliefs and of ideal ethical standards.

We must not, however, forget the pioneer character of Austin's work and how little time he was able to devote to it. He may not have

E

the expertise of the modern exponent of logical geography, but he was one of the first explorers of the logic of legal institutions, and he was permitted but few journeys. We cannot complain if he has not left us a complete map of the territory. He shows us what he considers to be the principal features: intrepid and skilful though he was, it is not surprising that he draws for us the main streams and indicates but roughly the mountains which feed them and the lands which they make productive. He concentrates on the rule element, and does not deal fully with the behaviour and ideal elements which also play their part in the complex of law.

Austin's model for his college was the faculty of law of German universities. This he did not slavishly follow. As we have already seen and shall consider further, he did not relegate English law to postgraduate professional studies. Moreover, as is to be expected in so slight a treatment, natural to its introductory function, he does not deal with problems concerned with the teaching of social sciences within a faculty of law. Nor can I fully consider them. However, it may be pointed out that continental experience since Austin's day is relevant to one problem. Subjects, such as political science and economics, developed there within faculties of law. Thus arose the problem of whether the disciplines of political science and economics were best developed within a faculty of law. It was a negative answer which emerged in the course of time. The President of the University of Pittsburgh, in quite a different connection, has recently said: "There are few institutions which at one time or another, have not permitted a basic disciplinary department to become the captive of a single professional school, with consequent neglect of the needs and interests of the discipline itself." This was broadly the argument used on the continent for the separation of social sciences from faculties of law. But it is by no means conclusive of all the problems involved. The complete exclusion of social sciences from faculties of law cannot be justified.

It is a triviality perhaps to point out that a university faculty of law is not a professional school, but it is fundamental to assert that the concept of legal institutions as instruments of government, as means of social control for the attainment of social purposes, compels attention to the need for the student of law to be acquainted with the social sciences. When should they be taught? Logic was regarded by Austin as a preparatory subject, so that doubtless it would have been assigned by him to the first year. In our sister faculty, medicine, as the Vice-Chancellor explained to Convocation last year, the pattern has been for the basic pure sciences, such as chemistry and zoology, to be studied in the first year, for the applied sciences, such as biochemistry and anatomy, to be studied in the next two years, and for the student then to proceed to hospital for practical training and further instruction. But there are important differences in the stages of development of the natural sciences which are basic to medicine and the social sciences which are basic to law. It by no means follows, therefore, that the social sciences should be studied in the faculties of law in the first year.[5]

What of the theory of justice? I have already said that Austin was much concerned with this; for him the doctrine of utility was no irrelevance. Sarah Austin has told us that " justice and humanity were part of his nature." It is doubtful whether the " political " and " moral sciences " of his day were thought to be as value-free as later scholars would have social sciences. It is, however, in the subject of " legislation " where Austin probably considered that the theory of justice should be most fully studied. It is noteworthy that in his table of a complete legal education we find set out instead of the two subjects of jurisprudence and legislation, which appear in the essay, the names " jurisprudence " and " ethics *stricto sensu* ". General jurisprudence was, of course, considered by him an essential prerequisite to the study of legislation.

We now finally turn to the distinction between the university study of law and professional training. Again, we cannot expect a full discussion of this vital topic from Austin. Nor can I do more than consider one or two aspects. Basically Austin agrees with Lord Douglas of Kirtleside, who, rejecting a proposal that courses in air transport should be given at universities, said : " A university is very different from a place to which you go to learn a trade—even if the trade is dignified by being called a profession." But a separation of university study from preparation for a profession is a different thing, and is certainly not an *a priori* necessity. Everything depends on the character of the profession, and on what the profession considers to be requisite preparation.

Academic lawyers join with leaders of the legal profession who have often encouraged the academic study of law as a necessary basis of training for the learned and liberal profession of the law. Nevertheless, Austin, and his successors also, had to deal with two somewhat contradictory types of professional criticism of the academic study of law. In the first place, it is sometimes said that the basic preparation for the profession is a liberal university education, but this is not to be obtained from the study of law. Secondly, it is said that what is required is a grounding in " practical " subjects, and for this purpose subjects like Roman Law, Legal History, Jurisprudence, Comparative and International Law are too academic.

Austin accepted neither type of criticism. In his time academic specialisation had not been carried to the extremes of today, and it was still possible to argue that an undergraduate should not specialise at all.

---

[5] It is not intended by the use of the phrase " social sciences " to suggest that " social psychology " alone, as opposed to psychology in general, was included by Austin in a complete legal education. Whether or not there is a particular subject of " social psychology ", it may be urged that the law student should be aware of the inquiries into the existence of psychic factors independent of social environment, of which one aspect is the study of the different responses that individuals make to similar environmental situations. This is in accordance with Michael and Adler's view (in *Crime, Law and Social Science*) that the basic sciences for the applied science of criminology are psychology on the one hand, and sociology on the other. Their doctrine extends to all the technologies involved in legal institutions.

But Austin rightly contended that an attempt at too extensive a study would result in a student failing " to know anything well ". Along this line of thought I hope for even more selection to be allowed to a law student within the field of legal studies.   Austin had also to contend with the doctrine that the classics and mathematics were the best, if not the only, vehicles for the development of mental powers.   With regard to classics, Austin's reply was to distinguish the subject of classical litera- ture from its language : the subject-matter was to be found in the various disciplines, its language was best studied at school.   With regard to mathematics, Austin denied its superiority either to logic or law as a training of the mind.   For him, as for Burke, the study of law did " quicken and invigorate the understanding ", and for him its proper academic study would have not a narrowing but a liberal and widening influence.   For this reason he hoped to see men not " intending to practise " attending law lectures in the faculty of law.   For future lawyers a preliminary arts course was, according to him, quite unneces- sary.   If a man wants to walk from London to York, there is no need for him first to go to Exeter.

Austin departed from his German model in bringing the detailed study of English law within his college.   But, as we have seen, this was not a concession to professional criticism, but a consequence of his belief in its inherent educational value.   Both general jurisprudence and parti- cular jurisprudence were within the curriculum. Particular jurisprudence, it will be remembered, was for him the study of the actual rules of legal systems.   Within his curriculum he included not only English law, but other legal systems.   The study of English law included the study of its history, and the outlines of Roman, canon and feudal law were in one place introduced as sources of English law.   But the general picture is that of a detailed and critical study of English law which necessarily involved its history and its purpose, accompanied by a dogmatical and historical outline of other systems, including modern continental systems.   Austin firmly believed in the value of his academic curriculum as a preparation for the practice of the law.   He devoted particular attention to the practical value of general jurisprudence, not only as a training for legal practice but for the conduct of all public affairs.   He assumed that the practical value of legal history and comparative law was self-evident, but what is evident today is a continued need to convert lawyers to such a belief.

It is clear that the curriculum outlined by Austin is far too extensive for an undergraduate course.   To some extent the defect may be remedied by giving to the student a choice among the various subjects, provided that a balance is preserved between the various so-called " theoretical " and " practical " branches.   In particular, I do not see any need for a university student to traverse more than in broad outline many of the particular topics of English law.   I have the highest regard for the academic standards of American law schools, but I consider that their coverage of legal topics imposes far too heavy a task on the student. The average student cannot penetrate very deeply into each subject. Austin should have followed more closely the German model of his day. The post-graduate professional course should include not only a training in professional skills, such as advocacy, drafting and office management, but also the study of all the branches of law with which, in the view of the profession, a practitioner should be acquainted at the outset of his career. But it is not necessary for them all to be studied at the university. Perhaps the profession may require a more ample acquaintance with the branches it considers requisite than a student may have obtained at a university in any introductory outline course. Nevertheless, for the purposes of professional qualification, though not necessarily for the purposes of subsequent professional utilisation, it will not be requisite for the future practitioner to study those branches as thoroughly and critically as the subjects selected for the degree course. His university education will have given the student an awareness of how an outline may be elaborated.

Indeed, it might be questioned whether there need be any teaching, as opposed to study, of professionally required subjects. My answer to this question involves a dream of my own, which I relate before concluding this address. It is five years ago that I suggested as an alternative to fusion of the two branches of the legal profession fusion of their legal education, with consequent easier transfer from one branch to the other. I have subsequently developed that idea. I saw a university degree in law as the basis of a common legal education; but I do not envisage this as the only common part. I envisage future members of the Bar spending some time in a solicitor's office. Nor is this by any means all. The idea of common education for barristers and solicitors is being separately considered by the Bar Council and the Law Society. My dream is of a joint organ of both branches of the profession administering a scheme of common professional education. The four Inns of Court have demonstrated the fruits of co-operation in the Council of Legal Education: the local law societies work together with the Law Society of England and Wales.

Has not the time come for wider co-operation in some institution of education for lawyers, which might one day become a Royal College of Barristers and Solicitors or a General Legal Council? Such a body need not be restricted to organising the training in professional skills, whether through apprenticeship or through direct instruction, which the Council of Legal Education has shown possible in its practical classes. It might also organise courses of lectures and other classes in the various branches of law. The university study of law must be directed towards its scientific and philosophical basis. The professional study of law may be properly oriented towards practical application, and this without in any way controverting the thesis of Plato, restated by both Bentham and Austin, that theory and practice are not opposed, but interdependent. I envisage such a college not only providing instruction to candidates for the profession, but also " refresher " courses to members of the profession. Nor need such an institution neglect research both into basic legal theory and the efficiency of practical administration of law. For such purposes there may well be co-operation with university faculties in particular projects. But I would also wish for co-operation with academic teachers of law in all aspects of the work of the institute : the governing body of the college might well include representatives of such university teachers.

My journey is almost complete. We have not been able to inspect at all thoroughly all that could have been seen. Perhaps I should have spent more time with international law. Though Austin did not include it within the class of law " properly so called ", he did include classes on the subject with the curriculum of his dream college. Clearly, it could not be excluded from a study concerned with the happiness and welfare of mankind. Can there be any doubt that ultimately this was Austin's concern? In this perspective his theory of law makes it not an instrument of power but a means for the control of power in the interest of " peace and good government ". His teaching is directed towards making law more effective for those ends. This is the message of Austin and his fellow jurists which comes down to us through the ages. It is not always delivered in the eloquent language of passion. It is the quiet voice of reason which is chiefly used—the still small voice of logic and justice. But it tells of human drama—of our hopes and fears. The chances are that if we fail to heed it we shall go out with many bangs and many whimpers.

5

General Principles of Law[*]

(1) Had the title of this paper found a place in the statement of claim of a litigant under the English legal system, I apprehend that the opposing party would have asked for further and better particulars of the scope and content of the subject. One who has voluntarily accepted a request by the organisers of a conference to write on such a subject finds himself without any such procedural aid. Though the conference is an international one, neither public nor private international law can help. The matter is regulated by the conventions of scholarship. By such conventions, moreover, it is the writer of the paper who is under an obligation to provide the table of contents of the paper. I shall endeavour to do so. Indeed, my first specification of the heroic title is that this paper is concerned with an author's search for the characters which constitute the notion of general principles of law.

(2) I begin by observing the principal features of the landscape which surround the scene. We are assembled at a comparative law conference. Can we derive help from this fact? I have drawn a distinction between comparative law and what I have called transnational additive law, that is to say between, on the one hand, a scientific study of the material provided by the existence of various legal systems and, on the other, a compilation, or even classification, of the rules of the various systems. In comparative law we seek for the principles common to different systems of law, perhaps those common to mature systems as opposed to primitive systems, as Austin might have said, or those common to capitalist systems as opposed to communist systems, as Marx or McCarthy might have said, or those common to all systems— the *jus gentium* of Roman legal ideology.

This approach, however, suggests rather than solves problems. In comparative law are we not seeking to identify common principles as opposed to expounding them? Can we follow the Romans and point to some broad principles about human behaviour, and say that these belong either to the *jus gentium*, or are common to a number of different legal systems? Can we say that countries have common principles of

* Rapport delivered at the Sixth Congress of the International Academy of Comparative Law, Hamburg, 1962. Unpublished.

65

contract and property law (substituting " property " for Justinian's example of slavery) making comparative law " scientific " by finding explanations for such uniformity, either by reference to the Justinian anticipation of Darwin as the adaptation of human beings, to similar environments, or by reference to Roman imposition of culture or other modes of cultural diffusion?   Do we find such common principles by looking for direct identity or similarity, a one-to-one correspondence of one law with another, among the verbal propositions which are assumed by the Institutes to form the laws of diverse countries—an anticipation of the Benthamite doctrine that law is an aggregate of rules of law?   We know that similarities may be found by comparing a group of rules with another group—one institution with its complex of rules with a similar institution having verbally different rules.   May we not have to think yet again about the nature of the " law " we are examining, and, perhaps, reject the Benthamite assumption of law as but a complex of verbal propositions about the behaviour of citizens? Lord Radcliffe, writing of the English common law, says, with apparent approval of the description, that " The law has been described as a mode of treating legal problems rather than a fixed body of definite rules ".   Is he not here perhaps referring to patterns of judicial behaviour? What I hope emerges from this discussion is that there may be general empirical principles of law common to various countries dealing with the ways of life of rulers, judges, officials, lawyers, or groups of citizens, as distinct from general analytical principles of law common to various countries, which latter may be discovered by that inductive process favoured by Holmes of following rules of law into their highest generalisations.   I should also make clear that in this paper I am not going to enter on an exposition of alleged general principles, such as *pacta sunt servanda, nullum crimen sine lege, audi alteram partem* or, to turn to the English tongue, " no liability without fault " or " no deprivation of property save by due process of law." I am not even going to consider whether they exist as principles common to different systems.

(3) Indeed, I am now going to turn from the wider perspectives of comparative law to consideration of general principles of law within particular legal systems—believing, however, that such a discussion is not irrelevant to the problems of comparative law.   Indeed, I would be prepared to contend that such consideration is *essential*.

Unlike Radin, I am convinced that a proper humility requires us to continue the search for a definition of law, aware however that any definitions we adduce may be no more definitive than those of previous thinkers who have sought to encompass the philosophy of law within a nutshell.   Austin laid down for English jurists the proposition that every rule of law must contain a sanction—a proposition which English judges find irrelevant to their examination of the problem (which is by no means uncommon) whether statutory rules are mandatory or directory, compulsory or optative. The Austinian thesis appears in the Marxian hagiographa as the doctrine that bourgeois law is the apparatus of coercion of a non-communist society. However, the doctrine that " law " is necessary even in communist societies joins hands with the assertion that certain systems, (such as those of the Jewish diaspora and International law before the millennium), are legal systems despite the absence of coercion. The effect of all this is to contradict the Marx-Austin power-realist conception of law. This aspect of a very important controversy concerning the definition of law appears to me, however, to be less significant than the aspect arising from the rejection of the imperative theory of law and the substitution for it of the thesis that a rule of law asserts a *normative* relation between one set of facts and another. In Kelsen's theory rules of law are of the form: " If there are legal antecedents there ought to be legal consequences ".

According to this view what we have is a relation between the possible actions of individuals and actions that others are authorised to take if such possibility is actualised. In this conception *a rule* of law is a verbal proposition, and we are referred solely to its mode of operation by virtue of the structure of its content. In this conception a rule of law is not concerned with any question of evaluation, nor with any empirical statement about the function of law in society: we are not concerned with the nature of legal systems, but with the logical structure of single rules of law. It is thus theoretically possible to contend that " law " as a social institution is a means of social control, but at the same time, to eliminate from the definition of a rule of law any reference whatsoever to its function within the society of whose law it is a part. This logical formula depicts a rule of law (which is in fact an instrument for the achievement of a social objective,) but omits any explicit reference to its instrumental character. It is, of course, true that in the presentation of the rules of law of various countries—in case law as well as in codified systems—the ordinary statements of the rules do generally accord with the abstract antecedent —consequent relationship of Kelsen's formula. Herein perhaps lies a reason why the bare comparison of such verbal formulations help but little in the comparison of legal institutions. Ought we not to recast our formula of the logical structure of a rule of law? Should not the policy of a rule of law be included within the logical framework of the scheme for a rule of law? The result would be that the formula for a rule of law should be, in accordance with the Ihering-Stammler view of law as a teleological directive—To achieve a particular social objective as a particular legal incentive (which may be a sanction, permission or reward) is authorised in respect of specified behaviour of specified individuals.

It is my submission that such a formula would be more truly descriptive of the operation of legal rules within the English system

than those formulae which are usually found in textbooks both of
jurisprudence and law which consist of the bare statement of impera-
tives or of attributions of consequences. I submit as evidence for this
view: (a) in the case of statute law, the extent to which in interpretation the policy of the statute is controlling through the invocation of the
Rule in *Heydon's Case* : (b) in respect of case law, the extent to which
the words of a judgment are limited as to their binding authority by
judicial consideration of the purpose of the decision in the light of the
issues being litigated.

This suggested analysis of the logical structure of a legal rule may,
of course, require amendment: the formula proposed may be lacking
in felicity in more than one respect. The suggested correspondence of
the formula with the sentences in legal discourse, usually called rules
of law, may not be absolutely accurate. Nevertheless, our analysis does
serve to indicate that in a discussion of general principles, both within
the sphere of municipal law and the sphere of comparative law, we
cannot ignore policies. Indeed it may well be that what is to be found
in common in different communities are policy objectives, and that the
variations of legal rules arise but from the common experience of a
multiplicity of causes. The repeated rules of different systems may be
but different means of securing identical ends.

When attention is directed to the instrument-policy relationship
in legal rules as opposed to the relation of antecedent and consequent,
it becomes evident that we must include within the sphere of legal
study the problem of cause-effect generalisations about social behaviour.
In the antecedent-consequent relation of the Hohfeld-Kelsen analysis
the consequent is *attributed* to the antecedent by virtue of the law-
derived verbal nexus. No predictions are made as to the probability
of the behaviour in the consequent following in fact from the antecedent
behaviour. It is, of course, possible to enquire into such probabilities,
and such enquiry may lead to the formulation of so-called sociological
" laws ": e.g., that in countries with a police force recruited on the basis
of educational qualifications of type x, paid on a salary scale y, and
organised in accordance with method z, the percentage of known
offences of burglary which result in convictions before legal tribunals
will be of the order of a. In the English language, as far as I am aware,
such probability statements would not be called principles of law. On
the other hand, a policy statement may well be called a legal principle.
And the policy formulation does call for a casual connection between
the social objective and the legal means. We are compelled to consider
not merely the *validity* of laws, but also their *efficacy*. Enquiring into
such efficacy involves consideration of the varying conditions within
each legal system—variations which may explain why different rules
have been developed to achieve the same purpose. There is also a
much more fundamental enquiry, which, though unencumbered by
varieties in economic, demographic and other social facts, is no less

arduous. It is the enquiry into human psychology, especially into the basic drives and external influences which determine or distort human behaviour.

(4) The above stated distinctions between legally recognised policies, sociological generalisations about legal behaviour, and normative prescriptions do not exhaust the rich potentiality of the broad notion of legal principles. Again, I refer to the English language, and note that therein the word " principle " is sometimes used to refer to a specific legal " doctrine ", a rule, and sometimes to a generalisation lying behind and unifying a number of detailed rules. When Lord Mansfield said that precedents do but serve to illustrate principles, he had in mind no wide sweeping generalisation, but specific rules. Yet the distinction between the general and the particular is made by contrasting the terms " principle " and " rule ". The rule-principle of a case is a proposition transcending the particular facts of the case: and the principle behind a rule is one which transcends the factual concepts which are embodied in one or more rules. Lord Mansfield discerned that wise use of the dependence of rule on principle would enable a case law system to adapt itself to changing social circumstances. In the *Maxim-Nordenfeldt* case, the House of Lords in this fashion transmitted the concept of geographical generality, in the old rule about restraints of trade, into one of economic reasonableness, and was thus able to adapt a law of the stage coach period into one valid for an era of railways and telegraphs. This notion of generality, which was already inherent in the concept of principle itself, applies not only to discourse about the verbal propositions of lawyers' law, but also to sociological discourse about legal institutions. The principle of official regulation of sexual intercourse is illustrated by a variety of marriage institutions.

This contrast between rule and principle is paralleled to some extent by the contrast between the detailed precepts of primitive law (now echoed in much social legislation, such as that concerned with percentages of fat in milk and alcohol in blood) and, on the other hand, the broad terms of modern rules, which leave so much scope for discretion in their application to particular circumstances. The Constitution of the United States regards vagueness in criminal statutes as a defect, but even their statutes are expressed in broad terms. The wide, flexible terms of the Constitution, e.g. " equal protection of the laws "— " due process "—have been praised by Mr. Justice Holmes as the embodiment of two thousand years of civilisation. It is to the great American jurist, Roscoe Pound, that we must still turn for the best analysis so far made of the varieties of what he terms " authoritative materials for decisions." But his analysis in terms of detailed precepts, standards, and conceptions, now some fifty years old, is surely in need of further analysis. At one time he included " ideals " as on a par with " conceptions " and " standards ". I think this earlier analysis of his was correct. And, of course, I have affirmed that view in my thesis concerning the part that policies should play in the formulation of a definition of law.

(5) There is yet another line of enquiry to be pursued. To what extent is any principle entitled to be called specifically legal? Is not the principle of no liability without fault an ethical principle, the doctrine of prohibition of restraint of trade an economic principle, the assertion of freedom of association a political principle? If we analyse the reasoning by which we seek to justify legal principles, to what extent do we discover among the premises psychological and sociological theories?

What are legal policies but approximations to the wisdom of a philosopher-king? We may, perhaps, perceive this more clearly by thinking of those definitions of law in which it is equated with social welfare; or with social justice; or with justice simply. Is social welfare or justice the concern only of jurists? An answer from the opposite point of view is that lawyers are not concerned as such with social welfare or justice, but merely with the administration of rules which may embody any set of values whatsoever. To this a rebutter comes again from Lord Radcliffe in his North-western University Lectures; and I quote the passage : " We cannot learn law by learning law. If it is to be anything more than just a technique, it has to be so much more than itself: a part of history, a part of economics and sociology, a part of ethics and a philosophy of life ". But at the close of these pleadings we are still left with the issue: what specific elements in a legal system may be said to be the exclusive province of jurists?

This question has long been debated, and I do not presume here to deliver even an interlocutory judgment. We may, however, derive some insights by looking again at one of the first formulations of the debate. Aristotle tells us that in addition to the Platonic conception of justice as equivalent to the good in general—the concept for which English translators use the term " general justice "—we must recognise also, " particular justice "—that element of good which belongs particularly to the judicial process.

The Platonic conception presents law as a goddess who weighs in the balance the contributions made by the particular social sciences and humanities, by economics and sociology, by history and ethics—and then resolves what is best for a society as a whole, and, indeed, for humanity. Such a view, while it attributes a final responsibility to law, nevertheless imposes also an immediate duty to acquire knowledge of the results of special disciplines. Let me illustrate by a consideration of the defence of insanity in criminal law. The psychiatrist supplies the evidence of sanity or insanity, but it is for the legislator in general, or for the judge in a specific case, to determine the social responsibility of the criminal and his liability to the processes of the criminal law. The psychiatrist presents but a part of what is relevant to the general problem of how society should deal with insane persons whose actions constitute an external infringement of society's criminal code. In

England judicial legislation has determined that some insane persons may yet be responsible according to the standards of criminal law, (though Parliament has recently provided for the different treatment of insane criminals, who may be sent to mental hospitals and not to prisons). Here we see the legislator weighing in the balance the character of the individual mind, as portrayed by the psychiatrist against the general impact on society of exempting the insane from all responsibility. But though the legislator has in consequence a superior task to that of the psychiatrist, he has, nevertheless, the preliminary task of acquiring accurate knowledge of the conclusions of psychiatry.

From Aristotle we derive the thesis that the specific legal element of justice is the notion of equality. Aristotle does not depict a merely mechanical notion of equality, though there are situations in which " arithmetical equality " is the appropriate criterion: this is true in the areas of what he calls " commutative justice ". He presents also the notion of geometrical equality in the area of " distributive justice ". Here, the basic idea is that of equality of merit. In other words, men are not to be regarded as equal, irrespective of their actions, for then we would be all equally guilty or equally innocent in respect of all crimes. Nor are they to be regarded as unequal irrespective of their actions, so that one man is guilty of a crime in a particular situation and another in precisely the same situation is adjudged innocent. What we have, in effect, is a specific contribution of law to the complex idea of justice, consisting in the notion now widely known as the rubric " The Rule of Law ". It has two aspects: on the one hand, the notion expressed in the Bill of Rights—that of the grant to all citizens of the " equal protection of laws "; and, on the other, the notion, which alone justifies the blindfolding of the goddess of justice—that of the " impartial administration of law ".

(6) We may also find in the Fifth Book of the Ethics some consideration given to that mode of approach to our present problem, which is indicated by the controversy being carried on, both in Britain and the United States, in the language of the relation between law and morals. For Aristotle law is limited in its operation to external behaviour in so far as it involves the relations of man to man. In a closely knit society it may be difficult to discern how far the behaviour of one man can be without some effect on his fellow men. But those today who assert that there is a private sphere of individual thought and action which should not be the concern of laws base their attitude on something other than the limits of the physical effects of an individual's actions. We have, indeed, passed from a doctrine of tolerance of variations of thought and actions, irrespective of their social consequences, to a doctrine of encouragement of variety of thought and action because of the enrichment of social and individual life which is its social consequence.

There is, however, one distinction between law and morals which is independent of the consideration of any difference between legal and moral objectives. It is concerned with the efficacy of legal means to attain social objectives. One of the great advantages of a comprehensive survey of the legal systems of the world is that it enables us to see what a great variety of legal instruments have been fashioned and how they may be employed to achieve a variety of human purposes. It has often been stated that the spheres of justice and benevolence are distinct because men cannot be made kind by law. I believe that anthropologists can supply evidence from so called " primitive " communities, and penologists evidence from methods of treatment of modern crimes, to show that " legal " institutions may induce varieties of dispositions in the plastic human being. Nevertheless, there always exists the problem of whether a specific social objective is best attained by means of a legal institution or in some other way, e.g. by the pressure of public opinion or by education. This is the character of natural law which distinguishes it from moral law. " Moral law " sets out a way of life for the individual, to which his will should be directed, whether as ruler or citizen. " Natural law " is concerned not only with a philosophy of life, but also with a philosophy of government: it is concerned both with legal ideals and with the efficacy of legal rules as instruments for the realisation of those ideals.

(7) This reference to Natural law reminds us of the age-old problem of the relation between *jus gentium* and *jus naturale,*—a problem which surely should be borne in mind in any comparative law study. But I shall conclude this examination of the characteristics of general principles of law by considering the stage in the history of natural law which produced the language of natural rights. Are not general principles of law but an elaboration of the rights of man? If this be dismissed as too idealistic a notion, we have yet to consider that the question has not to be asked in relation only to natural rights, but also in relation to those " rights " which have been recognised by a legal system, and which are enforced thereby. These are the " interests " of Ihering's theory of law. Are these " interests " anything more than statements of what legal policies signify in terms of their impact on men and women? The language of " interests ", public, social, or individual, provides a convenient method of grouping together rules which form part of the total complex of " *droit objectif* ". But the rules themselves are conceived not only as means for the realisation of " *droit objectif* ", they are also conceived as creating in men and women a complex of " *droits subjectives* ". Is not the significance of rules of law for men and women to be found not only in the interests which such rules protect, but also in the totality of individual rights and duties which the rules create? Perhaps the comparative lawyer should seek not only for common principles of law, but also for common rights and duties? Kocoureck envisages the judicial process as concerned with *three* distinct areas of inquiry: into the relevant laws: into the relevant facts: and into the relevant " jural relations ". In my opinion, however, we have here the third wheel of a bicycle in the sense of a

fifth wheel of a coach. " Jural relations " are not independent of laws and facts: they are but convenient ways of describing the application of general laws to particular facts. The abstract rule of law *alterum non laedere* confers, directly, rights on all persons not to be assaulted and, indirectly, rights of action if they are assaulted. The principle *pacta sunt servanda* confers rights *in rem* in English law on all that others shall not conspire maliciously to interfere with their privileges of entering into contracts; rights *in personam* against parties with whom they have contracted; and also rights of action for breaches of contract. Primary rights and sanctioning rights, rights and remedies, are but concepts employed in relation to the various stages of application of rules of law to particular situations. In primitive law rules are stated in terms of remedies; later, rules are often stated in terms of rights and duties; and finally, in terms of abstract relations of factual, antecedent and consequent. But whether the language employed be in terms of rules or rights or remedies the basic notions are identical. The comparative lawyer, seeking for common principles, should seek these among propositions concerned with remedies and rights as well as among " laws ".

(8) I conclude by proffering the table of contents which earlier I said convention required me to produce. I shall not follow precisely the order in which the items appear in the paper. Nor shall I supply an index under the guise of a table of contents. The order I follow is that of the words in the title of the paper.

(i) *General.* How general? Principles behind a particular complex of rules, or which are at the base of systems of law? of one country; or many countries; or all countries? How are such common principles related to " natural " law?

(ii) *Principles.* How are policies of rules related to inductive generalisations from rules; or to the " interests " of Ihering and Pound? What is the relation of policy to rule, and of principle to rule? And how do such relations take account of the varying conditions in different political units and of the changing circumstances within any one legal system? What is the logical structure of a rule of law? What account should be given of types of legal rules in terms of detailed precepts, general standards, flexible conceptions? To what extent should be disregarded the variety of formulations of principles in terms of rules or rights or remedies?

(iii) *Law.* To what extent are we concerned with sociological generalisations about behaviour, and to what extent with normative verbal propositions? How are legal principles distinguished from those of morals and politics? How are such principles related to propositions discussed in the social sciences about human nature and actions— sciences, such as economics and sociology, psychology and anthropology. How are they related to propositions discussed in the humanities, such as history and philosophy, ethics and metaphysics? Are they principles of legal means as well as principles of legal ends?

6

The Use of Legal Categories in Problems Concerning Compilation of Customs and of Codification*

(1) The two papers presented to this group deal only with particular aspects of the topics.[1] The exact scope of the topic is not clear. It may well be that since the topic falls under the more general title of " Legal Ethnology ", it was not conceived as extending to the enormously wide problem of codification in general, but was restricted to the codification of customs. This is how the topic was interpreted by Dr. Müller, who entitled his paper " The problem of the use of legal categories in the adoption and codification of native law." Nevertheless, the wider interpretation of the title does present a unified topic. There is a single problem of the manner in which legal categories are employed whenever " unwritten law " is converted into " written law ". It matters not whether the " unwritten law " be the rules of a common law system or of a customary law system. There is a cognate problem in the codification of statutes, when " written " laws promulgated at different times in relation to different social problems, and consequently employing varying terminology and concepts, are re-written at one time in the form of a code employing throughout a uniform terminology and system of concepts.

(2) Only the second half of Dr. Müller's paper falls strictly within the scope of the topic (even if widely interpreted), and this report will be largely concerned with the subject of that half.

(3) The paper submitted by Mr. A. G. Chloros of the University of London was entitled " The Relationship between Law and Custom in England : a Comparative Approach ". It dealt with the extent to which custom is considered either as law *per se,* or as a source of law in the legal systems of England, Rome, France, Germany and Switzerland.

---

*Rapport delivered at the Sixth Congress of the International Academy of Comparative Law, Hamburg, 1962. Published by Établissements Émile Bruylant, Brussels, and reprinted by kind permission.
[1] A. G. Chloros (London): *The Relationship between law and custom in England: a comparative approach*; Ernst W. Müller (Heidelberg): *Problematik des Gebrauchs juristischer Kategorien bei der Aufnahme und bei der Kodifizierung von Eingeborenenrecht.*

Legal customs are distinguished both from judge-made rules and from trade usages. It is shown that in English law " trade usages " operate as contractual terms, and are to be distinguished from the *usages conventionnels* of French law, and the *Verkehrsitte* of German law. Reference is also made to the subjection of contracting parties to statutory rules, whose content is derived from commercial practice or convenience.

Finally, the existence of custom as a source of law is attributed to the movement of society from a charismatic to a rational stage.

(4) The first half of the paper submitted by Dr. Ernst W. Müller of the University of Heidelberg is largely concerned with the age-old problem of the definition of law. What is specifically considered is how far it is proper to describe the régime of social order in " ethnological societies " as one of " law " : how far can the institutions and organisation by means of which social cohesion and stability are achieved be said to be of a legal character. Müller prefers the approach of Karl Llewellyn to that of Geiger. Geiger limited the concept of law to those societies where there existed some institution which represented superior and centralised power, whose function, however, was the expression of public reaction to the behaviour of members of the society. On the other hand, Llewellyn had a much broader concept of " law ". Law existed wherever effective means existed of dealing with situations of conflict and maintaining order in accordance with public opinion. " Law " exists, however, at several levels : under the comprehensive notion of law-stuff may be subsumed law-ways, which are concerned with the specific character of legal relations. Müller discusses the problem not only in relation to " ethnological societies " of today, but also in relation to " *mos* " of early Roman Law. But while " early Law " and the contemporary law of " Natur-völker " appear to fall equally within the province of " legal ethnology ", Müller does later warn against assuming that they share like notions.

The phrase " Ethnologie Juridique " has a German equivalent of " Rechtsethnologie ", which Müller uses to refer to the discipline whose subject matter is the law of societies where customary law prevails. Müller refers to the laws of various African societies (he has himself studied the Ekonda and the Mongo Bokoté), the laws of North American Indians, and the laws of Polynesian societies. I am not sure that " Legal Ethnology " is a satisfactory English translation of these phrases. The nearest phrase in general use is perhaps " Historical Jurisprudence ". This is the term which was used to cover the studies made by Maine in *Ancient Law, Early Law and Custom and Village Communities;* it was also applied to the theories of Savigny and his followers. Thus the term covers three distinct topics :

(i) exposition of past systems of law, such as early Roman Law;

(ii) exposition of contemporary systems of customary law;

(iii) theories of the genesis and evolution of law.

F

The phrase " primitive law " has been used in a more or less similar way. The appellation of " primitive law " for contemporary societies is, however, not only politically undesirable because of its pejorative character, it is also scientifically false. Though used by Hoebel in his major work, *The Law of Primitive Man,* it is likely that it will cease to be used both by anthropologists and jurists. English legislation of the " imperialist " era in referring to the customary law of " colonial " peoples used the phrase " native law and custom ", indicating a unity between " law and custom " in harmony with Müller's acceptance of Llewellyn's theory. Müller, as is seen from his title, employs the phrase " Eingeborenenrecht ". He also uses the term " Natur-völker " when speaking of societies where customary law prevails. It is doubtful whether such terms will survive in the new era where countries which were once " colonies ", and subject to the non-native law of the colonial power, have achieved sovereign independence.

(5) Dr. Müller has himself divided his paper into two parts. Part A is entitled " Terminological Problems of Research in Legal Ethnology ", and Part B " European Terms in the Codification of Native Law ". These titles themselves indicate the problem of the difference of approach of an " ethnologist " and of a lawyer *stricto sensu.* This difference, which is referred to in Müller's discussion of the definition of law, indicates the existence of a basic problem in the theory of legal categories, and will be considered later. I am concerned now to suggest that Dr. Müller's own division into Part A and Part B does not correspond with the logical division of the problems discussed in his paper. Part A deals both with the definition of law, and with the application of the special concepts of European legal systems made in the description of customary law systems. The second topic of Part A is closely linked with the topic of Part B. Identical problems concerned with the character of legal categories arise whether one is expounding customary law or codifying it. A lawyer trained in English law may become a judge in a colony, and be required to enforce the customary law of the colony. He will use the English language in his statement of customary law. What are the consequences of his use of English legal terminology in that statement? For ease of administration the customary law may be codified. The code is expressed in the English language devised by a draftsman trained in English law. Here we have the same problems of the consequences of the use of English legal terminology.

(6) As Müller indicates, the problems connected with the use of European legal concepts in the compilation and codification of customary law cannot be adequately considered without further examination of the concept itself of " legal category ". There are many problems which have to be considered in the use of legal categories in relation to advanced legal systems. The problem of the transferability of concepts from European legal systems to customary legal systems is paralleled by the problem of the transferability of concepts employed in one

branch of English law to another branch of English law. (See Hancock : *The Fallacy of the Transplanted Category*: 37 Can.B.R. 535.) Enlightenment may come from consideration of the more general philosophical problem of the nature of " category " itself. (This may seem doubtful at first sight, for the problem of " universals " has an even longer and more controversial literature than the problem of " definition of law ". But much of the controversy concerned with the definition of law might have been avoided if more attention had been given to the general philosophical problem of the nature of definition.) Is it not relevant to Dr. Müller's plea for the construction of " type-concepts ", concepts which are to be available for the description of different systems of law, to pay regard to Wittgenstein's theory of concepts derived from " family resemblance "? A concept, such as " acid " in chemistry, or " horse " in ordinary language, may be derived from consideration of the characteristics common to the various particulars classified together by means of the concept. Here we have a true generic concept defined by reference to those common characteristics : it is *l m*, while the various members are *l m a b, l m c d, l m e f* and so on. On the other hand, a concept may not be capable of being defined by reference to a set of common characteristics because one does not exist. The members of the class designated by the concept are linked through resemblances *l m a b* resembles *m n b c,* and *m n b c* resembles *n o c d.* There is nothing common to *l m a b* and *n o c d,* nevertheless they may both be comprehended under the same class name, that name indicates a family resemblance. John Stuart Mill considered that the manner in which words in ordinary language extended their range of application by such a use of analogy made them of little value for scientific discourse, but the recognition of the character of concepts of family resemblance is necessary if they are not to be employed in a misleading manner.

(7) The general problems concerned with the nature of legal categories raised by Dr. Müller are these :

(i) The problem of the construction of concepts which may be used in the description of any legal system. Are categories like public law and private law, criminal law and delict, marriage and property, true universals? Or does their indiscriminate use in relation to different legal systems result in a misleading picture of the law existing in particular societies?

(ii) The problem of the character of legal categories arising from the manner in which the operation of rules falling within a particular category is affected by the existence of rules classified under another category. The most general example of this, with which, however, Müller does not deal, is the way in which rules of substantive law are modified by rules of procedural law.

(iii) The problem of the character of legal categories arising from the manner in which changes occur through time in the character of legal rules in the process of their application without any formal alteration in the rules. The same terms continue to be employed, but the substance of the concepts is altered. Changes may be brought about by alteration in judicial ideas, which may, or may not, be the product of altered social conditions.

(8) The first problem, that of universal categories, is cognate to Austin's consideration of the existence of necessary or common notions of law. Müller considers that Hohfeld's "fundamental legal conceptions" have a universal character, but with Austin one may doubt whether the concept of "right" is a true universal. Müller, however, examines the concept of "*Eigentum*" and considers that this does form a universal *Typus-Begriff*.

The problem of such universal concepts is not only the concern of the legal ethnologist, it is also the concern of the comparative lawyer. Müller refers to Esser's work on the problem of comparing rules of law of societies which confront different social problems. What is the utility of a category so comprehensive that it embraces rules concerned with different social objectives? Is the "ownership" that exists in customary law societies with a simple economy the same as the "ownership" of European societies with their complex economic organisation? Do not the differences of functions of powers of disposition indicate real differences of concepts, which are concealed by using the same term for both concepts?

(9) The second problem is illustrated by Müller by an examination of the concept of "ownership". The definition of "ownership" in para. 903 of the B.G.B. acknowledges the existence of general legal limitations on the powers of an owner. But the character of such limitations greatly modifies the substance of ownership. Ownership of urban property is greatly modified by the extensive character of the modern law of Town Planning. The enormous literature on the "eminent domain" and "due process" clauses of the Constitution of the United States testifies to the way in which "ownership" may not be merely limited but "taken" and the owner "deprived" of his property. A useful illustration of the problem is provided by the Northern Ireland case of *Belfast Corporation* v. *O.D. Cars*.[1]

Müller gives an example where the limitation of ownership, though equally important, is not achieved in so direct a manner. In German Family Law the duty of maintenance is now borne equally by both spouses. The law making that change in Family Law makes no direct reference to the ownership of land or goods, but there can be no doubt about the change effected thereby in the extent of the powers of disposition of the spouses.

(10) The last illustration serves also as an example of the manner in which change in the substance of concepts is affected by historical changes in law. Müller's treatment of this problem draws attention to

---

[1] [1960] A.C. 490.

the manner in which judge-made law may produce contrast between " law in books " and " law in action " recognised by American sociological and realist jurisprudence in relation to modern law. An aspect of this gap arises from the manner in which concepts continue to be defined in the old terms despite the fact that they no longer correspond with the social realities of the administration of law. In this respect customary systems of law do not differ from modern systems, as is shown both in Pospisil's researches in Papua, and Müller's in the Belgian Congo.

(11) One way in which " native law " may be changed is through its administration by judges trained in the imperialist law of the colonial power, who use the language of that colonial power in expounding the indigenous law. The use of a different language in an unreflective manner may by itself be sufficient to introduce different concepts into the native law, and such a possibility is strengthened if the judges unconsciously assume that the concepts of their imperialist law are universal. Changes brought about by judicial belief in the superiority of what are the judges' native legal concepts and rules are in a different class. Müller shows how the use of an imperialist term in the administration of native law may even bring about a change in social practice. In African societies a marriage ceremony includes a payment made by the bridegroom and his " family " to the " family " of the bride. In the Belgian Congo where the French language was used by the Belgian administration the word " dot " was used to describe this payment. (In English colonies the word " dowry " is sometimes used.) Moreover, the verb " *acheter* " came into use also. The " *dot* " was the payment " to purchase " the bride, and was a " bride-price ". The Belgians thought in commercial terms of the transaction, and thought of a bride being bought and becoming the groom's property, in the same way as goods and chattels are bought. This was indeed at first a complete misdescription of the transaction, but in some areas in course of time the influence of these erroneous ideas brought about a change in the customary practices. What was misdescription of the original practice became description of the new practice.

I have set out this example at length because the problem arises whether linguistic usage is a sufficient explanation of the error. Müller is prepared to accept Dr. Allott's description of a corresponding marriage practice in Nigeria in terms of the English concept of " marriage consideration ". But is not the principal cause of error the failure to penetrate sufficiently deeply into the institution which is being considered and to be content with a superficial view? We need to use a microscope in our analysis in order to distinguish between actions which may have an external resemblance : we need to see the institution from within as it is seen by those whose practices create the institution. We need also a telescope in order that actions and institutions should be seen in a proper perspective, modified by the total context in which they operate. In his dissertation for his Master's degree at Queen's University, Okunniga presents a very different picture of the Yoruba *Idana* from that of "bride price" or "marriage consideration". A suitor in European societies will make gifts to his beloved to win her affection, to persuade her to abandon other attachments and engage herself to him. Family ties are very strong in the Yoruba, and the family has to be persuaded as well as the bride, if the bride is to attach herself to the bridegroom. The *Idana* as a payment represents such an inducement to the parents to release in some measure the family ties. It is not a necessary requirement for a valid marriage, as it would be if marriage were a sale of the bride, and the *Idana* were the consideration.

(12) The errors which are created by the use of the conceptual terms of one legal system in the exposition of another legal system do not arise from the mere employment of the terms, but from the association with the terminology of a legal system of the rules of that system. The result is to incorporate into the second legal system which is being expounded in the language of the first legal system rules which belong to the first legal system alone. This erroneous procedure has been judicially noted by the British tribunal dealing with appeals from the colonies. Thus Viscount Haldane in *Amodu Tijen* v. *Secretary for Southern Nigeria,*[2] refused to use the language of "property" and "possession" in stating the relevant Nigerian law. He said: "There is a tendency operating at times unconsciously to render [native] title to land in terms which are appropriate only to systems which have grown up under English law". What he rejected was the attempt to introduce into Nigerian law distinctions which were made in English law by those terms, but which were not made in Nigerian law. Other distinctions made in Nigerian law could doubtless be made by using the words "property" and "possession". But what relation would the words "property" and "possession" used in the description of Nigerian law have to the words "property" and "possession" used in the description of English law? Ought we not perhaps to distinguish the concepts despite the similarity of the words by calling one set $property_1$ and $possession_1$, and the other set $property_2$ and $possession_2$? In consequence may we not create meta-legal concepts of property and possession which form "*Typus-begriffen*", of which $property_1$ and $property_2$, $possession_1$ and $possession_2$, are species? It will be noted that Viscount Haldane in his dictum has used a meta-legal concept, capable of being applied both to English and Nigerian law, when he spoke of "title".

(13) How far are meta-legal concepts necessary only when we use a telescope to survey the legal systems of the world and to seek to compare them with each other? Or when we seek to restate the legal rules of one system in the language of another country? Does not a jurist need such concepts in the juristic exposition of the rules of law of his own

---

[2] [1921] 2 A.C. 399.

country? He cannot merely report the language of the legislator and the judge without falling into the errors already noted : (i) of failing to make clear that the rules of law under one category are modified by the rules of law under another category; (ii) of failing to note that categories defined on the basis of the rules of law of one historical period are inappropriate to the rules of law of a later period. The jurist expounding the laws of his own country also needs a telescope so that he can comprehensively survey at one time the different categories of his legal system. An instrument has yet to be invented to enable one to survey contemporaneously events at two different historical periods! But perhaps the nature of meta-legal concepts may be understood if we use a microscope to examine legal concepts themselves.

(14) Legal categories, such as murder, theft, *mens rea*, attempt, assault, nuisance, negligence, promise, offer, sale, bill of exchange, are not all of one type. I make a distinction between law-embracing concepts and law-constituent concepts. This is not the place to examine at length the problem of the logical structure of a rule of law. The Hohfeld-Kelsen formula posits a relationship between factual antecedents and legal consequences. If any person intentionally kills another person then a legal tribunal is empowered to order the death of the killer.[3] I would incorporate in the statement of the rule a reference to the social objective for which the rule in the Hohfeld-Kelsen scheme serves as an instrument of social control. But this, and other differences of formulation, do not affect the present point. Some concepts signify the entirety of the relationships between the constituent elements whose relatedness forms the rule of law : some concepts signify but a constituent element. The former I call law-embracing concepts, the latter law-constituent concepts. A law-embracing concept is but one example of the " compacted-doctrine " words, discussed by Empson in the chapter of *The Structure of Complex Words* dealing with " statements in [single] words ". The concept of " murder " refers to the entirety of the rule, whereby a form of killing is made punishable. On the other hand, " homicide " may be used as a concept referring to but one constituent of the law of murder, viz. the element of killing a man. Homicide with " malice aforethought " is punishable by law in a specified manner : and the complex is known as murder. When, however, we say that " homicide with malice aforethought " is murder, " homicide " is used as meaning " unlawful killing ", and in this case " homicide " becomes a law-embracing concept, though what rule of law is embraced is not specified. Homicide is then a multi-law-embracing concept : and we may say homicide is either murder or manslaughter. Another example of a law-embracing concept is provided by statute. In section 1 of the

---

[3] [In many jurisdictions capital punishment for murder has been abolished; in Great Britain by the Murder (Abolition of Death Penalty) Act, 1965. Ed.]

Larceny Act, 1916,[4] there is a " definition " of stealing. That section specifies a set of behaviour characteristics, and we must turn to section 2, where the behaviour is made unlawful, and where the law-embracing concept of " simple larceny " is introduced. Larceny is the name of a type of crime : it is the embodiment in one word of the rule that stealing is punishable with imprisonment.

The language of law may not be clear enough to ensure definite classification of a word as a law-embracing or a law-constituent concept. Judges sometimes use the word " negligence " to indicate a tortious situation : that there has been carelessness resulting in damage where there was a duty to take care to avoid the damage. Sometimes it is used to signify merely carelessness, and its use does not indicate that there has been a breach of a duty. The ambiguity sometimes permits the word to be used as a law-embracing concept without specifying the characteristics of the rule of law embraced. We are not told what rule of law creates the duty, and we do not know what factual antecedents are specified as giving rise to the duty. The controversy surrounding the word " cause " in English law is concerned with the problem of whether it is used to embrace a rule attributing legal responsibility without specifying the basis of such attribution.

(15) Law-embracing concepts, like the fee simple of English law, are clearly derived from the rules of particular legal systems. Multi-law-embracing concepts are also thus related. " Homicide " as the general concept for murder and manslaughter in English law is thus related. " Ownership " as a concept of English law is related to rules concerning the fee simple, the leasehold interest, " property " in the Sale of Goods Act, the equitable interest. Does the word indicate more than a family resemblance among a number of particular concepts? If not, what are the characteristics of this " true generic " concept? Certainly, though in the usage of judges and lawyers it may be no more than a " family resemblance " word, it may be possible for the jurist to construct a concept transcending the particular rules, and to give it the label of " ownership ". There has been no lack of such endeavours : but this is not the place to comment on their success and failure. How far are these juristically created concepts of " ownership " legal or meta-legal?

Dr. Müller raises the problem of the existence and the need for a concept of " ownership " which applies to all legal systems. How far does the actual usage of the word " ownership " in reference to legal systems in general correspond with a *Typus-begriff*, a true meta-legal concept : or is there here any more than a " family resemblance "?

(16) The present discussion is, however, not immediately concerned with the problem of the " type-concept ". It is still necessary to say

---

[4] [This Act is unlikely to survive 1968 in its present form. A new simplifying Theft Bill, based on the recommendations of the Criminal Law Revision Committee (whose formation owed much to Montrose's efforts (see Introduction to this volume p. 2). being now before Parliament. Ed.]

something about law-constituent concepts, where perhaps such type-concepts may have their proper home. If, as I consider, social objectives are constituents of rules of law, then the categories which denote such objectives are " legal categories ", but of a different kind from law-embracing concepts. They are the " interests " of Ihering's and Pound's schemes, the " policies " of United States jurisprudence. Though legal rules may differ, there may be common characteristics of human beings and social organisations everywhere which may serve as the basis for universal objectives. There may be a common humanity, of a psychological as well as a physiological character. There may be, as Dr. Müller's reference to Korn's work on *Raumanspruch* indicates, a common " human instinct " for the expression of our personality in relation to some things around us. In such a case a concept of a common social objective to permit such " instinctive drives " to be realised may not only be the imaginative creation of a " theorist ", like the " golden mountain " of much logical investigation, but have a correspondence with reality. " Personality-extension-realisation " as a universal concept is, however, not identical with " ownership " as a *Typus-begriff*. It represents but an interest, a policy, a social objective, which may be a constituent of the rules of law of many countries. Dr. Müller's type-concept of " ownership " is that of the possibility of the realisation of extension of personality by legal means. The various legal means of different countries are not specified : they are united under one concept by reason of having a common objective. A law-embracing concept may thus have a " true generic " quality, as opposed to family resemblance, by reason of having a " true generic " law-constituent concept as an element.

(17) The inclusion of a social objective as a constituent element of a rule of law is controversial. Let us consider the constituent element of " factual antecedents ". An important distinction exists between the kinds of factual antecedents included in rules of law. If we look at the English law of murder, we observe the term " malice aforethought ". (This term may be an example of a concealed law-embracing concept in so far as it refers to " objective " states of mind, whose objectivity is determined by unspecified legal standards.) This is as an example of a technical-legal " factual concept ". Such a concept has as its elements facts, and not legal relationships, but the grouping of those facts together under one concept is contrived by legal process. What facts constitute " malice aforethought " is not determined by combining the ordinary notion of " malice " in the English language with the ordinary notion of " aforethought ". For the purposes of the law of murder " malice aforethought " has to be specially defined. So, too, " domicile " in English conflict of laws has to be specially defined, though it is reducible to a complex of facts. On the other hand, " residence ", for the purposes of rules of law containing the word, once retained the meaning it had in ordinary language. It was a non-technical factual concept. The

practice of saying that " domicile is a question of law and residence is a
question of fact " is doubtless due to the technical-legal character of the
one and the non-technical character of the other. But both are concepts
of " facts ". We may contrast the statement that ownership is a question of law and possession one of fact. Here analysis shows that
" possession " may be as much a question of law as is ownership.

In the interpretation of statutes the question often arises whether
a particular word has a special technical-legal meaning, or is to be read
with the meaning it has in ordinary speech. For a long time English
judges dealing with income tax law maintained that the word " income "
had to be interpreted in accordance with usages of ordinary people
using that word in their daily lives. This is the meaning of Lord
Macnaghten's *dictum* " Income tax is a tax on income ". The position
is now more doubtful in view of the many statutory provisions dealing
with various receipts and saying they are to be treated as income. Now-
adays it may be said that what is income is no longer a " question of
fact " but a " question of law ". Nevertheless, there are, of course,
many rules of law where the constituent element of " factual antec-
dents " is stated in terms of ordinary language and not in any technical
language of law. What, however, is of importance for our present purpose is not the mere use of words, but the manner in which they are used
to group facts together. The words " malice aforethought " are but
legal shorthand for a collection of ordinary words. It is true that " stealing " in the Larceny Act has not the meaning of ordinary language, but
a technical meaning defined by section 1 of the Larceny Act. It is,
nevertheless, a factual concept, the corresponding law-embracing concept
is " larceny " as defined in section 2. " Larceny " obtains its peculiar
characteristics by the use of the ordinary words of section 1 by which
stealing requires " an intent permanently to deprive " an owner of his
things.

A further word may be said about " ownership " and " possession ".
The statement that " Ownership is a question of law : possession is one
of fact ", has to be contrasted with the statement that " possession is a
question of law and occupation is one of fact ". These statements lose
their contradictory appearance when they are analysed by means of the
concepts we have been considering. In a particular sense of the word,
" possession ", as used in English law, refers but to a complex of facts,
whereas " ownership " embraces the notion of legal regulation of facts.
The complex of " possession " however is not determined by reference
to ordinary language. The complex is defined by law through the rules
which place that complex of facts in relation to legal consequences.

(18) The construction of type-concepts from the factual antecedent
constituents of rules of law would permit the grouping together under
the same concepts of rules of law which attribute different legal consequences to identical or similar factual antecedents. In the construction
of such type-concepts care must be taken in examining the factual ante-

cedent concepts of the particular systems of law to see whether or not they are of a technical-legal character. We should not be misled by mere similarity of terms based upon " ordinary language ". In so far as ordinary languages are based upon similar reaction of our " common humanity " to similar environments, it is perhaps from factual antecedents defined by ordinary words, not grouped together in a technical manner, that the type-concepts that Dr. Müller appears to envisage may be found. At this stage, however, we should note a point of view which arises from the fundamental question asked by Dr. Müller as to the aim of an inquiry into the propriety of applying European legal concepts in the exposition of customary systems of law.

Dr. Müller distinguishes between (i) inquiry conducted with the practical aim of setting out the customary law so that it may be administered by the officers of a colonial power, and (ii) an inquiry conducted with the aim of making a contribution to the empirical discipline of intra-tribal relations—an aspect of the sociology of social control. The distinction appears to have more wide-reaching consequences for the problem of legal categories than he perhaps envisages. We have here an aspect of the Kantian doctrine that the nature of our knowledge is determined by the nature of our inquiry: our concepts, by means of which we comprehend phenomena, are determined by ourselves, not by the phenomena. We may approach the legal systems of the world without the aim of looking for common concepts in them, but we may, nevertheless, construct common concepts which we use in examining them. We may construct a concept of ownership as the recognition by the legal machinery of society in some manner of a human claim to the expansion of personality by physical control of objects in environment, and then ask in what societies such a claim is recognised. We may note that in non-nomadic societies individuals and groups remain in occupation of land for considerable periods of time, and with such a concept of " occupation " ask what legal effect is given to occupation in various societies. Concepts of such a character have a validity independent of their existence within the rules of law of various societies. The concepts of " ownership " and " occupation ", as defined above, would be " valid " even though neither figure in the legal rules of any society. The utility of such concepts, however, depends on the nature of the inquiry that is made.

(19) The principle we have sought to establish is that an investigation which is concerned with the rules of law of the societies of the world is not bound to accept as its conceptual framework the concepts which are to be found in, or derived from, the rules of law themselves. If the object of a sociological inquiry is to discover generalisations concerned with the etiology of rules of law, or how social characteristics result from rules of law, it may be that a different set of concepts may have to be constructed. An objective pattern of relations may perhaps only be discovered by separating facts which are grouped together in

legal rules, or combining facts which are separated in legal rules. There
is a parallel with the empirical science of criminology. If we seek for
the causes of crime, we must not assume that relationships are to be
found capable of being expressed in terms of murder and manslaughter,
larceny and embezzlement, rape and carnal knowledge. Only by constructing other concepts may significant correlations be found.

(20) It may be useful to restate some of the conclusions I have come
to in this report. As I read his paper, Dr. Müller's basic theme is a
consideration of the problems encountered in an examination of the effect
of using the language of an advanced society, the language employed in
a European legal system, when discussing the legal system of a customary law society. I concur with his view that the problems encountered
have a far wider application than the subject matter of the particular
examination: they include the problem of legal categories employed in
comparative law, for example. I go further, and say that also included
are the general problems of the nature of legal categories *per se* in any
legal discourse, and the general problems of the nature of categories
per se in any type of discourse. In my opinion, examination of these
general problems is relevant to a consideration of the more particular
problems of comparative law and legal ethnology. Dr. Müller draws
attention to the need for further investigation of the problem of framing
legal categories comprehensive enough to be used in the description of
all legal systems. I go further, and say that we require further investigation of the manner in which general theory of categories is relevant to
particular problems of the conceptual framework of comparative law
and legal ethnology. I have submitted some suggestions in relation both
to general and legal categories. I do not, of course, regard these suggestions as definitive, and I am sure that further investigation will produce more useful analyses and syntheses. My suggestions are: (1) that
regard be paid to the distinction between " true generic " concepts and
" family resemblance " concepts in the area of categories *per se*: some
of the concepts regarded as of universal application in comparative law
may indicate no more than a " family resemblance " between the concepts of particular systems; (2) that regard be paid to the distinction
between what I call law-embracing and law-constituent concepts in the
area of legal categories: it is from law-constituent concepts that comprehensive categories are more likely to be constructed; (3) that regard be
paid to the distinctions between the various types of law-constituent
concepts—(a) social objectives (interests, policies), (b) concepts which
combine facts in a manner determined by legal specifications, (c) concepts
which combine facts in accordance with the modes of classification of
ordinary language, language which reflects the " natural " combinations
of social factors made in unconscious fashion by people: it is from social
objective concepts and social classification concepts that comprehensive
categories are more likely to be derived.

I am fully in agreement with Dr. Müller's view that attention should be paid to the purpose of a discourse in considering the nature of the categories used in that discourse. I concur with the distinction he draws between (a) discourse about customary law societies which has as its object the accurate restatement of the legal systems of those societies in the terminology of a foreign language, and (b) discourse about customary law societies which is conceived as a contribution to empirical sociology concerned to discover correlations having a similar character to laws of the natural sciences. Again I go further, and think it *a priori* unlikely that the conceptual framework for one discourse will be well suited to the other. On the other hand, I do not see any basic distinction between discourse concerned with the description or compilation of customary laws, and discourse whereby the substance of customary laws is embodied in a code. Similar problems arise in both, and a conceptual framework suitable for one may be well suited for the other.

I express too my agreement with Dr. Müller's view that misdescription and misunderstanding may often result from the restatement of customary law in the language of an advanced society embodying the concepts employed in its legal system. Great care is needed to ensure that rules associated with the concepts of the legal system of the advanced society are not injected into the description of the customary law. I see no reason, however, to limit this doctrine in the above fashion: a similar danger arises whenever the law of one society is being described in the language of another society. It is certainly desirable to have comprehensive concepts which will permit accurate description in any language of the various legal systems of the world. Dr. Müller uses the phrase " *Typus-begriff* " for these concepts: but since a concept or category is *ipso facto* concerned with types, perhaps the phrase " metalegal concepts " may be preferable. Presumably such concepts operate by facilitating the subsumption under one term of the particular concepts of various legal systems. The construction of such concepts is no easy task, as Dr. Müller makes very clear. One difficulty, however, may be removed by saying that it is not a necessary condition of the construction of such meta-legal concepts that they have to be manifested in every legal system. Dr. Miller appears to consider that a *Typus-begriff* is one which " appears " in all legal systems. He considers that " ownership " may exist everywhere. His concept of " ownership " is carefully framed so that it does not connote the possibility of private property in all kinds of things. Even so, its universality is doubtful. He is doubtful about the value of Hohfeld's scheme of fundamental legal conceptions, even though he agrees with many anthropologists that it is of universal application. (Max Gluckman is not cited by him: he thought that the Hohfeldian concepts were exemplified in the legal system of the Barotse.) I doubt whether the Hohfeldian scheme, linked as it is with the individualist, natural-right ideology of the United States, can be of universal application. I suspect that what is found to be of universal application is a simple logical truth. This may be what Dr.

Müller indicates when he speaks of the " analytical " character of the concepts. The " truth " of the Hohfeldian scheme is that there may be situations in which there is a duty to act, situations in which there is a duty not to act, and situations in which there are neither duties to act nor duties not to act. Incidentally, Dr. Müller refers to Radin's refinement of Hohfeld's scheme. This refinement reduces Hohfeld's scheme of eight concepts to one of four. The power-liability and immunity-disability conceptions exist on a different plane from the others. A power-liability concept is a combination of a claim-duty relation and the factual conditions whose existence is a condition of the existence of the claim-duty relation. If the distinction between legal and factual relations be taken into account, and full use be made of the processes of affirmation and negation, Hohfeld's scheme can be reduced to one concept—that of claim-duty. The insistence by Hohfeld on paying regard only to biological human beings states a truth of nature, but the truths of social organisation do not show that claims by individuals as such necessarily receive social recognition in legal institutions. " Rights " presuppose a social organisation which recognises the claims of individuals as such, as opposed to claims made on behalf of a group, or of the entire society. They are not a necessity of social organisation.

For the purposes of description it is not necessary to have a set of meta-legal concepts, such that within every legal system there is an example of every one of them. Meta-legal concepts are not confined to the concepts of some " jus gentium ". A valid meta-legal concept of " ownership " may be constructed, even though there may be societies where there is no particular legal concept falling within that general meta-legal concept. From such societies there will be a nil return to an inquiry about their type of " ownership ". Furthermore, since concepts may exist as logical entities without any empirical extension, there may be a valid meta-legal concept which forms a " null-class ". Legal reformers may speak of a " right to privacy ", even though no society recognises any form of such a right. The range of exemplification of meta-legal concepts in the various legal systems of the world is a matter for empirical observation. In a changing world legal changes may provide examples of meta-legal concepts which at an earlier time were without exemplification. In progressive societies jurists will fashion new meta-legal concepts capable of describing and transforming legal systems.

7

Law, Science and the Humanities*

In another year our Society will be celebrating its jubilee. It will then be the time for voices more eloquent than mine to sing the praises of the famous men, both those who were our founding fathers and those who continued their work. Minds more discerning than mine will then assess the impact that our Society has had on law teaching, and the effect that developments in society itself have had on our character and function. Our Society unites both teachers in universities and teachers in professional law schools; and the future judge of our work will consider both academic education and professional training. I have already indicated that it would be presumptuous for me to prescribe our jubilations. The honour and privilege of my Presidency is due to the accident of my position in a university law school. For these reasons I wish to direct my remarks to the task of the university faculty of law, and to say of the relation between academic education and professional training no more than this. I think it a great mistake for academic education to be too professional and for professional training to be too academic: as I think they too often are. I also think that the best preparation for the legal profession is a truly academic education in a faculty of law followed by a truly professional training.[1]

It is a tribute to the advocacy of my predecessors who have dealt with this subject that it is now a commonplace to say that a university faculty of law has to provide a liberal education. For myself I find this formula requires two glosses. In the first place the character of a liberal education is the subject of keen debate: the growth of science

---

* Presidential Address to the Society of Public Teachers of Law, in Belfast, on 18th September, 1957. It is reprinted from the *Journal* of the Society of Public Teachers of Law by kind permission.

[1] A " truly professional training " should, in my view, include instruction and practice in the skills and techniques of the profession, such as a medical student receives. Apprenticeship as an articled clerk in a solicitor's office, or as a pupil in a barrister's chambers, are examples of such training. Such training could be improved; for example, a bar student should be trained in advocacy through his own efforts as well as by listening to his master. Part at least of such training could be given in a law school. In my opinion the course given by the Council of Legal Education to recently called barristers should be given before call, or before a right to practise is deemed to exist.

and technology has challenged many conceptions formerly expressed. In the second place research is an integral part of the task of a university,[2] and we may neither ignore it, nor ignore the truth that the character of legal research, like that of a liberal education, provides scope for argument. To these controversies I address myself, but in an address of this kind I can but proceed by way of sweeping generalisations which may not only appear as, but be, imperfect inductions. I trust they will not be regarded as dogmatic assertions to be accepted without question, but as tentative hypotheses to be tested by critical consideration of the details to which I have not referred. Since, moreover, it would be too tedious for me to define all the terms I use, or analyse all the concepts I employ, perhaps in some cases it may be assumed that definition and analysis are not impossible, and my remarks be not immediately dismissed as that " vague clap-trap " for which the French have now coined the word " blablabla ". May I conclude these self-accusations by asking to be excused for confining my address to secular debate? The issues to which I refer have theological implications. My mishandling of their lay aspects may raise heat enough to scorch me. I fear that I have not the tact to make the most nonsectarian reference to religion without being withered by fire from believers and non-believers alike.

Teaching and research are in close-knit relationship. It is not merely that they interact, as is shown by the manner in which difficulties encountered in teaching indicate a problem for research, and research work so inspires teaching that the infective enthusiasm of the researcher is often more effective than pedagogical competence in making the undergraduate a true university student. It should be realised that both are aspects of a common university function and their common qualities illuminate the character of university work. The student is a researcher and the researcher is ever a student: they are engaged in a joint " adventure of ideas ". In the ideal university clear-cut distinctions appropriate to an adolescent stage disappear. It is not true that the undergraduate deals with the known while the researcher explores the unknown: the undergraduate is brought face to face with many an unsolved problem and dark mystery: the teacher looks again and again at the work of his predecessors, seeking for new meaning or old error. It is not true that the undergraduate is the passive recipient of facts, while the teacher is intellectually active as to their connection and significance: the student must learn how to pursue facts and how to evaluate them; the teacher must ever be humble before old and new truths. It is not true that the undergraduate studies law as it is

---

[2] Those who prefer judicial authority to academic dogmatism should note that there are *dicta* in charity cases on which an argument might be founded that research is not part of " education ": see *per* HARMAN, J., in *Re Shaw*, [1957] 1 All E.R., pp. 752D to 753H, citing *Whicker* v. *Hume* (1858), 7 H.L.C. 124 and *Re Macduff*, [1896] 2 Ch. 451.

while the researcher seeks to discover law as it ought to be: that *is* and *ought* are not more easily divorced than teaching and research. Often the law is what it ought to be and the law ought to be what is, because of the need for stability. Austin recommended that the use of the word " jurisprudence " be limited to analysis and synthesis of positive laws, but he also recommended that the student in a faculty of law should study both jurisprudence and legislation, both what is and what ought to be the law. If it be thought that the jurist expects too much from the undergraduate it should be remembered that a great judge, Lord Atkin, in our Society's *Journal*, presented no very different view of the task of the law student when he insisted that university law teaching must be the education of adults.[3]

It is this insight that at a university the undergraduate assumes responsible adult status—acquires freedom to think for himself, rejecting subordination to mere authority, liberating himself from prejudice but accepting bondage to truth—that provides perhaps the most important characteristic of liberal education. It is the critical approach to his subject, making full use of creative imagination, which leads the student of law, as of every subject, to philosophy and sociology. It is the antithesis of indoctrination, whose baleful effects are too well known: and it is the antidote to that rejection of learning which is not only amusingly seen in those who rapidly forget what they have crammed for an examination, but which we have been seriously told is widespread among those who have had to endure a half-baked education

" of the piling up of received opinions, of the acquiring of facts rather than of the use and handling of facts." [4]

As this writer tells us, this is not a new problem. Herbert Spencer spoke of it fifty years ago.

" The established systems of education, whatever their matter may be, are fundamentally vicious in their manner. They encourage *submissive receptivity* instead of *independent activity*." [5]

If that statement was then true of universities we have learnt much in fifty years. One great merit of the case method of legal education, outweighing many suggested defects, is its elimination of mere passive

---

[3] *Law as an Educational Subject*, 32 *J.S.P.T.L.*, p. 28. Cf. Cragg in *The Case Method of Teaching Human Relations and Administration* (Ed. K. R. Andrews) (1953): Harvard U.P., p. 5 : " Thinking out original answers to new problems or giving new interpretations to old problems is assumed in much undergraduate instruction to be an adult function and, as such, one properly denied to students. The task of the student commonly is taken to be chiefly of familiarising himself with accepted thoughts and accepted techniques, these to be actively used at some later time. The instruction period, in other words, often is regarded by both students and teachers as a time for absorption ".

[4] Hoggart : *The Uses of Literacy*, p. 243.

[5] Spencer : *Autobiography* (Watts edn.), p. 338.

G

absorption by the student of pre-digested opinion.[6]   In my opinion, however, the case system, where cases are not supplemented by " other material ", fails in the ultimate use of the method of criticism.   Criticism leads to philosophy and sociology because it is linked with scientific method and tests the validity of the general principles used in legal reasoning, and is not restricted to consideration of their genesis and purpose, their significance and application.   We fail in the maintenance of university values if we ignore scientific method in this endeavour. The critical spirit must be aware of, and participate in, scientific development.   Criticism in law cannot ignore the social sciences.

May I examine the notion of liberal education again from a slightly different point of view?   The understanding that liberal education is the education appropriate to a free man, the meaning appropriate to the etymology of the word, has in the past been confused with the misunderstanding that it is the education of " gentlemen ".   The one consideration may lead to the notion of responsible freedom of thought: the other may degenerate into the view that liberal education is useless education.   It is indeed healthy to protest against the shortsightedness of some utilitarian pleading, but the part played by law teaching in the foundation of the university system of Europe is a demonstration of the error of believing that knowledge utilised by a profession has no part in a university.   It is but another formulation of this error to believe that university teaching in law is liberalised by adding such subjects as Roman Law, Jurisprudence, Legal History, Comparative Law and International Law because they are of no professional use: and that one becomes a jurist as opposed to a mere lawyer by acquiring learning in one or more of these subjects.   The inclusion of any one of the subjects I have listed could be justified, if necessary, by its practical value, and this does not merely mean that the literature of the subject is sometimes quoted in a judicial opinion.   Juristic research may be directed to lawyer's law, and, indeed, the limited amount of such research in " practical " subjects such as Procedure and Conveyancing, Revenue Law and Divorce Law is to be regretted.   I should like to say that the confused and archaic character of many branches of these subjects is largely due to their exclusion from academic consideration. I should like to prophesy that the scandal of our retention of an expensive and energy-wasting system of conveyancing would be ended if academic lawyers were to investigate the subject more fully and recommend its replacement by a modern system of registration of title.   But

---

[6] It is an error to consider the case method as tied to a case law legal system and deriving its merit, in accordance with the doctrine of its founder, from the belief that where law is found in cases it is in cases that it is best studied. This is appreciated in the Harvard School of Business Administration, which has adopted the case method : it is the main lesson of the School's papers in its symposium *The Case Method of Teaching Human Relations and Administration*. The " blurb " on the jacket of the book begins with the sentence : " Passive absorption of information and theory has no place at Harvard's Graduate School of Business Administration ".

I remember how complacent many academic lawyers have been about defects in more academic subjects, how limited have been their proposals for reform, and how even their moderate proposals have not always been fully implemented. It is here in connection with the nature of legal research that we approach what I regard as the nub of the problem of the function of a university faculty of law. I do not conceive research in law as being limited to the task of systematising the work of judges or of presenting statutes in more " cognoscible " form. Such tidying up of the raw material produced by the great social processes of legislation and adjudication is indeed of great value. There is, it is true, a stage in the teaching of undergraduates, particularly those in faculties other than law, where it may be essential. It is my belief, too, that more legal journalism is required for the wider adult education of citizens if democracy is to be more than a label for our political institutions. So, too, a knowledge of foreign law is usefully imparted at the level of journalism. But legal journalism is not enough, either for a university, or for the community which a university best serves by maintaining university ideals. Comparative law as a university discipline surpasses the level of journalism: the various legal systems but serve as data for an empirical science of law.

It is my hope that a solution of the problem I have indicated may emerge if we remember that legal education in a university, while it seeks to liberalise the mind, stimulating intellectual development through the material of law, also directs the mind to the character of that material, which is no less than the efforts of humanity to organise the lives of men in society. This " theorem-definition " of " law " might well be the starting point for discussion about meanings of the English word " law ", and the nature of the world phenomena which are referred to by one of the meanings of that word. But this is not the time to discuss the adequacy of my generalisation about the nature of " law ": though to prevent misunderstanding I have to ask that organisation should not be confused with regimentation. The English word " law " in many contexts signifies a concept one of whose elements is the idea of the freedom of the individual, and the English legal system in many of its parts has the realisation of that ideal as one of its great ends. The history of law everywhere points to origins in the use of public power to restrain the abuse of private power, and to later developments whereby institutional means are devised to support individual vigilance in the restraint of the abuse of public power. The ideal of law rejects the tyranny of anarchy and the anarchy of tyranny.

The purpose of my theorem-definition is to state that the subject-matter of law is humanity: that in faculties of law we join hands with the other humanities which inquire into the nature of man and of his responses to the universe. I have indicated that we students of law live mainly by the use of words describing our private experiences and by our examination of the words of others, and this though we can no longer be accused of confining study to the verbal opinions handed down by appellate courts. It is such literary treatment by the humanities of their subjects that is one of the issues in the great debate today between science and the humanities. We in faculties of law have to participate in that debate: the challenge that no man can be considered fully educated who knows nothing of science cannot be declined by us. Nor should we misconceive the fundamental character of the general challenge. We are not asked merely to learn about the achievements of the natural sciences in penetrating the mysteries of inanimate nature or about the processes created by technology for man's exploitation of natural resources. We do not have to leave the subject matter of the humanities to become concerned with science.

The ultimate challenge of science is to the validity of the traditional methods by which we are satisfied as to the truths of our beliefs and the rightness of our practices. The Savigny of to day should say that the vocation of our age is for the fuller use of science in all affairs of government. We can no longer afford in the complex societies of to day to ridicule the social sciences by pointing to expressions of obvious truths or trivialities in strange terminology and by concentrating on their failures and exaggerations in ignorance of their real achievements and aspirations.[7] Ehrlich's statement that the centre of gravity of legal development lies in society itself can, I think, be modified by saying that the growing point for rational law lies in the social sciences. There is, of course, a great debate as to what is involved in scientific methods and about their applicability to human affairs. I plead, nevertheless, for the participation by law teachers in the activity of the utilisation of the scientific spirit in the examination of legal problems. I am bold enough to explain the hypothetical-deductive method of science by saying that scientific thought has at its centre the readiness to recognise general propositions as hypotheses and the readiness to submit them to the test of crucial experience. In law we are familiar with the necessity of evidence for the establishment of a finding of fact. But are we sufficiently aware of the relation between evidence and the general propositions about man and society utilised in legal thought even in the establishment of findings of particular facts? Science deals with particular facts and with general propositions: but the propositions do not frame themselves by simple contemplation of particular facts: science tests general propositions by particular facts but such testing facts are not always readily at hand. The framing of appropriate general propositions may require the creation of new concepts, and their testing by appropriate experience may require the construction

---

[7] Even a supporter of social science like Jerome Hall can say of some of the terminology : " bizarre professional vocabulary whose least function is not implementation of status and prestige ", *Principles of Criminal Law*, p. 566.

of new experiments. The concepts of mass and acceleration were not imaged forth until the Middle Ages, but Galileo tested his theory of uniform acceleration by experiment. Newton's laws were based on the imaginative extension to the universe of explanations for phenomena observed in the earth's gravitational field; they were derived from and tested by astronomical observation, and modified eventually when observation did not fit theory. The Michelson-Morley experiment was designed to test a theory which had almost become dogma and led to its abandonment. In the realm of biology Pasteur conceived the possibility of germs and destroyed the theory of spontaneous generation of all diseases: the microscope has shown the existence of germs, but cannot establish that all disease is due to hostile organisms. Are we yet ready in law to accept the permanent achievements of scientific method in the exposition of error, and to expel from our beliefs those which can be demonstrated to be erroneous? Logical analysis is required to ascertain our inarticulated premises, but scientific method cannot be ignored in the examination of their truth.

I know you will want me to restrict myself to but a few aspects of the great debate. I hope I will be forgiven for my choice. I turn now to the general relation between science and the humanities: and later I shall consider what I consider to be connected with this whole question, the relation between jurist and judge in the development of society.

The very differences among Greek philosophers manifested their general agreement in a belief that was their supreme contribution to European tradition—their faith in reason. The practice of that faith through the use of the dialectical method in education was later to affect our universities, and to spread beyond Europe, influencing the methods of teaching in American law schools. Though European universities came into being in an age of faith we can discern from their very foundation the seeds of the rejection of mere authority, whether it was of Aristotle or Galen or Papinian. The scholastic philosophers in their disputations showed that Dryden erred in saying " our ancestors betrayed Their free born Reason to the Stagirite ". Recent research has shown that the modification of Aristotelian logic, praised as an achievement of this century, had been anticipated in the fourteenth century. The law school of Bologna early castigated the Valentinian Law of Citations for preferring the counting of authorities to reasoned argument. The scholastic doctrine that the foundation for the task of man's intellect is in his senses played its part in the development of experimental science whose beginnings, we now know, long preceded the writings of Bacon and others who thought that the middle ages did not adequately distinguish words and things. The broader vision sees intellectual life in the universities of the middle ages rejecting a divorce between faith and reason; man's reason was not opposed to man's values—the latter would be preserved and enhanced the more fully the former was stimulated and developed. We ought all of us to consider today whether a broader vision will not reject as exaggerated the antithesis so often proclaimed between science and the humanities, and will assert that it is derived from mistaken conceptions of their character. I make no claim to be able to summarise at all, let alone accurately, the literature which has grown up around the discussion of the limitations of science, of the logical gap between description, which has been suggested as the province of science, and evaluation, which, it is said, is the task of the humanities. Even if we turn to science to tell us about the causes and consequences of human action we do not gain knowledge of more than the means to be employed in human endeavour. The humanities may still retain their sovereignty in the area of the goals of human action, in the values we seek to establish and preserve.[8] Can science say what justice is; can we know what justice is without scientific knowledge of man and his environment? I put forward but two comments in support of my faith in the validity of the application of scientific matter to human affairs, where we need so much more knowledge of facts, and more judgment as to the correct mode of their evaluation.

A recent writer has said :

" If human values are not the business of science they would appear to be left to the mercies of poetic ecstacy and emotional whimsy." [9]

One truth in this that I accept is the rejection of mere assertion, even though it be in the melodious language of poetic vision, as an adequate foundation for truth. If I reject authority in favour of reason I cannot accept mere intuition and eloquence. But the statement does not bring out a number of important distinctions. There may be no inherent limitation in scientific method which renders it incapable of application to human values, and yet it may be that actuality discloses little, if any, scientific knowledge of human values. The social sciences are no longer embryonic, but few would say that they are no longer in their infancy. Again, when we speak of human values do we refer to what is valued, to subjective ideologies, to the actual faiths that men profess and the hopes they cherish, or do we refer to the process of evaluation, to the value judgments about men's operative ideals? If we attend to the many problems of the evaluation of values we may find that there is still in this century truth in the proposition that " poets are the unacknowledged legislators of the world ". It is to the poets'

---

[8] " Science can discuss the causes of desires, and the means for realising them, but it cannot contain any genuinely ethical statements, because it is concerned with what is true or false. " Russell : *Religion and Science* (1935), p. 237. This belief led Russell to say later : " Since no way can be imagined for deciding a difference as to values, the conclusion is forced upon us that the difference is one of tastes, not one as to any objective truth", p. 238. Russell was still influenced in his work by his atomistic doctrines. Once, however, general facts and general propositions are considered, and science is primarily concerned with these, then it is no longer a simple matter to say that science is restricted to the language of " true or false " as Russell used it : see Urmson : *Philosophical Analysis*, p. 67.

[9] Donald Wills : 47 *Journal of Philosophy*, p. 435.

power of creating in others their imaginative sympathy that we largely owe our will to make real their vision of Jerusalem, the city of peace. The poets still remain the experts in effective communication, even though the modern poet does not write for the voters who control our modern legislatures. But poets have not only excelled in narrative, in re-creative expression of the moods and desires of themselves and their fellow men: they have gone far beyond prosaic common sense in sensitivity to the many colours of life and to the need for judgment on them. Poetry has its basis in both experience and intellectual activity. The poet describes Helen's " cheek of just that grain ", the nose of just that length, on the particular face which uniquely " launched a thousand ships ". Aware that individual things differ in innumerable ways he reminds us that you may " Hold infinity in the palm of your hand ". But poets also discern the universal qualities exhibited by the patterns of things and people and events. The recurrent similarities of events enable us to see " eternity in an hour ". Beauty did not lose its appeal when Helen became old and died: behind the transient passions of men poets have seen a common humanity. But poetry is not enough: poets work in isolation. It is true they submit their statements to a test of experience—public approval down the corridors of time. But this gives us no more than the folk wisdom of common sense: there is no testing by means of objective logical involvement of their statements with genuine public experience.[10] The sensitivity to facts, the imagination and the intellectual judgment of poetry are required for the discussion of values, but they are not absent in natural science. The complexity of the subject-matter of social sciences makes even greater demands on these qualities than does natural science: the social sciences require wider sensitivity and deeper judgments.

It is in relation to the question of judgment that many see another alleged irreconcilable conflict between science and the humanities. The scientific judgment, it is thought, is concerned with definite concepts within a limited field of our experiences. But life calls for decisions in situations where knowledge may be limited and vague, the factors

---

[10] Cf. the comment by Jerome Hall on reliance on " literature " for explanations of the mental processes of criminals. " If it offends one's scientific sensibilities to probe sympathetically into this inner realm of personal experience for further insight into criminal behaviour, the major source of such knowledge will continue to be the imaginative portrayals of the novelist and the playwright. But literature, however suggestive, is not social science. However valuable as penetrating insight and as a repository of possible theories concerning criminality, its limitations, aside from exaggeration of the facts, are those of many avowed criminological researches—the theories employed are not expressed or they are not tested : no serious efforts are made to generalise from the particulars examined, and there is, of course, hardly any summation which can even remotely be called a ' systematisation ' of knowledge " (*Principles of Criminal Law*, p. 564). Jerome Hall himself thinks that " free-will " is a limitation on scientific handling of the mental processes of " the thinking, aspiring, problem-solving personality " because " the process is not limited by preceding or accompanying conditions ". Nevertheless, he believes explanations of criminal behaviour may be criticised on the basis of " objective standards of truth and morality " by reliance on " common sense, trained imagination, and experience, the arbiters of truth in any field ". His remarks, of course, are limited to criminal behaviour solely by reason of his universe of discourse.

many and complex, and the consequences far-reaching and potent.
It is said that it is to the humanities and not to science that we must
turn for the judgment needed for such decisions. But it is surely but a
caricature of scientific judgment to view it as so limited. Even pure
science, which abstracts from the manifold of history in search for
regularities, deals with many a complex situation, and is aware that
analysis may omit the relations which belong to a whole. The applied
scientist has to deal with the uniqueness of particular things, individual
persons and actual events in historical situations, which do not repeat
themselves: and his judgment may require the awareness of the interrelation of laws from different branches of science. Even he may have
to deal with unknown factors, but his ideal of knowledge of all relevant
laws and facts does not entail a mechanical but a human judgment.
Many lawyers, and more non-lawyers writing about law, have seen the
ideal for legal judgment as something like the Arts man's caricature of
scientific judgment: the notion of

> " the mechanical and logical application of clearly formulated legal norms
> of inescapable authority " [11]

is, indeed, what some conceive as a government of laws and not of
men. We find, however, in actuality, that judges have to exercise
quite other kinds of judgment. From a United States case I take this
description:

> " an intuition of experience which outruns analysis and sums up many un-
> named and tangled impressions: impressions which may lie beneath conscious-
> ness without losing their worth ".[12]

It is old learning that the spirit of justice requires consideration of all
circumstances, and it remains true that in human affairs many
circumstances and their patterns are unknown. It is from Mr. Justice
Holmes that I derive my belief that the life of the law and the law of life
require the judgments of both logic and experience—both analysis and
synthesis are needed. The judgment based on mere intuition is a

---

[11] This phrase is taken from Bryan King's stipulative definition of the concept of
" judicial function " used by him as a theoretical model for the study of the actual mode of
operation of courts, usefully called by him the " judicial process " to contrast it with
" judicial function " : " Concept of a Lawyer's Jurisprudence ", 11 Camb. L.J., p. 411.
Bryan King points out carefully that this concept of a judicial function is not his ideal of
what the judicial process ought to be. It was Austin's ideal : it is conceived by many non-
lawyers as the ideal of all lawyers, and, indeed, as corresponding with the judicial process :
see, for example, Nowell-Smith : *Ethics* (Pelican Series), pp. 236 *et seq.* The Judicial
Committee of the Privy Council in *A.-G. of Australia* v. *Reg.*, [1957] 2 All E.R. 45 appears
to have assumed the equation of the " judicial power " under the Constitution of Australia
with the " judicial function " (C.J.C. McOustra, 3 *B.J.A.L.* 46). The Supreme Court,
on the other hand, appears to have rejected so limited a view of " judicial power " : see
Textile Workers v. *Lincoln Mills*, [1957] 353 U.S., p. 448. The Court's attitude is pointed by
the dissent of Frankfurter, J., see p. 464.

[12] 204 U.S. at p. 598: quoted in 353 U.S. at p. 248. Cf. Holmes' well-known *dictum*
in *Lochner's case* (198 U.S. 76): " General principles do not decide concrete cases. The
decision will depend on a judgement or intuition more subtle than any articulate major
premise."

necessity arising from our ignorance, not a duty. The poetic and scientific task is to make explicit what is often inarticulate. The pre-eminence of man over beast lies in fuller consciousness. Greater scientific knowledge leads man nearer to the attainment of rational and human judgment.

It needs but little analysis of our legal rules to see how implicated they are with propositions in psychology, in economics, in sociology—in the social sciences generally. We have been made aware of the scientific aspects of the law of crime. The problem of criminal responsibility, though not determined by the psychologists' account of insanity, yet involves it. Nevertheless, some judicial opinions have come near to dogmatic assertions about the solution of a purely medical problem of the existence of irresistible impulse. In this field we readily see that common sense is not enough: the experience on which is based our common-sense opinions about physical disease is as great as the experience on which is based our common-sense opinions about social disease. The Royal Commissions have shown how the deterrent worth of corporal and capital punishment may be estimated by statistical investigation: and the Home Secretary has made available finance for further scientific research into the aetiology and therapy of criminal behaviour. But psychological propositions are not restricted to criminal law: nor is social science restricted to psychology. The problems concerning money which have come before the courts have required consideration of doctrines of economics. Not least of these cases has been the Domestic Gold Clause case, which surely involved a judicial view of the cause and control of inflation. When the Australian High Court considered the validity of Commonwealth laws for credit control, it had before it in an affidavit an economic survey of the operation of such controls. In *Lister* v. *Romford Ice Co., Ltd.*,[13] views were expressed about the impact of laws on industrial relations. When the United States Supreme Court dealt with race relations the now " notorious " footnote eleven at least acknowledged the work that sociologists had done in that field. The social sciences are relevant to every branch of law.[14] A quarter of a century ago

13 [1957] 1 All E.R. 125.

14 It would require volumes to prove this assertion by cataloguing the points of contact between the various rules of law and established propositions in the social sciences. Many would find it tedious to read again the well-worn ground of sociological jurisprudence. There is, however, still need for work in legal sociology; see my article on " The Nature of Legal Sociology ", 19 *Journal of the Statistical and Social Inquiry Society of Ireland*, p. 122. In the realm of matrimonial relations valuable " scientific " work has been done by Max Rheinstein: see his " Law of Divorce and the Problem of Marriage Stability " (1956), 9 *Vanderbilt L.R.*, p. 633. The sociological work by O. R. McGregor, *Divorce in England* (1957), stimulated the following remarks in a *Times* review (September 12, 1957): " Since law regulates social conduct, arguments about changing the law cannot ignore the relevant social facts, even though in the last resort decisions have to be reached on ethical grounds. The royal commission on mental health laws and the Wolfenden committee are good examples of recent official inquiries, which were careful to ascertain social facts pertinent to their subjects, to define the areas of ignorance, distinguish between fact and opinion and state the ethical reasoning behind their proposals. Through disregard of these rules, Mr. McGregor argues in his lively book, the recent Morton Commission on divorce has

Viscount Sankey stressed the growing relevance of social science to law and legal education, and his words have been echoed in later inaugural lectures of law professors.[15] I would but re-echo their words of the need for greater integration of the social sciences in legal teaching. I would for myself be prepared to see a reduction in the number of law subjects studied in order to make this possible. Perhaps the time has come for various honours schools and departments to be created within faculties of law even at the undergraduate level. But I would also urge that consideration be given to the place of social science in legal research. I refer to two aspects of this problem. First of all, there is the question of the part to be played by the law researcher in the basic scientific work. I think he has some part to play: and I am, of course, supported in that view by the work which has been done by the Department of Criminal Science of the Faculty of Law of the University of Cambridge.[16]

Perhaps more important is the second question, viz., that of the application of social science to the administration of law. One of man's great intellectual achievements is the creation of the English common law. The judges applied the reasoning of the Middle Ages, its logic and science, its philosophy of men and society, to the judicial problems presented to them in litigation. But it is no longer possible for judges adequately to perform unaided this task of legislation, of remoulding old law or creating new law in accordance with prevailing knowledge. The press of litigation is too great, the burden of scientific knowledge is too heavy. It is, of course, contended by many that this task is for the legislature, that judicial legislation has a humbler role to perform,

---

produced a report which is only a ' soufflé of whipped conjectures '. He shows how prone the commission's witnesses were to adduce as self-evident assertions they had not attempted to verify by reference to the facts."

Over fifty years ago Holmes had gone further, for he asked for examination not only of expressed assumptions but also of the inarticulate premises of legal reasoning. " An ideal system of law should draw its postulates and its legislative justification from science. As it is now, we rely upon tradition, or vague sentiment, or the fact that we never thought of any other way of doing things, as our only warrant for rules which we enforce with as much confidence as if they embodied revealed wisdom." *The Holmes Reader*, p. 107.

[15] Professor H. Street: 1 *Political Studies*, p. 97. Professor L. A. Sheridan: *University Law* (University of Malaya Publications).

[16] The desirability of participation by Faculties of Law in " field work " has, of course, not yet been universally recognised. It was, nevertheless, most discouraging for the members of the Faculty of Law of the Queen's University of Belfast to have been told by one of the Foundations, whose objects, it was believed, included the encouragement of new work in the social sciences, that activities which had been suggested for financial support were not within the proper field of a Faculty of Law, even though the scheme put forward provided for co-operation with other faculties in the University. Three projects were submitted to the Foundation. The first was an investigation, on the lines of some already conducted in the United States, on the actual need for a scheme of Legal Aid in Northern Ireland. The second was an investigation into the actual administration by magistrates' courts of the provision in the Northern Ireland Summary Jurisdiction Act which permitted the prohibition of reports of preliminary hearings. The third was an investigation into the actual effect on family life and agricultural development of the Land Purchase Acts, which are so important an element in the history of Northern Ireland. A great deal of preliminary work was done in connection with the last project, which was, of course, the most complex and ambitious of the three. How much valuable information for the Tucker Committee would have been gained if the most modest encouragement had been given to the second project!

viz., that of fashioning rule to accord with established principle.[17] But the contrary opinion is also widely held, and in my opinion is correct, that the task of judicial legislation is the greater one, and that consciously or unconsciously the judge incorporates the newer learning into law. We must ever call in new learning to redress the unbalance of the old. The Restrictive Practices Court is one model of how science may contribute to legal development: lawyer and scientist may together form the bench of the newer courts. But I suggest the possibility, and the desirability, of another mode of legal development. It surely is one of the great tasks of the legal researcher to keep himself in touch with developments in the social sciences, to see how they necessitate corresponding changes in our laws, and to make himself proposals for legal reform.[18] It may be that the task is too great for the individual jurist: the social sciences may witness the rise of the research team which already exists in the natural sciences. The task will certainly require increases in the staffs of faculties of law, and in the finances of these faculties. It will require the maintenance of the highest intellectual standards among law teachers. They will have not merely to attend to scientific development but to keep in perspective also both the permanent and the changing standards of justice.

I do not think that my plea for the judges of the future to pay more regard to academic work involves any derogation by the judges from their proud traditions of shaping the law to ideals of freedom and justice. I have earlier said that the task of the university teacher should not be limited to legal journalism. Will the judge who receives from the jurist the results of the impact of new scientific knowledge on past rules and translates them into new laws, communicating them to citizens through judgments, become the legal journalist? Such a task is indeed no journeyman's, and to call it journalism removes from that name any pejorative element. But I conceive of judge and jurist as partners in the task of statesmanship called for in adapting laws to the march of science and society. The immediacy of contact with the actualities of life in forensic experience has its contribution to make beside that of the relative detachment of the intellectual processes of

---

[17] This is a less metaphorical way of stating the declaratory theory of precedent. Von Mehren has shown that where social change takes place without a corresponding change in legal rules, there is automatically a change in legal principle: the old principle can only be re-established by changing the rule. " Applying ' existing ' law to resolve a conflict of interests to which that law was not addressed results, realistically speaking, in new law just as inevitably as if a new legal precept had been formulated. As our society changes, its law changes with it, even if the law may appear to stand still " (" Judicial Process in the U.S.A. and Germany," *Festschrift für Ernst Rabel*, 1. 84). In *Textile Workers* v. *Lincoln Mills*, [1957] 353 U.S. at p. 456, the Supreme Court asserted that " judicial inventiveness " would enable the creation of new federal law " which the courts must fashion from the policy of our national labour laws ".

[18] In the context of the text the proposals for legal reform are in respect of changes which judges may make. But, as Austin stated long ago, the science of legislation, which is a branch of legal study, is by no means limited to judicial legislation. The principles to be considered are those to be applied by legislatures as well as by courts. We should recognise, as so many United States teachers have done, that in faculties of law we train future statesmen as well as future judges.

academic contemplation. Such experience may well be used to serve as scientific tests of the validity of general propositions propounded by the social scientists. It is, however, ill used if it be made the sole basis for the formulation of generalisations about human nature.

In this address I have endeavoured to attend to the part that science has to play in the humanities and law. I trust that I have not committed myself to the view that we can ignore logic and philosophy. Indeed, one of my objects has been to suggest the interdependence of all three, of logic, science and philosophy. If I believe that the vocation of this age is for science I am not unmindful that in this age we have seen a great flowering of linguistic analysis, and I recall that Austin was among the sowers of the seeds, though he thought they had fallen in stony soil. I am mindful also that in this age philosophy is no longer limited to linguistic analysis, and we have seen a rebirth of natural law ideas which more than ever seek to unite the justice of man with the science of nature. And if it seems that in asking the student of law, be he professor or undergraduate, to consider the relations of law to logic and science and philosophy I impose too great a burden, I ask whether any less is commensurate with the burden on humanity in this age. More than a century ago, under the impact of Benthamite ideas, and stimulated by the dawn of the technological revolution, Austin saw that the student of law, the student of an instrument of government, of social control through official rules for human conduct, should be acquainted with the disciplines investigating what is basic to law. He advised that in faculties of law there should be studied what were then the infant sciences concerned with the nature of man and of society. He urged also the study of logic—the inquiry into the validity of methods by which we determine the truths of propositions concerning man and nature. Today the world situation is more exigent. Through our progress in learning we have acquired control of world destructive power; through our political developments the world contains two hostile power blocs. Our imperative task is to make what is potent for destruction active for the constructive tasks of humanity. National frontiers are unknown to the scientific tradition. In this International Geophysical Year we witness the greatest demonstration of scientific co-operation ever seen. The laws of nations are not immune from the influence of an ideal of law for nations. If some jurists have seen state and law as linked concepts, the learning of the comparative law of primitive and advanced, of ancient and modern, societies has shown the uniformity of concepts and goals in diverse systems. *Laissez-faire* and communism can be seen as mutations in the evolution of the common stock of the European beliefs in individual freedom and social justice. International law is a reality, even if it be no more than the recognition of man's yearning for peace. I have faith that science and law together may yet bring us nearer to humanity's desire for national welfare and international concord.

8

The Scope of Jurisprudence*

PART A

Semantic problems

The word " Jurisprudence " is a verbal symbol which is part of a language structure used by an élite of scholars in English-speaking countries.[1] Nevertheless, like the word " law ", which is part of the language of the ordinary man as well as the scholar, it has a range of " meanings ". It is a task of linguistic surveying, which I have not carried out, to catalogue and compare the many meanings of the symbol. However it appears to me that there is usually associated with the symbol the characteristic of theoretical consideration. Even when the word is used, in Holland's phraseology, as an " imposing quadrisyllable " instead of the word " law "[2] it carries with it the notion of learned exposition,

---

*Reprinted from *Me Judice*, 1965, by kind permission. In the original publication Professor Montrose added the following note: "This paper was drafted in the Cameron Highlands without any 'authorities' being available. It is accordingly not a model for 'legal writing', but it will help students considerably if they look up the authorities themselves and note the corrections which require to be made to my text! "

[1] The United States is included in the description " English-speaking countries." There are, however, significant differences between American-English and English-English even among scholars. Thus in the United States " jurisprudence " has been used to denote a wide range of academic subjects connected with " law ", grouped together merely because they were considered at one time by legal practitioners to be of no direct (and, by some, of no indirect) use to them. A " classic " example is the statement by Professor Freund of Chicago University at the beginning of this century. Levy tells us: " Freund called this collection jurisprudence: Criminology, Relation of State to Industries, Finance, Railroad Transportation, Accounting, Banking, Experimental Psychology, History of Political Ethics, Comparative Politics, Diplomatic History of the United States, Diplomatic History of Europe, Municipal Sociology, the Government of the Colonies, and American Political Thought."
In England many legal practitioners, and some academic lawyers, also consider (most mistakenly I think) jurisprudence to be of little use as a training for the legal profession. They quote out of context, and with no realisation that the author intended the judgment to be a condemnation not of jurisprudence but of the practising barrister, Dicey's dictum: " Jurisprudence stinks in the nostrils of the practising barrister."

[2] Holland did not specify whether the word " jurisprudence " was used as a substitute for one only of the meanings of the word "law ", and if so for which one.

as in such titles as " Equity Jurisprudence ", " Medical Jurisprudence ".[3]
The notion of rationality also occurs when the English word " jurisprudence " is used as the equivalent of the European counterparts " la
jurisprudence " and " die jurisprudenz ". It then means *principles* of
law developed by courts of law in the judicial process.[4] Sometimes the
word is used for the study of law in general. More often it is used for
the study of a particular branch of law—as the name for a particular
course in a Faculty of Law. It is with its use in this latter sense, in other
words, with the contents of a course in " jurisprudence ", that this
paper is concerned.

The doctrines of academic freedom and autonomy permit a university to prescribe any contents for a " jurisprudence " course. So too the
doctrine of freedom of " speech " permits an author to include any
topics within a book which he entitles " jurisprudence ". Moreover,
in the past it was true that the liberty of choice of universities and authors
was not restrained by the existence of a general agreement among
scholars as to the nature of the subject of " jurisprudence ". It is, however, submitted that there has now developed a consensus of opinion
among scholars of the English-speaking world as to the contents of
" jurisprudence ". It is accordingly now " improper " to include some
matters within, and to exclude other matters from, a course, or book
on " jurisprudence ". What this consensus appears to me to be has to
be stated.

PART B

The historical development of jurisprudence

(a) *Austin*

English scholars have always maintained some contacts with the
learning of the mainland of Europe. Nevertheless it is justifiable to

---

[3] The phrase " medical jurisprudence " was often used as a title of courses in Faculties
of Medicine, and sometimes in Faculties of Law, whose content was primarily the consideration of those branches of medicine which often arose in litigation or forensic discussion.
Examples are the characteristic of wounds, the causes of death, the nature of insanity, the
indicia of female virginity. There were also included, discordantly, also branches of law
concerned with the medical profession. Hence the subject is now more " properly " called
" forensic medicine ". I defend my use of the word " proper " against the criticisms of the
followers of Glanville Williams who state that there are no " proper " meanings of words.
I am aware of the symbolic character of words, and that they are human artefacts, dependent
for meaning on common convention or private stipulations. Because of the existence of
conventions I may be guilty of an impropriety, à la Mrs. Malaprop, for using a word in an
unconventional sense. I may even if I expressly stipulate for a private meaning be " properly "
criticised, i.e., rationally criticised, for creating a misleading situation. " Medical Jurisprudence " suggests a branch of the study of " law ", not of the facts with which courts
of law may be concerned. Consequently the " proper " descriptive phrase (or if the epithet
be preferred the " better " descriptive phrase) is " forensic medicine ".

[4] Some judges, believing that courts proceed rationally and legislatures arbitrarily,
and also wishing to capture for the word " law " a connotation of rationality, have suggested
that the word " law " be used for principles propounded by judges, and words like " decree "
for rules enacted by legislature.

begin our consideration of the historical development of the concept of jurisprudence with Jeremy Bentham.[5] Bentham did not coin a new word for the theoretical study of law, as he did in other fields of learning, for example in the realm of " international " law. Instead he used the existing word " jurisprudence ". The subject, he said, was divided into two branches: (i) expository jurisprudence, the exposition of existing rules of law, (ii) censorial (or critical) jurisprudence, the study of what ought to be the rules of law—the rules which should be enacted by legislators. He thought that the word " law " should be used only to refer to enacted rules, whether the rules were made by parliaments or by judges. The use of the word " law " to refer to ideals, such as in the phrase " natural law ", led, in his opinion, to nonsense statements.[6]

Bentham's disciple, John Austin, accepted his master's teaching with regard to the use of the word " law ". But he suggested a different use of the word " jurisprudence ".[7] In the first place, in order to make more abundantly clear the distinction between " is " and " ought ", he suggested that the word " jurisprudence " should not be employed for the study of what ought to be the law. He proposed, borrowing from Bentham,[8] that the phrase " the science of legislation " should be used instead of " censorial jurisprudence ". Moreover he distinguished two aspects of " expository jurisprudence ". Exposition of the detailed rules of law was not in his view even " particular jurisprudence ". The word " jurisprudence " was to be used for the discipline in which basic concepts and principles were extricated from detailed rules and then expounded.[9] When this process was applied to a particular legal system it yielded " particular jurisprudence ", and when applied to the legal system of all maturer societies it yielded

---

[5] Jeremy Bentham himself had close contacts with France, and much of his work was first published in France.

[6] It follows from Bentham's postulate that the use of the word " law " to refer to modes of behaviour, as in the phrase " customary law ", leads also to nonsense statements. It should be noted that Bentham rightly discussed the confusion which may result from verbal symbols which apply equally to normative and descriptive statements. He saw, for example, the confusion resulting from the use of the word " right " to apply both to a legal relation and to a natural " faculty " of man. This confusion exists in Hohfeld's concept of the " privilege: no-right " relation. It should also be noted that the phrase " customary law " is used not only to refer to actual patterns of behaviour, but also to statements of required behaviour.

[7] Austin's best known work is that in which he fashions a concept designated by the word " law " and constructed by the formula: " general command of a sovereign containing a sanction ".

[8] The title of an essay by Bentham showing the relation of utilitarianism to law-making is " Principles of Morals and Legislation ". For Bentham " utility " was the criterion for good law. Austin accepted the same criterion.

[9] Austin was influenced by the Kantian philosophy which underlay the " Allgemeine Rechtslehre " he studied in Germany. Kant's doctrine of " transcendental categories " was applied by him to the rules of English and Roman Law. The " transcendental method " consists in discovering the categories presupposed by types of discourse. Thus Austin's extrication of " common notions " is not a simple inductive process; there is involved an *a priori* procedure which leads to "necessary notions". Austin, however, does not make his distinctions, or epistemology, clear.

"general jurisprudence". When "jurisprudence" was used without any qualifying epithet the reference was to general jurisprudence.

Unfortunately Austin was for a long time misunderstood. There were two main causes for this arising from the method of publication of his work. In the first place what was published while he was teaching was but part of the course he gave. Though the book was entitled *The Province of Jurisprudence Determined*, its content was the exposition of the concept of law he deemed to be most fruitful for the study of "law" in general. In it was set out the command theory of law. This in itself was misunderstood as being a thesis similar to that of pessimists[10] like Hobbes and Hume who thought that order could only be maintained in society by a concentration and exercise of force in governmental hands. Another analogy is the theory of Karl Marx that in capitalist societies "law" is an "apparatus of coercion". Though there are passages in Austin which support such a "realist" view, on the whole his theory is logical rather than sociological and is consistent with different views as to the sociological causes for social stability.

In the second place Austin's actual delimitation of the scope of the discipline of jurisprudence, and his programme of the courses which should be provided for students in a Faculty of Law, were not published until after his death. They then appeared in the two volume collection of his lectures entitled *Jurisprudence or The Philosophy of Positive Law*. They were set out in his introductory lectures to his course. Those lectures however were printed at the end of the second volume, and they were omitted entirely from the much more widely read abbreviation of the lectures made by Campbell, and published as *The Student's Austin*. In Jethro Brown's *Austinian Theory of Law* they were not discussed. Indeed not until Stone criticised Austin's delimitation in his *Province of Jurisprudence Redetermined* were Austin's views of the scope of jurisprudence widely known.[11]

The consequences of the neglect of Austin's views about the contents of courses on "jurisprudence" and law were unfortunate. His thesis that the student of law should concern himself both with what law is *and* what it ought to be was ignored. So too his view that for a full appreciation of both topics a student should be aware of general principles of logic, ethics and social science was also ignored. Instead, Faculties of Law concerned themselves with rather a technical exposition of branches of English Law, "leavened" by courses on Roman Law, International Law, and "Jurisprudence" as Austin used that latter term. Moreover the courses on jurisprudence too often degenerated into a series of "pinpricks" of the Austinian concept of law.

---

[10] Those who favour the thesis may call them "realists".

[11] It is one of the many merits of Stone's *Province and Function of Law* that his examination of Austin's views was reprinted in it as its introductory part. The preliminary lectures are also reprinted in Hart's edition of Austin for students.

(b) Maine

The picture drawn in the last sentence is too sombre. Books like those by Amos, Holland, Salmond, and Gray made significant contributions to the development of " analytical jurisprudence ", the name most often given to the field of study described by Austin under the title " general jurisprudence ".[12] Moreover the area of jurisprudence was considerably widened by the influence of Sir Henry Sumner Maine.

Almost contemporaneously with the publication of Austin's lectures there appeared Maine's *Ancient Law*, shortly followed by *Early Law and Custom*, and *Village Communities*. These added a new realm to the empire of jurisprudence, viz. the territory which came to be called " historical jurisprudence ". Later scholars have too often presented too limited a view of Maine's contribution.[13] He has been regarded as presenting a criticism of the Austinian concept of law. This he certainly did. Austin had limited his concept to the systems within advanced societies in which political organisation had developed to a stage where the community was divided into " sovereign " and " subjects ", and " law " was the command of the sovereign to the subjects. Maine challenged the utility of such a concept: it was too narrow. It obscured the working of social forces. It was " false " to call societies " lawless " in which the bearers of physical power were not considered as having law-making powers. He postulated, though he never constructed, the existence and value of a concept of law applicable to " immature " as well as mature societies. In immature societies there existed traditional beliefs as to desirable modes of behaviour influential enough to be a means of social control and not identical with religion or ethics.

The greater significance of Maine's work is that he drew attention to neglected fields of study for jurists which could be embraced by

[12] The criticism by Dias of the use of the phrase " analytical jurisprudence " to refer to this field of study cannot be supported. He offends the canon, to which he himself attaches so much importance, that there can be no proper meaning of words. Of course " analysis " as the name of an intellectual operation is to be found in all branches of jurisprudence. It is also to be found in all branches of all disciplines. It is found in all mathematics, though the name " mathematical analysis " is used for one branch of mathematics. A more important criticism of the name " analytical jurisprudence " is that it is as much concerned with " synthesis " as with " analysis ", also an intellectual operation found in all disciplines. " Analytical jurisprudence " is a conventional label. What is important is to perceive the distinction between the study of rules of law conceived as conglomerates of verbal symbols and the separate, though related, studies of behaviour on the one hand and values on the other. " Analytical jurisprudence " is a convenient label to effectuate this distinction, not only because of the tradition but also because it draws attention to the predominance of logic in this branch of jurisprudence. Analytical jurisprudence has as its subject matter linguistic data. It must be an exercise in logic because the discipline which examines verbal statements and their propositional connections as such is logic. Nevertheless this thesis is not the equivalent of Stone's doctrine that analytical jurisprudence is the examination of law in the light of logic. The jurist must be more than an " extrovert ". There is no completed discipline of logic ready made by " logicians " for application to legal discourse, though great scholars, like Kant, have from time to time thought that there was. The analytical jurist has much work to do for himself in the construction of the appropriate logic as well as in the application of the logic of others.

[13] This remains true despite the appreciation of his genius and his literary merits. Holmes in his lecture " The Path of the Law " stated that those who read Maine's *Ancient Law* would find " their path strewn with diamonds ".

H

the term "jurisprudence" and which were different from the "analytical jurisprudence" of Austin. There was first the study of legal forms of social control in "primitive" societies.[14] The second was that of the evolution of legal institutions. He posited the doubtful thesis, based almost entirely on the history of Roman law, that in all societies the development of law was from one type of code to a different type of code. He posited also another doubtful thesis that it is to the Romans that we owe the institution of conscious legislation. Nevertheless, what is of great value is the formulation of models of patterns of development, and the recognition of the importance of "planning" in the area of law. Marx has been more influential with his hypothesis of the relation of law to economic forces and of the capitalist "take over" of legislation. But his views are intellectually no more persuasive. Maine did not subscribe to the views of Savigny, who has in my view less claim to the title of the father of historical jurisprudence than Maine, that law which gradually evolves through social customs, or in the course of the judicial process, by "the silent anonymous forces of nature" is the best kind of law. He was too good an Indian Civil Servant to believe that. But the significance of a "school of jurisprudence" is not the content of the hypothesis about law that its members frame. It is that of the field of study undertaken by its members. Maine found jurisprudence in England confined to the logical analysis and synthesis of the concepts and propositions within the verbal formulae of legal systems. He extended its area to include consideration of the operation as an empirical, historical process of legal institutions, and to the study of the development of those institutions within the wider march of history.

(c) *Roscoe Pound*

Austin and Maine are the pioneers of the jurisprudence of the English-speaking world. But the real founder of jurisprudence as it is conceived today is Roscoe Pound. He was a scholar of immense breadth and depth of learning who also achieved much in the world of practical affairs. He was an effective Dean of the Harvard Law School in the days of its great expansion. More importantly his unceasing efforts aroused the American Bar to the importance of legal education and research, and led to its encouragement of, and indeed participation in, both those enterprises. It was not until he was over eighty years of age, and had retired from the Chair of Jurisprudence he had held for some forty years, that he published, in five volumes, his *magnum opus* on jurisprudence. But long before then by his teaching and writing he had greatly extended the scope of jurisprudence as it was studied and taught in English-speaking universities.

---

[14] The term "primitive" is now loosely used to apply not only to "truly" primitive societies but also to societies with a different type of civilisation from that of modern Europe. Intellectual snobbery exists as well as social.

He made many important contributions both to analytical and historical jurisprudence.[15] But his dominating message was that of a " call for sociological jurisprudence ".[16] In his text-book on jurisprudence Holland had already introduced Ihering's doctrine of the nature of rights as legally protected interests.[17] But Pound adopted and developed the entire Ihering philosophy[18] of law as a means of social control whereby the interests of society in general and men in particular were maintained and regulated. He failed, it is true, to make an adequate distinction between careful scientific studies of human behaviour and general assertions about the empirical character of law as an instrument for achieving social purposes.[19] Nor was it always clear whether he was urging that law in general, and laws in particular, did in fact operate as policy tools and consequently should be so regarded by jurists, or whether he was urging that they ought to operate as such and be so regarded by judges in their role as legislators. But there is no doubt that he brought within the scope of jurisprudence a wide range of topics from the examination of the social origin of rules to the need for organised law reform under a Minister of Justice.

His learning and teaching were by no means confined to German scholarship[20] in the area of legal theory. He brought a knowledge of the contributions of Greek philosophers both to his readers,[21] and to his classes,[22] which contained many law graduates among whom were present and future teachers of jurisprudence. He examined the

---

[15] His *Introduction to Legal History* is one of the relatively few books published by him while the holder of the Chair of Jurisprudence, and that was originally conceived as a series of lectures.

[16] This was the title of his epoch-making article in 25 H.L.R.

[17] Holland presented both an Austinian analysis of " right " as a capacity to affect the legal relations of others, and the Ihering analysis as an interest recognised and protected by law apparently without recognition of their difference or consistency. They are consistent since Ihering was concerned with the purpose of " rights " and Austin was content to examine the instrumental character of " rights ".

[18] Ihering has been criticised by German scholars for his lack of " philosophy ". But the reproach is largely terminological. It reveals a dislike for a writer who did not base his views on Kantian or Hegelian epistemology, but ventured on common sense generalisation. about law and society.

[19] He was aware of the need for scientific study, and organised a criminological operation in his Cleveland Survey of Crime.

[20] His knowledge of German legal literature was by no means confined to Ihering. Stone has rightly pointed out that Pound's views as to the nature of law were greatly influenced not only by Ihering's social utilitarianism but also by Kohler's neo-Hegelianism.

[21] His *Introduction to Legal Philosophy* taught that the permanent contributions of Greek philosophy was the distinction between positive rules of law and the general view of law as the realisation of justice. It will of course be remembered that his readers included the students of his very many writings in legal periodicals to which he contributed throughout his life.

[22] There is a story told of the two students from Chicago who attended his lectures They sat patiently through the lectures in which he presented an annotated bibliography of the English literature. They tolerated his *catalogue raisonée* of French and German literature. However, the end came for them when during his survey of European literature he referred to a Russian work and said that the class would be happy to learn that it was available in a translation—into Portuguese!

character of the theories of Roman jurists. He did not adhere to the condemnation of the scholastic philosophy of the middle ages as worthless casuistry and verbal quibbling made by writers who were ignorant of the actual literature or only superficially acquainted with it. He regarded their theories of natural law as demanding serious study. It is not surprising that he regarded the natural right schools of the seventeenth and eighteenth centuries as important, for they influenced so greatly the founding fathers of the United States. He examined Kantian and neo-Kantian, Hegelian and neo-Hegelian theories of law. He studied the legal philosophy of the twentieth century, and was ready with an appraisal of the " realist jurisprudence " of his own pupils: an appraisal whose merits are now more generally appreciated. His own pragmatism led him to regard particular philosophies as responses to the social needs of time and place rather than as statements of eternal verities.[23] Nevertheless he had revived interest in the problem of the existence of " absolute " justice.[24] He added the field of " philosophical jurisprudence " to the domain of the discipline. He proclaimed that the empire of jurisprudence embraced the four schools of analytical, historical, sociological and philosophical jurisprudence.

PART C

The schools of jurisprudence

(a) The ambiguity of " law "

Pound's classification of jurisprudence into four schools of analytical, historical, sociological and philosophical jurisprudence was largely based on a principle of division according to different theories of the nature of law. The analytical school, according to this categorisation, subscribed to the doctrine that law was but the aggregate of rules enacted by those with legislative power (Austin's " command of the sovereign "). For the historical school law was an organic response to social needs (Savigny's " silent anonymous forces of nature " and Carter's " law is custom "). The sociological school held to the view that the function of law was to protect social and individual interests. Finally the philosophical school maintained that law was the

---

[23] In his later writings, however, he was prepared to consider the existence of a " natural law " and of criteria of value judgments whereby public, social and individual interests were not merely catalogued but arranged in a hierarchy.

[24] Salmond's theory that law was based on ideal justice has been perverted, and Salmond has been classified with the " positivists " by treating his phrase " the administration of justice " as equivalent to its use by parliamentary draftsmen in providing a title for Acts of Parliament dealing with the structure of courts and the judicial process. In fact Salmond was opposed to the view of Gray, with which it has nevertheless been equated, that law is but the rules adopted by courts.

administration of justice. (Salmond's formulation, though Salmond's work was analytical.) A more natural mode of classification is to proceed by reference to the different subject-matters with which the various branches of jurisprudence are concerned, and not to tie schools of jurisprudence to any particular theory of law. In the classification I suggest an analytical jurist, for example, does not necessarily have to believe that law is but an apparatus of coercion. He may instead believe that law is the inevitable result of basic social responses to human needs, or that it is the realisation by man of transcendent ideals. What distinguishes analytical jurisprudence is that the subject matter for analysis, and synthesis also, is that of the verbal propositions for the regulation of life in a society regarded within that society as having authoritative status. The classification is based on the different types of " law " with which each branch deals.

The ambiguity of the word " law " in the English language and of corresponding words in other languages, has long been recognised. It was, however, Pound who first fully demonstrated the full range of meanings the word possesses.[25] He recognised three main uses. (1) The word " law " referred to the authoritative rules for the official decision of disputes existing within a community.[26] (2) The term embraced the judicial administrative and legislative *processes* found within a community. A still wider use but also referring to empirical behaviour was that in which it referred to the " legal order ", the entire process of controlling society by diverse " legal " institutions.[27] (3) The term " law " embraced also an ideal element in social life. Such an ideal element is a constituent even of the authoritative rules themselves. In the English language the notion of justice may be involved in the word " law ". An historical origin for this may be found in the fact, demonstrated by Gough, that in the seventeenth and eighteenth centuries the notion of " fundamental law " was commonly used by scholars, and they often used the abbreviation of " law " for the concept of " fundamental law ". The ethical significance of the concept often symbolised by the word " law " is seen more clearly in the languages of the continent of Europe. For example the French " *droit* " and the German "*recht* ", though they may refer to an aggregate of legal rules or to a purely ethical notion of " right ", also refer to legal institutions interfused with the ethical sense of justice.

---

[25] It is nevertheless doubtful how far he himself always fully appreciated the significance of his own study. At one time he stated that all that could be said about the various meanings of " law " was that they all fall within the scope of jurisprudence.

[26] One of Pound's many important contributions to analytical jurisprudence was to show that such rules are of various types. Not only were there the detailed precepts traditionally regarded as the model of all legal rules, but there were also broad concepts and standards, and the even more general notion of the requirement of advancing some broad policy. Holmes also recognised the existence of different types of rules of law when he said that between the detailed provisions of the *leges barbarorum* and the flexible concepts of the Bill of Rights lay two thousand years of civilisation.

[27] The concept of the " legal order " is not a very precise one: it sometimes seems to be as broad as " a way of life ".

(b) Analytical jurisprudence

The above cataloguing of three different meanings of the word
" law " discloses three different subject matters which form the bases
for three different branches of " jurisprudence ". The subject matter
of one branch is that of the verbal propositions concerned with the
regulation of behaviour which constitute Bentham's aggregate of rules
of law. Rules of law are distinguished from other prescriptive verbal
propositions concerned with human behaviour, such as those of ethics,
by criteria varying from society to society but all comprehended within
a general criterion of " official " or " authoritative ". To this branch
the label " analytical jurisprudence " is for traditional reasons appropriately annexed. The problem of the delimitation of the area of
" analytical jurisprudence " has bulked so large in juristic literature
that there is no need here for further consideration.

(c) Sociological jurisprudence

The subject matter of a second branch is that of human behaviour
itself. The problem of demarcation of the juristic field of study within
this area has not been so widely discussed as the corresponding problem
for " analytical jurisprudence ". A study of the totality of human
behaviour would include religious, artistic, economic, cultural, military,
political and leisure behaviour with which the anthropologist, the
sociologist, the economist, the social psychologist and other social
scientists are concerned.[28] However, the distinction between the " legal
behaviour " to be studied by the jurist, and other forms of behaviour
is not easily stated. It will be the subject of study and debate for a
considerable time. One field of behaviour for juristic study can be
comparatively simply delimited. It is that of the behaviour of
" officials " engaged in the judicial, administrative and legislative
processes. Even here, of course, there may be boundary disputes
between " political science " and jurisprudence, for the area of the
behaviour of those concerned with the legislative process, such as members of parliament and voters, has been considered by some as belonging
peculiarly to " political science ".[29] A more difficult problem is that of
distinguishing the behaviour of the citizen in his engagement in the
" legal order " from other aspects of his behaviour. However, there is
much useful work to be done in legal sociology even though its boundaries be undefined.

To this second branch of jurisprudence the label of " sociological
jurisprudence " may be affixed, again largely for traditional reasons.

---

[28] There are no hard and fast boundaries between the social sciences. Nor indeed does
the sociological jurist claim any monopoly for any particular field of inquiry. Rather does
he complain of the neglect by other social sciences of " legal " behaviour.

[29] The boundaries between " political science " and constitutional law, as well as those
between political science and jurisprudence, and indeed also constitutional law and jurisprudence, are still undrawn. Perhaps the time has come for federation or union. I recognise
no distinction between political philosophy and legal philosophy.

It should, however, be noted that this phrase has also been used as a description of theories which assert the connection of law with social needs and maintain that its function is the advancement of social welfare.

(d) *Philosophical jurisprudence*

The third branch of jurisprudence is the study of the concept of justice, and of its realisation within society. Those who study this topic are not, *a priori*, committed to a thesis that there exists any form of absolute, transcendent justice. The notion of justice delimits a field of study: it does not involve acceptance of any ethical or metaphysical doctrine. A particular jurist may conclude that absolute justice is a conceptual hypostasis—a myth : or he may assert that it is a supreme reality. It is appropriate within this field to study existing ideologies about an ideally just system of law, though actual ideologies are, of course, empirical phenomena falling also within the field of sociological jurisprudence. Movements for the reform of positive law so that it be replaced by newer laws more in conformity with conceived ideal law also fall within the fields of both sociological jurisprudence and the study of justice and its realisation. So too the boundaries between this third branch and analytical jurisprudence are not rigid. The study of actual policies underlying existing rules are revealed by a penetrating analysis of positive law. But the aims of laws are relevant to a study of the notion of justice. Moreover, since such policies are part of the empirical phenomena of society they fall also within sociological jurisprudence. Within what branch of jurisprudence such topics as policies and ideologies should be included may well be a matter of pedagogical convenience varying from university to university. In my opinion the consideration of the total ideology of a legal system, its overall goals, seems most appropriate for the general study of justice.

The label " philosophical jurisprudence " may well be affixed to this study. The reason is largely historical. The phrase " philosophical jurisprudence " has been properly used for any study which raises philosophical issues. Accordingly, the work of Kelsen and his followers concerned with basic logical issues has sometimes been styled philosophical. Indeed the publishers of Austin's lectures employed the sub-title " The Philosophy of Law ". The phrase has also been used for studies in which there has been a conscious application of doctrines of " pure " philosophy. Again the work of Kelsen furnishes an example, for it involves the conscious application of Marburg Neo-Kantianism. Another use of the phrase is for the study of the ends of law, though this is now also called teleological jurisprudence. The use of the label " philosophical " can however be justified for such a study by reference to the teleological character of Aristotelian philosophy. Despite these other uses the phrase is appropriately used for the study of the concept of justice. Ethics still remains the most important branch of

philosophy. If further justification for this use of the phrase is required
it may be found in the propriety of a tribute to the scholarship of
Roscoe Pound who used the phrase "philosophical jurisprudence" in
this sense.

PART D

The unity of jurisprudence

(a) Basic diversity

The different branches of sociological, analytical and philosophical
jurisprudence, as we have defined those phrases, are concerned with
the cosmologically diverse entities of facts, relations and values. These
are the different ontological and epistemological areas of "Hume's
trident". His categories were the result, on the one hand, of his
consideration of the distinction between the contingency of natural
phenomena and the necessity of logical inference involved in his study
of causation, and, on the other hand, of his consideration of the relation
between "is" propositions and "ought" propositions. His discussion
of the latter distinction has often been misunderstood by those who
thought that he denied the validity or meaningfulness of "ought"
propositions.[30] All that Hume did was to show that as a matter of pure
logic no conclusion containing an "ought" can be drawn from premises
concerned only with "is". Value judgments cannot be derived by
logical inference from existential propositions. But this does not constitute a denial of the "validity" of "ought" propositions: on the
contrary their meaningfulness is assumed. Moreover, it is for the study
of values to consider how far existential concepts are involved in value
judgments. Value judgments may be about facts without being themselves judgments of factual correlations.[31]

(b) Methodological differences

The three branches of jurisprudence not only deal with very
different subject matters; they also require different methods for their
inquiries and the development of their theses. For analytical jurisprudence logic is a sufficient tool. But sociological jurisprudence
requires techniques for the study of empirical phenomena which are at
least analogous to those employed in the physical sciences, particularly
the biological sciences. The study of philosophical jurisprudence
requires the use of methods developed in the areas of ethics and meta-

---

[30] For example, by Friedmann in his *Legal Theory* where he stated that Hume
demonstrated the illusory character of natural law.

[31] In my opinion just as the concepts and propositions of "relations", both of logicians
and ordinary people, are about relations between facts, so too " values " are concerned with
a higher degree of relations between relations. They are thus ultimately concerned with facts.

physics.[32] There is thus much to be said for the view that the term " jurisprudence " has been used to embrace what are in reality three quite distinct disciplines. Indeed I have suggested that in order to emphasise the differences between the different fields of enquiry and their methods the terms legal analysis, legal sociology and legal philosophy be used instead of analytical, sociological and philosophical jurisprudence.

(c) Basic unity

Despite the differences between its three branches " jurisprudence " does constitute a unified discipline. The unity of the subject arises from the interrelations of the three branches, all of which are required in a complete study of law and discourse about law. Pound's dictum that the referents for all meanings of " law " are studied within jurisprudence can be reversed. The unity of jurisprudence is to be found in the truth that all three branches are about " law ". This proposition does not ignore the ambiguity of the symbol " law ". What it does is to assert that for a full understanding of law in any of its meanings it is necessary to consider the inquiries made in all branches of jurisprudence. Thus full comprehension of the significance of those verbal propositions which are classified as legal rules cannot be obtained merely by considering them in the light of logic. Certainly a logical study will achieve clarity of comprehension not only through clarification of terminology and concepts, but also through discernment of common concepts and general principles and examination of the validity of reasoning. Such achievements, and others, which logic may gain will not result in an understanding of the truth that rules of law are empirical phenomena possessing historical reality, and so will not yield that comprehension of their operation which can only result from sociological study.

Nor will logical and sociological study suffice. There still remains the problem of what values are realised by legal rules and systems, and what values are ignored or denied. Just as logical study must be supplemented by sociological and philosophical study, so philosophical study must be supplemented by sociological and logical study. A

---

[32] Logic is of course required both in the empirical studies of sociological jurisprudence and in the ethico-metaphysical study of philosophical jurisprudence. Nevertheless, a common use of logic does not unify the various branches of jurisprudence. The natural sciences depend to a very large extent on the use of logic in the form of mathematics. Nevertheless, though they are sometimes confused, mathematics and physics are very different disciplines. St. Thomas has rightly said that it is a " sin against the intellect " to confuse the two. So too he said it is a " sin against the intellect to confuse physics and metaphysics ". Nevertheless, it does not follow that the study of metaphysics and of values is not dependent on physics and mathematics, on the natural sciences and on logic. As has already been noted, the view of Dias that " analytical jurisprudence " is an inappropriate name for the particular branch of jurisprudence, because " analysis " is required in all branches, not only contravenes the semantic principle of the artificial character of words but also ignores the consideration that whereas " analysis " is the dominant characteristic of " analytical jurisprudence " it plays a subordinate role in the other branches of jurisprudence.

discussion of justice, to be complete, presupposes a sociological study of relevant behaviour and a logical examination of the legal rules related to that behaviour. It asks how the behaviour and the rules measure up to standards of justice. Again, no sociological study will achieve complete comprehension of legal behaviour without consideration, on the one hand, of the legal rules involved in and related to such behaviour and, on the other hand, of all the related problems of value. No branch of jurisprudence is self-sufficient for a complete study of the complex phenomena of " law ", nor is understanding complete without realisation that " law " operates within the different cosmological fields of facts, relations and values, requiring study by the distinct method of science, logic and ethics.[33]

(d) Stone's unification of jurisprudence

The above account of the unity of jurisprudence differs from that provided by Stone in his *Province of Jurisprudence Redetermined*.[34] That notable attempt was based on the thesis that jurisprudence is " the lawyer's extraversion ". All branches of law, it states, are related to law, and the specific character of the thesis is the mode of relationship. It should be noted that though no attempt is made to define " law ", nevertheless the discussion proceeds on the assumption that the law involved in the relationship with jurisprudence is the aggregate of

---

[33] The themes in the text can be illustrated from any branch of the law. I illustrate them by reference to the interpretation of statutes. Too often writers fail to make the appropriate distinctions, and thus confuse factual, logical and value questions. They state in the form of alleged legal rules what they believe the rules ought to be and sometimes what they believe the rules ought not to be. They allege that judges behave in various ways without adequate evidence to support their views since the relevant judicial behaviour is very often of a private character. Sometimes they allege that judges behave in a way inconsistent with judicial explanations of their own behaviour. The inquiry into what legal rules exist for the interpretation of statutes should be based on an examination of the verbal propositions enacted in statutes such as Interpretation Acts and propounded in the words of judgments. The jurist may properly restate the rules in his own terminology in order to clarify the official language, and he may expose the area of discretion permitted by the official language. But he cannot, without breach of allegiance to truth, substitute what he conceives to be better rules, though of course he can recommend the adoption of such rules. The question of what the rules are, and what is involved in logical application of them, is a different one from that of how in fact judges arrive at decisions concerning the interpretation of statutes. It is possible that judges in their decision-making ignore the verbal rules, or use them only when seeking to justify *ex post facto* their decisions. But how far the possibility is actualised depends on a total examination by psychological and other methods of the relevant judicial behaviour. It requires techniques which historians, psychologists and sociologists have by no means perfected. Too often jurists have given us dogmatic assertions instead of scientifically derived hypotheses. Again, how judges ought to behave is a separate inquiry into complex practical and social values. Conclusions in this field ought not to be presented in the guise of descriptive statements of behaviour.

Actual examination of statements of English judges shows that they have propounded different rules such as the *Rule in Heydon's Case* and the *Golden Rule*. At various times the majority of judges appear to subscribe to one set of rules rather than another. Though exceptions may be found, there is a pattern of dominant rules at any one time. There is neither entire homogeneity nor complete anarchy. I believe that full examination of judicial behaviour would show a considerable variety of decision procedures, though possibly some patterns of behaviour would emerge. The standards available for desirable rules and behaviours are many, and no patterns of juristic statements are discernible by me.

[34] Reprinted as part of his Swiney Prize opus *The Province and Function of the Law*.

official rules for behaviour in a society.[35] The relationship of jurisprudence to these rules is that they are examined in the light of disciplines other than law, and the unity of jurisprudence is achieved by this common method of treatment of law. Jurisprudence is thus the critical jurisprudence of Bentham. Analytical jurisprudence is the examination of law in the light of logic, sociological jurisprudence is the examination of law in the light of general sociology, and philosophical jurisprudence the examination of law in the light of philosophers' theories of ethical justice.[36] Such a theory presupposes that there is no distinctive field of legal logic or of legal sociology, or of justice considered as specifically legal ethics.[37]

Each of the propositions involved in Stone's thesis is doubtful. In the first place there is no ready-made logic of logicians, sociology of sociologists, or theories of justice of philosophers capable of dealing with all the problems which face the jurist. This is emphatically so in the case of theories of justice. It has been the responsibility of jurists throughout the ages to create their own theories of justice and their own systems of ideal law, a task often performed under the name of natural law. Philosophers have had relatively little to say about justice. Consequently a limitation of " philosophical jurisprudence " to a criticism of law in the light of the pure philosopher's theory of justice will omit a vast amount of juristic literature concerned with theories of natural law or the nature of justice. It will fail to arouse the jurist to the need for more work by them in these fields. To ask whether legal rules measure up to standards of justice desiderated by philosophers is indeed an important task. But it is only one of the tasks to be carried out within the scope of " philosophical jurisprudence " as I conceive that field of inquiry.

A similar comment may be made about the province of analytical jurisprudence as redetermined by Stone. There is, of course, much valuable work to be done in the examination of legal rules in the light of the logic already developed by pure logicians. Nevertheless

---

[35] Stone has sought to justify the failure to define his use of the word " law " by reference to the semantic doctrine that the meaning of words depends on the manner of their usage. This is inadequate in a scholarly treatise employing a word whose ambiguity may be a considerable source of confusion.

[36] Plato taught that the Greek word for " justice " had as its referent the totality of good. Aristotle raised the question whether there was any " particular justice" as distinct from virtue in general. He thought that lawyers did have a concept of " particular justice ". He examined the legal concept, and discerned that its characteristic was that of equality— the equality of arithmetical proportion in commutative justice, and the equality of geometrical proportion in distributive justice. Aristotle's theory of distributive justice was derived from forensic practice, but the phrase is now used for governmental distribution of the national income. It has yielded eventually the " socialist " formula of " to each according to his merit " and the " communist " formula of " to each according to his need ".

The concept of " particular justice " has recently been reasserted by Fuller under the name " inner morality of law " with a very different content from that ascribed to it by Aristotle in *The Morality of Law*.

[37] The phrase " legal ethics " has been appropriated by the legal profession for the concept of professional etiquette.

there is equally valuable work to be done in the creation of logical theories more appropriate to the vague concepts of legal rules and to the actualities of legal discourse and reasoning than has yet been developed by logicians. They have generally sought for a logic of discourse analogous to that of mathematics, capable of application to a cosmology of fixed species conceived in Aristotelian fashion. Jurists should themselves respond to the call for a logic more appropriate to law.[38] The value of traditional logic for lawyers should not however be minimised. The discipline of logic has been developed by logicians to such a degree that much of it is directly applicable to legal and juristic problems. Often when judges have purported to reject " logic " as an aid to decision-making, what has been really repudiated has been pseudo-logic. Judges have too often been unaware of the true character of logic, and have wrongly thought that logicians claim to answer questions of fact and questions of value. Nevertheless, it remains true that a limitation of analytical jurisprudence to an examination of law in the light of logic omits much important literature, and fails to arouse students to the need for further logical inquiry by jurists themselves.[39]

Finally, the limitation of sociological jurisprudence to an examination of law in the light of " general " sociology ignores the truth that sociology (which in this context includes also psychology) has not yet developed an adequate range of theories applicable to legal and juristic problems. Moreover, much of the sociological work which is relevant has been the creation of lawyers and jurists. It is sufficient to cite the writings about early law of Maine and other " historical " jurists, and the many discussions of crime and punishment by jurists from Beccaria and Bentham onwards. On the continent of Europe criminology is not only studied in faculties of law but is sometimes only studied there. Criminology is still in its infancy, and while the subject is not the monopoly of lawyers and jurists, indeed the concept of monopoly finds no place in scholarship, it is an area in which lawyers and jurists have much to contribute. Criminology is but one topic within the domain of legal sociology. What is true of criminology is perhaps more true of other areas of legal sociology. Thus it can also be said of " sociological jurisprudence " that the limitation of its

---

[38] There has, of course, already been some work done by pure logicians in the area of vagueness of concepts: a notable example is Körner's study in his *Conceptual Thinking*. It is noteworthy also that logicians have begun to realise that legal provisions and judicial speech provide them with models for logical theory more adequate than traditional logic (or the modern mathematical logic) for application to ordinary discourse. It is in this area that Hart's most valuable work is to be found; but see also Stephen Toulmin's recent writings.

[39] It should not be thought that the text denies the universality of logic. Formal logic asserts truths about concepts and propositions and their relations independent of the subject-matter of the concepts and propositions. It is applicable to all fields of study. It is, however, still incomplete, and needs to be supplemented by the development of theories more applicable to types of discourse such as are found in legal and juristic discourse.

province to the examination of law in the light of the sociology developed by non-lawyers is to ignore a considerable amount of relevant literature, and to fail to arouse lawyers and jurists to the need for greater efforts by them in the field of sociological inquiry.

PART E

The tasks of jurisprudence

(a) Legal analysis

Legal analysis may be carried out at various levels of comprehensiveness. Austin thought that " general jurisprudence " which was derived from, and applicable to, *all* legal systems of maturer societies was the more important study, and it was to such a general study that he applied the name " jurisprudence " when used without any qualifying epithet. Nevertheless, the legal analysis of particular legal systems—the " particular jurisprudence "—of Austin is of great significance. Much of this is done in the course of exposition of the various branches of law. On the whole, relatively little has been accomplished in respect of English law,[40] and doubtless the same is true of the law of Malaysia. There is needed for any legal system an examination of the language of the rules thereby revealing ambiguities and unnecessary vagueness with consequent suggestions for a new terminology with the precision required by the subject matter. Here it should be noted that there is a distinction between generality and vagueness. Law needs general terms (indeed Austin would only admit *general* commands within the category of legal rules), and while general terms may be precise so that the task of judicial application is quasi-mechanical it may be the right policy to employ general words of such a character to enable judges either to construct a series of subordinate rules for their application or to retain a discretion in application. There is real need for the construction of a logic of both general and vague concepts, distinct from the logic of " mathematical " classes which is our inheritance from the philosophy of physics.[41] The characteristics of legal concepts require much further elaboration than they have received from

---

[40] One of the achievements of " particular jurisprudence " is Holland's exposure that the theory of subjective agreement which Anson presented as characteristic of the *consensus ad idem* of the English law of contract, was not in truth the doctrine of the courts. Analysis revealed that two theories of agreement were possible, and observation showed that English judges adopted the theory of objective agreement. Anson had assumed that only one theory could exist, and had accepted the theory of Pothier.

[41] The creation of exceptions to general rules is part of the " logic " of judicial discourse. Hart has made a valuable contribution to the required logic in his discussion of " defeasible " concepts. See also my own discussion of the problem in *Law-Making and Law-Applying* in the memorial number to Jolowicz, of Butterworth's *South African Law Journal*, 1956.

Hohfeld and Kocoureck. I naturally consider my distinction between law-embracing and law-constitutive concepts, and between technical and non-technical law-constitutive concepts to be very significant.[42] The elements of concepts actually employed in legal discourse require determination. When they are catalogued relations between various concepts may be seen, and their classification under wider categories facilitated. It may be advisable to propose the use of different concepts, both to prevent the confusion between law and fact so often made in existing concepts with its consequent concealment of the legislative function involved in the use of those concepts,[43] and to enable more systematic and rational categorisation. Legal analysis should not stop at the analysis of specific propositions and the synthesis of their constituent concepts. It should proceed to an examination of the relations between various propositions. When the propositions are related in discourse yielding conclusions their consistency or inconsistency should be considered, and thus the logical validity of the reasoning in the discourse determined.[44] When the propositions are not related in such discourse a logical examination may nevertheless permit their classification under more comprehensive principles. The value of such logical operations for more efficient classification with the consequent facilitation of law finding, and better restatement and codification is clear.

Analysis is concerned with more than the immediate content of rules. It should also disclose the policy of rules by placing the rules within a wider verbal and non-verbal context. Such analysis leads to consideration of alternative rules which on *logical*[45] grounds may be more efficient means of advancing the revealed policies. The determination of overall policies of a legal system lies within the peripheral areas of the various branches of jurisprudence. It may be regarded with equal rationality as a task for legal analysis, legal sociology or legal philosophy.

The higher level of legal analysis is that which involves relations between various legal systems, and falls within comparative law equally with jurisprudence as a matter of pedagogical classification. Much

---

[42] See my paper contributed to the Hamburg Conference on Comparative Law in 1962, published by the Max-Planck Institute. [*Ante*, Ch. 6. Ed.]

[43] For example the existing concepts of " negligence " and " cause " used by judges conceal a legal element. " Negligence " as used by judges often means "carelessness where there is a duty to take care", but the rule of law which specifies the limits of the duty is not articulated. So too " cause " means very often " action antecedent to subsequent harm for which responsibility is to be attributed to the actor ", without any specification of the rule of law providing for the attribution of responsibility.

[44] The ethical validity of a conclusion is not dependent on the logical validity of the reasoning, or indeed on the ethical validity of the premises employed in the reasoning.

[45] When rules are regarded as operational instruments for achieving a policy, as empirical factors in social control, then the determination of efficiency is a problem in human behaviour in which means and ends are related to scientific consideration of cause and effect. Such scientific consideration depends on sociological knowledge transcending logical analysis. It is a task for legal sociology.

of Austin's work was done at the level of formulation of "common notions" derived from comparison of Roman and English law. Concepts of right, duty, ownership, possession, contract, delict, crime, substantive law and procedural law have been evolved and delimited in this fashion. Hohfeld's work in the formulation of basic concepts involved in all legal transactions and regulations falls also within this operational field. It derives from a consideration of these legal systems at a time when private interests and private property were dominant notions.[46] The appropriate analysis and synthesis may reveal also principles common to many legal systems. It is submitted that what will be found more common are policies, the ends being attained by a variety of different legal instruments.

The tasks of comparative law may be assisted by the formulation of concepts, principles and policies, which are more adequate than others for revealing similarities and differences between various legal systems. The comparative lawyer asks, for example, whether or not a system possesses a particular constructed concept. The various legal systems are compared with each other by reference to the presence or absence of such a concept.

One of the problems falling within the task of legal analysis is that of "necessary notions" of law. This problem is related to the problem of the definition of law whose consideration has bulked so large in the literature of analytical jurisprudence. Any pronouncement that the concept of "law" should be constructed (or defined) in a particular manner entails as a consequence that the elements of that particular concept (or definition) are themselves necessary legal concepts. Thus when Austin defined law as the general command of a sovereign, command in terms of sanctions, and sovereign in terms of the relation of a determinate group within a society to the remaining members of the society, it followed that generality, sanctions and absolute duties were necessary elements of law. Rights were not necessary notions, but were notions that might be found in particular legal systems. An "absolute duty" was a necessary notion because it was the concept derived from the necessary concepts of sovereignty and command by positing the relation of a member of a society to his sovereign who has issued a command. The problem of the definition of "law" is of course a problem of legal analysis at the highest level of comparison of all legal systems. The practitioner within a particular legal system is rarely concerned with that problem. He will however be concerned with the problem of the interpretation of the

---

[46] The most valuable contribution made by Hohfeld's *Fundamental Legal Conceptions* lies within the field of "particular jurisprudence" disclosing the ambiguity of the word "right" in English and United States law. Even in that area he failed to take note of the use of the word "right" as referring to the notion of "interest". This failure vitiates his finding of a logical fallacy in Lord Lindley's reasoning in *Quinn* v. *Leathem*. Hohfeld's scheme of concepts basic to all legal situations is subject to many defects. These have been pointed out in the United States literature, and the scheme largely abandoned.

word " law " when it occurs within a rule of positive law, as it sometimes does within the Constitution of Malaysia.[47]

A final note on legal analysis concerns the problem of the definition
of the law. It is that much of the controversy arises not from the
ambiguity of the word " law " but from the ambiguity of the word
" definition ".[48] Legal analysis is concerned not only with technical
legal words but also with non-technical legal words. Much recent
analytical literature deals with the ambiguities of the " logical
constants "—and, or, if—then.

(b) Legal sociology

Perhaps the most important division of legal sociology, though
it is not adequately recognised in the literature, is by reference to
the method of enquiry adopted. On the one hand there is the method
of statistical enquiry, sometimes involving experimentation. This is the
same method as that employed in other social sciences, and is analogous
to methods used in the physical sciences, particularly in those of
biology.[49] On the other hand there is the method of common-sense
generalisation from a variety of " evidence ", which is similar to the
methods of many historians. Despite the prophecy of Holmes that
the lawyer of tomorrow would be the man of statistics, it is the latter
method which is dominant in current literature except within the field
of criminology. The existence of diverse methods is an illustration of
the existence of a problem of methodology in legal sociology which it
shares with the social sciences in general. I do not agree either with
those who think that methods analogous to those in the biological
sciences cannot be employed in studies of human behaviour, nor with
those who think that discussion of method is largely sterile, and should
be set aside to allow " progress " to be made in active research. Too
many of the intuitive generalisations of those who reject statistical
and experimental methods are but hypotheses which require to be
tested. They do not cease to be dogma because they may happen to
possess rhetorical appeal. Further discussion of methodology, I believe,
will establish the superiority of a truly scientific approach.

An important aspect of methodological discussion is that of the
place of values in the area of social science. I find myself opposed
to those who think that facts and values are so inextricably interwoven
that they cannot be conceptually divorced or distinguished in scholarly

---

[47] In the Constitution of India this problem has given rise to judicial differences of
opinion: see Gopalan v. State of Madras A.I.R. 1950 (S.C.) 27.

[48] The definitive work on the ambiguity of " definition " is Robinson on Definitions.

[49] Today medicine in its research into the aetiology of disease is using such methods
more widely than heretofore. The most widely known example is the investigation of the
connection between smoking and lung cancer.

discussion. While I do not think Max Weber's idea of *wert-frei* social science can be attained, yet I think we can realise Holmes' desideratum of a science in which the postulates of value judgments involved are fully articulated.

A classification of legal sociology by reference to the number of societies embraced by an enquiry is of less significance than in the area of legal analysis. Holland thought that such a mode of classification, which is that involved in the distinction between " particular " and " general " jurisprudence, was of no importance in the area of legal analysis. The aim of jurisprudence, he thought, was the discernment of general doctrines. In the natural sciences the adequate study of rocks from one area would produce geological generalisations valid for the entire earth. In the same way the examination of the concepts and rules of one legal system would produce generalisations valid for all legal systems. However, this ignores the basic difference between the verbal artifacts which are the data for legal analysis, and the natural phenomena which are data for the physical sciences. A postulate of the uniformity of nature is a reasonable assumption which experience has raised to the level of a " working " hypothesis. Consequently, though generalisations derived from the logical study of the verbal rules of one legal system should not be thought to be of universal application, the position is different with regard to the empirical studies of legal phenomena of legal sociology. Legal sociology falls within the same class of inquiry as geology. The assumption that valid generalisations based on a study of behaviour within one society will be true for other societies is based on the reasonable postulate of the basic uniformity of human nature.[50] It is of course true that varying historical experiences and environmental characteristics may produce different conditional states for different individuals and indeed different groups. Such differences, of course, must be taken into account when generalisations based on studies within one society are applied to other societies.[51]

There is a distinction within legal sociology, drawn by reference to the character of the societies whose legal systems are the subject of study, which has been of great importance. It is that between

---

[50] The descriptive postulate that all human beings or races are basically alike can be distinguished from an ethical postulate of the brotherhood of man. One states a physical equality: the other states the desirability of treating all men as if they were equal.

The thesis of equality does not of course deny a distinction between infant and adult or between sane and insane. It merely asserts that such differences have a universal character.

[51] The thesis in the text underlies Aristotle's discussion of natural law in Book V of the *Ethics*. Aristotle notes that though fire burns in the same manner in Greece and Persia yet the peoples are governed in different ways. Nevertheless the difference between the laws of different countries is not inconsistent with the existence of uniform principles of government; in other words with the existence of natural law. The differences may depend on different circumstances. The identity is revealed by making the appropriate abstraction. A common principle of weights and measures is not contradicted by the existence of different units for wholesale and retail markets.

I

primitive societies and advanced societies. A considerable literature exists dealing with the law of primitive societies. Much of it has been classified under " historical jurisprudence " and indeed the formula whereby primitive law was equated with historical jurisprudence was a close approximation to reality. The problems of primitive law have not been merely those of description. The functioning of law as a means of social control has been in the views of some writers easier to discern in such societies, and consequently studies in primitive law have attracted the attention of sociologically oriented jurists. The problem of the relation between primitive law and the law of advanced societies has become a subject of political importance in the modern world as the situation in the " developing countries " has been seen to be fundamental to the preservation of world peace.

Another mode of classification of legal sociology produces yet another way in which the subject may be regarded as including within it historical jurisprudence.[52] Scientific propositions have often been regarded as probability statements about the future. They may be verified (or falsified if the Popper thesis be preferred) by testing the accuracy of the prediction through observation of the event foretold. The discernment of trends of legal development, of lines of change, is an important task of legal sociology. When consideration is given to long term trends over past stretches of time we are in the area of historical jurisprudence traversed by Maine and Marx and their followers. Such studies are of course relevant for the future. Extrapolation from past to present is always possible. Moreover one may predict (not necessarily accurately) that an evolutionary chain established for one society may be found to operate in the future in another society.[53]

The usual division of the task of legal sociology is into areas determined by the character of persons whose behaviour is studied. We have broadly a distinction between investigation of the behaviour of officials and the behaviour of citizens. A more detailed classification distinguishes between various types of official behaviour. Much of the " realist jurisprudence " of the nineteen-thirties is concerned with the behaviour of judges. More recently their sentencing function in criminal cases has aroused interest, and drawn attention to the conduct

---

[52] The treatment of " historical jurisprudence " as a separate species in addition to analytical, sociological and philosophical jurisprudence offends the logical canon of classification by reference to a single criterion. It introduces a principle of classification by reference to the factor of time in addition to that of classification by reference to character of subject-matter upon which the division into three branches is based.

[53] Scientific productions may be verified (or falsified) by reference to the past. Let t_1, t_2 and t_3 represent different periods of time arranged in chronological order. A prediction is of the form " given facts a b c at time t_1 then facts d e f will probably occur at t_2 ": t_1 and t_2 may both be in the past relative to t_3, the time when the statement is made that there has been verification (or falsification) of the prediction.

of judges in inferior courts. Judicial behaviour is but one aspect of the larger field of the whole process of litigation. Litigation may be described as an " institution ", and we are thus reminded of the sociological tasks involved in the study of institutions. The converse of this proposition is that the approach to the study of law of the " institutionalists " is basically that of legal sociology. Within the field of litigation we have not only to consider the behaviour of judges but also of juries and advocates: the " Brandeis brief " was the work of advocates. We have to consider the entirety of the organisation and functioning of " courts " as a whole which includes a study of the behaviour of all court officials, and not merely their superior officers. Nor should we continue to neglect perhaps the most important of all, the *dramatis personae*—the litigants themselves, or witnesses.

There are types of the administration of law other than through courts. There are of course the administrative tribunals. But further, we have the entire " executive branch " of government to consider, from the higher echelons of the civil service to the lower ranks of the police and such officials as clerks of licensing authorities. The entire legislative process provides yet another wide area for study, which, as has been previously noted, is shared with political scientists.

When we turn to the consideration of the investigation of the behaviour of citizens we are confronted with the difficulty of distinguishing the conduct appropriate for legal sociology from that appropriate for other legal sciences. The problem of demarcation is indeed one of the topics of legal sociology, as also are the problems connected with the relations between law and jurisprudence and the other social sciences. The most developed study of a type of behaviour falling within legal sociology is that of anti-social conduct with which criminology is concerned. Here we have also a problem of demarcation. Some legal criminologists would limit their study to conduct related to the criminal law. It is however *prima facie* unlikely that significant behaviour patterns will be discerned through a study of behaviour based on the arbitrary categories of the criminal law. We shall have to construct new concepts and postulate a variety of possible relations before significant correlations will be discovered.

The study of anti-social conduct is not the only field of inquiry into non-official behaviour. The subject of commercial law suggests many kinds of enquiries. For some business practices we may find the categories of the commercial law inadequate for the efficient handling of affairs. This may suggest the need for legal reform. There may be also discovered areas of " undesirable " practices also suggesting the need for legal reform. The study of restrictive practices in commerce and industry is another field of enquiry. Clearly there are many other fields of non-official behaviour with which law is concerned, and therefore which suggest topics for legal sociology.

Finally for the purpose of this paper, though the list of tasks for legal sociology has not been exhausted, there are two topics which have received considerable attention in the discussion of law in action as opposed to law in books. Both are Pound's phrases. They are: (i) The study of the origin of legal rules—the problem of legal aetiology. This is not the study of legal history nor the study of legal evolution, but the study of the sources of rules in the nature of man and the forces of society. Marx's theory of a social substructure of economic activity with law as one of the ideological components of the superstructure is but one of many competing hypotheses. (ii) The study of the consequences of legal rules—their effects on society. In this study falls the problem of the efficiency of rules as means of attaining desiderated ends. Such studies of course suggest questions of law reform both by means of substituting more efficient rules and more desirable or practically attainable ends.

(c) Legal philosophy

A description of the tasks of the legal philosopher as the consideration of justice presents a wide vista of some of the most important contributions to the dialogue of the human spirit. It is possible to enumerate various chapters of that conversation between hearts and minds. There is the problem of whether justice has to be expressed in terms of values independent of time and space or whether analysis reduces it to a series of ideologies current from time to time within particular societies. It is, of course, for legal sociology to say whether those ideologies relate to the felt needs of time and place. The presentation of values as " absolutes " opens up a debate whether from those absolutes there can be isolated directives[54] which immediately produce applicable rules, universal and eternal, or whether the absolutes are only to be found within sets of principles which are always relative to the varying circumstances of different societies.

The study of justice has been often carried out in terms of an examination of " natural law ": and this has produced many different accounts of natural law and theories about it. The classical theory of natural law of Aristotle and St. Thomas Aquinas was relativist in the sense that it stated a series of directives to legislators, who were empowered to enact rules of positive law by applying those directives[55]

---

[54] In *Hedley Byrne* v. *Heller* Lord Devlin presents the common law as containing a series of directives which are not directly applicable to the decision of particular cases, but require the intermediation of rules produced by applying directives to particular areas of social problems. The neighbour principle of Lord Atkin laid down in *Donoghue* v. *Stevenson* is thought by Lord Devlin to be such a directive; the name he gives to such directives is " conceptions ".

[55] When directives are applied to particular areas a choice of rules or decisions is available. The process of proceeding from directive to rule or decision, says St. Thomas, is not a quasimathematical one of *deductio*, but one involving " judgment ", *sapientia*, in making a *determinatio* among possibilities whose range is limited by the directive.

to the communities entrusted to their care and whose common good was the purpose of their legislation.

In the language of the discourse of St. Thomas a distinction was drawn between enquiry into the doctrine of natural law, and enquiry into the nature of justice. This may be restated by stating that there is a distinction between general principles upon which government by law should proceed and the particular ethical requirements to be observed because government proceeds by " law ". The distinction is not identical with, but is derived from, Aristotle's discussion, in Book V of the *Ethics*, of the distinction between general and particular justice, with its consideration of the principles of commutative and distributive justice, and his rejection of the denial of the existence of principles of natural law. " Natural law " in the classical theory is not equated with the entirety of ethical virtue since it envisages limitations arising from the practical problems of government, and the cultural requirement of government by law. That theory does not equate law with morals, but the relation of law to morals is one of the great topics of legal philosophy. One of the problems involved in that topic is that of the moral duty of the citizen to obey an immoral or unjust law. The medieval discussion of the " right " of rebellion has its contemporary counterpart in the discussion of the existence of a " legal duty not to obey an unjust law ".

The classical theory of natural law is but one of the theories to be considered in legal philosophy. It was followed by theories of natural rights, and theories which may be termed those of " natural rules ". The latter theories produced blue-prints of detailed codes for adoption as positive laws—" anytime, anywhere ". Scholars are constantly producing new examinations of the problem of natural law, and indeed new theories of natural law.

The problems considered in the Thomistic examination of justice also continue to demand attention. The principles of distributive justice have been widened to produce socialist and communist theories of government and state. There is still debate as to whether any, and if so what, elements of justice should be included in the definition of the concept of law. The problem of the definition of law has indeed been considered by some as the most important task for legal philosophy.

It is sometimes forgotten that St. Thomas' " eternal law " is not identical with " divine " law. While the universe, including the processes of government, is subject according to him to " eternal law ", those processes yield many problems for which the revelations of " divine " law provide no solution. The problems of the distinction between " divine law " and " natural law " are further topics for legal philosophy. They are one aspect of the wider problems of the relations between law and religion, between philosophical jurisprudence and theology. Though in this catalogue they appear last, they are not the least important.

PART F

The uses of the study of jurisprudence

It was under this heading that Austin really determined the
province of jurisprudence in the sense of considering the main tasks
of jurisprudence as he conceived them. He did not seek to advance
utilitarian inducements for students to embrace such study or pursue
such tasks. Nor is there any need to do so for students who are truly
students.[56]   Sir Edmund Hillary's answer to the question why he
undertook the arduous and perilous task of climbing Everest exists for
those who ask why they should study jurisprudence. The tasks are
there, and the spirit of man will find a response to the existence of the
tasks in the determination to overcome all their difficulties. Commentators on Austin have suggested that Austin advertised jurisprudence as a help to the study of the other branches of law. Manning
suggests that Austin conceived jurisprudence as a means of obtaining
knowledge of general principles of law.[57]   The critics of the study of
jurisprudence have been met by defenders who have said that it is only
in jurisprudence that students learn to think, and thinking is the
lawyer's trade. I agree that jurisprudence provides the most practical
training for the future practitioner. But nevertheless the thesis that the
study of legal rules directly does not produce " thinking " is an unfair
generalisation from the existence of courses of a purely mnemonic
character in particular branches of law. It is true that it is difficult to
produce a course in jurisprudence of a purely dogmatic character which
exercises but the memory of the student: nevertheless it has been
achieved. All courses in law are capable of stimulating intellectual
enterprise of the widest character.

Other claims put forward for jurisprudence are that it introduces
the student to branches of the law of which he would otherwise have
no knowledge. He studies but few branches, and in jurisprudence
he is presented with a synoptic view of the entire legal system. Again
it is said that only through jurisprudence will the student become
acquainted with foreign systems of law. These claims are doubtful,
but even if well founded they are concerned but with incidental aspects
of the subject. The proper advocacy of jurisprudence is that its study
produces a fuller, not an easier, understanding of the problems of law
and justice, of man's place in society and in the universe.

---

[56] There were very few such in the London of Austin's days. His lectures were discon-
tinued after very few years for lack of support. What is the realistic view of enthusiasm for
jurisprudence in the Singapore of to-day?

[57] Not a picture postcard of the view of the entirety of legal rules obtained by climbing
the holy stairs of detailed study of legal rules: but an aid to those who are prepared to perform
the arduous task of critically examining the legal rules.

9

The Treatment of Statutes by Lord Denning*

Case law derived from what judges say

In this article I am concerned with a description of what one of our foremost judicial thinkers *says* about the manner in which statutes should be treated by courts of law. I am not seeking to probe into any unstated grounds for his decisions of cases, to discover how far his expressed reasons are but rationalisations of pre-determined decisions. I am not seeking to discover any pattern of behaviour which will enable predictions to be made about what he will do or say in the future. On the basis of a common-sense approach I consider that what judges say in one case influences what they, or other judges, will do and say in later cases. That is why the examination of judicial opinions is of importance in a description of the practice of the courts. This is, of course, in no way inconsistent with the doctrine, so often insisted on by " realist " jurists, that what judges *do* is of perhaps greater importance. Indeed it is worth emphasising one aspect of that doctrine. Judges do not continue to say the same things: the judicial doctrines (the principles they enunciate, or which may be logically derived from what they say) with regard to some subjects are long-lived; others change more rapidly. Some change may be explained as the result of changed social circumstances: indeed this is part of judicial doctrine.[1] Thus, when the House of Lords in the *Maxim-Nordenfeldt* case said that general restraints of trade could be valid the judges themselves pointed out that they were not really over-ruling old cases in which it was said that general restraints were invalid: they were taking note of the relation of the old statements to the commercial practices and communications systems of the times, and of the impact on those state-

---

* Reprinted from the *University of Malaya Law Review*, July, 1959, by kind permission.

[1] It is this type of change to which Lord Radcliffe referred when he said: " No one really doubts that the common law is a body of law which develops in process of time in response to the developments of the society in which it rules . . . I do not think we need abandon the conviction of Galileo that somehow, by some means, there is a movement that takes place." *Lister* v. *Romford Ice Co., Ltd.* [1957] 1 All E.R. 142E. He had spoken of the " implications in a society which has been almost revolutionised by the growth of all forms of insurance."

ments of modern commerce and communications. But other changes occur which do not appear to be accounted for by such an explanation.[2] We may not, for example, entirely ignore a " great man " theory in consideration of legal history.

Judicial doctrine as the dominant pattern of opinions

It will be noted that I have not been severely " realistic " in talking about judges and judicial doctrines. My statement that " judges do not continue to say the same things " referred not only to different statements by the same judge but to statements by different judges: a judge of a later period does not say the same things as a judge of an earlier period. But, moreover, this latter statement involves the abstraction of " a judge ", as if one judge is interchangeable with another. And this, I believe, is largely true: we do have in considerable measure a government of laws and not of men. Judges do not all speak with the same voice, but, nevertheless, it is often possible with regard to a particular topic to discern a dominant pattern of judicial opinion in the reported cases. This may be styled the judicial doctrine of that subject. Thus, for a considerable period most judges dealing with " frustration " cases spoke of an " implied term " theory: and it was possible to describe the judicial doctrine as involving that theory. But because of the speeches in *Davis Contractors Ltd.* v. *Fareham U.D.C.*[3] it is no longer possible to speak with such assurance. There may be in process a change in the judicial doctrine of frustration. In the treatment of statutes a change of judicial opinion appears definitely to have occurred within the last few years. This is not to say that there is complete uniformity now, any more than there was fifty years ago. Some judges do sometimes make statements which repeat the judicial doctrine of the past, just as some judges fifty years ago made statements in line with the judicial doctrine of today.[4]

---

[2] Glanville Williams suggests changes brought about by changes in policy notions when he says: " to support the doctrine of precedent by reference to precedent is to suspend it on its own boot-straps. How far the courts will follow precedent is a matter of judicial practice founded on notions of policy: but the interpretation of this policy may change with the times." 70 *L.Q.R.* p. 471.

[3] [1956] A.C. 696. *Cf.* the remarks of McNair J. in the *Suez Canal* case, [1958] 3 All E.R. at 120D.

[4] The view has been advanced that no pattern of judicial opinion can be discerned: Jennings and Llewellyn, writing in 1936 and 1946, saw only a chaos of contradictory rules. " Courts and Administrative Law ", 49 *Harvard L.R.* at p. 435; " Counselling and Advocacy", 46 *Columbia L.R.* at p. 181. Some of the contradiction between so-called " rules " of interpretation is due to the expression as mandatory rules of what are not even " directory rules," but only reminders of the ways in which words may be used. Many of the " canons of construction " only state *possibilities* of the meaning of words. A canon which says that it is possible that general words may have a meaning restricted by the context of particular words is not contradicted by one which says that they may not be restricted: a canon which says that every word may have special significance, and there should be construction *ut res magis valeat quam pereat*, is not contradicted by a canon which reminds one of the use of words " *ex abundanti cautela.*" *Cf.* Lord du Parcq, *Cutler* v. *Wandsworth Stadium Ltd.* [1949] 1 All E.R. at 550A: " not rigid rules but principles which have been found to afford some guidance "; Frankfurter J., *U.S.* v. *Universal Credit Corporation* 344 U.S. at 227: " Generalisations about statutory construction are not rules of law but merely axioms of experience."

General doctrine of " statutory interpretation "

In quite a short time judicial doctrine with regard to the " interpretation " of statutes has changed twice. The development of Baron Parke's " golden rule " had resulted in the doctrine of the first quarter of this century being approximately this: (i) courts were to give the words of statutory clauses their ordinary meaning; (ii) if this first procedure did not resolve difficulties then aid was to be sought in the policy of the statute, the " intention of Parliament ", which, however, was to be sought only in the words of the statute including, of course, other statutes *in pari materia*; (iii) if difficulties still remained the judges were to select that meaning, consistent, however, with the words, which achieved more desirable consequences than alternative meanings: this generally meant choosing the narrower meaning of words so that the statute departed least from the common law. The canons of construction might also be invoked as if they were mandatory and provided mechanical solutions.

It was perhaps the political development of democracy and the social development of welfare legislation, combined with juristic criticism, which brought about new attitudes to the interpretation of statutes. By the end of the second quarter of the century judges were more aware than previously that it was quite ordinary for words to be " ambiguous ", and more ready to co-operate with government by resolving ambiguities in the light of the policy of the statute, to be discovered by an examination of the social context of the statute: they no longer restricted themselves to the verbal context or mechanically applied " canons of construction ". The judicial doctrine could be approximately described as this: (i) words in one part of a statute were to be read in the light of the statute as a whole;[5] (ii) if, so read, ambiguities

---

Even if a canon expresses a " presumptive " rule it is not contradicted by the existence of exceptions. Of course, there is a contradiction between the proposition which says that there is no " presumption " that general words are to be construed *ejusdem generis*, and a proposition that there is such a " presumption ". *Cf.* Devlin J., [1950] 1 All E.R. at 771H, with the dictum of Lord Tenterden, cited with apparent approval by Lord Evershed, [1958] 1 All E.R. at 213F. But there are many unresolved contradictions particularly at a higher level than that of the minor canons of construction, *viz.*, at the level to which Lord Radcliffe perhaps referred when he distinguished " a rule of construction " from " a rule of policy ": see *Galloway* v. *Galloway* [1955] 3 All E.R. 437A. The Rule in *Heydon's Case* is contradicted by the principle that the intention of Parliament is to be gathered from the words of the statute alone; the " rule " that penal statues are to be construed strictly contradicts the words in *Heydon's* case that its rule applies to all statutes "be they penal or beneficial". I have elsewhere suggested that the basic conflict is between a policy of protecting the citizen against government, and of co-operating with government in achieving its constitutionally approved objects: see "Judicial Implementation of Legislative Policy", 3 *Univ. of Queensland L.J.*, p. 146. The Rule in *Heydon's* case, it should be noted, may protect the citizen against a claim by the executive that a statute has a wider operation than that intended by the legislature.

[5] It was not until 1957 in the *Prince Ernest Augustus* case that it was " conclusively " determined that the preamble forms part of the statute for the purpose of this principle. Even in that case there are indications in some of the opinions that the preamble is only to be considered if the enacted words to be interpreted are ambiguous when considered in isolation from the preamble. It is not easy to say what the present doctrine is with regard to cross headings, marginal notes and punctuation.

existed, then they were to be resolved by reference to the intention of Parliament: the Rule in *Heydon's Case* was to be implemented; the mischief to be cured sought for in the social history of the statute;[6] and the remedy for the mischief was to be advanced, rather than the attempt made to maintain the harmony of the legal system by reading the statute in the light of the common law it was designed to alter;[7] (iii) if, however, the ambiguity was not resolved by consideration of the intention of Parliament then Blackstone's " tenth rule " was still to be applied, and the judges were to select the meaning considered the more desirable in the light of their view of justice; for example, penal statutes might still be construed " strictly ";[8] the rule still prevailed that statutes were not to be construed so as to take away the property of the subject without compensation.[9]

A powerful influence in the creation of the newer doctrine was that of Lord Wright.[10] The doctrine also appears in comprehensive fashion in the speech of Viscount Simon in *Nokes* v. *Doncaster Amalgamated Collieries*.[11] It is this now conservative, and perhaps outdated, doctrine which appears in the judgment of Denning L.J. (as he then was) in *Seaford Court Estates* v. *Asher*.[12] As he himself said : " The English language is not an instrument of mathematical precision,"[13] and it is possible to interpret what he said, as Lord MacDermott did in the House of Lords, in such a way that " the principles applicable to the interpretation of statutes . . . are stated rather widely ".[14] There are references to sets of facts not foreseen by the draftsman, and these might contemplate

---

[6] The phrase " social history of the statute " is used to refer to a concept distinct from the parliamentary history: the judicial doctrine is clear that parliamentary history is not admissible in interpretation. The term " parliamentary history " covers a number of different processes, but the distinctions do not appear in judicial discussion. A second reading statement of the social origins of a bill is, *e.g.*, in a different category from parliamentary exposition of the meaning of the clauses in a bill: the strongest arguments against admission of parliamentary history are concerned with the latter type of history. The former is hardly " parliamentary history " at all. Why should a historian's account of the reasons for the introduction of a measure be admissible and not the minister's account? The historian may well take his account from Hansard, or the minister become the historian.

[7] *Cf.* Lord Wright's strictures on " a tendency common in construing an Act which changes the law, that is, to minimise or neutralise its operation, by introducing notions taken from, or inspired by, the old law which the words of the Act were intended to abrogate and did abrogate:" *Rose* v. *Ford* [1937] 3 All E.R. 370G.
In *Rowell* v. *Pratt* [1937] 3 All E.R. Lord Wright said at 662A: " if the words of an enactment are fairly capable of two interpretations, one of which seems to be in harmony with what is just, reasonable and convenient while the other is not, the court will prefer the former." But it is clear that, as he said in *Rose* v. *Ford* [1937] 3 All E.R. 367H, there has first to be considered " the existing law, and the existing mischief, in view of which the measure was enacted."

[8] See the speeches in *London & N.E. Rly. Co.* v. *Berriman* [1946] A.C. 278: followed in *Howell* v. *Falmouth Boat Construction Co., Ltd.*, particularly by Viscount Simonds [1951] 2 All E.R. 281C.

[9] *e.g. Bond* v. *Nottingham Corporation* [1940] Ch. 429; *Billings* v. *Reed* [1945] 1 K.B. 11.

[10] See his speeches in *Rose* v. *Ford* [1937] 3 All E.R., 370G; *Rowell* v. *Pratt* [1937] 3 All E.R. 662A; *Pratt* v. *Cook* [1940] A.C. 452.

[11] [1940] A.C. 1022.

[12] [1949] 2 K.B. 481.

[13] [1949] 2 All E.R. 164E.

[14] *Asher* v. *Seaford Court Estates Ltd.* [1950] 1 All E.R. 1029H.

THE TREATMENT OF STATUTES BY LORD DENNING 133

legislative as opposed to linguistic gaps. This matter is dealt with in
the next section. In what immediately follows I have endeavoured to
" iron out the creases ".

There are two elements in the passage. The first is that it is not
within human powers to provide for all the manifold sets of facts which
may arise in terms free from all ambiguity.[15] Ambiguities are part of
the ordinary meaning of words. The second principle comes into
operation when the judge finds that different meanings are consistent
with an ordinary reading of the words. To resolve the ambiguity
there is required the constructive task of finding the intention of
Parliament in accordance with the procedure of the Rule in *Heydon's
Case*. This may involve qualifying the actual words of the statute so
as to bring out the specific meaning intended, but this is the time-
honoured practice of " necessary implication ". " Necessary " has
never been rigidly construed, and Lord Denning avers that the " implication " is from the statute read in its social context.[16]

Linguistic and legislative gaps

The above account of the views of Denning L.J. in the *Seaford*
case[12] presents the task of discerning the intention of Parliament as one
which arises after an ambiguity has been discerned when the words of
the statute alone have been considered. When a year later in the
Magor case he came to repeat what he said in *Seaford Court Estates
Ltd.* v. *Asher*, he gave primacy of place to finding out the intention
of Parliament.[17] This appears to mark a change in judicial doctrine,

---

[15] " Whenever a statute comes up for consideration it must be remembered that it is
not within human powers to foresee the manifold sets of facts which may arise, and, even if
it were, it is not possible to provide for them in terms free from all ambiguity. The English
language is not an instrument of mathematical precision. Our literature would be much
the poorer if it were. This is where the draftsmen of Acts of Parliament have often been
unfairly criticised. A Judge, believing himself to be fettered by the supposed rule that he
must look to the language and nothing else, laments that the draftsmen have not provided
for this or that, or have been guilty of some or other ambiguity. It would certainly save the
judges trouble if Acts of Parliament were drafted with divine prescience and perfect clarity."
[1949] 2 All E.R. 164E. The remainder of the quotation is in the next footnote.

[16] " In the absence of it, when a defect appears a judge cannot simply fold his hands
and blame the draftsman. He must set to work on the constructive task of finding the intention of Parliament and he must do this not only from the language of the statute, but
also from a consideration of the social conditions which gave rise to it and of the mischief
which it was passed to remedy, and then he must supplement the written word so as to
give ' force and life ' to the intention of the legislature. That was clearly laid down [3 Co.
Rep. 7b) by the resolution of the judges [Sir Roger Manwood, C.B. and the other barons
of the Exchequer] in *Heydon's* case, and it is the safest guide to-day. Good practical advice
on the subject was given about the same time by Plowden in his note (2 Plowd. 465) to
Eyston v. *Studd*. Put into homely metaphor it is this: A judge should ask himself the question
how, if the makers of the Act had themselves come across this ruck in the texture of it, they
would have straightened it out? He must then do as they would have done. A judge must
not alter the material of which the Act is woven, but he can and should iron out the creases."
[1949] 2 All E.R. 164G.

[17] " I would repeat what I said in *Seaford Court Estates Ltd.* v. *Asher*. We do not sit
here to pull the language of Parliament and of Ministers to pieces and make nonsense of it.
That is an easy thing to do, and it is a thing to which lawyers are too often prone. We sit
here to find out the intention of Parliament and of Ministers and carry it out, and we do
this better by filling in the gaps and making sense of the enactment than by opening it up
to destructive analysis." *Magor R.D.C.* v. *Newport Corp.* [1950] 2 All E.R. 1236A.

which will be later considered. What is proposed for present consideration is the reference to "filling in the gaps", which is the language substituted for the previous talk about straightening rucks and ironing creases.

The phrase "gap in the law" has long been used to describe the situation which exists where no rule appears to exist for a particular topic. The "sense of wonder" described by Cardozo at "the gaps in the system" of law[18] is being continually stimulated. Rules have recently been framed by trial judges to answer such "elementary" questions in the law of infancy as whether an infant intervener aged twelve can be guilty of adultery,[19] whether an infant beneficiary is entitled on marriage to the capital of a trust fund to which she was entitled "when she shall attain the age of twenty-one years or shall marry".[20] In a recent case the very words "supplying a gap" were used in relation to a proposed interpretation of statutory rules which would have made them deal specifically with a state of affairs for which otherwise no specific provision would have been made.[21] The notion of judicial legislation for a particular topic on the analogy of a statutory provision for similar topics has often been advanced.[22] This is the conservative method of developing law in countries where a code exists: *Au-delà du Code civil, mais par le Code civil.*[23]

It would appear that Lord Simonds thought that Denning L.J. had in mind such a "filling in the gaps" when in the appeal before the House of Lords he said of the dictum of the Lord Justice: "It appears to me to be a naked usurpation of the legislative function under the thin disguise of interpretation."[24] But the phrase "filling in the gaps" may refer to a gap in the wording in the sense that the actual words are ambiguous—it is not absolutely clear whether or not they apply to a particular state of affairs—and additional words are used merely in order to make clear whether the existing words do or do not apply.[25] Their function is to resolve an ambiguity, not to deal with a *casus improvisus*. Romer L.J. calls this procedure "filling a hiatus",

---

[18] *Paradoxes of Legal Science*, pp. 76-77.

[19] *Barnett* v. *Barnett* [1957] 1 All E.R. 389G.

[20] *Re Somech* [1956] 3 All E.R. 524I.

[21] Viscount Kilmuir L.C. in *Canadian Pacific Ltd.* v. *Bryers* [1957] 3 All E.R. 577A.

[22] It is suggested by Roscoe Pound as the law of the future in *Common Law and Legislation*, 21 *Harvard L.R.* at pp. 385-6. See also p. 407.

[23] Saleilles: Preface to the first edition of Gèny: *Méthode d'Interprétation*.

[24] [1951] 2 All E.R. 841G. He also expressed in relation to the earlier part of the passage from Denning L.J. the "out of date" doctrine: "the general proposition that it is the duty of the court to find out the intention of Parliament . . . cannot by any means be supported. The duty of the court is to interpret the words that the legislature has used. Those words may be ambiguous, but, even if they are, the power and duty of the court to travel outside them on a voyage of discovery are strictly limited." *ibid.*, 841E.

[25] See also my discussion in *Judicial Implementation of Legislative Policy, op. cit.*, p. 142.

which is, of course, but a latinised form of " gap ". He said : " When
we find . . . that the legislature has expressed itself elliptically . . . then
that is a hiatus which the court is entitled to fill, and in doing that to
have regard to the purpose of the Act as a whole, the history of the
matter and the probabilities."[26]
    That Denning L.J. had in mind a linguistic and not a legislative,
a formal and not a substantial gap, is indicated by his metaphor " A
judge must not alter the material of which an Act is woven."[27]   He
has himself specifically repudiated a doctrine of legislation by analogy,
citing for this purpose Lord Simonds' criticism in the *Magor* case,[17] and
using the language of " filling in of gaps ".   " . . . [A] fundamental
principle in all Acts . . . is this—the judges have no right to fill in gaps
which they suppose to exist in an Act of Parliament, but must leave it
to Parliament itself to do so. "[28]

Juristic criticism

    It is noteworthy that Lord Denning, in common with English
judges generally, makes little reference in his judgments to juristic writings.   He has neither called in aid of his advocacy of the rule in
Heydon's Case juristic approval of historical interpretation,[29] nor been
deterred from speaking of the intention of Parliament by juristic criticism of its fictional character.[30]   The scope of this article does not require
me to enter into explanations of this " neglect ", nor does it require me
to examine the juristic writings on the subject of interpretation of
statutes.[31]   But some " jurisprudential " analysis cannot be avoided of
the key terms used by Lord Denning in his judgments.   It is perhaps
desirable that it be presented at this stage before entering on the description of his later thought which had been influential in the creation of
current judicial doctrine.
    The words selected for consideration are " intention of Parlia-

---

[26] *British Transport Co.* v. *L.C.C.* [1953] 1 All E.R. 813D.

[27] Geoffrey Marshall, in an unpublished comment on my paper " Judicial Implementation of Legislative Policy," rightly says that it is not always possible clearly to distinguish
between linguistic and legislative gaps. He thinks that the metaphor of Denning L.J. is
not precise enough to decide which kind of gap is in question. " One can darn a hole perhaps
without altering the material." He draws attention to other passages in the judgment which
suggest a legislative gap, e.g., " I cannot help feeling that the legislature had not specifically
in mind a contingent burden such as we have here. If it had, would it not have put it on
the same footing as an actual burden?" [1949] 2 All E.R. 165A.

[28] *London Transport* v. *Betts* [1958] 2 All E.R. 655D. The gap seen by Lord Denning
was the case of " a single hereditament which was not part of a larger whole". In his opinion
the section :" envisaged a place within a factory", and could only be extended to an isolated
place by a rewriting which was, in effect, an additional clause dealing with a different
subject matter: see [1958] 2 All E.R. 652 I *et seq.*

[29] Outstanding in English writing have been Eastwood: *Pleas for Historical Interpretation
of Statute Law* (1935) *J.S.P.T.L.* 1, and Laski's note on *Judicial Interpretation of Statutes* appended
by him to the Donoughmore Committee Report: Cmd. 4060, p. 35.

[30] It is perhaps sufficient to refer for English criticism to Payne, " The Intention of the
Legislature in the Interpretation of Statutes", (1956) *Current Legal Problems*, p. 96.

[31] In view of the great importance of the subject there has been remarkably little
writing on the subject in the United Kingdom.

ment ", " ambiguity " and " interpretation ", and their associated concepts. The problems involved are interrelated, and are connected with fundamental problems of the meaning and function of words. It is not suggested that more is done than to " stir up " some semantic considerations, and ultimate solutions are left to " wiser heads than mine ".

If a speaker describes a feature of the surroundings to a hearer it it useful to discuss this situation, in the terms of Ogden and Richards,[32] by saying that the words of the speaker are but symbols for the thought of the speaker which refers to a referent, the thing which is the particular feature. It is " word-magic " to believe that a speaker's word is in some way directly linked with the thing. " Between the symbol and the referent there is no relevant relation other than the indirect one, which consists in being used by someone to stand for a referent." If in the surroundings there is a cup and a painting of a ship, and the speaker remarks on " the beautiful silver of that vessel ",[33] it is appropriate in the above language to say that the symbol " vessel " was used by the speaker to refer to the silver cup, and understood by the hearer to refer to the cup, and not to the blue ship. But the " reference " was not made by pointing or by the use of a proper name. It was by means of a descriptive phrase; and " the thing which a description describes " is not " what the description means ".[34] The meaning of the word " vessel " is not identical with the silver cup. " Description is by kinds and sub-kinds," says Sidgwick,[35] and the word " vessel " is a general word which can be said to " refer " to a class of objects of which the silver cup is but a member. Indeed it can be used to refer to more than one class. A dictionary tells us that " current English " gives to the word " vessel " four " meanings " of which the first two are " 1. Hollow receptacle esp. for liquid, e.g., cask, cup, . . . (2) Ship, boat, esp. large one."[36] The existence of several possible meanings for a word entitles us, according to the dictionary, to say that it has " ambiguity ".[37] Though perhaps stilted, we could say of the above situation that the speaker used an ambiguous word, but that the hearer had no difficulty, in the context of the actual surroundings, in giving to the statement an interpretation of " receptacle " in accordance with the speaker's intention, and, moreover, of applying the statement to the

---

[32] *Meaning of Meaning* (10th ed.), p. 11.

[33] The example is suggested by Hart in an unpublished comment on my paper on *Judicial Implementation* where he says: " if in a will a testator ' gives all my vessels to X . . .' the question whether this means his boats or his drinking cups shows its ambiguity." He also shows that the word " vessel " is *vague*: does it include flying-boats?

[34] Ryle: *Systematically Misleading Expressions*, p. 26 (Flew: *Logic and Language*, First Series). This is the nominalistic error of reducing " connotation " to "denotation".

[35] " Rules and Interpretation," 37 *Mind* 161.

[36] *Concise Oxford Dictionary of Current English* (4th Ed.).

[37] *ibid.*

silver cup.[38] We could note that, though the word "vessel" has a number of dictionary meanings, in the actual use of it by the speaker there was no ambiguity. But, of course, we can easily imagine a situation in which there would be ambiguity in actual user, as, for example, if the ship in the picture were painted silver: in such a situation the hearer might ask the speaker whether he was referring to the cup or the ship.

How far are the terms and concepts "interpretations", "ambiguity", "intention" appropriate in discussion of the very different problem of the words of the general rules contained in statutes? A full discussion would proceed through consideration of particular commands, like a sergeant-major's orders to troops, and general descriptive statements, like those of scientific laws. We have to bear in mind that statutory rules are not often considered in isolation from particular facts. In ordinary litigation the question is concerned with the legal position of the parties arising from particular facts, and the statutory rule is brought in as the law governing the situation.[39] It is asked whether the statute applies to the facts—do they fall within the provision? The particular facts most likely had not occurred when the statute was passed, and though it is possible, like a sergeant-major on the barrack square, to foresee and command future movements, it is not likely that the particular facts were in contemplation of anybody at the time the statute was passed.[40]

Despite the great differences between descriptive and normative sentences some similarities exist, and in consequence some of the terminology appropriate in the one case is appropriate to the other. The word "vessel" in our example is a common noun, a general word, and only an extreme nominalism holds that it has no "meaning" other than that it is applied in fact, without rhyme or reason, to various objects.[41] Even if the speaker used the word as a token[42] to refer to a specific

[38] " The audience is expected to fill in part of the meaning from the context, from their own previous knowledge or from the nature of the occasion. The context helps us to see the purpose of the statement, and so appreciate its intended purport." Sidgwick, op. cit., p. 154. In this article the problem of application is considered: but the terminology employed makes it part of "meaning". It is consistent with this that " ambiguity " in the articles includes "vagueness".

[39] Procedures do exist for determining the general meaning of a statute: e.g., the reference of sections of the Government of Ireland Act, 1920, to the Judicial Committee of the Privy Council: see s. 51 thereof.

[40] The distinction between the commands of a sergeant and those of a legislator is perhaps one of degree only: the sergeant's " contemplation " when he says " right turn " has elements of generality; he is not likely to picture precisely the specific men executing the movement in a specific manner.

[41] It would appear that it is this extreme nominalism which, according to Woozley (Theory of Knowledge, p. 89), " has never been seriously held by anybody except Humpty Dumpty," which is adopted by Payne when he says of general words: " we apply them to this particular and that particular not by reference to any general idea, but simply because we find them so applied by others." (1956) Current Legal Problems, p. 100.

[42] A token refers to the actual word on a specific occasion: it is opposed to a "type", the class of similar shapes. Each time " vessel " has appeared in these pages a different " token " has been used, but it has been the same type word. See, e.g., Woozley, op. cit., p. 90.

object, it is not absurd to conceive of the hearer receiving it as a type word in fact related to a common mode of user, which he applies to the specific object, and this without embarking on an inquiry into the problem of universals. It is appropriate to say that the words of a statute may be potentially ambiguous, that the ambiguity may be resolved by consideration of a context, or remain unresolved.[43] We can draw the distinction made by De Sloovere between interpretation and application. " Interpretation may be defined as the making of a choice from several possible meanings. Application is the process of determining whether the facts of the case are within the meaning."[44]

It is not, however, possible to draw a precise parallel between a speaker's intention and an intention of a legislature. In one case we have a psychic reality, in the other we have none in the sense of a single mind or a set of identical states of mind unless we refer perhaps to the actual draftsmen, or the minister responsible for the bill. But ambiguous as the phrase " intention of Parliament " is, rarely, indeed, is it used to refer to a real intention. What is involved is not so much a fiction in the sense of an assertion that some non-existent phenomenon does exist, but a fiction only in the sense of something to be created by following a stipulated procedure.[45] The question to which the courts are directed by the formula of the intention of Parliament is, what do the words mean having regard to the actual circumstances in which they were enacted, to the historical conditions of the times, to the realities of social mischiefs and proposed remedies? The parallel may perhaps be drawn not with the speaker of the descriptive statement, but with the hearer. We assumed in our example that the hearer had eyes as well as ears, and used them. In a consideration of the meaning of the words of a statute it is not fantastical to ask the interpreter to inform himself of the actual social history in the context of which the statute was passed. This is what the rule in *Heydon's Case* requires : and

---

[43] Stebbing confines the use of the term " ambiguity " to ambiguity within a context. " Reference to the context within which the word is being used is necessary in order to ascertain whether a word is ambiguous or not. No word in isolation is properly ambiguous." *Modern Introduction to Logic* (6th ed., 1948), p. 204. *Cf.* Schiller, *Logic for Use* (1924), p. 63.

[44] 46 *Harvard L.R.* at p. 1095. Lord MacDermott has indicated the existence of this distinction. " A precise definition of a regular minister appears impossible, and to search for one is to wander about between the realms of interpretation and application." *Walsh* v. *Lord Advocate* [1956] 3 All E.R. 135B. What is more, he relates questions of interpretation to issues of law, and questions of application to issues of fact.

[45] This apparently represents juristic and judicial doctrine in the United States. While Kocoureck (*Science of Law*, p. 201) and Radin (43 *Harvard L.R.* 870) are not alone in denying the reality of legislative intent, and its relevance, Newman and Surrey (*Case Book on Legislation*, 1955) say that view " has generally been rejected both by judges and by scholars". For the judicial doctrine they cited Judge Learned Hand: " When we ask what Congress ' intended ' usually there can be no answer, if what we mean is what any person or group of persons actually had in mind. Flinch as we may, what we do, and must do, is to project ourselves, as best we can, into the position of those who uttered the words, and to impute to them how they would have dealt with the concrete situation. He who supposes that he can be certain of the result, is the least fitted for the attempt." *U.S.* v. *Klinger* (1952) 199 Fed. 648, cited approvingly by Jackson and Frankfurter JJ. in *U.S.* v. *Henning*, (1954) 344 U.S. 79.

the phrase "intention of Parliament", whether regarded as metaphor or fiction, is often but a means of invoking that rule.[46] It would appear that judges when speaking of "ambiguity" have generally referred to the situation described above of a range of possible meanings which may be limited by the context.[47] It is by no means so clear that the term "interpretation" has been limited to the resolving of such ambiguities. The linguistic analysts have shown that a major difficulty in the use of words is *vagueness*. There may be agreement about the application of words to some particulars, but doubt about their application to others. There is said to be a central core of clear meaning and a peripheral zone of doubt.[48] Some words are clearly vague, like few, many, crowd, or reasonable man, bolshevik, fascist: but most, if not all, ordinary general words have an "open texture", and border-line cases which resemble the central instances in some respects but differ in others may be imagined. Even chemists may have difficulty in classifying some particular substance as an isotope of an existing element or as a new element.[49] Some words are both ambiguous and vague: such, for example, as Hart has shown, is the word "vessel": in addition to the ambiguity we have already considered we may ask whether a flying-boat is a vessel.[50] The distinction between "ambiguity" and "vagueness" is itself not too clear as we sometimes think of meaning in relation to connotation and sometimes in relation to denotation.[51] When we say "three is a crowd" are we doing so because of the vagueness of the term, or because we

---

[46] Lord Watson's well-known reminder of the ambiguity of the phrase, nevertheless, postulates the Legislature as having a mind: "'Intention of the Legislature' is a common but very slippery phrase, which, properly understood, may signify anything from intention embodied in positive enactment to speculative opinion as to what the Legislature probably would have meant, though there has been an omission to enact it." [1897] A.C. at p. 38.

[47] Thus Lord Reid: "A provision is not ambiguous merely because it contains a word which in different contexts is capable of different meanings. It would be hard to find anywhere a sentence of any length which does not contain such a word. A provision is . . . ambiguous only if it contains a word or phrase which in that particular context is capable of having more than one meaning." *Kirkness* v. *John Hudson & Co., Ltd.* [1955] 2 All E.R. 366 D. *Cf.* n. 43, above.

[48] *Cf.* Glanville Williams, "Language and the Law", 61 *L.Q.R.*, p. 181: Payne, (1956) *Current Legal Problems*, p. 98.

[49] Waismann (*Verifiability: Logic and Language*, First Series, p. 120) says: "Vagueness should be distinguished from open texture," but he says also: "'open texture' is something like possibility of vagueness." It appears to me that the difference may be one of degree, depending on the size of the "central core". Though Mill does not use the term "vagueness", he in effect points out that some words may be completely vague and have no central core at all. "A name not unfrequently passes by successive links of resemblance from one object to another until it becomes applied to things having nothing in common with the first things to which the name was given; so that at last it denotes a confused huddle of objects, having nothing in common whatsoever; and connotes nothing, not even a vague and general resemblance." *Logic* (8th ed.), p. 173. "Justice" is given as an example.

[50] See n. 33, above. "Cat" is ambiguous and vague: it is ambiguous because sometimes it refers to the domestic pet: sometimes it refers to the whole genus of which the domestic animal is a species, e.g., to tigers and lions as well as to "cats": it is vague because, as Waismann says, we would be in doubt whether to apply the term to freak examples.

[51] So Payne, whose nominalism presents the meaning of general words solely in terms of their extension, discusses only vagueness and not ambiguity: *op. cit.*, p. 98 *et seq.*

K

are using a different "meaning" of the word, *viz.*, too many people for the purpose in hand?[52]

It is suggested that problems arising from the vagueness of words are related to the application of statutes. The matter will be further considered in examining Lord Denning's views on the application of the doctrine of precedent to the "interpretation" of statutes. It would indeed be an aid to certainty if one could say that interpretation is related to ambiguity and is a question of law, and application is related to vagueness and is a question of fact.

The primacy of parliamentary intention

I have submitted that the judicial doctrine of the second quarter of this century was that if the words of any section read in the verbal context of the statute were ambiguous then recourse might be had to the entire social context at the time the statute was passed. It is very likely that the judicial doctrine of today is that the statute has to be read *ab initio* in the light of such social context.[53] This, at any rate, is the view of Lord Denning: " A statute is not passed in a vacuum, but in a framework of circumstances, so as to give a remedy for a known state of affairs. To arrive at its true meaning, you should know the circumstances with reference to which the words were used: and what was the object appearing from those circumstances which Parliament had in view."[54] " If I were to look at the words of the statute alone and take the word ' by ' literally I might be of the same opinion as Romer L.J. But when I look at the mischief which this section was passed to remedy, I come to a different conclusion. . . It is not so much a choice between a literal and liberal construction. It is rather a case of remembering that every statute must be read in the light of the circumstances in which it was made, and the object it was passed to achieve."[55] The opening words of a later judgment are : " My Lords, in order to under-

---

[52] Stebbing (*op. cit.*, p. 21) says that " ambiguity is to be carefully distinguished from vagueness." She also suggests that sometimes different words that have the same spellings are considered ambiguous. Certainly words of different etymologies may come to be spelt the same but are different type words: her example of " vice " can be so explained: as moral disposition it comes from *vitium*, as carpenter's instrument it comes from *vitis*. Dictionaries note this fact. But " fair " is etymologically the same word when " standing for the colour of a person's complexion: and for a just bargain". (As " market " it is etymologically different.) Is every shift of meaning by means of metaphor to be called the creation of a new word? This seems a matter of degree.

[53] Even Viscount Simonds, who in *Smith* v. *East Elloe R.D.C.* [1956] 1 All E.R. 859D said " the first of all principles of construction that plain words must be given their plain meaning " may be included as one of the creators of this doctrine. See the *Prince Ernest Augustus* case [1957] 1 All E.R. 53H and the *Parliamentary Privilege* case [1958] 2 All E.R 334A. Lord Evershed was prepared to say that the true meaning of " language precise and express " when considered in isolation was different " having proper regard to the historical matters ": *British Transport Co.* v. *L.C.C.* [1953] 1 All E.R. 806D. Lord Radcliffe is probably another creator: see *Re MacManaway* [1951] A.C. 178. Judges have generally found little difficulty in referring to history, *ab initio*, when dealing with " private law " statutes: see, e.g., the speeches in *Hickman* v. *Peacey* [1945] A.C. 304.

[54] *Escoigne Properties Ltd.* v. *I.R. Cssrs.* [1958] 1 All E.R. 414E.

[55] [1958] 1 All E.R. 416A, D.

stand s. 8 of the Rating and Valuation (Miscellaneous Provisions) Act, 1955, it is as well to know the background against which it was enacted."[56] Of course, considerations of administrative efficiency dictate that in most cases statutes will be applied without first embarking on a historical investigation of their origin,[57] but the newer doctrine is that when it is suggested that a problem of meaning exists then it is legitimate, and perhaps his duty,[58] for the judge to read the statute in the light of its social context without having first to discover an ambiguity in the verbal context.

The problem of how a court is to be informed of the history and policy of a statute has long been debated.[59] Lord Denning's view is: " All that the courts can do is to take judicial notice of the previous state of the law and of other matters generally known to well informed people."[60] He states, without comment, the rule excluding the use of legislative history including " the explanatory memoranda which preface the Bills before Parliament ". But he does say: " Thus one of the best ways I find of understanding a statute is to take some specific instances, which by common consent are intended to be covered by it. . . . When the draftsman is drawing the Act he has in mind particular instances which he wishes to cover. He frames a formula which he hopes will embrace them all with precision. But the formula is as unintelligible as a mathematical formula to anyone except the experts: and even they have to know what the symbols mean. To make it intelligible you must know the sort of thing Parliament had in mind. So you have to resort to particular instances to gather the meaning."[61] Two processes are combined in this passage. One is that of interpretation in the sense of translation from a set of symbols not understood by the reader to a set of symbols which are understood, like translation from a foreign language with the help of a dictionary. The other, relevant for the present purpose, is that of ascertainment of the object of a statute. The " instance " which the judge uses may be an example of the mischief under the old law, and drawn from the " history " of the matter. Such were the instances in fact used by Lord Denning in the *Escoigne Properties Ltd.* case.[60] He said they " by common consent,

---

[56] *National Deposit Co.* v. *Skegness* [1958] 2 All E.R. 610F.

[57] And nearly always the words will be read before anything else is done. *Cf.* " While literalness of construction does not conclude ascertainment of a statute's meaning, it certainly is the beginning." Frankfurter J.: *Master Plastics Corp.* v. *N.L.R.B.* (1956) 350 U.S. 287.

[58] The older doctrine said it was the *duty* of the judge to apply the Rule in *Heydon's Case* when an ambiguity was disclosed. The language of Viscount Simonds is not that of duty, nor, indeed, is the language of Lord Denning in the *National Deposit* case: but the logic of the *Escoigne Properties* judgment is that of duty.

[59] *Cf.* the debate over the " Brandeis Brief ", the collection of extracts from various reports of government committees, bureaus of statistics, commissioners of hygiene, inspectors of factories, presented to the Supreme Court in *Muller* v. *Oregon* (1908) 208 U.S. 412.

[60] *Escoigne Properties Ltd.* [1958] 1 All E.R. 414G. *Cf.* " It is legitimate to take notice of matters generally known to well-informed people." [1958] 2 All E.R. 610F.

[61] [1958] 1 All E.R. 414H; followed by him: *Shell-Mex and B.P. Ltd.* v. *Holyoak* [1959] 1 All E.R. 401H.

are covered by the section ".[62] Presumably " common consent " refers not to the agreement of the parties to the case, but to the common content of judicial notice.

As has been previously stated, Lord Denning constantly uses the language of parliamentary intention, and asks what Parliament had in mind, or in view, or intended, or meant. Nevertheless, though it may not represent his thought accurately, it is true that so far as results are concerned it would make no difference if one substituted for his references to the intention of the legislature references to the meaning of the words in their actual context : the same mental processes would have to be performed by the interpreter. Indeed it may be that Lord Denning is merely giving to the state of mind of the interpreter who performs the operations required by the Rule in *Heydon's Case* the name of " intention of Parliament ". It is true that he asks whether specific instances were in the mind of Parliament, and also how Parliament would have dealt with them had it then the mind.[63] But again, the same effect is produced by asking what do the words mean in their full context having regard to their possible application to the specific instances.

Primacy of the statutory words

In *Shell-Mex and B.P. Ltd.* v. *Holyoak* [63a] the question of the rateability of the underground petrol tanks of an ordinary roadside filling station depended on whether they were " tanks . . . in the nature of a . . . structure " within the meaning of the relevant statute and order. Lord Denning used the " method of instances " to discover " what Parliament meant ". He said : " To take illustrations is, I find, the most helpful way of understanding what an Act of Parliament means."[64] His purpose here was to elucidate the meaning of the statutory words, to make them more " intelligible ", as he explained in the *Escoigne Properties* case. We are here in the realm of the picture book and the parable as modes of understanding, rather than in the realm of resolving ambiguities. It is not that there is doubt as to which of the different clearly apprehended meanings is to be stated, but difficulty in comprehending any meaning. In this latter process of clarifying " meaning " an alternative method to the illustration is the paraphrase. Lord Denning deals with this method at the beginning of his opinion in the *Escoigne Properties* case.[60] " What is the meaning of the words ' the effect thereof '? Various interpretations are suggested. Do they mean

---

[62] [1958] 1 All E.R. 414I.

[63] Payne appears to have overlooked the remarks of Denning L.J. in *Seaford Court Estates* V. *Asher* (see notes 16 and 27, above) when he says;" So far as I am aware no English Court has ever suggested that the duty of a court construing general words in a statute is to speculate upon what the legislature would have done had the problem occurred to it.": *op. cit.*, p 102

[63a] [1959] 1 All E.R. 391.

[64] [1959] 1 All E R. 401H. He took as a specific instance one found in the statute itself: " water towers with tanks".

'the only effect thereof' or 'the substantial effect thereof', or 'an effect thereof'? I do not think they mean any of these things. It is a mistake to dignify these suggestions by calling them 'interpretations'. They are only substituted words. . . I look on the suggested interpretations only as attempts to elucidate it. When searching for the meaning of a statute, it is natural to try to put it into your own words— so as to express its meaning as it appears to you."[65]

It is not made absolutely clear why it is a mistake to call "substituted words" by the name of "interpretation", but I suggest that the distinction may be between the paraphrase or translation on the one hand and the resolution of an ambiguity on the other. However, the matter is not one of semantic analysis alone. Lord Denning states that no one has a right of "altering the words of a statute": "the function of the court is to apply not its own words, but the words of the statute to the given situation",[66] and he quotes Lord Reid's words in *Goodrich* v. *Paisner*:[66a] "No court is entitled to substitute its words for the words of the Act."[67] The point is whether a later court is bound by the substituted words; are they but guides to assist it in its own elucidation of the meaning of the words of the statute?

It would appear that Lord Denning is doing more than merely pointing out that the words of a judgment can never have the binding force of a statute.[68] It must also follow from what he says that where the problem before the court was that solely of "elucidation", of making clear what was not fully intelligible, the paraphrase into more easily understood words is not authoritative.[69] Again, if the task before a court is that of resolving an ambiguity, a translation into unambiguous words does not replace the statutory provision: it may have other effects than those of resolving the ambiguity, such as introducing different areas of vagueness. This would appear to be in line with Lord Denning's words, particularly in view of the fact that the problem in the *Escoigne Properties* case[60] may well be considered as that of ambiguity. But it does not follow that a later court is not bound by the resolution of the ambiguity. Current judicial doctrine is clear that the doctrine of precedent does apply to such a type of interpretation.[70] The later court applies the words of the statute to the situation before it, but it reads those words in the sense given them by the precedent court.

---

[65] [1958] 1 All E.R. 413I and 414B.

[66] [1958] 1 All E.R. 414A and C.

[66a] [1957] A.C. 65 ; [1956] 2 All E.R. 176.

[67] [1956] 2 All E.R. 185F: cited again by Lord Denning in *London Transport* v. *Betts* [1958] 2 All E.R. 655D. *Cf.* Lord Wright: "the danger of superseding the words of the Legislature by language used by judges." *Harris* v. *Associated Portland Cement Co.* [1939] A.C. at p. 89.

[68] *Cf.* Lord MacDermott in *Horton* v. *London Graving Dock* [1951] 2 All E.R. 14C.

[69] *Cf.* "Those are various phrases that have been used in the Court of Appeal or the House of Lords as glosses on the words of the Act. Judges of necessity have to find synonyms for the words they construe, but other judges' synonyms do not bind their brothers." Harman J., *Espresso Coffee* v. *Guardian Assurance* [1958] 2 All E.R. 694B.

[70] See Lord Shaw: *G.W.R.* v. *The Mostyn* [1928] A.C. 82; Lord Wright: *Cull* v. *I.R.C.* [1940] A.C. 68. In the recent case of *Brown* v. *Jamieson* [1959] 1 Q.B. 338, the court divided on the question of how a statute had been interpreted in the precedent case.

One more species of interpretation may be considered : *viz.*, where a court fills in a linguistic gap. Here Lord Denning's dictum has perhaps no application: the statutory words are applied, though they are applied together with those added by necessary implication. Judicial doctrine does not permit a later court to deny the " necessity " of the implication of the additional words: the words are added for the purpose of resolving an ambiguity.

However, though the doctrine of not substituting for the words of a statute the words a court has used in interpreting the statute, as expounded by Lord Denning in the *Escoigne Properties* case,[60] does not take interpretation out of the embrace of precedent, there is another exposition of that doctrine by him in which he does apparently seek to limit the operation of the doctrine of precedent. It is to that exposition I now turn. I believe that the explanation here is to be found in the distinction between interpretation and application.

The application of statutes and the doctrine of precedent

It is in *Paisner* v. *Goodrich*[66a] that we find Lord Denning expressly linking the doctrine of the primacy of statutory words with the doctrine of precedent. He said: " when interpreting a statute, the sole function of the court is to apply the words of the statute to a given situation. Once a decision has been reached on that situation, the doctrine of precedent requires us to apply the statute in the same way in any similar situation: but not in a different situation. Whenever a new situation emerges, not covered by previous decisions, the court must be governed by the statute and not by the words of the judges."[71] If this dictum be read in isolation it would appear to be far reaching. The later court apparently may ignore the consideration given by the earlier court to the meaning of the words of the statute: what a judge has said about the resolution of an ambiguity, though " one of the links in the chain of reasoning "[72] fashioned by him, leading to his conclusion about the facts of the case, is not of binding authority: it is as if the *ratio decidendi* is to be deemed restricted to the invocation of the statutory rule. But it is by no means certain that this is the true interpretation of the dictum. The dictum is preceded by the statement : " When the judges of this court give a decision on the interpretation of an Act of Parliament, the decision itself is binding on them and their successors: see *Cull* v. *Inland Revenue Comrs.*,[72a] *Morelle, Ltd.* v. *Wakeling.*[72b] But the words which the judges use in giving their decision are not binding." There is here, of course, an ambiguity : " a decision

---

[71] [1955] 2. All E.R. 332I.
[72] This is the criterion used by Denning L.J. in *Korner* v. *Witkowitzer* [1950] 1 All E.R. 573D to determine what is *ratio decidendi* as opposed to *obiter dictum*. In this article I shall use the phrase *ratio decidendi*, as the judges use it, to signify a legal principle propounded by a judge as the basis of his decision. Despite the criticism to which this " definition " has been subjected in recent controversy (which I have not yet had a proper opportunity of considering), I find no difficulty in what I consider to be the judicial usage.
[72a] [1940] A.C. 51.   [72b] [1955] 2 Q.B. 379.

on the interpretation of an Act of Parliament " could possibly refer to the decision of the case in which a question of interpretation was mooted. But it surely means, in view of the authorities cited, determination of the question of interpretation: and, if so, this statement says that the judge's *ratio decidendi*[73] dealing with the resolution of an ambiguity is binding.

Since *Paisner* v. *Goodrich*[66a] Lord Denning has not restated a doctrine of non-applicability of precedent to statutory interpretation. It is true that in *London Transport* v. *Betts*[73a] he cites Lord Reid's dictum " No court is entitled to substitute its words for the words of the Act ", in support of an argument for limiting the effect of a precedent House of Lords case. Moreover, he says: " The decision (about the paint shop) may be binding on your Lordships if there is another such paint shop elsewhere, but it is not, in my opinion, binding for anything else ".[74] This may at first sight appear to be an echo of the *Paisner* v. *Goodrich* dictum limiting interpretation precedents to cases with " similar " situations. But fuller examination results in a different conclusion. Lord Denning said of the earlier case: " That is a decision on the particular facts of the paint shop and nothing else ". He was thus basing his opinion on the generally accepted doctrine of *ex facto non oritur jus*, and denying that in the earlier case there was to be found a *ratio decidendi* dealing with the interpretation of the statute.[75] He continued: " If your Lordships were to elevate that particular precedent into a binding decision on the meaning of ' maintenance ' you would, I believe, carry the doctrine of precedent further than it has ever been carried before." This is a denial of authority to " that particular precedent ", and by implication an affirmation of the doctrine that other precedents on the meaning of statutory words may be binding on later courts.

One further dictum of Lord Denning's may be cited to show his support for the doctrine of precedent in relation to " true interpretation ". In *Shell-Mex and B.P. Ltd.* v. *Holyoak*[63a] he said: " That involves in this case a question of law, for the solution of it depends on the true interpretation of an Act of Parliament and the order made thereunder. . . . It is, moreover, a test case which will decide, once and for all, the rateability of all wayside filling stations."[76]

---

[73] See n. 72, above, for my use of this phrase.
[73a] [1958] 2 All E.R. 636.
[74] [1958] 2 All E.R. 655A.
[75] For a decision of the general doctrine, see my " Judicial Law Making and Law Applying," (1956) *Butterworth's South African Law Review*, p. 202. The article also contains a discussion of *Paisner* v. *Goodrich*.
[76] [1959] 1 All E.R. 401C. Of course, all wayside filling stations may be considered sufficiently " similar " to come within the *Paisner* v. *Goodrich* dictum.
Before *Paisner* v. *Goodrich* there is no indication that Denning L.J. might have thought that the doctrine of precedent did not apply to determination of problems of interpretation of statutes. On the contrary, his judgment in *Royal Derby Porcelain Co.* v. *Russell* [1949] 1 All E.R. 755C, is based on the assumption that, subject to the limitations arising from the hierarchy of courts, one court is bound to follow " a previous decision on the interpretation of statutes."

It is suggested that the dictum in *Paisner* v. *Goodrich*[66] can never-theless be supported provided that it be regarded as confined to that type of " interpretation " where the function of the court is limited to that of applying the words of the statute. There is a temptation, at any rate for counsel, to argue that the doctrine of precedent applies to the mode of applying a statute, as indeed they may argue that a precedent concerned with the application of a rule of the common law may generate a new rule of law. Judicial doctrine recognises that the doctrine of precedent does not treat a case as of binding authority for the manner in which a rule of law has been applied.[77] The manner of application is in the language of the courts a question of fact and degree and not a question of law.[78]

This approach to the dictum of Denning L.J. may perhaps not be doing very much violence to the language, for it should be remembered that the basis of the judgment of Denning L.J. was that the problem for the court was one of application as opposed to interpretation. It will be remembered that the case concerned a claim by a " landlord " to possession where the tenancy agreement covered four rooms of which the tenant had exclusive possession and a further room, " the back bed-room on the first floor ", in respect of which the agreement gave the tenant " the use in common with the landlord ". The landlord's claim failed if the rooms constituted " a house or part of a house let as a separate dwelling " within the meaning of the relevant statute. The statutory words had often been considered in relation to various circum-stances, and the judges had considered that there was no " separate dwelling " if the tenant shared with the landlord any of the essential living rooms :[79] and in applying the statute this preliminary test as to sharing was first used. In the court of Appeal in *Paisner* v. *Goodrich* the majority assumed that they were bound by this test. It was from this view that Denning L.J. dissented. In his view it was " a misuse of the doctrine of precedent " to substitute the judicial test of " sharing a living room " for the statutory words " let as a separate dwelling ".[80] This

---

[77] The " leading case " for common law rules is now *Qualcast (Wolverhampton) Ltd.* v. *Haynes* [1959] 2 All E.R. 38. For statutory rules it is perhaps sufficient to refer to Lord Radcliffe's opinions in *Edwards* v. *Bairstow* and *Goodrich* v. *Paisner*: see particularly [1955] 3 All E.R. 58F.; [1956] 2 All E.R. 1861. The problems of law applying are discussed in my article on *Judicial Law Making and Law Applying*: see n. 75, above.

[78] The dichotomy of judicial language which recognises only the two categories, " fact " and " law," obscured the difficulties involved in law applying. Thus Austin: " The difficulty is in determining not what the law is, or what the fact is, but whether the given law is applicable to the given fact." *Jurisprudence* I:273. A stronger view is Sidgwick's: " All disputable matter . . . turns upon the uncertainty of applying rules to cases." 37 *Mind* 167.

[79] When first formulated by Morton L.J. in *Cole* v. *Harris* the word " essential " did not appear, but nothing very much appeared to turn on the distinction. See Lord Morton in *Goodrich* v. *Paisner* [1956] All 2 E.R. 180E.

[80] See [1955] 2 All E.R. 332G.

was the view of Lord Radcliffe and Lord Somervell, and possibly also of Viscount Simonds, in the House of Lords, where the decision of the Court of Appeal was reversed.[81] It is, however, Lord Radcliffe who made articulate what appears to have been the assumption of all the judges, that the test was concerned with answering the question of degree which the words of the statute themselves raised, *viz.*, what constituted separateness. He said: " What circumstances amount to such a sharing of the house as to negative the constitution of a separate dwelling must be a question of degree . . . [the] test may be very helpful in deciding the question of degree that has to be solved afresh in every individual case."[82] In other words, he is saying that the problem for the court was one of application, and that the test was concerned with a manner of application, and so was not binding on later courts. Lord Radcliffe makes this even clearer by saying " it seems to me impossible to say that such a test can be presented as a construction of the statutory phrase."[83]

It is submitted, therefore, that the doctrine of Denning L.J. in *Paisner* v. *Goodrich*[66a] is that the problem of the application of statutory words to particular instances, arising from the vagueness of the words, is one of " fact ". The reasoning of the court in arriving at its categorisation of the instance, as within or without the words, does not constitute a rule of law, and so does not create a binding precedent. But he denies that a later court is free to categorise the facts before it unrestricted by previous decision. Where the facts before a later court are similar to those before the precedent court then a similar categorisation of the facts

---

[81] [1956] 2 All E.R. 176.

[82] [1956] 2 All E.R. 1861.

[83] In my opinion, however, it is very possible that the judges had considered the test as one determining the interpretation of the statutory phrase. On the one hand, the words " let as a separate dwelling " may be considered as deriving their meaning from their use by laymen as part of the ordinary English language: but, on the other hand, they may be considered as deriving their meaning from the technical usages of property lawyers dealing with leases. The test of sharing is surely attributable to the notion of exclusive possession associated in property law with leases. Is it purely coincidental that Scott L.J. and Morton L.J. were largely the creators of the test? One of the common sources of ambiguity in statutes (and other documents) is the existence of technical words of English legal language identical in shape and sound with words of the ordinary English language. It is a problem of interpretation, in the stricter sense, and thus a question of law, whether such words in a statute are to be considered as technical legal words or words of ordinary language. Once that problem has been solved then a problem of vagueness may arise.

The situation is illustrated by *Edwards* v. *Bairstow*. There the issue was whether a certain transaction was an " adventure . . . in the nature of trade " within the meaning of the Income Tax Act, 1918. Viscount Simonds emphasises that " it is a question of law, not of fact . . . what the statutory language means." [1955] 3 All E.R. 54F. Lord Radcliffe makes the same point but continues: " the law does not supply a precise definition of the word 'trade '; much less does it prescribe a detailed or exhaustive set of rules for application to any particular set of circumstances." [1955] 3 All E.R. 55I. But here the relation between technical legal words and ordinary words is a little more complex than outlined above. Lord Radcliffe says: " Here we have a statutory phrase involving a charge of tax, and it is for the courts to interpret its meaning, having regard to the context in which it occurs, and to the principles which they bring to bear on the meaning of income." An ordinary word is incorporated into a legal rule with much of its ordinary vagueness, but legally coloured to harmonise with its legal surroundings. The problem of vagueness is one of fact, the problem of colour one of law. An excellent illustration of this is to be found in the *Shell-Mex* case: see n. 87, below.

in relation to the statutory words must be made. One leading case before *Paisner* v. *Goodrich*[66a] had dealt with the sharing of a kitchen, and another with the sharing of a bathroom. Denning L.J. said: " I accept that the kitchenette takes away the protection of the Act, whereas the sharing of a bathroom or W.C. does not."[84]

Application of statutes and appellate courts

In *Paisner* v. *Goodrich* there were two problems for Denning L.J. The first was that which we have been considering, to what extent was he bound by what earlier judges had said about the statutory words. The second was whether he agreed with the decision of the lower court. An appellate court follows earlier cases so far as questions of law are concerned, it will not disturb the decision of a lower court where questions of " fact " are concerned. Thus, the question whether a particular problem in relation to a statute is one of law or one of fact is related to both functions of an appellate court. There are a number of cases in which Lord Denning has dealt with the problem of application of statutes when considering the relation of an appellate court to the tribunal of first instance. The general doctrine expounded by him in these cases recognises a distinction between interpretation as a question of law and application as a question of fact. Accordingly, it supports the view previously stated that he recognises such a distinction in relation to the doctrine of precedent.

The case in which Lord Denning, perhaps, best expounds his views is *B.P. Refinery Ltd.* v. *Walker*.[84a] It was concerned with the rateability of the components of certain plant, and this turned on whether they could be said to be " in nature of a . . . structure " within the meaning of an order made under the Rating and Valuation Act, 1925. The problem is, of course, typical of the very large number of cases arising under all sorts of statutory provisions in which the problem is whether some particular is to be classified as within the category designated by statutory words.[85] The Land Tribunal had considered the matter in detail and held that some of the components were rateable and others were not. The matter was taken to the Court of Appeal. There, in the words of Denning L.J., " Counsel for ratepayers submitted that the findings of the tribunal were findings of fact which could not be challenged in this court ". But Denning L.J. thought that the concept of " fact " in that proposition required analysis, and this he supplied. In the first place, he distinguished between particular facts and their classification within the category of the statutory words. " The primary facts are all found by the tribunal and are not in dispute. The only question

---

[84] [1955] 2 All E.R. 333B. This view may be compared with Viscount Dunedin's as to the effect of a decision where no " *ratio decidendi* " has been propounded. *The Mostyn* [1928] A.C. at p. 73: discussed by me, " Judicial Law Making and Law Applying," p. 203.

[84a] [1957] 1 All E.R. 700.

[85] For a general discussion see Hart: *Aristotelian Society: Supp.* vol. 29, p. 259.

is what is the proper inference or conclusion from the primary facts."[86] The nature of the category depends on the interpretation of the statutory words. " If the tribunal in coming to its conclusion, discloses by its reasoning that it has misunderstood or misinterpreted the words of the statute then it falls into error in point of law."[87] But there is a problem of application as well as of interpretation. " There is, however, a considerable area where two reasonable men, each of whom properly understood the statute, could reasonably come to different conclusions. In such cases the mere fact that the tribunal comes to a different conclusion from that to which some of the members of this court might come does not mean that the tribunal falls into an error in point of law. The question is then one of degree in which the tribunal of fact is supreme so long as it does not step outside the bounds of reasonableness."[88]

The general doctrine thus propounded needs two glosses. The first is to note the legal parallel between the separate processes of categorisation of facts and establishment of facts, which arise from confining the discretion of the tribunal of facts to the " bounds of reasonableness ". Just as an appellate court may reverse a finding of " primary " fact on the ground that there was no evidence to sustain such a finding, so too it may reverse a categorisation of fact on the ground that " no person acting judicially . . . could have come to the determination."[89]

---

[86] [1957] 1 All E.R. 715F. The terms " primary facts " and " inference from facts " have also been used in connection with the different problem, within the realm of evidence, of inferring one set of particular facts from another set: e.g. inferring an intention to dedicate a right of way from failure to obstruct people walking openly over a path: *Chivers Ltd.* v. *Cambridge C.C.* [1957] 1 All E.R. 885H, where counsel considered this type of inference was identical with that of statutory application: see *ibid.*, 888B. The evidence problem was discussed in the House of Lords in *Benmax* v. *Austin Motor Co., Ltd.*, [1955] 1 All E.R. 326, using the language of " simple " and " specific " facts.

[87] [1957] 1 All E.R. 715G. This was the view Lord Denning took of the situation in *Shell-Mex and B. P. Ltd.* v. *Holyoak* [1959] 1 All E.R. 402 F. That was a case where the same words " in the nature of a structure " fell to be construed as in the *B.P. Refinery* case. Lord Denning considered that the Land Tribunal had used an improper test in the determination of the nature of the statutory category. The full question, it will be remembered (see n. 76, above), was whether an underground petrol tank was a " tank . . . in the nature of a structure". Lord Denning attached no importance to the interpretation of the word " tank " (403B), but Lord Reid did. He asked: " What then is the ' tank ' within the meaning of the order? It has not been argued that any technical meaning attaches to the word ' tank ' in the order, and it must therefore be taken as an ordinary word of the English language to be construed in the light of the context in which it is found." (399B). The majority of the House of Lords considered that the Land Tribunal were dealing solely with the application of the word " tank."

[88] [1957] 1 All E.R. 715H. The distinction between " interpretation " and " application " was adverted to by Denning L.J. in *British Paste and Cement Manufacturers Ltd.* v. *Thurrock U.D.C.* (1950) 114 J.P. 582, where he said: " Once the principles of interpretation have been settled . . . the particular application of them to any particular set of facts is essentially a matter for quarter sessions."
Denning L.J. asserted that authority for his doctrine was to be found in *Edwards* v. *Bairstow*, which, he said, " seems to confirm authoritatively the principles laid down in a series of cases in which he had participated:" see [1957] 1 All E.R. 715I.

[89] The citation is from Lord Radcliffe in *Edwards* v. *Bairstow* [1955] 3 All E.R. 57H. But his analysis appears inadequate. He refers to " primary facts " and inferences from them, and speaks of " no evidence to support a conclusion." He does not distinguish as clearly as does Denning L.J. between unreasonable classification within a properly interpreted

The second gloss is also concerned with a limitation on the discretion of the tribunal of first instance. In 1948 Denning L.J. propounded a test of what matters would be left by an appellate tribunal to such discretion, and it was in terms of the distinction between primary facts and the conclusions from them. In *British Launderers Association* v. *Middlesex Assessment Committee*[89a] he classifies the matters for the inferior tribunal under two heads. (1) Primary facts: " facts which are observed by witnesses and proved by oral testimony, or facts proved by the production of a thing itself . . . the only question of law that can arise on them is whether there was any evidence to support the finding."[90] (2) Conclusions from primary facts, " if and in so far as those conclusions can as well be drawn by a layman (properly instructed on the law) as by a lawyer . . . the only questions of law that can arise on them are whether there was a proper direction in point of law and whether the conclusion is one which could reasonably be drawn from the primary facts."[91] In my opinion the qualification suggested under the second head is too indeterminate, and seems to involve the notion that a lawyer is a better " logician " than a layman. I consider this dictum as superseded by the fuller analysis provided in *B.P. Refinery Ltd.* v. *Walker*.[92] But the Court of Appeal in a yet later case has left open the question of the validity of the dictum.[93]

Conclusion

This conclusion is only a whimpered substitute for the word " finis ". I wish to emphasise the inconclusive character of my discussion, and to point out that I have not referred to the whole of Lord Denning's thought on the judicial treatment of statutes. In particular, I have not referred to his doctrine of liberal interpretation, nor to his doctrine of rejection of absurdities.

---

category, and a classification which must be deemed to be based on an improperly interpreted category. The latter situation is thus described by Denning L.J.: " Even if [the tribunal] does not disclose its reasoning, but asserts a conclusion which could not reasonably be entertained by a man who properly understood the meaning of the statute, then again it falls into error in point of law." [1957] 1 All E.R. 715G.

[89a] [1949] 1 K.B. 434, 462; [1949] 1 All E.R. 21.

[90] [1949] 1 All E.R. 25H.

[91] [1949] 1 All E.R. 26A.

[92] [1957] 1 All E.R. 700. This is supported by the statement in the *Launderers* case of what matters a lawyer can do better than a layman: " If and in so far, however, as the correct conclusion from primary facts, requires for its correctness determination by a trained lawyer—as for instance, because it involves the interpretation of documents, or because the law and the facts cannot be separated, or because the law on the point cannot properly be understood or applied except by a trained lawyer—the conclusion is of a conclusion law on which an appellate tribunal is as competent to form an opinion as a tribunal of first instance." [1949] 1 All E.R. 26A.

[93] *Chivers Ltd.* v. *Cambridge C.C.* [1957] 1 All E.R. 888G. The dictum was applied by Diplock J.: *Tsakiroglou* v. *Noblee Thorl* [1959] 1 All E.R. 50B.

10

Ratio Decidendi and the House of Lords*

The Latinity of the phrase *ratio decidendi* has not preserved it from the ambiguity of English words: indeed it may be responsible for some of the ambiguity since as a mere matter of translation it may be rendered equally by the phrases " reason for deciding " and " reason of decision ". Judges and scholars alike use the phrase on some occasions for *any* reason which influences the ultimate decision,[1] whether it be a finding of fact, or a determination of law, or an opinion about social circumstance or public policy, and on some occasions for a rule of law, whether influencing the court or not, for which it is thought the case can be used as authority. While such flexibility is doubtless not wholly disadvantageous, it is often productive of confusion. The confusion surrounding the use of *ratio decidendi* is only slightly lessened by the convention under which it is more often used to refer solely to some *rule of law* which is connected in some way or another with the decision. This convention is properly recognised by Glanville Williams in his instruction to the student beginning to learn law when he " translates " *ratio decidendi* as " the rule of law upon which the decision is founded ".[2] But the translation is ambiguous, for while it might appear to mean " the rule of law upon which the judge founded his decision ", it is clear that Glanville Williams accepts the terminology adopted and the doctrine expounded by Goodhart in *Determining the Ratio Decidendi of a Case*,[3] whereby the *ratio decidendi* of a case is not the rule of law propounded by the judge as the basis of his decision. Paton asserts, in accordance with the language of many jurists but not with that of the judges, that *ratio decidendi* means the rule of law for which a case is binding. There is no ambiguity in his exposition; he says that " The classical view was that the *ratio* was the principle of law which the judge considered neces-

---

* Reprinted from the *Modern Law Review*, March, 1957, by kind permission.

[1] A recent example of *ratio decidendi* being used to denote something other than a rule of law is to be found in (1955) 71 L.Q.R. at p. 25. Coutts there asks, in reference to a case, " What then is the *ratio decidendi* ? " He proceeds to consider as a possible *ratio decidendi* a particular finding of fact.

[2] *Learning the Law* (3rd ed.) 1950, p. 57.

[3] *Essays in Jurisprudence and the Common Law*, p. 1.

sary to the decision."[4] This sentence does not embody an explanation of the *meaning* of the word *ratio,* but a *criterion* of the already defined *thing.* It is this " classical " view which Goodhart controverted. I have argued that it is better to use the phrase *ratio decidendi* to mean exclusively the principle of law propounded by the judge as the basis of his decision, a usage which would correspond with judicial usage;[5] and to dispense with a succinct term for the rule of law for which a case is of binding authority. But the question of terminology, though not unimportant, is a subsidiary one. The main question is whether, to use Paton's language, the " classical view " is still correct. According to the doctrine of precedent, is " the principle of law which the judge considered necessary to the decision of the particular case before him " binding or not?[6] There has been very little judicial authority on this point. Most jurists have, like Goodhart,[7] said it is not binding. But now a Northern Ireland case has appeared in support of the doctrine, accepted by the South African courts,[8] that the classical view is still law.

In *Walsh* v. *Curry and others*[9] the Court of Appeal of Northern Ireland considered the authority of *George Wimpey & Co., Ltd.* v. *British Overseas Airways Corporation*[10] in relation to section 6 (1) of the Law Reform (Married Women and Tortfeasors) Act, 1935, because it was dealing with the interpretation of a precisely similar enactment, *viz.,* section 16 (1) (*c*) of the Law Reform (Miscellaneous Provisions) Act, Northern Ireland, 1937. *Wimpey's* case is a decision of the House of Lords, and we all say in that simple, lucid, uncritical and unrealistic style, which is perhaps the main characteristic of legal speech, " The

---

[4] *Jurisprudence* (1st ed.), p. 159.

[5] " The Language of Precedent," 2 West. Aust. L.J. at p. 323.

[6] The " classical view " may be regarded as true even though the principle stated by the judge is subsequently held to be too broadly expressed as a binding rule of law. There is abundant authority for reading a judgment *secundum subjectam materiam.* The important question is whether the proposition propounded by the judge may, so far as its binding character is concerned, be entirely ignored. That it can be so rejected is, *pace* Paton, the thesis of Goodhart.

[7] Glanville Williams accurately summarises Goodhart's thesis in the following sentence. " The *ratio decidendi* of a case can be defined as the material facts of the case plus the decision thereon": *Learning the Law* (3rd ed.), 1950, p. 57.

[8] The Goodhart thesis was specifically considered and rejected in *Pretoria City Council* v. *Levinson* 1949 (3) S.A. 305 (A.D.), see *per* Schreiner J.A. at p. 315. In *Fellner* v. *Minister of Interior,* 1954 (4) S.A. 523 (A.D.) the difficulties are considered of determining for what rule of law a decision of a multi-judge tribunal is of binding authority when the *rationes decidendi* of the individual judges differ. See the illuminating note by Honoré: (1955) 71 L.Q.R. 196.

[9] [1955] N.I. 112.

[10] [1955] A.C. 169. At the time of the hearing of *Walsh* v. *Curry, Wimpey's* case had not been heard in the House of Lords. " As that case was then under appeal to the House of Lords we thought it well to defer our determination of the present appeal until the conclusions of their Lordships had been published ": *per* Lord MacDermott L.C.J. [1955] N.I. at p. 121. It is submitted with respect that the argument of counsel could also have been adjourned, since so much was thought to turn on the examination of the speeches of the Lords. The procedure adopted by the Court of Appeal led to their consideration of the difficult problem of the legal consequences of *Wimpey's* case without hearing counsel. Certainly such a procedure is not consistent with the " umpire " theory of the judicial function.

House of Lords is the highest judicial authority for the United Kingdom. Its decisions absolutely bind all lower courts."[11] But when our thinking caps are firmly on we realise the need for qualification, even at the expense of conciseness, and we ask : (i) are decisions of the House of Lords from the English Court of Appeal binding on the courts of Northern Ireland, and *vice versa*?[12]; (ii) what is meant by a "decision" of the House of Lords? *Walsh* v. *Curry*[9] provides authority for answering both these questions.

An atomistic view of the nature of the common law, the approach of Lord Buckmaster in *Donoghue* v. *Stevenson*,[12a] of the United States Supreme Court in *Erie Railroad Co.* v. *Tompkins*[13], leads to the argument that since Northern Ireland is an independent legal system there is a Northern Ireland "common law".[14] Northern Ireland has its own courts, and its separate courts, producing their own decisions, lead to a separate law, the aggregate of those decisions. The House of Lords is only part of the system of Northern Ireland courts when determining appeals from Northern Ireland. Decisions of the House of Lords on appeal from the Court of Appeal of Northern Ireland are binding on the courts of Northern Ireland. England has its own courts, its own decisions, its own "common law". Decisions of the House of Lords on appeal from the Court of Appeal of England form part of the English "common law", not of Northern Ireland "common law", and are not binding on the courts of Northern Ireland. On the other hand, acceptance of the common law as an integrated set of principles, without any acceptance of any "brooding omnipresence in the sky", leads to a contrary conclusion. There is one common law. Different courts may come to different conclusions about the development of this dynamic, living system. But where a doctrine of precedent exists and a principle of the hierarchy of courts, there is no difficulty in accepting the highest court's decisions about the common law as authoritative, even though there are in theory two Houses of Lords.[15] In fact the courts have adopted a practice with regard to precedents without consideration of such arguments. The practice has been for English and Irish courts to consider themselves bound by decisions of the House of

---

[11] Hughes, *Jurisprudence*, p. 223.
[12] There are, of course, the questions whether decisions of the House of Lords on appeals from the Court of Session are binding elsewhere than in Scotland, and whether decisions of the House of Lords on appeals from the Court of Appeal of England and Northern Ireland are binding on Scottish courts. But Scotland is not a "common law" country, and so very different considerations apply.
[12a] [1932] A.C. 562.
[13] (1938) 304 U.S. 64. It is submitted that the rejection of an alternative view does not lead, as Holmes J. proclaimed it did in *Black & White T. & T. Co.* v. *Brown & Yellow T. & T. Co.* (1927) 276 U.S. at 534, to the adoption of "a transcendental body of law outside of any particular State."
[14] *Cf.* Holmes J., *Kuhn* v. *Fairmont Coal Co.* (1909) 215 U.S. at p. 372. "The law of a state does not become something outside of the state court and independent of it, by being called the common law. Wherever it is cited it is the law as declared by the state judges and nothing else."
[15] It may well be contended, of course, that there is but one court both for England and for Northern Ireland.

Lords on points of common law, whether the House of Lords was sitting on appeal from an Irish or an English court. Who has ever expressed doubts, from this point of view of the hierarchy of the courts, about the authority in England of the decisions of the House of Lords in *Cundy* v. *Lindsay,*[15a] *Quinn* v. *Leathem,*[15b] *McCartney* v. *Londonderry and Lough Swilly Ry. Co.*[15c] [16]. The doctrine behind the practice, however, has hitherto existed *sub silentio*. There are now dicta which can be quoted. In *Walsh* v. *Curry* each member of the Court of Appeal of Northern Ireland used language which, though it does not explicitly state, nevertheless expressly recognises, the doctrine that " decisions " of the House of Lords, though on appeal from English courts, are binding in Northern Ireland. Each judge said that the House of Lords in *Wimpey's* case[10] might have laid down a rule of law which would have been binding on him. Thus Lord MacDermott L.C.J. considers whether " the construction adopted by the majority in the Court of Appeal has not been conclusively established by the House of Lords ".[17] Porter L.J., though apparently in favour of " the interpretation put upon the paragraph by Denning L.J. in the Court of Appeal and by Lord Porter and Lord Keith in the House of Lords ",[18] nevertheless was unable to adopt it, because " The majority of the House of Lords . . . took a different and narrower view of the scope of the paragraph ".[19] Black L.J. said " Unfortunately, as the Lord Chief Justice has pointed out, the decision in the House of Lords does not give us authoritative guidance ".[20] If that reason had not existed the decision would have presumably been binding.

The reason stated by Lord MacDermott L.C.J. why the House of Lords in *Wimpey's* case had not " conclusively established ", gave no " authoritative guidance " for, a rule of law was that the members of the House of Lords expressed different opinions about the correct interpretation of the relevant statute. Lord MacDermott L.C.J. did not seek for some *ratio decidendi*, as Goodhart advises, by looking merely at " the material facts of the case plus the decision thereon ".[21] He carefully considered the *ratio decidendi* of each speech. He said " The House of Lords affirmed the decision of the Court of Appeal. This was a majority ruling, Lord Simonds, Lord Reid and Lord Tucker taking the view that the appeal of *Wimpey's* should be dismissed and Lord Porter and Lord Keith of Avonholm being of the contrary opinion." He then

---

[15a] [1878] 3 App. Cas. 459.
[15b] [1901] A.C. 495.
[15c] [1904] A.C. 301.
[16] All of these were " Northern Ireland " cases.
[17] [1955] N.I. at p. 125, line 5. The line numbers printed on each page by the *N.I. Reports*, the letters printed by the *All England Reports*, are most valuable. They save the search through an entire page for a particular sentence.
[18] [1955] N.I. p. 129, line 34.
[19] [1955] N.I. p. 130, line 6.
[20] [1955] N.I. p. 135, line 8.
[21] See n. 7.

proceeded to examine carefully the speeches of the Law Lords to see on what principles of law they based their decisions. It is clear that had all the members of the majority of the Lords agreed as to the interpretation of the statute, he would have considered himself bound by that interpretation, being the rule of law on which they had based their decisions. He found, however, that the majority were not agreed, for Lord Reid, though he came to the same ultimate decision, did not accept the interpretation adopted by Lord Simonds and Lord Tucker. Since the minority also rejected that interpretation Lord MacDermott did not consider it was " binding on this court ".[22] He concluded the question of the authority of the House of Lords by saying " For these reasons I think this court is in a position to form its own judgment on the matter."[23]

Enough has been said to show that *Walsh* v. *Curry*[9] is an authority for rejecting the thesis that the *ratio* propounded by the judge is not authoritative. But, as has often been pointed out, the classical view leads to many difficulties of application, particularly where multi-judge tribunals are concerned.[24] *Walsh* v. *Curry* deals with one of the problems. As has been seen, Lord Simonds and Lord Tucker in *Wimpey's* case[10] adopted one interpretation of the relevant section: Lord Reid adopted another. Lord Porter and Lord Keith, like Lord Reid, rejected the interpretation of Lord Simonds and Lord Tucker, but adopted yet another interpretation, leading to a different final order from that of the others. There were thus three judges in favour of rejecting the interpretation of Lord Simonds and Lord Tucker: they formed a majority of the House on that point. Lord MacDermott L.C.J. thought that he was in consequence not bound to accept the interpretation of Lord Simonds and Lord Tucker, even though they formed part of the majority of the House. On the other hand, he did not think that he was bound to reject their interpretation, even though on that point they were in a minority. The reason for this latter view was that " so to hold would be to reckon the views of the minority on which their dissent was founded ".[25] Honoré has stated a *rationale* for this dictum. " The fundamental reason why the opinions of minority judges cannot form part of the *ratio decidendi* of a case is that they are not reasons for the order made by the court : a *ratio decidendi* is entitled to authority not as the opinion of one or more judges, but as the reason for a judicial

---

[22] [1955] N.I. p. 124, line 36. " I do not think it can be said that the view taken by Singleton and Morris L.JJ. in the Court of Appeal has been adopted by the House of Lords, for although the House of Lords affirmed the decision of the Court of Appeal, which was based on that view, the view itself did not find favour with the majority of the Law Lords. I say this because I have no doubt from what Lord Reid says that he did not share the view taken by Lord Simonds and Lord Tucker."

[23] [1955] N.I. p. 125, line 11. The sentence concludes " in the light, of course, of the opinions evoked by *Wimpey's* case." But this is a reference to persuasive, not to binding, authority.

[24] See Paton and Sawer, (1947) 63 L.Q.R. 462: Coutts (1948) 64 L.Q.R. 463: Lord Asquith 1950, J.S.P.T.L. 358.

[25] [1955] N.I. at p. 125, line 8.

L

order."[26]   But this *rationale* is inconsistent with Lord MacDermott's reasoning. He did take into account the opinions of minority judges when seeking to determine the authority of *Wimpey's* case:[10] he relied on the views of Lord Porter and Lord Keith to show that the interpretation of Lord Simonds and Lord Tucker had not been " conclusively established ".

Lord MacDermott's reasoning leaves open the situation where though there is no unanimity in favour of a particular *ratio* there is no majority of the court against it. Thus, supposing the House in *Wimpey's* case had consisted solely of Lord Simonds, Lord Tucker and Lord Reid, would the view of Lord Simonds and Lord Tucker have been binding? Porter L.J. considered himself bound by their interpretation[27] : he did not, however, expressly take into account the fact that Lord Reid had not agreed with Lord Simonds and Lord Tucker.

The situation in *Walsh* v. *Curry*[9] must also be distinguished from that where though there is no unanimity in favour of a particular *ratio*, yet there is no rejection of it. The opinions of the judges may be different but not inconsistent. Thus in a three judge court, J_1 and J_2 may hold for the plaintiff by relying on rule of law x, and J_3, without rejecting x, may not adopt it, but may find for the plaintiff by relying on rule of law y. It may well be that in such a case both x and y are binding.[28] If there are two further judges, J_4 and J_5, who reject both x and y and hold for the defendant, what is then the position? *Walsh* v. *Curry* is distinguishable, since in that case J_3 rejected x; this, indeed, was a vital factor in Lord MacDermott's judgment.[29] Accordingly, *Walsh* v. *Curry* cannot be cited for the general proposition laid down by the South African Appellate Division in *Fellner* v. *Minister of the Interior*.[30] This is that in a five judge court " there is no *ratio decidendi* of the court

---

[26] (1955) 71 L.Q.R. p. 198. An interesting case illustrating the difference, and the relation, between the reasons for a decision and the final order of a court is *Lake* v. *Lake* [1955] 2 All E.R. 538 (*cf. Commonwealth of Australia* v. *Bank of New South Wales* [1950] A.C. 235, *per* Lord Porter at 294). While I agree with the substance of Honoré's statement, I would reaffirm that it is more convenient to use the phrase *ratio decidendi* solely for the rule of law propounded by the judge. In this terminology one would not speak of " the *ratio decidendi* of a case," or of a court, except as an elliptical way of referring to the *ratio decidendi* of a single judge constituting a court, or to the *rationes decidendi* of the judges of a multi-judge tribunal where they all propounded the same rule. This terminology may be correlated with Honoré's own view that " The notions of a *decision* and a *reason for a decision* apply primarily to individuals ": (1955) 71 L.Q.R. 201. He includes " a decision " in his statement; but the decision of a court is a perfectly clear notion: it is the final order of the court: see Lord Porter in the *Commonwealth Banking* case.

[27] [1955] N.I. p. 130, *passim*.

[28] This would follow from the analogy of *Jacobs* v. *L.C.C.* [1950] A.C. 361. Viscount Dunedin's speech in *G.W.R.* v. *The Mostyn* may be regarded as supporting this conclusion, because he thinks that a majority *ratio* is binding. See [1928] A.C. at p. 73.

[29] [1955] N.I. p. 124, line 41. A very large number of possibilities exist, and are actualised. The doctrine of precedent is far too complex for effective operation: it persists because its complications are overlooked.

[30] [1954] (4) S.A. 523 (A.D.). The quotation is taken from the note by Honoré in 71 L.Q.R. p. 196. The shift in the meaning of " *ratio decidendi* " is interesting.

unless at least three judges propound the same *ratio decidendi.*" Indeed the judgment of Porter L.J. is opposed to such a wide doctrine.

Lord MacDermott's view that the court was not bound either to accept or reject the interpretation of Lord Simonds and Lord Tucker led him to say " this court is in a position to form its own judgment on the matter." This dictum might be interpreted to mean that the court was free to adopt any construction of section 16 it pleased. This would be to wipe *Wimpey's* case[10] " off the slate ",[31] save for the persuasive authority of the speeches. In fact, all the members of the Court of Appeal adopted the interpretation of Lord Simonds. It is certainly not clear that Lord MacDermott considered himself free to adopt an interpretation which, applied to the facts of *Wimpey's* case, would have led to a contrary result in the House of Lords in that case.

---

[31] This is what Viscount Dunedin said could not be done with a decision of the House of Lords.

I I

Some Problems about Fundamental Terms*

PART I

The problems

The doctrine of " fundamental term " has been recently invoked in yet another case concerned with the hire-purchase of a car in order to enable the borrower to obtain damages despite the presence in the agreement of an exemption clause. In this case, *Charterhouse Credit Co., Ltd.* v. *Tolly*[1] a new point of law was decided. It may be said to be established law that a party to a contract who commits a breach of a fundamental term cannot escape liability for such breach by reliance on an exemption clause. But is the position altered if the innocent party, notwithstanding discovery of the breach, acts in a manner consistent with the continuance of some contractual relations? In the *Charterhouse*[1] case the borrower of the car, on discovering the breach, instead of returning the car, retained it, and indeed entered into negotiations about the time of payment of instalments. The Court of Appeal held that notwithstanding the borrower's conduct, the lender could not rely on the exemption clause in the agreement. In this note it is not desired to criticise the justice of this decision. One purpose is, however, to draw attention to the need for further consideration of

---

* Reprinted from the *Cambridge Law Journal*, April and November, 1964, by kind permission.

[1] [1963] 2 Q.B. 683; [1963] 2 All E.R. 433. The case will hereafter be called the *Charterhouse* case. All references for dicta will be to the *All England Reports* both for this and other cases in order to make clear, by means of the lettering system employed, the part of the page to which reference is made.

The legal point had previously arisen in *Handley* v. *Marston* (1962) 106 S.J. 327. However, in that case the Court of Appeal found that there was no " fundamental breach ", and consequently it was not necessary to decide whether the exemption clause had been kept alive merely by reason of the defendant not repudiating.

[I am indebted to my friend Mr. G. Treitel (Reader in English Law at the University of Oxford) for pointing out that the case would now fall within the financial limit of £2000, established by the Hire-Purchase Act, 1967, and so the exclusion clause would almost certainly be invalid under section 18. The case is much criticised in the *Suisse Atlantique Case* [1967] A.C. 361, whose impact on it is discussed by Treitel in 29 M.L.R. 546, 550 (Ed.).]

the terminology and concepts employed in the reasoning leading to the final decision—terminology and concepts which are by no means confined to the reasoning in this case. It is suggested that they do not exhibit the clarity and consistency and adequacy which is desirable in order to attain a realistic analysis of situations with which courts have to deal. Such linguistic questions are of course subordinate to the attainment of justice. The *Charterhouse* case[1] illustrates the general ability that judges possess of achieving just decisions despite the deficiencies of existing linguistic aids. But linguistic analysis has an intrinsic value of its own,[2] and, moreover, an improvement in terminology and the corresponding conceptual framework helps rather than hinders in the quest for justice.[3]

The terminology and concepts which call for review are to be found in the following passages from the judgments in the *Charterhouse* case. Upjohn L.J. stated the issue before the court in these terms: " The authorities establish that where there is a breach of a fundamental term the person in breach cannot rely on clauses of exclusion to protect him as against the other party: but the finance company [the lenders] said with some force that that is so, no doubt, when the innocent party treats the contract as repudiated, yet if he elects to affirm the contract, then he must take the benefit of the contract, subject to all its provisions, including a clause of exclusion, and he can no longer plead that the other party, though in breach of a fundamental term, cannot rely on a clause of exclusion." [4] The language of election and repudiation is to be found in section 11 of the Sale of Goods Act, 1893, in connection with " conditions " of a contract of sale.[5] One of the problems to be examined in this note is that of the association of fundamental terms with this concept of " conditions ". While none of the judges in the *Charterhouse* case expressly applied the language of " conditions " to a fundamental term, yet such application is by no means uncommon. In *Yeoman Credit Co., Ltd.* v. *Apps*,[6] for example, all the judges speak of

---

[2] The following remarks of Tarski, though about science, are nevertheless relevant to analysis of legal reasoning and the development of social welfare which is one of the aims of justice: " It is inimical to the progress of science to measure the importance of any research exclusively or chiefly in terms of its usefulness and applicability. We know from the history of science that many important results and discoveries have had to wait centuries before they were applied in any field. . . . I do not think that a scientific result which gives us a better understanding of the world and makes it more harmonious in our eyes should be held in lower esteem than, say, an invention which reduces the cost of paving roads, or improves household plumbing." " Semantic Conceptions of Truth " reported in *Semantics and the Philosophy of Language* (ed. Linsky), pp. 41-42. *Sed quaere*—should it be held in higher esteem?

[3] An ambiguous terminology and inadequate concepts may help to prevent a doctrine of precedent from becoming too rigid. But the prevention of rigidity is better achieved by reform of the doctrine of precedent than by perpetuation of imperfect analysis.

[4] p. 442C.

[5] It will be recalled that s. 11 (1) (*a*) recites, " Where a contract of sale is subject to any conditions to be fulfilled by the seller, the buyer may waive the condition or may elect to treat the breach of such condition as a breach of warranty and not as a ground for treating the contract as repudiated."

[6] [1962] 2 Q.B. 508; [1961] 2 All E.R. 281. This case will hereafter be called the *Apps* case. There are a number of cases in which the Yeoman Credit Co. Ltd. appear as plaintiffs.

a fundamental term as being a "fundamental condition".[7] Even the important dictum of Devlin J. in *Smeaton Hanscomb* v. *Sassoon I. Setty*[8] may be interpreted as regarding a fundamental term as a species of condition: "a fundamental term . . . must be something narrower than a condition."[9] This dictum, however, does draw attention to what is perhaps the major problem, that of distinguishing fundamental terms from conditions. Unfortunately there appears to have been no judicial consideration of this problem in the ten years since Devlin J. adverted to it.[10]

The approach of Donovan L.J. to the issue in the case employs the language not of "fundamental term" but of "fundamental breach". He says:[11] "a fundamental breach of contract, that is, one which goes to its very root, disentitles the party in breach from relying on the provision of an exempting clause. That principle will apply here unless an argument which the finance company has put forward ought to be sustained. It is this: that when the hirer elected not to treat the fundamental breach as ending the contract, but chose instead to treat the contract as still subsisting, then he 'affirmed' or 'approbated' the contract, with the result that he is bound by the [exemption clause] as much as by any other clause of the contract." He referred to the judgment of Denning L.J. in *Karsales (Harrow), Ltd.* v. *Wallis*, where "fundamental breach" was put forward as a generic concept, of which "breach of a fundamental term" was but a species.[12] This judgment was relied on also by Ormerod L.J. who used both the language of "fundamental breach" and "fundamental term".[13] It is submitted that it is problematical whether the notion of "fundamental term" is but a species of fundamental breach.

What exactly was the fundamental term in the *Charterhouse* case[1] was another subject of disagreement among the judges. While Ormerod L.J. thought that a fitness for purpose term was fundamental, Upjohn

---

[7] Holroyd Pearce L.J. at p. 289 I; Harman L.J. at p. 291 I; Donovan L.J. at p. 292 H See also Pearson L.J. in the *Astley* case (*q.v.*) at p. 44 G.

[8] [1953] 1 W.L.R. 1468; [1953] 2 All E.R. 1471. This case will hereafter be called the *Hanscomb* case.

[9] At p. 1473 C.

[10] Nor has there been much juristic consideration. Cheshire and Fifoot continue to repeat, without reference to the *Hanscomb* case, the statement in their early editions that "condition" must be distinguished from the fundamental object of the contract; they rely on the peas and beans dictum of Lord Abinger in *Chanter* v. *Hopkins*. Melville in (1956) 19 M.L.R. 26 gives the fullest consideration to Lord Devlin's dictum. But even he does not consider the appropriateness of applying the word "conditions" to promises. His discussion does not, with respect, go beyond my consideration of the problem in (1937) 15 Can.B.R. 764 *et seq.*

[11] At p. 483 F.

[12] [1956] 1 W.L.R. 936; [1956] 2 All E.R. 866, 869 C: "These are all comprehended by the general principle that a breach which goes to the root of the contract disentitles the party from relying on the exempting clause." Guest in (1961) 77 L.Q.R. 98 deals under the title of "Fundamental Breach of a Contract" with "fundamental terms" without any suggestions of the concepts being different.

[13] At pp. 444 E and 444 H.

L.J. thought it was not.[14]   Involved in the case also was the nature of
the content of a fitness for purpose term in a hire-purchase contract.
Discussion of these problems requires consideration of the earlier cases
of *Apps*[6] and *Astley Industrial Trust, Ltd. v. Grimley*.[15]

The problems arising from the *Charterhouse* case[1] thus fall into
two distinct groups, the first group being concerned with general
questions of fundamental terms, the second being concerned with
particular questions about the fitness for purpose term.   Accordingly,
after a statement of the facts of the *Charterhouse* case the remainder of
this note is divided into three further parts.   In Part II we consider
the general questions: (a) to what extent is there a significant distinction between concepts of fundamental breach and fundamental term;
(b) what is the concept of repudiation, and what is its relation to
breach of a fundamental term; (c) what is the concept of " affirmation " of a contract and what is its relation to breach of a fundamental
term; (d) what is the relation between fundamental terms and
" conditions "?   It should be emphasised that the object of the note
is to suggest the need for further consideration of terminology and
concepts; no comprehensive survey of all the authorities is made.   In
Part III the questions considered are: (a) whether a fitness for purpose
term in a hire-purchase contract is a fundamental term, and (b) what
are the contents of a fitness for purpose term.   Finally, some questions
of policy are considered.

The facts of the Charterhouse case

Though the discussion in this note is concerned with the conceptual
framework employed in the resolution of conflicting claims arising from
particular facts it is nevertheless desirable that the particular facts of
the *Charterhouse* case be stated in order that by giving a content to the
concepts the discussion may be better appreciated.

The plaintiffs were a finance company who had entered into an
agreement with the defendants for the hire of a specific motorcar.   The
defendant, the borrower, undertook to make, and made, an initial payment of £90;   he agreed to pay monthly rentals amounting to
£377 12s. 0d., and he was given an option to purchase the car at the
end of the hire by a further payment of £1.   The hire-purchase
agreement contained the following exemption clause: " The [finance
company] do not supply the vehicle with or subject to any warranties
or conditions either express or implied by statute, and the hirer shall
have no claim against the [finance company] arising directly or
indirectly out of any defect in the vehicle."   After taking delivery of
the car the hirer had two new tyres put on it and went for two short
drives and discovered that the back axle was defective.   He had it

---

[14] At pp. 444 F and 441 I.
[15] [1963] 1 W.L.R. 584; [1963] 2 All E.R. 33 hereinbefore and hereafter called the
Astley case.

stripped, and it was found that it required an expensive repair. The hirer did not return the car, but expressed his willingness to repair the car himself. Since, however, the cost of the repair would exhaust his resources he asked for postponement of the first three rentals. He did not claim to be free from the obligation of paying the rentals. This was granted. However, he fell ill, and after four months had expired, during which no rentals had been paid, the finance company seized the car and sold it for £250. They then sued for the balance of the hiring charges, *viz.*, £127 12s. The hirer counterclaimed for general damages for the finance company's breach in lending him a defective car, stating as one item of damage the £11 he had paid for the new tyres. He also claimed the return of the £90 he had paid. The finance company asserted that the counterclaim could not succeed by virtue of the exemption clause in the agreement.

PART II

Breach of fundamental term and fundamental breach

It is a feature of ordinary language and thought to group together facts and events because each has the quality in some circumstances of producing consequences similar to those produced by the others. Legal language, too, employs the same term to cover different situations to which similar consequences may be attributed. Quite disparate situations, *e.g.*, are covered by the term " agency " or " trust "; though comparison may be avoided by the use of qualifying epithets such as " actual " or " constructive." Such a method of classification may be convenient for many purposes. But it becomes a source of error if it leads to the belief that similar legal consequences are to attach to the different situations in all circumstances. May there not be a source of error in creating a concept consisting of a class of acts which are called fundamental breach and including a breach of fundamental terms as one instance of such a class? It may be true that both where there is the breach of a fundamental term and where there is a fundamental breach by one party the other party is free from obligations to perform his promises. It may also be true that in both cases the guilty party is unable to rely upon an exemption clause. But it is still necessary to inquire into the character of the two situations and how the consequences are brought about. It may be that a fundamental breach terminates the operation of an exemption clause because of the operation of some principle of justice, such as not being allowed to approbate and reprobate. On the other hand an exemption clause may not operate in relation to a breach of a fundamental term because the construction of the clause is such that breaches of fundamental terms are not included within its terms. Such differences should not be ignored.

Of course if the phrase "fundamental breach" is only applied to the breach of a fundamental term we have but an example of a verbal difference between synonyms, and not an example of a genus comprehending different species. So too a spurious uniformity could be brought about by "implying" in every contract a fundamental term not to commit a fundamental breach. This is the language of fiction, which judges now agree should be exorcised from the law, as is witnessed by the criticism in the House of Lords recently of the doctrine of presumed intention.[16]

The judgments in the *Charterhouse* case[1] may be illustrations of the use of the two phrases as synonymous, or they may be illustrations of what Treitel in his *Law of Contract* calls "indiscriminate" use. Treitel's view is that there are two different concepts which can be distinguished by the terms "fundamental breach" and "breach of fundamental term." It is submitted that this is the correct view. There may be a fundamental breach though there is no breach of a fundamental term, and it may well be that a breach of a fundamental term should be placed in a separate category from a fundamental breach.[17] Further arguments in support of this view are stated in the remainder of this article. In Part IV the differences of concept are related to basic differences of policy.

The suggested distinction is derived from the equation of the new phrase "fundamental breach" with the older phrase "total breach": this in its turn is associated with the word "repudiation." A "total breach" is one which manifests an intention not to perform the entirety of the contract. Where this happens the courts hold it to be unjust for the innocent party to be required to perform his obligations under the contract. A total breach may be constituted by a series of breaches, no one of which by itself is total. A well-known example of such a situation occurs in instalment contracts. Another example is furnished by *Pollock & Co.* v. *Macrae*,[18] where on a sale of marine engines there were a number of defects, each of which singly would have constituted

---

[16] See *per* Lord Reid in *Gollins* v. *Gollins* [1963] 2 All E.R. 966, 973 F: " we base ourselves on a fiction and that is bound to lead to trouble."

[17] Treitel states: " Although the two phrases ' fundamental breach ' and ' breach of a fundamental term ' are used indiscriminately, the two concepts appear to be distinct." *Law of Contract* (1962) p. 148. Treitel also has a concept (see p. 144) of " acting outside the contract ": this, however, is not a distinct concept: he himself relates it to " the true construction of the contract."

A valuable article on " Warranty, Condition and Fundamental Term " by Reynolds (1963) 79 L.Q.R. 534 has appeared after this article was written. He adopts the view opposed to that of Treitel and myself, but in accordance with Lord Denning, in thinking that there is but one doctrine of fundamental breach; the differences of language do not preclude a unity of doctrine (see particularly note 59). However, he has produced no arguments which have been able to convince me that the view contended for in the text of this article is incorrect. It is noteworthy that counsel in the *Charterhouse* case has considered that " fundamental breach " is inapt to describe the true doctrine. " As a matter of terminology it is more correct to speak of a fundamental condition rather than a fundamental breach " [1963] 2 Q.B. at p. 697.

[18] 1922 S.C. (H.L.) 192.

a breach covered by an exemption clause. Lord Dunedin said there was, however, "such a congeries of defects [as] amounts to a total breach of contract." [19] The translation from "total" to "fundamental" is shown by the *Apps*[6] case, in which reliance was placed on Lord Dunedin's speech. Holroyd Pearce L.J. speaks of "an accumulation of defects which, taken singly, might well be within an exception clause, but which, taken *en masse*, constitute such a non-performance, or repudiation, or breach going to the root of the contract, as disentitles a party to take refuge behind an exception clause."[20] Harman L.J. cited *Pollock & Co.* v. *Macrae*[18] when describing the situation in *Apps*[6] case as one of "fundamental breach." [21] The use of "fundamental breach" as the equivalent of total breach is of course older than the *Apps*[6] case. It is to be found in *The Albion*,[22] where the question is discussed whether two breaches of specific terms together constitute a fundamental breach.

The equivalence of "fundamental breach" with "total breach" may be further asserted by noting that the identical test has been suggested for both, *viz.*, whether the breach goes to the root of the contract. This was the test of "total breach" which was considered as well established by Lord Macmillan in *Heyman* v. *Darwin's Ltd.*[23] It is the test for fundamental breach propounded by Denning L.J. in *Karsales (Harrow), Ltd.* v. *Wallis.*[24] The main reason for considering the different phrases to refer to identical concepts is, however, that whatever term is used the notion involved is that of a breach which makes it unjust to require the innocent party to perform his promises. The guilty party cannot reprobate the contract so far as performance of his obligations is concerned, but approbate it when performance of the innocent party's obligation is concerned. This rationale prevents the guilty party from relying on an exemption clause in the contract.

The notion of a "fundamental term" as opposed to fundamental breach is derived from the actual agreement of the parties as to the obligations to be performed, not from a judicial evaluation of the character and effect of non-performance. The parties themselves show that they regard particular terms as so fundamental that without them there is a basic difference in identity. Thus a contract of sale or hire of goods will contain a promise to deliver and accept goods conforming to certain basic characteristics which determine the identity of the

---

[19] The buyer was in consequence held to be entitled to compensation notwithstanding the exemption clause. The case furnishes an early example of the modern practice whereby a so-called guarantee operates as an exemption clause for the benefit of the seller.

[20] [1961] 2 All E.R. at pp. 289 I and 290 A.

[21] *Ibid.* 292 C. Both Holroyd Pearce and Harman L.JJ. speak also of there having been a "breach of a fundamental condition."

[22] [1953] 1 W.L.R. 102; [1953] 2 All E.R. 679. Somervell L.J. speaks as if he considers a question of fundamental breach as equivalent to the breach of an implied fundamental term: p. 683 G.

[23] [1942] A.C. 356, 373.

[24] [1956] 2 All E.R. at 869 C.

contract;[25] delivery of goods without those characteristics cannot be classified as a mode of performance or malperformance, but is outside the scope of performance. There is no need for any inquiry into the quantum or substantiality of a breach of a fundamental term: one asks merely whether there was conformity or not with the required characteristics. The classical example of a fundamental term is the contract to sell peas of Lord Abinger's dictum in *Chanter* v. *Hopkins.*[25a] If the seller who promises to sell peas sends beans, he has exceeded the scope of the contract. The buyer has promised to accept peas, and because of this fundamental term is under no obligation to accept beans. The absence of a buyer's obligation to accept beans is not dependent on any release by reason of the consequence of a breach by the seller: it arises from an initial absence in the contract of any obligation to accept beans. So too the reason why an exemption clause cannot be relied on where there has been the breach of a fundamental term is that the content of the clause does not include the situation of the breach of a fundamental term. It is a question of construction of the contract, not of reparation for its breach.[26]

The view that we should employ two different concepts signified by the phrases " fundamental breach " and " breach of a fundamental term " is not in accordance with the dictum of Lord Denning in *Karsales (Harrow) Ltd.* v. *Wallis*[24] which was cited with approval in the *Charterhouse* case.[1] He said: " The principle is sometimes said to be that the party cannot rely on an exempting clause when he delivers something ' different in kind ' from that contracted for, or has broken a ' fundamental term ' or a fundamental contractual obligation. However, I think that a breach which goes to the root of the contract disentitles the party from relying on the exempting clause."[27] The remaining sections of this part, however, will show that a more reliable chart for the journey of judicial exploration will show not one stream for the submersion of exemption clauses but an estuary in which two different streams may be traced.

---

[25] In (1937) 15 Can.B.R. 764. I suggested the use of the concept of *definition* of contract goods; such a concept serves to distinguish fundamental terms from other terms of a contract of sale or hire.

[25a] (1838) 4 M. & W. 399, 404 : " .... as if a man offers to buy peas of another, and he sends him beans, he does not perform his contract ; but that is not a warranty that he should sell him peas; the contract is to sell peas, and if he sends him anything else in their stead, it is a non-performance of it."

[26] In *The Albion* [1953] 2 All E.R. 679, a claim that an exception clause did not apply was not accepted by the court. The reasoning of the judgment of the court, delivered by Somervell L.J., was based on (a) the absence of fundamental breach; (b) the construction of the exemption clause. Reference is made to an argument treating fundamental breach as breach of an implied term (683 G).

[27] [1956] 2 All E.R. at p. 869 C. The language of "fundamental breach " was used in the Judicial Committee of the Privy Council in *Boshali* v. *Allied Commercial Exporters Ltd.* (1961) 105 S.J. 987, where the opinion of the Board (Lords Hodson, Guest and Devlin) was delivered by Lord Guest. It is also the language of Willmer L.J. in *Handley* v. *Marston* (1962) 106 S.J. 327.

Repudiation

One ambiguity of the word " repudiation " is well known. It is that in which, speaking generally, repudiation sometimes has the meaning of manifestation of intention not to perform and sometimes has the meaning of rescission. Lord Macmillan in *Heyman* v. *Darwin's, Ltd.*[28] distinguished the two meanings by saying that one was " a refusal by one of the parties to perform his obligations under the contract," and the other " putting an end to the contract." While such formulae are sufficient to describe the distinction they are not adequate to bring out the full significance of each type of " repudiation." If we consider first what kind of rescission constitutes " repudiation " in the second sense we may see how the ambiguity arises. The two meanings of repudiation are related: repudiation in the second sense is the name given to rescission which may be effected by the innocent party where there has been repudiation in the first sense by the other party. The general principle that there cannot be a unilateral termination of a contract is subject to exceptions and does not apply where there is a provision in the contract, or where there is a specific rule of law, conferring such a power on one party. There is a rule of law that where there has been " repudiation " by one party then the other party can rescind. This type of rescission has come to be called also repudiation. Nienaber has described the manner in which the courts attached such a power to rescind to the situation of anticipatory repudiation by treating that situation as an offer to rescind.[29] Perhaps this contributed to the lack of a clear distinction between repudiation and rescission. But the major cause of the present ambiguity lies in Chalmers' draftsmanship of the Sale of Goods Act, 1893. It will be recalled that section 11 provides that " the buyer . . . may elect to treat the breach of such condition as a breach of warranty and not as a ground for treating the contract as repudiated." In attempting a literal construction one asks (a) who has repudiated, and (b) what does repudiation mean? Though the general sense is that the buyer may elect to treat the contract as terminated no clear answer to either question appears. The result of this lack of clarity is the emergence of repudiation as equivalent to rescission.

The judgments in the *Charterhouse* case[1] illustrate the ambiguity of the term. Donovan L.J. reports the county court judge as saying that " the finance company [the plaintiffs] had repudiated the contract," while Ormerod L.J. reports the judge as speaking of " a fundamental breach entitling the defendant to repudiate or rescind." Upjohn L.J. repeats the language of the Sale of Goods Act, and says the judge

---

[28] [1942] A.C. at p. 373.

[29] " The effect of Anticipatory Repudiation " [1962] C.L.J. 213, an article based on *White & Carter Ltd.* v. *McGregor* [1962] A.C. 413; [1961] 3 All E.R. 1178, hereafter called *McGregor's* case.

spoke of " a fundamental breach entitling the hirer to treat the contract as repudiated."

A more significant question than that concerned with the character of repudiation in the sense of rescission is that concerned with the use of the word in connection with refusal to perform. That use at present is neither precise nor consistent. One can discern the development in the nineteenth century of a particular concept for which the term was used as a designation. This was allied with, if not identical with, that of total breach. It is the manifestation of an intention by the repudiator not to perform the entirety of his obligations. This is the concept referred to by Lord Macmillan when he speaks of " a refusal . . . to perform his obligations under the contract," [30] and by Lord Reid when he speaks of a " refusal to carry out his part of the contract." [31] It is repudiation of this kind which gives the other party a power of rescission. There are two elements in the concept: (i) repudiation is distinct from mere non-performance, though non-performance may be the mode of manifestation of the intention;[32] (ii) repudiation must be of " total " performance:[33] a refusal to perform a single promise will not constitute repudiation, nor will a willingness to perform a single promise negative repudiation: unless the single promise by itself relates to a substantial part of the promised performance,[34] which involves the

---

[30] *Heyman* v. *Darwin's Ltd.* [1942] A.C. at p. 373. In this passage Lord Macmillan equates repudiation with total breach. Dealing with the effect of repudiation he says: " The contract stands, but one of the parties declined to fulfil his part of it. There has been what is called a total breach or breach going to the root of the contract, and this relieves the other party of any further obligation to perform what he has for his part undertaken."

[31] *McGregor's Case* [1961] 3 All E.R. at p. 1181 C.

[32] Nienaber ([1962] C.L.J. p. 224, note 61) employs the word repudiation to denote the concept described in the above text. He speaks of " anticipatory repudiation " not only to distinguish repudiation before the time for performance has arrived from repudiation at or after that time, but also to distinguish repudiation from " actual breach "—the breach of a promise. Repudiation for him is not the breach of a promise. He assumes that promises are undertakings to act or forbear: and that a breach of promise is a failure to carry out the undertaking. He refers to Lord Wrenbury's analysis of " anticipatory breach " in *Bradley* v. *Newson Sons & Co.* [1919] A.C. 16, 53. There Lord Wrenbury said: " He is recalling or repudiating his promise, and that is wrongful. His breach is a breach of a presently binding promise, not an anticipatory breach of an act to be done in the future." This restates the doctrine *solvendum in futuro, debitum in praesenti.* But repudiation of a promise is different from failure to carry out the undertaking in a promise: and to call both by a single name may produce confusion : *Sane commodius erat singulas causas singulis appellationibus distingui.* Nienaber uses the phrase " breach of contract " to cover both breach of promise and repudiation. It is clearer to say that damages may be obtained both for breach of promise and for repudiation. We still lack a clear analysis and a consistent terminology for elementary contractual notions. Nienaber is, of course, justified by judicial usage: thus Lord Keith in *McGregor's* case said: " Repudiation is nothing but a breach of contract " (1187 G).

[33] Hence the often made equation of " total breach " with " repudiation." " Total breach," of course, usually manifests an intention not to perform, and since objective considerations dominate in our law of contract when there is " total breach " there will normally be " repudiation." But there may be circumstances in which the breach does not manifest an intention not to perform. Nienaber rightly distinguishes repudiation from other breaches of contract by pointing out that " repudiation alone is ever said to be entirely a matter of intention." [1962] C.L.J. 223, citing *Freeth* v. *Burr* (1874) L.R. 9 C.P. 208; *Consorzio Veneziano di Armamento* v. *Northumberland Shipping Co. Ltd.* (1919) 88 L.J.K.B. 1194.

[34] The phrase is Nienaber's, used by him to indicate another characteristic for distinguishing repudiation from other breaches of contract. He cites *Johnstone* v. *Milling* (1886) 16 Q.B.D. 460; *Re Rubel Bronze Co. Ltd. & Vos* [1918] 1 K.B. 315.

notion of a fundamental term. There is wanting, however, a specifically and fully authoritative statement of such a concept, and of its relation with " total breach," " fundamental breach " and " breach of a fundamental term." Two factors may be mentioned as contributing to the present obscurity attached to the use of the term " repudiation ". (i) The emergence of the doctrine that anticipatory repudiation constituted a breach of contract for which damages could be immediately recovered diverted attention from the situation where repudiation was connected with a breach committed after the time for performance had arrived. (ii) The Sale of Goods Act linked " repudiation " with the breach of a single term—a " condition ". Judges have only recently realised the inadequacy of Chalmers' dichotomy of contractual terms into " conditions " and " warranties ", and have yet to realise that " repudiation ", as the term designated for giving effect to the contractual provisions for the consequence of non-performance, refers to a different concept from that which denotes the situation under which a judicial remedy of rescission is imposed for a refusal to perform contractual obligations. At present the word " repudiation " is used in connection with four different situations: (i) the manifestation of an intention not to perform the entirety of the repudiator's obligations; (ii) total breach; (iii) the breach of a Sale of Goods Act " condition "; (iv) the breach of a fundamental term. There is need for further analysis and discrimination, which would be assisted by changes in terminology.

Affirmation of contract after repudiation

It will be recalled that in the *Charterhouse* case[1] the borrower did not return the car on discovering that it had a defective back axle, but instead expressed his willingness to repair it and entered into negotiations about the time for payment of instalments.[35] The county court judge categorised this situation in a manner variously stated in the Court of Appeal. Donovan L.J. said: " the hirer elected to treat the contract as still on foot." Ormerod L.J. said: " the hirer did not repudiate . . . the hirer chose to treat the contract as still in being." Upjohn L.J. said: " the hirer did not treat the contract as repudiated but affirmed it." [36] The Lords Justices moreover agreed with these findings, which Ormerod L.J. said: " involved questions of mixed law and fact." Indeed there was no appeal against them. Nevertheless it is submitted that this mode of categorising the " brute " facts is unsatisfactory. Is it not at least inelegant to say that though there has been a breach of a fundamental term (or a fundamental breach), so that what is performed is fundamentally different from what was promised,

---

[35] There is no suggestion that there was a bargain with consideration, and that the borrower was offering to repair in return for the postponement of payment of instalments.

[36] See [1963] 2 All E.R. at pp. 437 B, 444 G, 441 E.

nevertheless the contract may be affirmed and still subsist? An example given by Upjohn L.J. makes this self-contradiction still more apparent. " Suppose the lender contracts to hire a tractor to a farmer and in purported performance of that contract delivers, not a tractor, but three fine Suffolk punches which take the fancy and for which he can find a use." The resulting situation he described as one of " the farmer's affirming the contract and accepting these horses in lieu of the tractor." [37] The purpose of the illustration was to show that despite the " affirmation " the farmer could not be bound by an exemption clause and could obtain compensation for taking the horses in lieu of a tractor. The conclusion is just, but the reasoning which assumes that the lender's and the farmer's actions can be related to a contract for the hire of a tractor is surely unsound. The farmer has entered into a new contract for the hire of horses, he has not affirmed a contract for the hire of a tractor.[38] Where a seller contracts to sell peas but delivers beans the buyer who retains the beans enters into a new contract for the sale of beans. The rights and duties under the new contract depend upon its terms which are derived from the circumstances. Those circumstances may vary. For example, if the seller manifests in intention that the new contract should contain the same terms as the old apart from the substitution of beans for peas, then the new contract will incorporate terms of the old. But if the seller manifests no such intention, then the terms of the new contract may have to be stated in terms of reasonableness. In *Gabriel Wade & English* v. *Arcos* [39] Acton J. in dealing with a delivery of goods different in kind from those bargained for said: " The sellers were in effect offering to the buyers a new contract which the buyers accepted, and the new contract was to sell to the buyers . . . in circumstances which made it plain that both the buyer and the seller knew perfectly well these facts. Directly the buyer had accepted these goods and the contract, there was a performance of the new contract which had sprung into being between these parties." He rejected a claim by the buyers for the difference between the original contract price, which they had paid, and the market value of the goods delivered. He took the view that the price under the new contract was identical with that under the old contract. But this is a finding of fact. There is authority for the view that the price under the new contract may be equal to the market value of the actual goods delivered—the reasonable price.[40]

---

[37] At p. 442 E.
[38] The doctrine of *Morris* v. *Baron* [1918] A.C. 1, and *British and Beningtons* v. *N.W. Cachar Tea Co.* [1923] A.C. 48, avers that for the purpose of s. 4 of the Sale of Goods Act [repealed by Law Reform (Enforcement of Contracts) Act, 1954 (Ed.)] an alteration of a contract does not necessarily constitute the entering into a new contract in substitution for the old contract, but may constitute a mere variation. But this doctrine does not apply where the alteration is fundamental.
[39] (1929) 34 Ll.L.R. 306.
[40] *Lomi* v. *Tucker* (1829) 4 C. & P. 15; *Okell* v. *Smith* (1815) 1 St.N.P. 107.

Upjohn L.J. attached importance to the hirer delivering the horses " in purported performance of the contract." It was this which entitled the farmer to retain them as a borrower. The implication appears to be that where the delivery is clearly a mistake then the farmer could not retain the horses. This is right for the reason that in those circumstances there would be no manifestation of a new offer.[41] But, of course, an express declaration of intention is not required. It is sufficient if there is a reasonable belief by the acceptor that a new offer has been made.[42] The extent to which rights and duties under the old contract are terminated by the delivery of the wrong goods again depends on the circumstances. The buyer who has received beans may remain entitled to receive peas though he has " accepted " the beans. He may in an appropriate case be entitled to damages for non-delivery of the peas and bound only to pay the market price for the beans.

The view expressed in the *Charterhouse* case,[1] that the original contract alone subsisted was based on an application of the principles relevant to anticipatory repudiation. In accordance with current terminology the judges described the action of the finance company as one of repudiation, and assumed that all types of repudiation were governed by the same rules. In the case of anticipatory repudiation where the innocent party does not exercise his power of rescission of course the original contract subsists. There has been no offer of a new contract. The guilty party cannot by his refusal to perform put an end to the contract. It is still possible for there to be complete performance of the acts and forbearances originally promised. The innocent party may most aptly be said to affirm the contract by refusing to rescind, and that language has often been used by judges. Difficulties, however, exist in the description of the consequences of anticipatory repudiation. Where the innocent party affirms the contract does he thereby deprive the repudiation of all effect? If the repudiation is a " breach of the contract " then, according to general principle, consideration is required for the termination of the guilty party's liability. Liability for breach cannot be unilaterally " waived " by the innocent party. This appears to be the significance of Lord Keith's dictum: " a repudiation can never be said to be accepted by the other party except in the sense that he acquiesces in it and does not propose to take any action." [43] On the other hand we have Lord Asquith's " graphic

---

[41] If " in purported performance " meant that the hire of the horses was to be on the same terms as the hire of the tractor, then the exception clause would be introduced into the new contract. The *Charterhouse* case could have been decided on the basis that the new contract did not contain an exception clause.

[42] Nienaber points out that plaintiffs used to plead both a failure to perform and a refusal to perform. The breach, as he says, was the failure, but by pleading a refusal it was made clear that the failure was no mistake.

[43] *McGregor's* case at p. 1187 G.

phrase," " an unaccepted repudiation is a thing writ in water."[44] Lord Keith's dictum criticises the established terminology whereby the innocent party who rescinds is said to " accept " the repudiation. This language is derived from the now obsolete doctrine that repudiation operated as an offer to rescind, so that the innocent party could effect rescission by accepting the offer. The contract was thus discharged by agreement.[45]

Difficulties are not confined to the situation where the innocent party does not rescind. If he " accepts the repudiation " he does not thereby make the contract one " writ in water ". *Hochster* v. *De la Tour*[45a] established that he may sue for breach. Lord Macmillan described this by saying : " The contract stands . . . for the wronged party still has his action for damages under the contract which has been broken, and the contract provides the measure of those damages."[46] However, the general view must be right that the contract is rescinded : one may sue for breach of a contract which has terminated. Theoretically one would ask why cannot the innocent party, while affirming the contract, still claim damages for repudiation. If repudiation is a breach the innocent party is entitled to nominal damages at least: and in some circumstances he may suffer substantial damages even if the guilty party were subsequently to perform.[47]

However, whatever the precise rules may be governing anticipatory repudiation, the problem is whether they should apply also to other situations where the term " repudiation " has been applied. It is submitted that to assume they do is to commit what Hancock has called " the fallacy of the transferred concept ".[48] In particular it is submitted that where the breach of a fundamental term is committed by the delivery of goods different in kind from those designated in the contract, the retention of the goods should not automatically be designated as affirmation of the contract.

---

[44] The description " graphic phrase " is Lord Keith's in *McGregor's* case. The phrase is from the judgment of Asquith L.J. in *Howard* v. *Pickford Tool Co.* [1951] 1 K.B. 417. The principle is expressed less figuratively by Lord Evershed (at p. 420): " if the conduct of one party amounts to a repudiation, and the other party does not accept it as such, but goes on performing his part of the contract and affirms the contract, the alleged act of repudiation is wholly nugatory and ineffective in law."

[45] Nienaber regards the development of the doctrine that the innocent party could sue for a breach as inconsistent with the doctrine of an offer to rescind. [1962] C.L.J. at p. 220 *et seq.* But the older doctrine survives not only in the language of acceptance of repudiation, but also in many judicial dicta.

[45a] [(1853) 2 *E.* v. *B.* 678. Ed.]

[46] *Heyman* v. *Darwin's Ltd.* [1942] A.C. at p. 373.

[47] The following situation may be envisaged. A seller of goods to be delivered at a future date announces he will not deliver. The buyer says he will require delivery, but to safeguard himself against the possibility of the seller's non-delivery, he enters into a contract with another merchant for delivery of similar goods at the due date with power to cancel on payment of £x if the seller delivers. The seller delivers, the buyer cancels and pays the other merchant the £x. If the substituted contract is reasonable cannot the buyer claim the £x as damages for the unaccepted repudiation?

[48] 37 Can.B.R. 535 (1959).

M

Fundamental terms and conditions

As has already been stated, one cause of the indiscriminate use of the word " repudiation " is to be found in the Sale of Goods Act, 1893. In section 11 the term " repudiated " is applied to the breach of what the Act calls a " condition ". The contention contained in the last section is that the repudiation consisting in a refusal to perform a contract should be distinguished from other situations to which the term has been applied. The present contention is that the language of the Sale of Goods Act is particularly inapt in making the term applicable to the entirety of a contract. That language contributes also to the failure to realise the precise significance of a fundamental term. In this respect, however, it is equally important to consider the manner in which the word " condition " is used in the Act.

The terminology of the Act provides a simple dichotomy of contractual terms into " conditions " and " warranties ". This classification has been judicially considered to be inadequate. Specific condemnation is to be found in the judgments in *Hong Kong Fir Co., Ltd.* v. *Kawasaki Kisen Kaisha Ltd.*[49] Diplock L.J. commented on " treating all contractual undertakings as falling into one of two separate categories: ' conditions ', the breach of which gives rise to an event which relieves the party not in default of further performance of his obligations, and ' warranties ', the breach of which does not give rise to such an event." He says, " Lawyers tend to speak of this classification as if it were comprehensive . . . But it is by no means true of contractual undertakings in general at common law."[50]   He regarded the dichotomy as limited to the statutory implied terms in contracts for the sale of goods. Upjohn L.J. also spoke of the inadequacy of the classification,[51] and in the *Astley* case he again " pointed out the danger of using the words ' condition ' and ' warranty ' except under the Sale of Goods Act, 1893 ".[52]   It is not quite clear what these interesting suggestions precisely are. Are the words " condition " and " warranty " to be confined in their use to discussions of Sale of Goods Act applications? And for such discussion are those words to be used exclusively? Or are we merely to recognise that the words have a special meaning in the Sale of Goods Act, so that we can use them with other meanings both in other contexts and in discussing problems of sale of goods? In such latter discussions we shall have to make clear when " condition " is used in the Sale of Goods Act sense, and when it is used in what will be its more general sense. At present a Sale of Goods Act meaning colours most uses of the word. There can be little doubt that the draftsman of the Act thought that he was giving statutory precision to an existing

---

[49] [1962] 2 Q.B. 26; [1962] 1 All E.R. 474. This case will hereafter be called the *Hong Kong* case.

[50] At p. 487 D.

[51] At p. 483 D.

[52] [1963] 2 All E.R. at p. 46 I.

terminology. The better way to deal with the inadequacies of that terminology is to repeal the Act and to re-enact its substance in other language.

In the *Hong Kong* case[49] the court drew attention to a class of " contractual undertaking . . . which cannot be categorised as ' conditions ' or ' warranties ' if the late nineteenth century meaning adopted in the Sale of Goods Act, 1893, . . . be given to these terms. Of such undertakings all that can be predicated is that some breaches will, and others will not, give rise to an event which will deprive the party not in default of substantially the whole benefit which it was intended that he should obtain from the contract: and the legal consequences of the breach of such an undertaking, unless provided for expressly in the contract, depend on the nature of the event to which the breach gives rise and do not follow automatically from a prior classification of the undertaking as a ' condition ' or ' warranty '."[53] The shipowner's promise to provide a seaworthy ship was classified as such an undertaking. The basic notion underlying the dictum is that of the judicial determination of a remedy for a breach as opposed to the parties' own contractual regulation of action to be performed in stipulated circumstances. Moreover, the notion appears to be indentical with that of " total breach " unless a distinction can be drawn between deprivation of substantially the whole benefit the other party is to receive and non-performance of substantially the entirety of the guilty party's obligations.

The *Hong Kong* case did not consider the relation of " fundamental terms " to " conditions " under the Sale of Goods Act. The reasoning in the dictum of Diplock L.J. is, however, in accordance with the view that there is a basic distinction between a " fundamental term " and a " fundamental breach ". The legal consequences of the breach of a fundamental term follow automatically from the contractual character of the term, while the notion of fundamental breach is that of a judicial determination of consequences dependent on the character of the breach. But every " condition " of the Sale of Goods Act is not a fundamental term according to Devlin J. in *Smeaton Hanscomb* v. *Sassoon I. Setty.*[8] He said : " a fundamental term . . . must be something narrower than a condition ".[54] His reasoning was that exemption clauses would embrace " conditions " though " fundamental terms " were not covered by them. He did not, however, venture upon an examination of the distinction, although he stated: " I do not think what is a fundamental term has ever been closely defined ". But an explanation of the difference between fundamental terms and " conditions " is available in the juristic criticism which Williston had

---

[53] *Per* Diplock L.J. in the *Hong Kong* case at p. 487 H.

[54] [1953] 2 All E.R. at 1473 C. In the *Apps* case Davies L.J. said: " Not every breach of condition, not every sort of unfitness would amount to a breach of what has been called the fundamental condition " [1961] 2 All E.R. at p. 292 H.

propounded of the terminology of the Sale of Goods Act.[55] This involves the entire abandonment of that terminology: a task carried out in the American Restatement of Contract and the Uniform Commercial Code.

Williston's criticism is not directed to the inadequacy of a dichotomy of contractual terms into "conditions" and "warranties" because it does not provide a broad enough spectrum of contractual colours. It is far more fundamental. It is an attack on the manner in which the word "conditions" is used because it confuses promises, the constituent elements of contracts, with matters which are not promises at all. The word "condition" has a well recognised use in legal language for the designation of clauses in legal documents which are not promises, as witness the learning with regard to estates in the law of real property. Recent cases have drawn attention to the distinction between "covenants" and "conditions" in leases of land.[56] Moreover, the word "condition" has also been applied to "facts" as opposed to legal clauses. Diplock L.J. in the *Hong Kong* case[49] stresses that in relation to "dependent covenants" in the law of contracts it was really the event resulting from the breach which relieved the other party of further performance of his obligations. Diplock L.J. made this comment in reference to Lord Mansfield's language in *Boone* v. *Eyre*,[56a] in which the mutual covenants are described as "conditions". In effect he is saying that it would be better to describe the event—the consequences of the breach—as a "condition" rather than the covenant or promises, whose breach is the basis of the event. This is indeed the substance of Williston's remarks. He rejects Chalmers' view that, "In conveyancing a distinction was drawn between 'conditions' and 'covenants' which, in contracts, has now become obliterated."[57] On

---

[55] This criticism enables one to state the nature of a fundamental term as opposed to a condition. I have ventured in 15 Can.B.R. at p. 264 (1937) to describe the nature of "the definition of contract goods"—the subject-matter of what is now called the fundamental terms of such a contract. Stoljar's criticism in (1951) 15 M.L.R. at p. 443 appears to me to be misconceived. He appears to be asking for a "closed definition" having the character of the precise terms of a medical prescription. No criterion is to be expected which will enable a mechanical judgment to be performed. Stoljar's own use of the epistemological distinction between "knowledge by acquaintance" and "knowledge by description" seems to me more adapted to a psychological study of learning by an individual than a legal study of transactions. We cannot in the latter study usefully draw a distinction between "knowledge of things" and "knowledge of *truths* about things." The basic problem is what is the "thing" which is the subject-matter of the transaction.

[56] See *infra*, p. 176 and notes 64 and 65.

[56a] [(1779) 1 Hy. Bl. 273n. Ed.]

[57] This statement in Appendix II, note II, to Chalmers' *Sale of Goods Act*, 1893, follows upon a definition of condition which corresponds with the "conveyancing" distinction, *i.e.*, the definition in the American Restatement based on the work of Williston and Corbin, and which is inconsistent with the use of the word in the Act where it applies to one of two kinds of "contractual undertakings." In this note Chalmers also says: "Though the Act uses the term condition, it does not define it. The definition belongs to the general law of contract" (a passage not cited by Diplock and Upjohn L.JJ.). The definition in this note is: "The term 'condition' as applied to contracts appears to mean indifferently (a) an uncertain event on the happening of which the obligation of the contract is to depend, and (b) the stipulation in the contract making its obligations depend on the happening of the event." This definition by use of the phrase "the obligations of the contract" obscures the fact that one, some, or all of the obligations in a contract may be dependent on a condition.

the contrary he says: " The distinction between a promise or covenant
on the one hand and a condition on the other, both in their legal effect
and in their wording, is obvious and familiar ", and he adds: " The
difference between conditions and promises is so radical in its consequences that there is no excuse for a nomenclature which fails to
recognise the distinction. In the English books there has sprung up an
astonishing usage of the word ' condition ' in the law of sales as meaning
a certain kind of promise. . . . It cannot be too strongly deprecated."[58]
Corbin's strictures on the use of " condition " to denote a type of
promise are no less trenchant: his description of a condition has often
been judicially approved to the United States.[59]

" Promise and conditions are very clearly different in character.
One who makes a promise thereby expresses an intention that some
future performance will be rendered . . . A promise in a contract
creates a legal duty in the promisor and a right in the promisee; the
fact or event constituting a condition creates no right or duty and is
merely a limiting or modifying factor."[60]

My language has been: " A promise is an undertaking to act or
forbear in some specified way in the future. The promisor is under a
duty to act or forebear: the promisee has a right to the act or forbearance. A condition states the event on the happening of which the
promisor has the choice of not acting or forbearing."[61] It does not
impose any duty on the promisor or promisee. The event may indeed
be the performance by the promisee of some act. But unless that act,
in addition to being the subject-matter of the condition annexed to the
promise of the promisor, is also the subject matter of a promise by the
promisee, the promisee is under no duty to perform the act and the
promisor has no right to performance of the act. What the promisor
has, in the event of non-performance, is a " right " not to perform the
undertaking contained in his own promise.[62]

The cancellation clause in a charterparty is an illustration of a
condition involving an act to be performed by a party who does not
promise to perform it. The shipowner undertakes to sail to a particular
port and the charterer undertakes to load a cargo when the ship arrives.
But there may also be a clause providing that if the ship is not at a
specified point by a stipulated date the charterer may cancel the

---

[58] See Art. 665, *Williston on Contract* (1936) 2nd edn. Vol. 3 p. 1911 (unaltered from
1st edn.).

[59] *e.g., Lach* v. *Cahill*, 85 Atl. (2nd) 481.

[60] Corbin, *Contracts,* (1951) Vol. 3, p. 521; (1953) One Vol. ed., p. 592.

[61] 15 Can.B.R. 311, p. 312 (1937). I drew a distinction between limitations and
conditions. This has not yet been the subject of judicial consideration.

[62] It is convenient to distinguish between the condition annexed to a promise and the
promise: but such a separation overlooks the essential unity of promise and condition.
The promisor promises to act in specified circumstances—the condition is part of the specification. It will be noted that since we are considering contractual terms we are using the
word " condition " to refer not to the event specified but to the clause specifying the event.

charter. The charterer's promise to load is modified by the condition of the cancelling clause. The shipowner is not in breach if the ship does not arrive at the specified point on time. No rights or duties arise from the cancelling clause except the charterer's " right " to cancel.[63]

The recent cases in which the distinction between promise and condition was drawn were Privy Council cases; one was concerned with the sale and the other with the lease of land. In *Aberfoyle Plantations, Ltd.* v. *Cheng*[64] a contract for the sale of a rubber plantation contained a clause : " The purchase is conditional on the vendor obtaining a renewal of the seven leases described in the schedule hereto." The Board held that the clause contained no promise, only a condition. In *Bashi* v. *Commissioner of Lands*[65] the Board had to consider whether provisions in a building lease requiring an hotel to be built were " covenants " within the meaning of a Crown Lands Ordinance, though in the lease they were described as " building conditions ". The Board drew a distinction between covenants and conditions, but held that the building provisions embodied both a promise to build and a condition of the lease: and constituted " covenants " within the meaning of the Ordinance.

A fundamental term is a promise and not a " condition " in the strict sense as used in the American Statement of Contract, or in the recent Privy Council cases. Of course, judicial usage describing fundamental terms as " fundamental conditions "[66] has in mind the wider meaning of " condition " in the Sale of Goods Act; and clearly a fundamental term confers rights and imposes duties. Yet the specific character of a fundamental term is obscured by the Sale of Goods Act

---

[63] In *Nelson* v. *Dundee East Coast Shipping Co.*, 1907 S.C. 927, where the provision in the cancellation clause referred to non-arrival of the ship at the port of loading within seven days of her expected readiness, Lord McLaren said (at p. 934): " If it could be shown that the shipowners have used their best endeavour and that the delay was due to unavoidable accident or perils of the sea, I should be of opinion that no damages were due. The contract would be cancelled, but damages would not be due." The shipowners had not sent the ship to the port of loading, but had chartered it to other charterers. This was the breach of a promise to which no condition was annexed. The cancellation clause constitutes a condition annexed to the charterers' obligation to load. This is clearly stated in the judgment of Kennedy, L.J. in *Moel Tryvan Ship Co.* v. *Andrew Weir* [1910] 2 K.B. 844, 856, where a similar cancellation clause was contained in the charter-party. He said that the shipowner's right " is to have the ship loaded by the charterers after her arrival at the loading port as and with the cargo, and within the time fixed by the charterparty, subject always to a stipulated risk of defeasance, namely that if the ship's arrival is delayed beyond an agreed date the charterers' obligation to load ceases to be enforceable against them. In that case they may load the ship as they please. I seek in vain for any words in the cancelling clause . . . which entitles the shipowner to say that the charterers are not to have the full benefit of the undertaking of the shipowners that the ship shall proceed to the port of loading because she failed to get there at the named date."

[64] [1960] A.C. 115; [1959] 3 W.L.R. 1011; [1959] 3 All E.R. 1910, noted (1960) 23 M.L.R. 434. The Board relied on *Re Sandwell Park Colliery* [1929] 1 Ch. 277, in which Maugham J. said: " There is no promise or undertaking by the vendor that the condition will be fulfilled." In this case, however, the " condition " was not an act to be performed by the vendor.

[65] [1960] A.C. 44; [1960] 1 All E.R. 117; noted (1960) 23 M.L.R. 550.

[66] *e.g.*, in the *Apps* case, Holroyd Pearce L.J. at [1961] 2 All E.R. 289 I, Harman L.J. at 291 I, Donovan L.J. at 292 H: in the *Astley Case* [1963] 2 All E.R. Pearson L.J. at 44 G.

usage.[67] The mere fact that the " conditions " of the Sale of Goods Act include many promises which are not fundamental, does not by itself produce confusion in this context, for the phrase "fundamental conditions" makes the required distinction. What is needed is an explicit statement of the characteristics of non-fundamental " conditions ", and none seems to be available. It is true that we know that they are embraced by exemption and rejection [68] clauses, but this is merely the converse of saying that fundamental terms are not so embraced. Judicial consideration of the distinction between " condition " and " warranty " has produced the criterion of " going to the root of the contract " which is difficult to distinguish from the concept of "fundamental." [69] The handicap of the Sale of Goods Act terminology makes it unlikely that clarity can be obtained. What appears to be significant is the recognition (a) of the possibility of a " condition " affecting only some of the promises of the other party, and " some " includes one, (b) that specific evidence is required of the annexation of the requirement of performance to the promises of the other party. In the case of breach of a fundamental term all the promises of the other party are necessarily affected, and the other party's promises are affected without the need of any specific annexation of a requirement of performance of the fundamental term.

A party who has promised to accept peas is not discharged from his obligation when beans are delivered because his promise was subject to a requirement that peas be delivered: he simply is in no position to accept peas. It is otherwise when a contract for peas provides they be of a particular species. Here if the species is not fundamental to the contract, a right of rejection depends on the specific annexation to the promise to accept peas of a " condition " of performance of the " condition " to deliver peas of that species. It follows from what has been said above that there may be no promise to deliver peas, and yet there may be a condition (*stricto sensu*), annexed to the buyer's promise to accept, that the peas be of the particular species. The buyer in such a case has the right of rejection but no claim to damages if different peas are delivered. If, however, there is a promise to deliver peas of a particular species and performance is a condition (*stricto sensu*) of the buyer's promise he may both reject different peas *and* claim damages for breach of promise.

---

[67] Confusion is increased by the provision of s. 13 that in sale by description there is an " implied condition that the goods shall correspond with the description." Not all " description " is fundamental.

[68] Recent discussion has been concerned with exemption clauses. But the operation of rejection clauses is also relevant. A usual type of rejection clause is: " Buyers shall not reject the goods herein specified but shall accept or pay for them in terms of contract." An exemption clause prevents a " specification " from having any contractual effect; a rejection clause prevents it operating as a condition. See (1937) 15 Can.B.R. at p. 780 *et seq.*

[69] Wedderburn [1957] C.L.J. 16 criticises the adoption, for the criterion of " fundamental ", of the phrase " going to the root of the contract."

It is abundantly clear in principle that where there is a contract for the sale of peas and beans are delivered the buyer may refuse the beans and also claim compensatiton for non-delivery of peas. But the language of section 11 of the Sale of Goods Act does not readily permit this result to be achieved. It divides the terms of a contract into " conditions " and " warranties " and annexes a " claim to damages " to a warranty. No definition is provided of " condition ", and the terms of the section invite the construction placed on them by Fletcher Moulton L.J. that where there is a failure to deliver " the kind of goods stipulated for " the buyer has a " choice of the two remedies, either of rejecting the goods and treating the contract as repudiated or suing for damages for delivery of the inferior article ".[70] At first sight this dictum suggests that if the goods are rejected there is no claim for damages. Nevertheless closer inspection reveals that it is not inconsistent with the view that the buyer may sue for damages whether or not he rejects the goods delivered. An incident of treating a contract as repudiated is the right to damages for repudiation. However, whether or not the " condition " of the Sale of Goods Act is to be regarded as putting a buyer to his election *either* to reject *or* sue for damages, the breach of a fundamental term gives the buyer a right to reject *and* to claim damages for breach.

PART III

Is fitness for purpose a fundamental term in hire-purchase contracts?

The need for clarification of concepts and propositions in the area of the position of exemption clauses has already been demonstrated by the discussion of the difference between " fundamental terms " and " fundamental breach ". In the *Charterhouse* case[1] we have seen one variety of judicial approach arising from this difference. But there is a further conflict of judicial opinion in the case which calls for further clarification of doctrine. The three members of the Court of Appeal agree that apart from the limited provision of the Hire-Purchase Acts there is to be implied in all hire-purchase agreements a fitness for purpose term. But while Ormerod L.J. describes such a term as fundamental, Upjohn L.J. denies that it possesses this character. Donovan L.J. is probably in accord with the view of Upjohn L.J. though he makes no explicit statement. Upjohn L.J. envisages hire-purchase agreements as containing a fundamental " correspondence with description " term in addition to a non-fundamental " fitness for purpose " term. These judicial opinions are derived from the precedents. These are few in number and can be examined separately. This examination, it is submitted, will show that much of the conflict is terminological and that the subject is in need of further theoretical analysis.

The three principal cases are the *Apps*[6] case, the *Astley*[15] case and the *Charterhouse* case.[1] But in the *Astley* case Pearson L.J., after speaking of an " obligation . . . as to the fitness of the vehicle for the defendant's purpose ", referred to the *Karsales* case as authority for the implication of " a condition or fundamental term ".[79] It is necessary therefore, to see what was said in the *Karsales* case[71] about this topic. In that case, it will be recalled, the car was delivered, a week after it had been inspected during the negotiations, in a very different and " deplorable state ". Denning L.J. founded his judgment on the doctrine of fundamental breach, but he also referred to an implied " obligation on the lender to deliver the car in substantially the same condition as when it was seen ".[72] The argument of counsel was that there should be implied a term " similar to that in the Sale of Goods Act dealing with description of the article hired ".[73] Birkett L.J., who applied the reasoning of fundamental breach, used the language " the thing delivered was not the thing contracted for ".[74] Parker L.J., who reasoned that there was a fundamental term, employed similar language. He said, " The vehicle delivered is not properly described as a motor vehicle . . . the same result is achieved by saying, in effect, that what was delivered was not what was contracted for ".[75] This is the formula subsequently used by Upjohn L.J. for his " correspondence with description " term : it is not the language of a fitness for purpose term.[76]

The *Apps* case has been treated as establishing the proposition that a fitness for purpose term is to be implied in every hire-purchase agreement, but it is not absolutely clear that this is so. The county court judge found that the car which had been hired was " in an unusable, unroadworthy and unsafe condition ". It appears that in one passage

---

[70] [1963] 2 All E.R. at p. 44 G. Origin: *Wallis* v. *Pratt* [1910] 2 K.B. 1003, 1014.

[71] [1956] 1 W.L. R.936: [1956] 2 All E.R. 866: see also the notes in [1957] C.L.J. at p. 12 and p. 17.

[72] p. 868 G.

[73] p. 870 B.

[74] p. 870 H.

[75] p. 871 E.

[76] In *Sze Hai Tong Bank, Ltd.* v. *Rambler Cycle Co., Ltd.* [1959] 3 All E.R. 182, Lord Denning, giving the judgment of the Board of the Judicial Committee of the Privy Council, said at p. 186 E: " In *Karsales (Harrow), Ltd.* v. *Wallis* the agent of the finance company delivered a car which would not go at all in breach of its obligation to deliver one that would go." Lord Jenkins and Mr. de Silva were the other members of the Board. The case was one in which the court held that the defendants could not rely on an exemption clause because according to the wording of the clause it did not apply to what had happened: " as a matter of construction their Lordships decline to attribute to it the unreasonable effect contended for." Lord Denning gave as a reason for this construction that unless so limited " the exemption clause . . . would run counter to the main object and intent of the contract." He appears to have considered that there was a general doctrine that exemption clauses " must . . . be limited and modified to the extent necessary to give effect to the main object and intent of the contract " (p. 185 G). He then proceeded to refer to fundamental breach as the disregard of " the prime obligations of the contract " (p. 185 H).

this was considered as a breach of a fitness for purpose term, but he also appears to have spoken of a fundamental term that the car should be roadworthy,[77] and of " a fundamental term of the contract to hire a motor car suitable for use on the highway ".[78] These may have been alternative ways of describing the same fundamental term. The formulation of the term in the language of fitness for purpose was the main subject of argument in the Court of Appeal. It was contended that the county court judge was wrong in law in holding that there was " an implied term of any hiring agreement that the goods hired should be as reasonably fit and suitable for the purpose for which they are expressly hired as reasonable care and skill can make them ".[79] To this contention there was a specific reply by Harman L.J. : " I take it to be quite clearly the law that the hirer of a chattel does warrant that it is reasonably fit for the purpose for which he hires it."[80] This passage was adopted by Donovan L.J. in the *Charterhouse* case[1] as the *ratio decidendi* of the *Apps* case,[81] and it is true that similar passages to that of Harman L.J. can be found in the *Apps* case[6] in the judgments of the other judges. But scrutiny reveals differences. It should be noted that Harman L.J. adds to the passage already quoted this description of the particular term in the *Apps* case : " in this case that the car should be a viable motor-car."[14] Holroyd Pearce L.J., though earlier he agrees with the county court judge in holding there is a fitness for purpose term, finally based his judgment on the holding of a breach of a fundamental term to hire a motor-car suitable for use on the highway.[82] Davies L.J. spoke of a " term of fitness and roadworthiness."[83] It is not easy to see that the court drew a clear distinction between " fitness for purpose " and " correspondence with description ".

In the *Astley* case[15] a six-year-old tipping lorry was hired. The agreement with the finance company contained an exemption clause which specifically excluded warranties but also stated: " the hirer's acceptance of delivery of the vehicle shall be conclusive that he has examined the vehicle and found the same to be complete and in good order and condition and in every way satisfactory to him." The borrower used the lorry on heavy work over a period of three months during which on a number of occasions, some being at the outset, he had to have substantial repairs done. He then wrote a letter to the finance company saying he was unable to continue payments. It was assumed that the letter " constituted a repudiation of the agreement ".[84]

---

[77] [1961] 2 All E.R. p. 285 A. The account of what the county court judge said is taken from the judgments in the Court of Appeal.
[78] p. 290 B.
[79] p. 285 D.
[80] p. 291 F.
[81] [1963] 2 All E.R. at p. 436 B.
[82] [1961] 2 All E.R. at p. 290 B. The Lord Justice relied in his judgment on the *Karsales* case (p. 287 G *et seq.*). This confirms the view that he regarded the fundamental term as a " correspondence with description " term.
[83] p. 292 E.
[84] *Per* Pearson L.J. [1963] 2 All E.R. at p. 40 F.

When sued by the finance company for the balance of the instalments, the borrower pleaded that it was " a fundamental term of the hire-purchase agreement that the vehicle was reasonably fit for the purpose for which it was hired ", and that there had been a breach of the term which entitled him to repudiate, and he counterclaimed for damages. The court affirmed the county court judge's holding that there had been no breach of any fundamental term, but they rejected the contention of the finance company that by virtue of the exemption clause they could be under no liability for any defects in the lorry.   Each Lord Justice affirmed that the exemption clause did not apply to a breach of a fundamental term, but no Lord Justice agreed absolutely with the existence of the term pleaded.

It is true that Pearson L.J. stated that the finance company had an obligation " as to the fitness of the vehicle for the [borrower's] purpose ".[85]   But he stated its contents as follows, " They were letting on hire to him a Bedford tipper, and it had to be a Bedford tipper, *i.e.*, a lorry of that make, and a tipper : it had to be an automobile, capable of self-propulsion along a road, and it had to be capable of receiving and carrying and tipping loads of material."   The Lord Justice cited the *Karsales* case[12] and the *Apps* case[6] as authorities for the implication of such a term.   It is not surprising therefore that Ormerod L.J. in effect considers that in the following dictum he is but affirming the views of Pearson L.J. : " In my judgment it is a fundamental term of a contract of this kind that the goods hired must correspond with the description of the goods which are contracted to be hired."[86]   Upjohn L.J. denied that the fundamental term was a fitness for purpose term. In his view the fundamental term was one of correspondence with description, and though a term of fitness for purpose was also to be implied it was not a fundamental one.   It should be noted that he carefully circumscribed the situation in which such terms are to be implied : " In general on a hiring of an ordinary motor vehicle, whether a car, lorry or van which the parties are intending shall be let and hired for normal use on the road for ordinary purposes for which the vehicle appears to be suited and capable, there are in my judgment, subject to any express terms as to the state of repair or condition and so forth, two stipulations to be implied in any contract of letting and hiring."[87]   This is the manner in which he states what I have called the correspondence with description term : " there is an implied stipulation that the vehicle hired corresponds with the description of the vehicle contracted to be hired, or to put it in another way, the lender must lend that which he contracted

---

[85] p. 44 F.

[86] p. 48 D.   Ormerod L.J. commenced his judgment by saying: "I agree with the judgments which have been delivered."   The headnote to the All England Reports, however, goes too far in saying that he agreed with the views of Upjohn L.J. about the existence and character of the two stipulations which Upjohn L.J. said were to be implied.   Ormerod L.J. specifically refers to the description by Pearson L.J. of the tipping lorry.

[87] 46 C., and see n. 23.

to lend, and not something which is essentially different."[88]   This term
is a fundamental one, which cannot be excluded, he says, by any exemption clause " however widely phrased ".[89]

The second stipulation which he thought was implied was one
" that the vehicle must be as fit for the purpose for which it was hired
as reasonable care and skill can make it ".   This term was not fundamental, indeed he says he would regard it " as a stipulation in the nature
of a warranty ".   But he makes it clear that breach of this stipulation
might in some circumstances entitle the borrower to put an end to the
contract.[90]   He thought that it was possible that the lorry had not been
fit for the purpose for which it was hired, but the operation of the
exemption clause prevented liability from attaching to the lender.[91]

Only a week elapsed between the delivery of judgment in the *Astley*
case[15] and the delivery of judgment in the *Charterhouse*[1] case.[92]   But while
Ormerod L.J., as we have seen,[86] said in the former case that a fundamental term in a hire-purchase contract was one of correspondence with
description, in the latter case he said : " There was an implied term that
the car would be fit for the purpose for which it was hired.   The car
was not so fit, and there was, therefore, a breach of the implied term,
which was a fundamental one."[93]   A possible inference is that Ormerod
L.J. considers that fitness for purpose is equivalent to correspondence
with description.   This, however, is contrary to the view expressed by
Upjohn L.J. in the *Astley* case.   Upjohn L.J. restated his doctrine of
two stipulations in the *Charterhouse* case, but no reference is made to

---

[88] Though he cites no authority this statement is surely derived from the judgment
of Parker L.J. in the *Karsales* case, see n. 9.   The learned Lord Justice does not directly
expand on the meaning of " essentially different " : but he does discuss the question of when
the motor vehicle delivered complies with the fundamental obligation.   This, he says, " is
very largely a question of fact and degree and must depend on the circumstances of each
case."   One of the factors he refers to is " the impact of unknown defects not merely on
the roadworthiness of the car but on its general condition and the ability to perform the
tasks for which it is hired " (p. 46 G).   The manner in which description involves fitness
for purpose may be noted.   It should also be noted that all " description " in a contract
does not deal with matters which are " essential."   The distinction drawn between
" definition " and " description " is relevant: see notes on the *Karsales* case in [1957] C.L.J.
at p. 12, and (by K. W. Wedderburn) at p. 16.

[89] This indicates that the phrase in his circumscription " subject to any express terms
as to the state of repairs or condition " requires consideration.   Perhaps Upjohn L.J. had
in mind specific references to particular defects, or the phrase only applies to the fitness
for purpose term.

[90] He classifies the term as one of those described in the *Hong Kong* case, breach of
which does not automatically give a right to terminate a contract, but which may do so
according to the nature of the breach: see above p. 172 and n. 53.

[91] It could be said that the exemption clause prevented the implication of a fitness
for purpose term: see nn. 21 and 23.   What Upjohn L.J. said was: " it is possible that the
hirer might originally have had some claim for damages against the lender for the defective
condition in which he found the vehicle but for the fact that by clause 3 of the agreement
the lender excluded liability " (p. 47 G).   There was another answer, he said, to a claim
based on breach of the fitness for purpose term. This depended on a more detailed
consideration of the nature of the term: see *infra*, p. 185.

[92] The *Astley* case was heard on November 13th, 14th and 15th, 1962, and the *Charterhouse* case on January 21st, 22nd, 23rd and 24th.   Judgments were delivered on March 8th,
1963, and March 15th.

[93] [1963] 2 All E.R. at p. 444 F.

t in the judgments of Ormerod L.J. and Donovan L.J. It is interesting
o note how Upjohn L.J. applied his doctrine. The defective back axle
ell under the correspondence with the description term, and the bor-
ower was entitled to damages notwithstanding the existence of the
exemption clause. The failure to have roadworthy tyres did not constitute a breach of the correspondence with description term, but only
of " the implied obligation of fitness [and] liability for breach of that
obligation (not being a fundamental term) was . . . excluded by [the
exemption clause]."[94]

The judgment of Donovan L.J. was based rather on the doctrine of
fundamental breach than that of fundamental term. However, he considered that the *Apps* case[6] established " that at common law it was an
implied term of the contract that the car should be reasonably fit for
the purpose for which it was hired ".[95] The mere breach of such a term
is not *ipso facto* fundamental : " a car with defective steering might be
' unfit to be used ' and ' quite unroadworthy ' and yet the task of putting it right might be simple and inexpensive. Nobody would describe
such a defect as involving a fundamental breach."[96] It is the character
of the defect which determines whether there has been a fundamental
breach. He thought the defect in the back axle constituted a fundamental breach. " A defect in the back axle can be an extremely serious
and dangerous matter." It involved " a substantial outlay on repair " :
" delivery of such a car was not a performance of the contract at all."[97]
This approach is consistent with the view of Upjohn L.J. expressed in
the *Astley* case,[98] that a fitness for purpose term is not a fundamental
term and is neither a " condition " nor " warranty " as those words are
used in the Sale of Goods Act, but belongs to that class of terms described
in the *Hong Kong* case[99] where the character of the legal consequences
depends on the nature of the breach.

Equivalence of fitness for general purpose and correspondence with description

It is submitted that some at least of the apparent conflict between
statements as to the fundamental character of a fitness for purpose term
arises from a failure to analyse sufficiently the nature of the concept of
" fitness for purpose ". The term implied by section 14 (1) of the Sale
of Goods Act speaks of " the particular purpose for which the goods are
required ". Upjohn L.J., it will be recalled, circumscribing the situation

---

[94] *Ibid.* 444 D. Upjohn L.J. said "probably excluded": but that is because there was no
full argument—" this matter was really treated in argument as *de minimis.*" He also gave
another reason for the failure of the borrower's claim in respect of the replacement of the
defective tyres: this was based on the nature of the fitness for purpose term, see *infra*, p. 185.
[95] p. 436 B.
[96] p. 463 I.
[97] p. 437 A.
[98] See n 90.
[99] [*Hong Kong Fir Co. Ltd.* v. *Kawasaki Kisen Kaisha, Ltd.* [1962] 2 Q.B. 26 ; [1962] 1
All E.R. 474. Ed.]

in which terms are implied in contracts of hire-purchase referred to "normal use . . . for ordinary purposes ".[21] The distinction between general purposes and particular purposes is significant. Two examples may help to make this clearer. The description of an object as a lorry carries with it the connotation of " automobile ", *i.e.,* that it is capable of self-propulsion along a road. This is what all the judges said in the *Astley* case.[15] But a lorry may be hired for the purpose of taking heavy loads over a specific steep hill. If there is a clause in the agreement stating that the lorry is capable of taking loads up to a certain weight over the specified hill is this " description "? However, suppose that while the purpose is known to the lender there is no such clause in the agreement. The lorry, by reason of lack of horsepower, cannot take heavy loads over the hill : but it can take light loads over the hill, and heavy loads over less steep hills. Here, we have a situation of unfitness for a particular purpose. It may well be that the courts would hold that in a contract for hire-purchase of the lorry a term would be implied of fitness for the particular purpose; but the *Apps* case does not appear to be binding authority for such a proposition. The dicta of Upjohn L.J. in the *Astley* and *Charterhouse*[1] cases provide persuasive authority both for the existence of such a term and for the character of the term as non-fundamental. Let us now suppose that the lorry was hired for the particular purpose for one specific journey. Would not the particular purpose then become essential and an implied term of fitness for such purpose a fundamental term or at any rate a " condition "?

Upjohn L.J. in the *Astley* case suggests an affirmative answer. He discusses a hypothetical situation which provides the second example of the distinction between general and particular purposes. He also distinguishes between a hire-purchase contract and a contract for hire for a specific occasion, but he posits deficiencies which, unlike the lack of adequate power, prevent the vehicle from being roadworthy at all while being capable of speedy remedy. He supposes a car without tyres or sparking plugs and with an unserviceable carburettor. A borrower who has entered into a hire-purchase agreement would be entitled to have tyres and sparking plugs fitted and a new carburettor : and claim damages for a late delivery. On the other hand a borrower who hired a car for " 9 a.m. sharp for the express purpose known to the lender of carrying the hirer 150 miles to lunch in the country and back the same afternoon " would be entitled to treat the delivery of a car at 9 a.m. without tyres or sparking plugs as repudiation of the contract of hire.[100]

It appears reasonable to consider a statement of general purpose as involved in the description of the contract. Ordinary language contains many descriptive words which refer to purposes : older logic referred to the teleological character of words such as hammer or table : the dispositional concepts of modern logic are logically related. Thus

---

[100] *Astley case* [1963] 2 All E.R., p. 47 C.

vhen goods are described by means of words which themselves connote
a relation to some function the statement that the goods must correspond with the description refers to the same proposition as the statement
:hat the goods must be fit for some general purpose. It is when par-
:icular purposes are under consideration that a distinction exists between
:orrespondence with description and fitness for purpose.[101]   The cases we
have considered have dealt with general purposes only, and it is submitted establish no more than that in contracts for hire-purchase a
fundamental term exists that the goods must correspond with essential
elements of their description in the agreement, which may include their
fitness for the general purposes for which such goods are ordinarily used.

The content of the implied term of fitness for purpose

There can be little doubt that the "source" for the suggestion
that a fitness for purpose term is to be implied in a hire-purchase
contract is to be found in the statutory provision in the Sale of Goods
Act for the implication of a fitness for purpose term in a contract for
the sale of goods.[102]   This has provided an analogy, but there has been
no suggestion that the term in a hire-purchase contract should be precisely parallel. Indeed we have already seen that the limitation in
section 14 to "particular purpose" has not been repeated in the language
of the judges. It remains to be seen how far the other limitations in

---

[101] Even so far as particular purposes are concerned it may be contended that a statement
of such purpose is part of description. Again authority is to be found in the judgment of
Upjohn L.J. in the *Astley* case. After asserting that the hirer of the car for driving to the
luncheon engagement could repudiate the agreement he added: " It may be that it would
also amount to a breach of the fundamental term [of description] for the lender has contracted to deliver a car capable of starting at 9.00 a.m. sharp and this is of the essence
of the contract. This shows that these two implied stipulations may in some cases tend to
merge " (p. 47 D). This emphasises the vagueness of the term " description " : though
it may be doubted whether a statement that a car would be ready at 9.00 a.m. would,
ordinarily, be regarded as " description."
    Support for the view that a fitness for purpose term is not fundamental is to be found
in *Handley* v. *Marston* (1962) 106 S.J. 327. There a car, which was the subject of a hire-
purchase agreement, had defective brakes, defective steering, badly worn tyres, excessive
oil leakage. the handbrake was inoperative and the footbrakes not in good order. Willmer
L.J. said:" However unsafe and unroadworthy the car, and however deteriorated its condition, it did and could still function as a car, and the plaintiff had not supplied something
different in kind from that which he had contracted to hire." In the brief report of the
judgments there is no reference to any discussion of a possible distinction between fitness
for purpose and description. Willmer L.J. finds that there was no fundamental breach of
contract, and we are told that Ormerod and Danckwerts L.JJ. delivered concurring
judgments.

[102] The provision in the Sale of Goods Act is to be found in s. 14. It provides as follows :
" Subject to the provisions of this Act and of any statute in that behalf, there is no implied
warranty or condition as to the quality or fitness for any particular purpose of goods supplied
under a contract of sale, except as follows:—
    (1) Where the buyer, expressly or by implication, makes known to the seller the
particular purpose for which the goods are required, so as to show that the buyer
relies on the seller's skill or judgment and the goods are of a description which it is in
the course of the seller's business to supply (whether he be the manufacturer or not),
there is an implied condition that the goods shall be reasonably fit for such purpose;
Provided that in the case of a contract for the sale of a specified article under its patent
or other trade name, there is no implied condition as to its fitness for any particular
purpose."

section 14 will be followed by judges who consider that a fitness for purpose term should be implied in contracts for hire-purchase. Already one limitation is to be found in the judicial dicta.

In the *Apps case,* as we have seen, the county court judge merely followed the requirement of section 14 that the buyer " expressly or by implication makes known . . . the . . . purpose for which the goods are required ".[103] Holroyd Pearce L.J. added a limitation derived from the clause requiring reliance on the seller's skill or judgment. He said, after surveying the authorities: " Those cases clearly establish that such a warranty, condition or undertaking exists in the hiring of specific chattels, except in the cases where the defect is apparent to the hirer, and he does not rely on the skill and judgment of the owner."[104]

This limitation of reliance has twice been applied by Upjohn L.J. In the *Astley* case he held that one answer to the hirer's claim in respect of a breach of a fitness for purpose term " is that the hirer never relied on any implied obligation of fitness by the lender when he took the vessel ".[105] In the *Charterhouse* case dealing with the borrower's claim for the replacement of defective tyres he gave as one reason for the failure of the claim : " the defect must have been apparent to him, and he cannot have relied on the implied obligation of fitness."[106]

PART IV

Some policy considerations

The main object of this article has been to consider the difficulties involved in the exposition of the law dealing with " fundamental terms " in, and fundamental breaches of, contracts arising from the inadequate analysis of the fundamental concepts of the law of contract. The inconsistencies and lack of *elegantia,* it has been suggested, are largely due to the use of terminology which obscures important distinctions, and is inadequate to comprehend the complexities of actual situations. But even clarity and adequacy cannot be completely obtained without the

---

[103] [1961] 3 All E.R. p. 285 D: " there is an implied term of any hiring agreement that the goods hired shall be as reasonably fit and suitable for the purpose for which they are expressly hired, or for which, from their character, the owner must be aware that they are intended to be used, as reasonable care and skill can make them."

[104] p. 287 F. The limitation that the defect must not be apparent is not to be found in s. 14 (1) of the Sale of Goods Act, but a similar limitation is found in the proviso to s. 14 (2): " Provided that if the buyer has examined the goods, there shall be no implied condition as regards defects which such examination ought to have revealed."

[105] [1963] 2 All E.R. at p. 47 G. This answer was seen to involve also knowledge of the defects. Upjohn L.J. added: " He knew of the principal defects, yet took the vehicle, relying on the collateral agreement with the dealers to rectify those defects." It may be noted that the borrowers obtained damages from the dealers for their failure to remedy the defects.

[106] [1963] 2 All E.R. at p. 444 C.

consideration of the policies it is sought to implement. Without such consideration, of course, it is not possible to hope for a just solution of the various legal problems.

Attention to underlying policies throws light on a policy distinction which appears in the terminological and technical difference between fundamental terms and fundamental breach. Two different basic policies are relevant to all branches of the law of contract. On the one hand there is the policy, consistent with the philosophy of *laissez-faire* and free enterprise, but based on the morality of *pacta sunt servanda,* of enforcing the agreement of the parties. They are deemed to have autonomous powers, but since they may not have the technical capability of adequate draftsmanship of their self-binding rules, the law articulates the categories by which the intention of the parties is expressed in legal terms. For such an autonomic policy to be effective, rules of law should be framed which embody a range of concepts adequate to give effect to the multifarious desires of parties. The concepts should be flexible, but should not confuse important distinctions : and the language should incorporate a terminology which corresponds to, and makes clear, the differences of concepts. The intention of the parties should not be frustrated merely because there is a lack of an adequate conceptual framework, and a corresponding terminology. Distinctions made by the parties should be recognised and made effective by legal procedures.

This autonomic policy underlies the doctrine of fundamental terms. The parties themselves distinguish between terms which are fundamental, such as those in the sale or hire of goods, which are " definitive " of the goods, and terms which do not have this fundamental quality even though they may operate as " conditions " of promises. The parties themselves agree to exemption and rejection clauses, and such clauses should only be given effect in accordance with the intention of the parties. On the other hand there is another policy operative in the law of contract. It is the public policy which declares certain kinds of contracts to be unenforceable or illegal—which declares that the intention of the parties is subordinate to higher considerations of justice. This policy is not confined to doctrines such as those of illegality, based on the conduct of parties entering into a contract, but extends to the regulation of the consequences of the conduct of the parties after they have entered into a contract. It is this heteronomic concept which underlies the doctrine of fundamental breach. The court does not seek to give effect to the intention of the parties. As has so often been judicially stated parties to a contract contemplate performance rather than breach. What the consequences of a breach should be is based on the court's own view of what justice requires, though of course the circumstances of the contract and the intention of the parties are material factors in the determination of justice.

Explicit recognition of the operation of the two different autonomic and heteronomic policies will, it is submitted, assist in the clarification

N

of the law of fundamental terms and breach, a task which can be carried
out by judicial recognition and exposition. But further recognition
of underlying policies is required, and full recognition of these further
policies probably requires legislative and not merely judicial action.
Relevant to both the case law and statute law of sale and hire of goods
is a concept which is, perhaps, best named by the politico-economic
term of consumer protection. There can be little doubt that such a
policy has been operative in the judicial search for the limitation of the
operation of exemption clauses and in the implication of the terms now
recognised by section 11-15 of the Sale of Goods Act, as well as in the
provisions of the Hire-Purchase Act. But there appears to be a need
for closer examination of the policy of consumer protection and of
the adequacy of its implementation by the law. Is not the " consumer "
the ordinary citizen who cannot be expected to be an expert in the goods
which are the subject-matter of the transaction, and who cannot be
expected by his own bargaining powers to obtain variations in the standard terms offered by sellers and lenders? The provisions of the Sale of
Goods Act, however, extend to the owners of chain retail stores with
their vast bargaining powers as purchasers, and since they are subject
to the agreement of the parties do not assure even the humblest citizen
complete protection. The protection afforded by the Hire-Purchase
Act is absolute, but is subject to a financial limitation, which excludes,
for example, most transactions by ordinary citizens for the acquisition
of a motor car. Clearly the definition of an " ordinary citizen " or
" consumer " is no easy task. Nor is it easy to draft other provisions
which will assure adequate consumer protection. But difficulties of
draftsmanship are challenges to, not denials of, the provision of adequate
laws of consumer protection. Such provision, it is thought, will be
assisted by distinguishing between the aspects of commercial law
designed to facilitate the enterprise of merchants and producers and the
aspects of that law designed to protect the welfare of the ordinary citizen
and consumer.

12

The Contract of Sale in Self-Service Stores*

While in Germany during last summer, I read an article in one of their legal journals on the contract of sale in self-service stores.[1] On my return to Northern Ireland, the first legal writing I happened to read was on the same subject. It was a comment[2] by my colleague, D. C. Williams, on *Pharmaceutical Society of Great Britain* v. *Boots Cash Chemists*.[3] I found these articles interesting illustrations of the German and English approaches to identical problems. This note also contains an English approach to the problem of when a contract of sale is concluded in a self-service store.

It may be helpful to give a brief résumé of the English case. The facts which appear in the report are these.[4] The defendants were owners of pharmacies against whom the plaintiffs brought an action for a declaration that a breach of the Pharmacy and Poisons Act, 1933, had been committed. Under that Act, it is not lawful for prescribed poisons to be sold unless the sale is effected by, or under the supervision of, a registered pharmacist. The declaration sought was to the effect that offences were committed when customers bought at one of the defendants' shops two bottles of medicine containing small amounts of prescribed poisons. The particular shop was conducted as an ordinary self-service store, but with a registered pharmacist on duty at the cash desk. Customers had open access to shelves on which medicines and other commodities were set out. The customers brought their selected

---

* Reprinted from the *American Journal of Comparative Law*, April, 1855, by kind permission. A German version appeared in *Juristische Rundschau*, February, 1955.

[1] Otto C. Carlsson, " Nochmals ' Kaufabschluss in Selbstbedienungsladen,' " JR, 1954, p. 253.

[2] 10 N.I.L.Q. (1953) 117.

[3] [1953] 1 Q.B. 401; [1952] 2 All E.R. 456 (Q.B.D.); [1953] 1 All E.R. 482 (C.A.).

[4] The background to the case is that the plaintiffs were the professional association of pharmacists concerned to see that the employment of pharmacists is not diminished. The self-service system reduces the number of registered pharmacists involved in the sale of drugs. The defendants were the owners of a large chain-stores organisation whose shops sell pharmaceutical goods.

189

goods to the cash desk where they paid for them the amount specified
by the cashier. The pharmacist present at the cash desk saw the goods
bought by the customer and had power to prevent any customer from
removing any drugs from the premises. The contention of the plaintiffs
was that the sales were complete before the customer took the medicine
to the cash desk: the contention of the defendants was that the sale was
not " effected " until the customer arrived at the desk where it was
effected under the supervision of a registered pharmacist. In the
Queen's Bench Division, Lord Goddard L.C.J. refused the declaration,
holding that " There was no sale until the buyer's offer to buy was
accepted by the acceptance of the purchase price, and that took place
under the supervision of a pharmacist,"[5] i.e., at the cash desk. The
reasoning of the Lord Chief Justice, as well as his decision, was
approved in the Court of Appeal. Indeed the judgments there largely
restated or cited the words of Lord Goddard. Somervell L.J. stressed
the point that there was no sufficient difference between the modes of
conducting transactions in an ordinary shop and in a self-service store
for the law to distinguish between contracts of sale in them.[6]

The object of Dr. Carlsson's article is, of course, different from
that of Mr. Williams' note, and this to some extent accounts for their
difference of treatment. It is, nevertheless, noteworthy that Dr.
Carlsson does not cite the decision of any German, or indeed European,
judicial tribunal. Eight-ninths of his article is devoted to a juristic
consideration of the problem, in the course of which his references are
to two previous articles in German journals[7] on the same subject, and
to the views of four commentators on the German Civil Code:[8] there
are also three mentions of paragraphs in the code.[9] The remaining
one-ninth of the article consists in a brief discussion of United States
case law, which he considers to be of special value because of the many
years' experience which the United States has had of self-service
stores.[10] Mr. Williams gives a brief account of the case which he is
" noting ", and adds a brief comment, accepting the court's conclusion
but rejecting its reasoning. According to Lord Goddard L.C.J. and the
Court of Appeal, it is the customer who makes an offer: Mr. Williams
prefers to say that the store owner makes the offer, which, however, is
not accepted by the customer until he produces the goods to the cashier.

The possibility that the analysis supported by Mr. Williams is
correct is considered by Dr. Carlsson, but he states that he prefers the

---

[5] [1952] 2 All E.R. at 459B.

[6] See [1953] 1 All E.R. at 483 H; and per Lord Goddard C.J. [1952] 2 All E.R. at 458F.

[7] Recke: NJW, 1953, p. 91; Bögner: JR, 1953, p. 417.

[8] See n. 13 *infra*.

[9] Art. 158 and Arts. 823 ff. (twice).

[10] He makes specific reference to *Lasky* v. *Economic Stores* (1946) 319 Mass. 224 and
Gargaro v. *Kroger Grocery & Bakery Co.* (1938) 22 Tenn. App. 70.

analysis according to which the offer is made by the customer. His main concern is not to decide between these two doctrines, but between two different doctrines concerned with the point of time when the contract is made. According to one thesis, the contract is made " when the purchaser places the goods in the carrier and it is clear that he has turned to the selection of other goods ".[11] The other thesis contends that the contract is made at the cash desk.[12] Dr. Carlsson supports the latter thesis. The former thesis, he considers, lays down a rule which is too vague to be practical, and which is also unrealistic. The nature of a self-service store makes it clear, he considers, that neither the customer nor the shopkeeper is contractually bound until the goods are paid for at the cash desk. A rule of law should correspond with social realities, and, moreover, the rule which he favours is in the interests of both storeowner and customer. The storeowner is interested in selling the maximum amount of goods, and psychological studies have shown that a customer who can freely handle goods is very likely to buy them. There would be far less sales if the law were that the customer was bound to buy goods which he had taken from the shelves. Romer L.J. expressed the same point of view when he said : " If that were the position in this and similar shops, and that was known to the general public, I should imagine the popularity of such shops would wane a good deal." Dr. Carlsson contends that not only has the customer freedom to change his mind after selecting an article, but that also the shopkeeper may do so. He lays stress on the fact that the customer has to place the selected goods in the carrier provided by the shop and take the carrier with the goods to the cash desk. The customer is not entitled to put the goods into his pocket. Control of the goods remains with the shopkeeper.

Dr. Carlsson points out that two different analyses may lead to the view that the contract is made at the cash desk. The one he prefers is derived from the general principle that it is the customer in a shop who makes an offer to the shopkeeper.[13] Applying this general principle to self-service stores, he says that the customer makes the offer when he places the goods in the container provided by the shop, and continues to make it so long as he keeps the goods in the container. This is in accordance with the dictum of Lord Goddard L.C.J.—" the mere fact that a customer picks up a bottle of medicine from the shelf . . . is an offer by the customer to buy ". Nevertheless, I think it more realistic to say that the customer has not passed beyond the stage of

---

[11] Bögner: JR, 1953, p. 417.

[12] Recke: NJW, 1953, p. 91.

[13] He cites as authority the views of two commentators, Von Oertmann and Soergel, and of the editors of the RGR-Kommentar. The contrary view, that the display of goods with a marked price constitutes an offer by the vendor, is held by two other commentators on the B.G.B.—von Staudinger and Palandt.

preliminary negotiation until the goods are taken to the cash desk. This is the view of Somervell L.J., who described a self-service store as " a convenient method of enabling customers to see what there is for sale, to choose, and, possibly, to put back and substitute, articles which they wish to have, and then to go to the cashier and offer to buy what they have chosen."

Dr. Carlsson points out that there are German jurists who consider that in all circumstances where goods are displayed with marked prices there is an offer by the vendor. Applying this principle to self-service stores, he contends that the customer who takes the goods from shelves " accepts " the offer subject to a condition that he will not put the goods back.[14] There is no complete acceptance until the goods are taken to the cash desk. This is the doctrine supported by Mr. Williams.[15]

In my view, the better opinion is that which treats the customer as making the offer when tendering the goods at the cash desk. This makes it possible for the shopkeeper to reject the offer in all cases, and not merely in cases like the *Pharmaceutical Society* case,[3] where there is a sale of drugs, and the pharmacist supervising the cashier is " authorised to prevent a customer from removing drugs from the premises ". According to the analysis of Mr. Williams, the customer could insist on purchasing the goods at the marked price, except perhaps where he was aware that a mistake had been made. One of the arguments which has been put forward for saying that display of goods at marked prices only amounts to an invitation to treat is that it is unfair to hold the vendor to a mistake in the pricing. In a self-service store, it is not inconceivable for the cards displaying the prices to get mixed by the actions of customers.

It is valuable to consider under what logical category the judgment as to the nature of the transaction falls. Is it a mere question of fact? Is it necessary merely to consider the factual character of the circumstances and proceedings in a self-service store in order to decide by whom and when the offer or acceptance is made? Or is a policy judgment, a judgment of value involved? The judgments in the *Pharmaceutical Society* case consider questions of value. Thus, Lord Goddard L.C.J. says: " One has to apply common sense and the ordinary principles of commerce in this matter. If one were to hold that in the case of self-service shops the contract was complete directly the purchaser picked up the article, serious consequences might result." The reason why value judgments are involved is the following. The question whether an offer or acceptance is made does not depend on the

---

[14] In English law, of course, acceptance must be unconditional.

[15] He cites *Wiles* v. *Maddison* [1943] 1 All E.R. 315, but it is difficult to regard that case as being concerned with more than the interpretation of a wartime price regulation order.

actual state of mind of the particular shopkeeper or customer: the question is one of objective not of subjective intention. It is whether an offer or an acceptance has been reasonably manifested. Would a reasonable man have thought there was an offer or an acceptance? The character of the reasonable man in contract has not been precisely determined. Either he is a logical construct, a statistical creature, like the " average taxpayer ", " the normal household ", or he is the man who acts reasonably, i.e., in such a manner as to do justice. In the first case, his reaction is a matter of conjecture, and the judges' view of justice can properly be brought into the balance where conjecture alone yields no decision. In the second case, the criterion involves an immediate use of the sense of justice. In either case, therefore, the rules as to offer and acceptance and the completion of a contract in the case of self-service store transactions, as in other transactions, involve considerations of justice.

The various factors to be taken into account include the public interest in self-service stores as well as the just regulation of the relations between shopkeeper and customer. Dr. Carlsson in his article dogmatically asserts that the rules of law which German judges have to construct, because specific provision for self-service stores is not to be found in the BGB, should not obstruct or hamper the development of the new sales system. A common sense judgment of economics suggests that it is in the public interest to encourage, or at any rate not to hinder, the development of self-service stores because they lower the costs of distribution of goods. There was, however, a clash of interests in the *Pharmaceutical Society* case[3] between, on the one hand, the storeowners' interest in minimising costs of distribution in order to some extent to increase profits, combined with the interest of the general public in keeping prices low, and, on the other hand, the interests of pharmacists to see that they are employed in the distribution of pharmaceutical goods, an interest which to some extent subserves the public interest of protection against improper distribution of dangerous goods. The judgments in the case, however, were confined to considerations of the relations of the individual interests of shopkeeper and customer.

Consideration has already been given to some of these interests. There have already been discussed the interests of freedom of choice of the customer and of control of the goods and prices by the shopkeeper. Problems of loss or damage to the goods and to the customer also call for a solution. In *Lasky* v. *Economic Grocery Stores*,[16] a customer was injured by the explosion of a bottle of mineral water that she had taken from the shelf in a self-service store. A claim in contract

---

[16] *Supra* n. 10. My reading has been confined to the very brief statement in Dr. Carlsson's article.

was rejected.   The court said: " It is plain upon the plaintiff's own
testimony that it was optional with her to return the article she selected
or to keep it and later become the purchaser."   Clearly, the court
treated the question as one of fact.   In the opinion of the court, moreover, there was no contract until the goods were taken to the cash desk.

Mr. Williams concludes his note by hoping that the House of
Lords will one day decide that a display of goods in a shop may, in
certain circumstances, be an offer.   Does the *Pharmaceutical Society*
case[3] decide that the display of goods in a self-service store is not an
offer?   Are the dicta to that effect *obiter dictum* or *ratio decidendi*?
I think they are *ratio decidendi,* but I am not sure.   What is clear,
however, is that English textbook writers now have " clear " authority
for their proposition that a display of goods in a shop amounts merely
to an invitation to treat.

13

The Basis of the Power of an Agent in Cases of Actual and Apparent Authority*

The polemics of legal literature were enriched by the pyrotechnically illuminating controversy which took place some thirty years ago between Cook and Ewart dealing with the question whether estoppel is a proper explanation of the doctrine of apparent authority. Ewart in his book on Estoppel had dealt with apparent authority as an illustration of the doctrine of estoppel. Cook denied that apparent authority was based on estoppel and Ewart replied.[1] Cook's thesis is that the liability of a principal for acts within the apparent authority of his agent is a " true contractual liability ". Though there can be little doubt that some of the arguments with which Cook supported his proposition are fallacious the proposition itself has been generally accepted. It was supported by Seavey in his well-known article *The Rationale of Agency*,[2] and it reappears in the American Law Institute's *Restatement of Agency*.[3] Wright has also recently approved this thesis.[4] It is proposed in this article to consider afresh the basis of actual and apparent authority, and in so doing to survey the past controversy. Some of the differences between the protagonists are purely verbal, and it is necessary in the first place to consider the terminology of the subject.

The Definition of Agent

In legal terminology it is important that concepts relating to factual situations should be clearly distinguished from concepts which relate to

---

*Reprinted from the *Canadian Bar Review*, 1938, by kind permission.

[1]Cook, *Agency by Estoppel* (1905), 5 Col. L.R. 36; Ewart, *Agency by Estoppel* (1905), 5 Col. L.R. 354; Cook, *Agency by Estoppel: a Reply* (1906), 6 Col. L.R. 34. Another article by Cook on the same subject is *Estoppel as Applied to Agency* (1903), 16 Harv. L.R. 324. Other articles by Ewart are: *Estoppel: Principal and Agent* (1902), 16 Harv. L.R. 186: *Estoppel by Assisted Misrepresentation* (1905), 5 Col. L.R. 456; *ibid.*, 35 Am. L.R. 707.

[2] (1920), 29 Yale L.J. 859.

[3] " Apparent authority conforms to the principles of contracts"—Art. 8 Comment c. " Apparent authority . . . is to be distinguished from estoppel."—Art. 159 Comment e. It should be remembered that Seavey was the reporter, and largely responsible for the Restatement.

[4] *Restatement of Contract and Agency* (1935), 1 Univ. of Tor. L.J. 17 at p. 41.

195

legal rules referring to or embodying such factual situations. Unless this is done it will be difficult to explain or justify a rule of law; for the terminology will itself introduce the rule, and the attempted explanation or justification will involve a circular argument or an *ipse dixit* of the law. For example the term " negligence " is sometimes used as embodying a legal rule making certain conduct actionable and connotes therefore that there has been a breach of a legal duty, that the conduct has been the legal cause of damage, and that the conduct has not been that of a reasonable man. On other occasions the term " negligence " is used as referring only to careless conduct. The result has been that many are confused as to the basis of the " Rule in *Davies* v. *Mann* ". [4a] The rule has nothing to do with the doctrine of " contributory negligence " : it is an illustration of the doctrine of causation. Where A and B are both careless and the consequence of their antecedent want of care is damage, then if B had the last chance of avoiding the damage and did not avail himself of it A's carelessness is not the legal cause of the damage. It follows that A has not been guilty of negligence in the sense in which that term is used in the phrase " contributory negligence ". In contributory negligence the acts of both parties cause the damage. Once it is seen that the problem in *Davies* v. *Mann* is one of causation it is possible to realise that the temporal order of the acts of carelessness is not always conclusive on the question of causation. A's action may be a cause of the damage or even the cause notwithstanding subsequent carelessness on the part of B.[5]

In the law of agency it is equally important not to confuse factual situation and legal rule. In his article on *The Rationale of Agency*, Seavey defined agency as " a consensual relation in which one (the agent) holds in trust for and subject to the control of another (the principal) a power to affect certain legal relations of that other ". This was indeed a confusion of factual situation and legal rule, without any precise delimitation of either. The Restatement to some extent separates factual situation from legal rule. Its definition of agency, and consequently of principal and agent, deals entirely with a factual situation, and may be accepted.[6] The legal rules applying to the factual situation are then set out in Arts. 12-14. For example, Art. 12 says : " An agent or apparent agent holds a power to alter the legal relations between the principal and third persons and between the principal and himself." However, in

---

[4a] (1842) 10 M.X.W. 546.

[5] Hence the decision in *Loach's Case*, [1916] A.C. 719, and the *dicta* in *Swadling* v. *Cooper*, [1931] A.C.1.

[6] Art, 1, subsections 1, 2 and 3:.

(1) " Agency is the relationship which results from the manifestation of consent by one person to another that the other shall act on his behalf and subject to his control, and consent by the other so to act.
(2) " The one for whom action is to be taken is the principal.
(3) " The one who is to act is the agent."

discussing the power of the agent the separation of factual situation from legal rule rather breaks down. I deal with this in dealing with the definition of " authority ".

It is important to note that the term " agent " is only properly applicable to a person in connection with the relationship in which he stands to the principal, and that that relationship is limited to the acts to be done on the principal's behalf. The word " agent ", therefore, properly connotes the character in which a person acts. It is, however, sometimes applied to a person irrespective of the character in which he acts, merely because in respect to other acts he stands in the relationship of agency to the principal. If P agrees with A that A should do acts *a—g,* he thereby constitues A his agent for the purpose of doing those acts. It is true that A is P's agent, but if A does any act *h—l,* he does not do it as agent of P. It can be said that in doing the act he was not an agent of P. Yet it can also be said the act was the act of P's agent. In this last sentence " agent " does not refer to the character in which the acts were done. This equivocation incidental to the word " agent " must not be allowed to lead to error. The courts distinguish between " agent " as descriptive of a person and descriptive of a function. The difference between signing a document " John Smith, agent ", and " John Smith as agent ", is well-known.[7]

The phrase " as agent " is also equivocal. It may mean that the act was in fact done in the character of agent in the sense that it fell within an actual agency relationship: or it may mean that the actor was purporting to act as if there were an agency relationship. Though A does an act he had not agreed with P to do he may yet represent to T that there is an agency relationship between him and P covering that act. In such a case it can be said that A was acting as agent.

In the definition of " apparent authority " in the *Restatement of Agency*[8] it is not clear in what sense the phrase " as agent " is used. Is it necessary for the apparent agent to purport to be an agent? Consider this case. L says to M, " X is authorised to sell you my horse Bess upon terms to be agreed upon between you and him ". There never has been any agreement between L and X. L and X in fact are negotiating about the sale of the horse from L to X, and X has possession of the horse. X offers to sell Bess to M for £100, and M accepts. Is this a case of apparent authority within the article even though X has not purported to act as L's agent? It may be that the Restatement contemplates an appearance of agency coming from the actions of the apparent principal

---

[7] See *Fleet* v. *Murton* (1871), L.R. 7 Q.B. 126; *Universal Steam Navigation Co.* v. *James McKelvie & Co.,* [1923] A.C. 492.

[8] Art. 8 " Apparent authority is the power of an apparent agent to affect the legal relations of an apparent principal with respect to a third person by acts done in accordance with such principal's manifestations of consent to such third person that such agent shall act as his agent."

alone: so that X will appear to M as an apparent agent in the transaction. The concluding words of the article may have to be read: " that such apparent agent shall act as his apparent agent ". X's action may be considered as one consistent with his being an apparent agent and therefore done " as apparent agent " and so within the article.

Most writers would consider the case as one of apparent authority if X purported to act as L's agent; but Cook would say that L's statement to M constituted X not merely an apparent agent of L, but an agent of L. His definition of agency appears to be that the relationship exists wherever one person has a power to affect the relations of another with third persons. This is similar to the one already cited of Seavey's: but it eliminates all questions of agreement and control. It destroys the distinction between actual and apparent authority by concentrating on the fact that in both cases the agent has a power to affect the principal's relations with third persons. Cook says: " Our law recognises that while as between principal and agent the relation of agency may in a given case not exist, it may and often does exist as between third parties." The words " principal and agent " require some qualifying epithet, for otherwise the statement involves a repetition: if the parties are principal and agent the relation of agency must exist: and if it does not exist *inter se* it must exist as regards third persons.

It may seem to be flogging a dead horse to deal further with Cook's view of agency, but his obvious fallacy does appear in more subtle forms. Ewart dealt with Cook's view by a *reductio ad absurdum*. Suppose in the above case L had not said to M, " X is authorised to sell my horse ", but " You may buy my horse upon terms to be agreed between you and X ". In this new case Cook, to be consistent, would have to regard X as agent of L. Yet X would be merely an arbiter or referee: the case would have nothing to do with agency.

The Definition of Power

The term power has been given a precise meaning by Hohfeld. It is a legal relation, one which exists by virtue of a legal rule. The power of an agent is not strictly conferred by the principal but by the law: the principal and agent do the acts which bring the rule into operation, as a result of which the agent acquires a power. If A agrees with P to do certain acts *a—l* for and on behalf of P and also agrees that he shall be subject to the control of P as to the doing of those acts, then the factual situation which thus arises is important enough to be given a special name and it is said the relationship of agency exists between P and A. It is clear law that A has power to affect P's relations with third persons and himself by doing those acts *a—l*. It is, however, conceivable that the law might have been otherwise. It is a question of law, not of agreement between P and A, how far A has power to affect P's relations by doing acts other than *a—l*. As such it is a question not merely of logic but of social policy.

The Definition of Authority

A most important factual matter in the problem of agency is the content of the agreement between the principal and agent as to the acts the agent is to do on behalf of the principal. P and A agree that A shall do acts *a—l*. It is expedient to have some name for the sum total of the agreed acts. The term " authority " has been used for that purpose : I see no objection to its use, and I will use " authority " in this article as meaning the sum total of the acts it has been agreed between principal and agent that the agent shall do on behalf of the principal. When it is said that P confers authority on A this means that P and A have agreed that certain acts should be done by A on behalf of P. That A has acted within his authority means that he has done one or more of such acts. That A exercises his authority similarly means that he has done one or more of the acts agreed upon. That he has authority means that it has been agreed he should do certain acts. The verb " authorise " is used with the same significance. To authorise A means to agree with A that he should do certain acts.

What the legal consequences of a grant of authority are is a matter quite distinct from the agreement between P and A. The terminology here adopted does not confuse question of fact with legal rule. It enables the legal rules, moreover, to be stated quite simply. Thus if P confers authority on A (factual situation) then A will have a power to affect P's relations by an exercise of his authority (legal consequence).

The authority of an agent, since it is governed by the agreement between him and the principal, can obviously be limited in any way. It is independent of what third persons reasonably or unreasonably believe it to be. That certain instructions are secret does not in any way prevent them from operating in limitation of the authority. There is, however, another meaning of the phrase " limiting the authority of the agent " which has to be considered. The agency agreement provides for control by the principal of the acts the agent is to do. The authority originally conferred can, therefore, be limited by subsequent instructions from P. P and A agree that A shall do acts *a—l*. P subsequently informs A that is not to do acts *h—l*. A's authority is limited to the acts *a—g*. It is immaterial whether A agrees *ad hoc* to the subsequent limitation. There has been a prior agreement in entering into the agency relationship that P shall control his acts. So the fact that P can by an unilateral act delimit the authority does not prevent the relationship from being consensual.

The extent of the authority, being dependent on the agreement, is governed by the ordinary rules for the interpretation of agreements. P may have thought that the authority he was conferring was confined to acts *a—g* : A may have thought the authority he was accepting referred to acts *h—l* : P may have acted so that a reasonable man in A's position would have thought he was conferring authority to do acts *m—v* : A may have acted so that a reasonable man in P's position would have thought he was accepting authority to do acts *s*—*z*. There is no special agency rule applicable: the ordinary contract rules apply.[9] I may repeat that what a third person, however reasonable, believes cannot affect the authority. P and A use a code according to which their language denotes authority to do acts *a*—*g*. To a third person, unaware of the code, it denotes *h*—*l*. A has authority to do acts *a*—*g*. He may have a power to bind P by doing acts *h*—*l*, but his authority is to do acts *a*—*g*.

Unfortunately the term " authority " has been used as meaning the power which an agent has arising from the fact of agency. Used in this wide sense the distinction between actual and apparent authority disappears. Thus Cook writes, " If P says to T ' A is authorised to sell you my horse upon terms to be agreed upon between you and him ', A thereby has authority to bind P." Ewart replies, " We do not agree that he (the agent) had authority for the fact is otherwise ". The difference here is really verbal: the protagonists are using " authority " in different senses; Cook in the sense of power, Ewart in the sense of agreement between P and A. The ineptness of Cook's terminology will be noticed if for the words " A is authorised " there be substituted what should be synonymous, " A has authority ". Cook would then use " authority " in two different meanings in the same sentence. As it is his verb has a different significance from his noun.

Seavey stated that " authority should be limited to its primitive meaning of a power which can be rightfully exercised ", *i.e.*, a power to do the acts agreed upon. Cook's definition was, nevertheless, adopted in the tentative draft, but Seavey's modification prevails in the Restatement.[10] The defects due to the use of authority in the sense of power are these : —

(a) Art. 7 sandwiches two propositions (*i*) a definition of the term " authority ", (*ii*) the statement of the legal rule that an agent has a certain power. The comment on the article reads as if by some mystical process legal rules could be deduced from an inherent meaning of the term " authority ". It is often difficult in reading the Restatement to know whether a statement is a definition for the purpose of subsequent exposition, a proposition of logic, or a legal rule.

(b) The Restatement is left without a simple term to denote the content of the agreement between principal and agent, to which it often has to refer. It sometimes uses the phrase " manifestations of consent ". More frequently it uses the word " authorisation "; which perhaps etymologically should refer to the act of conferring authority. But often

---

[9] The rule in *Ireland* v. *Livingstone* (stated in Art. 44 of the Restatement) is not, it is submitted, a special agency rule. It applies wherever it is agreed that one party shall state a contractual term without an *ad hoc* agreement to that term by the other party. S sells goods to B and it is agreed that the goods are to be delivered in instalments according to the directions of B. B's directions are governed by the rule.

[10] Art. 7: " Authority is the power of the agent to affect the legal relations of the principal by acts done in accordance with the principal's manifestations of consent to him."

it uses the word " authority " not as meaning the power resulting from the legal rule dealing with the agency relationship but in the meaning adopted in this article of the content of the agreement between principal and agent.[11] The Restatement therefore uses the same word in different senses. The verb " to authorise ", moreover, is nearly always used in the sense of actual agreement.

(c) Since " authority " as used in the Restatement is limited to the power conferred in respect of authority the same legal rule may be stated whichever meaning is given to the word " authority ". The Restatement, however, rather disregards the fact that " authority " in the sense of power is created by law, e.g., Art. 26 says "authority . . . . may be created by written or spoken words ".

Definition of Implied Authority[12]

The distinction between express and implied authority is not fundamental, but depends merely on whether the authority is delimited by words or by conduct. The distinction is sometimes difficult to draw. If P tells A that he is to act as manager this is really a compendious way of stating that he is to do all the acts a manager would ordinarily do. Those acts might well be termed his express authority. However, it is often said that if an agent is placed in a certain position he has implied authority to do all the acts a person in that position ordinarily does.[13] The law does not confer such implied authority. The proposition expresses a judgment of fact.

Definition of Apparent Authority[14]

It has been rightly said that apparent authority " denotes no authority at all ".[15] Apparent authority is really equivalent to the phrase " appearance of authority ". There may be an appearance of authority whether in fact or not there is authority. There is only one kind of authority; but since the phrase " apparent authority " has come into existence it is not unusual to use in opposition thereto the phrase " actual authority ". The adjective " actual ", however, adds no qualification to the noun " authority " : all authority is " actual ". When it is said that an agent's act was within the scope of his apparent authority all

---

[11] The title of Chapter 2 is " Creation of Relationship ". The page headings are " Creation of Authority ". Chapter 3 is called " Creation and Interpretation of Authority and Apparent Authority ". Topic 1 is entitled " Methods of manifesting consent ". Art 28. speaks of " sealed authority ". Topic 2 is entitled " Interpretation of Authority etc.". The Articles generally speak of " authorisation ", and in the comments " authority " appears to be interchangeable sometimes with " authorisation ". Art. 45 reads: " If authority is stated to be conditional upon the existence of specific facts . . ."

[12] The Restatement uses the term " incidental ".

[13] Article 35 of the Restatement says: " Unless otherwise agreed, authority to conduct a transaction includes authority to do acts which are incidental to it, usually accompany it, or are reasonably necessary to accomplish it."

[14] Sometimes termed " ostensible authority ".

[15] Smith and Watts, *Mercantile Law*, 8th ed., 1924, p. 177, note S.

that is meant is that the act appeared to be authorised. An act which falls within the scope of the apparent authority but without the actual authority is one which is not authorised but appears to be so.

The notion of apparent authority raises two questions: apparent from what? and apparent to whom? The necessity of asking the second question has been sometimes overlooked, and there has grown up in the English cases a use of the term " apparent authority " in an objective sense, in which " apparent authority " is conceived to exist independently of its subjective perception by somebody. The notion of perception is not regarded as inherent in the phrase " apparent authority " but as additional, so that there may or may not be a " reliance on an apparent authority ".[16] This judicial phraseology is possibly linked up with an occasional use in ordinary language of the word " appearance." An appearance involves two factors, the matters to be perceived and their perception. Sometimes, however, appearance is used to denote only the matters to be perceived and the connotation of their perception by somebody does not receive attention. Thus an actor may be said to appear on the stage though he is only rehearsing and nobody sees him. Nevertheless the potentiality of being perceived is always connoted by the word appearance. It is perhaps worth while examining closely the judicial phraseology. P places A in a position in which an agent would ordinarily have authority to do acts a—l. It follows that a third person, aware of A's position and of the authority ordinarily possessed by a person in that position, and unaware of the actual agreement between P and A, might reasonably consider that A had apparent authority to do acts a—l. This potentiality certainly always exists in the circumstances. The phraseology we are considering stresses this; it says that A always has apparent authority to do acts a—l. It may be that to a particular person, T, there was no appearance of authority to do acts a—l; he may not have known A was an agent, or he may not have known that the ordinary agent in the position of A had that authority, or he may have known that P had restricted A's authority to acts a—d. Nevertheless even so far as T is concerned it is said A had an apparent authority to do acts a—l.[17]

Another possible explanation of the judicial phraseology is that it is a survival of the old notion of " holding out to the world ".[18] How-

---

[16] See e.g., the language of the judges in *Underwood* v. *Bank of Liverpool*, [1924] 1 K.B. 775.

[17] Let us apply this to a hypothetical case, put forward in the Agency Restatement in another connection. P appoints A his general wheat selling agent for Philadelphia, instructing A not to give the usual market warranties with wheat sold. A deals with T, a stranger to the Philadelphian market, who is unaware that a warranty is customary, and moreover A tells him a warranty is not customary. The English user of " apparent authority " would result in it being said that A had apparent authority to give the usual warranty.

[18] In *Martin* v. *Gray*, 14 C.B.N.S. 839, Erle C.J. said: " Formerly it was considered sufficient if the party was held out to the world as a member of the firm. Now, however, it is necessary that there should be direct evidence that the holding out should come to the knowledge of the plaintiff." In *Dickinson* v. *Volpy*, 10 B. & C. 125, Parke J. said at p. 140: " If it could be proved that defendant had held himself out not ' to the world ', for that is a loose expression, but to the plaintiff himself ".

ever, it is now clear law that an agent will not have a power to bind the principal merely by doing an act within this kind of " apparent authority " : there must have been a reliance by the third party on such apparent authority.

There is no necessity to apply the phrase " apparent authority " to the concept of the authority which an agent occupying the position in question would ordinarily have. Another name exists for that concept and is always used in the law of tort, to wit " the course of employ-ment " : it should be used also in the law of contract : the judicial usage whereby apparent authority is used in a peculiar objective sense should be discarded.

The above discussion answers the question " apparent to whom? " Apparent authority only exists—there is only an appearance of authority —when it is apparent to the person with whom the agent deals. We have now to deal with the question " apparent from what? " It is clear that T is concerned with the acts not only of P but also of A : nevertheless neither Cook nor Seavey considers the effect of A's actions : they assume that he will purport to act as agent and thus contribute to the appear-ance of authority. But suppose he does not. L says to M, " X is author-ised to sell Blackacre to you ". There has been no agreement between L and X. X offers Blackacre to M for £1,000 but states he has no authority to do so, or that he is the owner himself, or that he will be the owner at the date of conveyance. M accepts. It is possible to argue that L is bound : but it is difficult to see how there is an appearance of authority to T.[19]

The usual case of apparent authority occurs when P puts A in a certain position giving him an authority less extensive than the course of employment. T is aware of the position and the course of employ-ment and A purports to be authorised to do some act within the scope of employment but beyond his authority. By putting A in that position P represents that A's authority is co-extensive with the course of employ-ment.[20] Since T is aware of P's act there is a representation to T by P. But can there be an appearance of authority based on A's conduct alone? P appoints A his manager but with restricted authority. T knows nothing of P or A. A approaches T, informs him that he is the manager of P's business, and a contract is concluded within the course of A's employment but not within his authority. It is submitted A has apparent authority. T would have acquired knowledge of the appoint-

---

[19] The question whether such a case falls with the definition of apparent authority in the *Agency Restatement* is discussed above. I am of the opinion that the case is not one of apparent authority and that L is not bound.

[20] In *Dawn* v. *Simmins* (1879), 41 L.T. 783 the report suggests that Bramwell L.J. doubted whether there was any representation at all. He is reported as having said *arguendo :* " The only way in which there was a representation was by putting in Clarke as manager. How is that a representation? " If putting a person in the position of manager is not a representation at least that he is manager, the position of manager is a very curious and precarious one. The report is probably incorrect.

O

ment of A as manager and of the course of employment of such a position from many sources; A's intimate connection with the matter does not pollute the information he supplies. The appearance of authority is derived in such a case from the acts of both A and P.

In the above case P's appointment was considered to be of a public nature. Let us consider a case in which that is not so. P privately appoints A to sell goods. T, a stranger to A and P, has no means of ascertaining whether A has been so appointed, save by asking P. He concludes a contract with A without any enquiry of P but relying on A's assertion of authority. The contract was in the course of A's employment but unauthorised. In this case one cannot, merely by forming a judgment of a factual situation, say there was an appearance of authority. For such appearance must be derived from the acts of A and P. But the case can be brought within apparent authority by the assistance of a legal rule. A is authorised to disclose the fact of his appointment. A legal rule makes the disclosure by A equivalent to a disclosure of P.[21]

I have already referred to the definition of apparent authority in the *Restatement of Agency,* and pointed out an ambiguity in its concluding words. The *Restatement* defines authority as a power: nevertheless apparent authority is not an apparent power but a real power : there can be no such thing as apparent power. Again, according to the *Restatement* definition, where P authorises A to act *a—l,* and P represents to T that A has authority to do acts *a—l,* A has *two* powers. Surely it is better, using authority in its factual sense, to say that whether there is actual or apparent authority or both A has *a* power.

The Definition of Contract

The concept of contract is usually considered as being that of an agreement directed to the creation of rights and duties between the parties; this may be called the jurisprudential concept. In English law, however, there are various kinds of contracts : the technical term " contract " is not the equivalent of the jurisprudential concept. In using the term " contract " in connection with English law it must be borne in mind that it has a technical meaning in addition to the jurisprudential one.

The technical terminology of English law applies " contract " to the contract of record, the specialty contract, the simple contract, and also to the relation between principal and third person brought about by the agent. This technical terminology is based on the history of the procedure of English law. The action of assumpsit was available for various relations, it was the form of action which had to be invoked by

---

[21] It follows that the legal rules as to apparent authority could not be made applicable in the following case. A agrees to sell goods for P but not to disclose the existence of the agency. He contracts with T within the scope of employment but beyond his authority. In breach of his agreement he discloses the existence of the agency.

the principal or third person. Since the Common Law Procedure Act personal actions are divided into actions of contract or tort. The action of contract applies to different relationships including that of principal and agent. A contract is said to exist whenever there is a relationship in respect of which an action of contract lies. It is important, therefore, to realise that when it is said that a contract is made by the agent between the principal and the third person no more may be meant than that the relationship between them is one in respect of which an action of contract lies. It does not follow from the terminology that the relationship is one which is governed by the same principles as govern that existing where there is a contract formed by agreement between the parties themselves. The single terminology does suggest that there may be a unifying principle applicable to the various relationships which are those of contract, but the terminology alone does not prove there is such a single principle. In fact it is submitted that the terminology is misleading.

The Basis of Contractual Liability

Owing to the various kinds of contracts in English law the phrase " contractual liability " can only refer to a single concept if the various kinds of contracts are based on a single principle. As already stated, a proposition that the various kinds of contracts are based on a single principle is not self-evident; it requires proof. Nevertheless we find Cook speaking of contractual liability as if it were a single concept. The explanation, no doubt, is that he has in mind what I have called the jurisprudential concept of contract.

The jurisprudential concept is probably derived from the Kantian theory of contract which was generally adopted in the 19th century. As Pound has pointed out,[22] Kant based contract on a conveyance of property, the promisor delivering his freewill to the promisee. Kant stressed however that this could only take place by the combined wills of both,[23] and his notion of a common will as the basis of a contract is to be found in most theories propounded during the last century. It is submitted that where a contract is made through an agent the theory of a common will is inapplicable: the principal and third person even " under abstraction of . . . empirical conditions " have not common wills except in the case of the *nuntius*.[24]

Lewis considers that the principles governing liability under the forms of action of covenant, debt, and assumpsit were distinct, and he therefore puts forward three bases of contractual liability.[25] He does not accept the notion of a common will as applying to any action of contract.

---

[22] *Introduction to the Philosophy of Law*, p. 260.
[23] " It is neither by the *particular* Will of the Promisor nor that of the Acceptor that the property of the former passes over to the latter. This is effected only by the *combined* or united Wills of both."—*Philosophy of Law*, tr. Hastie, p. 102.
[24] This is discussed more fully later.
[25] *Undisclosed Principal*, 9 Col. L.R. 116 at p. 132.

The first principle he submits is that of the unilateral will, the willingness of the promisor to be bound by what he has promised: he cannot complain of injustice if he is required to do that which he has said he is willing to do. One can also subject the unilateral will to liability on the ground of the moral obligation to keep one's word. It must be pointed out, however, that English law never subjects a unilateral declaration of will to liability. In the action of covenant there must be a formal act— the sealing or signing. The unilateral will is not, of course, an adequate explanation of the liability arising from a simple contract. There must be an agreement for consideration to which the promisor is a party. If M and N together agree that L should do a certain act, a statement by L that he is willing to do the act would not involve him in liability even though made before the agreement between M and N, unless either M or N was an agent for L.

Lewis considers that the doctrine of unjust enrichment underlies the action of debt. The receipt of the *quid pro quo* makes it unjust to retain the thing or money without doing the act promised. This principle is not of universal application; it cannot be easily applied to an executory contract.

Pound's postulate that reasonable expectations must not be defeated is considered to be the basis of assumpsit. This links up with the theory of the objective nature of agreement. Lewis says the plaintiff recovers because " he would not have promised had the defendant not so acted as to cause him to promise, in the expectation of a benefit which the defendant has failed to give him ".

We thus have four principles which may be considered in relation to contract, and so it is pertinent when the *Agency Restatement* comment says that apparent authority " conforms to the principles of contract " to ask to which of these four the commentary refers. We shall discuss these principles in connection with both actual and apparent authority.

Actual authority. (1) The undisclosed principal

It is submitted that the case of the undisclosed principal is governed by considerations peculiar to itself. The relations of the principal are not directly affected by the agent treating with the third person. The agent alone acquires immediate rights and immediate liabilities as regards the third person. Under the contract of the principal with the agent the principal is entitled to the benefits which the agent obtains from his contract with the third person. The principal could indeed compel the agent to bring an action against the third person. He could thus obtain the name of the agent for the purpose of an action. The law shortens the proceedings by enabling the principal to sue the third person in his own name; this is in accordance with the principle of preventing circuity of action. That the action by the principal is one to enforce the agent's rights is shown by the fact that the principal is bound by the state of accounts between the agent and the third person. As regards the action by the third person against the principal it cannot be said that the third person has a contractual right to the agent's rights against the principal. The position nevertheless is that the third person has a right against the agent and the agent has a right to an indemnity from the principal in respect of the liability corresponding to the third person's right. Is it not a form of the doctrine of subrogation which enables the third person to sue the principal?[26]

(2) The nuntius

I think the case of the *nuntius* must be distinguished from other cases of agency. The *nuntius* is in fact and not metaphorically a channel of communication between the principal and the third person. He carries to a third person, specified by the principal, either (a) an offer, the terms of which have already been formulated by the principal, or (b) the acceptance of an offer, of which the principal is already aware. In such a case the offer or acceptance is in fact made by the principal himself and not by the *nuntius* for the principal. The principal is in direct agreement with the third person. The *nuntius* is not only " legally the mechanical contrivance by means of which the minds of the principal and the third person meet ", he is so in fact.[27] The principal acts *per se* in accepting or offering, it is only the communication which is *per alium*. The case is exactly the same as a contract by correspondence, there is no room for the application of the maxim *qui facit per alium facit per se.*

The situation in the case of the *nuntius* calls for little comment. No agency principle is in fact involved. It is true that the *nuntius* does fall within the definition of an agent given in the *Restatement,* but it would not be unreasonable to restrict the definition to the case where an agent exercises a discretion. It is conceivable that a legal system might require the parties to conduct their negotiations in the presence of each other. A transaction concluded by telephone might be legally unenforceable, *a fortiori* a human messenger might not be allowed, but even Roman Law, which had no general doctrine of agency, allowed contracts to be concluded through a *nuntius.*[28]

---

[26] Seavey expresses the point of view in the text thus: " Ames objects that logically the undisclosed principal is a *cestui que trust* and that a *cestui que trust* cannot sue or be sued at law. Admitting that he is a *cestui* he may as such realise through proceedings in equity upon the claim held by his trustee (agent) against the third party, as Ames pointed out. If the rights of the third party are properly taken care of, as in fact they are, the only abnormality is the informality of allowing a direct action at law. The same is true in the case of suit against the principal; there should be no objection simply on the ground that a short cut has been taken."

[27] The quotation is from a note on *Kinahan* v. *Parry,* [1910] 2 K.B. 389 in 19 Col. L.R. at p. 764. It is represented as being the basis of the operation of agency generally, the case of a *nuntius* not being discussed. The note is in effect only a lengthy paraphrase of the maxim *qui facit per alium facit per se.*

[28] The following case perhaps merits some consideration. T makes an offer to P and dispenses with the necessity of any communication of acceptance to him. P writes to A telling him to accept P's offer. Before A communicates with T, P cancels his instructions. Is

(3) Qui facit per alium facit per se

Where the agent has a discretion either as to the person with whom
he is to deal or as to the terms he may offer or accept or as to both he is
not a contrivance for conveying the state of mind of the principal to the
third person. By exercising his discretion the agent produces a state of
mind which does not psychologically correspond to any state of mind of
the principal. It follows that the offer is made by the agent and not by
the principal; there is no agreement between the principal and the third
person. The result of the agent's dealings may be that the principal is
legally bound to the third person, but we are in the realm of fiction if
we say that this is so because the offer or acceptance is made by the
principal. The maxim *qui facit per alium facit per se* read without any
qualification is obviously a fiction. Seavey treats it as such, but while
Cook speaks of the fiction of the identity of principal and agent he considered that the maxim is not necessarily fictitious, for, he says that " in
1304 the maxim meant just what it said ". If so the maxim can only
be regarded as a tribute to mediaeval witchcraft. One must read the
maxim as meaning that the legal consequence of a person acting *per
alium* is the same as if he had acted *per se*. Whether such a proposition
is true or false depends obviously upon legal rules and not upon the facts
of nature.

A rule of law regulates human conduct by prescribing certain consequences for stated factual situations. It sometimes happens that the
same or similar legal consequences may be prescribed for two different
factual situations. Sometimes such a happening is described by saying
that " in law " the two factual situations are the same or similar. The
qualification " in law " may not be expressly stated : this happens in the
maxim *qui facit per alium facit per se*. It appears by use of the epithet
" legal " in Holmes' statement of the maxim which is " the characteristic
feature which justifies agency as a title of the law is the absorption *pro
hac vice* of the agent's legal individuality in that of the principal ".[29]

The equation of two different factual situations, though it be a
defiance of reality, will not produce legal error if it be true that the
same legal consequences follow from the two situations. Though some
people's sense of accuracy may be offended by saying that recklessness
is the same as intention no error will result in law if in fact the law
always attaches the same consequences to them. But because in some
circumstances the law does attach the same consequences to recklessness
as to intention it does not logically follow that it should not differentiate

there a completed contract? It can be argued that P's letter to A being more than a mere
mental assent is a sufficient acceptance. It is submitted that P's letter can mean either
(a) I have accepted T's offer, please inform him of that fact, or (b) I intend to accept T's
offer as from the time of your communication to him. In case (a) there is clearly a contract.
Case (b) raises the question whether it is possible to qualify an acceptance by making it
operate as from a future event or date. But in either case, it is submitted, it is correct to
say that the acceptance is in fact made by P.

[29] *The Common Law*, p. 232.

between them in other circumstances. The device of equating two factual concepts should be used cautiously.[30] Psychologically human beings, including lawyers, having treated diverse things similarly on some occasions may tend to treat them again in the same way despite altered circumstances. This tendency is strengthened, or it is perhaps more correct to say evidenced, by language which equates the diverse things. The law however should, and very often does, pay regard to the points of difference and does not always attach the same consequences. The phraseology may hamper the law in doing this or may make exposition of the law difficult when it is done.

The maxim *qui facit per alium facit per se* merely states the legal rule that if A agrees with T, relations between P and T result just as if P had personally agreed with T. It does not explain or justify the rule. The maxim itself perhaps requires a little explanation. What is meant by " *per* "? If P pushes A so that A falls on T, has P pushed T *per* A? Has P pushed T *per* A where P and A agree that A should push T and A does so? Where P sends an offer through a *nuntius,* A, is the offer made *per* A? Or is it only where A exercises a discretion that the offer is made *per* A and not *per* T?

Cook insists that the offer or acceptance is made by the principal. True, he regards the identity of principal and agent as a fiction, and he admits that the offer or acceptance actually emanates from the mind of the agent. Nevertheless he says that the doctrine of the objective nature of the agreement justifies him in considering that the legal view is that the offer or acceptance is that of the principal.[31] He says " in law the manifestation " (by the agent) " is of the intention of the principal ". By this he may mean that the legal consequence of the act of the agent is that the principal is bound in law as if he had himself manifested the intention. If this is his meaning it is merely a statement of the doctrine of agency and not an explanation of it. If he means that the courts consider that the offer by the agent is in fact a manifestation of the principal's intention he is wrong. It is strange that he does not support his statement by any quotation from a judg-

---

[30] The maxim " every person is presumed to intend the natural consequence of his acts " is based on the same device. It represents a person's relation to the natural consequences of his acts as being the same as his relation to intended consequences. All the maxim means is that a person will sometimes be treated in relation to the natural consequences as if he had intended them. It is not surprising that Holmes (*Common Law*, p. 147) says the maxim is " very inaccurate ".

[31] " It is fundamental in the law of contract that a person is bound not by his real but by his manifested intention. One may manifest his intention not only by his own words or acts but also through the words or acts of another called in law an agent. In the latter case the complete expression of the intention is left to the agent: he is often given a discretion to fix the terms of the offer, but when he does fix them, in law the manifestation is of the intention of the principal . . . Let us never forget that our law of agency does not say that the agent makes a contract and that by some process of transfer the rights and duties thus executed are transferred to the principal: but that on the other hand it does regard the contract as made by the principal through the agent, the agent being treated only as a medium of transaction. It is the mind of the principal which meets the mind of the third party, just as much where the medium of conversation is an agent, or where for example it is a letter." (From the article in 6 Col. L.R. 34.)

ment. It is merely playing with words to say that the act of the agent manifests the principal's intention. It is true that the principal intends the agent to make an offer, and that when the agent does so he acts in accordance with the principal's intention. But the actual offer was never conceived by the principal, he never has a specific intention as to that; the agent's state of mind is not a psychological development of the principal's mind. The offer is not even a manifestation of the principal's intention that the agent should make an offer. The law rejects the view that the mere fact that the agent purports to be authorised is evidence that he was authorised.

It is true that according to the objective theory what matters is not the principal's actual intention but his conduct. This is sometimes loosely stated by saying that what matters is not his real intention but his manifested intention, *i.e.*, the intention which his conduct reasonably manifests him as having. But the conduct of the principal consists in agreeing with the agent, and his intention is fully manifested by the grant of authority to the agent. The conduct of the agent is not that of the principal; it manifests his state of mind alone.[32] The specific offer made by the agent is a product of his mind alone. It cannot be regarded as in any way a product of the principal's mind; the grant of discretion to the agent shows that the principal had no specific offer in *his* mind.

Seavey's demonstration of the view that the law does not regard the agreement between agent and third person as being an agreement between principal and third person is based on the doctrine of *Collen* v. *Wright*.[33] His argument is that if the law regarded the agreement as made by the principal himself there would be no room for saying that the agent warranted he had authority.

> In exchange for the undertaking of T to enter into a contract with P, A guarantees that he has a power to make P a party. If the agent is regarded merely as a channel of communication, or if the promise of the agent is the promise of the principal, no such agreement would exist, and the agent could be held only upon a representation that the principal consents to the existence of the contract. . . . The doctrine of *Collen* v. *Wright* . . . recognises the real facts of the situation and disregards the fiction of the identity of principal and agent.

---

[32] It looks to me as if Cook's statements involve an obvious fallacy. His argument appears to be: (i) According to the objective theory the actual state of the party's mind is immaterial in deciding whether he has entered into a contract. (ii) In a contract through an agent the actual state of the principal's mind is not necessarily the same as that of the agent's mind which conceived the contract. (iii) As a conclusion from the two above premises we have the proposition that, according to the objective theory, in a contract through an agent, though the principal's mind did not conceive the contract, he may be a party to it.

But of course no conclusion can be validly drawn from two negative premises. The argument neglects the positive factor of the objective theory that there must be conduct by the one party leading the other to believe that the former is entering into a contract. When the agent makes a contract there is, as stated in the text, no conduct by the principal leading the third person to believe that the principal is entering into that specific contract.

A similar argument is put forward by Seavey in dealing with apparent authority. See *infra*.

[33] (1857), 7 E. & B. 301; and in the Exchequer Chamber, 8 E. & B. 647.

It should be pointed out that consistently with his argument Cook regards the doctrine of *Collen* v. *Wright*[33] as anomalous.

The accuracy of the proposition that the contract is always made by the agent can perhaps be demonstrated more clearly by considering the following case which is very nearly one where the contract is made by the principal. T makes an offer to P and dispenses with the necessity for communication to him of acceptance of the offer. P writes to A authorising him to accept if he thinks fit. A accepts. Even in such a case it cannot be said that the acceptance was by P : the contract was made by A not P. P's intention is that A should accept if A thinks fit. A, by accepting, does not effect telepathically an alteration in P's state of mind so that it becomes an intention to accept. A's conduct in accepting does not manifest P's intention in the sense of making externally perceptible P's state of mind. It is in accordance with the content of P's intention but there is a different meaning from that which even Cook gives to manifestation of intention. Cook's definition of manifested intention is " an intention which one man led another to believe irrespective of whether he had such intention or not ". It is of course no part of the doctrine of agency that T in dealing with A should consider that P had the specific intention of accepting. In law, to use Cook's phrase, it is quite immaterial what T thought about P's intention. In fact it is likely T will only think that the offer was authorised by P. Why should he think A is a mere messenger?

The case just considered was an extreme one; let us now consider one on the other side of the boundary. P makes an offer to T to sell at a price to be fixed by A. A price is fixed by A and T accepts. The contract in such a case is without doubt made by P; but as Ewart has pointed out, this is not a case of agency at all : T could have accepted before A fixed the price. Where the agency relationship is involved and P authorises A to make the offer to T at a price to be fixed by A then T, even if he knows of this, cannot accept before A makes an offer to him.

The discussion of the maxim has, it is submitted, made it quite clear that it cannot be said that the contractual principle of agreement between the parties is the basis of the doctrine of actual authority. Whether agreement be subjective or objective there is no agreement between the principal and the third person : the agreement is between the agent and the third person.

(4) The unilateral will

Seavey agrees that in the case of actual authority " the contract comes into existence through the independent will of the agent " but he adds " the contract does come into existence in accordance with the expressed will of the principal and there is no departure from the theory of contracts ". This is surely tantamount to saying that the unilateral will is the basis of contract. Yet Lewis considers that it applies only to formal contracts. Even there the form is as important as the intention of the promisor. Moreover the doctrine of unilateral will is inconsistent with the following well-established principle of agency. If T, knowing of the agency relation between A and P, gives exclusive credit to A, *i.e.*, deals with A as if A were the principal, he cannot make P liable. P's willingness to be liable is of course unaffected by T's conduct; it cannot be said that in all cases P is only willing to be liable if A contracts as agent.

When it is said that " the contract does come into existence in accordance with the expressed will of the principal ", all that is being said is that the contract was authorised by the principal. We have to explain why the fact that the principal authorises the agent to enter into agreement with a third person should involve the principal in relations with the other party to the agreement.

(5) Reasonable expectations must not be defeated

Both the principal and the third person doubtless expect that the one will be liable to the other. In the case of the principal it is probably correct that his expectation is always reasonable, because it is based on the knowledge that T will undertake to be liable to him. But T's expectations cannot confidently be said to be always reasonable. If A is a special agent and T relies solely on A's statement that he has authority to do a particular act, is it reasonable for T to expect P to be liable?

(6) Suggested basis of liability

The basis of a legal rule can always be expressed by reference to some such term as justice or public policy. Such terms are, however, properly used to indicate either a metaphysical concept transcending all rules of law or a teleological concept generalising the ends of all rules of law. The jurist dealing with a particular rule must point to the particular vestment by means of which the metaphysical concept makes its material manifestation in that rule or to the particular end of that rule; he must then go further and show that the particular vestment does indeed clothe a manifestation of justice or that the particular end is one of justice. To perform the latter part of his task he may have to consider the fundamental problems of jurisprudence. However, he may escape that task by using the argument of analogy. He may refer to some matter in connection with the rule which is accepted as a justification of some other rule. Thus the doctrine of actual authority would be justified if it were based on the principle underlying the enforcement of simple contracts. The principle underlying simple contracts is accepted as being in accordance with justice, and so any doctrine referring to that principle will also be accepted as being in accordance with justice.

Sometimes a rule of law is justified by showing its practical necessity for maintaining given social conditions. A doctrine of agency is clearly required to meet the needs of commercial life today: commerce involves transactions with persons geographically remote, and the extensive capital involved demands organisation of many people in commercial units. Business would be impossible unless agents could bind principals to third persons and *vice versa*. Yet practical necessity cannot be accepted as a juristic basis. Legal technique consists in creating particular concepts for the handling of the complex circumstances of life. Vague as the general idea of justice may be it is nevertheless the touchstone of the jurist, and the technical concepts of law are not governed merely by the ordering of social facts but are moulded also under the influence of the idea of justice. The theme of the play is the idea of justice. The technical concepts are the characters in the play. To many, however, the appearance is that of a modern play in which there is no theme—only a discussion of the characters.

The problem of finding a basis of liability consists in determining the particular concepts into which agency may be fitted. The concepts of English law are affected by the Roman law background of juristic science and its own terminology. Both combine in suggesting an agreement between principal and third person as the basis of actual authority. We have already seen that according to the terminology of English law the relation between principal and third person is said to be that of contract; this suggests the dominant kind of contract in modern days, *viz.*, that arising from agreement. But it is misleading in so far as it suggests an agreement between principal and third person. The existence of slavery in Rome made it unnecessary for Roman law to develop rules whereby, in all cases, one free man should be bound by the acts of another free man. Mediaeval Roman law accepted the concepts of the classical law and applied them to the new conditions. It treated a person making a contract through an agent in much the same way as the classical law treated the person making a contract through a slave. The doctrine of agency was regarded only as an extension of the Roman law of contract and its underlying principle was that the contract was made by the principal.

We have rejected the notion of agreement between principal and third person as being the basis of the doctrine of agency. It is submitted, nevertheless, that the basis is that of agreement, but not between the principal and the third person; it is that of agreement between the agent and the third person. Combined with this we have the well-known concept of a power; the principal has granted the agent a power to affect his relations with third persons. The agreement between the agent and the third person provides that the principal shall acquire rights against and be subject to obligations to the third person and *vice versa*. English law enforces this agreement and the principal and the third person do acquire those rights and are subject to those obligations.

Why has this simple basis of an agreement between A and P combined with a power given by P to A not been recognised? The answer appears to be that it has been thought to be a fundamental rule of English law that X can neither acquire rights nor be subject to liabilities by reason of an agreement between Y and Z. A doctrine of the personality of contracts may have been a universal doctrine of Roman law; certainly the modern law of contracts appears to have been formulated in the belief that it was. But when the doctrine was formulated as part of English law it was really inconsistent with cases of agency with which English law had dealt from its earliest times. The fiction of the identity of principal and agent was possibly an attempt to resolve the inconsistency. Justice may require that a third person may not be subject to liabilities nor acquire rights as a result of agreement between others—*res inter alios acta alteri non nocet.* But the doctrine of personality is not a necessary concept of universal application : it certainly does not apply in the case of agency. A third person may acquire rights under an agreement between others, for example, a *cestui que trust* and the principal may be bound by the acts of his agent.

T's liability depends on the ordinary principle of agreement. He has agreed to be bound with the agent's principal. P is bound because he has granted A a power to enter into an agreement specifying that P shall be bound. The concept of a power is not confined to cases where the donee has authority to enter into a contract; under a power of appointment the donee makes a grant of the donor's property. Underlying the concept of power is doubtless the principle of the unilateral will, so that it can be said that P is bound because he was willing to be bound. But this principle has to be combined with that of the agreement made by A under which the obligations of P are defined.

The Nature of the Agreement between the Agent and the Third Person

I have called the transaction between A and T an agreement. It is tempting to say that it is a contract whereby A promises that P will be liable to T and T promises to be liable to P. If that were so, since the law will only make P liable if P has authorised A, A will be liable to T should it turn out that he (A) had in fact no authority. The doctrine of *Collen* v. *Wright*[33] would thus follow from the essential nature of the transaction between A and T. There are two matters to be considered in connection with this theory of a contract which may not however prove to be flaws in the theory. The first arises from the case of an executed contract. A supplies P's goods to T. What is the consideration for T's promise to pay for the goods? The consideration of the goods moves from the principal, not the agent. This is the converse case to *Dunlop Pneumatic Tyre Co.* v. *Selfridge*,[34] and the decision in that case makes it difficult to argue that the consideration moving from the principal will support a promise to the agent. On principle there is no reason why it

---

[34] [1915] A.C. 847.

should not—for it cannot be said that the doctrine of consideration moving from the promisee is a necessary concept of justice. It might further be argued that consideration consists in a promise by the agent, not indeed that the principal will be liable in any respect, but that the goods are the goods of the principal, which is another way of saying the warranty of authority. There would thus be mutual promises of the agent and the third person.

The other matter to be considered is also concerned with the " warranty of authority ". Suppose that unknown to A the principal is an infant. It is clear that the principal will not be liable to the third person. Is the agent liable? According to the contract theory under which the agent promises that the principal will be liable the agent of course does become liable.[35] The *American Restatement* suggests that there is no liability.[36] English case law based on *Collen* v. *Wright*[33] is not decisive: but it would be consistent with the authorities that the agent should be liable.

The real objection to the contract theory, however, is that it is factually incorrect. The legal consequences of such a theory may coincide with established rules and may supply that *elegantia juris* which on the formal side is so desirable. It may also supply a solution for problems hitherto undecided. But it is submitted it is not in accord with an accurate judgment of the facts. The agent does not promise the third person that the principal will be liable, nor does the third person promise the agent that he (T) will be liable to the principal. Neither the agent himself nor the third person considers the agent as participating in the content of the liabilities to which the principal and the third person are subject.

The factual nature of the transaction, it is submitted, is that there is an agreement that P will be liable to T and T to P. There is a difficulty in calling the agreement a contract in the sense of a contract being an aggregate of promises. With regard to the actual subject matter of the liability neither the agent nor the principal undertakes anything. Can a statement by the agent that the principal will do certain things be said to be a promise of the principal? It is certainly not a promise *by* the principal. The transaction is really *sui generis*. A consensual relation not amounting to a contract is, however, not peculiar to the transaction of the agent and the third person. It may indeed exist in the setting up of the agency relation between the principal and the agent, *e.g.*, where the principal is an infant.[37]

In addition to the agreement between the agent and the third person dealing with the subject matter of the relation between principal and third person there is a collateral contract between the agent and

---

[35] Strictly the contractual liability, it is submitted, only arises when the agent refuses to compensate the third person.

[36] See Art. 332 and comment (a).

[37] *Agency Restatement*, Art. 20 comment (b).

the third person. This contract consists in a promise by the agent to compensate the third person if the agent was not authorised. The general consensus of opinion is that this " warranty of authority " is not a legal fiction, but depends on a judgment of fact that the agent does by his conduct warrant that he has authority from the principal. Since it is based on the agent's conduct, the warranty may be excluded by the circumstances of the transaction. It is a question of fact whether the warranty covers the case of incapacity of the principal unknown to the agent.[38]

Apparent authority
A contract between principal and third person

The ordinary statement of the doctrine of apparent authority is that though A exceeds his authority in dealing with T there will nevertheless be a contract between P and T if T reasonably believed that A had authority.[39] A consequence of the doctrine is that even if A had no authority P is liable. This is sometimes put in the form that the actual agreement between P and A does not affect T. According to this reasoning it is clear that the latter proposition is not the basis of the doctrine of apparent authority but a deduction from it: if the doctrine did not exist the actual agreement between P and A would concern T. Yet we find Cook, in explaining the doctrine, saying: " The third party cares not and need not trouble himself about the state of affairs as between agent and principal, that is no concern of his ". In fact the doctrine of apparent authority assumes that the third person has concerned himself about the agreement between principal and agent, for an essential part of the rule is that the third person reasonably believes the agent was authorised.

We have seen that when it is said that there is a " contract " between P and T the statement does not necessarily mean that the relationship between them is that of other species of contract. Both Cook and Seavey however consider that there is a " true contract ", by which they mean a simple contract based on agreement between the parties. They both justify their attitude by reference to the objective nature of agreement.

Seavey says, " The situation is not different from that where P makes an offer personally to T. P's actual consent is unnecessary. The offer is made by the speaking of the words or the doing of an act with communication through authorised channels. With P's mental processes we are not concerned." This reasoning transcends ordinary logic which does not allow a conclusion to be drawn in positive terms from a negative proposition. A similar argument to Seavey's would show that a " true contract " results between P and T because T is not concerned with the

---

[38] *Yonge* v. *Toynbee*, [1910] 1 K.B. 215 suggests that it does.

[39] The *Agency Restatement* is careful to say that the principal is liable on " contracts made by the agent ".

colour of P's eyes, neither when dealing with A nor when dealing personally with P.

Perhaps I may be forgiven still further repetition in stating Cook's application of the doctrine of manifested intention to the case of apparent authority. Cook writes:

> A says to B, " X is authorised to sell you my horse upon terms to be agreed upon between you and him." Privately A instructs X not to sell for less than $150. X offers the horse to B for $100 and B accepts. We all agree that A is bound, but why? By estoppel? So says the new school. A has not contracted with B, for he has not assented: there has been no meeting of the minds. To be sure there has not in fact. I contend there has been in law. A's statement to B is nothing more or less than an offer to contract with him leaving the terms to be fixed by X.

Ewart deals trenchantly with this statement, pointing out that A's statement to B is certainly not an offer to B, it is a statement that A is willing to be bound by an offer to be made by X. To say that there is " a meeting of the minds in law " is merely an incorrect statement of the legal rule itself—it is not an explanation of it.

The *Agency Restatement,* though it avoids saying there is a contract between P and T, says " apparent authority conforms to the principles of contracts; there is a manifestation of consent by the principal to the third person, and in the case of a bilateral transaction, a counter-manifestation which completes the transaction ". But the " principles of contracts ", as I understand them, require in the case of a simple contract that there shall be a consent to the specific terms of the contract. If L and M " contract to make a contract " they are not bound by the future " contract " until its terms have been agreed. In the case of apparent agency, moreover, there is no original agreement at all between P and T. P's representation that A is authorised does not necessarily result in a contract between P and T that P will be bound by the dealings between A and T. Of course there may be such a contract between P and T, but it does not arise from T's consent to the arrangement with A. That consent does not also operate as consent to such a contract with P. In any case such a contract is quite different from the contract whose terms are settled between A and T. The fallacy of the *Restatement* comment is the equivocacy of " consent ". As used there it means merely a unilateral willingness to be bound by the contract between A and T. In the " principles of contracts " it means a bilateral willingness to be bound by specific formulated terms.

Equivalence of cases of apparent and actual authority

Cook, in his reply to Ewart, put forward the argument that apparent authority is in fact equivalent to actual authority. He said: "Agency is a question of fact, but we must not forget that the external relationship may exist as a fact, even though the internal one does not. So far as the persons to whom I have held a given person out as possessing certain authority are concerned the relationship of principal and agent does exist : he is authorised, has authority to act for me to that extent : he is in fact my agent, with that authority and I am bound, if at all, because through my agent I have entered into those contracts which have been duly accepted." Though he speaks of " fact " his definition of the terms " agency " and " authority " involve legal rules. They, in fact, embody the rules he is attempting to explain : and his argument is merely tautology.

Seavey says " if P represents to T that A has authority to contract the legal result is exactly the same as if A had authority ". Even if this is true it does not follow that the factual situations in apparent and actual authority are identical : they are *ex hypothesi* different. Nor does the proposition imply that the legal causes are the same. But is the proposition true? Is the legal result *always* the same? Suppose, to consider one point only, A enters into a contract for which he has apparent authority but no actual authority; will he not be liable under the doctrine of *Collen* v. *Wright*?[33] Should not A be liable for a wrongful assertion of authority even though no damage result to T because P does become liable? Damage is not required to sustain an action of contract.[40]

The theory of estoppel

Ewart's thesis is that the principal does not make the contract, neither does the agent " make the contract for him . . . for he had no authority to do so. . . . One of the requisites of a contract is missing, namely the authority of the agent to make it ". The principal is, however, he maintains, estopped from traversing an allegation by the third person that the agent had authority, because the third person contracted with the agent on the faith of a representation by the principal that the agent had authority.

This argument assumes that the case of actual authority is familiar and explains apparent authority by reference to it. Its factual aspect is that the third person deals with the agent because he believes the agent had authority and that that belief was induced by the principal. The legal rule it introduced is that in these circumstances the law should deal with the principal as if the principal had authorised the agent. It maintains that this legal rule is an exemplification of the doctrine of estoppel. It is the last proposition which is generally controverted. It is said that the rule is not an application of the doctrine of estoppel, for the doctrine of estoppel requires that there must be some detriment sustained by the person misled, *i.e.*, in the case of apparent authority, by the third person.

" Has the third person changed his legal position[41] in any way?"

---

[40] This point is further discussed below.

[41] It is not clear what Cook means by " legal position ". Does he mean that the estoppel-assertor must have changed his legal relations either with the person making the representation or with others? The doctrine of estoppel has no such requirement. Or does he mean a change of position which the law recognises? What changes of position are not recognised?

asks Cook. In the formation of an executory contract where is this change of position? asks Wright. The *Agency Restatement*[42] says: " Apparent authority, which creates contractual relations between principal and third person, is to be distinguished from estoppel which operates to permit suit by the third person if he has changed his position." Of course it cannot be said that T's liability to P is for the change of position which makes the doctrine of estoppel applicable. The hypothesis is that the liability to P comes into existence because of the application of the doctrine of estoppel: there must be a change of position *before* there is liability. Ewart accepts the view that there must be detriment sustained by the third person, but he says it does exist. Suppose the contract is in writing and T " does nothing except sign something ". T, because of the representation of P, does change his position: he makes an offer to A or accepts one made by A. That is a change of position precedent to the existence of the contract. Cook, however, denies that the mere act of offering or accepting is a detriment. " Surely he does not mean the labour of speaking the words or signing the memorandum (if he did so) is the change in position," says Cook. This, however, is precisely what Ewart does mean: and he claims that the law recognises such labour as a change of position, not only by estopping P but also by giving T a right of action against A for wrongful assertion of authority. That right of action depends on a contract between A and T for which there must be consideration. The only consideration moving from T to A is the labour of T in making an offer to contract with P or in accepting such an offer. Consideration consists in a detriment, hence such labour must be a detriment.

This appears a rather strained view of detriment. Moreover, is consideration in the sense of a detriment sustained by a promisee always necessary to a contract? Is not the case of a promise for a promise one where no such consideration is necessary? If so the argument from the doctrine of breach of warranty of authority does not help. Again, if the labour of offering or accepting is a detriment then will it not exist in every agreement, so that consideration is not an additional requirement of English law? X says to Y: " I offer to give you £100 if you will accept ". Y says: " I accept ". Is Y's labour of speaking these words consideration?

A possible answer to this last argument is this. The speaking or writing of words which constitute an undertaking[43] is a very different thing from speaking or writing words which do not constitute an undertaking. The strain on the vocal cords or on the muscles of the hand may be the same in both cases. But that does not constitute the detriment. There is a moral obligation to keep one's word which

---

[42] Sec. 159, Comment.

[43] I use undertaking here to mean the factual promising to do something without assuming that the promise is enforceable in law.

P

applies in one case and not in the other—and there is a social recognition of this obligation apart from law. It is this which the law regards as the detriment and which is present in the speaking or writing of an undertaking. Such a detriment exists in the case of apparent authority by the undertaking by T to A to be liable to P. It exists in every executory contract, so that there is no need to say that the case of a promise for a promise is one where the doctrine of consideration in the sense of detriment does not apply.

This argument is of course far from convincing; it is akin to the doctrine of moral obligation which Lord Denman in *Eastwood* v. *Kenyon*[44] said, " would annihilate the necessity for any consideration at all ", though of course it does not involve any past consideration as did the doctrine discussed in *Eastwood* v. *Kenyon*.

The case of a promise for a promise is one where no detriment is required. The true answer to the objection against estoppel as the basis of apparent authority because no detriment exists is to say that the existence of detriment is not universally necessary in the doctrine of estoppel. It is true that it is stated as a requisite in Lord Tomlin's recent statement of the doctrine of estoppel;[45] but it will not be found in the statement of Parke B. in *Freeman* v. *Cooke*.[46] The modern doctrine of estoppel was first formulated in a case of apparent authority,[47] and in *Freeman* v. *Cooke*[46] apparent authority is given as an example of the doctrine.

Cook calls the view that the doctrine of estoppel explains apparent authority a " new theory ". It must have a youthful vitality if in 1905, when Cook wrote, it was still novel, after having been stated, as we have seen, in 1837. Cook said also, " the courts are beginning to base the doctrine in question upon principles of estoppel ", but surely for some seventy years the doctrine of estoppel was the accepted explanation of apparent authority in the courts. Cook's chronology can perhaps be understood when it is realised that he traces the doctrine of apparent authority back to the Year Books.[48] This historical perspective makes him consider the 19th century as unimportant. The earlier cases were certainly decided before the modern doctrine of estoppel was formulated. But an examination of them reveals no express statement of any theory on which they were decided. The mere fact that the doctrine of estoppel was formulated later does not mean that they cannot be regarded as examples of it. In fact the doctrine of estoppel, as we have seen, was formulated with express reference to the case of apparent authority, and with no reference to a requirement of detriment. Just

---

[44] (1840) 11 A. & E. 438 at p. 450.
[45] *Greenwood* v. *Martin's Bank*, [1933] A.C. at p. 57.
[46] (1848), 2 Ex. 654.
[47] *Pickard* v. *Sears* (1837), 6 A. & E. 469.
[48] Cook cites Y.B. Lib. Ass. pl. 5 fol. 133 (1353); *Seignior and Wolmer's Case* (1623), Godb. 360; *Anon.* (1691), 1 Shower 95; *Anon.* v. *Harrison* (1698), 12 Mod. 346; *Nickson* v. *Barham* (1712), 10 Mod. 109.

as detriment may not be a universal requirement for contract so too it may not be for estoppel.

The controversy on this point is largely terminological. Some writers would confine the term " estoppel " to cases where there is a detriment. Others would apply it to all cases where the law refuses to allow one man to prove that in fact there does not exist the situation which he led another to believe did exist.[49]

Even according to the narrower terminology the doctrine of estoppel only requires that there be some detrimental action in consequence of P's representation. It does not require that there should be some action in consequence of T's agreement with A. In *Reo Motor Car Co.* v. *Barnes*,[50] A, the plaintiff's salesman, sold and delivered a motor car to the defendant and agreed to take the defendant's old car in part exchange. A had previously completed a similar transaction with the defendants without objection from the plaintiff. In fact A was authorised to make only cash sales. Before the defendant had given up his old car or made any payment the plaintiff sued for return of the motor car. It was clear that A had apparent authority; but the court considered that the principal might repudiate the transaction so long as the third party had not acted in reliance on it. This is clearly a misapplication of the theory of estoppel. The third party had acted in reliance on P's representation that A was authorised.

The *Agency Restatement* says " estoppel . . . . . does not operate to permit the apparent principal to maintain an action ". Wright asks: " If we say the principal is estopped how can the principal ever sue on the resulting ' contract '? We have yet to find a case where conduct creating an estoppel gives rights to the person estopped." It is submitted that there is little difficulty in answering the question. If P sues T no question of apparent authority arises: P has ratified A's acts. If T sues P, P can counter-claim without being deemed to have ratified A's act. The estoppel theory says that P cannot set up the defence that A was unauthorised but it goes no further. T, in suing, alleges P is liable on the contract made through the agent: he does not have to plead estoppel; he does not sue on the estoppel; estoppel only operates *in limine* to prevent P saying the agent was unauthorised. But T cannot blow hot and cold; he cannot set up the contract made through an agent for the purpose of enforcing his rights thereunder without conceding to P rights which P would have under such a contract.

The agreement between agent and third person as the basis of liability

In order to show that the agent has a power to affect the principal's relations the theory of estoppel takes two bites at the cherry. It assumes a power exists in the case of actual authority and then shows

---

[49] Thus in *Smith* v. *Hughes*, L.R. 6 Q.B. 597, Blackburn J. deals with the doctrine of manifested intention in creating a contract as an application of the doctrine of estoppel.

[50] 9 S.W. (2d.) 374, noted in (1929), 42 Harv. L.R. at p. 570.

that the parties should be treated as if actual authority existed. Can a more direct basis not be found? Is not the representation by P to T in itself sufficient to give A a power without calling in aid the position where there is actual authority? The factual situation is that A and T agree with each other that P will be liable to T and T to P. Can it not be said that this agreement will be enforced so as to make P liable because P has shown a willingness to be liable, not as in actual authority by his agreement with A but by his representation to T? Moreover, P has led T reasonably to expect that he (P) will be liable. There appears to be good reason for enforcing the agreement between A and T.

How far, nevertheless, does this view of the position take account of what must usually be a factual element in the transaction, namely that the third person deals with A because he believes that A was authorised? One can only conjecture about the probable state of T's mind: but it appears likely that if P's representation is that A is authorised T will think he is authorised. Of course if T does not in fact usually concern himself as to whether A is authorised, but is content to agree that P will be liable without caring whether A was authorised to make such a contract, the theory of agreement between A and T is realistic enough. In law it matters not if T has or has not concerned himself —but in fact it is likely that he has and that he only agrees with A because he only believes A to have authority. The theory of estoppel does take account of that likelihood. Is the omission of T's belief a serious defect in the theory of agreement between A and T?

Apparent authority and the doctrine of Collen v. Wright

An agreement between A and T is an inadequate treatment of all the facts; but it must be realised that there also exists a contract between A and T under which A promises that he has been authorised by P. This contract does take into account the fact that T contracts with A believing that A had authority. The existence of this contract, as we have seen, depends on a judgment of fact based on A's conduct. Since A's conduct is the same whether apparent authority exists or not it would appear that the doctrine of *Collen* v. *Wright*[33] applies to both cases.[51]

The consequences of the contract are not however the same whether apparent authority exists or not. If no apparent authority exists P is not liable to T and T may incur substantial damage. When apparent authority exists P becomes liable to T and T suffers no actual damage from the fact that A was not authorised. It is a purely theoretical question to consider whether T can recover nominal damages from A.

In so far as T's action is based on the tortious character of assumpsit

---

[51] This assumes that T does not disclose to A that P has represented to T that A had authority. If, however, T does disclose this fact and A deals with T as agent for P then, it is submitted, *actual* authority exists. The agreement between P and A is based on an offer to A conveyed by T and accepted by A by dealing with T.

it is submitted he must fail for want of damage. In so far as his action is contractual the problem raises the question whether the subject matter of a promise is necessarily an act or forbearance. If Holmes' view be correct that the subject matter of a promise is not necessarily an act or forbearance,[52] then T can recover nominal damages from A, for A commits a breach of promise by reason of the fact that he had no authority. If, however, Holmes' view is incorrect then A's promise is only one to compensate T for the damage T suffers. Since T suffers no damage it follows that he cannot sue A. A always takes on himself when purporting to act as agent, when in fact he has no authority, the risk of P not ratifying his action. Where P has already represented to T that A has authority A's risk is already nullified and there is no need for ratification.

Conclusion

The conduct of a person in acting as agent has a dual significance. On the one hand it amounts to a representation that rights and liabilities are not to be acquired by the person himself, but by another, his principal; and on the other hand it is an offer of a promise that the person acting as agent has authority so to act. For example, where a person enters into an agreement as agent for the sale of goods then (1) there is an agreement that the principal will be liable to the third person to deliver certain goods and that the third person will be liable to the principal for the payment of the price. (2) The agent promises that he has authority from the principal to enter into the agreement.

Apart from the warranty of authority an agent, in so far as he acts as agent, incurs no liabilities and acquires no rights, for the agreement is that the liabilities shall be those of the principal against the third person. The simile of the conduit pipe is, however, misleading. The principal is not active in leading his legal bonds into confluence with those of the third person through the medium of the agent as a passive conduit. The agent is the active force, in combination of course with the third person. The principal, by agreeing with the agent or making a representation to the third person, endows the agent with power, and the exercise of power by the agent generates a force which brings the principal into contact with the third person.

The principal is affected by an agreement between the agent and the third person, not because he can be said to be a party to that agreement but because his own conduct has made it just that he should be bound in accordance with the terms of the agreement. In the case of actual authority he has agreed with the agent so to be bound; in the case of apparent authority he has shown the third person an intention so to be bound and he has led the third person reasonably to believe that he will be so bound.

---

[52] *Common Law*, pp. 289-290. The contrary view is taken in the *Restatement*.

14

Liability of Principal for Acts Exceeding Actual and Apparent Authority*

The English analytical jurists of the nineteenth century were convinced that they had proved that the declaratory theory of precedent was a fiction. It is not surprising that they ignored the question of the logical pre-existence of rules, for their prevailing metaphysic was anti-metaphysical and they thought only of historical existence. It is, however, surprising that having satisfied themselves that judges do make law they did not direct more attention to the question of how the judges make law. It was left to the lawyers of the twentieth century to investigate what Cardozo has termed the nature of the judicial process.

It is clear that law making by a judge is not a purely logical process. This proposition does not only state an empirical truth based on observation of the actual behaviour of judges, it states also a rule of logic. The most cautious judge, he who always looks within the existing corpus of the law for some principle by which to decide the case before him, transcends logic in arriving at that principle. The new principle is discovered by abstracting certain elements from one or more of the existing principles. This process of abstraction is not strict logical induction, for the latter does not justify the derivation of a rule wider than the particular cases, and the process of abstraction yields a rule to be applied to a new case. The process of abstraction, moreover, is capable of yielding more than one new principle. The selection of the one in fact applied by the judge is not a logical process. It may be said that the principle chosen is one which conforms with the idea of justice which the judge thinks implicit in the legal system. Such idea is rarely made articulate, but even if it is, it is either an *a priori* concept from the point of view of law, or one arrived at by a process of abstraction carried still further so that it is one of several ideas which are implicit in the legal system. Logic can establish the consistency of a set of propositions but it cannot demonstrate the truth of an

---

* Reprinted from the *Canadian Bar Review*, December, 1939, by kind permission.

isolated proposition.   In making law for the new case the judge has a choice among several principles consistent with the legal system, and his choice of a particular principle cannot therefore be a logical process. The importance of logic must not, however, be overlooked: it does restrict the choice of a new principle to one which is consistent with existing legal rules.[1]

Having regard to the importance of the idea of justice in legal development it is reasonable to expect that consideration of the concept should be part of legal training.   It is doubtless true that a judge's sense of justice is not entirely subjective but is to some extent the product of legal training.   Some writers deny or ignore or minimize the effect of legal training, but the extent of agreement among lawyers of a particular system, though drawn from different surroundings, is a proof that such training has some effect.   Nevertheless, the formation of the sense of justice by such means is largely unconscious, for it is rare that attention is paid in Anglo-American legal education to the nature of justice or the relation between rules of law and the idea of justice.   Legal philosophy is neglected.   Bentham's exclusive order against " natural law ", which he himself abrogated by his doctrine of utilitarianism, is observed by his disciples.   Judges may use the phrase " contrary to natural justice ", but its use is emotional and persuasive rather than rational, for there is no attempt to analyse it.

However, the law is largely administered by judges with this Anglo-American legal education, and it is their decisions which, owing to the doctrine of *stare decisis,* determine the law for the future.   But this doctrine does not require that the reasoning of the judge as well as his decision be incorporated in the law.   Were the occupants of the bench " philosopher judges " both their decisions and their reasoning would always be acceptable.   Since they are not, it is only so far as their reasoning does enunciate a sound legal philosophy that it is accepted.

Sometimes, therefore, a decision introduces a desirable rule into the legal system as a result of faulty reasoning on the part of the judge. It is afterwards that the true reasons are found for the decision.   It may be that the judge has blundered into a good decision, or it may be that a sound sense of justice has prompted the decision, and moreover, the faulty reasoning need not be due to inexpertness in handling the legal material but may be due to the fact that the judge by concentrating

---

[1] Lord Halsbury in *Quinn* v. *Leathem* [1901], A.C. 495, appears to deny any place to logic in legal development.   If rules of law were inconsistent there would be no legal order but legal chaos.   The conflict between law and equity was only superficial.   In fact the legal rule was abrogated by the equitable rule.   The major function of logic in the law is to prevent contradictions in the rules.   Opposing "principles" there may be.   Law like life is hospitable to inconsistent principles.   But, with all respect to the dictum of Lord Halsbury in *Quinn* v. *Leathem,* that the law is not logical, it is the task of the lawyer with the aid of logic to delimit the sphere of operation of such principles by the forming of consistent rules. All that Lord Halsbury needed to say was that the process of analogy must not disregard significant distinctions.

on the decision has not paid sufficient attention to the means by which he supports the decision.

The position in English law with regard to the liability of a principal where the agent has exceeded his authority presents an interesting example of a case where a decision was the result of unsound reasoning, the errors in which involved a misstatement of the existing law. Moreover, it is one of those not infrequent situations in our law where a legal problem of an important and recurrent character remains unsolved for want of litigants.

Watteau v. Fenwick—the facts and decision

The case to which I refer is that of *Watteau* v. *Fenwick*,[2] the facts of which were quite simple. One H transferred the business he carried on at a hotel to the defendants, a firm of brewers; but he remained at the hotel as their manager. The licence was taken out in his name, and it was his name which was painted on the door as licensee. The defendants arranged with the manager to supply all the goods required for the hotel except bottled ales and mineral waters. The manager had authority to buy the latter but he had no authority to buy other goods. Nevertheless he did buy other goods on credit from the plaintiffs. The plaintiffs were quite unaware at the time of the sale that the defendants had any connection with the business: they considered that H was the owner not the manager and they gave credit to him alone. Nevertheless, on discovering the actual state of affairs, they sued the defendants and the judgment which they obtained in the county court was upheld in the Divisional Court.[3]

It is quite clear that the manager in contracting for goods other than bottled ales and mineral waters was exceeding his actual authority. It is equally clear that he was acting within the course of his employment;[4] (for it was assumed that the manager of a hotel business would, as such, apart from special instructions, have authority to buy all the goods required for the business).

It is, however, disputed whether a question of apparent authority arose. Goodhart and Hamson say: " There is in *Watteau* v. *Fenwick*[2] an excellent example of pure estoppel by conduct ".[5] Wright's disagreement with this is, in my opinion, correct, though I cannot agree with his view that " the only possible representation was one of ownership and not agency ".[6] Once it is considered that H's acts had some relation to another person they can be equally explained by regarding him either as a purchaser from that person or as the agent of that

---

[2] [1893] 1 Q.B. 346.

[3] Lord Coleridge C.J. and Wills J. The judgment was delivered by Wills J.

[4] I mean by this phrase the authority which an agent in the same position would ordinarily have. See (1938), 16 Can. Bar Rev. 757.

[5] *Undisclosed Principals in Contract*, 4 Camb. L.J. 310 at p. 336.

[6] *Restatements of Contracts and Agency*, 1 Univ. of Tor. L.J. 17 at p. 48 n. 108.

person. In so far, therefore, as there can be said to be any representation by the defendants it might possibly be one of agency. But it is difficult on the facts to see that there was any representation at all made by the defendants.[7] Even if there were a representation of agency the plaintiffs did not rely on it and so there was no agency apparent to them. There was no case of " estoppel by conduct "; the manager's acts exceeded his apparent as well as his actual authority.

The case therefore did raise the question whether a principal can be liable where the agent has exceeded his actual and apparent authority; and it was on this point that it was argued. Finlay, Q.C., counsel for the defendants, maintained that the principal can only be liable, in the absence of actual authority, where the agent has been held out as such to the third person. The court however held that, provided the act is within the course of employment, it is immaterial whether the doer appears to be authorised by the principal. " The principal is liable for all the acts of the agent which are within the authority usually confided to an agent of that character, notwithstanding limitations as between the principal and agent put upon that authority."

The proposition laid down by the court (subject to the qualifications required by the facts of the case, that the principal must be undisclosed and the acts must be done for the benefit of the principal) has become established law in many of the United States and it appears as Art. 194 of the Agency Restatement.[8] It cannot, however, be said to be established law in England. It has been subject to extra-forensic criticism and has been followed on one occasion only and then by another Divisional Court.[9] Its authority in the Court of Appeal is doubtful, especially as the Supreme Court of Ontario has refused to accept it.[10]

Wills J. found authority for the proposition he stated in two places. He said: (a) " This principle appears to be identical with that enunciated in the judgments of *Edmunds* v. *Bushell*.[11] There was no

---

[7] Goodhart and Hanson, *op. cit.*, speak of the principal doing " an external notorious act: *e.g.* he may put him in charge of a beer house ". The external notorious act in *Watteau* v. *Fenwick* was surely that the agent was in charge of the beer-house, not that he had been put in charge by the principal. Moreover even if the principal's act was external and notorious it is not sufficient to make him liable to a third person who was unaware of it.

[8] "A general agent for an undisclosed principal authorised to conduct transactions subjects his principal to liability for acts done on his account, if usual in such transactions, although forbidden by the principal to do them." Art. 195, which is a special application of Art. 194, lays down a rule dealing more closely with the facts of *Watteau* v. *Fenwick*. " An undisclosed principal who entrusts an agent with the management of his business is subject to liability to third persons with whom the agent enters into transactions usual in such businesses and on the principal's account, although contrary to the directions of the principal."

[9] I deal with the criticism in text books and periodicals later. The case in which *Watteau* v. *Fenwick* was followed is *Kinahan Ltd.* v. *Parry*, [1910] 2 K.B. 389 (Div. Court.) The case was taken to the Court of Appeal where the decision of the Divisional Court was overruled, but on the ground that there was no evidence of any agency at all [1911] 1 K.B. 439 (C.A.).

[10] *McLaughlin* v. *Gentles*, 51 D.L.R. 383.

[11] L.R. 1 Q.B. 97.

holding out, because the plaintiff knew nothing of the defendant; "
(b) "It is clear law that no limitation of authority as between the
dormant and active partner will avail the dormant partner as to things
within the ordinary authority of a partner. The law of partnership
is in such a question nothing but a branch of the general law of
principal and agent."

Edmunds v. Bushell

The facts of *Edmunds* v. *Bushell*[11] were that Jones, one of the defendants, employed Bushell, the other defendant, as the manager of a
business. The business was carried on in the name of Bushell and Co.
There was, however, no express finding of fact as to how far the
connection of Jones with the business was known. The report states
that the plaintiff did not know anything about Bushell and Co., which
means that he did not know that Jones had any connection with that
business. But the action was brought by the plaintiff as an indorsee
for value of a bill of exchange and the vital question therefore was
whether the original holder knew anything of Jones. On this the report
is silent. A writer in the Solicitors' Journal says:[12] "we gather from
the wording of the judgment rather than from the somewhat bare
statement in the report of the facts that Jones was generally known by
the trade (if not by the particular indorsee for value) to have some
interest in the business." To this question I must return after completing the particulars of the case.

Bushell was authorised by Jones to draw cheques in the name
of Bushell and Company, but he was expressly forbidden to draw or
accept bills. Nevertheless he did accept four bills, on one of which the
action was brought against Bushell and Jones by an indorsee for value.
The bill was drawn by one Britten payable to his own order and
indorsed by him to Taylor and by Taylor to the Birmingham and
Midland Banking Company of which the plaintiff was the public
officer. Taylor had had previous dealings with Bushell and Co. in
the way of business.

For Jones it was argued that it was not shown that the plaintiff
was aware of Jones' connection with Bushell and Co., and he could
not therefore recover. The main point of the argument appears to have
been directed to destroying the already annihilated argument of a
holding out to the world. It is surprising that according to the report
the plaintiff does not appear to have pointed out that he was entitled to
recover if Britten or Taylor could have recovered.

The judgments were very brief. The fullest was that of Cockburn,
C.J. He said: "Bushell was the agent of the defendant Jones, and
Jones was the principal, but he held out Bushell as the principal and

---

[12] 37 Sol. J. 280.

owner of the business. That being so the case falls within the well established principle that if a person employs another as agent in a character which involves a particular authority he cannot by a secret reservation divest him of that authority. . . . Bushell cannot be divested of the apparent authority against third persons by a secret reservation." Mellor J. said: " It is not a question of partnership but whether Bushell who had been held out to everybody as a partner had authority to bind."

It is a fair deduction from the report that Taylor at any rate was aware of Jones' connection with Bushell and Co., so that the decision was a simple application of the ordinary doctrine of apparent authority. Even if there were no *direct* evidence to show Taylor's reliance on Bushell's agency there can be no doubt that the " well established principle " to which Cockburn C.J. referred was that of apparent authority. Moreover, the facts that it was generally known that Bushell was the agent of Jones and that Taylor had had dealings with Bushell and Co. were surely sufficient evidence from which the court must have inferred, in the absence of all rebutting evidence, that Taylor knew of Jones' connection.

Edmunds v. *Bushell*[11] therefore is no authority for making a principal liable in the absence of actual and apparent authority.[13] The law of partnership also presents very slippery ground on which to base such a liability.

The Liability of Dormant Partners for Unauthorised Acts. Sec. 5 of the Partnership Act 1890

In the case of a dormant partner the doctrine of apparent authority is inapplicable, for the person dealing with the actual partners is unaware of any agency relation between them and the dormant partner. If, therefore, a dormant partner is liable for acts done exceeding the actual authority we have an instance of liability being independent of authority and being a risk incidental to participation in a business.

In practice it cannot frequently happen that the authority of the active partners does not extend to the doing of all acts " carrying on in the usual way business of the kind carried on by the firm ". As between active partners, restriction of authority is generally merely a division of function: their separate functions together cover everything

---

[13] The anonymous writer in the Solicitors' Journal explains *Edmunds* v. *Bushell* thus: " Bushell was generally known to have authority to bind, not only himself, but also Jones, whether as a partner or not was immaterial: and that being so the plaintiff himself, although personally ignorant of the facts, was entitled to take advantage of this general reputation". This is only an attempted resuscitation of the doctrine of holding out to the world. The explanation by Cotton L.J. in *Daun* v. *Simmins* is equally unsatisfactory. " A carried on business under the mask B & Co.: B & Co. being really A and the business being carried on by B for A's benefit." Despite the invocation of reality this is a restatement of the fiction of the identity of principal and agent, unless it makes a recognition of a doctrine that the principal is always liable for the contracts of his agent within the course of employment because the business is that of the principal and the principal employs the agent for his own benefit.

usually done in the business, and, of course, jointly they can do anything. In the case of a dormant partner, restrictions limit the activities of the firm. Of course the partners jointly could still do anything, but a partner who is consulted as to the ordinary activities of the firm is hardly a dormant partner.

The proposition of Wills J. "that no limitation of authority as between the dormant and active partner will avail the dormant partner as to things within the ordinary authority of a partner " is by no means the clear law he says it is. So far as authorities are concerned, my, perhaps not sufficiently exhaustive, research has failed to discover any; and if the proposition be viewed as one of reason, it is no more self-evident than the doctrine he was seeking to establish as to the liability of a principal for the unauthorised acts of an agent.

In fact, as a universal proposition it is inconsistent with s.5 of the Partnership Act which recites: " Every partner is an agent of the firm and his other partners for the purpose of the business of the partnership; and the acts of every partner who does any act for carrying on in the usual way business of the kind carried on by the firm of which he is a member bind the firm and his partners, unless the partner so acting has no authority to act for the firm in the particular matter, and the person with whom he is dealing either knows that he has no authority or does not know or believe him to be a partner." [14]

There can be little doubt that the provision in the section was an attempt to fix in the law of partnership, beyond the possibility of judicial development, the doctrine, in which the draftsman believed and which was the prevalent one in the profession, that a principal could not be liable in the absence of actual or apparent authority. It was but a corollary to this doctrine that an undisclosed principal such as a dormant partner could only be liable for acts actually authorised.

Where a firm is composed of only two partners the attempt is successful. X is a dormant partner of Y in a hotel business. It is agreed that Y shall obtain all goods other than bottled ales and mineral waters from X. Y purchases whisky on credit from T. T cannot make X liable; for, by the express words of the Partnership Act, " the partner acting has in fact no authority to act for the firm in the particular matter, and the person with whom he is dealing does not know or believe him to be a partner ". This illustration is of course analogous to *Watteau* v. *Fenwick*,[2] and if the authority of the law of partnership be accepted that case should be decided differently.

Where a firm is composed of more than two partners the attempt in s. 5 not only fails, but the section introduces the contrary doctrine and in some cases makes the dormant partner liable even though the active partners exceed their authority. Neither Lindley nor Pollock

---

[14] The Partnership Act was, of course, in operation when *Watteau* v. *Fenwick* was decided.

refers to such liability, and in my opinion the anomaly is due to an oversight in the drafting. X is a dormant partner of Y and Z in a hotel business. It is agreed that all foods other than bottled ales and mineral waters shall be obtained from X. T sells whisky to Y knowing that he is a partner of Z, but without any knowledge of the agreement as to buying goods from X. Since Y has done an act " for carrying on in the usual way business of the kind carried on by the firm " that act will " bind the firm and his partners ". Thus X is liable. He is not saved by the proviso, for while Y had no authority to purchase the whisky it cannot be said that T " did not know or believe Y to be a partner ". T did consider Y to be a partner of Z. The draftsman should have added the following words which it is submitted the courts cannot add, viz., " of the partner that person is seeking to make liable ".

The anomalous character of the liability discussed in the last paragraph will be more clearly perceived when it is realised that it does not always exist where the firm is composed of more than two partners. X is a dormant partner of Y and Z in a hotel business. It is agreed that all goods other than bottled ales and mineral waters should be bought from X. Y and Z *jointly* purchase whisky from T who knows nothing of the agreement to buy goods from X, and of course does not know X is a partner, but does know Y and Z are partners *inter se*. In applying s. 5 to this case the plural has to be read for the singular. " The acts of the partners (A) . . . . . bind their partners (B) . . . . . unless . . . . . the person with whom they are dealing . . . . . does not know or believe them to be partners (C) ". Now it is true that T does know that Y and Z are partners *inter se*. That, however, it is submitted is insufficient to exclude the proviso. The partnership referred to in the proviso by the word " partners " (C) is not a partnership *inter se* such as may be indicated by the word " partners " (A), but is a partnership with somebody other than the actors such as is indicated by the word " partners " (B). Otherwise the proviso would never operate. The proviso requires T to know and believe that Y and Z have a partner or partners and this he does not know since he is unaware that X is a partner. Consequently by virtue of the proviso X is not liable.

Agreements Excluding the Liability of Dormant Partners

It is possible that Wills J. had in mind in stating his proposition about dormant partner cases like *Pooley* v. *Driver*.[15] In these cases a person enters into an agreement whereby he becomes a dormant partner, but it is provided that the other partners shall alone assume liability as regards those dealing with the firm. Such an agreement does not protect the partner from liability at the suit of third persons, though it may bind the active partners to indemnify the dormant

---

[15] 5 Ch. D. 458.

partner against the consequence of the suit. The dormant partner who authorises the active partners to do certain acts is by law liable for those acts, and his private agreement cannot derogate from the general law. The existence of such an agreement may be evidence from which the court may deduce that the relation is that of lender and borrower and not of dormant and actual partner: but if the court finds that a partnership relation exists, the dormant partner is liable despite a contrary agreement.

If, however, the partnership agreement restricts the authority of the active partner, then a different question arises. If the active partner is authorised only to conduct the business on a cash basis the liability of the dormant partner for a credit transaction is no longer governed by cases like *Pooley* v. *Driver*:[15] for in those cases it was assumed that if the partnership relation existed the acts were within the actual authority of the active partners.

Restrictions between dormant partners and undisclosed principal

It may be of value to consider whether the assumed liability of a dormant partner for unauthorised acts is as Wills J. contended "nothing but a branch of the general law of principal and agent". It is true that a partner is an agent for the firm, including dormant partners, but are there any material distinctions between a partnership relation and an ordinary agency relation?

Partnership involves the "carrying on of a business in common". Active participation in the management is not essential for there may be dormant partners: on the other hand, merely sharing the profits does not amount to partnership even if the sharer has also financed the business. Despite the large number of cases following *Cox* v. *Hickman*[16] no precise test of the partnership relation has emerged. Lindley suggests: "No person who does not hold himself out as a partner is liable to third persons for the acts of persons whose profits he shares unless he and they are really partners *inter se,* or they are his agents".[17] This is decidedly not helpful. Lindley's reference to agency is, of course, not intended as a test of partnership, but only to include the liability of a principal for the acts of his agent. The sharing of profits coupled with agency is not a sufficient test of partnership: an agent who is paid a commission is not necessarily his principal's partner. Moreover, the argument from agency is often circular when the position is doubtful: the relation of principal and agent is just as much an inference from that of partnership as the relation of partnership from that of agency.

Yet ultimately, it is the test of agency which distinguishes a dormant partner from a lender. Partners stand in a position of

---
[16] 8 H. L. C. 268.
[17] *Partnership,* 9th Ed., p. 64.

equality; the dormant partner must have such an intimate connection with the business that it can be said to be as much " his " as that of the other partners. This entails equal control by him of the business: and control, of course, is the test of agency. A person may refuse to lend money unless certain alterations are made in the mode of carrying on the business, and despite this requirement he may be only a lender. If, however, the borrowers yield up their sole control, so that any change of the defined method requires the co-operation of the lender, then a relation of partnership is constituted.[18]   The arrangement whereby the dormant partner leaves the management to the other partner can be viewed as an exercise of the control of the business.

In so far as control of the business and participation in profits determine the liability of a dormant partner for unauthorised acts, the argument is even stronger for the liability of an undisclosed principal in respect of unauthorised acts of an agent. But the equality of position which is the characteristic of partnership, and which entails control by all the partners of the business, also distinguishes partnership from agency. An agent is not on a footing of equality with his principal. He is not entitled to a share in the profits except by virtue of and subject to the limits of a specific agreement for his remuneration. Consequently, an agent who commits a breach of his agreement, *e.g.* by exceeding his authority, may forfeit all share in the profits through wages or commission or other remuneration. A partner, however, is still entitled to share in the profits despite breach of agreement. Another consequence of the distinction is that, whereas an agent may be expected to act solely within the limits of his authority, a partner is more likely to exceed the limits of his authority and to do all acts usually done in his kind of business despite partnership restrictions. Pollock's reason for distinguishing a dormant partner from an undisclosed principal appears to be based also on the same distinction. " Is a dormant partner liable merely because he is an undisclosed principal? Is it not rather that he is by the partnership contract liable to the same extent as the known partners? " [19]

It may even be contended that the actual authority of a partner always extends to all acts within the usual course of the business. An agreement between partners as to how losses are to be shared has no effect on the liability to third persons. So too, partners may allocate various functions to each other *inter se* without affecting the authority of each partner to bind the firm by performing any function. X and Y carry on a silk and woollen business. They agree that X should deal with silks and Y with woollens. Why should that preclude the firm from being bound if Y deals in silks with T? A limitation of function

---

[18] No partnership would arise where the alteration of the defined method merely made the loan immediately repayable.

[19] 9 L.Q.R. 111. This cryptic statement is made in a criticism of *Watteau* v. *Fenwick*.

is quite a different matter from authority to bind the firm.   The
Partnership Act itself draws a distinction between " authority to act
for the firm " which is dealt with in s. 5, and " power to bind the firm "
which is the subject matter of s. 8.[20]   Owing to the equality of position
implicit in the relation of partners, the firm agree to be bound by any
act done by a partner in the ordinary course of the business.   An agreement that one partner should not do certain acts would not affect his
power to bind the firm except where the person with whom he dealt
had notice of the restriction.   If, therefore, the third party was unaware
of the existence of the partnership he would be unaware also of the
restriction; and the firm would be bound by an act done within the
power of a member to bind it.

This argument is of course inconsistent with the proviso in s. 5
of the Partnership Act.   But it does show that any liability of a dormant
partner for unauthorised acts is based on reasons which are not
necessarily applicable to the ordinary relations between undisclosed
principal and agent.

Existing criticism of Watteau v. Fenwick: Miles v. McIlwraith

The decision in *Watteau* v. *Fenwick*[2] has been the subject of much
adverse comment in periodicals and text-books.[21]   Much of it, however,
is based on the ground that the decision is not fortified by the old
doctrines of actual and apparent authority.   This is correct, but
nevertheless, though the principles which underlie those doctrines may
not be capable of extension to a case where there is neither actual nor
apparent authority, some other principle may apply there.   All the
principles may moreover be capable of subsumption under some wider
postulate.   Holt C.J. long ago in *Ashby* v. *White* [21a] demolished the argument that " never the like case was heard before ".   The criticisms
do, however, reflect the general opinion that the liability of a principal
is confined to cases where there is actual or apparent authority.

Some of the criticism is based on authority.   It is contended that
Watteau v. *Fenwick* is inconsistent with *Miles* v. *McIlwraith*,[22] a decision
of the Judicial Committee of the Privy Council, which though not
binding on the Court of Appeal might well be preferred to a decision
of a Divisional Court.

An action was brought to recover a statutory penalty from the
defendant M, a member of the Legislative Assembly of Queensland,
for having, in the words of the statute, " entered into a contract or
agreement for and on account of the public service."   M was a ship-

---

[20] " If it has been agreed between the partners that any restriction shall be placed
on the power of any one or more of them to bind the firm, no act done in contravention of
the agreement is binding on the firm with respect to persons having notice of the agreement."
[21] See 37 Sol. J. p. 280: 8 Harv. L. Rev. p. 50; 9 L.Q.R. p. 111: Pollock, *Partnership*,
8th Ed. p. 30: Halsbury, *Laws of England*, Vol. 12, p. 25. To these may be added the
doubts expressed in Lindley, *Partnership*, 9th Ed., p. 178.
[21a] [(1703) 2 Ld. Raym. 938. Ed.]
[22] 8 App. Cas. p. 120.

owner, and he employed as his ship brokers the firm of A.B. & Co. A, one of the partners, was registered as managing owner of one of M's ships. A.B. & Co. were contractors with the Government for the carriage of immigrants. M had expressly instructed A.B. & Co. not to employ any ship in which he had shares for the purpose of carrying immigrants. Nevertheless, as the jury found, " contrary to the express directions of the defendant ", A.B. & Co. fixed the *Scottish Hero* to carry immigrants for the Government. The charter party was signed by them " for and on behalf of the owners of the *Scottish Hero* ", but it was no part of their agreement with the Government that they should establish privity of contract between the Government and the ship owners. There was no suggestion that the Agent-General of the Government, who carried out the negotiations for them, knew either that A.B. & Co. were the general agents of the defendants or that A was registered as managing owner. Thus there was neither actual nor apparent authority.

The opinion of the Judicial Committee[23] was in favour of the defendants. Lord Blackburn said : " The principle on which a person, having clothed an agent with apparent general authority but having restricted it by secret instructions, is bound (if the other party chooses to hold him so) to one who, in ignorance of the restrictions, contracts through the agent in the faith of the agent having the authority he seems to have is well explained in *Freeman* v. *Coke*.[23a] The principal does not actually contract, but the person who thought he did, has the option to preclude him from denying that he contracted if the case is brought within the very accurate statement of the law by Parke B. . . . . . It is enough to say that there is no evidence that the Government or their agent ever knew that the firm[24] or any individual of it had general authority to bind the defendant and acted upon the belief that such authority continued unrestricted. It is not, therefore, shown that the Government could have held the defendants bound to them."

It will be observed that Lord Blackburn's reasoning was wider than was necessary. Even though the defendants may have been liable to the Government it may not have been because of a " contract or agreement ". Even those who consider that liability in the cases of actual and apparent authority is " truly contractual " do not think that liability under the *Watteau* v. *Fenwick*[2] rule is based on " contract principles ".[25] Lord Blackburn however stated that there could not be liability in the absence of apparent authority, which, incidentally, he based on estoppel. With respect to this opinion of so great a master of

---

[23] The members of the court were Lord Blackburn, Sir Barnes Peacock, Sir Robert Collier, Sir Richard Couch and Sir Arthur Hobhouse.
[23a] [(1848) 2 Ex. 654. Ed.]
[24] A.B. & Co.
[25] Wright, *op. cit.*, p. 43, says "agency doctrine is broader than contract principles". He considers " the recognition of such doctrine by the *Restatement* . . . one of the most useful aids to an understanding not of what the courts said they were doing, but of what they have actually done in practice."

Q

commercial law, it is merely an *ipse dixit*. Because apparent authority can be based on estoppel, it does not follow that in a case where estoppel cannot exist, there may not be liability based on some other principle. A dictum of Lord Blackburn however would be seriously considered, especially since it was in accord with general opinion. We have to consider whether the American decisions and writings are entitled to greater weight.

Holding out to the world

It is worth considering how far support for the view that liability is confined to cases of actual or apparent authority is to be found in those authorities which allege that a holding out to the world is insufficient and that there must be a holding out to the person seeking to make the principal liable.

In the case of partnership, s. 14 of the Partnership Act enacts that liability as a partner by holding out only exists to " one who has on the faith of such representation given credit to the firm ". This is declaratory of the established common law. Thus in *Martyn* v. *Gray*,[25a] Erle C.J. said: " Formerly it was considered sufficient if the party was held out to the world as a member of the firm. Now, however, it is necessary that there should be direct evidence that the holding out should come to the knowledge of the plaintiff." [26]

With regard to this necessity for a holding out to the specific person suing, in principle " the law of partnership is in such a question nothing but a branch of the general law of principal and agent." There can be little doubt, that where there is no actual authority at all, a man cannot be liable as a principal, merely because another has purported to a third person to be the agent of the former, even though the alleged principal has represented " to the world " that the purported agent is his agent, if the third person was not aware of that representation.

The distinction between this proposition and that of *Watteau* v. *Fenwick*[2] is that the latter requires there be some actual authority: according to the statement in the American *Restatement* a general agency must exist. But there is of course no authority with regard to the act in respect of which the principal is sued. The distinction, however, is vital, for it is to the authority given by the principal to the agent that the doctrine of *Watteau* v. *Fenwick* attaches a power to bind the principal by acts within the course of employment.

McLaughlin v. Gentles [27]

Though *Watteau* v. *Fenwick* was followed by the Divisional Court in England in *Kinahan Ltd.* v. *Parry*,[27a] it was not followed by the Ontario Supreme Court (Appellate Division)[28] in *McLaughlin* v.

[25a] [(1863) 14 C.B.N.S. 824. Ed.]
[26] 14 C.B.N.S. 824 at p. 839.
[27] 51 D.L.R. 383.
[27a] [(1910) 2 K.B. 389. Ed.]
[28] Meredith C.J.O., Maclaren, Magee and Hodgin, JJ. A.

Gentles.[27] In this case the court considered that *Miles* v. *McIlwraith*[22] was inconsistent with *Watteau* v. *Fenwick*[2] and preferred to follow the earlier case.

One Chisholm had been authorised by a syndicate of which he was a member, to undertake certain mining and exploration operations. His authority, however, was limited to the expenditure of $2,000. He continued his operations after that sum was expended and it was during this period that he bought goods from the plaintiff in respect of which the syndicate were sued. The plaintiff had no knowledge that Chisholm was a member of any syndicate or acting for anybody.

The court considered the case as one where an agent had exceeded his authority while acting within the course of his employment, but refused to follow *Watteau* v. *Fenwick*. There appears to have been no reference to United States cases. Hodgins J.A., who delivered the judgment of the court, concluded with the following remarks:

> It appears to me that the fact that there was a limitation of authority is at least as important as the fact that the purchaser was an agent. The vendor did not know either of these facts and so did not draw any conclusion involving the principal when he sold and delivered the goods. Should he be permitted, when he elects to look to the principal, to do so upon any other terms than in accordance with the actual authority given at that time? It is entirely different where there is a holding out as agent and the fact of agency is known, but where neither is an element in the bargain nor the reason why credit was given, and so not an additional security known to the vendor at the time, no equity should be raised in favour of the vendor as against the principal so as to make the latter liable.

Earlier in the judgment he says: " It seems to be straining the doctrine of ostensible agency, or of holding out, to apply it in a case where the fact of agency and holding out were unknown to the person dealing with the so-called agent at the time." It should be pointed out, however, that Hodgins J.A. does not appear to have realised that *Watteau* v. *Fenwick* might be based on some new principle.

There can be little doubt that Chisholm was a general agent,[29] but it has been suggested to me by the learned editor of this *Review* that the agency relationship had terminated when the $2,000 had been expended. Hodgins J.A. certainly dealt with the case on the footing that the agency relation was in existence at the time of the transaction with the plaintiff, and he considered that the limitation of expenditure to $2,000 was an ordinary restriction of power and not a limitation of the duration of the agency. Even if Hodgins J.A. were incorrect, his judgment has the authority of an *obiter dictum* dealing carefully with the actual point. I respectfully agree, however, with Hodgins J.A. Chisholm was a partner and the partnership was not to terminate upon

---

[29] Art. 3 (1) of the *Agency Restatement* defines a general agent thus: " A general agent is an agent authorised to conduct a series of transactions involving a continuity of service." It is necessary in order that the doctrine of *Watteau* v. *Fenwick* should apply that the agent be general, for otherwise there would be no course of employment.

the expenditure of $2,000. But, apart from that, his authority was to undertake mining and exploration operations: the syndicate as such were prepared without further consultation to spend $2,000: when that amount was expended Chisholm had no power to pledge their credit. But he still had authority to conduct such operations as entailed no expenditure, or he could have financed the operations himself. He could not have kept the benefit of subsequent operations himself. Was he not in the position of an agent without authority to pledge his principal's credit, though such authority would have been in the course of employment?

Liability of a disclosed principal where the agent exceeds actual and apparent authority

The proposition enunciated by Wills J. in *Watteau* v. *Fenwick*[2] was not in its terms restricted to the case of an undisclosed principal. Let us consider the authorities dealing with the application of the proposition to a disclosed principal.

In *Kinahan Ltd.* v. *Parry*[27a] the Divisional Court considered that *Daun* v. *Simmins*[30] was an authority against the application of the proposition to a disclosed principal. They were pressed with that case, a decision of a Court of Appeal,[31] as an authority in effect overruling *Watteau* v. *Fenwick,* but they distinguished it on the ground that the principal was disclosed. The facts in *Daun* v. *Simmins*[30] were that the defendants owned a public house of which one Clarke was the manager : but unlike the situation in *Watteau* v. *Fenwick* here the licence was taken out in the name of the defendants, and it was the defendants' name which was printed on the door. The manager had instructions to buy goods only from a certain firm. He nevertheless bought goods from another firm, the plaintiffs. He expressly told the plaintiffs that he was the defendants' manager. The court held that the defendants were not liable to the plaintiffs.

I have already stated that the court in *Kinahan Ltd.* v. *Parry* relied on the fact of disclosure of the principal as distinguishing *Daun* v. *Simmins* from *Watteau* v. *Fenwick.* They treated *Daun* v. *Simmins* as an authority for the proposition that where the principal is disclosed his liability must be confined to the agent's acts done within the actual or apparent authority. It is true that *Daun* v. *Simmins* is consistent with this proposition, but it is consistent also with existence of liability for acts done in the course of employment even though the principal is disclosed. The court in *Daun* v. *Simmins* paid no attention to the fact that the principal was disclosed. The proposition on which the court based its decision was thus expressed by Brett L.J. : " It is clear that the manager of a public house ordinarily orders the spirit of particular

---

[30] 41 L.T. 783.

[31] Brett, Cotton, Bramwell L.JJ.

persons ". Now since the course of employment of the manager was in that case co-extensive with the apparent authority, this proposition amounts to a statement that the act of Clarke in buying from the plaintiffs was neither within his apparent authority nor within the course of his employment. The *ratio decidendi* of the case may therefore be: (1) to render a principal liable the agent's act must fall within the actual or apparent authority, or (2) to render a principal liable the agent's act must fall within the actual or apparent authority or the course of employment, or (3) to render a principal liable the agent's act must fall within the course of employment. The case may be distinguished from *Watteau* v. *Fenwick*[2] not only on the ground of disclosure of principal, but also on the ground that the agent's act was not in the course of his employment.

I know of no English case which is inconsistent with the application of the *Watteau* v. *Fenwick* doctrine to facts where the principal is disclosed. The *Agency Restatement* adopts the doctrine in the case of the general agent of a disclosed principal, without, however, using the same phraseology as in the case of an undisclosed principal: and without expressly stating that the two cases are but an application of a general doctrine that a principal is liable for all acts of an agent within the course of employment.[32] There can rarely exist a case, however, in which, the existence of the principal being disclosed, the course of employment is different from the apparent authority. If the position of the agent is known to the person with whom he deals the case is one of apparent authority. That is so even if knowledge of the agent's position is derived from the agent himself. The appointment of an agent to a certain position must carry with it incidental authority to disclose the nature of the appointment: a contrary agreement must surely be one not to disclose the existence of the principal.[33] In my opinion illustrations (2) and (3) to Art. 161 of the *Agency Restatement* are examples of apparent authority.[34] In illustration (2), A's statement to T that he is P's general manager is equivalent to such a statement by P: and in illustration (3) A's signature means that he is P's agent for the purchase

---

[32] Art. 161 says: "A general agent for a disclosed or partially disclosed principal subjects his principal to liability for acts done on his account which usually accompany or are incidental to transactions which he is authorised to conduct if, although they are forbidden by the principal, the other party reasonably believes that the agent is authorised to do them and has no notice that the agent is not so authorised." Art 194 (undisclosed principal) speaks of acts " usual or necessary in such transactions ". Can a person who has notice that an agent is not authorised have a reasonable belief that he is? Can a person have a reasonable belief that an agent is unauthorised without knowing anything of his position? If the person knows the agent's position the case is one of apparent authority.

[33] *Cf.* Art. 40, *Agency Restatement.*

[34] Illustration 2 is: P appoints A as the general manager of his manufacturing business. instructing A to employ no one except those of Nordic origin. A employs a Semite, T P is bound by the employment of T, although T knows nothing of A's authority except A's statement to him that he is P's general manager. Illustration 3 is: P employs A as the general manager of his foundry, instructing A to purchase his alloys from a certain firm. A, finding the alloys to be unsatisfactory, and without consultation with P, purchases alloys from another firm, T, writing to T upon personal stationery, and signing the letter only "A, agent of P ". P is bound upon this transaction.

of alloys, and is equivalent to such a statement made to T by P. The mere fact of an agent negotiating with a third person amounts to a representation by him, equivalent to one by the principal, that he has authority to transact that class of business.[35]

It is, however, possible to envisage a case where the principal could only be bound under the doctrine of Art. 161. P appoints A as his general manager for the purchase of houses in Leeds, instructing A, however, not to disclose the existence of the agency, and not to purchase except on a surveyor's report. A discloses his position to T, withholding, however, the requirement of a surveyor's report and purchases houses in Leeds from T as agent for P without a surveyor's report.

Reasons for the doctrine of Watteau v. Fenwick

Seavey rightly points out in his well-known *Rationale of Agency*[36] that the liability of a principal for unauthorised acts must be based on public policy. Judicial legislation is just as much social legislation as is parliamentary legislation on any social welfare scheme. But what is the content of public policy? The accurate determination of what is socially desirable in the case under discussion depends on knowledge of the actual behaviour of business men. The promotion of commerce is a social interest: if the principal is made liable for all acts within the course of employment commerce may be restricted through people fearing to employ agents: on the other hand, in the absence of such liability commerce may be restricted through people fearing to deal with agents.

We have, however, the most scanty knowledge of the actual behaviour of business men, and so we must proceed as best we can with common-sense guesses and by the light of the traditional concepts of individual justice.

The principle it is sought to establish is that the law subjects the owner of a business to all the risks connected with the business, including contracts made by agents within the course of employment but in excess of actual or apparent authority. Seavey suggests that the reasons which have actuated the courts in upholding such a principle may be grouped under three heads.

(a) The principal has reposed more trust in the agent than has the third person. It is, however, a strange corollary that the principal should be liable for the breach of trust by the agent. The statement that " there is a trusting with a power, as in the case of a trustee there is a trusting with a title " begs the very question whether the agent has such a power.

---

[35] I have discussed this mode of constitution of apparent authority in 50 L.Q.R. at pp. 229 and 230, and in 16 Can. Bar Rev. 757. In 50 L.Q.R. I use it to explain *Hambro* v. *Burnand*, [1904] 2 K.B. 10. Consequently I cannot agree with Wright's suggestion that that case is an illustration of the *Watteau* v. *Fenwick* doctrine, (*op. cit.*, at p. 45).

[36] 29 Yale L.J. 859.

(b) Liability follows control. This again begs the question. If a moral proposition is being stated, this must be that there should be liability where there is actual control. A principal, however, has no actual control: he only has control in law, based on the agent's agreement. Seavey switches the argument under this head over to another line, viz., the analogy of *Rylands* v. *Fletcher*.[36a] Where a principal appoints an agent with less authority than the course of employment, he puts into circulation a source of danger to persons dealing with reference to the usual business methods. The connection with the basis of control is that the principal allows this dangerous thing to escape from his control. This reasoning is more ingenious than convincing. Restrictions which make the authority of the agent less than is usual are nevertheless not so unusual as to be dangerous. Moreover, by saying that the agent " may be expected to cause injury to third persons dealing with reference to the usual business methods " Seavey makes the argument applicable only to the case of apparent authority.

(c) The third person has not time or opportunity owing to the exigencies of business to investigate the authority of an agent. He must assume that the agent has the normal authority. This argument again is surely only applicable to a case of apparent authority.[37]

We can consider also an argument discussed by Seavey when considering the liability of an undisclosed principal for acts of the agent actually authorised. This liability he bases upon the canon that reasonable expectations ought not to be defeated. He denies that " the third person receives a godsend neither contemplated nor bargained for." " The principal," he says, " enabled the agent to invite the confidence of the third person. It was his credit which gave the agent assurance, and his support which gave the agent a standing in the mercantile world. To trust the owner of a business is not the same thing as to trust one who is not such owner and subject to the control of another in the transaction." We may restate this argument thus. In *Humble* v. *Hunter*[38] the court said : " A man has a right to the benefit which he contemplates from the character, credit and substance of the person with whom he contracts." Such " character, credit and substance," Seavey in effect contends, may not inhere in the agent but in the position in which he has been placed by the principal. A right of action against the principal is therefore necessary to enable the third person to obtain the contemplated benefit. The argument in this form is applicable to the doctrine of *Watteau* v. *Fenwick*.[2] The argument however is fallacious; for it proceeds on an inaccurate description of the facts of the mercantile world. The " character, credit

---

[36a] [(1868) L.R. 3 H.L. 330. Ed.]

[37] These reasons might be compared with those advanced for the liability of a master for the torts of his servant. See Baty, *Vicarious Liability*.

[38] 12 Q.B. 310 at 317.

and substance " may in fact inhere in the agent: it often happens that the agent's " standing in the mercantile world " is higher than that of the principal. In such a case the third party is not misled as to " the character, credit and substance " of the person with whom he is dealing.

There remains the point that in addition to the principal having control of the agent, he derives a benefit from his authorised activities and therefore in justice ought to bear the burden of unauthorised activities. But does not the third person also deal with the agent for the purpose of obtaining a benefit, and that from the very activity in question? It is difficult to say that, as between the two, one is less meritorious. Must we not say with Seavey that " one of two persons both innocent " must suffer?

Ultimately, therefore, we are driven, in order to uphold the doctrine of *Watteau* v. *Fenwick*,[2] to guess with Seavey " that it is good business sense to hold that when one employs another in the performance of acts for the benefit of a business that business ought to pay for the mistakes, negligence and errors of judgment of the one employed ", including wilful entering into unauthorised contracts. The owner of a business can foresee the possibility of an agent exceeding his instructions, and he can guard against such a risk by insurance, and by increasing the price of the commodities in which he deals, and so he can distribute the risk over the whole community of consumers.

The courts have adopted the doctrine of liability for all acts in the course of employment in the case of liability in tort: and both Seavey and Wright press this analogy. There is, however, an important distinction between the cases of contract and tort. This distinction is based on the conduct of the third person. Where a person is injured by an agent's tort he has not voluntarily entered into the specific relation with the third person: but when he negotiates with an agent relating to a contract does he not voluntarily incur the risk of the agent not being authorised? In the case of an undisclosed principal has he not voluntarily agreed to accept the liability of the agent?

That the courts may regard the conduct of the third person as material is shown by the doctrine of election. If the third person chooses to give exclusive credit to the agent he cannot sue the principal,[39] yet the business is the principal's, he has control of the agent and derives a benefit from his activities whatever the third person's conduct may be.

Again " if a person has notice that the principal does not consent to have the agent act for him, such person cannot acquire rights against the principal by dealing with the agent, although the agent reasonably believes that he has authority because of the principal's manifestations to him ".[40] Here, though actual authority exists, the third person is

---

[39] *Calder* v. *Dobell*, L.R. 6 C.P. 486.
[40] *Agency Restatement*, Art. 27, Comment b.

unable to sue because of his own conduct in having notice of the principal's unwillingness to be liable. If the liability attaches to the mere fact of agency would the third person's knowledge disentitle him?

Conclusion

The result, it is submitted, is that no conclusive argument can be drawn from partial surveys of facts or from the analogy with liability in tort. The adoption of a doctrine that a principal should be liable in contract for unauthorised acts of the agent merely because they are within the course of his employment would in the state of our knowledge be an experiment. But the adoption of the opposite doctrine is also an experiment. Perhaps the realisation that a great many legal rules are only experimental, that many are only probabilities, that as such they are not eternal verities, is the most fruitful state of mind for legal development.

15

The Apparent Authority of an Agent of a Company*

PART A

Introduction

The positive doctrine of constructive notice

Thirty years ago the dominant opinion of the legal profession in England appears to have been that a contractor[1] dealing with a company through one purporting to act on behalf of the company could hold the company liable merely by showing that there was provision in the articles of association empowering the company to confer authority on the purported agent to carry out the transaction. The doctrine was thought to be derived from *Turquand's* case.[1a] The absence of authority, it was considered, arose because the power to confer authority had not been exercised, but it was not necessary for the contractor to show it had been exercised. Whether or not it had been exercised was a matter of indoor management, and *Turquand's* case dispensed with the need to inquire into such matters.

The best exposition of the professional opinion was by Sir Arthur Stiebel in his article " The Ostensible Powers of Directors "[2] in which he surveyed the relevant authorities.[3] A judicial statement of the rule

---

* Reprinted from the *Malaya Law Review*, December, 1965, by kind permission.

[1] This is the terminology of Diplock L.J. in the *Buckhurst* case (considered later). Gower in his *Modern Company Law* adopts what he calls the "vivid American terminology" of "outsider", but he rightly draws attention to the difficulties associated with that terminology when members deal with the company.

[2] (1933) 49 *L.Q.R.* 350. The term "ostensible authority" is synonymous with "apparent authority". The term "apparent authority" is the more common, and is the one preferred by Diplock L.J. in his judgment in the *Buckhurst* case.

[3] Sir Arthur relied on a note by the learned reporter, Mr. Hussey Griffith, to his report of *British Thomson-Houston* v. *Federated European Bank, Ltd.* [1932] 2 K.B. 176 (hereafter referred to as the *B.T.-H.* case). The note is at p. 184. In it the reporter said: " It is submitted that actual knowledge on the part of the plaintiff of the contents of the articles of association is irrelevant except to an issue raised as to his *bona fides* ". This proposition is not quoted by Willmer L.J. in the *Buckhurst* case. He does quote with approval other propositions stated by the reporter in which a distinction is drawn between acts ordinarily beyond the powers of an officer of a company, and acts ordinarily within his powers.

supported by it, though there the rule is put on a different basis, is found in the judgment of Wright J. (as he then was) in *Kreditbank Cassel v. Schenkers', Ltd.*:[4] " The memorandum and articles are public documents, and everyone dealing . . . with a limited company is taken in law to be acquainted with their terms . . . He is bound by the articles if they are adverse to his claim : it seems that if the articles are in his favour he should be entitled to benefit by their terms."[4] This simple statement of some new equity goes back to an earlier principle than that of *Turquand's* case.[13] It is the doctrine established by the House of Lords in 1857 in the case of *Ernest v. Nicholls*.[5] There Lord Wensleydale laid down : " The stipulations of the [articles] which restrict and regulate . . . authority are obligatory on those who deal with the company; and the directors can make no contract so as to bind the whole body of shareholders, for whose protection the rules are made, unless they are strictly complied with."[6] This statement contains no reference to a fiction that the public are taken in law to be acquainted with the articles. But the doctrine soon became based on such a fiction, and known as the doctrine of constructive notice of the articles. One hundred years after it was established the doctrine was termed by Gower " wholly unrealistic ". He states the doctrine in the language of notice thus : " Anyone dealing with a company is deemed to have notice of its public documents ".[7] One of the merits of a new terminology for the formulation of the doctrine proposed by Diplock L.J. in the *Buckhurst* case [8] is that it accords more with Lord Wensleydale's language and does not resort to a fiction, thereby raising more clearly the issue as to what is the actual policy supporting the doctrine.

The doctrine propounded by Wright J. was by no means universally accepted. In the courts Sargant L.J. intervened in the argument in *Houghton & Co. v. Nothard, Lowe & Wills, Ltd.*[9] to say that he did not agree with it. In his intervention he created the terminology which has since been used in discussion of the correctness of the professional opinion propounded by Sir Arthur Stiebel. He said : " The doctrine of constructive notice is not a positive doctrine, but a negative one operating against the person who has not inquired."[10]

The view of Sir Arthur Stiebel could thus be stated as one asserting

---

[4] [1926] 2 K.B. 450 at p. 459. This case will hereafter be referred to as *Schenkers'* case. The decision of Wright J. was reversed in the Court of Appeal: [1927] 1 K.B. 826.
[5] (1857) 6 H.L.C. 401.
[6] *Ibid.*, at p. 419. Lord Wensleydale referred not to articles but to the deed of settlement which was the predecessor of articles of association. Lord Wensleydale prefaced the quoted dictum with the words: " All persons, therefore, must take notice of the deed and the provisions of the Act. If they do not choose to acquaint themselves with the powers of directors it is their own fault ". He thus related the doctrine to the social policy of legalising joint stock companies with limited liability in order to promote commercial enterprise and further the national economy. The doctrine is one of the means of protecting the shareholders of the new enterprises.
[7] *Modern Company Law* (2nd Ed.,) at p. 144.
[8] See Part D *infra*. [See note 15. Ed.]
[9] [1927] 1 K.B. 246.
[10] *Ibid.*, at p. 253.

the existence of a positive doctrine of constructive notice of the articles of association. It was regarded as a consequence of the statutory provisions of company law. There was little examination of the manner in which it was related to the doctrine of apparent authority of agents in general. Indeed that doctrine had not been subjected to any extensive scrutiny in England. In the United States Ewart in his work *Estoppel* had based apparent authority on the doctrine of estoppel.[11] This view, however, was not adopted in the *Agency Restatement*, where apparent authority was distinguished from estoppel.

The present position

In an article the present writer differed from Stiebel, and asserted " there is no positive doctrine of constructive notice ".[12] He disagreed with Stiebel's interpretation of the authorities, related the general doctrine of the apparent authority to the principles governing estoppel, and asserted that those principles applied in the realm of transactions with companies as elsewhere. The doctrine of constructive notice was traced to *Ernest* v. *Nicholls*,[5] and an examination was made of *Turquands'* case[13] in order to show that it in no way constituted authority for a positive doctrine of constructive notice. The view that there was no positive doctrine was firmly asserted in 1952 by Slade J. in *Rama Corporation, Ltd.* v. *Proved Tin and General Investments, Ltd.*[14] where there was a careful examination of the previous authorities. But the manner in which the view that there is only a negative doctrine of constructive notice has become universal is now strikingly illustrated by the case of *Freeman and Lockyer* v. *Buckhurst Park Properties (Mangal), Ltd.*[15] which it is submitted concludes the debate,[16]

---

[11] Cook disputed Ewart's thesis, and though Ewart made an effective reply, Seavey, the reporter for the *Agency Restatement*, intervened on Cook's side, which was thereafter favoured by academic opinion generally. See my review of the literature in (1938) 16 *Can. B.R.* 758, where I supported Ewart's view that apparent authority derives from the doctrine of estoppel.

[12] (1934) 50 *L.Q.R.* at p. 240.

[13] *Royal British Bank* v. *Turquand* (1856) 5 E. & B. 246: 6 E. & B. 327.

[14] [1952] 2 Q.B. 147; [1952] 1 All E.R. 554. This case will hereafter be referred to as *Rama's* case. All references in footnotes solely to the number of a page and a letter are to the report of this case in the All England Law Reports. Once again I plead that all publishers of law reports will sub-divide their pages so as to indicate where on a page a passage appears. An alternative to the All England Law Reports letter system is that used by publishers of poetry of printing the figures 10, 20 etc. against the tenth, twentieth etc. line

[15] [1964] 2 Q.B. 480; [1964] 1 All E.R. 630. This case is and hereinbefore and hereafter called the *Buckhurst* case.

[16] Gower in *Modern Company Law*, at p. 149 (text and n. 90) describes earlier discussion of the authorities in order to see whether they establish a positive or negative doctrine of constructive notice in these terms: " The vexed question whether the outsider is entitled to rely on a provision in the articles when he has never read the articles at all . . . is discussed *ad nauseam* by Stiebel (1933) 49 L.Q.R. 350; Montrose (1934) 50 L.Q.R. 224; and in *Houghton & Co.* v. *Nothard, Lowe & Wills, supra; Kreditbank Cassel* v. *Schenkers, supra; B.T.-H.* v. *Federated European Bank, supra* (where the reporter was moved to reject his normal reticence and to append a note giving *his* understanding of the law); *Clay Hill Brick Co.* v. *Rawlings, supra* (where Tucker J. approved the reporter's note); and finally (to date) *Rama Corporation* v. *Proved Tin & General Investments, Ltd., supra* (where Slade J. in an elaborate judgment dissented from Stiebel and the reporter's note, and agreed with Montrose)".

and provides a rationale for the apparent authority of an agent of a company. Counsel and court in the case accepted completely the view that there was no positive doctrine of constructive notice. The legal issue in the case arose over the contention of counsel for the defendants who maintained that the authorities did not merely establish that the doctrine of constructive notice was wholly negative, but went further and said that it negated all claims based on apparent authority unless there was actual knowledge of the existence of articles of association, either conferring authority or empowering the grant of authority. The Court of Appeal unanimously rejected that contention. This necessitated another examination of the authorities, and of the debate about their interpretation. The Court once again asserted that the doctrine of constructive notice was negative, but while asserting this considered its impact on the doctrine of apparent authority, and also affirmed that apparent authority is based on estoppel by representation. There is, moreover, an examination of the interaction between actual and apparent authority by Diplock L.J., and as has already been stated he proposed a new terminology to replace that of " constructive notice ".

PART B

The Buckhurst Case

The facts of the case

K was a property developer. He entered into a contract to purchase the Buckhurst Park estate for the purpose of its development. The purchase price was greater than the resources of K. Accordingly he entered into an arrangement with one H whereby a private limited company was formed, the defendant company. H invested in this company the sum required to complete the purchase, and the estate was conveyed to the company. K and H and two other nominees were the directors. He went abroad, and all the management of the estate, and the planning of its development and sale, were left in the hands of K. No properly called board meetings with the required quorum took place and in consequence there were no valid resolutions authorising K to act as he did. However, all the directors were aware that K was managing the estate. K employed the plaintiffs, who were architects and surveyors, to draw up the necessary plans for the development of the estate and to apply for planning permission. The hopes for development and re-sale came to nothing. K disappeared, and the plaintiffs sued the company.

The argument

Counsel for the plaintiffs argued that there was actual authority for K to employ the plaintiffs. This was based on the construction of the articles of association, and on the proceedings at so-called, but invalidly held, board meetings. Neither the county court judge, nor the Court of Appeal, agreed with this submission. Though Diplock L.J. was far from being so emphatic, Willmer L.J. said it was hopeless to contend that K was ever clothed with authority to do what he did.[17] Counsel, however, maintained that there was apparent authority. He based the existence of such authority on the fact that despite his not having been formally appointed K had in fact acted as managing director, and that the other members of the board knew that this was so and approved of his so doing. K's instructions to the plaintiffs were within the ordinary scope of the business and of a managing director. Counsel for the plaintiffs admitted that they were unaware of the provisions in the articles whereby K could have been appointed as managing director, and had made no enquiries about the articles.[18] Nor did they call in aid such provisions by maintaining that there was a positive doctrine of constructive notice. They based their case on the existence of apparent authority apart from the articles. The county court judge found as a fact that there was apparent authority, and his finding was accepted by the Court of Appeal.[19]

Counsel for the defendant, though challenging the county court's findings of fact on which the existence of apparent authority apart from the articles was based, said that the case was not concluded against him by those findings. He admitted that there were no restrictions in the articles of association preventing the company from conferring authority on K. Far from there being restrictions there were powers by whose exercise K could have been appointed. Consequently the negative doctrine of constructive notice, as it had been hitherto understood, could not prevent the plaintiffs from recovering. He maintained that the authorities established the existence of an extended negative doctrine. His contention was:[20]

> Even if K was acting as managing director to the knowledge of the company the plaintiffs could still not rely on K's apparent authority because they had no knowledge of the defendant company's articles of association, and had made no inquiries with regard to them, and so could not rely on any power of delegation contained in the articles.

The rejection of counsel's contention: general principles

Counsel's contention was a distortion of the principle that there is no positive doctrine of constructive notice of the articles. The positive doctrine asserted that a contractor could base a claim merely on the existence of a power to confer authority contained in the articles: the contractor was to be regarded as a person who had read the articles so

---

[17] [1964] 1 All E.R. at p. 645 E.
[18] See per Willmer L.J. at p. 638 B.
[19] Per Willmer L.J. at p. 636 I: per Pearson L.J. at p. 641 B. & E.; per Diplock L.J. at p. 643 C.
[20] [1964] 2 Q.B. at p. 482.

that there was an appearance of authority. A denial of the positive doctrine involves the proposition that a contractor cannot base a claim on a power to confer authority contained in the articles unless he has read them. This if properly understood may be accepted. A claim by a contractor that apparent authority existed by virtue of a power to confer authority requires proof that the contractor had knowledge of the articles. This follows from the nature of estoppel on which the doctrine of apparent authority is based. But the proposition may be misunderstood, and when misunderstood supports counsel's contention. Whenever a contractor is claiming against a company through a transaction with an agent he must show that there is in existence a power in the articles to confer authority on the agent. In the absence of such a power the negative doctrine of constructive notice comes into operation and the contractor must in consequence fail in his claim. But if he can only affirm that there is such a power in the articles if he has read them then counsel's contention is established. The answer to this argument is that properly understood the proposition that a contractor cannot base a claim on unread provisions in articles is confined to the situation where they are required in order to establish the existence of apparent authority. If at the time of the transaction the contractor did not know of a provision of the article how can he say that it appeared to grant authority? No invocation of the Rule in *Turquand's* case[13] will help him. On the other hand whether or not restrictions on authority exist in the articles has nothing to do with the knowledge of the contractor, either when he entered into the transaction or at any other time. If there are no restrictions the contractor is not affected by the negative doctrine of constructive notice. He need not wait for the company to allege that restrictions exist. He can assert at any time that they do not exist by pointing to the existence of powers to confer authority, whether he was previously aware of them or not. If the contractor can establish the existence of apparent authority at the time of the transaction apart from the articles, then his knowledge, or absence of knowledge, of provisions in the articles is quite immaterial. Counsel's contention was completely unsound in principle.

The rejection of counsel's contention: the authorities

An affirmation of basic principles establishes the unsoundness of the contention. In Part C we shall examine the judges' examination of the basic principles governing apparent authority. Counsel was, however, able to cite a number of judicial dicta in support of his contention. They were to be found mainly in *Houghton's* case,[9] *Schenkers'* case,[4] and *Rama's* case,[14] the authorities which before the *Buckhurst* case[15] were the principal ones for the rejection of the positive doctrine. It is undoubtedly true that there are difficulties in interpreting the judgements in these and in other cases. This can be illustrated by reference to the conflicting interpretations which have been placed on them.

We begin by noting that the members of the Court of Appeal in the *Buckhurst* case[15] differed as to the interpretation of the judgment of Slade J. in *Rama's* case.[14] Wilmer L.J.[21] and Diplock L.J.[22] thought that the contention of counsel for the defendant was supported by Slade J. On the other hand, Pearson L.J.[23] did not consider that Slade J. had adopted that view. Willmer L.J. and Diplock L.J. said they preferred to their view of what Slade J. decided the contrary doctrine enunciated in the *B. T.-H.* case.[24]

Slade J. in *Rama's* case interpreted the judgments of Scrutton and Slesser L.JJ. in the *B. T.-H.* case[24] and Sargant L.J. in *Houghton's* case[9] in a different manner from that in which they were interpreted by Willmer L.J. in the *Buckhurst* case.[25] So too Diplock L.J. disagrees with Slade J. as to the law laid down in *Houghton's* case and the *Kreditbank Cassel*[4] case.[26] Slade J. thought that Scrutton and Slesser L.JJ. in the *B. T.-H.* case had expressed a view inconsistent with *Houghton's* case, and in the conflict between the two Court of Appeal decisions he followed the earlier, *Houghton's* case.[27] Willmer L.J. thought there was no conflict between *Houghton's* case and the *B. T.-H.* case.[28] Diplock L.J. also thought there was no conflict, but if there were he said he would prefer to follow the later *B. T.-H.* case.[29]

This sketch of labyrinthine wanderings may be completed by stating that Slade J. in *Rama's* case[14] thought that Scrutton and Slesser L.JJ. had propounded an erroneous proposition in the *B. T.-H.* case, because they had misinterpreted what Atkin L.J. had said in *Schenkers'* case :[4] Greer L.J. on the other hand had rightly interpreted Atkin L.J.[30]

---

[21] [1964] 1 All E.R. at p. 638 D.
[22] *Ibid.*, at p. 674 H.
[23] *Ibid.*, at p. 642 I.
[24] This is my abbreviation for *British Thomson-Houston Co., Ltd.* v. *Federated European Bank, Ltd.* (see note 3 *supra*). Judges do now use abbreviations of the names of cases: *e.g.* in the *Buckhurst* case we read of *Mahony's* case, *Houghton's* case and so on. The *B. T.-H.* case is only once abbreviated: and then only as the *British Thomson-Houston* case by Diplock L.J. at p. 648 A.
[25] [1964] 1 All E.R., at p. 638 D.
[26] *Ibid.*, at p. 647 H.
[27] [1952] All E.R., at p. 569 C. Apparently he did not consider that he had a discretion of choosing between two inconsistent decisions. Contrary to the opinion of the court in *Young* v. *Bristol Aeroplane Co.* [(1944) K.B. 718 ; Aff. (1946) A.C. 163. Ed.] he thought he was bound to follow the earlier of two inconsistent decisions. A possible reason for such a view is that the latter of two inconsistent decisions must be wrong, for the court was bound by the earlier decision.
[28] [1964] 1 All E.R., at p. 638 D.
[29] *Ibid.*, at p. 647 B.
[30] Slade J. considered that the views of Scrutton and Slesser L.JJ. formed the *ratio decidendi* of the *B. T.-H.* case because they were the majority. He was only able to follow Greer L.J. because of the conflict with *Houghton's* case. Diplock L.J. also considered himself bound by the majority of a Court of Appeal. It should be noted that we are not dealing with situations in which a minority dissents, and the majority pronounce the decision of the Court, but situations where majority and minority pronounce different reasons for the same decision. It should be further noted that all the narrated search for the correct interpretation of earlier judgments illustrates the doctrine rightly expressed by Lord Reid in *Midland Silicones* v. *Scrutton's, Ltd.* [1962] A.C. 446 that the *ratio decidendi* of a case is arrived at by a process of interpretation of the actual reasoning, and that this *ratio decidendi* is usually binding.

An explanation of conflicting interpretations: the ambiguity of the phrase " rely on "

It is not proposed to enter on a consideration of the various interpretations of the various dicta in order to put forward submissions of correct interpretations. The " correct " doctrine it is considered has now been propounded in the *Buckhurst* case,[15] and it is not necessary to investigate thoroughly the earlier authorities. It is, however, submitted that much of the difficulty in interpretation of judgments and in the exposition of principles arises from incomplete comprehension of the ambiguity of the commonly used phrases connected with the clause " rely on the articles ".[31] The consequence has been confusion between different propositions denoted by similar language.

There are two different meanings of the phrase " rely on the articles ". (i) There is that reliance on the articles which exists when a legal contention is advanced. Thus, counsel relies on a provision in the articles to establish the existence of actual authority : or to show that the negative doctrine of constructive notice does not apply by pointing to a power to confer authority to be found in the provision. (ii) " Reliance on the articles " may designate a factual situation, such as a contractor acting on the faith of a provision in the articles of which he has actual knowledge. The result of this ambiguity is that two propositions may appear to be inconsistent when in substance they are not : and one proposition may be mistaken for a quite different proposition.

A simple example of the ambiguity, where the context makes clear the different uses, is found in the judgment of Sargant L.J. in *Houghton's* case[33] which Willmer L.J. said was " much relied on by the defendant company in the present case " :[32]

> Next as to the power to delegate which is contained in the articles of association. In a case like this where that power of delegation has not been exercised, and where admittedly Mr. Dart and the plaintiff firm had no knowledge of the existence of that power and did not rely on it, I cannot for myself see how they can subsequently make use of this unknown power so as to validate the transaction. They could rely on the fact of delegation, had it been a fact, whether known to them or not. They might rely on their knowledge of the power of delegation, had they known of it, as part of the circumstances entitling them to infer that there had been a delegation and to act on that inference, though it were in fact a mistaken one. But it is quite another thing to say that the plaintiffs are entitled now to rely on the supposed exercise of a power which was never in fact exercised and of the existence of which they were in ignorance at the date when they contracted.

There, it is clear, that when " rely on " is first used the reference is to what happened at the time of the transaction : in so far as the power

---

[31] Examples of such phrases in addition to " rely on the articles ", are " relied on the articles ", " reliance on the articles ".

[32] [1964] 1 All E.R. at p. 639 C. Note that Willmer L.J. is referring by his use of "relied on " to a legal contention submitted by counsel.

[33] [1927] 1 K.B. at p. 266.

R

in the articles constituted a representation it was not relied on, in the sense of action taken on the faith of the representation.   In all the subsequent uses of the phrase " rely on ", as is abundantly clear from its last use, the reference is to the submission to the court of a legal contention, and the sentences may be translated thus : (i) the contractor can assert the existence of actual authority, whether he had knowledge of it or not when he contracted; (ii) the contractor can assert that there was apparent authority, and to establish such authority he can point to the power as one of the factors constituting an appearance of apparent authority, but he cannot succeed in a claim based on apparent authority unless he can show reliance on the apparent authority in the sense of action taken in the belief that authority existed, which must include knowledge of the power; (iii) the contractor cannot assert an actual authority when there was no action taken in the belief that there was authority.

Another passage whose interpretation was disputed is that from the judgment of Slade J. in *Rama's* case : [34]

> I understand this case [the *B. T.-H. case*] to have been decided by Scrutton L.J. and Slesser L.J. on the footing that Atkin L.J. in his judgment in *Schenkers'* case had said that there were cases in which one could rely on the articles of association, and a power conferred by the articles, even when one did not know of the existence of the articles and, *ex hypothesi*, could not have relied on them.

Here it is clear that the first reference is to the submission of a legal contention.   It is also clear that the second reference is to actual behaviour, action taken by reason of knowledge of the power in the faith that it had been exercised.   But what is not clear is the character of the legal contention.   Was the reliance on the articles a submission that the existence of the power established, in accordance with the Rule in *Turquand's* case,[13] that the negative doctrine of constructive notice had no application?   Or was it a submission that apparent authority existed? The differences of interpretation of *Schenkers'* case[4] and *Rama's* case[14] arise from this latent ambiguity.   It is my opinion that Slade J. misinterpreted Scrutton L.J. and Slesser L.J. in the *B. T.-H.* case.[24]   They were not asserting that a contractor could call in aid an article of association containing a power of delegation, of which they had had no knowledge at the time of the transaction, in order to establish apparent authority.   On the other hand the judgment of Slade J. was wrongly interpreted by Willmer L.J. and Diplock L.J. in the *Buckhurst* case.[15] He did not, by rejecting what he erroneously believed to be the ratio of Scrutton L.J. and Slesser L.J. in the *B. T.-H.* case, assert that a contractor would not for the purpose of the Rule in *Turquand's* case point to a power of delegation, unless he knew of it at the time of the trans-

---

[34] [1952] 1 All E.R., at p. 569 C.

action. He clearly made no such assertion, for that would have contradicted the ratio of Greer L.J. in the *B. T.-H.* case[24] which he accepted as valid.

It is worth-while giving further examination to the latent ambiguity, referred to in the above paragraph, of the phrase " rely on the articles ". Without awareness of that ambiguity it may be believed for example that the two following propositions are inconsistent. The doctrine that an apparent authority cannot be asserted unless a contractor acted in the belief that authority existed may yield the proposition: a contractor cannot rely on provisions in articles of association whereby a power exists to delegate authority, unless he had actual knowledge of the provisions. One the other hand one aspect of the Rule in *Turquand's* case[13] can be expressed thus: a contractor can rely on provisions in articles of association, whereby a power exists to delegate authority, even though he had no actual knowledge of the provisions. Despite the apparent contradiction of the expressions there is no inconsistency between the propositions: they refer to different legal contentions. When the phrase " rely on the articles " is encountered we should ask what is the purpose of the reliance. If a contractor is seeking to establish the existence of apparent authority then the rule prohibiting reliance without knowledge applies. If apparent authority exists apart from the articles a contractor has no need to rely on the articles for that purpose. Nevertheless a contractor will not recover despite the existence of apparent authority if the articles prohibit the agent from acting as he did. He may however point to a provision in the articles to show there was no such prohibition. If a contractor is seeking to show that permission for the agent to act is found in the articles then the rule allowing reliance without knowledge applies.

The operation of knowledge of articles of association

One can state in the following manner the propositions established by the *Buckhurst* case[15] with regard to the operation of knowledge or absence of knowledge of provisions in articles conferring powers to delegate authority. (i) Knowledge of such provision at the time of the transaction is not required (a) for the purpose of rejecting a contractor's claim by virtue of the negative doctrine of constructive notice of *Ernest* v. *Nicholls*,[5] (b) for the purpose of allowing a contractor's claim by virtue of the Rule in *Turquand's* case. (ii) Knowledge of such provisions (a) is not required for the purpose of accepting a contractor's claim based on apparent authority existing apart from the articles, (b) is required for the purpose of accepting a contractor's claim based on apparent authority where no such authority exists apart from the articles. With regard to the fourth proposition it should be noted that knowledge of the provision is not by itself enough. Not only must there be " reliance on " the knowledge, the knowledge is but " part of circumstances " which may constitute apparent authority. Those circumstances should indicate that it is usual for the person with whom the contractor has dealt to have the authority on which the contractor relies. If the circumstances are such that there could not usually be authority then mere knowledge of the provision in the articles would be inadequate.[35]

PART C

*The present doctrine of the apparent authority of the
agent of a company*

Apparent authority and estoppel

All the judges in the Court of Appeal in the *Buckhurst* case[15] recognised that the doctrine of apparent authority was based on estoppel. Diplock L.J. provides a rationale for the doctrine in these terms, contrasting it with actual authority which is created by a consensual agreement between principal and agent, and by which a contractor may obtain rights against the principal even though " totally ignorant of the existence of any authority " :[36]

> An " apparent " or " ostensible " authority, on the other hand, is a legal relationship between the principal and the contractor created by a representation, made by the principal to the contractor, intended to be and in fact acted on by the contractor, that the agent has authority to enter on behalf of the principal into a contract of a kind within the scope of the " apparent " authority, so as to render the principal liable to perform any obligations imposed on him by such a contract. To the relationship so created the agent is a stranger. He need not be (although he generally is) aware of the existence of the representation. The representation, when acted on by the contractor by entering into a contract with the agent, operates as an estoppel, preventing

---

[35] The principle that the existence of unusual circumstances puts a contractor on inquiry as to the terms of the actual authority is to be found in *Underwood* v. *Bank of Liverpool* [1924] 1 K.B. 775; see *per* Bankes L.J. at p. 788 and Atkin L.J. at p. 797. See also the discussion of *Houghton's* case, *Schenker's* case and *Rama's* case by Willmer L.J. in [1964] 1 All E.R., at p. 638 E, where he said: "They were all cases of most unusual transactions, which would not be within what would ordinarily be expected to be the scope of the authority of the officer purporting to act on behalf of the company."

[36] It is worth reciting the whole of the passage on actual authority and noticing that he accepts the thesis of circuity of action I had propounded as the rationale for the liability of an undisclosed principal: "An 'actual' authority is a legal relationship between principal and agent created by a consensual agreement to which they alone are parties. Its scope is to be ascertained by applying ordinary principles of construction of contracts, including any proper implications from the express words used, the usages of the trade, or the course of business between the parties. To this agreement the contractor is a stranger; he may be totally ignorant of the existence of any authority on the part of the agent. Nevertheless, if the agent does enter into a contract pursuant to the ' actual ' authority, it does create contractual rights and liabilities between the principal and the contractor. It may be that this rule relating to ' undisclosed principals ', which is peculiar to English law, can be rationalised as avoiding circuity of action, for the principal could in equity compel the agent to lend his name in an action to enforce the contract against the contractor, and would at common law be liable to indemnify the agent in respect of the performance of the obligations assumed by the agent under the contract." [1964] 1 All E.R., at p. 644 D.

the principal from asserting that he is not bound by the contract. It is irrelevant whether the agent has actual authority to enter into the contract.[37]

Pearson L.J. succinctly says: " The expressions ' ostensible authority ' and ' holding out ' are somewhat vague. The basis of them when the situation is analysed, is an estoppel by representation."[38]

In order for apparent authority to exist there must be the appearance of authority. In other words, in terms of the theory of estoppel there must be a representation that the person purporting to act as agent was authorised to act on behalf of the company in the manner in which he purported to act. Thus, apparent authority is a question of fact concerned with the general circumstances of the transaction, and not merely with the terms of the articles of association. Indeed from the circumstances apart from any provision in the articles it may be reasonable for the contractor to infer that authority existed. In such a situation there is appearance of authority and knowledge of the articles is immaterial.[39] It is only where there is no apparent authority apart from the articles that knowledge of the articles becomes material. A provision in the articles may constitute a representation of authority. If there is knowledge of it, and the representation is " relied on " by entering into a contract with the company through the agent, then the company may be estopped from denying the existence of authority. But a provision in the articles, for example, of a power to delegate is not by itself sufficient to constitute an appearance of authority. The general circumstances, including the nature of the representation, may be such as to put a reasonable person on inquiry as to the existence of actual authority. They may indeed be such that a reasonable person would not believe that authority existed. For example, where a contractor has knowledge that a person purporting to sign cheques is but an office boy he could not assume merely from knowledge of a provision in the articles of a power to delegate to " any person " that the office boy has authority to sign cheques. Whenever an agent is purporting to exercise powers not in the ordinary scope of the powers of such an agent there is no appearance of authority. The provision in the articles has to be read together with the general circumstances as a whole in order that there should be a representation of authority.

The rejection of the positive doctrine of constructive notice follows from the doctrine of estoppel. A statement in the articles may constitute

---

[37] *Ibid.*, at p. 644 F.

[38] *Ibid.*, at p. 641 F. Later he says: " as against the other contracting party, who has altered his position in reliance on the representation, the company is estopped from denying the truth of the representation ". What is meant by alteration of position? It appears to be assumed by all judges of the Court of Appeal that merely agreeing with the apparent agent about the term of the contract "entering into the contract" according to Diplock L.J. in his condition (*c*), is a reliance and this constitutes an alteration of position. But this is not the general American view: see n. 11.

[39] " It is possible to have ostensible or apparent authority apart from the articles ". Slade J. in *Rama's* case [1952] 1 All E.R. 566 E, approved in the *Buckhurst* case.

a representation by the company that a particular person has authority, but the company cannot be estopped from denying that he has authority if such in fact be the case, unless the contractor knows of the representation and has acted on it. Thus, Willmer L.J. said: " the three decisions relied on by the defendant company are to my mind no more than illustrations of the well-established principle that a party who seeks to set up an estoppel must show that he in fact relied on the representation that he alleges."[40] Diplock L.J. in his rationale sets out "four conditions which must be fulfilled to entitle a contractor to enforce against a company a contract entered into on behalf of the company by an agent who had no actual authority to do so ". Two only of the conditions concern us now. They are: " (a) a representation that the agent had authority to enter on behalf of the company into a contract of the kind sought to be enforced was made to the contractor . . . (c) that the contractor was induced by such representation to enter into the contract *i.e.* that he in fact relied on it."[41] This is a restatement of the thesis that the doctrine of apparent authority is derived from estoppel, but later in his explanation of the authorities "relied on" by defendants' counsel he said:

> The contractor in each of the three cases sought to rely on a provision of the articles, giving to the board power to delegate wide authority to the agent, as entitling the contractor to treat the conduct of the board as a representation that the agent had had delegated to him wider powers than those normally exercised by persons occupying the position in relation to the company's business which the agent was in fact permitted by the board to occupy. Since this would involve proving that the representation on which he in fact relied as inducing him to enter into the contract comprised the articles of association of the company as well as the conduct of the board, it would be necessary for him to establish, first, that he knew the contents of the articles (*i.e.*, that condition (c) was fulfilled in respect of any representation contained in the articles) and, secondly, that the conduct of the board in the light of that knowledge would be understood by a reasonable man as a representation that the agent had authority to enter into the contract sought to be enforced, *i.e.*, that condition (a) was fulfilled.[42]

The modification of the doctrine of apparent authority arising from the provisions of the Companies Act.

The result of the doctrine of *Ernest* v. *Nicholls*[5] is that, notwithstanding that the contractor has relied on an apparent authority, he cannot recover if the articles do not permit the exercise of the purported authority. The Rule in *Turquand's case*[13] says that requirements of " household management " do not constitute a denial of such permission

---

[40] [1964] 1 All E.R., at p. 639 B.

[41] *Ibid.*, at p. 646 D. The dissection of the masterly discourse of Diplock L.J. and the presentation of isolated passages is a wholly inadequate acknowledgment of the great contribution to theoretical understanding as well as practical application which the judgment as a whole constitutes.

[42] *Ibid.*, at p. 647 D.

unless they have been fulfilled. On the contrary a provision stating that authority can be exercised when the "household management" requirements have been fulfilled constitutes permission. These propositions are enunciated in accordance with conventional terminology by Willmer L.J. He states:

> It is well established that all persons dealing with a company are affected with notice of its memorandum and articles of association, which are public documents open to inspection by all: see *Mahony* v. *East Holyford Mining Co.* However, by the rule in *Royal British Bank* v. *Turquand*, re-affirmed in *Mahony*'s case, it was also established, in the words of Lord Hatherley in the latter case.

> " that, when there are persons conducting the affairs of the company in a manner which appears to be perfectly consonant with the articles of association, then those dealing with them, externally, are not to be affected by any irregularities which may take place in the internal management of the company."

> Thus in *Biggerstaff* v. *Rowatt's Wharf, Ltd.*, where the articles of association conferred power to appoint a managing director, the company was held bound by the act of a person who purported to contract as its managing director, though he had never been formally appointed as such.[43]

Diplock L.J. also restates the propositions but he does so in accordance with the new terminology which he proposes and which is considered in Part D.

The modification of the doctrine of apparent authority arising from the nature of corporate personality: interaction of actual and apparent authority

A natural person himself makes representations about the authority of an agent. A corporation can only make representations through agents. This gives rise to problems which are for the first time analysed and expounded by Diplock L.J.[44]

The Lord Justice points out that to create apparent authority there must be a representation made by persons who have actual authority to make the representation. Actual authority may be conferred by the articles of association directly: quite often powers of the board of directors are specified. On the other hand there is often power to delegate authority, and the delegate by exercising such power may confer authority to make representations. Estoppel may be by words or conduct, and the commonest form of representation of apparent authority in general is by conduct, " *viz.* by permitting the agent to act in the management or conduct of the principal's business ". In relation

---

[43] *Ibid.*, at p. 637 C.

[44] Pearson L.J. acknowledges their existence when he says: " The identification of the persons whose knowledge and acquiescence constitute knowledge and acquiescence by the company depends on the facts of the particular case ". *Ibid.*, at p. 641 H.
Some preliminary discussion will be found in (1934) 50 *L.Q.R.* at p. 229.

to transactions with a company it follows that if a board of directors permit an agent to act in the management of the business they represent that he has authority so to act. Such a representation is usually within the actual authority of the board of directors. One who purports to be an agent cannot confer apparent authority on himself, " a contractor cannot rely on the agent's own representation as to his actual authority ". But if the board of directors know that he is purporting to be an agent, and permit him to act as agent, they may create an apparent authority. However, a representation by a board of directors as to the authority of the agent of a company, instead of being actually authorised as part of the board's function of management of the company's affairs, may in fact be inconsistent with the memorandum or articles of association. In such a situation, in accordance with *Ernest* v. *Nicholls*,[5] the company will not be bound by the board's permitting some one to act as agent, or permitting an agent with limited authority to act beyond the scope of such limited authority.[45]

These considerations lead to the formulation by Diplock L.J. of two further " conditions which must be fulfilled to entitle a contractor to force against a company a contract entered into on behalf of the company by an agent who had no actual authority to do so ".[46] These are : " (b) that such representation was made by a person or persons who had ' actual ' authority to manage the business of the company either generally or in respect of those matters to which the contract relates . . . (d) that under its memorandum or articles of association the company was not deprived of the capacity either to enter into a contract of the kind sought to be enforced or to delegate authority to enter into a contract of that kind to the agent."[47]

There is one situation which has a somewhat paradoxical character with which Diplock L.J. does not deal. That an unauthorised person cannot confer authority on himself seems to be a clear proposition. But it does not follow that an agent with limited actual authority cannot confer a wider apparent authority on himself. The dictum of Diplock L.J. that " a contractor cannot rely on the agent's own representation as to his actual authority " is not universally true. An agent whose actual authority is limited to certain classes of acts may also have actual authority to make representations as to the extent of his authority. He may abuse that authority to make representations by stating that his actual authority is wider than it is. If the contractor relies on such a misrepresentation, and circumstances are not such as to put a reasonable

---

[45] If the agent is permitted to do acts beyond the scope of acts ordinarily done by an agent in his position the company will not be bound because there is no appearance of authority in the circumstances. Diplock L.J. does not refer to that situation, but he does deal with the similar situation where the agent does acts outside the ordinary course of the company's business.

[46] The two other conditions (a) and (c) are set out at p.264.

[47] [1964] 1 All E.R., at p. 646 A to D.

person on inquiry,[48] then the company is estopped from asserting the original limitation of the agent's authority.[49]

PART D

Misleading Terms

" Constructive notice ". The new terminology of Diplock L.J.

As we have already stated Diplock L.J. has proposed a new terminology to replace that of " constructive notice " of the articles. He abandons the language of publicity with its concomitant of " constructive notice ", and adopts the language of public law with its concomitants of " constitution " and " ultra vires ". The reason he advances is that " the expression ' constructive notice ' tends to disguise that constructive notice is not a positive but a negative doctrine, like that of estoppel of which it forms a part ".[50] It is not clear that the phrase " constructive notice " does suggest a positive doctrine. Perhaps the rule that a contractor is deemed to have notice of all the provisions in the articles of association does suggest that he is so deemed for all purposes, and is to be treated as if he had knowledge of the articles when he entered into the contract. This is, of course, the positive doctrine of constructive notice. If so the rule is misleading and the phrase " constructive notice " which summarises the rule is misleading. But there are further reasons for abandoning the old terminology. In the first place the rule it suggests is a fiction. More importantly it obscures perception of the policies of the rules. The provisions of the Companies Acts requiring the powers of those in immediate control of the company's affairs[51] to be stated in the memorandum and articles of association are designed to protect the interests of shareholders against directors and others who might dissipate the funds of the company, derived from the investments of shareholders, by transactions outside the terms of the agreement on the faith of which the original shareholders contributed the funds, or subsequent shareholders purchased their shares.[52] The protection of shareholders, it is thought, would be inadequate if directors and their agents could exceed the stated powers. The publicity of memorandum and articles is for the benefit of those who contract with the company, so that they are able to know the nature of the company's enterprise and

---

[48] And there is no inconsistency with the memorandum or articles of association.
[49] This is the explanation proffered by me in 50 L.Q.R. 229 for the decision in Hambro v. Burnand [1904] 2 Q.B. 10.
[50] [1964] 1 All E.R., at p. 645 D.
[51] The shareholders are in ultimate de jure control of the company, though even such ultimate control may be exercised de facto by groups who use the company's resources or employ other means of de facto control. It is of course the directors who are in immediate control of the management of the company.
[52] The marketability of shares is one of the inducements leading the original shareholders to contribute funds.

the manner of its operation, and see the limits of the powers of those who have the immediate control and management of the company's affairs.[53]

Diplock L.J. extends the use of the language of *ultra vires* from its present use in connection with the memorandum of assocation. He uses the concept of the " constitution " of a company to include both the memorandum *and* articles of association. He states that the general doctrines of actual and apparent authority are affected where the principal is a corporation : " The capacity of a corporation is limited by its constitution, *i.e.* in the case of a company incorporated under the Companies Act, by its memorandum and articles of association. . . . This affects the rules as to the ' apparent ' authority of an agent in two ways. First, no representation can operate to estop the corporation from denying the authority of the agent to do on behalf of the corporation an act which the corporation is not permitted by the corporation to do itself. Secondly, since the conferring of actual authority on an agent is itself an act of the corporation, the capacity to do which is regulated by its constitution, the corporation cannot be estopped from denying that it has conferred on a particular agent authority to do acts which, by its constitution, it is incapable of delegating to that particular agent . . . these are direct consequences of the doctrine of *ultra vires*."[54]

It is rewarding to note how the various rules relating to the authority of an agent appear in the new terminology.

The rule of *Ernest* v. *Nicholls*[5] becomes simply that an act *ultra vires* the constitution does not bind the company. There is no need to refer to any doctrine that the documents of a company are public documents. The rule applies to both actual and apparent authority.[55]

The Rule of *Turquand's* case[13] becomes a rule concerning the interpretation of the constitution. Whenever a power to do any act, including the delegation of authority, is subject to some procedural requirement of " indoor management " action taken without complying with the procedural requirement is not *ultra vires* the constitution. In such circumstances, however, there will be no actual authority, but there may be apparent authority.

There is no necessity to state that a person is deemed to have notice of articles of which he is in fact unaware. There is thus no basis for a " positive doctrine of constructive notice " (to use the old terminology to designate a doctrine which never gets on its feet under the new terminology). Apparent authority of an agent of a company is a question of fact dependent on the circumstances in the same way as is the appar-

---

[53] The manner in which directors may deal only with general policy questions, and the day by day " control " be in the hands of the executive and technical management, is the subject of legal-economic and legal-sociological study. In the nineteenth century a divorce between ownership and control was envisaged. This dichotomy is insufficient to describe accurately the operation of modern companies in which separation exists between (i) ownership (ii) control and (iii) management. Nor are these concepts adequate.

[54] [1964] 1 All E.R., at p. 645 B.

[55] There is, of course, in a strict sense no actual authority where an agreement to create authority is *ultra vires*.

ent authority of an agent of a natural person, subject however to the doctrine of *ultra vires*. It may arise apart from the articles : actual knowledge of a provision of the articles may be a factor in its establishment. The actual authority of an agent of a company is a matter of interpretation of the constitution, or of the agreement between the agent and other agents of the company whose actual authority is derived from the constitution. There is no actual authority if an agreement involves action *ultra vires* the constitution.

" Rely on "

The problems concerned with this phrase have already been discussed.

" Apparent authority "

This phrase involves a fiction of hypostatisation. The phrase is an elliptical way of referring to " authority apparent to a contractor ". If a contractor is unaware of circumstances which, to those aware of the circumstances, would give rise to an appearance of authority it is clear that there is no appearance of authority to him. Yet current terminology states that there is apparent authority but that he cannot set up the apparent authority because he has not relied on it. Watts, the editor of *Smith's Mercantile Law,* stated the position accurately when he said : " The term ' ostensible authority ' denotes no authority at all."[55] It is a phrase conveniently used to describe the position [of] an appearance of authority ".[56] In current language " apparent authority " is often used as the maximum authority which may be reasonably apparent to some person dealing with the agent in some circumstances.[57]

---

[56] Smith & Watts' *Mercantile Law,* (8th Ed., 1924), at p. 177 n. (*s*). The note in full is as follows : " There is a clear distinction between the proper use of the two expressions, ' implied authority ' and ' ostensible authority.' The former is a real authority, the exercise of which is binding not only as between the principal and third parties, but also as between principal and agent. It differs only from an express authority in that it is conferred by no express words in writing, but is to be gathered from surrounding circumstances. The term " *ostensible authority* " on the other hand, *denotes no authority at all.* It is a phrase conveniently used to describe the position which arises when one person has clothed another with, or allowed him to assume, an appearance of authority to act on his behalf, without actually giving him any authority either express or implied, by which appearance of authority a third party is misled into believing that a real authority exists. As between the so-called principal and agent such ' ostensible authority ' is of no effect. As between such principal, however, and the third party it is binding, on the ground that the principal is estopped from averring that the person whom he has held out and pretended to be his agent is not in fact so."

[57] See the fuller discussion 50 *L.Q.R.* at p. 226 *et seq.* The following is an extract : " The apparent authority is treated as independent of a particular person dealing with the agent, and is derived from a consideration of the relation of the principal and agent only; though it is distinct from the actual authority, being the outward relation. In effect it is equal to the representation which may be said to be made by the principal to the world at large." See also the discussion in 16 *Can. B.R.* at p. 765 where I say (*inter alia*) : " When it is said that an agent's act was within the scope of his apparent authority all that is meant is that the act appeared to be authorised . . . there has grown up in the English cases a use of the term ' apparent authority ' in an objective sense, in which ' apparent authority ' is conceived to exist independently of its subjective perception by somebody. The notion of perception is not regarded as inherent in the phrase ' apparent authority ' but as additional so that there may or may not be ' reliance on an apparent authority '." [*Ante,* Introduction pp. 6-7. Ed.]

The operation of the doctrine of apparent authority involves two questions which are however obscured by the phrase " apparent authority " into which the doctrine is compressed. The language of appearance of authority raises the two questions more directly. They are: (a) from what does the appearance arise? (b) to whom is the appearance made? The asking of these questions brings out the two corresponding aspects of the doctrine: (a) the circumstances must be such as to constitute a representation, by words or by conduct, that the purported agent has the authority the contractor thinks he has, (b) the contractor must have been aware of the authority—it must have appeared to him —and he must have entered into the contract believing it was within the agent's authority to negotiate.

" Agent "

The pervasiveness of the power of language to mislead prevails within the pervasive word in this branch of law—" agent ". That word is often used to refer to somebody who is in fact no agent at all. It may be used to refer to a person with whom the contractor deals, and who purports to act on behalf of the company, but has no actual authority to do so. The term " agent " is but an elliptical way of saying " one who purports to be an agent ". This ellipsis is not easily perceived because of the use of the phrase " apparent authority ". We say " A has apparent authority ", though A in fact has no authority whatsoever, when it appears that A is authorised. We say that A is an " apparent agent ", and, regarding apparent agency as a species of agency, we feel justified in saying that A is an agent.

The phrases " agent " and " apparent agent " have misleading effect not only in relation to the factual situation they describe but also in relation to the legal consequences. It is as we have seen important to distinguish, on the one hand, between a " true " agent, one who has been actually authorised, but whose authority is limited to certain clause of acts, and on the other hand, a so-called " agent ", a person who has no authority at all. Indeed our common language often describes as " agent " one who is not even an " apparent agent "—who does not reasonably appear to be one—but who nevertheless purports to be one.[58]

Where an agent is actually authorised, then in such a case he may also have authority to make representations as to the extent of his authority. If a contractor relies on such a representation, and enters into a contract outside the scope of the agent's actual authority but within the ambit of the authority the agent purported to have, the company will be estopped, and in consequence bound by the contract.[59]

---

[58] Indeed ellipsis sometimes results in describing one as " agent " who is not an apparent, and does not even purport to be one, but who is believed by the contractor to be one.

[59] See my discussion of *Hambro* v. *Burnand*, *supra* n. 49.

16

The Cheques Act, 1957*

The notion that the law of a country can be changed by human action is not one that appears to have been developed early in the history of all communities. Early legislation is said to have been no more than a restatement of existing custom. The Roman emperors introduced the practice of conscious legislation to Europe, and since the days of Jeremy Bentham the more usual process of legal development in the United Kingdom has been that of statutory change. Yet even here the reform of lawyer's law by Act of Parliament is still regarded as something exceptional; a new reason for this attitude is the fact that the time of Parliament is occupied to such a large extent by the consideration of high policy and the newer social legislation, matters which are the principal concern of governments who now have to a very great extent control of parliamentary time. One of the reasons why the *Cheques Act,* 1957, which we are to consider tonight, commands general interest is that it is an example of desirable legal reform brought about by the initiative and persistence of a Member of Parliament availing himself of the limited opportunities which exist for presenting Private Members' Bills to Parliament.

Social and legislative history of the Act

For many years men engaged in commerce and industry and banking have complained of the waste of time that resulted from the practice of endorsing cheques which a payee never negotiated to any other person but paid directly into his own account. There was the time spent by the payee in endorsing the cheques : there was the further time spent by bank officials in examining the endorsements. It was calculated that in 1956 some four million man hours were consumed in these activities. This figure was derived from the fact that 780 million cheques were drawn of which 97 per cent were paid direct by the

---

*5 & 6 Eliz. 2, Ch. 36. This article is reprinted from *Journal* of the Institute of Bankers in Ireland, October, 1958, by kind permission. It was a lecture delivered to the Institute of Bankers in Ireland, in Belfast, on 23 October, 1957.

payees into their banks. In 1950 both the Federation of British Industries and the London Clearing Banks had gone on record as being in favour of the abolition of such endorsement.

It was not however until 1954 that any action was taken in Parliament. In that year Mr. Graham Page introduced a Private Member's Bill under the Ten Minutes Rule with the object of abolishing endorsements on cheques. The scheme he adopted was the creation of a legal fiction to the effect that in certain circumstances there had been an endorsement. It was an ingenious plan, but the attacks by Jeremy Bentham on the legal fictions which were a feature of our legal system right up to the nineteenth century have rightly made every one suspicious of such devices. When Mr. Eden went to the country in 1955 Mr. Graham Page's Bill died, and it has never been revived. But the idea of abolishing unnecessary endorsements survived. Mr. Graham Page did succeed in making the Government aware that an absurd situation existed, and Mr. Butler, who was the Chancellor of the Exchequer, before Parliament ended, set up a Departmental Committee. Its terms of reference were:

> To consider (a) whether, and if so in what circumstances and to what extent, it is desirable to reduce the need for the endorsement of order cheques and similar instruments received for collection by a bank, (b) what, if any, amendment of the Bills of the Exchange Act, 1882, or other statutory provision should be made for this purpose.

The Chairman of the Committee was Mr. A. A. Mocatta, Q.C.,† one of the leaders of the Commercial Bar, and another distinguished member was Lord Chorley, the author of the well-known text-book on the law of banking. The Committee received a great deal of evidence from many representative bodies, including the Institute of Bankers. One of the individual experts who gave oral evidence was Dr. J. Milnes Holden, whose admirable thesis *The History of Negotiable Instruments in English Law* was more than once referred to in the Committee's Report.[1] The Report was published in November 1956; it is an elaborate document of twenty-six pages which I commend for careful study by every one. Mr. Nigel Birch, the Economic Secretary to the Treasury, has described it as " thorough, painstaking and deep-thinking ". It recommended the abolition of cheque endorsements in certain circumstances, and considered several cognate matters, such as the special problem of receipt forms on the backs of cheques which have become so popular. The Report also contained a draft of a suggested Act of Parliament to amend the existing law.

The Report was presented to Mr. Macmillan, who had succeeded Mr. Butler as Chancellor of the Exchequer. It was not made the

---

† [Now Mr. Justice Mocatta. Ed.]

[1] *Report of the Committee on Cheque Endorsement:* Cmnd. 3 H.M.S.O. 1s. 3d. See the *Journal* for January 1957, Vol. LIX, Part I, pages 21-23.

subject of Government legislation.   Mr. Graham Page had been fortunate in the ballot for Private Member's Bills, and he took advantage of this opportunity for presenting a further bill to Parliament on the subject of endorsement of cheques.   He did not adopt the draft prepared by the Committee, but submitted an entirely new bill, which he rightly described as embodying " a more straightforward method."[2] It contained provisions giving effect to recommendations in the Report dealing with matters cognate to the endorsement of cheques.   The original bill was amended on Mr. Graham Page's own motions in one or two respects.   The debates on its second reading and in the committee stage are of considerable interest,[3] but it is an established doctrine of case law that the parliamentary debates cannot be referred to by Courts when they are considering the interpretation of an Act of Parliament.   The bill received the Royal Assent on July 17, 1957,[4] and in accordance with the provisions of s. 8(2) it came into operation on October 17.   By s. 8(1) it was given the short title of the *Cheques Act, 1957*.   But the provisions of the statute are not confined to cheques, as is clear from the long title, which is *An Act to amend the law relating to cheques and certain other instruments*.   The older method of citation by reference to the regnal year is " Chapter 36 of the Parliament holden in the fifth and sixth years of the reign of Elizabeth the Second," abbreviated to " 5 & 6 Eliz. 2, ch. 36 ".

Application to Northern Ireland

The more important sections of the Act are concerned with the substantive law of cheques, but here in Northern Ireland it is not inappropriate to deal first with s. 7, the marginal note to which reads " Provisions as to Northern Ireland ".   An Act of the Imperial Parliament will extend to Northern Ireland unless a contrary intention appears.   The matter is put beyond doubt by s. 7.   Were it not for this imperial enactment it would not have been possible for the law to be changed in Northern Ireland, since by s. 4 of the *Government of Ireland Act, 1920*, the Parliament of Northern Ireland has no power to pass laws relating to negotiable instruments.   Cheques are of course a species of negotiable instruments.   Some provisions of the Act apply however to instruments which are not negotiable.   The Parliament of Northern Ireland had legislative power with regard to such instruments, and, by

---

[2] I surmise that this bill was prepared with the assistance of parliamentary draftsmen. In presenting it for the second reading Mr. Graham Page spoke of a customer having a claim against a bank for " wrongfully debiting him ". (568 *Commons Debates*, p. 1507). The true position is that the customer's claim is in respect of the original loan to the bank, and the bank is unable to defend itself by setting off the payment of the amount of the cheque because there was no mandate to make it. In the Committee stage he confuses the discharge of a cheque, which discharges the *drawer*, with the discharge by a banker of his obligation to obey the drawer's mandate (569 *Commons Debates*, p. 1374).

[3] See 568 *Commons Debates*, p. 1504; 569 *Commons Debates*, p. 1364a; 570 *Commons Debates*, p. 1571.

[4] The date of the Royal Assent to an Act of Parliament is set out immediately after the long title.

virtue of the clause in s. 7 saying that the provisions of the Act with regard to instruments other than negotiable instruments shall be deemed to have been passed before the appointed day referred to in s. 6 of the Government of Ireland Act, the Northern Ireland Parliament retains such legislative power. By the *Government of Ireland Act,* 1920, the Parliament of Northern Ireland has no power to make any law with regard to a matter which has been the subject of legislation by the Imperial Parliament applying to Northern Ireland. This limitation is however restricted to Acts of the Imperial Parliament passed after the day appointed under the 1920 Act for the carrying into force of that Act: it has no application where the Act of the Imperial Parliament was passed before the appointed day.[5]

Necessity for the endorsement of cheques

A cheque is defined in s. 73 of the *Bills of Exchange Act,* 1882, as the linguistic symbol for " a bill of exchange drawn on a banker payable on demand ", and it is used with that meaning in the *Cheques Act,* 1957, for s. 6(1) provides that the Act is to be construed as one with the Act of 1882. It will be remembered that part of the definition of " bill of exchange " contained in s. 3 of the 1882 Act is " an unconditional order in writing addressed by one person to another ". These definitions should be remembered in considering the provisions of the *Cheques Act,* 1957, which apply to documents other than cheques. In the law relating to cheques we have to bear in mind two sets of legal rules, those deriving from the " bill of exchange " element of definition, and those deriving from the " banker " element. The relation between banker and customer may be regarded as governed by a set of rules other than those concerned with negotiable instruments, to use another term important in the legal discussion about cheques. A paying banker's duty to obey his customer's order or mandate contained in the cheque derives from the contractual relations between banker and customer: it is not determined by a provision in an Act of Parliament. Similarly, a collecting banker's duties to his customer with regard to the collection of cheques are determined by contract. Both paying banker and collecting banker are guilty of the tort, or civil wrong, of conversion if they deal with a cheque belonging to one person in a manner inconsistent with the owner's title. Both the contractual and tortious obligations of bankers have however been modified by statutory provisions contained not only in Bills of Exchange Acts, but also in Stamp and Revenue Acts. When John Brown draws a cheque payable to " James Smith or order " the paying bank is usually under a duty to Brown to honour the cheque and to pay Smith or his order. It is however under no duty to Smith, or to Smith's bank which seeks to collect the cheque for him, nor is it obliged to pay any endorsee of the cheque

---

[5] See Halsbury's Statutes of England, 2nd ed., Vol. 17, p. 23.

or the endorsee's bank. Let us look at what is the position in some 97 per cent of cases, *i.e.* where Smith will not have negotiated the cheque; and first where he seeks to cash it over the counter. If the paying bank insists on Smith's endorsing the cheque it commits no breach of contractual duty to Smith, nor does it commit a breach of statutory duty. On the other hand there is no statutory obligation requiring endorsement. It may be however that the bank commits a breach of contractual duty to John Brown, the drawer. I know of no Court decisions saying that the banker's contract is only to pay customer's order cheques if the payee endorses them, and of course there is no statutory requirement. But the practice of bankers may have to be considered in saying what are the terms of the contract between banker and customer; certainly banking practice is to require endorsement, and it will continue to be so after the Act of 1957 has come into force. There is a problem whether under such a practice the document called a cheque is one which contains only a conditional order, *i.e.* pay John Smith if John Smith endorses. As a conditional order it ceases to be a " cheque " within the meaning of the *Bills of Exchange Act.* The answer may be that the practice affects the relations between banker and payee, and does not modify the relation between banker and drawer-customer, and that the document remains as between them an unconditional order and so a cheque.

Reasons for endorsement

But why does the paying bank want the endorsement? The answer arises from consideration of the situation where the cheque has come into the hands of some person other than the payee. Look at the consequences if the paying bank pays William Robinson and not James Smith. It should be remembered that the teller at the counter has generally no means of knowing whether the person before him is James Smith or William Robinson. The bank cannot set off the amount of the payment in John Brown's account; it has had no mandate to do so. On the other hand it is liable to an action for conversion at the suit of James Smith, the payee and true owner of the cheque. How can the bank avoid such liability? It does so by requiring endorsement, because then there comes into operation the special statutory provision giving the bank protection: not, it should be noted, the general law of bills of exchange. An order cheque does not become a bearer cheque if it is endorsed without authority by somebody other than the payee. The banker's authority to debit the customer's account derives from s. 60 of the 1882 Act. So too does his immunity from action by the payee, since he is deemed to have paid the payee. He derives no immunity from s. 80 which deals only with crossed cheques paid through a collecting bank. That section, it should be noted, by its reference to " payment . . . to the true owner ", is drafted so as directly to eliminate any question of an action of conversion.

s

Of course, most cheques are not cashed over the counter, but are paid by the payee into his own bank, which only in a minority of cases is the same bank as that on which the cheque is drawn. Let us now look at the position where James Smith pays his cheque into his own bank for collection from John Brown's bank. Once again a requirement for endorsement can only arise from banker's practice. If the paying bank will not honour the cheque without one it becomes requisite for the collecting bank to require James Smith to endorse even though endorsement converts a fairly innocuous order cheque into a dangerous bearer cheque. We see therefore that need for endorsement can derive only from the situation where someone other than the true owner has obtained the cheque. Under the law before the *Cheques Act,* 1957, the paying banker could only be protected by s. 60 where there was an endorsement. It is true that s. 80 was so worded as not specifically to require endorsement, but it applied only to crossed cheques, and moreover the banker had to pay " without negligence ". Since the practice of requiring a payee's endorsement on order cheques was firmly established as part of the ordinary course of business it is very doubtful whether s. 80 would have applied in the case of payment of an unendorsed order cheque. We have also to consider the liability of the collecting bank. A collecting bank's liability for conversion was subject to s. 82 of the 1882 Act which had been amended by the *Bills of Exchange (Crossed Cheques) Act,* 1906, in consequence of the decision in *Capital and Counties Bank* v. *Gordon.*[6] Once again, the words " without negligence " appear. While the same argument about banker's practice applies, we have here the further consideration that the collecting bank can be expected to know its own customers. It cannot be said to act without negligence if it collects from William Robinson a cheque which appears to be that of James Smith.

One further comment has to be made before we turn to the consideration of the various provisions of the Act of 1957. Supposing our payee's name is James *Smyth* and the cheque is made out to James *Smith,* then the banker's practice was (and still will doubtless be for counter paid cheques) to have two endorsements " Smyth " and " Smith ". The reason for this is that the banker must comply with the specific instructions of the customer. There is a legal maxim *falsa demonstratio non nocet* : a mere error in spelling does not affect the legal position, nor does any other mere error of indication.[7] But

---

6 [1903] A.C. 240.
7 It is sufficient to refer to the discussion of the doctrine in *Arab Bank Ltd.* v. *Ross* [1952] 1 All E.R. 709. The legal position is concisely stated by Somervell L.J. (as he then was) at p. 712E. " Precise correspondence is not required." Lack of correspondence, however, was said in that case to make the endorsement " irregular ", even though it was valid and operative: see per Denning L.J. (as he then was) at p. 716A. The irregularity of an endorsement is important for the purpose of the definition of a holder in due course under s. 29 (1) of the 1882 Act. It was decided in the *Arab Bank* case that an irregular endorsement prevents a bill of exchange from being " complete and regular on the face of it." (Of course in that section " face " includes back.) See the discussion of the case in the text *infra* p. 270.

banks do not want the responsibility for investigating whether or not there may be merely an error of designation, and multiple endorsements seemed to give complete protection. S. 32(4) of the Act of 1882 makes specific reference to wrong designations or mis-spellings. I do not agree with the Mocatta Committee Report which suggests that this section requires the practice of multiple endorsements.[8] Moreover in my opinion if a cheque is made out to a specific payee, the mere existence of an endorsement in his name does not exempt a bank from negligence. If there are two firms, one *Black & Green,* and the other *Green & Black,* and a cheque is made out to *Black & Green* and paid into the account of *Green & Black,* there may be negligence in paying the cheque even though there has been written out the endorsement *Black & Green.* It depends on all the circumstances. The artificiality of the well-known multiple rubber stamp endorsements needs no further comment from me.

The paying bank: section I

The first sub-section is in one sense the main provision of the Act since it deals with the problem of unnecessary endorsements and their inspection. It is however concerned only with the paying bank: the provision relating to collecting banks is to be found in s. 4(3). If the conditions set out in the subsection are fulfilled, it is clear to me that the paying bank incurs no liability: the sub-section says so twice. The banker is deemed to have paid in due course. This, as we have seen, discharges him from liability by reason of s. 59(1) of the 1882 Act, not because the cheque is discharged, since the banker is not liable under it, but because he is deemed to have paid the payee or the endorsee in possession, or the bearer.[9] The sub-section also says the banker does not incur any liability by reason only of the absence of, or irregularity in, endorsement. I cannot however see the significance of the word " only " in view of the complete exoneration given by the concluding words.

But we have to look at the conditions to be fulfilled before the immunity arises. We can make our first division of them into two: (i) the cheque must be an unendorsed or an irregularly endorsed one, and (ii) the banker must pay in good faith and in the ordinary course of business. With regard to the first of these divisions, if the cheque is endorsed and the endorsement is not irregular, then the sub-section does not permit the bank to ignore the endorsement. It will not carry out its customer's mandate if it pays somebody other than the endorsee; it will also be liable in these circumstances to him as he is the true

---

[8] See paragraph 14 of the Report.

[9] It will be remembered that s. 59(1) speaks of payment to the " holder ": a " holder " is defined in s. 2 as the payee or endorsee of a bill or note who is in possession of it, or the bearer thereof. I do not think that the effect of these provisions is that the bank is deemed to have paid the payee, or endorsee, provided he was in possession: rather the effect is that the bank is deemed to have paid the payee, or endorsee, who is deemed to have been in possession.

owner of the cheque. I cannot see therefore how the sub-section eliminates the need for the paying bank to turn over a cheque to see whether there is an endorsement. If however, it finds no endorsement it will be completely protected. Certainly the section fully guarantees the position of banks who do not require cheques to be endorsed by payees. And so the Act does save the time of business men who no longer need endorse their cheques.

If the cheque is endorsed and the endorsement is " irregular ", the bank is fully protected. What does " irregular " mean? The Act of 1882 speaks of forged and unauthorised endorsements. It does however in s. 29(1), defining a holder in due course, speak of a bill regular on the face of it, on the face includes on the back: and we know that the sections relating to irregular endorsements were introduced in view of the case of *Arab Bank Ltd.* v. *Ross*[10] decided in 1952, where the distinction was drawn between invalid and irregular endorsements. In that case promissory notes were made in favour of " Fathi and Faysal Nabalsy Co. or order ". The company was an ordinary partnership in which the two Nabalsys were the sole partners. The notes were endorsed by one of the partners to the plaintiff bank with the full authority of the other partner and the endorsement was the usual partnership one, omitting the word " Co ". It was held that the bank could recover as holders for value because the endorsement was valid, but not as holders in due course because the endorsement was irregular.[11] Presumably, though not certainly, the Courts will give to " irregularly " and " irregularity " the meaning to be derived from the decision in this case. If so the paying bank will only be protected by the sub-section if the endorsement is a valid one, though not in " precise correspondence " with the payee's name appearing on the cheque.[12] If the endorsement is invalid, this will be because it is forged or unauthorised, and the paying bank must turn for protection to s. 60 and s. 82 of the Act of 1882. Under s. 60 it will be remembered that the bank must pay " in the ordinary course of business ", and from the context it may not be " in the ordinary course of business " to pay where there is a discrepancy between the payee's name and the endorsement.

The second division brings in the requirement of " the ordinary course of business ". It is because of this requirement that banks will not get protection in respect of cheques cashed across the counter which contain no endorsement. And they will not get the protection because they have themselves decided that it will be their " ordinary course of business " to require cheques tendered at the counter to be endorsed.

---

[10] [1952] 1. All E.R. 709. See also Note 7 p. 268.

[11] Mr. Page was, I think, incorrect in saying that the case " clearly shows that the Courts view a bad endorsement as an endorsement " (569 *Commons Debates*, p. 1364).

[12] per Somervell L.J.: See also Note 7 p. 268.

The Mocatta Committee reported that protection should not be given to cheques cashed across the counter: and their draft bill specifically excluded in terms such cheques. During the committee stage of the bill an attempt was made to introduce an amendment specifically confining it to cheques paid through a collecting bank. The amendment was defeated, though in my opinion the reasons advanced for its rejection were largely spurious. It is the sense of public responsibility exercised by bankers which gives to the public protection in respect of cheques lost by them or stolen from them, provided they have not converted them into bearer cheques by endorsement. It remains to be said that the protection given to paying banks by s. 80 of the 1882 Act does not extend to cheques cashed across the counter.

Instruments resembling cheques

Sub-section 2 was added in committee when attention was drawn to the fact that certain instruments which strictly speaking are not cheques were nevertheless in practice required to be endorsed. The sub-section deals with two classes of instruments. In paragraph (a) reference is made to instruments which are not cheques because they contain no order; *e.g.* some dividend and interest warrants. Such instruments have to be stamped like cheques, and by virtue of s. 17 of the *Revenue Act*, 1883, banks have the same protection in respect of them as arises under ss. 76-82 of the 1882 Act. Paying banks are by this sub-section given a wider protection than they are accorded under s. 80 of the 1882 Act, and collecting banks are also given similar wide protection by s. 4(2)(b).

Paragraph (b) deals with documents which are not cheques because they are not addressed by one person to another as is required for a bill of exchange by s. 3 of the 1882 Act[13] They are dealt with by the *Bills of Exchange Act* (1882) *Amendment Act,* 1932. That Act is now repealed because of the protection given to paying banks by this paragraph and to collecting banks by s. 4, ss.2(d).

It should be noted that Government Payable Orders are not included in s. 1. The Mocatta Committee reported in paragraph 70 against general dispensation of signatures. On the other hand, they are included in the protection given to collecting bankers by s. 4: see sub-section 2(c) of that section.

Protection of the collecting bank: section 4

Two objects are achieved by this section. In the first place, in order to ensure that the practice of requiring payees to endorse their cheques will not be continued as a result of the requirement of collecting banks, those banks are protected. In the second place, the opportunity was

---

[13] See *Capital & Counties Bank* v. *Gordon* [1903] A.C. 240.

taken of extending the protection of collecting banks to uncrossed cheques and to documents which are not cheques.

Sub-section 1 is but a restatement of s. 82 of the 1822 Act suitably modified because of the extension created by paragraph (b) and by sub-section 2. S. 82 is itself repealed, as is the *Bills of Exchange (Crossed Cheques) Act*, 1906, which is replaced by paragraph (b). The Act of 1906, it will be remembered, was passed because of the decision in *Capital & Counties Bank* v. *Gordon*[6] to the effect that if a collecting bank credits its customer's account with the amount of the cheque so that he can draw on it, it does not receive payment of the cheque for the customer and so was not protected by s. 82. Paragraph (b) of ss. 1 makes it clear that in such circumstances the bank is protected.

It will be realised that a bank may collect a cheque for its customer who is not the true owner of the cheque. Thus, if a cheque is made out to another James Smith than the collecting bank's customer, and the wrong James Smith gets it and pays it into his bank for collection, the bank is guilty of conversion unless protected by statute. Before October 17 the bank could only rely on s. 82: the cheque had to be crossed, and the bank had to act in good faith and without negligence. The collecting bank is not normally negligent for not knowing which James Smith was intended by the drawer of the cheque. But if the collecting bank did not require an endorsement, not only might it have found itself not receiving payment from the paying bank, and perhaps not protected for that reason,[14] but also it might have been held to be negligent for departing from the usual practice of requiring an endorsement. If the cheque had been made out to James Smyth and the customer, James Smith, either did not endorse it or endorsed it but once in his own name, again the collecting bank might have been held negligent. Now however by reason of s. 4(3) the bank is not to be regarded as negligent merely because of the absence of an endorsement or because of an irregular endorsement. The word " only " in this sub-section is vital: there may well be circumstances other than the absence of an endorsement or an irregular endorsement which will make a bank negligent in collecting a cheque for its customer.

No lengthy comment is required on sub-section 2. It is because of paragraph (a) that the protection formerly restricted to crossed cheques now applies to uncrossed cheques as well. The other instruments specified in paragraphs (b), (c) and (d) have already been considered.

A collecting bank which gives value for a cheque becomes the

---

[14] S. 4 of the 1957 Act, like s. 82 of the 1882 Act, only applies where the banker " receives payment". Tendering a cheque for payment is a dealing inconsistent with the title of the true owner and is a technical conversion for which the collecting bank gets no protection if the paying bank refuses to pay. In that case, however, no loss would be incurred, and it is submitted that the damages would be merely nominal, and a plaintiff would not recover costs.

" holder in due course " if the cheque has been endorsed. It is not a holder of the cheque if there is no endorsement. Thus the new practice of not requiring endorsement may deprive banks of rights which they held under the old practice. This situation is put right by s. 2, which applies also to banks having a lien on a cheque.

Extension of protection of crossing cheques: section 5

As we have seen, certain instruments are very like cheques and they are dealt with by banks in the same way as they deal with cheques. Under s. 4(2) they are treated like cheques for the protection of the collecting banker. But the protection which the public got from crossing cheques could not be got from crossing such instruments, since such protection is the creation of statute, and no statutory provision dealt with crossing instruments other than cheques. This position is altered by s. 5.

Cheques and receipts: section 3

It appears to me that the provision which will give rise to most misunderstandings is s. 3. This is the section which is supposed by many to dispense with the need for giving and getting receipts for payment of debts. It is no longer necessary, it has been said, to put a receipt form on the back of a cheque and to require the payee to sign the receipt.

It is undoubtedly true that a practice has developed during this century whereby large firms when paying sums of money do so by means of a cheque form on the front of which there is a statement that the payee must sign a receipt form on the back. Insurance companies have gone further and placed not only a form of receipt on the back of the cheque, but also a waiver of all claims against the company. Certainly s. 3 does not make an unendorsed cheque amount to a waiver of claims by the payee. A requirement that a " cheque " is not to be paid unless the payee signs a receipt form prevents the instrument from being an unconditional order and therefore from being a cheque.[15] It is not certain that a signature can operate both as a receipt and as an endorsement. It is also not certain how far, apart from specific agreement, a debtor can require a creditor to give a receipt for the payment by the debtor. S. 103 (2) of the *Stamp Act*, 1891, certainly suggests that receipts must be given.[16] All that is certain is that to give an unstamped receipt is an offence under s. 103 of the *Stamp Act*, 1891.

---

[15] *Bavins & Sims, Ltd.* v. *L. & S.W. Bank* [1900] 1 Q.B. 270.

[16] Where the original agreement creating the debt provides that the creditor should give a receipt then it is clearly a breach of contract to fail to give a receipt. If there is no such provision then it is clear that a mere request for a receipt would not, apart from statute, impose an obligation to give one. It may well be contended that a restrictive interpretation should be placed on s. 103(2) of the *Stamp Act*, 1891 : and that it should apply only to failure to give a receipt where an obligation to give one existed before the request for the receipt. In other words, the *Stamp Act* makes the failure not only a breach of contract, but also a criminal offence.

It is also true that in the report of the case of *Egg* v. *Barnett*[17] decided in 1800, Lord Kenyon said where the defendant has tendered evidence of an endorsed cheque:

> Here the money had been actually received by Egg (the plaintiff) and his servant for their names are put on the back of the cheques as receiving the money.

Moreover, though the reporter can be accepted as accurate, the reporter was Isaac d'Espinasse who was born in Cork, and of whom it was said that he was deaf and only heard half of what went on in Court, and reported the other half. But it is clear from the report that Lord Kenyon held only that the endorsed cheque was relevant as evidence. " I think it evidence of payment " is another passage in his judgment. He did not say that it was conclusive evidence, or even *prima facie* evidence of payment of the debt in respect of which the action was brought. He drew attention to the need for relating the cheque to the particular transaction in respect of which the action was brought. This is often done in receipt form put on the back of cheques. The Mocatta Report says:

> a simple receipt for payment by cheque, not linking the payment with the relative transaction, has no greater value as evidence than the paid cheque itself. This is so whether the receipt is printed on the cheque or is issued separately.[18]

I do not agree. A receipt is not conclusive evidence; it can be rebutted. But it does raise the presumption of receipt and needs to be rebutted. I am not convinced that an endorsement on a cheque, while relevant evidence, does raise a legal presumption of receipt. The distinction is a very real one.

In my opinion the existence of an unendorsed cheque which appeared to have been paid by the banker on whom it is drawn was always relevant to the issue of whether the payee had been paid the sum payable by the cheque. The matter has now been removed from any area of doubt on this point by s. 3. But that section does not make the unendorsed cheque conclusive as to the receipt, nor does it raise any legal presumption: it is only evidence of receipt. It certainly does not provide a means of connecting a particular cheque with a particular transaction. Where, however, a cheque is collected by a bank it is always possible to call the collecting bank to give testimony of placing the proceeds of the cheque to the account of the payee.

---

[17] (1800) 3 Esp. 196. See also *Skaife* v. *Jackson* (1824) 3 B & C. 421; *Farrar* v. *Hutchinson* (1839) 1 Per. & D. 437; *Keen* v. *Beard* (1860) 8 C.B.N.S. 372.

[18] See paragraphs 86 and 90(1) of the Report.

17

The *Ostime* Case*

The learned commentator in a previous number of this journal on *Ostime* v. *Australian Mutual Provident Society*,[1] has asked whether the decision of the House of Lords is authority for a general rule " or is no more than authority for its own particular rule which is, of course, extremely specialised." This is an interesting question from the point of view of the doctrine of precedent. But the case also gave rise to other problems within the field of precedent which are relevant to that question. For these reasons further consideration of the case from that point of view is merited.

Lord Radcliffe, with whose speech three other Law Lords concurred, was able to come to a decision by discussing only the interrelation of two statutory provisions. The arguments in the case, however, were concerned also with the effect of previous decisions of the House of Lords. While Lord Denning dissented from the statutory construction, his views on these arguments did not diverge so widely from those of Lord Radcliffe. Both agreed in differing from the judgment of the Court of Appeal that one of the House of Lords cases compelled a decision for the respondents. The discussion of these arguments is the principal topic of this note, but it is necessary to present the background to them.

The two statutory provisions are Rule 3 of Case III of Schedule D to the Income Tax Act, 1918,[2] and Article III of the Double Taxation Relief (Australia) Order, 1947, made under the authority given by section 51 (2) of the Finance (No. 2) Act, 1945.[3] The Rule deals with all " foreign " assurance companies carrying on business in the United

---

* Reprinted from the *British Tax Review*, May/June, 1960, by kind permission.

[1] [1960] A.C. 459 ; [1959] 3 W.L.R. 410 ; [1959] 3 All E.R. 245. The previous note on the case is in [1959] B.T.R. 451.

[2] In fact, some of the assessments in issue were made under s. 430 of the Income Tax Act, 1952, which re-enacted the provisions of Rule 3. The speeches, however, dealt only with the Rule, for it was the Rule alone which was considered in the earlier House of Lords cases decided before 1952.

[3] This section has been repealed by the Income Tax Act, 1952, and replaced by s. 347 (1) of that Act. By virtue of s. 528 (2) the Relief Order operates as if it had been made under the powers conferred by s. 347 (1). No reference, however, to the repeal is made in the case. The effect of this oversight is considered at the end of this note.

Kingdom through a branch here. It requires a calculation to be made of the proportion of branch policy premiums to the total premiums received by the company from its global activities. This fraction is then applied to the income of the company from the investments of its life assurance fund, and the result is a sum on which income tax is paid.[4] The exact words of the rule are important: they say that the sum so calculated " shall . . . be deemed to be profits comprised in this Schedule and shall be charged under this Case."

By the Relief Order provision was made for the payment of tax by any " Australian enterprise " in respect of " industrial or commercial profits." The order did not apply to " income in the form of dividends, interests, rents, . . ." *i.e.*, to ordinary income on investments. So far as " profits " were concerned, tax was to be payable only if the Australian enterprise had a " permanent establishment " in the United Kingdom, and then tax was to be payable only on such a sum as was attributed to that establishment by a method of calculation requiring " the hypothesis that the branch is an independent enterprise dealing as an independent entity at arm's length with the head office."

The respondent society was a " foreign " assurance company for the purpose of the Rule and an " Australian enterprise " within the Order. It had a " branch " within the United Kingdom according to the Rule, which was a " permanent establishment " for the purpose of the Order. It had investments in United Kingdom securities and paid United Kingdom tax on the dividends and interest received from those investments. The Crown, however, contended that such tax was inadequate since the amount arrived at by the calculation described in Rule 3 was greater than the total of United Kingdom dividends and interest. The Court of Appeal decided that the Order prevented the application of the Rule, and the appeal to the House of Lords was dismissed.

As has already been indicated, Lord Radcliffe was able to come to a decision merely on the wording of the Rule and the Order. The basis of his judgment is this. The Order deals comprehensively with the tax liability of " Australian enterprises " with a " permanent establishment " in the United Kingdom. Income in the form of dividends, interest, etc., is to be subject to United Kingdom taxation rules and procedures. All other tax liability is to be calculated by the method of attribution in the provision dealing with " industrial and commercial profits." The notional sum determined by the Rule is

---

[4] The reason for this mode of calculation is stated by Lord Denning ([1959] 3 All E.R. 245 at p. 254) as due to a need to prevent insurance companies from evading tax by investing abroad the profits they make on business done in the United Kingdom. Lord Radcliffe describes Rule 3 as " a unilateral solution of this particular aspect of double taxation " (p. 250). This policy statement is probably the basic reason for his decision. The Order supersedes the Rule because its policy is to substitute a bilateral solution, derived from international agreement, for a unilateral solution.

not dividends or interest within the meaning of the Order[5]: consequently tax on such a sum is not payable unless the calculation of the sum is consistent with the method of attribution in the Order. It is not so consistent: the calculation required by the Rule assumes a relation of connection between branch and society, which is inconsistent with the hypothesis of independence required by the Order.

Lord Denning's dissent is based on the view that Rule 3 does impose a tax on dividends or interest within the meaning of the Order, and that the method of attribution of profits to a " permanent establishment " has no application. The Court of Appeal took the view that Rule 3 had categorised the tax it established as a tax on " profits ": it assumed that the category of " profits " within the Order was identical with the category of " profits " in the Rule, and that the Order superseded the Rule. Lord Denning disagreed with this view. Lord Radcliffe said that the case did not require agreement with the reasoning of the Court of Appeal: all he determined was that the tax charged by the Rule was a tax on " profits " within the meaning of the Order[6]: whether it was a tax on " profits " for any other purpose did not arise.

The precedent problem: the 1947 case

The view that Rule 3 had categorised the tax it imposed as one on " profits ", and that the category of " profits " was a single one, comprehending all particular instances of the use of the word " profits " in tax law, was derived by the Court of Appeal[7] from the earlier House of Lords case between the Crown and the respondents: *Inland Revenue Commissioners* v. *Australian Mutual Provident Society*.[8] In that case Rule 3 had been considered, and particular attention had been given to the phrase " shall be deemed to be profits ". Lord Denning interpreted this phrase as a device for making a sum liable to tax as *if* it were profits " though not so in fact ".[9] Phrases such as " *a* shall be deemed to be *x* " occur in many statutes, and have often been criticised for their vagueness. Sometimes they have been interpreted, as Lord Denning did in this instance, as being fictional. But on other occasions they have been treated as extending a category, as altering the character of a concept, generally employed in the law. It was in the latter manner, according to the Court of Appeal, that the phrase in Rule 3 was interpreted in the 1947 case. Lord Radcliffe and Lord

---

[5] [1959] 3 All E.R. 245 at p. 251.

[6] [1959] 3 All E.R. 245 at p. 252. We are indebted to Hancock in 37 Can.B.R. 535 for the phrase " the fallacy of the transplanted category." Lord Radcliffe does not commit this fallacy: he notes that what may be " profits " for the purpose of the Rule may not be " profits " for the purpose of another statutory provision.

[7] [1958] 2 All E.R. 665.

[8] [1947] A.C. 605; (1948) 28 T.C. 388. The identity of the parties in the two cases is immaterial. No question of *res judicata* arose: the problems are those of *stare decisis*.

[9] [1959] 3 All E.R. 245 at p. 256.

Denning agreed.   Nevertheless, both considered that they were not compelled to adopt such an interpretation of Rule 3 for the 1959 case, though the reasons they gave for this attitude differ.   An explanation of the situation calls for an examination of the 1947 case.

The dispute between the Crown and the Society in the 1947 case concerned the question of how the Rule applied when some of the investment income of the Society was free of tax.   The dispute is simply illustrated by assuming that the global investment was £1,000 of which £400 was tax-free, and that the fraction resulting from comparison of branch policy premiums with total premiums was one-half.   The Crown contended that the £400 was to be deducted from the £1,000 before applying the fraction of one-half.   The notional sum, they said, that the Rule subjected to tax was thus £300.   The Society contended that the fraction was applied to the £1,000, and that from the resulting £500 the tax-free amount of £400 was deducted.   According to them the notional sum under the Rule was £100.   Macnaghten J. decided in favour of the Crown, and the Court of Appeal in favour of the Society. In the House of Lords the view taken by all their Lordships was that no deduction of the tax-free amount of £400 need be made at any stage. The Rule imposed a tax on " profits ", and in the determination of the amount of the profits of any enterprise the question of liability to tax did not arise.   Only after the amount of profits was determined did taxing profits have to be considered.   The argument that " the word ' profits ' in the Rule merely means income which is subject to tax under Case III " was presented to the House, and was specifically considered and rejected by Lord Porter.[10]   The Rule, he said, " does not mean that the charge is imposed on the income from investments and not on profits ".   Viscount Simon pointed out that there was no provision made by the Rule in its method of calculating profits for the deduction: " There is no justification," he said, " for reading ' any income of the company from the investments of its life assurance fund ' as though it ran ' any income of the company from such part of the investments of its life assurance fund as are [not] exempt from income tax '."[11]

The applicability of the 1947 case

Lord Radcliffe recognised that the " unanimous decision of the House " in the 1947 case " was directed to analysing and explaining the true nature of the Rule 3 charge . . . in order to determine the validity of the claim that was under the appeal ".[12]   In other words, he considered that the interpretation of the words of the Rule—" shall be

---

[10] [1947] A.C. 605 at p. 624.

[11] *Ibid.* at p. 618. The " not " is accidentally omitted from the report. The House did not give full effect to its view. It allowed the appeal, but did not modify the order made by Macnaghten J. The Crown had only asked for the restoration of that order.

[12] [1959] 3 All E.R. 245 at p. 252.

deemed to be profits "—as an enlargement of the category of profits was part of the actual reasoning of the House. That interpretation was thought to be a necessary link in the chain of reasoning leading to a decision.[13] It was not *obiter dictum*, but part of what in judicial language is called *ratio decidendi*.[14] Moreover, Lord Radcliffe thought the interpretation to be correct: "my own reading of the statute leads to the same conclusion ".[15] Nevertheless, he did conceive it possible for a different interpretation to be put on the Rule. In effect he said: " I should . . . think it right to propound in this case [an] analysis of Rule 3 that was materially different from the explanation then given [if] I was convinced that it was unmaintainable."[16] The reason for this view appears to be the absence of any objective necessity in the 1947 case for the adoption of the particular interpretation of the Rule. " It would have been sufficient for the decision of the earlier case if the House had merely confined itself to pointing out, as Lord Wright did, that the Rule 3 charge is not in any case a charge on any specific investments: for if that is so, it is very hard to see how to carry the relief on particular items of income into the unappropriated proportion."[17]

Lord Radcliffe's remarks do, therefore, constitute support for the negative contention of Professor Goodhart in his classic essay that the doctrine of precedent does not require a later court to adopt the actual reasoning of an earlier court.[18] On the other hand, they do not support his positive contention that the later court must construct the authoritative rule implicit in the precedent case from the earlier court's selection of the material facts of the precedent case. The facts of cases are matters to which statutes are applied, not materials from which the

---

[13] The criterion " one of the links in the chain of reasoning " is propounded by Denning L.J. (as he then was) as the test of whether a proposition expressed in a precedent case is *ratio decidendi* or *obiter dictum*: *Korner* v. *Witkowitzer* [1950] 1 All E.R. 558 at p. 573.

[14] The statement by Denning L.J. cited in note 13 is but one of many in which judges have used the phrase *ratio decidendi* to refer to the actual reasoning of judges in the precedent cases. Whatever may be the position about the authority attached to the actual reasoning in a precedent there is almost complete uniformity in judicial use of the phrase *ratio decidendi*. They use it in the manner that Professor Goodhart calls " misleading " (*Essays in Jurisprudence and the Common Law*, p. 2), and which accords with Professor Stone's expression " descriptive *ratio decidendi* " (1959) 22 M.L.R. p. 600. While juristic usage in England has, following Salmond, agreed with Goodhart, in the United States Llewellyn has not. He distinguishes between *ratio decidendi* and the *rule of the case*. The former is " the rule the court *tells you* is the rule of the case, the ground upon which the court itself has rested its decision." The latter is what the case " will be made to stand for by another court." *The Bramble Bush* (public edition) p. 45 and p. 52.

[15] [1959] 3 All E.R. 245 at p. 252.

[16] What he actually said was " I should *not* think it right . . . *unless* I was convinced . . . " [1959] 3 All E.R. 245 at p. 252. It is submitted that the two prepositions are logically equivalent.

[17] [1959] 3 All E.R. 245 at p. 252.

[18] This essay first appeared in (1930) 40 Yale L.J., p. 161. It was subsequently printed in the author's *Essays in Jurisprudence and the Common Law*. The debate on Goodhart's doctrine, triggered off by a brief reference of mine in (1957) 20 M.L.R. 124, has produced valuable contributions by Goodhart himself in (1959) 22 M.L.R. 117, and Stone (1959) 22 M.L.R. 597. The fuller statement of my views is to be found in 2 *West Aust. L.J.* pp. 301 and 504.

interpretation of statutes is created.[19] It is, however, submitted that
Lord Radcliffe's remarks which were professedly *obiter,* do not reflect the
dominant pattern of judicial attitudes. That is represented more by the
attitude of the Court of Appeal. However, Lord Radcliffe's view
provides another piece for the kaleidoscope of law. Further pieces of a
similar character may require a reassessment of the dominant pattern of
judicial thought on precedent. Nevertheless, the thesis that no proposition enunciated by a court is of binding authority unless it is absolutely
necessary for the decision runs into the difficulty that the wit of man may
always devise some other proposition which would justify the decision.
The acceptance of such a thesis involves a denial of the binding
authority of precedent.[20]

Lord Radcliffe did not deal explicitly with the assumption of the
Court of Appeal that the notion of profits indicated by the phrase
" industrial and commercial profits " in the Order was that of the
category of profits general to tax law, and, consequently, identical
with that involved in the Rule according to the 1947 case. All he did
was to negative that assumption by asserting " that there is nothing in
the earlier case that could amount to an interpretation of the words
' industrial or commercial profits ' ".[21] The learned commentator on
the case appears to approve of the position taken by the Court of
Appeal, and, indeed, he explains Lord Radcliffe's judgments as based
on the view that there was a notion of profits common to the Rule and
the Order. In his view, however, the result of applying the Order is
that " there was no profit chargeable ".[22] The thesis that the category
of profits is a general one derives from the view that it is a social and
economic category, to be determined according to " ordinary " usage,
rather than an artificial category or series of categories of tax law. A
profits tax is a tax on profits. The utility of the recognition of such a

---

[19] Of course, Professor Goodhart's essay may be regarded as restricted to the operation
of the doctrine of precedent in relation to the elaboration of common law rules.

[20] It is a pretty puzzle to contemplate the situation which would have arisen if the
House of Lords as a whole had thought the reasoning of the 1947 case unmaintainable
and had rejected it, and had announced that the rejection was the basis of a decision to
reverse the Court of Appeal. Would the judicial doctrine of the day compel the judges
to abandon the doctrine, since the rejection of the doctrine was involved in the reasoning
of the House?

[21] [1959] 3 All E.R. 245 at p. 252.

[22] As I see it all Lord Radcliffe said was that the Order prevented the imposition
of the charge under the Rule. Lord Radcliffe does not say that no life assurance profits
were attributable to the London establishment of the society because of the method of
attribution in the Order. Investment income was not " profits " at all. Surpluses on
assurance trading were also not " profits." There was no room for division of " profits,"
and attribution of some to a London establishment unless the Rule applied. Had there
been funds which were " profits," the method of attribution in the Order would have
produced a sum on which the London establishment could have been charged. But the
Rule did not apply, and so there were no " profits " to be divided. This is, doubtless, the
learned commentator's contention when he says; " we must answer the question as to what
would be the life assurance profits of the London branch of the respondent company if it
were trading with the head office as an independent enterprise. Lord Radcliffe's answer
is ' none,' since the only statutory basis for computing the profits assumes that the branch
is not independent of the whole but a part of it."

general category, despite its vagueness, is evident. Unfortunately, as experience has shown with the concept of " income ", one cannot assume that legislators or judges will continue to accept its value. The 1947 case regarded the legislator as extending the category of profits in tax law beyond the facts of a socio-economic category to embrace one artificial legal class. Lord Radcliffe, in the 1959 case, is not prepared to assume that " profits " in the Order is identical with the socio-economic category, or the extended category resulting from the 1947 interpretation of the Rule.

Was the 1959 decision made per incuriam?

Lord Denning, too, denies that the 1947 interpretation of the Rule applies to the Order. " I invite your lordships to say that the decision of this House in 1947 has no application to the meaning of the word ' profits ' in the Double Taxation Agreement."[23] But his reasoning is the converse of that of Lord Radcliffe. The latter conceived of the possibility of some special meaning for the word " profits " in the Order. Lord Denning considered that the word " profits " in the Order had the meaning of profits " in fact ", and that the word " profits " in the Rule should be regarded as having a meaning applicable only to the Rule and not operative outside the Rule. It was his opinion that the interpretation put on the Rule in 1947 was wrong, and that, therefore, the decision of the House was " not to be followed from step to step regardless of consequences ". With his usual felicity he states his view in metaphor: " The doctrine of precedent does not compel your Lordships to follow the wrong path until you fall over the edge of the cliff. As soon as you discover that you are going in the wrong direction, you must at least be permitted to strike off in the right direction, even if you are not permitted to retrace your steps."[24] Apparently he accepts the view that there should be but one category of " profits ", viz., the socio-economic one of profit in fact. Had the decision of the House in 1947 been correct, he would have said that Rule and Order dealt with the same category of " profits ". But he was coerced by the decision in 1947 to hold that an artificial category of " profits " did exist, restricted, however, in its operation to the application of the Rule for purposes such as those dealt with in the 1947 case.

It will perhaps be more generally admitted that Lord Denning is not conforming to the general pattern of judicial behaviour in relation to the doctrine of precedent. It has, indeed, been stated by jurists and judges that a decision which is thought wrong is confined within narrow limits by a series of artificial distinctions. The history of the doctrine of common employment is cited as evidence of this judicial process. But it has also been thought that this was a nineteenth-century attitude

---

[23] [1959] 3 All E.R. 245 at p. 256.
[24] Ibid., at p. 256.

which is no longer adopted in the twentieth century. Discussion of the subject would, however, transcend the limits of this note.

What Lord Denning might have done was to assert that the 1947 decision was not binding because it was given *per incuriam*. It is true that the doctrine that a decision given *per incuriam* is not binding has not been specifically laid down in relation to decisions of the House of Lords. But, in principle, the doctrine should apply where the House of Lords is considering the effect of an earlier House of Lords case. Indeed, authority for such a doctrine can be found in cases where earlier cases have been distinguished because they dealt with different issues and did not constitute precedents *sub silentio*. This has been done where the attention of the earlier court was not drawn to a relevant statute.[25] The principle is thus identical in such cases with that laid down in *Young* v. *Bristol Aeroplane Co.*[25a] for cases in the court of Appeal decided *per incuriam*.

Failure to advert to a relevant House of Lords decision is equivalent to failure to advert to a statute. Lord Denning points out that " the House in 1947 was never referred to a very relevant decision of its own. It was never referred to the decision in *Styles* v. *New York Life Assurance Co.*, which holds that a mutual life insurance society does not make profits."[26] How relevant, however, was the principle of that decision? Undoubtedly if it had been fully considered the House might have interpreted the Rule differently. Lord Denning, indeed, considers it must have done so. He says: " That case is quite inconsistent with the notion that the tax under Rule 3 is truly a tax on ' profits ' as that word is used in English law. At most it is a tax on a calculated figure that is ' deemed to be profits ' though not so in fact."[27] If the decision in the 1947 case had indeed been to the effect that the notional sum determined by the Rule represented " profits in fact " then the decision indeed could be said to have been given *per incuriam,* and, in consequence, not binding. But, as has been seen, the principle laid down in the 1947 case might well be regarded as constituting an extension of the category of " profits ", applicable wherever a tax was charged on " profits ". The issue before the House in 1947 was not whether the surplus resulting from a mutual assurance society's activities was " profits ", as that term was understood in earlier income tax statutes, but whether the Rule extended the significance of the term. Of course, a clearer apprehension of the nature of this issue would have been obtained by consideration of the cases dealing with the nature of a mutual assurance society's surplus. Nevertheless, a decision is not given

---

[25] See *e.g., Kidd* v. *Liverpool Watch Committee* [1908] A.C. 330; *Lochgelly Iron Co.* v *McMullen* [1934] A.C. 11.

[25a] [1944] K.B. 718.

[26] [1959] 3 All E.R. at p. 255. *Styles'* case is reported *sub nom. New York Life Insurance Co.* v. *Styles* in 14 App Cas. 381. It was followed by the House in *I.R.C.* v. *Ayrshire Employers Mutual Assurance Ltd.* [1946] 1 All E.R. 637.

[27] [1959] 3 All E.R. at p. 255.

per incuriam merely because all the relevant authorities have not been cited, and a better argument might have been presented. As Evershed M.R. said, discussing this question in *Morelle, Ltd.* v. *Wakeling*,[28] the criterion is " one of degree ". Perhaps one day the House of Lords will itself give consideration to the problem of how far it is bound by earlier House of Lords cases decided *per incuriam,* and what is meant by *per incuriam* in this connection.

Was the 1959 decision made per incuriam?

There was unanimity that in any conflict between the Rule and the Order the latter should prevail. Since the Rule was enacted in 1918 and the Order in 1947, the superiority of the Order could be based on the doctrine that later enactments impliedly repeal earlier ones. But some of the assessments were based not on the Rule, but on section 430 of the Income Tax Act, 1952, which expressly repealed and re-enacted the provisions of the Rule. The doctrine was inapplicable to a conflict between the Order and the Act of 1952. However, neither Lord Radcliffe nor Lord Denning paid any regard to chronology: the superiority of the Order was derived from a proposition which, if correct, is a constitutional innovation. Lord Radcliffe said: " unilateral legislation of the United Kingdom must give way " to legislation giving effect to a bilateral agreement.[29] Lord Denning declared: " arrangements about taxation which have been made between the governments of the United Kingdom and Australia . . . override any other enactment ". What has happened to the doctrine of the sovereignty of Parliament? Is it not an absolute consequence of that doctrine that international agreements have no legal effect except as embodied in legislation, and that an Act of Parliament embodying an international agreement has no greater effect than any other Act? A later Act of Parliament, inconsistent with an earlier one, repeals the earlier one, even though the earlier Act is based on bilateral or multilateral international agreement. It is chronology, not subject-matter, that is determinative.

Of course, the proposition that one Parliament cannot bind a successor, which is another corollary to the sovereignty of Parliament, merits closer examination than that given to it by Dicey. Is it absolute, as he states? The application of an Interpretation Act to subsequent statutes cannot be easily reconciled with the proposition. We appear to accept the view that one Parliament can compel the use of words in a particular way by later Parliaments. It is true that an Interpretation Act only provides for a prima facie interpretation: its provisions are to apply unless the context other requires. But this still creates a limitation on the sovereignty of the later Parliament: it cannot be a perfect Humpty-Dumpty. An argument may perhaps be based on the thesis

[28] [1955] 2 Q.B. 379.
[29] [1957] 3 All E.R. at p. 248.

T

that an Interpretation Act is directed to the judges, and that they are bound by its terms until it is repealed. However, if it be said that Parliament must be presumed to use words in accordance with the rules of an Interpretation Act, are we not modifying the amplitude of the doctrine that one Parliament cannot bind a successor?

Another restriction may also be found in the maxim *generalia specialibus non derogant*. This is, however, more doubtful. Where a statute providing for relief against double taxation to non-residents is followed by another statute which is general enough in its terms to apply to both residents and non-residents, the relief provided by the earlier statute continues to apply. This, however, depends on principles of the interpretation of general words fully consistent with the " intention of Parliament " when enacting the later statute. A definite limitation of the sovereignty of Parliament is to be found in the thesis that some Acts of Parliament may have constitutional status in the sense of a written constitution determining the validity of later statutes. It has been contended that the Statute of Westminster of 1932 might be so regarded. Would anyone contend that Canada is bound by an Act of the Parliament of Westminster, which did not comply with the provisions of the Statute of 1932? And what legal, as opposed to political, arguments exist to make Canada less bound than the United Kingdom? Parliamentary sovereignty was not confined to the United Kingdom.

It is thus conceivable that the doctrine of the supremacy of bilateral legislation proclaimed by Lord Radcliffe and Lord Denning may be accepted. It is, however, also conceivable that the proposition may be regarded as having been propounded *per incuriam* since its consistency with the sovereignty of Parliament was not considered. The older view that international agreements are subordinate to Parliamentary enactment is at the basis of the decision of the House of Lords in *Ellerman Lines* v. *Murray*.[30] Since the *Ostime* case that principle has been applied by Vaisey J. in *I. R. C.* v. *Collco Dealings, Ltd.*[31] He said : " as the statute is unambiguous its provisions must be followed even if they are contrary to . . . any international treaty or arrangements ". This dictum, however, is not concerned with inconsistency between two statutes, one of which gives effect to an international treaty.

Further support for the views of Lord Radcliffe and Lord Denning may be found in the principle that the operation of statutes *is* affected by their character. Private Acts of Parliament are regarded as subject to different rules of interpretation from public Acts. And now the contention, often urged unsuccessfully in the past, that constitutional statutes are to be interpreted differently from others has been accepted in the House of Lords. Lawyers in Canada and Australia have criticised the Judicial Committee of the Privy Council for dealing with their

---

[30] [1931] A.C. 126.
[31] [1959] 3 All E.R. at p. 351: affirmed [1960] 2 All E.R. 44.

basic constitutional documents, the British North America Act and the Commonwealth of Australia Act, as if they were statutes making some particular legislative change in the common law. Now an echo of Marshall's dictum that it should be remembered that it is a *constitution* that is being expounded is to be found in Viscount Simonds' speech in *Belfast Corporation* v. *O.D. Cars, Ltd.*:[32] " a flexibility of construction is admissible in regard to [constitutional] instruments which might be rejected in construing ordinary statutes ". A statute giving effect to an international agreement might similarly be regarded as having a different status from an ordinary statute.

Though it was assumed that the doctrine of supremacy of bilateral legislation was necessary for the decision of the case it was not so absolutely. It is true that the Income Tax Act of 1952 is later in date than the Relief Order of 1947. But the Relief Order can be regarded as having come into operation *after* section 430 of the Act of 1952. This arises in the following manner. The Order was made under the authority conferred by section 51 (1) of the Finance (No. 2) Act, 1945. That section was repealed by the Income Tax Act of 1952, and replaced by section 347 (1) of that Act. By virtue of section 528 (2) of the Act of 1952 the Order operates as if it had been made under the powers created by section 347 (1). Since the sections of the Act came into operation simultaneously, and the Order may be regarded as coming into operation after section 347, it may be regarded as coming into operation after section 430. In this manner the Relief Order would prevail over section 430 by virtue of their chronology and the doctrine of implied repeal of earlier statutory provisions. Nevertheless, it cannot be said that the statements of Lord Radcliffe and Lord Denning were but *obiter dicta*. They were essential parts of their reasoning.

---

[32] [1960] 1 All E.R. at p. 69.

18

Basic Concepts of the Law of Evidence*

PART I—HISTORICAL INTRODUCTION

It may be said to be traditional for commentators on the English law of evidence to complain about its unsatisfactory character. Lord Mansfield's thesis that precedents do but serve to illustrate principles is said to be particularly inapplicable to this branch of the law, where it is alleged that there are multitudes of cases but few clearly enunciated principles.[1] It is submitted that perhaps the principal cause for this state of affairs is the failure to give adequate attention to the basic concepts which are required for the satisfactory elaboration and exposition of the rules of evidence. It is submitted, moreover, that there are but a few concepts underlying the law, and that their characteristics have already been discerned by writers on the subject: in particular they are described by Wigmore in his monumental treatise on *The Law of Evidence*.[2] It is the strange neglect in this country of American literature on the subject which justifies this article. In it an attempt is made to state the presuppositions for rational discussion of the law of evidence. This, it is considered, involves a scheme of four basic concepts. The scheme is the outcome of the work of many jurists, among whom Thayer and Wigmore are predominant, and its general adoption would help to eliminate much of the confusion which now exists.

Sketch of the historical development of doctrine

A presupposition of discussion of the law of evidence is that courts of law are seeking to determine " facts " by means of " rational " processes. Early forms of procedure, such as trial by battle, by ordeal, by compurgation, in so far as they involved the determination of facts

---

* Reprinted from *Law Quarterly Review*, October, 1954, by kind permission.

[1] A recent number of the L.Q.R. contains two repetitions of the complaint: Carter, 69 L.Q.R. at p. 80; Megarry, 69 L.Q.R. at p. 141.

[2] All subsequent references to Wigmore are to the third edition of his work; the first edition was published in 1904.

286

did so by divine guidance or in some arbitrary manner. These procedures were replaced by newer methods in which courts sought to apply laws to facts, and there was gradually developed a set of principles for the finding of facts. The rules of evidence which were thus brought into operation, like other rules of common law, were elaborated by busy judges in the course of deciding the issues brought forward by litigants. Indeed it is reasonable to conjecture that judges have given much less time to consideration of points of evidence than to questions of substantive law. The law of evidence has been in greater need of systematisation by juristic commentary, and the need has not gone entirely unsatisfied. The system of evidence has been derived from judicial good sense and practical understanding,[3] but the judicial work has been supplemented by juristic exposition of the principles implicit in it.

The first substantial exposition of the law of evidence was by Gilbert.[4] Though he prefaced his work with some considerations derived from Locke's *Essay Concerning Human Understanding,* they do not form the basis of his treatment[5] which, valuable as it is, is largely a digest of case law. The one rule which is advanced as a general principle of the law of evidence is the best evidence rule. It is necessary to turn next to Bentham, whose *Rationale of Evidence* was published in 1827. It is not concerned with the principles of the English law of evidence, which he criticised as being irrational,[6] but with the principles on which any law of evidence ought to be based.[7] He did, however, use terms and concepts which were subsequently adopted by Best in his treatment of the English law. According to Bentham, the law of evidence deals with " persuasion concerning the existence of . . . matter of fact ". He defines " facts " as " events or states of things ", and classifies them as either " primary " or " evidentiary ". Evidence is not

---

[3] " A system of evidence like this, thus worked out at the forge of daily experience in the trial of causes, not created, or greatly changed, until lately, by legislation, not the fruit of any man's systematic reflections or forecast, is sure to exhibit at every step the mark of its origin. It is not concerned with nice definitions, or the exact academic operations of the logical faculty. Its rules originate in the instinctive suggestions of good sense, legal experience, and a sound, practical understanding."

Thayer, *Preliminary Treatise on the Law of Evidence,* p. 3. All subsequent references to Thayer are to this work.

Cf. p. 509: " Our law of evidence is a piece of illogical, but by no means irrational, patchwork; not at all to be admired, nor easily to be found intelligible, except as a product of the jury system, as the outcome of a quantity of rulings by sagacious lawyers, whilst settling practical questions, in presiding over courts where ordinary, untrained citizens are acting as judges of fact."

[4] The first edition of Lord Chief Baron Gilbert's *The Law of Evidence* was published in 1756. Morgan (62 Harvard L.R. p. 182, n. 5) says it was written before 1726.

[5] *Cf.* Stephen who said " Gilbert's work . . . is founded on Locke's ' Essay ' much as my work is founded on Mill's ' Logic.' " *Digest of the Law of Evidence* xii.

[6] " In the map of science, the department of judicial science remains to this hour a perfect blank. Power has hitherto kept it in a state of wilderness; reason has never visited it." *Works* (ed. Bowring) Vol. VI, p. 209.

[7] Accordingly he says: " The species of reader for whose use this book is really designed is the legislator." *Ibid.,* p. 209.

conceived by Bentham as a concept employed only in courts of law: on the contrary, he considers that we rely on evidence in all human activities, scientific and non-scientific. He defines " evidence " as " a word of relation " meaning " any matter of fact the effect, tendency or design of which, when presented to the mind, is to produce a persuasion concerning the existence of some other matter of fact ".[8] In this definition " evidence " is equated with " evidentiary fact ": the " other matter of fact " evidenced by the " evidentiary fact " is, in Bentham's language, the primary fact. Bentham's distinction between " primary fact " and " evidentiary fact " is more generally expressed as the distinction between *factum probandum* and *factum probans*. The relation between the two has subsequently been called that of relevance.[9]

While Best adopted Bentham's basic notions, he rightly pointed out that Bentham was wrong in assuming that some unitary view of evidence, applicable " in all human activities, scientific and non-scientific ", was capable of dealing with all problems of evidence in courts of law. He affirmed that there was a distinction between the approach required for any determination of facts by any human being —historian, scientist, judge, business man or ordinary citizen—and the qualified approach which courts of law must also adopt because of the conditions of litigation and the policies which courts of law carry out. This distinction gives rise to the concepts which he called " natural evidence " and " judicial evidence ". He criticised Bentham for failing to consider the problem of " judicial evidence ". He said that Bentham's work " embodies several essentially mistaken views relative to the nature of judicial evidence, and which may be traced to overlooking the characteristic features whereby it is distinguished from other kinds of evidence ".[10] Best does not assert, however, that courts of law are concerned solely with " judicial evidence ". In his view they have to take account of both " natural evidence " *and* " judicial evidence ". He discusses the general problem of establishing facts by what he calls " historical proof ": this is the function of " natural evidence ". Courts of law, however, have to take into account also many factors which give rise to " judicial evidence ". The relation between the two is stated in a proposition which expresses the basic distinction from which the framework of concepts for the law of evidence is derived. " Judicial evidence is, for the most part, nothing else more than natural evidence, restrained or modified by rules of positive law."[11]

---

[8] *Ibid.*, p. 208.

[9] For a criticism of Bentham's introduction of psychological factors into the concept of relevance see *post*, p. 297.

[10] *Principles of the Law of Evidence*, Art. 34. The first edition was published in 1849. In the preface Best asserts that previous writers on evidence had produced but digests of case law: he was seeking to set out the principles behind the cases.

[11] *Ibid.*, Art. 34. There is no need for the qualification " for the most part."

Best did not make the distinction between natural evidence and judicial evidence the basis of his treatment of the law of evidence. The distinction, though not completely ignored, is little stressed in his subsequent exposition. The principle which he uses as the framework for the exposition is the one to which Gilbert had already attached importance, *viz.*, the best evidence rule. It is in the later work of Stephen and Thayer that basic importance is attached to the distinction; in their writings it is discussed in the language of " relevance " and " admissibility ".

Stephen first published a theory about the nature of the law of evidence in 1872 in his *Introduction to the Indian Evidence Act*. But his views are best known from his very influential *Digest of the Law of Evidence,* which first appeared in 1876, and has been through many editions. In the *Digest* Stephen modified his first theory; and it is his revised theory which is stated here.[12] Stephen introduces the language and concept of " relevancy " by considering the various meanings of the word " evidence ". He speaks of " the ambiguity of the word ' evidence ' (a word which sometimes means testimony and at other times relevancy) ".[13] The ambiguity can be illustrated by sentences like " similar fact evidence is not generally evidence ", " hearsay evidence is not evidence ", but the concept of " relevancy " as used by Stephen is not sufficient to explain both those sentences. For Stephen " relevancy " is the principle of " natural evidence " of Best. Proffered testimony, he says, may not be given of facts which are not relevant to " facts in issue ". This is a reference to the relation between the " evidentiary facts " and the " primary facts " of Bentham, a relationship not determined by law, but by " the common course of events ", by science and " inductive logic ".[14] Certain classes of facts, however, " which in common life would usually be regarded as falling within this definition of relevancy, are excluded from it by the Law of Evidence ".[15] The four classes are similar facts, hearsay, opinion and

---

[12] All subsequent references to Stephen are to the 5th edition. The pagination of the introduction is, however, the same in subsequent editions. (The latest edition is the 12th revised, reprinted with additions, 1948. Thayer and Wigmore, in my submission, misinterpret Stephen's later thesis.)

[13] p. xi. Four different meanings of the word " evidence " are listed by Stephen in *The Indian Evidence Act*. A distinction exists between testimony, the utterances of a witness, and the facts asserted in the testimony. The process of accepting a fact (a), because it has been asserted by a witness merits examination, but discussion about evidence may not be concerned with this subject. Discussion is often concerned with the relation between (a) the fact asserted, and some other fact (b) which the proponent of the testimony is seeking to establish. Such discussion is concerned with the relevance of (a) to (b); it considers whether (b) can be inferred from (a) and assumes the inference of (a) from the testimony. The distinction between testimony and fact asserted by testimony is not considered, and the word evidence may be used to refer to both. Stephen says (p. 3): " It sometimes means the words uttered and things exhibited before a Court of Justice. At other times it means the facts proved to exist by those words or things, and regarded as the framework of inferences as to other facts not so proved."

[14] " When the inquiry is pushed further and the nature of relevancy has to be considered in itself, and apart from legal rules about it, we are led to inductive logic, which shows that judical evidence is only one case of the general problem of science." p. xii.

[15] p. xiv.

character. The principle asserted by Stephen, though his formulation is not felicitously worded, is that evidence is generally receivable by courts if relevant, but that relevant evidence may not be received by virtue of " exclusive rules " of law. Unfortunately, Stephen adopted a terminology which has produced considerable confusion, and has obscured the nature of relevance and its relation to receivability. Where relevant evidence is excluded by a rule of law, he says that such evidence is " deemed to be irrelevant ". We must turn to the United States for a clearer statement of the basic concepts of the law of evidence.

It was Thayer[16] who demonstrated most fully the basic distinction between the rejection of evidence by a court of law because of want of relevance, and the rejection of evidence, even though relevant, because of some specific policy of the law. He introduced the language which stresses the distinction by the use of the words " relevance " and " admissibility ", language, which though widely used in England is not yet universally adopted here.[17] To indicate that the concept denoted by the term " relevance " was an extra-legal concept, the " natural evidence " and " historical proof " of Best, Thayer often employed as a synonym for " relevant " the phrase " logically probative ". This phrase does carry out the purpose of its author, but may be misleading, and the term " relevant " is by itself adequate.[18] In Thayer's view, though the concept of relevance was a presupposition of a rational system of evidence, it was not the function of the law of evidence to determine whether particular kinds of evidence were relevant or irrelevant. He characterised the function of the English law of evidence as being the formulation of rules for the exclusion of relevant evidence. However, he stated two principles connected with relevance which lie at the basis of the law of evidence. The first is the principle " which forbids receiving anything irrelevant, not logically probative ".[19] The second is: " Unless excluded by some principle or rule of law all that is logically probative is admissible." [20]

---

[16] Most of Thayer's work was originally published as separate essays in the *Harvard Law Review*: see Vols. 3-7 (1889-1893) and Vol. 12 (1898). The chapter in the *Preliminary Treatise* from which the majority of my quotations are taken is Chapter VI, which is entitled " The Law of Evidence and Legal Reasoning as Applied to the Ascertainment of Facts." This chapter had not been previously published in the *Harvard Law Review*.

[17] See for example Hammelmann's criticism of the terminology employed by Nokes in *An Introduction to Evidence* : B.R. 16 M.L.R. at 256.

[18] " Logically probative " may indicate that relevance is an affair of deductive logic, which Thayer certainly did not think was the case. Wigmore substitutes the phrase " rationally probative." Either phrase is preferable to the misleading uses of the phrases " legally relevant " and " legally irrelevant." In *Noor Mohamed* [1949] A.C. at 194, Lord du Parcq ventured on some unhappy criticisms of the phrase " logically probative." These criticisms, and much subsequent juristic and judicial comment on them, appear to have been uttered in ignorance of the source and original significance of the phrase.

[19] It is this principle which he describes as being " not so much a rule of evidence as a presupposition involved in the very conception of a rational system of evidence." *Preliminary Treatise*, p. 265.

[20] *Preliminary Treatise*, p. 265.

Thayer excluded from the scope of the law of evidence some topics which other writers classified as belonging to it. Thus for Stephen " the most important of all questions that can be asked about the law of evidence " is " what facts are relevant?"[21] But for Thayer that question was for science, not for the *law* of evidence. He examined the nature of " admissibility ", not " relevance ", though, of course, it was one of his fundamental tenets that on the answer to Stephen's question depended the receivability of evidence. In a similar manner he considered the question " what are the facts in issue?" as lying outside the scope of the law of evidence, and depending on " substantive law or the law of pleading ", though again he realised that on the answer to the question depended the receivability of evidence.[22] Wigmore, however, rightly considers it necessary to emphasise the distinction between (a) the rejection of evidence because it is not relevant to facts sought to be established thereby and (b) the rejection of evidence because it is not relevant to a fact in issue; two matters which were often confused. He distinguished the two by employing the name " materiality " in relation to the latter, reserving " relevancy " strictly for the former.[23] This is not the place to review Wigmore's many contributions to the law of evidence. In relation to basic concepts all that has to be added is that he differed from Thayer by asserting that judicial decisions on questions of relevance were as binding as other decisions of courts, so that for him " relevancy " was within the scope of the law of evidence.

The scheme of concepts that thus emerges in Wigmore is, at any rate so far as names go, a threefold one : the names used being relevancy, materiality and admissibility. The scheme proposed in this article is a fourfold one, the extra term being " receivability."

Part II—The Four Concepts

The logical derivation of the four concepts: receivability

The brief historical sketch has indicated the evolution in juristic writing of the basic concepts of the law of evidence. It is now proposed, despite the repetition involved, to approach the question of basic concepts in a synchronistic manner, amplifying somewhat the examination of the concepts, though not attempting a complete treatment of each. All that it is sought to do is to explain the character of each concept; it is not sought to demonstrate the various theorems concerning the matters to which these concepts apply. It is hoped to show what

---

[21] *Indian Evidence Act*, p. 4.

[22] " The greater part of statements denying admissibility to evidence are not related to these basic problems of relevance, but are really reducible to mere propositions of sound reason as applied to points of substantive law or pleading." *Preliminary Treatise*, p. 269.

[23] Vol. I, p. 7.

"materiality" and "relevance" are, not to propound theorems involving "materiality" and "relevance", still less to establish rules for saying what particular facts are material or relevant.[24] In this examination the "admissibility" of Thayer and Wigmore is resolved into two elements, for one of which the term "admissibility" is retained, while the other receives the name "receivability".

Writers are agreed that the law of evidence is concerned with the procedure whereby courts of law determine the "facts" which are in dispute. The term "facts" is in ordinary language possessed of multiple meanings[25] : e.g., Cohen and Nagel in their *Introduction to Logic* list four different meanings.[26] Within the context of the law of evidence the word is generally employed with the meaning of discriminated parts of the totality of existence, sections of history, empirical phenomena. Bentham's "events or states of things" has been considered a satisfactory definition; it doubtless is adequate if it be taken broadly to include properties of events and things, such as shapes and colours, and relations between diverse events and things, such as comparative size and spatial or temporal order.[27] But even within the context of the law of evidence ambiguity exists, and it is important to distinguish between the use of the term "fact" in Bentham's sense, and the use of the term to denote a "proposition"; for example, a true proposition such as "twice two are four" or "beer as a beverage is not necessarily harmful."[28] "Brute facts" must be distinguished from propositions of fact; and it is, moreover, necessary to distinguish between a particular proposition of fact, one which asserts the past or present existence of *a* fact,[29] and a general proposition of fact such as a scientific law.[30] The

---

[24] Compare Carnap's distinction between the classification of an *explicandum* and the formulation of an *explicatum*. *Logical Foundations of Probability*, arts. 2 and 3.

[25] "A word of universal use, carrying such different meanings, cannot be used in rational thinking and argument without causing immense confusion. That is why all who hope to use reason fruitfully must make it their first duty to agree upon a clear definition of ' fact.' " Brown: 28 *Philosophy* 154.

[26] (1934), p. 217.

[27] The fourth category of Cohen and Nagel is "those things existing in space or time, together with the relations between them, in nature of which a proposition is true. Facts in this sense are neither true nor false; they simply are: they can be apprehended by us in part through the senses." Epistemological questions are raised when this meaning of "fact" is compared with their first meaning which is "discriminated elements in sense perception." Lawyers do not usually distinguish between sense data and things-in-themselves, between the "references" and "referents" of the scheme of Ogden and Richards. But they are often concerned with the problem of discriminating between the totalities involved in sense perception. The difficulty of defining *res gesta* is that of drawing boundaries between "facts."

[28] The latter example is cited by Thayer as a "fact" of which a U.S. court held it could take judicial notice. His thesis was that "judicial notice" was often not concerned with the proof of "facts" but with judicial reasoning.

[29] Propositions asserting the future existence of a fact are in a separate category: and their character is complex.

[30] Cohen and Nagel give as their second and third meanings of "fact" :— (2) "propositions which interpret what is given to us in sense experience. *This is a mirror.*" (3) "propositions which truly assert an invariable sequence or conjunction of characters. *All gold is malleable.*"

subjects of dispute between parties are particular propositions of fact. They are the issues: one party asserts the truth of one or more particular propositions of fact, the other enters a denial. General propositions are the means which may be invoked, explicitly or implicitly, in argument about particular propositions: they may be in issue, but they do not state the facts in issue. They determine whether evidence is relevant.

For a law of evidence to be " rational " the proof of the particular proposition of fact containing the *factum probandum* must be rational. It is considered to be so if there is a rational connection between the proposition containing the *factum probandum* and another proposition containing the *factum probans,* which latter proposition is made self-evident by " evidence ". There is, however, duality of meaning of the word " evidence ", arising from this rational character of litigation. Parties who seek to establish or deny facts in issue ask the court to receive " evidence " which they tender: for example, they may proffer the testimony of a witness. It is, however, an important judicial function, performed in English judicial administration by the judge, to say what tendered evidence is to be received and relied on in the proof of facts in issue. The judge may say : " You must not tell us what the soldier said . . . it's not evidence." The word " evidence " is sometimes used to mean (a) " tendered evidence ", statements of witnesses or documents,[31] proffered by the parties and sometimes to mean (b) " received evidence ", statements of facts which the courts receive in proof of facts in issue as being in accordance with the law of evidence.

Thus arises the basic concept of " receivability ", which is that of tendered evidence being in accordance with the law of evidence. It follows, moreover, that " receivability " is a complex concept depending on the principles under which the rules of the law of evidence can be classified. The law of evidence is composed of various rules, and by virtue of its character of being a rational method of determining facts for the purpose of settling disputes and of being part of the legal system maintaining various public policies, the rules do not necessarily fall under a single principle. There are, it is submitted, three broad principles involving three further basic concepts. In the first place evidence is only received in proof of facts to which it is " rationally " related: this gives rise to the concept of " relevance ". Secondly, evidence must be related to facts in issue before the court. Hence arises the concept of materiality. Furthermore, evidence may be excluded by reason of a rule of law taking note of the conditions of litigation or some specific policy of the law: there is, in other words, also the concept of

---

[31] It is not necessary for the present purpose to consider the nature of " real evidence," nor to comment on the difference between Bentham's definition of " evidence " as being " matter of fact " and Stephen's definition as being " statements made by witnesses in court " and " documents produced for the inspection of the court." This difference is referred to above in note 13.

admissibility. While it is possible to conceive of a system of law ignoring some of these concepts, English law does employ all three concepts. Before evidence is receivable it must in English law satisfy the conditions of each of these concepts : it must be relevant *and* material *and* admissible.

In Wigmore's scheme the word " admissible " has to perform the dual function of signifying both the specific concept denoted by admissibility in the present scheme, and the general concept of being in accordance with the law of evidence, which I call " receivability ". In his terminology evidence is inadmissible if it is irrelevant. It is, however, important to distinguish the general concept from the specific elements of which it is composed, and to specify why evidence is not received. It is important to distinguish rejection of evidence for irrelevance from rejection for inadmissibility. This requires four terms. With this terminology it is possible to construct sentences such as the following which have significance and clarity. " Evidence, though relevant, is not receivable because it is not admissible." " Evidence, though admissible, is not receivable because it is not relevant to a material fact."

The significance of such sentences depends, of course, on the meaning of the terms used for the three concepts. The nature of these three concepts is now discussed.

Materiality

As has been stated, the concept of materiality was considered by Thayer as falling outside the scope of the law of evidence. This is, however, largely a matter of terminology and classification; as he admitted, questions of receivability do involve what is here called the concept of materiality. Other writers, such as Taylor,[32] have included it within the scope of evidence, and have applied the name " relevance " solely to it. Still others use the word " relevance " to apply to the two distinct concepts which Wigmore rightly separates by means of the terms " materiality " and " relevance ". " The two problems," he says, " are wholly distinct, and yet the inaccuracy of our usage tends constantly to confuse them." [33]

Materiality of evidence signifies that the evidence is concerned with an issue before the court. The question of materiality is not whether the evidence is adequately related to the facts sought to be established thereby, but whether those facts are adequately related to the case made by the party. As Wigmore says, materiality defines " the status of the proposition " sought to be proved " to the case at

---

[32] See the index for the references to relevance, and note pp. 211 *et seq.*, particularly p. 222 (12th ed.).

[33] Vol. I, p. 7.

large." [34] A court is not concerned with the entirety of history, but only with that section of it which is being litigated. An important branch of legal procedure is concerned with provisions requiring the parties to specify issues to be decided by the court. Such requirements may be detailed or general, rigid or flexible. In the course of the development of English law its requirements have varied considerably in character, and today they are more elaborate in civil cases than in criminal cases. These requirements determine what facts may properly be proved by the party who wishes to succeed in his claim or by the party who wishes to succeed in his defence. Unless evidence is concerned with establishing such facts it is not received: and the reason for rejection is usefully termed want of materiality.

Relevance

I propose in this section to attempt an elucidation of the concept designated by the use of the word " relevance " here proposed, and also to state a number of propositions about facts and litigation which embody the concept of relevance.

It is essential for the theoretical construction of possible systems of evidential rules, and for the critical evaluation of any actual legal system, to conceive of the relationship which facts have to each other in history itself, in the actual stream of events, aware, of course, of the limitations of man's knowledge of such matters. It is to such a conception that it is suggested the word " relevance " be limited. The concept of materiality derives from the division of history by the litigants into sections for investigation by the court, a division which takes note of the facts required by law to be established for a legal remedy to be granted or denied. It is concerned with the relation borne by the facts that those tendering evidence seek to establish *facta probanda* to the section of history thus constructed by the litigants, or, as Wigmore states, with their character in relation to the case as a whole. The concept of relevance is concerned with the relationship which the tendered evidence has to the fact it is sought thereby to prove because of the order of nature: it posits a " natural " connection between *factum probans* and *factum probandum*. Evidence is rejected as im-

---

[34] The relativity of the concepts makes the difference between materiality and relevance less clear-cut than might appear at first. Let fact T be the subject of tendered evidence and let M be the fact it is sought thereby to establish. If, in the opinion of the court, T does not tend to establish M then the evidence is rejected as irrelevant, (i). If, however, T does tend to establish M the evidence may still be rejected. For M may be neither a fact in issue nor related to a fact in issue. If no one contends that M is related to a fact in issue then the rejection of T is classified without difficulty as an instance of immateriality, (ii). But it may be contended that M does tend to establish a fact in issue, I; in such a case the rejection of T where the contention is not accepted by the court presents difficulties of classification. It may be said to be an instance of immateriality, as in (ii) above. On the other hand, it may be said to be an instance of irrelevance; for though tendered to prove M directly it was tendered to prove I indirectly through M. The concept of relevance is usually applied to take note of the contentions of the proponents, so that the case is one of irrelevance. But this reduces considerably the area of materiality in practice.

material because the fact it is sought to establish is not by reason of the choice of the parties, and man-made rules of substantive law, an issue before the court. Evidence is rejected as irrelevant because it does not " prove " the fact it is sought to establish by reason of its natural, " historical ", connection with that fact.

The determination of whether a particular fact is relevant, in the sense in which the word is here employed, is dependent on man's knowledge of historical relationships, a knowledge which includes the primitive science of inarticulate common sense as well as the formulated propositions of organised sciences. In order to make clear that the concept denoted by relevance was an extra-legal (pre-legal might be a better term) notion of natural connection, Thayer often used as a synonym the phrase " logically probative " and Wigmore used the phrase " rationally probative ". Stephen[35] qualifies " proof " by the more empirical phrase " common course of events " in his definition of relevance, but it is the same concept that he designates. He says:[36] " The word ' relevant ' means that any two facts are so related to each other that according to the common course of events one, either taken by itself or in connection with other facts, proves or renders probable the past, present or future existence or non-existence of the other."

While enough has been said to explain the nature of relevance, it is nevertheless desirable to state some propositions concerning the application of the concept, if only to challenge a number of misconceptions which are still often held. It is, however, not possible here to do more than present a number of dogmatic assertions. A much fuller exposition of the nature and operation of relevance is required. It is also necessary to point out that no examination, however full, of the nature of relevance, can ever provide " practical help " to enable anyone to determine whether one fact is relevant to another. Such an examination can only indicate the nature of the factual inquiry which has to be conducted in order to answer a problem of relevance. A definition propounded by Stephen earlier than the one set out above has been wrongly criticised for using terms which are not mechanically determinative of a problem of relevance.[37] Such criticism is indicative of a lack of understanding of the nature of both relevance and definitions. No definition of relevance can set out the infinite number of empirical propositions on whose existence the relevance of facts depends.

The following theorems are, it is believed, true. (1) The relevance of facts depends on objective order, not on subjective beliefs. (2) Relevance is an affair of science not of logic. (3) Relevance involves probability not certainty. (4) Relevance is relative; there is no relevance

---

[35] *Digest of the Law of Evidence, ante*, n. 12.
[36] p. 2.
[37] See Phipson's *Law of Evidence*, 9th ed., p. 48.

in the air. (5) The categories of relevance are never closed: it is impossible to say *a priori* that fact A is not relevant to fact B.

(1) Bentham employs the concept of relevance in his use of the word " evidence ". [38] In effect he says that one fact is relevant to another if the effect or tendency of the former " when presented to the mind, is to produce a persuasion concerning the existence of some other matter of fact ". This is to base relevance on subjective attitudes, not on the objective order of things. It is true, of course, that the objective order of things is only known to us through subjective constructs, but, in so far as we are rational, we endeavour to relate our beliefs to a natural reality. The ordinary usage of the word " evidence " indeed provides often the touchstone to distinguish between the myths and illusions of men and the objective reality of history. Relevance is based on objective order, not on psychological effect.[39] It is because the subjective attitudes of juries often incorrectly reflect the actual relationships between facts that much relevant evidence is excluded in law, and that judges withdraw from juries evidence which is relevant.

(2) The connection between facts which gives rise to relevance is neither psychological nor logical. Of course, if the word " logical " is used in the wide sense of " valid thought " then no objection can be raised to statements such as " relevance is an affair of logic and not of law." But " logic " often refers to deductive logic, to logical entailment, and connotes certainty of relations between propositions. But relevance is concerned with relations between facts: and what mediates between the facts is an empirical proposition. The " logic " which is involved is inductive logic, the reasoning being the inference of science, not the implication of logic.[40]

While relevance is an affair of science the matters of fact which come before courts of law range far beyond the boundaries of the organised sciences. The empirical propositions which are involved are rarely established in the recognised scientific departments: they are asserted by the primitive science of common sense, and, indeed, have only infrequently been made articulate outside courts of law. The presumptions of fact on which courts rely, and the generalisations about facts of which they take judicial notice, represent formulations based on common sense.

(3) Inasmuch as relevance is concerned with empirical facts the

---

[38] See above, pp. 287, 288, and footnote 8.

[39] Carnap has some valuable comments on psychologism in logic: see Arts. 11 and 12 *Logical Foundations of Probability*.

[40] The text incorporates, of course, Hume's theory, dealing with knowledge of facts, that " all the laws of nature . . . are known only by experience." The simplest statement by Hume of his theory is to be found in section IV of his *Enquiry*. It has been summarised by Ayer. " There can be no possibility of *deducing* the occurrence of one event from another. That the events are connected is a matter of fact, which is in no way necessary *a priori* . . . logical necessity is eliminated ": *British Empirical Philosophers*, p. 25. A Holmesian summary is that relevance is an affair not of logic but of experience.

relation is one of contingency. Moreover, the common sense generalisations often resemble statistical " laws " of many of the sciences. There is no complete assurance that observed uniformities can be extended, and what is frequently observed is not uniformities but frequencies. A *factum probandum* cannot be established with absolute certainty. In order for *factum probans* to be relevant to *factum probandum* it is not necessary that the former should conclusively prove the latter.[41]   Relevance is an affair of probability not of certainty.

(4) Though Bentham was wrong in introducing psychological factors into his treatment of " evidence ", he was right in stressing the relativity of " evidence ".   " Evidence ", *factum probans,* is always relevant to some *factum probandum*; there is no relevance " in the air ". Evidence may be relevant to one fact and irrelevant to another; it may be relevant to many facts.

Where there are different issues evidence which is relevant to one issue may be irrelevant to others.   It is a question of policy for each legal system whether to reject evidence which is relevant to one issue because it is irrelevant to a different issue.   The English law of evidence does not reject evidence for such a reason; evidence is received if it be relevant to any issue irrespective of its relation to other issues.[42]

(5) The parallel with negligence can be taken one stage further. Just as it is true that there is no relevance in the air, so it is true that the categories of relevance are never closed.   The relations between facts may be intricate and indirect.   It cannot be laid down *a priori* that members of one class of facts are never relevant to members of another class of facts, or are only relevant in a limited number of ways. Everything depends on the circumstances.   An instance of one kind of facts may be irrelevant in one set of circumstances to an instance of another kind of facts, and in different circumstances a similar instance of the former kind may be relevant to a similar instance of the latter kind.   Another reason for the difficulty surrounding similar fact evidence has been a failure to realise the validity of the proposition that similar conduct may be relevant to *factum probandum* not only through disposition, but in an unlimited number of other ways.[43]

---

[41] Stephen's definition does suggest that *factum probans* may sometimes " prove " *factum probandum*. But what is often regarded as proof is only a high degree of probability.

[42] The topic of multiple issues though neglected by English writers is dealt with fully by Wigmore: see Vol. I, pp. 712 *et seq.* Evidence may be relevant to more than one *factum probandum* and on grounds of policy it may be irreceivable in respect of a particular *factum probandum*. It will, nevertheless, be received in proof of another *factum probandum*. Failure to appreciate the existence of this rule has given rise to much of the confusion about evidence of similar conduct. The rule was the basis of the decision in *Sims,* and was expressly affirmed in *Noor Mohamed* (see [1949] 1 All E.R. at 372A). Yet commentators said *Sims* was upset by *Noor Mohamed* !

[43] Just what the other ways may be has only recently been the subject of investigation and needs further examination. In *Harris* Viscount Simon, commenting on the proposition of Lord Herschell in *Makin's* case that similar fact evidence may be relevant otherwise than through disposition, said: " It is, I think, an error to attempt to draw up a closed list of the sort of cases in which the principle operates " [1952] 1 All E.R. 1046G). But though the list must remain open there is no need for absence of distinction between the various kinds

Admissibility

The concept of admissibility is essentially negative and exclusively legal. It implies the existence of " canons of exclusion ", rules of law which say that evidence is not to be received even though it be both material and relevant. In the terminology here proposed, evidence is inadmissible if it be rejected for some reason other than immateriality or irrelevance: it is admissible if there is no rule for its rejection other than one dealing with materiality or relevance. It may be admissible and yet irreceivable, for it may be rejected because it is either immaterial or irrelevant. While the historian, for example, may take into account any evidence that is relevant a court of law must consider the public policy of the society of which it is an organ and the actual circumstances of its investigation. The possibility must be considered that a court of law may exclude material and relevant evidence. Thus, state documents may be excluded on grounds of public policy, and evidence of only slight weight may be excluded because of the need for some measure of speed in litigation. The broad concept under which rules for such exclusion may be grouped is that to which I give the name " inadmissibility ". I employ the word " admissibility " for the concept of the absence of an applicable rule of exclusion.[44]

Thus, while the concept of relevance is one of fact, the concept of admissibility is one of law. For Thayer the distinction is not only fundamental, it has the result of confining the law of evidence to the concept of admissibility. He says: " The excluding function is the characteristic one in our law of evidence ": the laws of evidence are not, in his view, concerned with what is relevant, but what " among really probative matters shall for this or that reason be excluded." [45] Wigmore provides a corporeal demonstration of the distinction. He has written two separate works. *The Science of Judicial Proof* embraces

---

of relevance. In *Sims, Hall,* and *Straffen* different kinds of relevance have been confused with the specific kind of relevance through identification which occurred in *Thompson.* Carter in 69 L.Q.R. 80 adequately distinguishes relevance *via* disposition from relevance depending on some other factor. But in my view he has not adequately dealt with *Thompson.* The " correct explanation " is not that the disputed evidence was relevant " to establish identity " ; this is much too vague and comprehensive a phrase, and indeed is little more specific than " to establish guilt," which provides no explanation at all: the correct explanation is that the evidence was relevant in corroboration of an act of identification as stated by Lord Finlay [1918] A.C. at p. 225. The correct explanation of *Sims, Hall,* and *Harris* is that the evidence was relevant to indicate the single causal factor responsible for the pattern exhibited by diverse events, an explanation which requires further elucidation, some of which is provided by Russell in *Human Knowledge* at p. 482. The correct explanation of *Straffen* is that the evidence was relevant to establish a technique of action characteristic of one individual: this explanation is rightly suggested by Treitel in 16 M.L.R. at 74, but he is wrong in saying that the case involves a new departure.

[44] It is the existence of the concept of " admissibility " which makes " receivability " an instance of the class of " defeasible concepts " examined by Hart in *The Ascription of Responsibility and Rights* (being Chap. VIII of *Logic and Language* ed. Flew), see p. 148.

[45] This thesis cannot be sustained in its entirety. Even after separating from the mass of so-called presumptions those which are not " true " presumptions, but rules of substantive law or rules concerned with burden of proof, there remain those which are propositions concerned with the relevance of the facts they deal with. One aspect of this question is dealt with below, see p. 310.

U

the topic of relevancy and is largely a work of science, referring to few legal authorities. His multi-volumed *Treatise on the Law of Evidence* deals mainly with canons of exclusion, and abounds with citations of case and statutes.

It is not the province of an explanation of the concept of admissibility to indicate the nature of " this or that practical reason," which is the basis of a rule of inadmissibility. Thayer was prepared to make a sweeping generalisation, and to say that the main reason for rules of exclusion was the existence of the jury. Experience had suggested to the judges that juries placed so much more weight on certain kinds of relevant evidence than they really merited that it was politic to exclude those kinds.[46] Hearsay evidence and character evidence were examples of such kinds. The rule recently laid down in *Harris* is a striking illustration of the operation of a principle of exclusion based on the reaction of a jury to evidence.[47] Wigmore considered that Thayer's generalisation was an over-simplification. It is submitted that the exclusion of character evidence, for example, is not solely due to a belief that juries give too much weight to such evidence—hang a dog because of a bad name—but is due in part to an appreciation by judges that Englishmen consider it a principle of justice to ignore character. Each rule of exclusion must be carefully related to the policy on which it is based, and such policies are in need of continuous examination. While definition of the concept of admissibility cannot provide a statement of such policies it does draw attention to their existence and emphasises the importance of the tasks just formulated. Much of the valuable work accomplished by American jurists dealing with the character and efficacy of the various rules of exclusion can be fairly said to derive from realisation of the distinctive character of the concept of admissibility.

Realisation of the policy behind a rule of exclusion helps to bring out the truth that while evidence may be inadmissible when tendered for one purpose it may, nevertheless, be receivable when tendered for another purpose in respect of which the policy of exclusion does not apply. Of course, in order that it should be receivable it would have to be relevant for the second purpose as well as for the first, but, as already seen, multiple relevance is not impossible. Similar conduct evidence furnishes many examples of the above proposition. An instance of such conduct may be relevant for many purposes, for example, to show disposition, to establish knowledge or intention, to

---

[46] In *Doe* d. *Wright* v. *Tatham* Bosanquet J. said: " By the rules of evidence established in the courts of law, circumstances of great moral weight are often excluded, from which much assistance might be afforded in coming to a fast conclusion, but which are, nevertheless, withheld from a consideration of the jury upon general principles lest they should produce an undue influence upon the minds of persons unaccustomed to consider the limitations and restrictions which legal views upon the subject would impose " (1838) 7 A. & E., at 375.

[47] For the rule laid down in *Harris* see *per* Viscount Simon [1952] 1 All E.R. at 1048A. The following dictum supports the view of Thayer in relation to hearsay evidence. " In England where the jury are the sole judges of the fact, hearsay evidence is properly excluded because no man can tell what effect it might have upon their minds " : *per* Mansfield C.J., *Berkeley Peerage Case* (1811) 4 Camp. at 415.

corroborate identification, to establish a characteristic technique of action, to suggest the causal factor producing a sequence of similarly patterned events. Exclusion of such evidence for the purpose of proving disposition does not entail the consequence of exclusion also for the proof of other facts to which it may be relevant.

It is theoretically possible for a rule to make a particular kind of evidence inadmissible irrespective of the purpose for which it is tendered. Where the policy of a rule of exclusion is based on the effect produced on the jury then it may be reasonable to ignore such purpose. Whatever be the purpose for which the evidence is tendered, the effect may be of a kind it is desired to prevent. An example of such a general rule of exclusion is that affirmed in *Harris*,[17a] *viz.*, evidence may not be received, irrespective of purpose, if its effect in prejudicing the jury against the prisoner is considered as far outweighing the probative value of the evidence.[48]

PART III—THE UTILITY OF THE SCHEME OF CONCEPTS

It is believed that the existence and nature of the four concepts have been made clear and an adequate terminology proposed. The utility of the scheme of concepts has perhaps also appeared, but further comment may be useful. In this comment attention is drawn to the manner in which in past literature the concepts have been confused and an inadequate terminology employed. It would, perhaps, be more orderly to consider terminology and concepts in the order hitherto followed, *viz.*, receivability, materiality, relevance, admissibility. But the confusion between relevance and admissibility has in many ways been the most dramatic, despite the fact that it was to the distinction between the two that Thayer directed so much of his energy. I begin, therefore, with the importance of distinguishing between relevance and admissibility.

Relevance and admissibility

Failure to appreciate the distinct character of the two concepts of relevance and admissibility has been the main reason for the confusion surrounding the subject of similar fact evidence, and for the many misinterpretation of *Makin*[48a] which have been entertained for more than fifty years. The subject has been conceived in terms of a general rule of undifferentiated irreceivability of similar fact evidence irrespective of the purpose for which it is tendered, subject to exceptions in specified

---

[17a] [1952] A.C. 694 ; [1952] 1 All E.R. 1044.

[48] Authority for this rule is to be found in *Makin* as well as in *Christie* and *Noor Mohamed*, which were referred to by Viscount Simon. Twenty years ago Stone stressed the importance of excluding similar conduct evidence, even though relevant otherwise than via disposition, where its effect was too prejudicial:—his words were " where the peg is so small and the linen so bulky and dirty that a jury will never see the peg, but merely yield to indignation at the dirt." *Exclusion of Similar Fact Evidence*, 46 H.L.R. at 984.

[48a] [1894] A.C. 57.

cases.   Considerable controversy has surrounded the nature and principles of the exceptions.   In terms which distinguish between relevance and admissibility the doctrine of similar fact evidence is clear.   To be receivable similar fact evidence must be relevant.   Mere similarity does not result in relevance, but similar conduct *may* be relevant in unlimited ways, examples of which are given by Lord Herschell in *Makin*,[48a] *viz.*, to show design or accident or to rebut a defence otherwise open to the accused.   Similar conduct is relevant where it shows disposition or propensity,[49] but there is a rule of admissibility which denies receivability to similar conduct tendered to show such disposition. Thus, in criminal cases, in the words of Lord Herschell, similar fact evidence is inadmissible where it is tendered to show " that the accused is a person likely from his criminal conduct or character to have committed the offence for which he is being tried."   The rule of inadmissibility does not extend beyond evidence tendered to show disposition; evidence is receivable even though its *effect* is to establish disposition if tendered to prove some relevant fact other than disposition.   Where, however, the effect of such evidence is to create prejudice out of proportion to the weight to be attached to the proof of relevant facts, it is a rule of practice not to receive it.   These principles are implicit, and to a large extent explicit, in Lord Herschell's speech in *Makin*.   The *locus classicus* for the analysis of that speech is Stone's article on the " Exclusion of Similar Fact Evidence ".[50]   The principles are implicitly affirmed by Lord du Parcq in *Noor Mohamed*,[51] and are authoritatively stated by Viscount Simon in *Harris*.[47a]   However, it is not certain that there may not be fifty years of misunderstanding of that speech. The dust of controversy still surrounds the subject of similar fact evidence, and the air will not be cleared until clarifying concepts are more widely

---

[49] I regard disposition and propensity as synonymous.   For Carter " ' disposition ' is assumed to differ in meaning from ' propensity ' in degree only " (69 L.Q.R. at p. 83). I regard " character " as largely identical in meaning with disposition, though it is often used to mean the totality of different dispositions an individual has.   Huxley gives to it a meaning equivalent to disposition when he says "character is the sum of the tendencies to act in a particular way " (*Evolution and Ethics*, p. 61). A reason why mere similarity does not establish relevance is that a single act does not establish disposition.   A driver is not " accident-prone " because he has been involved in a single accident.

[50] 46 H.L.R. 975.   The conclusion of his analysis is: " Here is no broad rule of exclusion with exceptions, but a broad rule of [receivability], except where the only relevance is via disposition " : p. 984.

[51] Attention is directed to one dictum: " If all that the court in *R.* v. *Sims* meant to say was that evidence of the kind specified in the first of the principles stated in *Makin's* case may be admitted if it is relevant for other reasons, then the dictum has no novelty " ([1949] 1 All E.R. at 372A). The court had indeed said this in *Sims*: " Evidence is not to be excluded merely because it tends to show the accused to be of a bad disposition, but only if it shows nothing more " ([1946] K.B. at 537). Wigmore states the proposition in these terms: " The fact that a defendant's act of misconduct could be inadmissible as showing his bad character does not in the slightest stand in the way of receiving the same acts in evidence if they are evidential for some other purpose " (Vol. I, p. 712).   The view that evidence relevant otherwise than through disposition is not to be received because its effect may be to show disposition is called by him a fallacy, and he adds: " No fallacy has been more frequently or more distinctly struck at by denial, by argument, by explanation on the part of the courts. It has been rebuffed, rebuked, repudiated, discredited, denounced so often that it ought by this time to be abandoned forever."

employed. It will then be seen that various tasks remain to be done: the policy of inadmissibility calls for investigation and elaboration; the manner in which similar fact evidence may be relevant has to be considered, and the nature of the various modes of relevance stated.

Perhaps the most striking illustration in the realm of similar fact evidence of the confusion which has followed from the absence of recognition of distinguishing concepts is the misunderstanding which has surrounded *Sims*.[51a] In *Noor Mohamed*[52] Lord du Parcq, confronted apparently for the first time with Thayer's language in the judgment of *Sims*, subjected the passage containing that language to a criticism in which he committed the " entire misconception " against which Wigmore had warned.[53] This misled one writer into saying that *Sims* had been disturbed;[54] another writer implied that the judgment in *Sims* was nonsensical.[55] *Sims* had been approved in *Hall*[55a] and *Harris*:[47a] but misunderstanding still exists and appears in the textbooks. In Nokes' admirable *Introduction to the Law of Evidence* he says that the dicta in *Sims* " reverted to the older law, reversing the approach to this subject of the last hundred years, by laying down that evidence of similar fact was relevant and admissible unless there was some ground for exclusion ".[56] This is erroneous. *Sims* does not lay down the principle that all similar fact evidence is relevant: this is the entire misconception of Lord du Parcq. It expressly affirms the hundred-year-old rule that evidence to show disposition is inadmissible. It is made clear that similar fact evidence must be relevant before it can be received. The principle on which *Sims* proceeds is that there is no rule of exclusion of similar fact evidence which is relevant otherwise than through disposition; there is here " no novelty ", no new approach.[57]

The value of the distinction between relevance and admissibility is by no means confined to the topic of similar fact evidence. One general value is that it keeps a concept of fact distinct from a concept of law. One of the great sources of fallacious reasoning in the law is the use of concepts which confuse law and fact, so that policies are not clearly revealed. A principle of legal policy that certain kinds of

[52] [1949] A.C. at 194; [1949] 1 All E.R. at 371.
[53] " This principle does not mean that everything which has probative value is admissible: this would be an entire misconception " (Vol. I, p. 293). The principle referred to is that evidence must be relevant before it can be received.
[54] Hammelmann, 12 M.L.R. 232.
[55] Seaborne Davies: 1951 J.S.P.T.L. at 432.
[55a] [1952] 1 K.B. 302.   [56] p. 89.
[57] The pessimistic statement in the text that *Harris* may be misunderstood for the same length of time as *Makin* is confirmed by a review of Nokes' *Evidence*, which not only accepts Nokes' statement about *Sims* but says that *Harris* rejected the approach approved in *Sims*: see Armitage, B.R. 1952, J.S.P.T.L. p. 58. Lord Oaksey in *Harris* expressly approved of the approach in *Sims* (expressly disagreeing with Lord du Parcq): see [1952] 1 All E.R. at 1052D. Viscount Simon makes express reference to the " approach," but does not disapprove. He merely refers to the possibility of misunderstanding the language: see [1952] 1 All E.R. at 1049 F and H. He fails to distinguish the questions of materiality and relevance which were confused in *Sims* (see below, p. 306). He expressly approves of the conclusion of *Sims*.

evidence should not be received by the courts may be concealed by statements which suggest that the evidence is not being received because it has no worth measured by extra-legal standards. The policy behind the exclusion of hearsay evidence is not discussed so long as hearsay is thought of only by means of notions which do not ask whether it is relevant and why it is inadmissible.

Current terminology: relevance and admissibility

One of the reasons for the lack of recognition of the distinct concepts of relevance and admissibility is to be found in current terminology. Powell states that relevancy is concerned with " what facts a party will be allowed to prove at the trial of any legal proceeding ",[58] and Cockle likewise uses the term in a manner which fails to make any distinction between materiality, relevancy and admissibility.[59] Taylor uses the word " relevancy " to denote " materiality ", and Roscoe ignores both the word and the concept.[60]

Stephen was aware of the distinction between the concepts of relevance and admissibility, but, unfortunately, he used a terminology which blurred the distinction. For the concepts of admissibility and inadmissibility he used the phrases " deemed to be relevant " and " deemed to be irrelevant ". These do not clearly manifest his intention : for Stephen " deemed to be irrelevant " meant " though relevant, nevertheless to be rejected as if it were irrelevant ". Isolated from a context, however, the phrase " deemed to be irrelevant " may well be taken to mean " adjudged to be irrelevant ", so that the phrase " evidence is deemed to be irrelevant " may be taken to assert that evidence is rejected because of want of relevance.[61] Nor did Stephen always supply an adequate context. Moreover, the phrases are sometimes abbreviated in Stephen's own *Digest* to the words " relevant " and " irrelevant ". The texts which contain the propositions that hearsay and character are " deemed to be irrelevant " appear under the headings " Hearsay irrelevant except in certain cases "; " Character generally irrelevant ".[62] It is not surprising that law students and others have taken their language and ideas from the headings and not from the text.[63]

---

[58] *Law of Evidence*, 10th ed., p. 3.

[59] *Cases and Statutes on Evidence*, 5th ed., p. 58.

[60] *Digest of the Law of Evidence*.

[61] Lord du Parcq, when he used the phrase " deems to be irrelevant," meant thereby " considers to be irrelevant." The dictum in which he uses the phrase is this " The expression ' logically probative ' may be understood to include much evidence which English law deems to be irrelevant." The passage in *Sims*, criticised in this dictum of Lord du Parcq, stated that " logically probative evidence might be excluded." His dictum would have been pointless if all he meant by " deems to be irrelevant " was " may be rejected."

[62] Headings (i) to Chap. IV (ii) to article 55.

[63] Nokes, like Stephen, is aware of the distinction between relevance and admissibility, but adopts a terminology which does not adequately bring out the distinction. Hammelmann rightly criticises him for such phrases as " irrelevant facts may be admissible " (B.R. 16 M.L.R. 256). See also *post*, note 78.

Receivability and admissibility

According to Hammelmann[64] the term " admissible " has a " strictly technical sense ". I do not agree. Current terminology uses " admissible " and " inadmissible " sometimes as general terms denoting receivability and non-receivability, and sometimes as specific terms, opposed to relevant and irrelevant, denoting absence and existence of rules of exclusion of relevant evidence. In current terminology, whether evidence is rejected on the ground of irrelevance, or whether it be rejected on the ground that it offends a canon of exclusion, it is said to be inadmissible. Both what the soldier said about battles long ago which are like the flowers that bloom in the spring, and what he said about the fight which is the subject of the proceedings for assault, are classified as inadmissible. It is true that the context often makes it clear how the term is used, but the adoption of a terminology of " receivability " and " admissibility " avoids ambiguity. Appreciation of the distinction between the concepts makes it clear that rules exist for the exclusion of evidence which is material and relevant, and emphasises the need for examination of the policy of exclusion of such evidence.

Materiality and relevance

The distinction between the two concepts is not always clearly stated, and confusion is sometimes the source of error. *Sims* provides an illustration of such an error. The question of joinder before the court depended on the receivability on a charge of sodomy of evidence of other acts of sodomy. The court held that the evidence was relevant otherwise than through disposition, and was, accordingly, receivable. In giving judgment the court said: " If one starts with the general proposition that all evidence that is logically probative is admissible unless excluded, then evidence of this kind does not have to seek a justification, but it is admissible irrespective of the issues raised by the defence."[65] (In my discussion of this dictum I translate the court's language into my terminology. I substitute " relevant " for " logically probative " and " receivable " for " admissible ".) The argument of the dictum is as follows. (i) All evidence that is relevant is receivable unless there is a specific rule of exclusion. (ii) As a consequence, since the evidence of the other acts of sodomy is relevant, it is receivable irrespective of the issues raised by the defence. Lord du Parcq singled out the first proposition for attack. In my opinion, the target he selected was not vulnerable to the weapons he employed. The dictum as a whole, however, is vulnerable, for it contains a *non sequitur,* and the first proposition, moreover, can be criticised for failure to take note of the necessity of materiality. Relevancy is a relative term; evidence is not just relevant " in the air ", it is relevant to some fact, and if the

---

[64] 16 M.L.R. 257.
[65] [1946] K.B. at 539. The judgment was read by Lord Goddard C.J., but was largely prepared by Denning J.: see p. 535.

evidence is to be receivable the *factum probandum* must be a fact in issue, or the evidence will be rejected as immaterial. What is in issue depends on principles other than those of relevance: it may well depend in a criminal trial on the issues raised by the defence. The question depends on consideration of rules relating to materiality, not relevance. It is true that Viscount Simon has said that where the accused has pleaded " Not Guilty " in a criminal trial issues exist irrespective of the particular issues raised by the defence, and that the evidence in *Sims*[51a] was relevant to an issue of this kind, and so was receivable irrespective of the issues raised by the defence.[66] But the agreement with the conclusion does not establish the validity of the reasoning in the passage quoted from *Sims*. Viscount Simon supplied the missing premise dealing with materiality. His judgment confirms the importance of careful attention to the distinction between the concepts of materiality and relevance.[67]

PART IV—THE ACTUALITY OF THE CONCEPTS

Theoretical exclusion of concepts

The scheme of concepts displayed in this article has been suggested by English law, just as concepts of straightness, lines and angles may be suggested by a roughly drawn triangle. The scheme has been presented as an ideal scheme, as a theoretical framework for any " rational " system of law. It has not been fully established that the concepts do actually lie behind the rules of English law, though it has been claimed that they may be employed in the juristic exposition and criticism of English law. In the section dealing with the utility of concepts it has indeed been assumed that they are embodied in English law. It is worth while, however, considering the scheme as one of possibilities and not as realised actualities, and to consider the nature of a system of evidence which did not exemplify all the concepts.

It is possible for a legal system not to make use of the concept of materiality. That concept would have no actuality in a system which permitted litigants once they were before the court to range over every topic that occurred to them. Such a system might also require the court to remedy all grievances which were established, irrespective of whether they formed part of the original complaint. The efficiency of a society where such a system existed might well be doubted.

It is possible for a legal system to ignore the concept of relevance. It might do so completely by providing for the proof of facts by arbitrary rules. It might do so partly by the use of a " tariff " of

---

[66] [1952] 1 All E.R. at 1049H and 1050B.

[67] The fallacy pointed out in the text exists only if the " condemned " passage be read in isolation. The passage is followed by one treating of relevance in relation to facts in issue, and the court itself supplied the missing premise by asserting that the evidence was relevant to an issue with which the court had to deal irrespective of the nature of the defence. Nevertheless, there is a fallacy in the passage which it is believed would have been avoided had the distinction between materiality and relevance been more generally recognised.

evidence, requiring specied modes of proof for various kinds of fact. In such systems the time spent in litigating each case might be reduced, but there might well be lack of confidence in the judicial process, producing harmful social consequences outweighing the social gain of reducing unproductive energy-consumption. Such legal systems would not be termed " rational ".

Finally, it is possible for a legal system to ignore the concept of admissibility. This would be the case if it were provided that all evidence that was material and relevant was *ipso facto* receivable. This indeed was the situation at Nuremberg, where the Tribunal was directed " to admit any evidence which it deems to have probative value ". It is clearly debatable whether under such a system the time spent in litigation would be increased or decreased.[68]

English law: materiality and admissibility

It is unnecessary to cite authority to show that in English law litigation is confined to particular issues. The Judicature Act has widened the number of issues that may be brought before courts, and simplified the manner in which they may be presented. Issues, however, have still to be specified. The case of the general issue which survives in the plea of " Not Guilty " in criminal trials may, however, still require clarification.

It is equally unnecessary to cite authority to show that there are rules for the exclusion of material and relevant evidence. The topic of privilege embodies the notion of admissibility. It is perhaps necessary to reiterate that the exclusion of hearsay and character evidence depends on the concept of admissibility, for there are still some who regard such evidence as irrelevant. Viscount Simon has said that they are relevant,[69] but subsequent to his judgment Devlin J. has repeated the view that character evidence is irrelevant.[70]

---

[68] Art. 19 of the Charter of the International Military Tribunal reads in full: " The Tribunal shall not be bound by any technical rules of evidence. It shall adopt and apply to the greatest possible extent expeditious and non-technical procedure, and shall admit any evidence which it deems to have probative value." It is not surprising to find that Lord Oaksey, who was a member of the Tribunal, found nothing wrong with the language of the judgment in *Sims*.

[69] *Harris* [1952] 1 All E.R. at 1049G. The relevance of hearsay evidence is discussed by Baker, *Hearsay Evidence*, p. 13: see also the dicta of Bosanquet J. and Mansfield C.J. cited in notes 46 and 47.

[70] " It is not normally relevant to inquire into a man's previous character, and particularly, to ask questions which tend to show that he has previously committed some criminal offence. It is not relevant because the fact that he has committed an offence on one occasion does not in any way show that he is likely to commit an offence on any subsequent occasion. Accordingly, such questions are in general inadmissible, not primarily for the reason that they are prejudicial, but because they are irrelevant " (*Miller* [1952] 2 All E.R. at p. 668H). There is *non sequitur* in this argument. An isolated previous offence may be irrelevant, but " character " depends on more than a mere isolated act. The strongest dictum asserting the irrelevance of character evidence is that by Lord Sumner in *Thompson* (13 Cr.App.R. at p. 78): " No one doubts that it does not tend to prove a man guilty of a particular crime to show that he is the kind of man who would commit a crime, or that he is generally disposed to crime and even to a particular crime." It is submitted that this is contrary to the commonsense view that character is a reliable test of conduct.

English law: relevance

It is submitted that Thayer's two basic principles are principles of English law. The first is the negative principle, that no evidence is receivable unless it is relevant; the second is the positive principle, that all evidence that is relevant is receivable unless excluded by a rule of admissibility.

The negative principle

A particular instance of the general principle is stated by Viscount Simon in *Harris*:[71] " Evidence of ' similar facts ' cannot in any case be admissible to support an accusation against the accused unless they are connected in some relevant way with the accused and with his participation in the crime." An excellent illustration is afforded by the case of *Maxwell*.[72] The case was concerned with the application of the statutory provision in the Criminal Evidence Act, 1898, that a prisoner " shall not be asked any question . . . unless . . ."[73] It was held that this provision was not the equivalent of a provision that " a prisoner may be asked questions . . . if . . ." Consequently the fact that the statutory conditions had been fulfilled did not result in absolute permission to ask the questions; there might be common law conditions which had to be fulfilled. The question whose validity was challenged was whether the prisoner had been previously charged with a similar offence. This was one of the questions which the statute said could not be asked unless certain conditions were fulfilled. Those statutory conditions had been fulfilled in this case. It was clear, as a matter of statutory interpretation, that the effect of the statute was that if those conditions were fulfilled the common law rule of exclusion of character evidence did not apply. But the overriding rule that evidence must be relevant before it can be received was not affected by the statute. In the circumstances of the case it was considered that the fact that the prisoner had previously been charged with a similar offence and acquitted could have no bearing on the issue of the commission of the offence on which he was arraigned.[74] Such evidence was irrelevant, and the question accordingly improper. Thus the court in effect interpreted

---

[71] [1952] 1 All E.R. at 1048E: see also *per* Lord Oaksey at 1052D.
[72] [1935] A.C. 317.
[73] " A person charged and called as a witness . . . shall not be asked, and if asked shall not be required to answer, any question tending to show that he has committed or been convicted of or been charged with any offence . . . unless:—
    (i) the proof that he has committed . . . such other offence is admissible evidence . . .
    (ii) he has . . . asked questions of the witnesses for the prosecution. . . .
    (iii) he has given evidence against any other person . . ."
                              —s. 1 (6) Criminal Evidence Act, 1898.
[74] In accordance with the doctrine of relativity of relevance, it does not follow that evidence of a previous charge that resulted in acquittal is always irrelevant. In *Waldman* (24 Cr.App.R. 204) the prisoner was charged with receiving stolen goods from X. Evidence that he had previously been charged with receiving stolen goods from X was held receivable, even though he had been acquitted. The evidence was relevant to the fact of the prisoner's knowledge that X was a thief, and that fact was relevant to knowledge of the goods being stolen goods.

the statute as dealing with the problem of admissibility, and affirmed the negative principle that no evidence can be received unless it is relevant.

The positive principle

As has already been seen, the positive principle, that all evidence that is relevant is receivable unless excluded, was expressly accepted by the court in *Sims*.[51a] There it was stated in these terms : " All evidence that is logically probative is admissible unless excluded." The manner in which this dictum has been criticised would appear to demonstrate that the positive principle is no self-evident and universally recognised principle of English law. That it is not self-evident is confirmed by Stephen's account in the introduction to his *Digest*[75] of his discovery of the principle. In effect he claims to have been the first to have realised that such a principle was the " unexpressed principle which forms the centre and gives unity to . . . the great bulk of the Law of Evidence ". How far the principle has been recognised in England since Stephen wrote is doubtful, though there has been no adverse reaction to Stephen. Criticism in England has been directed to his definition of relevance in terms of cause. In America the positive principle has, of course, been approved, and Stephen is criticised for failure to state it clearly, and to distinguish between relevance and admissibility.

The popularity of Stephen's *Digest* suggests that the principle is accepted in England. In the two works on Evidence written in England since Stephen,[76] the principle, though far from being emphasised, is adopted. Phipson does so expressly,[77] and Nokes does so implicitly.[78] If the principle is accepted, why the criticism of its statement in *Sims*? It may be that Viscount Simon is correct and that criticism is concerned with the language of the formulation of the principle, *viz.*, with the phrase " logically probative ".[79] Further explanations reconciling criticisms with acceptance of the principle are these : (i) The context in *Sims* appears to suggest there is a denial of the rule that evidence tendered to show disposition is inadmissible. The criticism says this denial is wrongful. (ii) The context appears to suggest that there is a denial of Lord Sumner's doctrine, laid down in *Thompson*,[80] that the prosecution has no right " to credit the accused with fancy defences " in order to adduce evidence that would otherwise be irreceivable. The criticism considers such denial wrongful. If these explanations be correct then the criticism

---

[75] pp. xi and xii.
[76] [Since this article was written, the classic work of Professor Cross has appeared. Ed.]
[77] English ed., p. 94.
[78] Chap. V *passim:* and in particular at p. 69. Nokes' qualifications are basically terminological. In my view, when he says " irrelevant facts may be admissible " (p. 70) he means facts indirectly relevant. He elsewhere specifically accepts Thayer's negative principle that evidence must be relevant: see pp. 15 and 68. It is unfortunate that he conceives of " logic " solely in terms of deduction.
[79] [1952] 1 All E.R. at 1049F.
[80] [1918] A.C. at p. 232.

is directed not at the particular dictum setting out the principle but at the fallacy in the passage as a whole,[81] and does not impugn Thayer's positive principle.

However, as already explained in Part III, an important factor in the misunderstanding of *Sims*,[51a] one which may have affected the general acceptance of the positive principle, is the lack of clear recognition of the distinction between the concepts of relevance and admissibility, which lack has been aided by the want of adequate terminology. If these deficiencies are overcome no citation of specific judicial authority is required for the positive principle, which has been asserted to be a principle of English law by Best and Stephen, by Thayer and Wigmore. Nevertheless, *Harris*[47a] and *Makin*[48a] should perhaps be cited.

Harris contains a dismissal of the criticism to which the dictum in *Sims* was subjected. Viscount Simon reduces the criticism to a comment on the phrase " logically probative ". Lord Oaksey's judgment approves of the " approach " in *Sims* and of the " general rule of admissibility "[82] stated in *Sims*. It is to be noted that his dissent is not from the general principles of evidence approved by the other members of the House of Lords but only with their application to the facts of *Harris*.[83]

Makin[48a] is an application of the general principle of relevance to the specific instance of similar fact evidence. The crucial passage in Lord Herschell's opinion is: " The mere fact that the evidence adduced tends to show the commission of other crimes does not render it inadmissible if it be relevant to an issue before the jury."[84] This is followed by a passage giving some examples of relevant evidence. It is preceded by a passage stating that evidence tendered *for the purpose* of showing disposition is inadmissible. The major premise behind the paragraph as a whole is that where any evidence is relevant it is receivable except where there is a specific rule asserting inadmissibility. This is the positive principle of Thayer.

PART V—LEGAL RELEVANCE AND LEGAL IRRELEVANCE

Though the concept of relevance is an extra-legal one, what is relevant being dependent on the order of nature not on the policy of

---

[81] See above, pp. 305, 306.

[82] [1952] 1 All E.R. at 1052D.

[83] Lord Oaksey thought that the evidence was relevant otherwise than through disposition, and important enough not to be excluded by the rule of practice excluding evidence over-prejudicial in relation to its weight. He thought that the other members of the Lords also considered the evidence relevant otherwise than through disposition, but slight enough to be caught by the rule of practice. His words were: " As I understand it your Lordships are of opinion that the evidence . . . was relevant, but so slightly relevant that it should have been excluded " ([1952] 1 All E.R. at 1051E). Unfortunately, it is not absolutely clear that this is the correct view of the majority speeches. There was, however, no dissent from his statement.

[84] [1894] A.C. at p. 65.

lawyers, it is, nevertheless, necessary for courts to judge whether tendered evidence is relevant or irrelevant. Since courts of law are human institutions, it is possible for them to err. Judges may find that tendered evidence is relevant when the better judgment is that it is irrelevant, and, *vice versa*, they may find that such evidence is irrelevant when the better judgment is that it is relevant. The problem that arises for consideration is whether decisions of courts of law on questions of relevance are binding on subsequent courts of law.

On this matter Thayer and Wigmore differ. Wigmore maintains that the area of the doctrine of precedent includes the field of relevance.[85] According to this view, if a court holds that fact x is relevant to fact y, and x is an instance of class X, while y is an instance of class Y, then the proposition " facts of class X are relevant to facts of class Y " is a proposition of law. If in a later case counsel tender fact x, to prove fact y, the court is bound to hold that it is relevant. According to Thayer, the doctrine of precedent is inapplicable since relevance is not an affair of law. " The law has no orders for the reasoning faculty, any more than for the perceiving faculty—for the eyes and ears."[86]

In my opinion, the teaching of Thayer is the sounder : *ex facto non oritur jus.* Courts of law ought not to stand committed to theories about natural happenings and human behaviour that have been discarded by science and common sense. But the possibility of courts considering themselves bound by decisions as to relevance or irrelevance cannot be ignored: and indeed courts do, in fact, consider themselves bound. Thus arise concepts of general legal propositions of relevance and irrelevance. These can be distinguished by the names " legal relevance " and " legal irrelevance ". These names, however, suffer from the defect that they may suggest that there is a different concept of relevance employed in courts of law from that employed outside courts of law. Thayer has warned against " the common but uninstructive distinction between legal and logical relevance." Those who make that distinction mean by " logical relevance " nothing but relevance, and by " legal rele-vance " reference is made to admissibility. By " legal relevance " in the terminology here proposed is indicated a combination of precedent and relevance—a concept that a court of law is bound by a finding of an earlier court law about a question of relevance.

---

[85] Vol. I, p. 298. " So long as courts continue to declare in judicial rulings what their notions of logic are, just so long must there be rules of law which must be observed. For these rules the only appropriate place is the law of evidence." He cites in support of his view the dictum of Cushing C.J. in *State* v. *Lapage*, 57 N.H. 288, that " the subject of the relevancy of testimony has become . . . matter of precedent and authority."

[86] 14 H.L.R. 139. This sentence occurs in a reply made by Thayer to a criticism expressed by Fox of Thayer's doctrine that relevance is not an affair of law. Thayer makes a half-concession to his critic. He says that decisions as to relevance " may stand as a precedent to half-settle other cases."

19

Broom v. *Morgan* and the Nature of Juristic Discourse*

I.   General discussion of juristic discourse.
II.   Discourse about *Broom* v. *Morgan*.
III.   Law in relation to logic, social welfare and justice.
IV.   Juristic discourse and extra-legal discourse.
V.   Conclusion.

PART I.—GENERAL DISCUSSION OF JURISTIC DISCOURSE

Ultimately this paper constitutes an inquiry into the kinds of activities which are being carried out in university faculties of law, or ought to be carried out—an inquiry into the studies proper for teachers and students.   I believe that such introspection into methods and purposes is valuable.   Professor Stone on a memorable occasion doubted whether introspection is always valuable.   He referred to the story of the centipede which asked itself the question how it walked, and thereafter did not move another step.   The same story has been relied on by those who criticise pleas for inquiry by science students into scientific method. Professor Dingle has replied to such critics by saying that while self-consciousness may be destructive of the activities of centipedes it is a means of improving higher ranges of activity.   There are not wanting those who say that full awareness of methods and purposes is an essential

---

*Reprinted from *Res Judicatae*, 411 (1954), by kind permission.
[Many of the author's most intimate professional friends thought that this was his best work, and he himself, though always a stern critic of his own writings, may have shared their opinion.   Accordingly, I took advantage of the publisher's generosity as to space, to preserve it from oblivion.   I took this course in spite of the Law Reform (Husband and Wife) Act, 1962, which provides that spouses, subject to certain discretionary powers of the Court, can sue each other. The English Act was reproduced in Northern Ireland by section 2 of the Law Reform (Husband and Wife) Act (Northern Ireland), 1964.   But the author's reasoning has a universal application, and so is independent of the actual case to which it is harnessed. And a wife might still sue her husband's employer rather than her husband himself, if he had insufficient means to pay damages, and was uninsured as to her injuries. Ed.]

312

characteristic for activity which is truly human : and that the development of such awareness is the characteristic of a liberal education. Of course, this is Professor Stone's belief : his masterpiece, *The Province and Function of Law,* has as its central plan an inquiry into what it is that writers on jurisprudence do and ought to do.

An enquiry into what this paper is about is called for not merely by the principle first proclaimed, but also by the vagueness of the title. " Nature " and " juristic discourse " are ambiguous terms often used ambiguously. Many are the counts which have been made of the different ways in which Aristotle used the Greek for " nature ", and of the different meanings of the phrase " law of nature ". " Juristic discourse " can mean the discourse of certain kinds of people called " jurists ", or a certain kind of discourse no matter who the discourser may be. Of course, the distinction breaks down if by " jurist " we mean one whose discourse is " juristic ".

It may well be asked why such a vague title has been selected. Even if it be legitimate sport for a writer to set up his own Aunt Sally to be bombarded by his own verbal sallies, why select a creature of such impure and indeterminate character ? The answer lies in the " purr-word " character of the word " juristic " in contrast with the " snarl-word " character of the word " legal ". It is often said that to be a good lawyer one must be more than a mere technician, a " working-mason "; one must be a " jurist ". In many contexts the word " jurist " stands to the word " lawyer " in the same relation as in other contexts does the word " statesman " to the word " politician ". It is accordingly true, though tautological, to say that it is valuable to know what distinguishes the " jurist " from the lawyer. And since jurists and lawyers act in words it is valuable to know what is the nature of " juristic " discourse. Yet I should be rashly presumptuous if I thought I could state the characteristics of the excellence of laws and lawyers, of discourses about laws and about lawyers, in any paper or number of papers. I am, however, bold enough to think that this paper is an approach, albeit hesitating, to some aspects of those problems. While the phrase " juristic discourse " does have a eulogistic overtone, its ordinary range is not limited to the note of eulogy. Though I have selected a title embodying the phrase " juristic discourse " because of its evocation of more fundamental problems, I shall endeavour to discuss in exploratory manner the two different questions : (i) What are the criteria by which the discourse called " juristic " is distinguishable from other discourse? (ii) What are the functions in fact fulfilled by some specific discourse which is accepted as " juristic " ?

Semantics and the Austinian definition of law

The second topic is akin to questions which " semantic logicians " ask : but it can be illustrated without calling on such writers by asking questions about the Austinian " definition " of law. A writer on jurisprudence is often called a jurist. John Austin was a jurist, and the following extracts from his lectures thus conventionally merit the name "juristic discourse". "A law is a command which obliges a person or persons generally to acts or forbearances of a class. . . . A command is distinguished from other significations of desire . . . by the power and the purpose of the party commanding to inflict evil or pain. . . . But every positive law, or every law strictly so called, is a direct or circuitous command of a monarch or sovereign number in the character of a political superior." These passages may be summarised in the familiar formula that a law is the general command of a sovereign entailing a sanction. The following questions may be asked about this discourse. (i) Is the statement of a linguistic character? Does it tell us about the way in which the word "law" is used, that it has the "meaning" assigned to it in the discourse of the majority of occasions when it is used, or at any rate on some of them? Does it tell us how Austin proposes to use the word, thus defining the limits of his proposed discussion? (ii) (which may not be correctly separated from (i).) Is the statement of a conceptual character? Does it tell us what are the elements required for the construction of a particular concept considered useful in the discussion of political and judicial discourse and activities? This concept, of course, may be one of the references the word "law" already has conventionally. (iii) Is it of an empirical character? Does it tell us of the common characters that are found if one examines the various "things" which are called law, thereby amounting to an inductive generalisation? (iv) Is it a statement of values? Does it tell us really about "good" laws, thus constituting basically a "programme"[1] for society, viz., that societies in order to promote the happiness of their members should be organised with sovereign bodies issuing general rules which contain sanctions, and with executive organs for enforcing the sanctions?[2]

The meaning of the nature of discourse implied by these questions is that of assigning the discourse to the logical types discussed by writers to whom I arbitrarily give the name "semantic logicians".[3] Charles Morris, for example, classifies discourse by reference to "modes of signifying" which may be "designative", "appraisive", "prescrip-

---

[1] The term "programme" was used by Corbett to characterise the discourse of economists in an essay in which he applied Hume's trident of "is", "must" and "ought" to determine the nature of such discourse. (*Aristotelian Society*. Supp. Vol. xxvii, 218).

[2] Such questions, of course, may be asked about any "definition" of law, or any discourse. It is my belief that Austin, for all his proper emphases on distinguishing between "is" and "ought", did not make explicit the type of statement he was making. There is, however, considerable scope for argument about the Austinian texts.

[3] The use of the label "semantic logicians" does not indicate any belief by me in the existence of identity of views among the authors. Though I am too often guilty myself of the vulgar error of assuming that "all Chinks are alike" I react strongly to a writer who ascribes a particular proposition (sometimes his own) to "the Greeks" or "economists" or "the semanticists".

tive ", " formative ", and to uses which may be " informative ", " valua-
tive ", " incitive " or " systematic ".[4]

The " semantic logicians " are but developing techniques which
have long been employed by jurists as well as philosophers. An appreciation of their work may be obtained by considering the perhaps simpler
approach of a modern jurist, Kelsen, and a not so modern philosopher,
Hume. Analytical jurisprudence has long been concerned with expos-
ing the deceptions committed by ordinary language which lawyers
use; and English analytical jurists, at any rate, have been influenced
by the empirical philosophers—Hobbes, Locke and Hume.

Though Kelsen did much of his work in Vienna, much of his
thought anticipated rather than derived from the logic of the Vienna
Circle. His basic teaching is concerned with the analysis of the significance of propositions employed by practising lawyers, and the fundamental analysis is of the proposition asserting that particular action is
legal or illegal. What is the real character of the predicate in such a
proposition? Classical logic shows that the sentences of ordinary speech
are related to propositions which can be expressed in a different grammatical form of words. The distinctions between sentences and propositions and between logical and linguistic grammar are inherent in
the traditional exercises of such logic. The various ways of expressing
the transience of human life are translated to propositions of the form
" All men are mortal ", which is expressed symbolically as " S a P ".
The form is that of the relation of a " subject " " all men ", and a
" predicate " " mortal " by means of a logical copula. It is true that
four different kinds of propositions are recognised, according as the
subject is universal or particular, " all men " or " Socrates ", and
according as the relation is one of affirmation or denial as in " all men
are mortal " and " Socrates is not immortal ". It is also true that from
the earliest times it has been recognised that predicates do not all function in the same way. Thus the Aristotelian teaching of categories
classifies different functions of predicates. But the effect of classical
logic is to divert attention from the different modes of operation of
different predicates. There are important distinctions between the
predicates in the following propositions: " this action is usual ", " this
action is praiseworthy ", " this action is illegal ". But they do not
affect syllogistic reasoning and were obscured by a logic primarily concerned with the syllogism.

Kelsen did point out the nature of the distinctions between those
propositions. He investigated what was involved when the ordinary

<hr/>

[4] *Signs, Language and Behaviour* at p. 123. Of " legal discourse " (by which he means
"the body of laws ") he says (at p. 130): " The language of the law furnishes an example
of designative-incitive discourse. Legal discourse designates the punishments which an
organised community empowers itself to employ if certain actions are or are not performed,
and its aim is to cause individuals to perform or not to perform the actions in question. Legal
discourse as such does not appraise these actions nor prescribe them. . . It does not even say
the community will take the steps signified ". This, of course, accords with Kelsen's view
of the nature of " a law ".

W

man or lawyer said human behaviour was legal or illegal.   His conclusion was that nothing was being affirmed about the intrinsic quality
of the behaviour, corresponding to the assertions made in sociological
or ethical statements, such as action is customary or is just.   All that is
posited by saying *the act x is illegal* is that there exists a rule of law
dealing with actions of a class under which x can be subsumed.   From
this beginning he proceeds to examine the character of a rule of law.
Analysis of the statement *p is a rule of law* leads to the doctrine of the
hierarchy of norms.   For that doctrine affirms only that a proposition
P exists which asserts that there may be created propositions of the form
p is a rule of law.[5]   The existence of the higher norm, P, is the test of
the validity of the postulated norm, p.

Throughout his writing Kelsen demonstrates the over-simplification and consequent confusion effected by the ordinary language and
thinking of lawyers.   The demonstration of the over-simplification and
consequent confusion created by ordinary language and the traditional
propositional logic is the task of the modern school of analytical philosophers.   An illustration of the difference between " grammatical and
logical form " given by one of their leaders is very much like Kelsen's
analysis of the proposition that an act is legal.   " ' Jones is popular '
suggests that being popular is like being wise, a quality : but in fact it
is a relational character and one which does not directly characterise
Jones but the people who are fond of Jones."[6]   Professor Ryle is contrasting the operation of the predicate in the proposition " Jones is
popular ", with the operation of predicates in other propositions.   He
makes no endeavour to classify the types of predicates.   " Jones is six
feet tall " is a different kind of proposition from " Jones is wise ", and
both are different from " Jones is popular ".   Sentences may have the
same linguistic form, and even appear to have the same logical structure, and yet analysis discloses differences.

The lack of correlation between linguistic form and logical substance is emphasised in different ways by traditional and modern logic.
Classical logic showed that despite different linguistic forms there might
be identity of logical substance; the more recent logic deals with differ-

---

[5] Kelsen has correctly analysed one of the possible meanings of sentences like *the action
x is legal, p is a rule of law.*   But he repeats in a more subtle manner the Austinian fallacy
of the proper meaning of law.   There are uses of *law* and *legal* which do not involve references
to a hierarchy of norms, but to customary behaviour and to principles to which the user
believes norms ought to conform.   The scholar should not ignore the folk-wisdom exhibited
by actual language (even if improper).   It is right to distinguish between custom, official
rule and justice.   It is right also to consider their interrelations.   Kelsen's statement that
his theory is an analysis of the " proper " use of the word law by lawyers is to be found in
his article " Law, State and Justice in the Pure Theory of Law " in (1948) 57 *Yale Law
Journal* 377, 378.   He says, " In defining the concept of law as a coercive order . . . The
Pure Theory of Law simply accepts the meaning that the term ' Law ' has assumed in the
history of mankind."   But according to the Oxford English Dictionary, in the English
language from the earliest times the word " Law " has been used with reference both to
natural law and to custom.

[6] Ryle, " Systematically Misleading Expressions " in *Logic and Language (First Series)*,
(ed. Flew), 11, 33.   A fuller discussion is to be found in Carnap: *Logical Syntax of Language*,
at p. 308, where the dangers of " transposed speech " are set out.

ence of logical substance which may be concealed behind similarity of linguistic structure. It is the task of semantic logicians to examine the different logical types of propositions. This involves the affirmation or elaboration of Hume's " trident ". He discloses three basic types of propositions, which may be characterised, by reference to their basic verbs, as *is, must* and *ought* propositions.[7] There are propositions which deal with *facts,* propositions which deal with the necessities of *logic,* and propositions which deal with what we now often call *values.*[8] Propositions of one kind cannot be educed from propositions of another kind, and propositions of each kind have their own methods of verification. The logical classification of propositions is, of course, related to ontological and epistemological doctrines. The threefold classification of Hume can be related to a world of basic space-time particulars and of perceiving and conceiving minds which discern the patterns formed by the particulars and the values exhibited by such pattern structures. This paper is, however, concerned with the nature of discourse. It is sufficient here to assert how important is that part of juristic discourse which is concerned with the analysis of discourse, allotting each part to its distinct logical type. Actual discourse, including both legal and juristic discourse, is made up of propositions of all types, and classification is often difficult as well as important. The importance of discerning that a proposition of value may be concealed behind an apparent statement of fact has often been asserted. I give priority to the task of making clear what sentences do express propositions of fact. In discourse propositions of fact are not too often based on conjectures. While conjecture may have to be accepted in the realm of values, or met by no more than counter-conjecture, there are well developed procedures for questions of fact: historical method can deal with existence of particular events and scientific method with propositions which assist the existence of uniformities. To return to the Austinian theory of law, there are often statements made that the official pronouncement of rules for the conduct of citizens has no effect unless sanctions are incorporated in the rules. The empirical investigation of such statements would be fruitful.[9]

---

[7] Mises classifies propositions about human behaviour by reference to the employment of the verbs " will ", " ought ", " may", " must ". See ch. 25 of *Positivism.*

[8] Hume's separation of *is* from *ought,* of fact from value, is to be found in Book III, Part I, Sect. I, of the *Treatise on Human Nature,* see particularly the last two paragraphs. His distinction of *is* and *must,* of fact and logical relation, is at the basis of his examination of the nature of cause and his denial of its necessity. This occupies Part III of Book I. In Sect. XI we find a distinction drawn between knowledge and probability. Knowledge— " The assurance arising from the comparison of ideas " is to be distinguished even from proofs —those arguments, which are derived from the relation of cause and effect, and which are entirely free from doubt and uncertainty ". I would refer the necessity of logical relation to *deductive* logic, but from his footnote to Sect. VIII it is clear that Hume would not distinguish deduction from other " acts of the understanding ".

[9] " Every proper statement of the form X is a means to Y can be supported by empirical evidence showing that X produces or tends to produce Y, and this evidence is statistical. It is of the form *n* per cent of the people who have headaches and who take aspirins find that their headaches are relieved." Weldon: *Vocabulary of Politics* at p. 163. Weldon's thesis is that " Aspirins relieve headache " is a " proper statement of the form ", but " Parliamentary institutions promote the general good " is not.

Juristic discourse as meta-legal language

Modern semantics may also be invoked in considering the first question of what are the criteria by which juristic discourse is distinguished from other discourse. Discourse on examination discloses that it exhibits different strata or orders. A distinction has been drawn between object language and meta-language. The sentences of an object-language deal directly with " things ", those of a meta-language are about sentences in the object-language. " Heute ist Montag " is a sentence in an object-language. " ' Heute ist Montag ' means ' To-day is Monday ' " is a sentence in a meta-language. " To-day is Monday " is an object-language statement. " ' To-day is Monday ' is true " is a sentence in a meta-language.[10] In a similar way discourses *about* " laws " may be opposed to " laws " themselves : it is the former which is sometimes called juristic discourses, while the phrase legal discourse may be reserved for the laws themselves and for language that is purely descriptive of the laws. That is to say " legal discourse " may be used to denote both the pronouncements of legislators of all kinds—parliamentary, judicial, ministerial—and the statements of others, including " jurists " and sometimes judges, who are merely translating the language of the men of law into other language for many reasons, such as for purposes of summary, to achieve greater lucidity, to attract more attention to them, or for didactic purposes, putting them into a form in which it is believed the rules may be more easily memorised or understood. In summary fashion it may be said that " legal discourse " can mean legislation and exposition of legislation. Incidentally, this approach throws some light on the nature of " laws ". In juristic discourse they are sentences or propositions and as such have no spatio-temporal qualities. It is absurd to ask about the location of " twice two is four ", or to ask when did the *proposition* occur that the first of July, 1953, fell on a Wednesday. As Hart says where a judge upholds the plaintiff's claim based on contract, " there is a contract in the timeless sense of ' is ' appropriate to judicial decisions ".[11] It is by looking at the propositional character of laws that Kelsen is able to " depsychologise " the Austinian command, and to separate the category under which law falls from those of " is " and (ethical) " ought ".[12]

It will be noted that meta-legal discourse is not identical with the discourse of jurists. On the one hand, any one can take part in meta-

---

[10] Waismann distinguishes between macrological and micrological features of a language —one deals with a system of statements as a whole, the other with single statements. " Language strata " in *Logic and Language* (Second Series), (ed. Flew). p. 11, at p. 18. This suggests other ways of classifying juristic discourses.

[11] *Logic and Language* (First Series) at p. 155.

[12] Mises regards a category of " being of the ought " as chimerical, *Positivism* at p. 332, but he misses the propositional character. So too the view that " laws " can only " exist " as ideas in minds, adopted by Glanville Williams in *Langauge and the Law* [(1945) 61 L.Q.R. 71, 179, 293, 384 and (1946) 62 L.Q.R. 387] is concerned with a different matter. Of course, " laws " can only be applied when administrators " think " of them: but attention is there directed to an element of psycho-physiological activity.

legal discourse; it is not confined to students of jurisprudence, but extends to students of any branch of law. Judges are often jurists in more than a merely eulogistic sense of the term. Politicians and soap-box orators may all utter meta-legal discourse. On the other hand, all discourse by students of jurisprudence is not meta-legal: it may be about human behaviour or about values such as justice and equity. It might in those cases still be said to be about " law ", for the word " law " has both empirical and valuational significations, but it would not be about " laws ": we should be passing from " the concepts of a lawyer's jurisprudence " to that of a jurist's jurisprudence.[13]

The analysis of legal reasoning and Stone's province of jurisprudence

The statement that juristic discourse is discourse about laws conveys no information as to what the sentences of the discourse say about laws. It is, of course, an over-simplification of Professor Stone's *Province and Function of Law* to say that its function is to convey that information: and in view of its lack of an explicit definition of the word " law " it may be a more erroneous over-simplification to say that Stone's thesis is that " jurisprudence " consists in the relation of rules of law to logic, sociology (in so far as sociology is concerned with " social control "), and philosophy (in so far as philosophy is concerned with principles of justice). Some attention has already been given to the light that modern logic may throw on the nature of juristic discourse. Classical logic may also be called in aid.

The problem of classification is one of the traditional topics of such logic, in which it embraced both deduction and induction, for the statement that a number of particulars are all members of one class is a form of induction. Discussion is generally confined to the classification of " things ", carried out, of course, by means of words signifying the things. Applied to law this process becomes one of classifying the various legal concepts, and yields the " common notions " of legal systems, whose examination was considered by Austin to be one of the main tasks of jurisprudence. In a similar manner propositions whose terms contain particulars, " Socrates is mortal ", " Plato is mortal ", can be classified as instances of wider propositions, " Some men (query all men) are mortal." Applied to law this process yields, when a single system of law is examined, the highest generalisations of legal systems, which Holmes envisaged in the *Path of the Law* as the fruit of jurisprudence.[14] When all (a task no one has carried out) or some legal systems are examined we find principles common to all legal systems or to some particular legal system, whose examination receives from Mabbott the name of

---

[13] See Bryan King " The Concept of a Lawyer's Jurisprudence ", (1953) 11 *Cambridge Law Journal*, 404.

[14] Tennyson's " broadening down from precedent to precedent " refers to judicial legislation employing inductive generalisation as part of its reasoning process. In *Rylands* v. *Fletcher* (1868) L.R. 3 H. L. 330, Blackburn J. induces the " rule " from particular propositions dealing with cattle trespass, liability for fire and nuisance.

" jurisprudence ", and is considered by him to be one of empirical inquiry by scientific method.[15] The language of English lawyers employs the terms " rules " and " principles " to indicate the distinction between particular and general propositions. It is to be noted, however, that these terms may also be used to indicate a different distinction, namely that between rules of law and the policies they implement or serve.

The main task, however, of classical logic was the examination of inference, of the relations between propositions which are linked in a chain of reasoning in order to determine whether conclusions were validly reached or not : and its bright star is the logic of the syllogism. Stone has brilliantly demonstrated many fallacies of logical form to be found in legal reasoning arising mainly from the unsatisfactory character of the terms employed in legal propositions. Holmes has been the inspiration for the task of examining legal reasoning in order to see what premises have been suppressed, which are, nevertheless, required for such reasoning to attain complete syllogistic or other valid logical form. He himself, of course, recognised that minor as well as major premises are often inarticulate. He has also been the inspiration for the task of examining the character of the various premises for the purpose of seeing into what branch of learning they fall, for, as Finch said long ago " the sparks of all the sciences are raked together in the ashes of the law ". Judges as well as other legislators make use of propositions which fall within the ambit, for example, of economics, medicine, political science and ethics. The criteria for the validity of such propositions, it has been suggested, are determined by " disciplines other than law ".[16]

The concept of " legal reasoning " which has been referred to requires some comment. It is distinct from that of legal discourse which has been conceived as merely the aggregate of rules of law, constituting separate propositions not linked in a general deductive or inductive system. It is necessary to go beyond the signification of the word " law " as an aggregate of rules of law if " law " is to be examined in the light of inferential logic. As Pound has shown, the word " law " bears a meaning beyond that of " authoritative grounds of decision ". It refers sometimes to the legislative and judicial process. The judicial process involves the application of rules of law to facts in order to arrive at decisions, and this process may be said to constitute " reasoning ", which may be logically examined. But, moreover, legislators and judges in many systems of law expound reasons for the rules of law they enunciate,

---

[15] *The State and The Citizen*, p. 172. Mabbott is concerned with delimiting the province of political philosophy, and his statement about " jurisprudence " is consequently terse. Presumably he would include within " jurisprudence " dynamic principles of evolution of legal systems, the subject matter of Maine's *Ancient Law*.

[16] In *Railroad Co. of Texas* v. *Rowan Nichols Oil Co.* 310 U.S. 573 at 583 Frankfurter J. said, " The record is redolent with .... matters of geography and geology and physics and engineering . . . Plainly these are not issues for our arbitrament." Professor K. C. Davis poses some stimulating questions in the *Notes and Problems* to this case in his case-book (Cases in *Administrative Law* at p. 940) e.g. " if instead of ' geography and geology and physics and engineering ' the problems had concerned economics and business . . . would the Court have taken the position that ' Plainly these are not issues for our arbitrament?' "

and it is such reasoning which can be examined in the light of inferential logic. By "legal reasoning" I mean the totality of reasoning used by legislators and judges in the formulation and application of rules of law. Closer examination of the concept is doubtless required, in particular, for example, to see whether all that a judge says is "legal reasoning", and to consider how much of it is juristic discourse. My immediate task, however, is to suggest a gloss on Stone's thesis that jurisprudence is the examination of law in the light of disciplines other than law. It is legal reasoning and not merely rules of law which can properly be so examined.

Let us consider, for example, the rules (a) that contracts in restraint of trade are void, (b) that irresistible impulse is no defence to a criminal charge.* Let us assume (i) that economists hold that non-enforcement of contracts in restraint of trade leads to diminution of the "national income", (ii) that psychologists hold that persons may suffer from conative disease of the mind so that some impulses are irresistible. (a) The legal rule that contracts in restraint of trade are void is condemned by the science of economics if the sole policy of the legal rule is that of augmentation of the national income. If, however, the policy of the legal rule is that of the maximisation of economic freedom, because of some ethical doctrine of "freedom", then the criterion for criticism is not to be found in economics but in ethics. What, however, if the policy of the law is not single but complex—if it is to augment the national income and to maximise freedom? The rule which according to the discipline of economics increases the national income may, according to moralists, decrease the amount of freedom. A rule of law may be affected by factors from many disciplines, some empirical and some valuational. Some synthesis is required of the relations between the rule and various disciplines. Is there a meta-discipline which provides this synthesis—history, perhaps, or philosophy? Does juristic discourse involve such synthesis on the basis of common sense or intuition, or on the basis of principles which jurisprudence itself must evolve? (b) The rule of law that irresistible impulse is no defence to a criminal charge is condemned by the science of psychology *if* the rule of law is based on the belief that empirically no impulse is irresistible. But this particular doctrine of the science of psychology affords no criterion whereby to judge a policy of attributing criminal responsibility to those who commit crimes as the result of an irresistible impulse. A science of eugenics might indeed indicate that if the policy were accepted of the desirability of a nation free from insanity all insane persons should be eliminated. But is the "major premise" good?

The supplementation of Stone's province

The debt of law teachers to Stone is very great, both of his insight into the task of jurisprudence and for his masterly exposition and criti-

---

*[Under the Homicide Act, 1957, it may reduce murder to manslaughter. Ed.]

cism of juristic theories. His major premise, which he has well articulated, can be expressed in the language of his lamented colleague, Professor Simpson: " Every good course in law is a course in jurisprudence." It is not the major task of juristic discourse to tidy up the statute book and the utterances of judges. In the language of Bentham, we must go beyond exposition to " censorial jurisprudence ", and in so doing should be perhaps readier than Bentham to give praise where praise is due: moral and intellectual virtues exist in the law as well as defects. In my view, however, juristic discourse cannot be limited to Stone's province of jurisprudence. I would not limit juristic discourse to the examination of rules of law in relation to extra-legal disciplines. I regard the empirical study of " legal " behaviour, the sociology of law, as rightly called a " legal " discipline. Surely studies of judicial behaviour and legal etiology are " legal " disciplines. Again, I consider the examination of the nature of justice to be a " legal " discipline. However fundamental the distinction between " natural law " and " positive law " may be, I do not consider the study of natural law to be an extra-legal discipline. Austin, it should be remembered, conceived that the study of the philosophy of positive law was but a stepping stone to the science of legislation, the examination of what ought to be the law. However, even if juristic discourse be limited to the evaluation of legal rules, the criteria to be employed in this task must often be determined by the jurists themselves. One reason for this has already been considered, *viz.*, that since other disciplines deal only with particular factors involved in a total judgment about a legal rule, some synthesis is required of the conclusions of the disciplines. But other reasons are to be found in the inconclusive character of extra-legal disciplines. Many of the social sciences are still in a rudimentary state. This situation has a two-fold operation. In the first place they have not yet proceeded to the stage of formulating hypotheses about the matters which are involved in the juristic criticism of laws. In the second place, many of their formulative hypotheses are not sufficiently established.[17] If we turn to philosophy, though much guidance is to be found,[18] we shall also find that the philosophers have given little attention to many matters with which laws are concerned, even though they fall within the bounds of social and political philosophy.[19] Jurists have often to make judg-

---

[17] Cf. " Summary of a Conference on Law and Psychology ". (1953) 5 *Journal of Legal Education*, 355.

[18] Is the legal practice of disparaging philosophy at an end? Even Pollock, an admirer of Spinoza, warned lawyers against " the deep water of philosophy ". But Lord Asquith has recently said " A philosopher—a term which I use in no disparaging sense, for what is a philosopher but one who, inter alia, reasons severely and with precision." (*Stapley* v. *Gypsum Mines Ltd.* [1953] 2 All E.R. 478, 489 F.)

[19] Oxford " philosophers" today appear to contend that judgments as to the goodness or badness of laws and legal institutions are for the lawyer or the statesman, not for the philosopher. The task of the " philosopher " is apparently that of explaining the logical character of political propositions. Thus Weldon denies in his stimulating *Vocabulary of Politics* that " the job of the professional political philosopher is to demonstrate that one variety of political organisation is especiallypraiseworthy and that the others are defective."

ments affecting laws which fall within the areas of psychology or sociology, morals or politics, but whose operation has not been formulated in propositions of those disciplines. In a similar manner judges have developed general principles of government and social welfare which are not paralleled in the works of social and political philosophers.

Juristic discourse in seeking to evaluate actual rules of law unites the two fields of what is and what ought to be. It is linked with the formulation of possible rules which are thought to be better than existing rules. Juristic commentary on proposals for changes in the law is basically no different from that on existing laws.

The task of the jurist is thus similar to that of the legislator, but the legislator, judicial or otherwise, has to observe limits in his proposals for new laws from which the jurist is free. The member of a government takes into account the attitudes of Parliament and the electorate: the judge is influenced by the analogies of existing laws, the pressures arising from the facts of the case before him, and the necessity for giving a prompt decision. The fundamental choice before jurists and legislators, however, appears to me to be between the formulation of judgments based on intuition, emotion and common feelings, and the formulation of judgments based on reflective thought, science and philosophy. In order to escape from intuitionistic judgments it is not sufficient to call in aid the empirical social sciences if the view be accepted that ultimate policies, scales of values, notions of justice, are themselves but matters of taste and arbitrary emotion. The rejection of the doctrine that justice is a rational concept, in other words the rejection of natural law, leaves the jurist ultimately with no function but logical analysis of positive law. There have, of course, always been jurists who have accepted positivism. Kelsen, who in Vienna anticipated the logical positivists of the Vienna school, has shown both the strength and the limitations of the positivist approach. In England the logical positivists have found disciples among jurists, and Glanville Williams' articles on *Language and the Law*[20] have been a stimulus to juristic thought, though their value lies more in their semantic analysis than in their ontological discussion. Outside

---

(at p. 9). It is not a philosophical question to ask whether the political institutions of Switzerland are better than those of Spain. The philosopher's task is " to show the logical character of political appraisal." It is a philosophical task, however, " to explain the resemblances and differences between ' The political institutions of Switzerland are better than those of Spain ' on the one hand and ' Smith is a better full-back than Jones ' on the other hand". (at p. 160). The jurist who passes the ball to such a political philosopher for guidance as to the justice of a law will get a return pass leaving him no nearer the goal. The first draftsman of this self-denying ordinance for philosophy appears to have been Wittgenstein who said, " All philosophy is Critique of language ". He was anticipated in the realm of legal philosophy by some analytical jurists, though Austin himself never thought that legal philosophy excluded the science of legislation.

[20] The articles are to be found in (1945) 61 L.Q.R. 71, 179, 293, 384 and (1946) 62 L.Q.R. 387. The change of attitude to morals undergone by other logical positivists has not yet apparently been experienced by him. In *Joint Torts and Contributory Negligence* he propounds a principle justifying vicarious liability and adds " Some may be inclined to reject this statement of policy, and it seems that whether one accepts it or rejects it is a matter of feeling and is not susceptible of argument ", at p. 433.

England the revival of natural law, heralded at the beginning of the century by Charmont, has become widespread since the war.[21] The jurist who seeks for a rational basis for his judgments on legal rules will, of course, call in aid the empirical social sciences, but he will also turn for assistance to the sciences of values. He will, however, find that the extra-legal disciplines are not sufficient for his task. He will, nevertheless, find some guidance in the theories of justice and human behaviour which have been the creation of lawyers, working both in courts and schools of law, even though they have sought no higher title for their views than that of organised common sense.

PART II.—DISCOURSE ABOUT THE PROBLEM OF BROOM V. MORGAN

Introduction

In this part instead of dealing in an abstract and perhaps *a priori* manner with juristic discourse, I shall consider three recent discourses, not for the purpose of dealing with their subject matter, but in an endeavour to show the character of the enterprise on which the authors were engaged and the methods they employed. The discourses are related by the fact that they are concerned with a common problem, which can be epigrammatically and misleadingly stated as this: is a master liable for the *torts* or for the *acts* of his servant? Two of the discourses are by law teachers writing in law reviews, the other consists in the complex judgments of the Court of Appeal in the case of *Broom v. Morgan*.[22] I must confess that my examination was not completely disinterested; I approached the task with certain hypotheses in mind. This may be described as either the scientific method, or as arguing from pre-established premises to pre-determined conclusions. What is certain, however, is that the conclusions, even if correct, apply only to the specific discourses examined: these discourses cannot be regarded as a " fair sample " of the opinions of law teachers and judges, and the characteristics they exhibit cannot be predicated generally of juristic and judicial discourse. The hypotheses were, however, general propositions; they were: (i) that much " juristic " discourse is description of

---

[21] Charmont in *La Renaissance du Droit Naturel* emphasises rather the contribution of Gény than that of Stammler. Neo-Thomism has been certainly a powerful influence in the general revival of natural law and is possibly the main factor in the present general interest in " natural law " in Western Europe and the United States. But Neo-Kantianism had its place; and it certainly is a curious classification which confines " natural law " doctrines to those deriving from St. Thomas. Renard's rejection of eighteenth-century so-called natural law is, however, reasonable. The tradition of natural law from Aristotle onwards has been that of a set of principles to be utilised in the making of positive laws. In the eighteenth century a detailed blueprint of "laws" derived from " reason " was propounded. Renard calls this " droit idéal ": see *Le Droit, L'Ordre et La Raison*, at p. 134. It is this " ideal law " which was discredited by Savigny and other jurists in the nineteenth century.

[22] [1953] 1 All E.R. 849.

what judges say, (ii) that much judicial discourse is " juristic " in character, going beyond exposition of what the law is to criticism and justification, (iii) that in connection with many of the problems with which juristic discourse deals little help is to be gained from the writings in other disciplines, from ethics or politics, from sociology or economics. I shall in connection with each discourse, first summarise it, then assess its character and, finally, examine its method.

The nature of a master's liability in the law of tort: Hughes and Hudson[23]

(i) Exposition

The first discourse to be examined is in an article in the *Canadian Bar Review*. The authors are concerned about the absence of any " convincing technical statement " dealing with the law relating to the liability of a master, and the article concludes with the formulation of a statement of the doctrine of master's liability. The lack of a technical statement is demonstrated (i) by showing that text-book writers are in conflict about the statement of the doctrine: some write of liability for the torts of a servant, others of liability for the acts of a servant, (ii) by constructing five hypothetical situations for which specific judicial authority is lacking, and which give rise to problems which cannot be determined while doubt as to the doctrine persists.

So far as space is concerned, the major part of the article is concerned with a review of cases. The " mass of case law on master and servant " in England is said to provide but " occasional and fragmentary assistance ". It is true that in *Twine* v. *Bean's Express*[24] there is a dictum that " the law attributes to the employer the acts of a servant done in the course of his employment ", but the authors submit " that the main trend of this passage is to emphasise that the employer is not necessarily liable simply because the servant is liable ",[25] and that the *ratio decidendi* of the case was that the act was not in the course of the servant's employment.[26]

---

[23] (1953) 31 *Canadian Bar Review* 18.

[24] [1946] 1 All E.R. 202, 204.

[25] At p. 25. There is no further examination of the distinction between master's liability for torts of the servant and acts of the servant in order to bring out that a proposition in terms of acts may both widen and narrow the master's liability. See post p. 329.

[26] This is asserted to be the *ratio decidendi* of the judgment of Uthwatt J. as well as of the Court of Appeal; and it is asserted that the Court of Appeal in *Conway* v. *George Wimpey and Co. Ltd.* [1951] 1 All E.R. 363 also considered this to be the ratio of *Twine* v. *Bean's Express*. Professor Baker considers that the dictum of Uthwatt J. cited in the text was the *ratio* for the decision of Uthwatt J. and was adopted in *Conway's* case. The Court of Appeal in *Twine* v. *Bean's Express*, he says, " complicated the issue by a ruling that the driver in giving a lift . . . was not acting in the course of his employment ". Glanville Williams supports Baker. These differences throw light on the certainty engendered by the doctrine of precedent. This certainty is assisted by the accuracy of reporters. The *All England Law Reports* sets out the account of *Twine* v. *Bean's Express* narrated by Asquith L.J. in *Conway's* case as if it were his own. ([1951] 1 All E.R. at 365 F). The *Times Law Reports* ([1951] 1 T.L.R. 587, 589) shows that Asquith L.J. was setting out the headnote drafted by the reporter of *Twine* v. *Bean's Express* for the *Times Law Reports:* See (1946) 62 T.L.R. 458.

Three English cases and one American case received particular attention. In *Dyer* v. *Munday*[27] the master was sued in respect of an assault committed by a servant. Criminal proceedings had already been taken against the servant, which, under s. 45 of the Offences Against the Person Act, 1861, amounted to a bar to civil proceedings against the servant. Nevertheless, the master was held liable. The authors reject the reasoning of the Court of Appeal based on the purpose of s. 45, but accept the decision: they say that the case can " be very easily explained on the ground that the servant was clearly liable in tort: the plaintiff was only procedurally barred ". *Smith* v. *Moss*[28] and *Broom* v. *Morgan*[29] were cases in which a wife injured by the careless act of her husband was held entitled to recover against the husband's employer, though she herself, because she was his wife, could not have recovered from her husband.* They accept the decisions as correct,[30] but consider them as " forming a particular decision on the law of husband and wife " justified by the " social expediency test ", and " not capable of forming the basis of the general principle of vicarious responsibility ". Nevertheless, they consider " the crucial difficulty is *why* the employer is liable in such a case ". In *Schubert* v. *Schubert Wagon Co.*[31] Cardozo J., in another case where a wife was held entitled to sue an employer, said " The liability of the master must remain until he satisfy it or be by rule of law relieved from the liability of his servant's wrong ". This reasoning is rejected : our authors say : " If the servant is not liable, how can his act be said to be wrong? Any test of ' wrongness ' outside the ambit of legal liability is a dangerous and uncertain one for a Court to adopt ".

The crucial difficulty of *Smith* v. *Moss* is overcome, and the technical statement formulated in the following manner. " In order to draw some conclusions from the case law considered, it is suggested that we use as our test a blend of legal logic and social expediency." Two " explanations " of *Smith* v. *Moss* and two technical statements may be considered. The first is that the master's liability is independent of that of the servant, and is based on an independent primary duty of his own : this is the doctrine of liability for *acts*. The second is that the master is liable if the servant is liable, but such liability includes the case where the servant has " committed a prima facie tortious act, even though he

---

[27] [1895] 1 Q.B. 742.

[28] [1940] 1 K.B. 424.

[29] [1952] 2 All E.R. 1007. This is the report of the case in the Court of first instance before Lord Goddard L.C.J.; the article was written before the decision of the Court of Appeal.

[30] They point out that Hanbury (*Principles of Agency* at p. 11) and Salmond (*Torts* 10th edn., 1945 at p. 66) consider *Smith* v. *Moss* in conflict with the correct doctrine of vicarious liability. Powell (*Agency* at p. 240) considered it an exception.

[31] (1928) 249 N.Y. 253.

*[Under the Law Reform (Husband and Wife) Act, 1962, spouses, subject to certain discretionary powers of the court, can sue each other. Ed.]

may be immune from an action based upon it ":[32] this is the doctrine of liability for *torts*: but torts are extended to include *prima facie* torts. The doctrine that a master has an independent primary duty is said to be " logically unsound ", and a logical demonstration of its unsoundness is presented. The alternative that the master is liable for the torts of his servant must, therefore, be accepted. This results in a rule of law which " appears to be socially equitable and expedient ". It is: " A master is liable in tort for the act of his servant, if the servant's act was a breach of duty imposed on the servant by the law of tort and was done in the course of the servant's employment: the fact that the servant enjoys an immunity from action does not protect the master ".

The " logical " argument, on which the authors rely, is discussed subsequently.

(ii) Type of Discourse

Attempts to classify discourse as descriptive of what is the law or prescriptive of what ought to be the law run into the difficulty of the ambiguity of " law ". In the discourse under review it could be said that the authors have drafted proposed legislation and submitted reasons for its acceptance. This legislation, in their view, is needed not in substitution for an existing rule of law but in order to fill a " gap ", because no rule of law exists dealing specifically with the topic. In their view judicial pronouncements deal with only part of the topic they consider, *viz.*, that part dealing with the factual situation giving rise to the litigation, and are indeterminate in relation to hypothetical situations, imagined by the authors but not yet the subject of litigation. This type of discourse formulating proposed rules of law for dealing with situations for which official legislation has made no provision, has a long tradition, being found in the discourse of Roman jurists who developed the classical law of Rome, and in the discourse of commentators on Roman law who developed the modern law of Europe. Persuasive devices employed by such commentators for the acceptance of their proposals have been the use of phrases such as " in accordance with right reason " or " natural law ": it will be noted that our authors do not use those phrases, but they do use the phrases—" legal logic ", " socially equitable ", " the interests of society ".

The discourse under review does, however, contain indications that the authors are purporting to state what the law *is*, not what it ought to be. They point to the absence not of " law ", but of a " technical statement ", and the rule they propose is called a " restatement of the law ". Their discourse is consistent with the acceptance by them of the view that " the law " consists not merely in already formulated " tech-

---

[32] The authors consider that by using the words " immune " and " immunity " they have adopted a " Hohfeldian classification ". This is not so. They envisage the servant being under a duty in respect of his acts and yet having an " immunity " from action against him. This is a departure from Hohfeld's use of " immunity " and ignores the Hohfeldian distinction between primary and secondary rights.

nical " rules, but also in principles or processes for the formulation of other rules.[33] They formulate the rule for master's liability in accordance with the official method—their argument is one which not only could be addressed to a court of law, but might be presented by a court. Discourses of such a kind may be described as prophecies of what courts of law are likely to say in the future, or statements of what they ought to say according to the common law doctrine of precedent. Such discourse contains much reference to past cases, to the distinctions between *ratio decidendi* and *obiter dictum*, to " explanations " of cases, and to " principles " behind cases. It may engender controversy because there is no agreement as to the nature of the judicial law-making process : if " the law " consists in principles for law-making, perhaps they are those of which the judge spoke when he said " the common law consists in half-a-dozen obvious principles, but nobody knows what they are ".

The dichotomy between what is the law and what ought to be the law dissolves if the rule-making principles which are part of " the law " are based on what the law ought to be; for example, if there be a principle that in some circumstances at least the judges are to formulate a rule " required by justice ". Differences of opinion as to the rules that judges will enunciate can, of course, be expected if the judicial law-making process involves reference to concepts such as justice and social welfare, for so far no agreement yet exists, either as to the content and mode of operation of those concepts or as to methods by which differences about those matters may be resolved. Thus there is a desire on the part of some to believe that the process is of a logical character derived from the entailments of existing rules, involving only principles about which there is as much agreement as about the rules for arithmetic. If this were so, one could rightly ask what is the law on a matter not covered by authority in the same way as one could ask what is the product of two numbers which had not previously been multiplied? Different answers might be forthcoming to either question, but with care one could see who had " got the sum right ". There is, however, an intermediate position between logico-legal rule-making for gaps and ethico-social, extra-legal rule-making. One may ask either what ought to be the law in a given situation positing freedom of choice, utilising only extra-legal notions, or what ought to be the law taking into account not only the extra-legal notions, but also existing rules of law. This is in essence the debate about *libre récherche scientifique*.[34] It also pre-

---

[33] This is a " restatement " of the declaratory theory of law. It was surely in relation to this theory, and this meaning of the word " law ", that Lord Jowitt was speaking when he said at the Seventh Legal Convention of the Law Council of Australia that if the problem of *Candler* v. *Crane, Christmas & Co.* came before the House of Lords, it would be decided in accordance with " the law " (1951) 25 A.L.J. 296. [It did not come before the House of Lords but was overruled by the House in *Hedley, Byrne* v. *Heller and Partners* [1964] A.C. 365. Ed.]

[34] The classical summary of the debate is to be found in the introduction by Saleilles to Gény's *Methode d'Interpretation.* Adapting Ihering's phrase " Through the Roman Law but beyond the Roman Law ", he says the two schools of thought are represented by (i) *Par le Code civil, mais au-dela du Code civil* (i.e. *libre récherche scientifique*), (ii) *Au-dela du Code civil, mais par le Code civil* (i.e. the use of analogy).

sents analogies to one of the debates among moral philosophers denoted by " absolute " and " relative " ethics.[35] The discourse of our authors is perhaps based on the intermediate position, for they give us reasons in support of their formula (i) that " it adequately explains all existing cases ", (ii) that it " appears to be socially equitable and expedient ".

(iii) Methods of Discourse

" Relativists " who maintain that new law should conform to existing law will in their discourse discuss existing law. Our authors, as has been seen, give much space to discussion of decided cases and to stating what they consider to be the principles behind the cases. They consider that cases can be " explained " not by reference to the actual reasoning of the judge, but by some principle they themselves elucidate. It is, of course, pertinent when submitting for acceptance a proposed rule of law to show that it produces the same beneficial results as a rule of law it is proposed to amend; but one does not repeal a rule of law by demonstrating that its effects can be produced in another way. It is a " technical " question of the doctrine of precedent whether the rule of law enunciated by a judge has binding authority. I have elsewhere supported the view of Hamson that the doctrine of precedent does not permit the " explanation " of cases by reference to rules not propounded by the judges. The authors appear to accept " explanation " as a method of exposition of case law.

The next stage in " relativist " law drafting is to consider the implications of existing law. This our authors do : and they reject a possible rule of law because, in their view, it is not " logically " consistent with existing law, or, in their own words, because it is not consistent with " legal logic ". In my view, their appeal to " logic " is actually an appeal to values more or less concealed, to policies for law of which they approve, but which do not appear to me to be accepted legal policy. I elaborate this assertion in a later section where, in considering the relation of law to logic, I consider also the general question of the distinction between logic and policy.

The last comment about the method of the discourse that I make at this stage is about the manner of extra-logical justification of rules. The authors refer to a range of terms. There are single words " convenience " and " expedience ", there are words qualified by the epithet " social ", so that we have the phrases " social expedience ", " socially equitable ", " interests of society ". Nowhere, however, is there any demonstration of the relationship of a rule to the concept : apparently the relationship is self-evident. The various terms are not even defined : again it may be that they have precise meanings known to everyone. I am not sure,

---

[35] Sidgwick uses " absolute ethics " to refer to the conduct of perfect men in an ideal society and " relative ethics " to refer to what ought to be the conduct of actual men in actual societies (as opposed to what is their conduct, which falls within the field of sociology). See *Methods of Ethics* (6th Edn. 1901), at p. 18. Spencer in his *Social Statics* had maintained that a system of relative ethics could not be devised.

however, whether the terms are synonyms or refer to distinct concepts: at any rate I shall use the phrase " social welfare " to refer to the single concept or aggregate of concepts. I shall endeavour to see how " social welfare " is involved in the problem of master's liability, and what light other social sciences throw on the relationship between master's liability and " social welfare ".

The Importance of a word in the respondeat superior doctrine: Baker[36]

(i) Exposition

Professor Baker in his article is content to describe the " puzzle ", as he calls it, which has arisen in connection with the doctrine of master's liability. He adds some comments, but makes no claim of solving the puzzle. The puzzle is the correctness of the new pattern of ripples caused by the effect on the previous uniformity of the dictum of Uthwatt J. in *Twine's* case.[24] Does *respondeat superior* mean that the *acts* of a servant are attributable to the master, or does it mean that the master is liable where a servant has committed a *tort* in the course of his employment? He finds a champion for the former view in Asquith L.J., who in *Conway's* case[37] exempted a master from liability because though the act causing damage was his responsibility, yet it created no liability since the master was under no duty. Professor Baker points out that this same view " solves " the difficulties which have been found in such cases as *Smith* v. *Moss*.[28] The act is the act of the master and the immunity the immunity of the servant. The fact that the servant could not be sued is irrelevant when considering the master's liability. Professor Baker puts forward Denning L.J. as a champion for the latter view, that of liability for torts, citing his judgment in *Young* v. *Edward Box & Co., Ltd.*[38]

In a survey of the case law Professor Baker deals with a number of authorities not cited by others, but finds no solution, though in his view such authority as there is supports the theory of responsibility for acts.[39]

---

[36] (1952) 2 *University of Queensland Law Journal:* 1. Professor Baker's later article in this journal was not available to me at the time of writing.

[37] [*Conway* v. *George Wimpey & Co. Ltd.* [1951] 1 All E.R. 363. Ed.]

[38] [1951] 1 T.L.R. 789. The case is not cited by Hughes and Hudson, nor in *Broom* v. *Morgan* ([1953] 1 All E.R. 849) where Denning L.J. champions most vigorously what Professor Baker calls the view of Asquith L.J., to which, according to Professor Baker, he was opposed in *Young* v. *Edward Box*. For the thesis that there is no inconsistency between the two judgments of Denning L.J. see the section in the text on law and logic, *post* 336 ff. There is a cleavage of judicial opinion in the cases of *Conway* v. *George Wimpey & Co. Ltd.* and *Young* v. *Edward Box & Co., Ltd.*: but Asquith and Denning L.JJ. are on the one side and Somervell and Singleton L.JJ. on the other. According to the former, a servant cannot license anyone to use his master's property unless he has actual authority. (See Asquith L.J. [1951] 1 All E.R. at 366 C and Denning L.J. [1951] 1 T.L.R. at 793). According to the latter, one who acts on the apparent authority of a servant may be a licensee. The Asquith-Denning doctrine is a strange one. One who acts on the apparent authority of an agent can clearly become a contractee. In the language of the law of property a contractee is a licensee, though not a " bare " licensee.

[39] He " misses " *Dyer* v. *Munday* [1895] 1 Q.B. 742, but this case, of course, should be counted as an " Asquith L.J. case." It had to be " explained " by Hughes and Hudson, whose views on the authorities are opposed to those of Professor Baker.

To throw light on the problem he turns first to the "history" of the doctrine and then to the "rationale". As regards history he finds that "digging in the past does not help us very much with this controversy" yielding only "isolated sentences".[40] The "rationale" is more helpful. He finds that "it is now generally agreed that notions of policy and justice are the only acceptable basis upon which the doctrine can rest". Where there is no rational scheme of accident insurance, he considers it socially desirable "that the operators of vehicles should be responsible for injuries negligently inflicted even upon uninvited passengers". He points out, as do other supporters of the "enterprise theory", that the owner of the enterprise can easily cover the cost by insurance and pass it on in the price paid by consumers.

Finally Professor Baker lends his support to the view expressed by Denning L.J. in *Young* v. *Edward Box & Co., Ltd.*[38] that since an owner of land may be under a duty to a trespasser, so too may an owner of a vehicle. In his view "logically there seems no ground for any differentiation".

(ii) *Type of Discourse*

The discourse is professedly mainly one of description of what the law is. The exposition of an alleged inconsistency between judicial statements does involve a reference to logic, albeit of a simple kind. On the other hand, the references to "history" and "rationale" are not necessarily extra-legal. The history referred to is very little more than a statement of early cases. There is no essential difference between exposition of early judicial statements and exposition of later judicial statements: nor does established usage of language prevent both being called "historical". The doctrine of precedent assumes that history is law.[41]

In order to decide whether discourse about "rationale" is descriptive of law or is meta-legal, it is necessary to attempt an analysis of the meaning of the word "rationale". A number of different meanings attach to the word and to its dictionary definition.[42] The reasons for a legal rule may be the social forces that have produced it, its historical causes, "rationale" being used to denote etiology. When "rationale" is used as equivalent to justification there may be a reference not to

---

[40] Professor Baker's findings are opposed to those of Hughes and Hudson. The latter state that "the earlier cases (for example, the judgments of Holt C.J. in *Hern* v. *Nichols* (c. 1700) 1 Salk. 289 and *Wayland's* case 3 Salk. 234) reveal a laconic readiness to accept the doctrine of a master's liability for his servant's acts as an unfortunately unnecessary solecism in the common law". Baker finds no such reluctance, and indicates that Holt was quick to recognise the needs of a century of expansion in commerce and industry for change in the law: he developed the law and based the new law on public policy.

[41] Some writers have entertained the view that early cases have greater authority than later ones. According to them the true law is to be found in the first case: any divergence from that law is unjustified legislation. Winfield's view, it will be recalled, was that the authority of cases was like wine; it improved with age for some time and then went off. Lord Goddard C.J. in *Terrell* v. *Colonial Secretary* has recently rejected the view that the content of a rule is fixed by its origin. See [1953] 2 All E.R. 490, 496 C.

[42] The Oxford English Dictionary merely substitutes (a) reasons (b) fundamental reasons for "rationale". A rationale of dictionary definition is needed.

causes but effects—to the results produced by the rule. Again the meaning of "rationale" may be that of teleology—what purposes had the legislator in mind, what effects did he hope to produce by the rule? The various meanings provide us with the fundamental questions of juristic criticism of laws. They are : (i) what is the purpose of a rule of law? (ii) does the rule achieve its purpose? (iii) what ought to be the purpose of a rule dealing with this particular topic? (iv) what rule of law would achieve such a desired purpose?[43]

Professor Baker begins his discussion of "rationale" by providing a definition when he says, "Many reasons have been put forward to justify this exception to the general principles of agency ";[44] nevertheless, it is clear that he has in mind purposes of the judicial legislator. He says, "It is now generally agreed that notions of policy and justice are the only acceptable basis upon which the doctrine can rest," and the context shows that the general agreement is that of the judges. But exposition of judicial purposes is not always equivalent to exposition of rules of law. A distinction exists between what may be called extrinsic purposes and intrinsic purposes. An intrinsic purpose delimits the ambit of a rule of law and is part of the content, just as is the "purpose" in any statutory rule which contains the phrase "for the purpose of ".[45] An extrinsic purpose is not part of the content of a rule; thus, so far as statutory rules are concerned, it may be set out in the preamble, and there is, of course, no compulsion to modify a section so that its effect may conform to the purpose expressed in the preamble,[46] though ambiguities may be resolved by reference to the preamble.[47] (Discourse about intrinsic purposes is exposition of law; discourse about extrinsic purposes may be considered meta-legal.) How far the distinction between intrinsic and extrinsic purposes can be made for rules of common law is doubtful. It can be argued that all judicial purposes are intrinsic : it has been said that *cessante ratione legis cessat lex ipsa* is a doctrine of the common law. On the other hand, a rule may be applied to circumstances in which its effects are different from those desired by its originators but are desired by the judge who applies the rule, and rules have been applied without regard to purposes. The purposes of the doctrine of *respondeat superior* mentioned by Professor Baker, *viz.*, the effectuation of "policy and justice" are, however, so vague that the

---

[43] Weldon points out that the discovery of the purpose of a rule is more difficult than the discovery of the purpose of particular action: see *Vocabulary of Politics* at p. 162. The difficulty is well known to lawyers in connection with " intention of Parliament ".

[44] Why " exception " ? Is it accurate to say that there is a general principle either in contract or tort that a master is liable only for the acts of a servant which were actually authorised?

[45] A random selection has produced s. 6, 15 Geo. III c. 62: " An Act for completing and maintaining the Pier at the Town of Mevagissey in the County of Cornwall ". An article could be devoted to the juristic character of this Act.

[46] This is the doctrine of *Ellerman Lines* v. *Murray* [1931] A.C. 126.

[47] Ambiguities may also be resolved by reference to purposes, even though they have not been expressed in the preamble. This is the *Rule in Heydon's Case.*

distinction between intrinsic and extrinsic purposes in relation to them is without significance.

The discussion of liability to trespassers does introduce a meta-legal note. Professor Baker appeals to a criterion of " logic " :[48] his use of the word " logic " is examined later.

(iii) Method of Discourse

Considerations of space have doubtless prevented Professor Baker from being able to do more than present in compendious manner the conclusions of his inquiry and from elaborating the exact character of the principles he has invoked. Judges are compelled to appear dogmatic in their reasoning through lack of time and jurists through lack of space. It is revealing to compare the full discussion that the analysis of a simple sentence of individual perception receives from the philosophers with the terse presentation by jurists of solutions of complex problems of social organisation. The bare invocation, as the rationale of master's liability, of the " notions of policy and justice " is insufficient in two ways. What exactly do " policy " and " justice " signify in this context, and in what manner does a rule of master's liability serve policy or achieve justice? Surely it is not only the doctrine of master's liability which has as its rationale " policy and justice ", but every rule of law : is there a specific manner in which the doctrine of master's liability operates in achieving these aims, or do all rules of law operate in the same manner?[49]

Professor Baker, after his discussion of the rationale, asks if it is " open to decide such an issue upon policy considerations ". This suggests that " policy " is used as a comprehensive term to include all purposes, all ends, all values to be achieved or maintained by rules of law. The phrase " policy and justice ", however, suggests that he may consider that policy is distinct from justice. It is certainly important to know whether an opposition of " justice " to " public policy ", which is asserted by some writers, is valid. Professor Baker considers that they co-operate : he says it might appear just that a master's burden should include responsibility for injury even to a trespasser, that it is socially desirable that operators of vehicles should be responsible for injuries inflicted upon even uninvited passengers. In this passage " policy " is replaced by " socially desirable ", without, however, adding much precision.

(i) Exposition
Broom v. Morgan[50]

This was a case where the plaintiff was injured by the careless act of her husband : (he had left open a trap door down which she fell). The

---

[48] Stone's doctrine that logic is extrinsic to law has been challenged. It appears to me that the terms of the proposition require analysis. The logic of inference appears to me an intrinsic part of legal reasoning. No judge would regard any reasoning as legally sound if he were satisfied that it was " logically " unsound.

[49] If, as the cynics say, justice is a matter of taste and feeling, there is no space for reasoning.

[50] [1953] 1 All E.R. 849.

act was in the course of her husband's employment and she sued his employer : (she also was employed by the defendant, but the defence of common employment has been abolished). She could not bring an action against her husband by virtue of s. 12 of the Married Women's Property Act, 1882. This was relied on by the master as a defence to the action against him. He said that a master is liable for the *torts* only of his servant; the husband had committed no tort, and so the master was not liable. All members of the Court of Appeal found in favour of the plaintiff.[51] Singleton and Hodson L.JJ. reasoned in a similar manner. Their initial premise is that the master would have been liable if the plaintiff had not been the spouse of the servant, or there had been no s. 12 of the Married Women's Property Act. The case thus turns upon the effect to be given to s. 12. They inquire into the content and the (extrinsic) purpose of the section. So far as content goes, the section presupposes that a tort has been committed, but denies suit to the spouse. Hodson L.J. (not using Hohfeldian language) says that this is " a substantive disability based upon public policy ".[52] So far as purpose goes the object is to prevent litigation between husband and wife because it would be " unseemly, distressing and embittering ".[53] The effect of the section should be limited to its purpose. If the effect were to deny suit to a plaintiff against someone other than the spouse, this would exceed the purpose : such litigation would not be " unseemly, distressing and embittering ". The sartorially surprising dictum of Cardozo J. is accepted : ". . . Though the law exempts the husband from liability for the damage others may not hide behind the skirts of his immunity.[54]

Hodson L.J. does in two sentences refer obliquely to the nature of a master's liability. He considers that the phrase " vicarious act " is more accurate than " vicarious liability ", and is apt to cover all cases

---

[51] They affirmed the judgment of Lord Goddard C.J. ([1952] 2 All E.R. 1007) and approved of the decision of Charles J. in *Smith* v. *Moss*.

[52] [1953] 1 All E.R. 856B. He disagreed with Denning L.J. who considered that s. 12 was purely procedural in the same way as the Statute of Frauds. I do not believe that there is any order of importance as between rules of substantive law and rules of procedure: both can be said to be based on public policy. But the difference is important: thus in conflict of laws different considerations apply to procedural and substantive rules.

[53] The quotation is from Winfield on *The Law of Tort* (4th edn. 1948) at p. 100. Winfield gives this as a better reason than what he calls the fiction of the common law that husband and wife are one flesh. Denning L.J. also calls the time-honoured phrase a fiction and says " that no longer has it any place in our law ". But surely even a fundamentalist would take the biblical quotation in metaphorical sense. What is meant is that husband and wife form a unity. Litigation between husband and wife is inimical to the integrity of family life. A denial of a general right to litigate is a recognition of the view that the welfare of the community is connected with the maintenance of the family as a unit.

[54] The quotation is taken from the judgment of Maxwell J. in *Waugh* v. *Waugh* (1950) 50 S.R. (N.S.W.) 210. The reasoning by reference to the purpose of the section is similar to that of the Court of Appeal in *Dyer* v. *Munday*. That reasoning, in the opinion of Hughes and Hudson, " evaded the issue ". They assume, however, that the effect of a section is always independent of its purpose. This is not so. Where there is doubt as to the application of a statute, it is well settled that regard may be had to the purpose, and the application limited to execution of the purpose.

whether the master is liable " directly or liable merely through the act of his servants ".[55] This recognises that a master may be liable both for the acts and torts of his servants.

The judgment of Denning L.J. is divided into two branches. In the first he affirms that a master's liability in respect of damage effected by the servant " is his own liability ", resulting from his being " morally responsible " for the damage. It is not a " true vicarious liability " arising from the liability of a servant though there is a " vicarious act ", because " the servant's act is his act ". Consequently, a master's liability " remains, notwithstanding, the immunity of the servant ".[56] The second branch deals with the situation on the assumption that a master " is only liable if his servant is also liable ". His reasoning in this case is similar to that of Singleton L.J. inasmuch as it is based on a consideration of s. 12 of the Married Women's Property Act. In his view, from which Hodson L.J. dissents, that section creates an immunity which " is a mere rule of procedure and not of substantive law ". The husband " is liable to his wife, although his liability is not enforceable by action, and as he is liable so also is the employer ".

Denning L.J. furnishes reasons for his view that a master is morally responsible for the harm done by a servant. " The reason for the master's liability," he says, " is the sound moral reason that the servant is doing the master's business, and it is the duty of the master to see that his business is properly and carefully done. He is himself under a duty to see that care is exercised in the driving of the lorry on his business. He takes the benefit of the work when it is carefully done and he must take the liability when it is negligently done."

(ii) Type of Discourse

These judgments all, of course, contain legal discourse, stating the judge's decision and the rule of law on which it is based. No one of the judges is, however, content to rely on authority for their views as to what is the law—neither their own judicial authority nor the authority of past judges: all give reasons. Singleton and Hodson L.JJ. consider the purpose of s. 12 of the Married Women's Property Act. That purpose is extrinsic to the section, but is perhaps intrinsic to a rule of law for application of statutes. Nevertheless, their discourse about purpose may be classified as juristic in the sense of meta-legal. The discourse of Denning L.J. about the basis of master's liability is clearly juristic:

---

[55] [1953] 1 All E.R. at 856 E. The judgment of Hodson L.J. followed that of Denning L.J. and the purpose of this sentence, as of that quoted above (see note 52), was to dissent from views expressed by Denning L.J. who appeared to have taken the view that a master was always " directly " liable.

[56] As already stated in note 38, Denning L.J. in this part of his judgment supports the doctrine of liability for *acts* of the servant, which Professor Baker has called the " view of Asquith L.J.", and to which he says Denning L.J. ran directly counter in *Young* v. *Edward Box & Co., Ltd.* Certainly, the two judgments of Denning L.J., the one in *Broom* v. *Morgan* ([1953] 1 All 849) and the other in *Young's* case, require some " explanations " if they are to be reconciled.

he is propounding a justification for the rule he enunciates, of direct liability of a master in respect of his servant's acts.

(iii) Method of Discourse

As already indicated, judgments, and particularly extempore ones, as were the judgments in *Broom* v. *Morgan*,[50] are not the place for a lengthy discussion of all the argument for and against the " goodness " of a rule of law. Singleton and Hodson L.JJ. briefly assert the purpose and justification of s. 12 of the Married Women's Property Act, 1882, without any inquiry at all into history or sociology. Denning L.J. makes a number of interesting comments about the morality of the doctrine of the liability of a master, but they are all assertions made without regard to consideration of the contrary view that a master who takes care to appoint competent servants, takes care to give them proper equipment and facilities, takes care to instruct them not to be negligent, is not morally responsible for his servant's negligence. He does not examine the meaning of morality, nor does he refer to any writer on morals. I discuss his notion of morality in the section on law and justice.

PART III.—LAW IN RELATION TO LOGIC, SOCIAL WELFARE AND JUSTICE

Law and logic

The above review of discourses had disclosed references to concepts which are considered in disciplines other than the law : there have been references to logic by the law teachers, to social welfare (under various other terms) also by them,[57] and to morality by Denning, L.J.[58] In the following sections I propose to consider the relation of law to logic, to social welfare and to justice, dealing with the treatment of these matters found in the articles and judgments and adding some general comments.

As Morris Cohen has shown, the difficulties as to the meaning of " law " and " jurisprudence " are equalled by those concerned with " logic ".[59] Nevertheless, there is one field which all agree falls within the field of logic, and whose character should be clearly appreciated when reference is made to logic. Morris Cohen has indeed limited all " logic " to this field. It is that of " the relation of implication between propositions ". In this sense logic does not concern itself with the truth

---

[57] Hodson L.J. also invokes " public policy ": [1953] 1 All E.R. 855 H.
[58] Professor Baker also refers to justice in his discussion of the rationale of master's liability.
[59] *A Preface to Logic*, Ch. 1 passim. The heading to the first section is " The subject matter of books on logic ". Collingwood attaches importance to the definition of a discipline by reference to the sentences that compose it. He would regard a definition of jurisprudence as " the subject matter of Professor Derham's lectures on Tuesday mornings " as possible, while " the science of law and justice " would be wrong because an understanding of what law and justice are is what it is hoped to achieve through jurisprudence. See *The New Leviathan*, ch. 1. passim.

of individual propositions but with the consistency of propositions asserted in reasoning.[60] There are axioms or postulates which logic employs; their validity is assumed, not demonstrated, by implicational logic: such an axiom is the doctrine of classical logic that a thing cannot be both A and not A. Their number is small, even in modern logic, which admits of some freedom in the choice of postulates.[4] Thus despite the differences among logicians as to the field of logic it is not a logician's practice to use the term " logical " as a criterion for the truth of an asserted proposition, unless the proposition is shown to follow " logically " from propositions whose truth is admitted, or unless the references be to the limited number of " logical " axioms.[61]

When, however, we turn to Professor Baker's article we find that he uses the term " logically " not in a logician's manner.[62] For logic " trespassers on land " and " trespassers on vehicles " are different terms, and from propositions involving one term no implication of propositions involving the other term can be made without the mediation of another proposition such as " trespassers on land are to be treated as trespassers on vehicles ", which, according to Professor Baker, is a proposition which is " logically " true. It is certainly not an axiom of logic, and Professor Baker makes no attempt to establish it as a conclusion from other propositions. Whether or not there is a ground for differentiation is a question of law not logic. Doubtless what Professor Baker means is that no valid argument can be asserted for differentiation between trespassers on land and on vehicles, but the validity of the premises used in the argument would not be determined by logic. So far as logic is concerned, it may be true that trespassers on vehicles are a greater source of danger to the community than trespassers on land, from which, with the aid of a number of other propositions no one would controvert, it could be " logically " shown that a ground for differentiation does exist.

The argument of Hughes and Hudson by which they purport to establish that a master's liability is a " true vicarious one in which he is only the automatic reflector of his servant's tort " also employs the words " logically " and, moreover, speaks of " inescapable conclusions ", a phrase reminiscent of logical necessity. They do, however, base some

---

[60] Cohen and Nagel: *Introduction to Logic and Scientific Method*, at p. 8.

[61] In ordinary language "logic" and " reason " are often synonymous. A note by Sidgwick is relevant to the statement in the text. " We do not commonly say that particular physical facts are apprehended by the Reason: we consider the faculty to be conversant in its discursive operation with the relation of judgments or propositions: and the intuitive reason (which is here rather in question) we restrict to the apprehension of universal truths, such as the axioms of Logic and Mathematics." *Methods of Ethics* (6th edn.) at p. 34, note 1. The note is on the passage in his text which says " the apprehension of moral truth is more analogous to Sense-perception than to Rational Intuition (as commonly understood)". Weldon dogmatically asserts that " The Law of Reason is logic "; he does provide a striking simile to explain that logicians' logic is not concerned with the truth of isolated propositions. Logical analysis, he says, can never prove or disprove the existence of anything, and this inability is not like the inability of an aged motor car to get over the Simplon Pass: it is like the inability of a motor car to write a poem or compose a symphony (*Vocabulary of Politics* at p. 116).

[62] See above p. 330 for the statement of Professor Baker.

of their premises on principles other than logic. The basis of their argument is that " it is socially inexpedient and legally nonsensical to hold a master liable for harm done by a servant for which the master could not be sued had he done the act himself ". [proposition (a)] : Whether or no it is socially expedient would appear to require some demonstration; is it not socially expedient to forbid the employment of agents for some purposes, e.g., because personality is important or to prevent the multiplication of acts; and if to forbid, why not to permit subject to liability for servants' acts more stringent than for one's own? But the question of social expedience comes later. What does " legally nonsensical " mean? The proposition so dubbed is certainly not illogical : " doing an act by a servant " is not identical with doing the act oneself : and so a legal proposition applicable to one may logically be inapplicable to another. If the phrase means contrary to a rule of law, the sentence merely affirms emphatically that the proposition is a rule of law. If so, what is the authority? The authors say—" *damnum sine injuria* done by the servant will obviously not fix liability on the master ". [proposition (b)] : Where there is no question of master and servant, the actions of one individual alone being concerned, it is tautology to say that *damnum sine injuria* gives rise to no liability. But where there is a question of master and servant, then the fact that an act of the servant is *sine injuria,* so far as the servant is concerned, does not " obviously " make it *sine injuria* for the master; nor does the fact that the act, if performed by the master, would have been *sine injuria,* make it obviously *sine injuria* so far as the master is concerned when performed by the servant. These are the very questions in issue in the argument. Proposition (b) is indeed the proposition the authors are setting out to prove. However, what they infer from proposition (a) is that a master is not " liable for any harm that the servant does in the course of his employment " [proposition (c)]. From this it certainly follows, as the authors say, that it must logically be only a certain kind of harm which can make the master liable [proposition (d)].[63]

The authors explain that by " kind of harm " they mean harm produced by a kind of act : and they proceed to examine " what quality must be present in the servant's act to render the master liable ". They then return to the reasoning of Cardozo C.J. for the purpose of repeating their rejection of it.[64] They cannot accept the view that the quality of the servant's act, which will render the master liable, is that of being " wrong ", for " there is extreme danger in any doctrine based on the idea of a ' wrong ' as opposed to a tort ". This looks like assuming that there is only one skittle to be knocked down. But have they knocked

---

[63] The sequence in the text attempts to follow the "logic " of the authors. It departs from their spatial order. They set out the propositions in the order: c, b, a, d. Proposition d does, however, follow directly from c. Proposition c, however, appears more " obvious " than either a or b.

[64] See above p. 326.

down the skittle by "logic"? Indeed the questions arise, whether they have knocked down the skittle at all and whether "logic" cannot demonstrate that their ball has missed the mark.

The doctrine that there is extreme danger in basing a rule of law on "wrong" is one of legal policy. Our authors do not state specifically what the danger is: but it may be conjectured, though they use the phrase "dangerous and uncertain", that the danger is that of uncertainty. The policy upon which they appear to rely is that legal rules must be in precise terms and cannot include such indefinite ideas as those of social or moral wrong. Their desire for a "technical statement" makes the conjecture more likely. But even if the policy is sound, it does not follow that legal doctrines cannot be "based on the idea of a 'wrong' as opposed to a tort". Nor does their conclusion follow, viz., "the servant's act cannot be legally regarded as a wrong unless we invest it with the technical apparel of a tort". The phrase "based on" contains an ambiguity: it may refer either to the internal content or the external origin of a rule. An indefinite moral notion may supply the unmapped underground sources of a rule which is canalised by legal processes: specific aspects of a moral notion may be selected to form the content of a legal rule. The moral notion thus forms the basis of the rule. If one asks why the rule contains those elements, the answer is a reference to the moral notion. A rule of law may say that the careless act of a servant imposes legal liability on the master: to the question why, the answer can be made that a servant is under a moral obligation not to be careless. Indeed, it has been contended that the specific character of the legal function is to put into precise rules extra-legal notions. Whence, it may be asked, come the concepts in legal rules? Are they not derived from such considerations as social and moral wrong, administrative convenience, characteristics of human nature? Is there a specific quality of legal wrong? It is possible to oppose benevolence to justice, but the doctrine that rules of law cannot be based on general notions of wrong isolates justice completely from law.

The logical defect in the argument appears more clearly when we examine their conclusion. This is, of course, logically "based on" the general proposition that no act can be legally regarded as a "wrong" unless we invest it with the technical apparel of a tort. This is, of course, a tautology if "technical apparel of a tort" means merely "legally regarded as a 'wrong'". If it means "gives rise to an action for tort", the proposition runs counter to the facts that acts may amount to crimes or breaches of contract without being torts. Even within the sphere of the law of tort, judges who do not accept the view that the categories of tort are closed, inquire whether acts are "wrong".

The question whether acts not covered by authority are tortious or not cannot be answered if the authors' proposition is followed, for it would lead one to say that they are tortious if they are tortious.

So far we have examined statements which have been explicitly said to be " logical ". Implicit, however, in the two articles is the view that there is an opposition between the principle that a master is liable for the torts of his servants and the principle that he is liable for the acts of his servants. This requires examination. As a preliminary point it should be made clear that it is not suggested that anyone contends that the two propositions thus formulated are completely exclusive of each other. The act of a servant may be the breach of a duty owed by the servant, and thus a " servant's tort ", and also constitute, when attributed to the master, the breach of a duty owed by him. This indeed may be the normal case : and those who maintain that the master is liable for the acts of his servant do not mean that a master is never liable if the servant's acts constitute a tort of the servant. The main point is that the formula of liability for acts is too general. There are two distinct propositions included in it, deriving as legal rules from two distinct classes of cases. On the one hand, there is the rule of *Smith* v. *Moss*[28] and *Broom* v. *Morgan* :[50] on the other, the rule of *Twine* v. *Bean's Express Ltd.*[24] and *Conway* v. *George Wimpey.*[37] When Denning L.J. says in *Broom* v. *Morgan* that the doctrine of master's liability is one of vicarious *acts,* he is asserting that a master may be liable notwithstanding that the act of the servant is not tort of the servant. When Uthwatt J. in *Twine* v. *Bean's Express Ltd.* says the law attributes to the employer the acts of a servant, he is asserting that notwithstanding that the acts of a servant constitute a tort of the servant within the scope of employment, the master may not be liable. The principle asserted by Uthwatt J. is inconsistent with the principle asserted by Denning L.J. in *Young* v. *Edward Box & Co., Ltd.*[38] that a master is always liable for the torts of a servant committed within the scope of his employment. The principle asserted by Denning L.J. in *Broom* v. *Morgan* is not inconsistent. It is thus both logically possible and impossible to have rules that a master is liable for the torts of his servant *and* for the acts of his servant : it all depends on what is meant by liability for acts.

The propositional logic of implications, as has been seen, cannot answer ultimate legal questions as what is or ought to be the rule of law on a given topic. It may demonstrate errors in reasoning, but so far as the truth of individual propositions is concerned it is confined to truths about the reasoning process. It is believed that these remarks are true for all types of logic, the logic of terms as well as the logic of propositions, inductive as well as deductive, modern as well as classical. This, however, does not, of course, deny the utility of logic for law, but it does help to refute the claims of pseudo-logic. " Logic " is not, however, entirely destructive : one of its uses is the construction of a scheme of logical possibilities, which is essential for release from routine and for the development of the faculty of invention. The construction of such a scheme in connection with the problem of the liability of a master may serve, not only as an illustration, but also as a means of providing a warning against the pseudo-logic of " the theory of deciding cases by the application of existing concepts " (a suggested translation of *Begriffs-jurisprudenz*).

Analysis of the problem of the liability of a master may lead to the view that three elements are involved : (i) the status of the plaintiff; is he a trespasser or licensee so far as the master is concerned? (ii) the relation of the servant's act to the scope of employment; is it within or without the scope? (iii) the nature of the servant's act; was it a tort of the servant or not? These are the elements suggested by the case law on the subject. Given these three concepts, it is a simple matter of " permuting " to see that there are sixteen possible rules of law. These are set out in the accompanying table.

TABLE OF RULES

	Status of Plaintiff	Relation of Act to Exployment	Nature of Act	Liability of Master
1	Trespasser	Outside the Scope	Tortious	Liable
2	,,	,,	,,	Not Liable
3	,,	,,	Non-tortious	Liable
4	,,	,,	,,	Not Liable
5	,,	Within the Scope	Tortious	Liable
6	,,	,,	,,	Not Liable
7	,,	,,	Non-tortious	Liable
8	,,	,,	,,	Not Liable
9	Licensee	Outside the Scope	Tortious	Liable
10	,,	,,	,,	Not Liable
11	,,	,,	Non-tortious	Liable
12	,,	,,	,,	Not Liable
13	,,	Within the Scope	Tortious	Liable
14	,,	,,	,,	Not Liable
15	,,	,,	Non-tortious	Liable
16	,,	,,	,,	Not Liable

The rules are *logically* possible : whether any particular rule should be accepted depends not on logical but legal considerations. Thus rule 3, that a master should be liable to a trespasser in respect of the non-tortious acts of a servant without the scope of his employment, is logically possible, though no one would suggest it for enactment. So too rule 14, that a master is not liable for the tortious acts of a servant within the scope of employment committed in respect of the licensee of the master, is logically possible, though, again, no one would suggest it for enactment. Though any one rule is logically possible, all are not logically possible as simultaneously valid rules : each pair of rules, e.g., 1 and 2 are contradictory. On the other hand, some of the rules may be simultaneously valid : thus rules 5, 7, 13 and 15 are cumulative.[65]

---

[65] Denning L.J. considers that rules 5, 13 and 15 are all valid. For rules 5 and 13 authority is to be found in his judgment in *Young* v. *Edward Box, & Co. Ltd.* For rule 15, there is his judgment in *Broom* v. *Morgan*, but that judgment does not extend to all non-tortious acts.

This cumulative possibility points to the possibility of the redundancy of some of the concepts: instead of three being determinative of a legal rule, it is possible to frame a rule incorporating only one or two of the concepts. It is logically possible to have as a rule that a master is liable in respect of all his servant's acts committed within the scope of employment, irrespective of whether the act be tortious or not and irrespective of the status of the plaintiff. The process of "widening down from precedent to precedent" takes the form of reducing the number of concepts in a rule. It is thus contrary to a theory of *fixed* concepts which is the evil aimed at when *Begriffsjurisprudenz* is condemned. Legal rules must embody concepts: but it is wrong to assume that the concepts hitherto employed are necessary. Like rules of law concepts are man-made and may be altered to suit man's needs. The raw material of life may be grouped in many ways to produce a variety of concepts. Whether or not there are fixed species is a matter of natural science: that there are no fixed concepts may be regarded as part of the "logic of terms": so that *Begriffsjurisprudenz* so far from being logical is only pseudo-logical. The facts of previous cases are capable of reclassification, and some later generation may find acceptable reasons for employing concepts other than those of trespasser, licensee, scope of employment and so on. There is no logical reason why the class of trespassers should not be sub-divided: thus there is no logical reason that all trespassers should be dealt with in the same way, nor is there any logical reason why they should not. Thus the master might be liable, as Denning L. J. and Professor Baker suggest, to some trespassers in some circumstances, but not liable in other circumstances. The bare classification in the table of acts as being tortious or non-tortious is clearly inadequate having regard to existing case law. While liability exists in respect of some non-tortious acts, it does not exist in respect of others. Hughes and Hudson have as their classification (a) acts which are either torts or *prima facie* torts, (b) acts which are neither torts nor *prima facie* torts. The construction of concepts involves the construction of rules of law, and the content of legal concepts is determined by legal policy, not logic. The error of "mechanical" or "conceptualist jurisprudence" (to provide other translations for *Begriffsjurisprudenz*) is to believe that there are concepts fixed in number and nature to which there can be neither addition nor change.

Law and social welfare

The theory that the purpose of law is the common good is one of the oldest doctrines of legal philosophy, and from it is derived the name of the Commonwealth of Australia. It is, however, by no means universally accepted, and among those who do accept it there are many differences of opinion as to what is the common good and how it may be achieved. Its critics, and some of its supporters, indeed regard propositions asserting that actions lead to the common good as being but matters of " opinion ". I cannot here examine fully the doctrine of social welfare (a phrase I regard as equivalent to " common good "), but what is said in the articles under review needs comment.

Hughes and Hudson, as has been said, neither use the phrase " common good " nor " social welfare ". They do, however, accept the view that the general doctrine of master's liability is based on " public policy " : the doctrine that an employer is liable for harm carelessly done by his servant to the spouse of the servant is justified by " social expediency ", and the particular principle they advocate is supported by the statement that it is " socially equitable and expedient ". The only hint as to the meaning of these phrases is supplied by the extract they quote from Fifoot's *English Law and its Background,* a passage which they say " sums up the traditional attitude of the Courts to the topic ".[66] Fifoot says that before 1852 " the judges were reverting to an open avowal of convenience as the basis of their doctrine. After that date the doctrine was accepted as a generalisation to be justified not as a deduction from legal premises but as a sacrifice to public policy." Our authors themselves said the doctrine was " long established on grounds of obvious expedience and convenience ". The reference supported by their desire to narrow the limits of the doctrine, is that they consider there is some opposition between legal policy and public policy, between some basic legal principle and social welfare. Certainly there are many who consider that " morality " and " social welfare " may be opposed, regarding morality as individualistic. But whether or no the English law is committed to individualism for its basic legal policy, making concessions to social welfare on grounds of expediency, should be expressly discussed. Holmes would surely say that the common law no more than the United States constitution incorporates the principles of Spencer's *Social Statics.* How far legal principles ought to be based on notions of individual morality or social welfare is a basic issue which lawyers can only neglect at the cost of being executives of policies created by others.

Professor Baker, it has been seen, uses both the term " justice " and " policy " : he speaks of social necessities and requirements of justice and of a rule being both just and socially desirable. It would appear that for him there is no opposition between " justice " and " social welfare ", but, of course, it is not possible from his brief remarks to say that he adopts the view that what is just is for the social welfare, and what is for the social welfare is just. He does furnish some indications as to what he means by socially desirable, though conjecture is also required. Presumably it is the sense of security of the individual against the financial consequences of injury which is considered socially desirable : those incapacitated from earning a living should be furnished with the means of subsistence. Against this view, of course, some have argued that

---

[66] It will be recalled that in their view Holt C.J. considered the doctrine of master's liability an " unfortunately unnecessary (sic) solecism on the common law ".

security leads to lack of effort by the individual. But the doctrine of employer's liability involves also the social desirability of the compensation payable to the injured plaintiff coming from the employer. The cost of this compensation, it is assumed, may be passed on to the consumer, but is it socially desirable to increase the cost to the consumer? If not, does a felicific calculus show that the social desirability of compensating the plaintiff outweighs the undesirability of increasing prices? If the cost of compensation cannot be passed on to the consumer is there a disincentive to the owner arising from the reduction in his profits? And is this disincentive socially desirable or not?

It is submitted that such questions as these, concerned with social welfare, do necessarily arise in the consideration of the problem of master's liability as in other legal discussions. How are these questions to be answered? By the common sense of lawyers, by lawyers adopting "scientific method", or by lawyers referring the questions to social scientists?

Law and justice

Long before the rise of modern logic and semantics the difficulties surrounding the use of the word "justice" were a commonplace of learned discourse.[67] Some of the difficulties are concerned with its range of meanings. The phrase "social welfare" has also many meanings, and thus there are many relationships which may be indicated by the phrase "the relation between justice and social welfare". For one set of meanings identity exists between the terms, for another, contradiction, while for others the relation is that of difference. Thus, for those who regard "justice" as indicating the quality exhibited by good laws and for whom, like Austin, utility is the test of goodness of laws, "justice" is identical with "social welfare". Some who hold this view consider that utility or social welfare may be determined by "experience", in other words, that the concept is ultimately of a factual character, and though they reject the "felicific calculus" of Bentham, accept as a criterion some combination of vital statistics like infant mortality rates, judicial statistics like crime rates, social statistics like numbers of houses built, and economic statistics like productivity indexes. There are, however, many who hold that the goodness or justice of a law or a legal system is not to be determined by the desirability of its consequences. They may not proceed to the extreme of saying *fiat justitia ruat coelum,* for their faith is that so long as justice is done the skies will not fall : but they do aver that the concept of justice represents a value judgment, dependent on the intrinsic character of the action required by a rule of law rather than on its social effects, a character which cannot be wholly stated in descriptive terms, but involves the category of "ought".

In this section I am concerned with the use of the term "justice"

---

[67] Cardozo—*Growth of the Law*, p. 81.

as indicating some quality other than that of social welfare.[68] I am, of course, not concerned with the analysis of all such uses of the term " justice ", but with the way in which the concept of justice was invoked in the three discourses under review. Nevertheless, a further general note is required. Aristotle stated that the Greek for justice, *dikaiosune, to dikaion,* had both a general and a limited meaning. In the broader sense it was equivalent to the whole of goodness : a " just man " was one who exemplified all the virtues of the good citizen. In the narrower sense " justice " referred to but one particular virtue. It is my view that the English word " justice " is used in a similar way in both a wide and a strict meaning. Sidgwick denies this,[69] but he must have ignored legal writings where often " justice " is the word used when a distinction is sought to be drawn between what is the law and what ought to be the law. In reading legal writing it is necessary to ask whether the writer means by " just " in accordance with what ought to be the law, or in accordance with a concept of " particular justice ", one criterion of many involved in a determination of what ought to be the law. A law may be said to be " just " in a wider sense though it offends a canon of " particular justice ". Thus it may be said that though a law involves hardship to innocent people (" unjust " according to one view of " particular justice "), it is, nevertheless, " just " in the wider sense. On the other hand, there are some who would say that if a law offends the canon of equality of incidence (a very commonly held notion of the nature of " particular justice "), it is to be described as " unjust " no matter what other merits it possesses.

I must confess that I am not sure whether Baker, in using the word " just ", had in mind a broad or a narrow meaning. Hughes and Hudson do not use the word " just ", but employ instead the equally vague term " equitable ", without affording me a clue as to the sense in which they employed it. Nor did Denning L. J. use the word " justice "; he employed instead the terminology of " morality ", but he did illustrate his use of that terminology. I discuss his language under the heading " law and justice ", for I apprehend that in the context he meant by " moral " a non-utilitarian view of " right ", and that his language was synonymous with that of " justice " as used by me in this section.

Denning L. J. was concerned to show that the doctrine of employer's liability was a just one, in the strict sense of that term. It was not justified as being socially desirable for reasons of social welfare; it

---

[68] It has already, I hope, been made clear that I am not using " justice " to indicate the quality of being in accordance with law.

[69] *Method of Ethics* (6th edn.), ch. v, at p. 264, note 2. " Aristotle, in expounding the virtue of *dikaiosune*, which corresponds to our Justice, notices that the word has two meanings: in the wider of which it includes in a manner all Virtue, or at any rate, the social side or aspect of Virtue generally. The word ' Justice ' does not appear to be used in English in this comprehensive manner (except occasionally in religious writings, from the influence of the Greek word as used in the New Testament), although the verb ' to justify ' seems to have this width of meaning."

was in accordance with justice. "The reason for the master's liability is not the mere economic reason that the employer usually has money and the servant has not. It is the sound moral reason that the servant is doing the master's business, and it is the duty of the master to see that his business is properly and carefully done."[70] On the other hand, he thought that "true vicarious liability" did not accord with morality. He described such liability as "a substituted liability whereby a person who is not morally answerable is made responsible for the liability of another". Both these propositions repay examination.

The injustice of vicarious liability has often been described, in language employed by Professor Baker, as consisting in the infliction of suffering on an innocent person.[71] This, however, is to limit the inquiry to the morality of punishment. It is necessary to consider whether A may be "morally answerable" to pay money to B, not because A has wronged B, but for some other reason. The award of damages to B may not be the punishment of A, but the enforcement of a moral duty on the part of A to care for B. A duty to protect the children of the poor is not necessarily limited to a duty to punish the wrongdoer.[72] There are moral notions which have been stated in the language of justice and which say that, though A is in no way to blame for the harm which B has suffered, yet it is just, and not merely benevolent or charitable, for A to relieve B's suffering.

Denning L. J. in seeking to show that a master is "morally answerable" to compensate a plaintiff for the loss he has sustained as the result of the servant's negligence, bases his argument on the morality of punishment: the master is not an innocent person, but one who has been guilty of wrongdoing since he has failed to carry out "a duty to see that care is exercised in the driving of the lorry on his business". In my opinion, however, the judgment does not take adequate account of the relevant distinctions. Three duties have to be distinguished: (i) a moral duty to see that no harm is caused to others, (ii) a "moral" duty to compensate others for harm they have suffered, (iii) a legal duty to compensate others for harm they have suffered. The justification for (iii) may be (i) or (ii), for they are not identical. According to an individualistic morality of an extreme kind no one is under a moral duty to compensate unless he has been guilty of the breach of a moral duty to see that no

---

[71] Hughes and Hudson consider that the principle they assert as lying behind the liability of a master is "socially equitable", but their article also cites, apparently with approval, the view of others that vicarious liability is to be justified only on grounds of expedience, "as a sacrifice to public policy".

[71] An Arabian condemnation of vicarious liability is related by E. V. Lucas in *A Boswell of Baghdad* (Methuen: 1917, at p. 37). "Al-Hajjaj said to the brother of Katari 'I shall surely put thee to death'. 'Why so?' replied the other. 'On account of thy brother's revolt' answered Al-Hajjaj." Al-Hajjaj did not, however, carry out his decree, for Katari showed that it was unjust; one of his arguments was: "The book of Almighty God says 'And no burdened soul shall bear the burden of another'".

[72] On the wall of the Central Criminal Court building in London (the Old Bailey) is inscribed the text "Punish the wrongdoer and defend the children of the poor."

harm is done. While such a view would be condemned by many as unduly selfish, doubtless there are many who would regard a duty to compensate, which did not arise out of the breach of a duty against harm doing, as being a duty of benevolence and not of justice. Among such persons there are those who accept a political doctrine that legal duties should not be based on benevolence but on " justice ". But there is another moral doctrine which has found many advocates. It has been said that " social justice "[73] may require one person to compensate another for the loss the latter has suffered though the former is not to blame for the occurrence of the loss. The " welfare state " imposes legal duties to pay taxes which are used to assist others in need through no fault of the taxpayer : and it may be that the doctrine of master's liability is based on the justice of the welfare state.[74]

The manner in which Denning L.J. has failed to pay regard to the distinctions between these duties is this. He has the first duty in mind when he says that the master " is himself under a duty to see that care is exercised in the driving of the lorry on his business ". Conceived as the statement of such a duty, the statement is elliptic. When expanded it becomes a complex of duties. They are (a) to employ only competent drivers, (b) to give drivers adequate instructions for the careful discharge of their tasks, (c) to give drivers adequate facilities for the careful discharge of their tasks. It is possible for a master to perform those duties and yet for the servant to be negligent. It is submitted, moreover, that even if the above catalogue of a master's personal duties be incomplete, nevertheless, there is no logical connection between the discharge of the master's personal duties and absence of negligence by the servant. The mere commission of negligence by a servant cannot necessarily involve the master in the breach of a personal duty. All moral duties are duties relating to the subject's own acts. Nevertheless, Denning L.J. continues : " If the driver is negligent there is a breach of duty, not only by the driver himself, but also by the master. In support of this view I would observe that the master and the servant are held in law to be joint tort-feasors ". This statement involves a transference from the first duty to the third duty. Denning L.J. is no longer juristically giving the reason for a rule of law, he is judicially declaring what the law is. He is asserting that a master is under a legal duty to compensate a plaintiff where his servant has been negligent; he is providing no justification for the rule. When we turn to the statement that the master " takes the benefit of the work when it is carefully done, and he must take the

---

[73] " Social justice " is, of course, also a vague term. See Lewis and Maude (*Professional People*, at p. 82). " The principles, and therefore the implication of this, are impossible to define for they depend entirely on the personal views or emotions of individuals. There are no absolute standards of social justice ". But such a statement can be made with equal truth or falsity of " justice ".

[74] Taxation for " welfare " purposes is, of course, much older than the welfare state. Specific legal duties of benevolence were enforced in the first state of Israel " Thou shalt not glean thy vineyard, neither shalt thou gather every grape of thy vineyard; thou shalt leave them for the poor and stranger ". *Leviticus* 19, 10.

Y

liability when it is negligently done ", it appears that it is a duty of the
second kind to which reference is made. I would agree that the basis
of the liability of a master can be explained in terms of the second class
of duty, but the nature of the duty requires more elaborate exposition than
that contained in the succinct statement of Denning L.J.

It is desirable in the first place to refer to a general principle involved in the relation between law and justice, between legal duties and
moral duties, which is often overlooked even by writers on the subject.
I will call the principle, using a name of a phrase suggested by the
Pirque Aboth, that of " the hedge round the law ".[75] Rules of law may
have a moral justification, even though they embrace proscriptions of
moral as well as immoral acts. The justification for the proscription of
moral acts arises from the necessity for generality in rules of law and
from the morality of proscribing the immoral acts. Thus it could be
argued that the justification for making an employer liable if the servant
causes harm is not that the particular employer has necessarily failed in
his own duty, but that there is applied to him a general rule aimed at
preventing employers generally from failing to observe their moral duties
to their neighbours. The particular employer is made liable because (a)
no practicable test exists for distinguishing the two types of cases, those
where the employer has behaved immorally and those where he has
behaved morally, (b) to allow the distinction to be made might lead to a
lowering of standards by employers.[76]

The doctrine of the " hedge " is required to supply the missing
premise in many theories where general principles are justified by means
of arguments applicable only to a narrow range of instances. The
" enterprise " theory of the liability of a master, invoked by Professor
Baker, is an example of such a theory. The argument is that the owner
of an enterprise is not harmed by a general principle of liability for the
negligence of his servants, for he can pass on that liability to the whole
body of consumers of the products sold by the enterprise, by the simple
means of including the amount of compensation in the costs of the enterprise. The consumers, moreover, do not suffer because the individual
cost to each of them is so small. But the principle of employer's liability
is not limited to the owners of " enterprises "; it extends also to the injury
which a plaintiff suffers through the negligent act of a single domestic

---

[75] The opening sentences of the *Pirque Aboth* (Sayings of the Fathers) say: " Moses
received the law from Sinai, and delivered it to Joshua and Joshua to the elders and the
elders to the prophets and the prophets delivered it to the men of the Great Synagogue. They
said three things. Be deliberate in judgment; raise up many disciples; and make a fence
about the law". The principle in this text is that of imposing additional restrictions on
men so that they are kept at a safe distance from forbidden ground. It they never break
any of the additional restrictions, they will certainly never break any of the provisions of
the law itself. If they endeavour to keep the additional restrictions, but fail through human
weakness, they may, nevertheless, not commit a breach of the law.

[76] On the other hand, it might be argued that knowledge on the part of an employer,
that the utmost care by him will not relieve him of liability is not an incentive to take care.
The discussion is, to some extent, unrealistic because of the practice of insuring.

servant committed in the course of duties discharged from an infirm and needy widow.[77]

The doctrine of the hedge suggests a possible mode of basing the doctrine of master's liability on the moral duty not to cause harm to others. The doctrine, however, appears more firmly based when it rests on a moral duty to compensate for harm done by one's blameless acts. Such a moral duty may be derived from the broader moral duty that " thou shalt love thy neighbour as thyself ", an injunction to be found even in the legalistic and ritualistic context of *Leviticus*.[78] The majority of jurists, however, deny that this moral duty can be the basis of a legal duty; and indeed would define a legal duty based on justice by contrasting it with a moral duty based on love. Lord Atkin in *Donoghue* v. *Stevenson*[79] regarded it as self-evident that the only legal correlative of the basic injunction of Judaeo-Christian morality was " thou shalt not harm thy neighbour ". But there have been jurists who have maintained that the moral duty of love can be, and has been, translated into legal regulations. A legal duty to compensate others for harm sustained in consequence of one's blameless actions can be regarded as one way in which the general moral obligation of positive action for the benefit of one's neighbour can be reduced to the legal rule. It is Stammler who has dealt most fully with the theory proclaimed by Shelley in the lines " . . . justice is the light of love and not revenge . . ."

For Stammler the " pure idea " of law consists in the duty of co-operation which exists among men in society.[80] Human life necessitates a struggle for existence in which men can only succeed as a result of social co-operation. The physical fact of interdependence is mirrored as the result of intellectual reflection in the idea of justice, which is made applicable by means of rules to the facts of everyday life, through the basic principles of respect of man for man as an individual and participation of man with man in social life. The social ideal cannot be fully set out if the principle of participation is ignored, and that principle is the legal correlative of the duty to love one's neighbour.

Stammler does not ignore the question " Who is my neighbour?" He did realise that a man has many neighbours and that duties may conflict. He dealt with this problem by the notion of different degrees

---

[77] At first sight it may appear that the doctrine of the " hedge " is merely that of administrative convenience and that it represents a device for the ease of administrators indifferent to the distinction between justice and injustice. The religious doctrine of the " fence about the law " calls attention to the duty of doing more than a religious obligation strictly requires in order to make sure the obligation is performed. There is a direct parallel to this in the political doctrine of the hedge, and also an indirect one. The latter arises in the following way. Where governors and governed, administrators and citizens, conceive themselves as co-operators in the maintenance of moral standards, then such social co-operation gives rise to a moral duty that the citizen accept a liability imposed on him though he personally has acted morally. The reason is that the liability is derived from a rule designed to ensure the observance of moral standards by others.

[78] *Leviticus*—19, 18.

[79] [1932] A.C. 562.

[80] *The Theory of Justice*, ch. v., passim.

of neighbourliness. A duty to a near neighbour may outweigh a greater duty to a remote neighbour. The degrees of neighbourliness are, in part, fixed by customary social practices, but they are also affected by the transactions in which a man participates and the circumstances in which he finds himself : the good citizen, like the good Samaritan, may find that his closest neighbour is not his next of kin, but the man " who cannot maintain natural existence " without assistance from him.

Stammler's theory and model of just law have been severely criticised as hopelessly vague and impracticable.[81] His critics forget that the " model " he suggested was not a geometry of neighbourly relations or an arithmetic of duties : in order to solve a problem of just law according to the model " *prout sapiens determinat* ". It operates not by differential equations, but by human judgment; a judgment, however, determined in its broad direction by the theory. Let us see if it helps at all in the consideration of the doctrine of master's liability. We must ask in the first place whether the master is a " neighbour " at all to a plaintiff injured by a servant. If he is a neighbour, a duty to assist arises from the mere fact of his having suffered an unanticipated loss. But in the United Kingdom, at any rate, if we consider that all members of the community are our neighbours, the obligations of a general community relationship are discharged through contributions by way of taxes to national welfare schemes. Does an employer stand in some special community relationship to the injured person? He certainly stands in relations of special community to his own employees : compensation paid to injured persons will diminish the fund available for distribution among employees. Where a person is injured by the negligence of an employee, the rough equity of common sense suggests that the claim of employees generally is deferred, though they are closer to the owner of the fund, to the claim of the injured person who usually has no claim on the fund. Thus an employer may be said to be justly liable to compensate a plaintiff injured by the negligence of a servant, but not justly liable to compensate a plaintiff whose injuries are not due to negligence.[82]

It may be considered that " *sapientia* " has not been displayed either in the selection of a model or in its application. Are there any other methods to be considered in an attempt to solve the problem of the justice of master's liability?[83] The " social engineering " of Pound

---

[81] Ginsberg on Stammler in *Modern Theories of Law* (ed. Jennings).

[82] The doctrine of the hedge has to be brought in to justify positive legal rules which make no inquiry into the financial status of the plaintiff, and give compensation of equal amount to the rich man, whose Rolls Royce is scratched and to the poor man whose, barrow, on which his livelihood depends, is ruined.

[83] Cardozo speaks of a judge having four methods available—the methods of logic, of history, of sociology, of philosophy. He warns against rigid adherence to the single method. " We must learn to handle our tools, to use our methods and processes, not singly, but together. They are instruments of advance to be employed in combination. The failure to combine them, the use of this method or that as if one were exclusive of the other, has been the parent of many wrongs ". *Growth of the Law* at p. 108. Is anything altered in substance if for Cardozo's language of the employment of the methods of logic, history, sociology and philosophy we substitute the consideration of claims of certainty, adaptability, welfare and justice?

has been criticised for neglecting concepts other than those of material welfare; such welfare claims, however diverse, may be regarded as basically similar so that their adjustments call but for quantitative treatment. But the theory can be extended to encompass notions other than those of " welfare " in the material sense. The structure to be built by social engineering may be regarded as having as its component elements spiritual as well as material welfare : corrective and distributive justice as well as happiness may have to be considered, freedom as well as security, peace as well as adventure. It could be argued (a) that the careful employer is morally blameless and morally irresponsible for the injury sustained by a plaintiff whether the servant causing the injury was negligent or not, (b) that it is socially desirable that an injured plaintiff receive assistance from the servant's employer, whether the servant was negligent or not, (c) that as a resultant of these considerations, the careful employer is not liable to an injured plaintiff when his servant has not been negligent, but is liable when the servant has been negligent. But in this extended task of social engineering, how do we ascertain that all the requisite components have been assembled? How is the strength of each estimated? How do we determine the design which combines them into a stable and function-fulfilling structure?

Jurisprudence, social science and philosophy

An examination of the possible justification of the doctrine of master's liability by reference to the concepts of social welfare and justice has yielded a series of questions, which, it is submitted, the discourses under review do not answer. The questions arise as the result of an attempted analysis of the concepts of social welfare and justice which have been invoked in the discourses. It is relevant to consider whether such analysis should be made in the course of a survey of a legal doctrine. If Stone's thesis be correct, that criticism of law is in terms of other disciplines, it may be that the analysis of the concepts under review is not for the lawyer or jurist but for the social scientist or philosopher. There is, however, in the discourses no explicit references to the work of social scientists or philosophers, nor does there appear to me to be any implicit reference. The thesis of this section of this article is that a reference to the work of social scientists and philosophers would not have proved fruitful. Social scientists and philosophers do not appear in dealing with these concepts to have considered such questions as a doctrine of master's liability, nor to have dealt with the concepts in such a way as to make it easy for a lawyer to apply their doctrines to legal doctrines.[84] There are, indeed, social scientists and philosophers who would deny that their work has any relation to the work of lawyers. The logical positivist considers that philosophising about " justice " leads but to the demonstration of the spuriousness of the word or concept when attempted to be used as something more than a cloak for the emotions. Other philosophers would say that philosophising about " justice " merely exposes the real character of various problems which it is for the jurist as such and not the philosopher as such to solve.[85] Such philosophers form part of a larger school of scholars, including social scientists as well as " pure " philosophers, who assign to jurisprudence an area of legal topics for which specifically legal methods and approaches are to be employed. But perhaps the majority of social scientists and philosophers do consider that legal issues involve questions of social science or philosophy. Nevertheless I am not aware of an economist or sociologist whose work would be helpful in relation either to the specific problem of *Broom* v. *Morgan*[50] or the general problem of master's liability. Nor are philosophers much more helpful: they are more concerned with the metaphysics and epistemology of morals than with practical moral issues. Even Sidgwick's book is entitled *The Method of Ethics*,[86] though we do find in it some examination of actual problems of human behaviour. While there is no treatment of the responsibility of a master for the acts of his servants, there is a discussion of the general problem of reparation for harm that has been blamelessly caused. The principle of reparation is distinguished from that of " corrective justice " which " requires pain to be inflicted on a man who has done wrong, even if no benefit result either to him or to others from the pain ". Thus distinguished, the principle is not tied to cases where harm has been caused by a blameworthy act; " the question arises whether we are bound to make reparation for harm that has been quite blamelessly caused: and it is not easy to answer it decisively ". Sidgwick inclines to the view that there is a moral obligation to make compensation for harm that one has blamelessly caused, but " perhaps we regard this as a duty of Benevolence— arising out of the general sympathy that each ought to have for others, intensified by this special occasion—than as a duty of strict Justice ". The moral obligation to make compensation for harm intentionally or negligently caused is, he says " a simple deduction from the maxim of general Benevolence ", and, since he regards such an obligation as

---

[84] Of course, one cannot expect complete " casuistry " from scientists and philosophers, nor are lawyers incapable of applying general doctrines of science and philosophy to the circumstances of legal problems: not all lawyers come from Vermont. The contention in the text is not merely that scientists and philosophers have failed to consider the kinds of facts which have given rise to litigation, but that they have not dealt with the general principles applicable to such facts.

[85] Cf. Part I, note 15.

[86] The quotations are taken from pp. 281-282 of the 6th Edition.

clearly an obligation of justice, it is clear that he does not draw a sharp line between justice and benevolence. Moreover, he adds, " If, however, we limit the requirement of Reparation, under the head of strict Justice, to cases in which the mischief repaired is due to acts or omissions in some degree culpable, a difficulty arises over the divergence between the moral view of culpability and that which social security requires ".

The treatment of the problem by Sidgwick is thus suggestive rather than conclusive and definitive, and by no means precludes the need for an independent examination of the problem by the jurist. This view is strengthened when it is borne in mind that what Sidgwick purports to do is to report the findings of Common Sense on the matter, and that he treats legal doctrines as representative of Common Sense.[87]

The submission which I make is that the problem of master's liability is one of a number of legal problems which do give rise to questions of social science and philosophy, and for which, however, no clear answer is to be found by reference to the writings of social scientists or philosophers. The jurist who would criticise the legal doctrine of master's liability in the light of social science or philosophy must himself become a social scientist or philosopher.

It is relevant to consider the cognate problem of the relation between law and psychology. Analysis of legal discourses will often reveal that involved in it are propositions falling within the scope of psychology. How is the lawyer to deal with them? What will the result be if he consults the psychologists? This last question can be answered not merely by reference to the writings of psychologists but also by reference to the proceedings of a conference attended by lawyers and psychologists at which lawyers did consult psychologists about psychological questions involved in legal problems.[88] Thus Professor Schwartz asked " Do threats of punishment deter? . . . Does ' motive ' have a separate existence from ' intent ' as a psychological phenomenon?" To these and other questions Professor Dennis, a psychologist, replied " There are no ready-made answers to these stimulating questions. Years of research would be required to approach answers." Doubtless a psychologist could show that many psychological errors are committed by lawyers, but it seems clear that phychologists are at present no more competent than lawyers in regard to the state-

---

[87] He refers to ch. III of Holmes' *Common Law* as illustrating "the perplexity of Common Sense ". He says that the doctrine which " has in the main prevailed in English Law ", that " the risk of a man's conduct is thrown upon him as the result of some moral-shortcoming " is " certainly in harmony with the Common Sense of mankind, so far as legal liability is concerned, but I do not think that the case is equally clear as regard moral obligation ".

[88] See " Summary of a Conference on Law and Psychology," (1953), 5 *Journal of Legal Education*, 355.

ment of many " psychological truths." Lawyers often have to be their own psychologists.[89]

Lawyers, social scientists and philosophers

The jurist who is concerned with the justification of rules of law, actual or possible, with their goodness or badness, has to deal with many problems. He has to consider to what extent criteria of goodness are to be found within a specifically juristic discipline. Stammler, for example, propounds the idea of law derived from reflection on the content and character of rules of law. The jurist is thus concerned with the lawyer's introversion. On the other hand he has to consider to what extent criteria of goodness are to be found within the extra-legal disciplines which I comprehensively entitle social science and philosophy. He is to that extent concerned with the lawyer's extroversion, as Stone terms it. He cannot ignore the practices of many lawyers, nor the doctrines of some philosophers according to both of which judgments of goodness of laws are intuitive, and jurisprudence, whether introvert or extrovert, is but a systematisation of such intuitive judgments, and not a collection of principles providing criteria for a rational judgment of goodness of specified laws. According to this latter view, it is good laws which are criteria for judging the soundness of juristic, scientific and philosophical doctrines, and it is not sound doctrines which are criteria for testing the goodness of law.[90]   In this section, however, I wish to deal with but one situation in which such a jurist may find himself, the situation which it is suggested arises in connection with *Broom* v. *Morgan*, viz., that of the jurist who considers that the problem with which he is concerned does involve considerations of social science or philosophy, but finds that it is a problem with which social scientists and philosophers have not dealt, and for which they provide no answer.[71]

I have said that the jurist concerned with the goodness of a law must himself in such a situation become social scientist, philosopher, psychologist. But it may be objected that a jurist cannot properly hope always to deal with a problem of social science, for example, as efficiently as would a social scientist—to do so would properly merit con-

---

[89] Lawyers are sometimes bad psychologists. Edith Swan, who was subsequently proved to have been the author of obscene letters, was acquitted at her first trial. " For the defence it was urged that nobody had ever heard Miss Swan use bad language. This appeared to impress the judge, Mr. Justice Bailhache, so greatly that he commented ' If I were on the jury I should refuse to convict '." O'Dounell, *Cavalcade of Justice*, p. 76.

[90] " The knowledge represented in law and its administration ... represents the testing and adaptation of psychiatry and other empirical knowledge to the solution of legal problems." Hall: " Psychiatry and the Law ", (1953), 38 *Iowa Law Review*, p. 689.

[91] By an " answer " I do not mean a proposition definitely establishing a final truth. The faith of a scholar is that it is always worth while re-examining the propositions of a discipline for unobserved error. I mean an answer given after a discussion of the problem. The lawyer who is dissatisfied with the answer of a social scientist is entitled to suggest that it is wrong, but has he a specifically legal method for demonstrating its error?

demnation as a megalomaniac.[92] It is proposed to consider a number of alternative courses open to such a jurist.

In the first place, he can say that until social scientists or philosophers do provide precise answers to the questions he would ask them, he must be content with the traditional methods of lawyers. He will seek to avoid mere verbalisms, dogmatism and pseudo-logic, but will rely on intuitive analogies with accepted doctrines when any new law has to be formulated, and justify an existing law by the manner in which it harmonises with the general body of laws.[93] In so doing, he may be supported by the faith that a system of positive law does embody proved values of society; he will escape the anxious doubts of those who wonder whether law is in accord with justice; he will avoid the " primal curse, the self-torture " of those who " at times . . . seem to have learned nothing and wonder whether there was profit in the labour and the sacrifice ".[94] On the other hand, he may keep before himself the belief that the right solution is not to be found within the verbal framework of legal rules and that questions of social welfare or justice have to be independently considered. He may, however, deal with such questions by his native wit, reflecting on what he considers to be the answers to them of " common sense ". In doing this he may be comforted by the thought that time winnows the chaff from the growth of new learning and adds the sound grain to man's store of common sense.[95]

In the next place, the jurist, without himself attempting to master all the learning of the social sciences and philosophy, may yet endeavour to understand their methods and apply them to the problems he discerns as falling within their scope. He may endeavour to employ a rigorous logic, to make what causal laws (or statistical generalisations about factual sequences) are presupposed by particular solutions of legal problems, and to ascertain what political and ethical postulates are in like manner involved in these problems. He will eliminate from consideration such propositions about " facts " and " values ", as one aware of the disciplines of social science and philosophy, though even a lawyer, will know have been emphatically repudiated as false by those disciplines. He may have to choose factual propositions and judgments

---

[92] I say " properly " for lawyers have improperly been called megalomaniacs merely for asserting that lawyers should be aware of the manner in which legal discourse may involve problems of social science or philosophy.

[93] He may even reflect that the law's unscientific approach to psychology is more likely to be in the right direction than the tottering steps of the infant science of psychology " Dealing as it does mainly with human behaviour, the law has very likely more to teach psychology than to learn from it. The law has had a long history and very able students and practitioners." Hall op. cit.

[94] Cardozo: Growth of the Law, at p. 108.

[95] Another simile may, however, be nearer the reality. Time deposits the detritus of brittle scientific and philosophical errors at the estuary of common sense: the wise man will seek for truth in the solid rock of scientific and philosophical doctrine or seek the source where fresh waters keep green the meadows of inspiration.

of value which have not been " established ", and are but hypotheses and expressions of faith. The choice must be made in partial ignorance, but if there be recognition of ignorance there is also a challenge for a better solution of the legal problem, a call to inquire into the facts needed to develop the scientific laws and for such reflection about values as may lead to settled principles of justice.

There is another course open to the jurist, one which may be pursued concurrently with the others. The challenge to jurists for the production of better solutions of legal problems based on consideration of the contributions of social science or philosophy is also a call for co-operation with social scientists and philosophers. The present barriers between law, the social sciences and philosophy are, to a large extent, not merely artificial but unreal: they are the results of pedagogical accident, not recognition of natural frontiers. In England, today, much of public law is taught outside faculties of law, while, on the other hand, in France economics is taught within faculties of law. There are said to be three separate disciplines of legal, political and social philosophy, and in Britain these subjects are found in faculties of law, arts and economics respectively: but wherein are the distinctions between the disciplines really to be found? Law, social welfare and justice may certainly be considered as distinct topics, but it does not follow that jurists, social scientists and philosophers may not be concerned with the same subject. Even if they be concerned with different aspects of one subject, or with different subjects, it yet remains true, in my opinion, that they may by collaboration assist each other. One of the themes of this article is that the jurist would be assisted by consideration of many problems jointly with the social scientist and the philosopher. It is also submitted that the social scientist or philosopher would be assisted in his work by co-operation with the jurist. Already in many places and in many ways such co-operation exists; law and philosophy at Oxford; the conference on law and psychology called by the Association of American Law Schools, to which reference has already been made is but one of many co-operative schemes in the United States; in Australia the National University has sponsored a number of joint discussions by lawyers, social scientists and philosophers, and, though there has not been wanting, at any rate in the United States, criticism of the value of general discussions, others have considered them extremely beneficial.[96] Such academic co-operation but mirrors the actual co-operation between lawyers and others in legislative commissions and assemblies. What is now required is the initiation and development of projects of academic co-operation on specific topics. What is also required is the education of new genera-

---

[96] " Research psychologists over the country ought to be told about areas in which lawyers need psychological data not now available." (Professor Dennis at the conference: (1953), 5 *Journal of Legal Education*, at p. 359,) This suggests another mode of co-operation.

tions of lawyers in awareness of the relations between law and the social sciences and philosophy, so that they may be ready to take part in or support such projects.

PART V.—CONCLUSION

Summary

This discourse has now returned to the assertion of its first paragraph, that it is all of it ultimately concerned with the nature of legal study in institutions which are concerned with more than merely routine learning. It has been specially concerned with the part that logic, social science and moral philosophy have to play in such study and in the juristic discourse which is the outcome of such study. I hope that my views have not been too dogmatically asserted, for they are but tentative. Among the hypotheses considered in the circular tour have been the following :

Classical and modern logic have much to contribute to understanding both of the exposition and criticism of legal rules, though neither is capable of solving problems. The logic of most logicians is concerned with the forms and not the contents of propositions, and, in so far as it is concerned with truth, is concerned with truths of inference and not with truth of facts or values. Its roles are principally the detection of pseudo-problems due to linguistic confusion, the rejection of errors in inferential reasoning, the indication of the non-logical and non-legal questions involved in legal thinking, the enumeration of the possibilities of legal rules which should be considered in the solution of legal problems. It is not the role of " logic " to provide criteria for the determination of the particular rule which constitutes the best solution, the right or just solutions, of a legal problem.

It is the tradition of lawyers, and particularly of judges of the Common Law, that discourse containing statements of legal rules should contain also statements of the reasons by which they may be supported. Moreover, the procedures of classical inferential logic enable inarticulated premises for legal rules to be suggested. It is a task associated with the older *speculum mentis*, and now pursued in modern logic, to indicate the type of the propositions which furnish the reasons for legal rules. The premises for legal rules often lie within the fields of recognised disciplines taught in faculties other than those of law. Partly, they lie within the field of disciplines concerned with description of social processes and of the causes of social welfare, a term whose denotation is here restricted to satisfactions of material needs, disciplines that I comprehensively term the social sciences. Partly, also, they lie within the fields of those disciplines concerned with the ethical evaluation of human behaviour, which might alternatively be phrased the examination of justice, disciplines that I comprehensively term philosophy.[97] It follows that any critical consideration of rules of law cannot ignore social science and philosophy. Such examination falls within the scope of jurisprudence. But for a number of reasons the scope of jurisprudence is not limited to the examination of rules of law in the light of extra-legal disciplines.

In the first place, the particular extra-legal disciplines too often deal with but particular aspects of a problem which the jurist has to survey as a whole. The task of synthesis has to be performed, and, despite the claims of some that disciplines such as history or sociology or philosophy should provide such synthesis, in fact they do not. Secondly, extra-legal disciplines often provide no definitive or no reliable guide to the jurist or no answer at all to his inquiries. The topic in which the jurist is interested is one which is still being debated in the extra-legal discipline or one which it has not yet considered. Next, the topic in which the lawyer is interested may not fall within the area which has been mapped out for the extra-legal disciplines: unless the jurist investigates the topic it is not likely that it will be investigated at all. Lastly, the critical examination of reasons for legal rules has long been undertaken by jurists themselves, and their writings form a large part of jurisprudence.

Two branches of " lawyer's jurisprudence " grow out of meanings for the word " law " other than that of official rules: meanings which are used in the phrases " natural law " and " customary law ". Jurists have themselves considered the nature of justice, and made contributions to theories of natural law. Indeed there have always been philosophers who, like the Oxford analysts of today, have considered that the determination of the general character of justice and of the justice of particular rules are matters not for the philosopher but for the jurist. Again, a sociology of law arises from the investigations of those aspects of human behaviour sometimes denoted by the word law. The " realist jurists ", who consider law to be official behaviour and thus produce a juristic sociology, have had predecessors who have regarded customary behaviour as a subject for study by lawyers. Doubtless, the methods of general sociology are those to be employed in the study of " legal " behaviour, whether of judges or law-breakers, but for many years to come it appears as if jurists will be the only scholars to explore many areas of behaviour.

These hypotheses have been tested by consideration of the writings of law teachers and judges dealing with a specific legal problem, viz., that which arose in *Broom* v. *Morgan*,[50] involving the explanation and

---

[97] I should emphasise again the rather vague character of this classification of disciplines; but it serves the present need of asserting the "extra-legal " character of propositions in juristic discourse. In particular, I should emphasise that there is much of what in the text is called philosophy with the disciplines of economics, politics and sociology, a fact to which writers in those fields often testify.

justification of the legal rules of employer's liability. It was seen that many parts of the discourses examined consisted but in exposition of legal rules and of the cases in which they were enunciated. But there was also critical evaluation of existing and suggested legal rules; and in such consideration there were references to logic, to social welfare and to justice. The law teachers were not content with dogmatic descriptions but sought for justification, and rightly so : the judges were not content with a judicial " sic jubeo ", but also sought for justification, and rightly so, and justification was expressed in language embodying the concepts of logic or social welfare or justice. Nevertheless, however sound the judgments of justification or condemnation of the legal rules may have been, it is submitted that they remained largely but bare assertions. It is my own conviction that the extra-legal references were relevant and indeed necessary, but it is my submission that they were inadequate. The reasoning, which was said to be logical, appeared to be based on unexpressed value judgments; the appeals to social welfare were not buttressed by facts or by the views of social scientists; the exposition of morality was not derived from any system of moral philosophy. If these were typical juristic discourse, it is pertinent to say that there is need of more study by jurists of logic, social science, and philosophy, and indeed it was possible to draw attention to fuller considerations of logic, social welfare and justice. A suggestion was made that the basic principle justifying the liability of an employer for the negligence of his servant was that asserting the positive duty of one person to care for the welfare of another, a duty derived, not from any fault of the employer, but from a social obligation of benevolence.

Yet, while the appeals by the critics to logic would have been rejected by logicians, it could not be said that the claims that specific rules promoted social welfare or justice would have been accepted or rejected by social scientists or philosophers. Social scientists have barely considered even broad questions of the law of tort, and philosophers largely draw their opinions from the rules of legal systems. My suggestion of a legal obligation to love one's neighbour is derived from juristic, not philosophic, writing. A solution to the problem of *Broom* v. *Morgan*[50] is not found in the writings of social scientists or philosophers. Certainly no specific solution is to be found, nor, it is believed, any general principle capable of yielding a solution by application to the characteristics of the particular problem. It is realised that the actual duty of an agent in a concrete situation is said by philosophers not to be capable of determination by simple deduction from a general moral principle, but for the particular problem of vicarious liability it is doubtful whether the moralists have suggested any *prima facie* duty, they have not suggested the general principles to be considered in the exercise of the specific moral judgment.

The problem thus arises for the jurist of how to proceed in questions of social welfare and morality in the absence of aid from the social scientists and philosophers. Some *via media* has to be found between the jurist endeavouring himself to become social scientist and philosopher and between ignoring completely the issue of the " goodness " of the law. It is suggested that more co-operation is required between jurists, social scientists and philosophers.

As the term jurist is commonly understood, a man cannot be a jurist and not be concerned with the goodness of laws. Implicit in what I have written is the view that a lawyer cannot be fully a man and indifferent to the problem of what ought to be the law. It is contrary to the obligation of a lawyer as counsellor to advise his clients not as to what the law is, but as to what he considers it ought to be. It is often contrary to the duty of a judge as a judge to determine a case not in accordance with what he considers the law is, but with what he thinks it ought to be. But as human beings both counsellors and judges are concerned with what the law ought to be, for it is believed that the specific nature of humanity is to seek for rationality in the control of man's actions.

It is, of course, not uncommon for statements to be made that lawyers are not concerned with this or that aspect of some matter. But attention should be given to a distinction well known to lawyers. A statement that a lawyer is not concerned with what ought to be the law may merely mean what is indicated by the more precise phrase, that as a lawyer he is not concerned with what ought to be the law: and clearly when the phrase " as a lawyer " means, as it often does, " as one concerned with what is the law ", then the statement under review becomes a tautology. If a writer states that as a lawyer he is concerned with what is the law, and that only as a jurist is he concerned with what ought to be the law, then, undoubtedly, he does employ a terminology apt to bring out differences in thought and reality. But these apt distinctions of words do not deny the unity of human personality, nor do they disprove the contention that for the full development of personality a lawyer must also be a jurist. It has been questioned whether a man can be efficiently both a lawyer and a jurist. An answer is supplied by Austin, who maintained that he who seeks to improve the law must fully understand what the present law is; thus to say that a man cannot be efficient both as a lawyer and a jurist is to deny that he can be an efficient jurist. This may well be so: for it is a commonplace that man cannot attain complete rationality. There is here, however, no denial of the obligation to seek for rationality.

The task of the law student

The affirmation of faith as to the obligations of jurist and lawyer may seem not to embrace the student of law. It is my belief that it does. I conceive a university not as a collection of individuals engaged in self-improvement, nor, indeed, as merely a fellowship of men engaged in scholarly activity but detached from their fellow-men. In my view a university is an organ of society dedicated to fostering the exercise of intelligence and the advancement of knowledge, ultimately for the common good of all in the society.[98] The ultimate task of a faculty of law is the improvement of rules of law: its instrumental tasks are the preservation and dissemination of knowledge of the law, through which cultural values of society are maintained and developed, and the education of the law student. Faculties of law are not the only agencies concerned with these tasks. Politicians, civil servants, the legal professions, various bodies of citizens—all are concerned with law reform; and indeed I have contended that all citizens should be so concerned. The family, the circle of friends, the churches, political organisations, the general sources of information, such as the press and broadcasting, the social organisations within and without universities, the professional organisations (to which the student may already belong)—all these and others play their part in the education of the law student. It is, indeed, my belief that neither the faculty of law, nor even the university as a whole, ought to be the sole educational influence affecting the student, for I believe that a university as such is not concerned with the whole personality of a student, but with his intellectual personality. His moral and artistic development, for example, are not the primary concern of the university; though a good university will provide education in morals and aesthetics, for it will contain " rounded " men and women who practise moral virtues and display artistic sensibility. In the same way a university will provide education in political activity and the religious life, for it will contain men and women who are politically active or who lead religious lives. But the university's responsibility extends to the whole of the intellectual activity of the student; it is not limited to the provision of information about the subject the student has elected to take. Law is the medium for the general intellectual development of the law student.

Intellectual activity is not limited to the memorising of propositions, but inquiries into the criteria by which they are to be judged as worthy of acceptance, and into the manner in which the propositions satisfy such criteria.[99] An initial task of the law student is to inquire into the validity of the propositions which are asserted to be rules of

---

[98] The maxim that scholarship knows no frontiers is regarded by me as evidence for the existence of a world society, and the development of universities evidence of the potentiality of development of more elaborate institutions of a world society. At present it must be recognised that there are not yet in existence all the institutions requisite even for the society of the members of the British Commonwealth.

[99] " When religion seeks to shelter behind its sanctity, and law behind its majesty, they justly awaken suspicion against themselves, and lose all claim to the sincere respect which reason yields only to that which has been able to bear the test of its free and open scrutiny." Kant: *Kritik der Reinen Vernunft*, Preface i.

law.[100] This is indeed a vast enterprise, requiring as part of it the study
of actual cases, rather than the study of the opinions of text-book
writers. Moreover, under our British system of law, (and under other
systems as well) inquiry into the validity of a proposition will lead the
student into questions of ethics and politics, of psychology and sociology.
For under that system criteria of validity often involve efficacy and
desirability.[101] But even were validity not associated with justice, the
nature of intellectual activity requires that the students do more than
merely list a number of rules, acquire knowledge of criteria of validity,
and check the validity of the listed rules. Merely to do that does not
advance the student above the status of Goethe's fact-grubber. Perception of a number of creatures and classification of them as earthworms
is not adequate intellectual activity.[102]

> " Dann hat er die Teile in der Hand.
> Fehlt leider nur das geistige Band."

The task of the university teacher is to stimulate the student to
inquiry into the interrelated topics of the nature of law, the origin and
function of rules of law, and their relation to social life in general. It
is true that this imposes a vast task on the law student, and the wisdom
of the policy has been denied. I do not doubt that much is sometimes
gained by attention to a single part of a complex in interrelated parts;
such a process of abstraction often merits the name of " practical ", and
much success has followed this procedure. But failure to realise
interrelations has led to pragmatic failures, and many successes have
attended those who have attempted to deal with complexes as a whole.
Analysis and synthesis have had their particular triumphs and disasters;
together they may be invincible: together they constitute intellectual
activity.

There is widespread agreement that students should examine the
function of laws. Analysis of that function exhibits its two components. In the case of laws these are what the laws were designed to
effect, and what they do effect. These are questions of fact which are
difficult to answer in many instances, but the attempt should be made.
We have learnt to appreciate the importance of efficiency, and the
efficiency of laws is the measure of the relation of the two components
of function. It may be seen that efficiency depends on a wide range of

---

[100] I am using the terminology of Kelsen with its distinction between the validity and
efficacy of a rule of law. It is valid if constitutionally authoritative: as an Australian lawyer
would say, if laid down in a statute or in some case which had binding authority. It has
efficacy when in fact the rule is enforced. A rule, of course, may be valid but not enforced.
A statute may be a " dead letter ".

[101] The proof of this dogmatic affirmation requires a series of articles. They have indeed
been written by many authors; the dynamic character of our law, so ably portrayed again
by Lord Denning in *The Changing Law*, derives in part from this quality of the legal system.

[102] " Whatever the world thinks, he who hath not much meditated upon God, the human
mind, and the *summum bonum* may possibly make a thriving earthworm but . . . a sorry
patriot and statesman " (Berkeley).

factors, among which clarity of formulation of the laws, skill in administration and adequacy of the technical legal procedures are important, but by no means paramount. Other factors are usually classified by such terms as biological, psychological, economic, political, environmental. Study of the function of laws leads to an examination of the social sciences which investigate many aspects of social life. Moreover, even this " scientific " approach leads to one aspect of the problem of law reform, viz., that of increasing the efficiency of laws.

Analysis of the relation of law to social life in general exhibits other aspects of the problem of what ought to be the law. We are faced with the problem of the purpose of social life, the problem of the good life and its involvement with social welfare. The pursuit of the good life is itself a moral activity, but rational consideration of the nature of the good life is intellectual activity. Unfortunately, such is the social and educational system of today, that many students entering the university are unaware that such rational consideration is possible. It is, however, an activity involved in the study of any of the humanities, for the great issues of ethics and politics, of metaphysics and theology are all intertwined.

The study of law includes, therefore, not only the examination of what is the law, but also of what it ought to be. Moreover, it has been seen that there are three problems in what ought to be the law : (i) what laws would most efficiently promote the ends, preserve the values, of existing laws? (ii) what ought to be the ends of the law, what are the values of the good life? (iii) what laws would most efficiently promote the values of the good life? In pursuit of what ought to be the law actual law cannot be ignored for many of the values of the good life are cherished and protected by existing legal systems. Nor can there be ignored the many suggestions for their improvement made by those who have reflected on legal systems and on the systematisation of ideals for the ends of law made by jurists in their theories of natural law. But, as has been seen, there must also be taken into account the contributions of social scientists and philosophers to the discussion of social welfare and moral conduct. The burden of learning is heavy, but it seems cognitively clear that for the wisest solution of the great problems of what ought to be the law the co-operation of many thinkers is required. Is it not also morally certain that the toil and sacrifice involved in the learning is merited by the causes of justice and the good life?

In what manner and to what extent a student may acquire critical and creative knowledge of what is the law and what it ought to be are, of course, difficult though compelling pedagogic problems. The attempt to answer them has to be made by both teachers and students. The student who feels a moral urge to lead the good life, to promote justice and social welfare, will find the study of the law more rewarding and enriching by reason of its inclusion of what ought to be the law, and

z

by its embracing the labours of scientists and philosophers in the field of understanding of social life. Even he may be frustrated or suffocated if too much is expected of him, though the danger is greater that he may be starved or lamed if too little is required of him.[103] The intellectually eager student may delight in the broader fields, and be stimulated by the thought of the many prizes for the explorer of unfrequented areas. His moral self may indeed be stimulated and he may feel the urge to preserve and advance the values in law. What of the students who have no such moral desires or intellectual comprehensiveness, or who feel themselves compelled to subordinate such feelings, if not to exterminate them, in the interests of acquiring the means of subsistence. There is indeed for the teacher a moral problem of the justification of imposing consideration of what ought to be the law on the student who is interested solely in what is the law. Suggestions for such a justification have already been made. It has been suggested that a technical knowledge of what is the law involves consideration of what it ought to be; and that an intellectual understanding of what is the law compels such consideration. Various writers have indeed stated that a juristic approach to legal study is a better approach for the actual practice of the law than one which ignores criticism in terms of social welfare and justice. But suggestions of this kind give to the consideration of what ought to be the law only an incidental and subordinate place in the study of law. I believe that the true position of such study is co-ordinate with the study of what is the law. I derive this belief from my thesis that a university is an organ of society having as one of its functions the improvement of laws by means of the exercise of intellectual ability. A university comprises the whole body of students as well as the teachers and governors. The student joins a university: he does not contract for the provision to him of information and training. He is a member of a fellowship dedicated to the objects of the association: he must play his part in the advancement of learning. But learning is not, any more than is law, an end in itself, as the medieval universities well knew. The advancement of learning is the care and prevention of sickness and disease, the advancement of bodily and mental health and all that medicine serves. It is the elimination of brute force and wasteful neglect, the advancement of order and welfare and justice and all that law serves. It is the advancement of the mind and soul of man and all that philosophy and theology serve.

---

[103] " The hungry sheep look up, and are not fed, But swollen with wind, and the rank mist they draw Rot inwardly, and foul contagion spread."

LIST OF OTHER WORKS BY THE AUTHOR

1. E E Bowerman: Law of Child Protection, (1934) 50 Law Quarterly Review 288. (Book review.)

2. E J Bullock: Law as to Children and Young Persons, *Ibid.* (Book review.)

3. A E Ilkin: Children and Young Persons Act, 1933, *Ibid.* (Book review.)

4. W C Hall: Law relating to Children and Young Persons, *Ibid.* (Book review.)

5. Apparent Authority of an Agent of a Company, (1934) 50 Law Quarterly Review 224.

6. Conditions, Warranties and other Contractual Terms, (1937) 15 Canadian Bar Review 309.

7. Operation of Description in a Contract of Sale of Goods, (1937) 15 Canadian Bar Review 760.

8. The Statutory Protection of the Collecting Banker, (1938) 40 Journal of the Institute of Bankers in Ireland 125.

9. *Miscampbell* v. *McAlister*, (1938) 2 Northern Ireland Legal Quarterly 38.

10. Registered and Unregistered Easements—Natural and Artificial Watercourses, (1938) 2 Northern Ireland Legal Quarterly 142.

11. Fee Farm Grants, (1938) 2 Northern Ireland Legal Quarterly 194, (1939) Northern Ireland Legal Quarterly 40, 81, 143, (1940) 4 Northern Ireland Legal Quarterly 40, 86.

12. *Miscampbell* v. *McAlister* Again *sub nomine Glover* v. *Montrose*, (1939) 3 Northern Ireland Legal Quarterly 68.

13. Legal Education and the War, (1939) 3 Northern Ireland Legal Quarterly 196.

14. Equitable Deposits of Title Deeds, (1940) 4 Northern Ireland Legal Quarterly 64.

15. Review of legal education during the War 1939-1945 (Various Universities including Queen's University, Belfast—J L Montrose contributor only), (1947) 1 Society of Public Teachers of Law (NS) 23.

16. Proof of Foreign Marriages, (1938) 11 Modern Law Reviews 326.

17. The Law of Agency: Some Elementary Considerations of Contractual Agency, (1948) 50 Journal of the Institute of Bankers in Ireland 259.

18. Bentham, (1948) 8 Northern Ireland Legal Quarterly 28.

19. Joint Deposit Receipts—a Reconsideration, (1951) 9 Northern Ireland Legal Quarterly 148.

20. Legal Aspects of Taxation and Grant under the Northern Ireland System of Devolution, (1952) Federalism, an Australian Jubilee Study, ed. G Sawer (Melbourne) 1.

21. Sale of Goods—Illegality (*V. and B. Viennese Fashions* v. *Losane* [1952] 1 All E.R. 909), (1952) 15 Modern Law Review 491.

22. Legal Education in Northern Ireland, (1952) 5 Journal of Legal Education 18.

23. A Specialist Approach to General Education, (1952) 7 Universities Quarterly 70.

24. General Education and the Law Student, (1952) 25 Universities Review 20.

25. Language of a Notation for the Doctrine of Precedent, (1952) 2 University of Western Australia Annual Law Review 301 and 504.

26. The Supreme Court of the US and Academic Freedom, (1953) 17 Universities Quarterly 348.

27. Negligence and Liability for Dangerous Premises (*Dunster* v. *Abbott* [1953] 2 All E.R. 578), (1954) 17 Modern Law Review 265.

28. Negligence as the Basis of Liability to Trespassers (*David* v. *St. Mary's Demolition Co. Ltd.* [1954] 1 All E.R. 578), (1954) 17 Modern Law Review 368.

29. Reasoning, *Ratio Decidendi* and Denning L.J., (1954) 17 Modern Law Review 462.

30. McNaghten Rules, (1954) 17 Modern Law Review 383, (1955) 18 Modern Law Review 505.

31. Contribution to a " Round Table " on " The Lawyer's Role in Modern Society ", (1935) 4 Journal of Public Law 1.

32. Noch einmal in die Bresche: Verkaufe im Selbstbedienungsladen Eine englische Gerichtsentscheidung, (1955) Juristische Rundschau. [German version of Chapter 12. Ed.]

33. Overseas Relations and the Exchange of Views by Practising Lawyers, Teachers of Law, Students, etc. (Commonwealth and Empire Law Conference, London, July 1955), (1955) 11 Northern Ireland Legal Quarterly 183.

34. G W Keaton and G Schwarzenberger: The Year Book of World Affairs, 1954, (1955) 3 Journal of the Society of Public Teachers of Law 128. (Book review).

35. Legal Theory for Politicians and Sociologists, (1955) Political Studies 211.

36. Do occupiers of land owe a lower duty than non-occupiers? (*Creed* v. *McGeoch and Son Ltd.* [1955] 1 W.L.R. 1005), (1956) 19 Modern Law Review 79.

37. Distinguishing cases and the limits of *ratio decidendi*, (*A V Pound and Co.* v. *M W Hardy and Co.* [1956] 2 W.L.R. 683), (1956) 19 Modern Law Review 525.

38. Occupiers Liability for Negligence (*Slater* v. *Clay Cross and Co.* [1956] 3 W.L.R. 232), (1956) 19 Modern Law Review 69.

39. K K Kagan: Three Great Systems of Jurisprudence, (1956) 19 Modern Law Review 712. (Book review.)

40. Taking Property without Compensation, (1956) 11 Northern Ireland Legal Quarterly 278.

41. Friedmann on Legal Theory, (1956) 5 Journal of Public Law 418.

42. Judicial Law Making and Law Applying, (1956) Butterworth's South African Law Review 187.

43. How should we control monopoly?, (1956) 66 Economic Journal 578.

44. Contract-exemption clauses—description or condition (*Karsales Ltd.* v. *Wallis* [1956] 1 W.L.R. 936), (1957) 6 Cambridge Law Journal 12.

45. To speak or not to speak (*Regina* v. *Agricultural Land Tribunal* [1956] 1 W.L.R. 1240), (1957) 20 Modern Law Review 285.

46. The *Ratio Decidendi* of a Case, (1957) 20 Modern Law Review 587.

47. *Jus Quaesitum Tertio,* (1957) 20 Modern Law Review 658.

48. Universities Law Libraries, (1957) 4 Journal of the Society of Public Teachers of Law 1.

49. Judicial Implementation of Legislative Policy, (1957) 3 University of Queensland Law Journal 139.

50. United Kingdom National Committee of Comparative Law (1957/8) 6/7 International and Comparative Law Quarterly 160/144.

51. Contract—Description of Goods—whether condition (*Oscar Chess Ltd.* v. *Williams* [1957] 1 W.L.R. 370), (1958) 16 Cambridge Law Journal 22.

52. Duties of non-occupiers (*Riden* v. *A C Billings and Sons* [1957] 3 All E.R. 1), (1958) 21 Modern Law Review 76.

53. Reasoned Judgements, (1958) 21 Modern Law Review 80.

54. Constitutional Provisions for Fundamental Human Rights, (1958) International and Comparative Law Quarterly 144.

55. Is negligence an ethical or a sociological concept? (1958) 21 Modern Law Review 259.

56. J W Gough: Fundamental Law in English History, (1958) 7 Journal of Public Law 186. (Book review.)

57. Vol 7, Halsbury's Statutes of England, 2nd Ed., Title " Northern Ireland ", Preliminary Note (Joint Contributor).

58. Different Reasons by Judges of Same Court (*Pyx Granite Co.* v. *Ministry of Housing and Local Government* [1958] 1 All E.R. 325).

59. Training for the Legal Profession, (1958) 4 Journal of the Society of Public Teachers of Law 175.

60. Some Impressions of the United States, (1959) 11 Journal of Legal Education 379.

61. A J R Kiralfy: Source book of English Law, 1957, (1959) 3 American Journal of Legal History 288. (Book review.)

62. J F Wilson: Principles of the Law of Contract, (1959) 22 Modern Law Review 217. (Book review.)

63. J C Smith: Casebook on Contract, (1959) 22 Modern Law Review 220. (Book review.)

64. Compensation for Victims of Criminal Violence (Contribution to a " Round Table "), (1959) 8 Journal of Public Law 197.

65. Mock Turtle: A Problem in Adjectival Ambiguity, (1959) Modern Use of Logic in Law.

66. Legal Logic and Philosophy, (1959) 5 Journal of the Society of Public Teachers of Law (NS) 29.

67. Dismissal of Professors, (1959) Yearbook of Education 441.

68. Natural Justice and the Courts, (1960) Public Law 8.

69. Ambiguous Words in a Statute (*I.R.C.* v. *Hinchy* [1960] 2 W.L.R. 448), (1960) 76 Law Quarterly Review 359.

70. Conditions and Promises (*Bashir* v. *Lands Commissioner* [1960] 1 All E.R. 117), (1960) 23 Modern Law Review 550.

71. Procedure for Investigation by Universities, (1961) 33 University Review 51.

72. The Academic Lawyer's " House of Intellect ", (1961) 14 Journal of Legal Education (devoted to the proceedings of the British-Canadian-American Conference on Legal Education in New York, September 1960, in General Session).

73. Syntactic (formerly Amphibolous) Ambiguity, (1962) Modern Use of Logic in Law.

74. Fact Finding and Law making, (1962) Public Law 399.

75. " L.C., L.C.J., L.J. " (1963) 79 Law Quarterly Review 187.

76. Bodenheimer: " Jurisprudence ", (1964) 15 University of Toronto Law Journal 463. (Book review.)

77. G R Rudd: The English Legal System, (1964) University of Toronto Law Journal 463. (Book review.)

78. Legal Philosophy and Social Democracy, (1965) 1 Demos (Organ of Democratic Social Club, University of Singapore).

79. Legal Education. Paper Third Commonwealth and Empire Conference, Sydney, Australia, 1965. (Summary presumably read at the conference on presentation of paper.)

80. Chinese Thought, (1965) 1 Law Times (University of Singapore); Expatriate (a poem), ibid.

81. Some impressions of the Free University of Berlin, (1965) 8 Journal of the Society of Public Teachers of Law 162.

82. The Three Fields of Jurisprudence, (1966) 26 University of Toronto Law Journal.

PUBLICATION UNCERTAIN

83. The Legal Relation between a University and its Professors. (The Orr Case in Tasmania).

84. " Our Motto " (Gray's Inn).

85. The House of Lords and the Declaratory Theory of Law.

86. The Nature and the Relevance of Similar Conduct.

87. Causation and Contributory Negligence: a Plea for " Metaphysics " (1946).

88. On the Nature of a Definition of Law (first draft known to have been written in 1947).

89. Legal Education in the United States and Europe. (Lecture delivered in 1954 or 1956).

90. Technology and the Universities: Presidential Address to the Association of University Teachers. (1956).

91. Relevance and Remoteness: Trials within Trials (on the decision of the Court of Criminal Appeal in R. v. Toohey [1964] 1 W.L.R. 1286, before that decision was reversed by the House of Lords, sub nom., Toohey v. Metropolitan Police Commissioner [1965] A.C. 595).